Handbook of Research on Emerging Perspectives in Intelligent Pattern Recognition, Analysis, and Image Processing

Narendra Kumar Kamila
C.V. Raman College of Engineering, India

A volume in the Advances in Computational
Intelligence and Robotics (ACIR) Book Series

An Imprint of IGI Global

Published in the United States of America by
Information Science Reference (an imprint of IGI Global)
701 E. Chocolate Avenue
Hershey PA, USA 17033
Tel: 717-533-8845
Fax: 717-533-8661
E-mail: cust@igi-global.com
Web site: http://www.igi-global.com

Library of Congress Cataloging-in-Publication Data

Handbook of research on emerging perspectives in intelligent pattern recognition, analysis, and image processing / Narendra Kumar Kamila, editor.
    pages cm
  Includes bibliographical references and index.
  Summary: "This book discusses the advances of image processing and pattern analysis and addresses how new innovations will cater to the demands of daily life"-- Provided by publisher.
  ISBN 978-1-4666-8654-0 (hardcover) -- ISBN 978-1-4666-8655-7 (ebook) 1. Pattern recognition systems. 2. Image processing--Digital techniques. 3. Computational intelligence. I. Kamila, Narendra Kumar, 1967-
  TK7882.P3.H364 2015
  006.4--dc23
                        2015015649

This book is published in the IGI Global book series Advances in Computational Intelligence and Robotics (ACIR) (ISSN: 2327-0411; eISSN: 2327-042X)

British Cataloguing in Publication Data
A Cataloguing in Publication record for this book is available from the British Library.

All work contributed to this book is new, previously-unpublished material. The views expressed in this book are those of the authors, but not necessarily of the publisher.

For electronic access to this publication, please contact: eresources@igi-global.com.

Advances in Computational Intelligence and Robotics (ACIR) Book Series

ISSN: 2327-0411
EISSN: 2327-042X

MISSION

While intelligence is traditionally a term applied to humans and human cognition, technology has progressed in such a way to allow for the development of intelligent systems able to simulate many human traits. With this new era of simulated and artificial intelligence, much research is needed in order to continue to advance the field and also to evaluate the ethical and societal concerns of the existence of artificial life and machine learning.

The **Advances in Computational Intelligence and Robotics (ACIR) Book Series** encourages scholarly discourse on all topics pertaining to evolutionary computing, artificial life, computational intelligence, machine learning, and robotics. ACIR presents the latest research being conducted on diverse topics in intelligence technologies with the goal of advancing knowledge and applications in this rapidly evolving field.

COVERAGE

- Machine Learning
- Evolutionary computing
- Brain Simulation
- Intelligent control
- Fuzzy Systems
- Synthetic Emotions
- Computer Vision
- Robotics
- Cognitive Informatics
- Cyborgs

IGI Global is currently accepting manuscripts for publication within this series. To submit a proposal for a volume in this series, please contact our Acquisition Editors at Acquisitions@igi-global.com or visit: http://www.igi-global.com/publish/.

Titles in this Series

For a list of additional titles in this series, please visit: www.igi-global.com

Research Advances in the Integration of Big Data and Smart Computing
Pradeep Kumar Mallick (Institute for Research and Development, India)
Information Science Reference • copyright 2016 • 380pp • H/C (ISBN: 9781466687370) • US $210.00 (our price)

Innovative Research in Attention Modeling and Computer Vision Applications
Rajarshi Pal (Institute for Development and Research in Banking Technology, India)
Information Science Reference • copyright 2016 • 457pp • H/C (ISBN: 9781466687233) • US $200.00 (our price)

Handbook of Research on Swarm Intelligence in Engineering
Siddhartha Bhattacharyya (RCC Institute of Information Technology, India) and Paramartha Dutta (Visva-Bharati University, India)
Engineering Science Reference • copyright 2015 • 744pp • H/C (ISBN: 9781466682917) • US $335.00 (our price)

Handbook of Research on Advancements in Robotics and Mechatronics
Maki K. Habib (The American University in Cairo, Egypt)
Engineering Science Reference • copyright 2015 • 993pp • H/C (ISBN: 9781466673878) • US $515.00 (our price)

Handbook of Research on Advanced Intelligent Control Engineering and Automation
Ahmad Taher Azar (Benha University, Egypt) and Sundarapandian Vaidyanathan (Vel Tech University, India)
Engineering Science Reference • copyright 2015 • 795pp • H/C (ISBN: 9781466672482) • US $335.00 (our price)

Handbook of Research on Artificial Intelligence Techniques and Algorithms
Pandian Vasant (Universiti Teknologi Petronas, Malaysia)
Information Science Reference • copyright 2015 • 796pp • H/C (ISBN: 9781466672581) • US $495.00 (our price)

Handbook of Research on Synthesizing Human Emotion in Intelligent Systems and Robotics
Jordi Vallverdú (Universitat Autònoma de Barcelona, Spain)
Information Science Reference • copyright 2015 • 469pp • H/C (ISBN: 9781466672789) • US $245.00 (our price)

Recent Advances in Ambient Intelligence and Context-Aware Computing
Kevin Curran (University of Ulster, UK)
Information Science Reference • copyright 2015 • 376pp • H/C (ISBN: 9781466672840) • US $225.00 (our price)

Recent Advances in Intelligent Technologies and Information Systems
Vijayan Sugumaran (Oakland University, USA & Sogang University, Seoul, Korea)
Information Science Reference • copyright 2015 • 309pp • H/C (ISBN: 9781466666399) • US $200.00 (our price)

www.igi-global.com

701 E. Chocolate Ave., Hershey, PA 17033
Order online at www.igi-global.com or call 717-533-8845 x100
To place a standing order for titles released in this series, contact: cust@igi-global.com
Mon-Fri 8:00 am - 5:00 pm (est) or fax 24 hours a day 717-533-8661

List of Contributors

Table of Contents

Section 1
Image Processing and Computer Vision

Gebeyehu Belay Gebremeskel, Chongqing University, China
Yi Chai, Chongqing University, China
Zhou Shangbo, Chongqing University, China
Su Xu, Chongqing University, China

Vania Vieira Estrela, Universidade Federal Fluminense, Brazil
Hermes Aguiar Magalhães, Universidade Federal de Minas Gerais, Brazil
Osamu Saotome, InstitutoTecnologico de Aeronautica, Brazil

Md. Imtiyaz Anwar, Dr. B. R. Ambedkar NIT Jalandhar, India
Arun Khosla, Dr. B. R. Ambedkar NIT Jalandhar, India

Jhih-Yuan Hwang, National Sun Yat-sen University, Taiwan
Wei-Po Lee, National Sun Yat-sen University, Taiwan

Section 2
Pattern Recognition, Watermarking and Face Recognition

Detailed Table of Contents

Section 1
Image Processing and Computer Vision

Chapter 1

Gebeyehu Belay Gebremeskel, Chongqing University, China
Yi Chai, Chongqing University, China
Zhou Shangbo, Chongqing University, China
Su Xu, Chongqing University, China

Mining techniques can play an important role in image decomposition, segmentation, classification and retrieval systems. As image data become more complex and growing at a fast pace, searching valuable information and knowledge implicit become more challenging than ever before. In this chapter, authors proposed a WT based DM techniques to optimize and characterize the unique feature of image retrieval, which is fundamental to optimize informative mathematical representation of image objects. Many software, including data exploratory tools such as DM packages contain fast and efficient programs that perform WT. Wavelets have quickly gained popularity among scientists and engineers, both in theoretical research and in applications. The authors discussed in details and introduced a novel method for image database analysis in different scenarios that foster the wide access of image data.

Chapter 2

Vania Vieira Estrela, Universidade Federal Fluminense, Brazil
Hermes Aguiar Magalhães, Universidade Federal de Minas Gerais, Brazil
Osamu Saotome, InstitutoTecnologico de Aeronautica, Brazil

The objectives of this chapter are: (i) to introduce a concise overview of regularization; (ii) to define and to explain the role of a particular type of regularization called total variation norm (TV-norm) in computer vision tasks; (iii) to set up a brief discussion on the mathematical background of TV methods;

and (iv) to establish a relationship between models and a few existing methods to solve problems cast as TV-norm. For the most part, image-processing algorithms blur the edges of the estimated images, however TV regularization preserves the edges with no prior information on the observed and the original images. The regularization scalar parameter λ controls the amount of regularization allowed and it is essential to obtain a high-quality regularized output. A wide-ranging review of several ways to put into practice TV regularization as well as its advantages and limitations are discussed.

Chapter 3

Md. Imtiyaz Anwar, Dr. B. R. Ambedkar NIT Jalandhar, India
Arun Khosla, Dr. B. R. Ambedkar NIT Jalandhar, India

Road accident is a serious issue in most of the countries due to degraded visibility in bad weather such as fog, haze and rain. A better visibility is a key requirement for passenger's safety while maintaining the speed of the vehicle. Researchers throughout the world are focusing to enhance the visibility through bad weather mainly due to fog or haze to minimize accidents. Many efforts are being put up to clearly visualize the scene using computer vision. Classifications of fog and analysis of de-weathering techniques are prime motive of research. This book chapter addresses and summarizes the progress in the development of vision enhancement techniques for road safety in turbid medium, particularly with fog which greatly affects the vision. This chapter also presents a brief comparative analysis on different weather conditions and classification of fog which is important for application point of view.

Chapter 4

Jhih-Yuan Hwang, National Sun Yat-sen University, Taiwan
Wei-Po Lee, National Sun Yat-sen University, Taiwan

The current surveillance systems must identify the continuous human behaviors to detect various events from video streams. To enhance the performance of event recognition, in this chapter, we propose a distributed low-cost smart cameras system, together with a machine learning technique to detect abnormal events through analyzing the sequential behaviors of a group of people. Our system mainly includes a simple but efficient strategy to organize the behavior sequence, a new indirect encoding scheme to represent a group of people with relatively few features, and a multi-camera collaboration strategy to perform collective decision making for event recognition. Experiments have been conducted and the results confirm the reliability and stability of the proposed system in event recognition.

Chapter 5

Abhijit Chandra, Jadavpur University, India
Srideep Maity, Indian Institute of Technology, Kharagpur, India

Digital images are often corrupted by various types of noises amongst which impulse noise is most prevalent. Impulse noise appears during transmission and/or acquisition of images. Intrusion of impulse noise degrades the quality of the image and causes the loss of fine image details. Reducing the effect of impulse noise from corrupted images is therefore considered as an essential task to be performed before letting the image for further processing. However, the process of noise reduction from an image should also take proper care towards the preservation of edges and fine details of an image. A number of efficient noise reduction algorithms have already been proposed in the literature over the last few decades which have nurtured this issue with utmost importance. Design and development of new two dimensional (2D) filters has grown sufficient interest amongst the researchers. This chapter attempts to throw enough light on the advancement in this field by illustratively describing existing state-of-the-art filtering techniques along with their capability of denoising impulse noises.

Ankit Chaudhary, Truman State University, USA
Sandeep Kumar, Government College of Engineering & Technology, Bikaner, India

Steganography is the technique which has been used in many fields for hiding information and many different versions for each application are available in the literature. This chapter demonstrates how to increase the security level and to improve the storage capacity of hidden data, with compression techniques. The security level is increased by randomly distributing the text message over the entire image instead of clustering within specific image portions. The degradation of the images can be minimized by changing only one least significant bit per color channel for hiding the message. Using steganography alone with simple LSB has a potential problem that the secret message is easily detectable from the histogram analysis method. To improve the security as well as the image embedding capacity indirectly, a compression based scheme is introduced. Various tests have been done to check the storage capacity and message distribution.

Karim Saheb Ettabaa, Ensi University, Tunisia
Manel Ben Salem, IsitCom, Tunisia

In this chapter we are presenting the literature and proposed approaches for anomaly detection in hyperspectral images. These approaches are grouped into four categories based on the underlying techniques used to achieve the detection: 1) the statistical based methods, 2) the kernel based methods, 3) the feature selection based methods and 4) the segmentation based methods. Since the first approaches are mostly based on statistics, the recent works tend to be more geometrical or topological especially with high resolution images where the high resolution implies the presence of many materials in the same geographic area that cannot be easily distinguished by usual statistical methods.

Piyush Kumar Shukla, UIT RGPV, India
Madhuvan Dixit, Millennium Institute of Technology and Science, India

Current image coding with image fusion schemes make it hard to utilize external images for transform even if highly correlated images can be found in the cloud. To solve this problem, we explain an approach of cloud-based image transform coding with image fusion methodwhich is distinguish from exists image fusion method. A fast and efficient image fusion technique is proposed for creating a highly generated fused image through merging multiple corresponding images. The proposed technique is based on a two-scale decomposition of an image into a low layer containing large scale variations, and a detail layer acquiring small scale details. A novel approach of guided filtering-based weighted average method is proposed to make full use of spatial consistency for merge of the base and detail layers. Analytical results represent that the proposed technique can obtain state-of-the-art performance for image fusion of multispectral, multifocus, multimodal, and multiexposure images.

Section 2
Pattern Recognition, Watermarking and Face Recognition

Chapter 9

Swaptik Chowdhury, VIT University, India
Pratik Goyal, VIT University, India
R. Hariharan, VIT University, India
Pijush Samui, VIT University, India

This article adopts Minimax Probability Machine (MPM) and Extreme Learning Machine (ELM) for prediction of stability status of rock slope. The proposed MPM and ELM models use unit weight (γ), cohesions (cA) and (cB), angles of internal friction (ϕA) and ϕB, angle of the line of intersection of the two joint-sets (ψp), slope angle (ψf), and height (H) as input parameters. For this chapter the determination of stability of rock slope has been adopted as classification problem. The developed MPM and ELM have been compared with each other. The results of this article shows that the developed MPM is robust model for prediction of stability status of rock slope.

Chapter 10

Suranjan Ganguly, Jadavpur University, India
Debotosh Bhattacharjee, Jadavpur University, India
Mita Nasipuri, Jadavpur University, India

Although, automatic face recognition has been studied for more than four decades; there are still some challenging issues due to different variations in face images. There are mainly two categories of face recognition based on acquisition procedure. One technology that deals with video based face recognition and another approach where different sensors are used for acquisition purpose of different stationary face images, for instance: optical image, infra-red image and 3D image. In this context, researchers have focused only on 3D face images. 3D face images convey a series of advantages over 2D i.e. video frame, optical as well as infra-red face images. In this chapter, a detailed study of acquisition, visualization, detail about 3D images, analyzing it with some fundamental image processing techniques and application in the field of biometric through face registration and recognition are discussed. This chapter also gives a brief idea of the state of the art about the research methodologies of 3D face recognition and its applications.

#### Chapter 11

Research emphasizes in face recognition has shifted towards recognition of human from both still images and videos which are captured in unconstrained imaging environments and without user cooperation. Due to confounding factors of pose, illumination, image quality, and expression, as well as occlusion and low resolution, current face recognition systems deployed in forensic and security applications operate in a semi-automatic manner. This book chapter presents a comprehensive review of face recognition approaches in unconstrained environment. The objective of this book chapter is to address issues, challenges and recent advancement in face recognition algorithms which may help novel researchers to do innovative research in unconstrained environment. Finally, this chapter provides the stepping stone for future research to unveil how biometrics approaches can be deployed in unconstrained face recognition systems.

Advances in technologies facilitate the end users to carry out unauthorized manipulation and duplication of multimedia data with less effort. Because of these advancements, the two most commonly encountered problems are (1) copyright protection and (2) unauthorized manipulation of multimedia data. Thus a scheme is required to protect multimedia data from those two above said problems. Digital Watermarking is considered as one of the security mechanisms to protect copyrights of multimedia data. The literature review reveals that the calculation of scaling and embedding parameters are not completely automated. In order to automate the procedure of calculating scaling and embedding parameters the computational intelligence need to be incorporated in the watermarking algorithm. Moreover the quality of the watermarked images could also be preserved by combining computational intelligence concepts. Thus watermarking schemes utilizing computational intelligence concepts could be called as intelligence based watermarking schemes and it is presented in this chapter in detail.

#### Chapter 13

The feature extraction is the process to represent raw image in a reduced form to facilitate decision making such as pattern detection, classification or recognition. Finding and extracting reliable and discriminative features is always a crucial step to complete the task of image recognition and computer vision. Furthermore, as the number of application demands increase, an extended study and investigation in the feature extraction field becomes very important. The goal of this chapter is to present an intensive survey of existing literatures on feature extraction techniques over the last years. All these techniques and algorithms have their advantages and limitations. Thus, in this chapter analysis of various techniques and transformations, submitted earlier in literature, for extracting various features from images will be discussed. Additionally, future research directions in the feature extraction area are provided.

Section 3
Bio Imaging and Applications

Chapter 14

Shrinivas D. Desai, B. V. B. College of Engineering and Technology, India
Linganagouda Kulkarni, Vivekanand Institute of Technology, India

Metallic implants are known to generate bright and dark streaking artifacts in x-ray computed tomography (CT) images. These artifacts cause loss of information, reduces the resolution, forms noise which hinders diagnostic capability. The reduction of metal artifact is of immense importance in the present scenario. We propose seeded watershed segmentation-interpolation based sinogram correction method to reduce the metal artifacts caused by metallic implants. We tend to find projection bins affected by the metallic objects in the raw projection data and to replace the corrupted values by appropriate estimates. The novelty of proposed method lies in segmentation of metal part from the CT image by seeded watershed segmentation method, using IlastiK tool. Proposed method is experimented using dataset pertaining to different clinical cases. Solution is studied for correctness by quantitatively as well as qualitatively. The result presents significant improvement in artifact reduction aiding to better diagnostic ability.

Chapter 15

Shiwangi Chhawchharia, Vellore Institute of Technology, India
Subrajeet Mohapatra, Birla Institute of Technology Mesra, India
Gadadhar Sahoo, Birla Institute of Technology Mesra, India

Light microscopic examination of peripheral blood smear is considered vital for diagnosis of various hematological disorders. The objective of this paper is to develop a fast, robust and simple framework for blood microscopic image segmentation which can assist in automated detection of hematological diseases i.e. acute lymphoblastic leukemia (ALL). A near set based clustering approach is followed for color based segmentation of lymphocyte blood image. Here, a novel distance measure using near sets has been introduced. This improved nearness distance measure has been used in a clustering framework for achieving accurate lymphocyte image segmentation. The nearness measure determines the degree to which two pixels resemble each other based on a defined probe function. It is essential as image segmentation is considered here as a colour based pixel clustering problem. Lymphocyte image segmentation algorithm developed here labels each pixel into nucleus, cytoplasm or background region based on the nearness measure.

Chapter 16

Tripti Rani Borah, Gauhati University, India
Kandarpa Kumar Sarma, Gauhati University, India
Pranhari Talukdar, Gauhati University, India

In all authentication systems, biometric samples are regarded to be the most reliable one. Biometric samples like fingerprint, retina etc. is unique. Most commonly available biometric system prefers these samples as reliable inputs. In a biometric authentication system, the design of decision support system is critical and it determines success or failure. Here, we propose such a system based on neuro and fuzzy system. Neuro systems formulated using Artificial Neural Network learn from numeric data while fuzzy based approaches can track finite variations in the environment. Thus NFS systems formed using ANN and fuzzy system demonstrate adaptive, numeric and qualitative processing based learning. These attributes have motivated the formulation of an adaptive neuro fuzzy inference system which is used as a DSS of a biometric authenticable system. The experimental results show that the system is reliable and can be considered to be a part of an actual design.

Chapter 17

Narendra Kumar Kamila, C. V. Raman College of Engineering, India
Pradeep Kumar Mallick, St. Peter's University, India

Fruit and vegetables market is getting highly selective and requiring their suppliers to distribute the fruits of high standards of quality and good appearance. So the growing need to supply quality fruits within a short period of time has given rise to development of Automated Grading of fresh market fruits. The objective of this chapter is to classify apples into three grades based on its attributes such as color, size and weight. Initially apple image database is created. Next each image is analyzed using image processing software where images are first preprocessed and useful features like color and size are extracted from the images. Fuzzy logic is used for classification. Color, size features are represented as a fuzzy variables which are used for classification. The apples of different classes are graded into three grades viz. Grade1, Grade2 and Grade3 on the basis of combination of parameters mentioned above.

Chapter 18

Yugal Kumar, Birla Institute of Technology, India
Gadadhar Sahoo, Birla Institute of Technology Mesra, India

This chapter presents a charged system search (CSS) optimization method for finding the optimal cluster centers for a given dataset. In CSS algorithm, while the Coulomb and Gauss laws from electrostatics are applied to initiate the local search, global search is performed using Newton second law of motion from mechanics. The efficiency and capability of the proposed algorithm is tested on seven datasets and compared with existing algorithms like K-Means, GA, PSO and ACO. From the experimental results, it is found that the proposed algorithm provides more accurate and effective results in comparison to other existing algorithms.

Chapter 19

The explosive growths in data exchanges have necessitated the development of new methods of image compression including use of learning based techniques. The learning based systems aids proper compression and retrieval of the image segments. Learning systems like. Artificial Neural Networks (ANN) have established their efficiency and reliability in achieving image compression. In this work, two approaches to use ANNs in Feed Forward (FF) form and another based on Self Organizing Feature Map (SOFM) is proposed for digital image compression. The image to be compressed is first decomposed into smaller blocks and passed to FFANN and SOFM networks for generation of codebooks. The compressed images are reconstructed using a composite block formed by a FFANN and a Discrete Cosine Transform (DCT) based compression-decompression system. Mean Square Error (MSE), Compression ratio (CR) and Peak Signal-to-Noise Ratio (PSNR) are used to evaluate the performance of the system.

Foreword

Image Processing and Pattern Analysis are the two areas in applied science that have become almost indispensable in modern day to day life. The application areas are many. Use of images in medicine for diagnostic purpose is well known. Remote sensing through satellite images, biometric authentication through face and finger print recognition, video surveillance, visual inspection, automated navigation, gesture recognition and anomaly detection etc. are only to name a few. All these applications use images or sequences of images in the form of video as inputs. In most of the applications the raw input image or the image sequence is processed to have an intermediate representation, mostly symbolic, before it can be used for understanding the content of the images or video sequences. That is where the theory of learning and recognition comes into picture.

In all these applications determining the authenticity of the input data, image or video, is very essential. Also some of the critical applications may require secrecy of the image/ video data to be maintained while transmitting from one place to another. This demands watermarking as well as data hide to be effective.

Handbook of Research on Emerging Perspectives in Intelligent Pattern Recognition, Analysis, and Image Processing provides a valuable insight into the science of image data analysis as well as content recognition. The chapters contributed by various authors and classified into three different subsections, namely Image Processing and Computer Vision, Pattern Recognition, Watermarking and Face Recognition, and Bio-Imaging and Applications describe the employed techniques from the basics. I believe that the book will not only motivate the beginners in the Image Processing and Pattern Recognition domain but will act as a handbook to the researchers.

P. K. Biswas
IIT Kharagpur, India

Preface

The topic of image processing and pattern analysis plays a vital role in engineering science. Without research, technology does not carry any meaning. Similarly, without information and engineering the word "grow" has no existence in every field of life. Technology makes life better and smoother. To achieve that objective we have to value the potential global contribution of our researchers. Every day new inventions are coming to limelight enriching human life. The above topic is interrelated. Hence, our endeavor is to capture new inventions and present those to cater to the demands of global scientists and human beings at large.

It gives me a great sense of pleasure to introduce this collection of chapters to the readers of the book series *Emerging Perspectives in Intelligent Pattern Recognition, Analysis, and Image Processing.* In computer science perspective, the core of imaging science includes three intertwined computer science fields, namely: pattern recognition, image processing and computer vision. This book covers the emerging trends in these three important areas.

This book discusses the advances of image processing and pattern analysis. Moreover it aims to address how new innovation will cater to the demands of human beings and how it will help them in daily life. For example: images are already in use in card-less ATM transactions. The chapters included in this book entitled *Handbook of Research on Emerging Perspectives in Intelligent Pattern Recognition, Analysis, and Image Processing"* encompass different aspects of recent image processing and pattern analysis innovations, ranging from mobile image tracking, motion picture analysis, image data mining, warehousing, pattern classification, mobile image classification, real time application, 3D image, supporting routing protocol, advance networking for communication of multimedia image, operating system to process such image, supporting hardware architecture, brain computer interface, image restoration, segmentation and enhancement and other related topics. Additionally, the book will explore the impact of such technologies on the day to day lives.

The objective of this book is to bridge the existing gap in literature and comprehensively cover the system, processing and application aspects of both pattern recognition and image processing. Due to rapid developments in specialized areas of pattern recognition and image processing, this book takes on the form of a contributed volume where well known experts address specific research and application problems. It presents the state of the art as well as the most recent trends both in coverage and applications. It serves the needs of different readers at different levels. It can be used as stand-alone reference for masters, researchers and practitioners. For example, the researcher can use it as an up-to-date reference material since it offers a broad survey of the relevant literature. Finally, practicing engineers may find it useful in designing and implementing various pattern recognition and image processing tasks.

Pattern recognition (or pattern classification) can be defined as a process of generating a meaningful description of data and a deeper understanding of a problem through manipulation of a large set of primitive and quantifying data. The set inevitably includes image data. As a matter of fact, some of the data may come directly after the digitization of a natural image. Some of that large data set may come from statistics, documents or graphics and some are eventually expected to be in visual form. Preprocessing of these data is necessary for error corrections, for image enhancement, and for their understanding and recognition. Preprocessing operations are generally classified as low level operations while pattern recognition including analysis, description and understanding of the image (or the large data set) belongs to high level processing. The strategies and techniques chosen for the low and high level processing are interrelated and interdependent. Appropriate acquisition and preprocessing of the original data would alleviate the effort of pattern recognition to some extent. For a specific pattern recognition task we frequently require a special method of acquisition of data and its processing. However, visual experience is the principal way through which humans sense and communicate with the world around them. We are visual beings and images are increasingly made available to us in electronic digital format via digital cameras, the internet and hand held devices with large format screens. Despite much of the technology introduced in the consumer market, digital image processing remains a hot topic and promises to be one for a very long time. Of course, digital image processing has been around us for a while and indeed, its methods pervade nearly every branch of science and engineering.

However, images are not self-explanatory. Their interpretation requires professional skill that has to grow with the number of different imaging techniques. Many case reports and scientific articles about the use of images in diagnosis and therapy administration bear witness to this. The task of computer science has been, and still is, the quantification of information in the images by supporting the detection and delineation of structures from an image or from the fusion of information from different image sources. Image processing is a rapidly growing field that deals with the manipulation of an image for the purpose of either extracting information from the image or producing an alternative representation of the image. Image analysis includes modeling and analysis of the original image itself (i.e. from image space analysis to different methods to represent the image). Some of the tools used in image analysis include spectral analysis, wavelets, statistics, level-sets, rough sets, fuzzy logic and partial differential equations. On the other hand, image processing is useful in modifying the original image to improve the quality or to extract information from the given image, for example, image restoration, compression, segmentation, shape, and texture analysis. There are the two twin fields that are directly connected to image processing in contemporary computer science. In the field of these techniques enable us vision to the reconstruct 3D world from the observed 2D images and through computer graphics do the opposite i.e. designing suitable 2D scene images to simulate our 3D world. Image processing can be considered the crucial between vision and graphics.

This book purports to serve as a research reference book in the area of pattern recognition and image processing by providing useful cutting edge research information to the students, researchers, scientists, engineers and other working professionals in this area. The book provides the latest research trends and concepts to develop new methodologies and applications in the area of image representation and reconstruction and bio applications. In addition, the book also incorporates chapters related to new challenging application area of pattern recognition and image processing. Above all, each and every chapter is designed in such a way as to incorporate the latest literature review, methods and models, implementation, experimental results, performance analysis, conclusion, future work and the latest relevant references.

Pattern recognition and image processing can be applied in diverse areas to solve existing problems. This is one of the major reasons behind the subject growing so fast. The other important reason behind the quick development of this discipline is the need for solutions to practical problems.

Theory and applications are both important in pattern recognition as well as image processing. They are treated equally well in this book on a pragmatic basis. Here different types of problems of scientists and engineers are addressed concerning pattern recognition and image processing scientists and engineers. The book comprises chapters contributed by highly qualified and diverse group of authors.

It is my pleasure to present this book which includes selected chapters of internationally recognized authors on Pattern recognition, image processing and analysis. The book is intended to provide a forum for researchers, educators and professionals to share their discoveries and innovative practices with others and to explore future trends and applications in the field of pattern recognition, analysis and image processing. However, this book will also provide a forum for dissemination of knowledge on both theoretical and applied research on the above areas with an ultimate aim to bridge the gap between these coherent disciplines of knowledge. This forum accelerates interaction between the above bodies of knowledge, and fosters a unified development in the next generation pattern recognition and image processing.

The broad spectrum of this book includes the topics but not limited to:

- Mobile image tracking
- Motion picture analysis
- Image data mining, warehousing
- Pattern classification
- Pattern recognition, face recognition
- Shape, range and motion analysis
- Mobile image classification
- Real time application
- 3D image
- Supporting routing protocol
- Advance networking for communication of multimedia image
- Operating system to process such image
- Supporting hardware architecture
- Brain computer interface
- Image restoration
- Segmentation and enhancement
- Multisensory data fusion
- AI application in computer vision
- 3D vision and perception
- Signal or image processing
- Parallel computer vision
- Signature verification
- Medical imaging
- Image matching
- Cognitive vision
- Wireless sensor network application on image processing
- And related topics

ORGANIZATION OF THE BOOK

This edited book entitled *Emerging Perspectives in Intelligent Pattern Recognition, Analysis, and Image Processing* provides an overview of recent research developments in the field of pattern recognition and image processing and related applications. This book contains 19 chapters arranged under three sections, namely, section 1: Image Processing and computer vision, section 2: Pattern Recognition, watermarking and face recognition and Section 3: Bio Imaging and Applications.

Section 1: Image Processing and Computer Vision

The first chapter entitled "Image Data Mining Based on Wavelet Transform for Visualization of the Unique Characteristics of Image Data" by Belay et al. has proposed techniques to optimize and characterize the unique feature of image retrieval, which is fundamental to optimize informative mathematical representation of image objects. The authors who introduced a novel method for image database analysis under different scenarios that foster the widely access of image data are discussed in detail.

The authors of second chapter entitled "Total Variation Applications in Computer Vision" have presented a concise overview of regularization and explained the role of a particular type of regularization called total variation norm (TV-norm) in computer vision tasks. They have set up a brief discussion on the mathematical background of TV methods and established a relationship between models and a few existing methods to solve problems cast as TV-norm.

The 3rd chapter is based on Vision Enhancement in Bad Weather. Better visibility is a key requirement for passengers in bad weather. The authors have discussed different weather conditions and done a classification of fog with a comparative analysis for application point of view. Moreover, they have focused on enhancement of visibility for a degraded image due to heavy fog using computer vision method.

In contrast, in Chapter 4 the authors have proposed a distributed low-cost smart camera system to detect abnormal events by analyzing the sequential behaviors of a group of people using machine learning techniques. Moreover, this system employs a multi-camera collaboration strategy to perform collective decision making for event recognition. Their experimental results confirm the reliability and stability of the proposed system in event recognition.

Chapter 5 entitled "A Review of the State-of-the-art Algorithms for Impulse Noise Filtering" attempts to throw sufficient light on the advancement in the field of image processing by illustratively describing existing state-of-the-art filtering techniques along with their capability of denoising impulse noises.

In chapter 6, the authors have demonstrated how to increase the security level and how to improve the storage capacity of hidden data with compression techniques. The security level is increased by randomly distributing the text message over the entire image instead of clustering within specific image portions.

In Chapter 7 Karim et al. have discussed an over view on anomaly detection in hyper spectral images. The overview presents statistical methods, kernel based methods, feature selection based methods and segmentation based methods for detection. These works tend to be more geometrical or topological especially with high resolution images where the high resolution implies the presence of many materials in the same geographic area that cannot be easily distinguished by usual statistical methods.

Chapter 8 presents Cloud Based Image Fusion Using Guided Filtering. A fast and efficient image fusion technique has been proposed for creating a highly generated fused image by merging multiple corresponding images. The proposed technique is based on a two-scale decomposition of an image into a low layer containing large scale variations, and a detail layer acquiring small scale details. Their analytical results demonstrate that the proposed technique can obtain state-of-the-art performance for image fusion of multispectral, multifocus, multimodal, and multiexposure images.

Section 2: Pattern Recognition, Watermarking, and Face Recognition

Chapter 9 discusses Minimax Probability Machine (MPM) and Extreme Learning Machine (ELM) for prediction of stability status of rock slope. The authors have considered determination of stability of rock slope as a classification problem. It is observed from their presentation and analysis that developed MPM is a robust model for prediction of stability status of rock slope.

Whereas Chapter 10 presents 3D Image acquisition and analysis of a range face images for registration and Recognition. In this chapter, the authors have made a detailed study of acquisition, visualization, 3D images, analyzing it with some fundamental image processing techniques and application in the field of biometric through face registration and recognition. This chapter also gives a brief idea of the state of the art about the research methodologies of 3D face recognition and its application.

In Chapter 11 the authors have presented a comprehensive review of face recognition approaches in unconstrained environment. The objective of this chapter is to address issues, challenges and recent advancement in face recognition algorithms which may help new researchers to do innovative research in unconstrained environment.

However, Chapter 12 presents Intelligence based adaptive digital watermarking for images in wavelet transform domain. In this chapter intelligence based watermarking schemes have been discussed in detail.

Chapter 13 tells us about the fundamental concepts on feature extraction. The goal of this chapter is to present an intensive survey of existing literature on feature extraction techniques over the last years. All these techniques and algorithms have their advantages and limitations.

Section 3: Bio Imaging and Applications

In Chapter 14 the authors have discussed the technology behind the topic entitled "Metal Artifact Reduction - A Problem of Tremendous Importance in Medical Imaging". They have proposed seeded watershed segmentation-interpolation based sinogram correction method to reduce the metal artifacts caused by metallic implants with an objective to find projection bins affected by the metallic objects in the raw projection data and to replace the corrupted values by appropriate estimates.

But the objective of Chapter 15 is to develop a fast, robust and simple framework for blood microscopic image segmentation which can assist in automated detection of hematological diseases i.e. acute lymphoblastic leukemia (ALL).

Also, Chapter 16 tells us about biometric identification system using neuro and fuzzy computational approaches. In a biometric authentication system, the design of decision support system is critical and it determines success or failure. But the authors have proposed such a system based on neuro and fuzzy system. The authors have performed experiment and found their system working well in a secure manner.

Chapter 17 deals with fuzzy logic classifier for classification and measurement of apple fruits. It is a kind of automatic system by which apples are classified into different grades.

Similarly, Chapter 18 presents a charged system search (CSS) optimization method for finding the optimal cluster centers in a given dataset.

And finally Chapter 19 concludes and talks about Learning Aided Digital Image Compression Technique for Medical Application. Learning systems like. Artificial Neural Networks (ANN), etc. have established their efficiency and reliability in achieving image compression.

This comprehensive and timely publication aims to be an essential reference source, building on the available literature in the field of image processing and pattern analysis to boost further research in this dynamic field. It is hoped that this text will provide the resources necessary for technology developers, scientists and policymakers to adopt and implement new inventions across the globe.

In short, I am very happy both with the experience and the end product of our sincere efforts. It is certain that this book will continue as an essential and indispensable resource for all concerned for some years to come.

Narendra Kumar Kamila
C. V. Raman College of Engineering, India

Acknowledgment

The editor would like to acknowledge the help of all the people involved in this project and, more specifically, to the authors and reviewers that took part in the review process. Without their support, this book would not have become a reality.

First, the editor would like to thank each one of the authors for their contributions. My sincere gratitude goes to the chapter's authors who contributed their time and expertise to this book. They are all models of professionalism, responsiveness and patience with respect to my cheerleading and cajoling. The group efforts that created this book is much larger, deeper and of higher quality than any individual could have created. Each and every chapter in this book has been written by a carefully selected distinguished specialist, ensuring that the greatest depth of understanding be communicated to the readers. I have also taken time to read each and every word of every chapter and have provided extensive feedback to the chapter authors in seeking to make the book perfect. Owing primarily to their efforts I feel certain that this book will prove to be an essential and indispensable resource for years to come.

As editor I would like to thank the pattern recognition and image processing community for recognizing the quality, effort and care that has been made (by many) in creating such a successful, wonderful and useful product.

Second, the editor wishes to acknowledge the valuable contributions of the reviewers regarding the improvement of quality, coherence, and content presentation of chapters. Most of the authors also served as referees; we highly appreciate their double task.

Last but not least the editor would like to thank all members of IGI Global publication for their timely help; constant inspiration and encouragement with friendly support make me able to publish the book in time.

Narendra Kumar Kamila

C. V. Raman College of Engineering, India

Section 1
Image Processing and Computer Vision

Chapter 1

Image Data Mining Based on Wavelet Transform for Visualization of the Unique Characteristics of Image Data

Gebeyehu Belay Gebremeskel
Chongqing University, China

Zhou Shangbo
Chongqing University, China

Yi Chai
Chongqing University, China

Su Xu
Chongqing University, China

ABSTRACT

Mining techniques can play an important role in image decomposition, segmentation, classification and retrieval systems. As image data become more complex and growing at a fast pace, searching valuable information and knowledge implicit become more challenging than ever before. In this chapter, authors proposed a WT based DM techniques to optimize and characterize the unique feature of image retrieval, which is fundamental to optimize informative mathematical representation of image objects. Many software, including data exploratory tools such as DM packages contain fast and efficient programs that perform WT. Wavelets have quickly gained popularity among scientists and engineers, both in theoretical research and in applications. The authors discussed in details and introduced a novel method for image database analysis in different scenarios that foster the wide access of image data.

1. INTRODUCTION

Data Mining (DM) is a process of automatically extracting novel, useful, and understandable patterns from a large collection of data. Over the past decade, this area has become significant in many fields naming from the retailer -marketing to DNA -bioinformatics. DM techniques involve diverse

dynamic and advanced tools, including wavelet to explore data sets as its nature and domain contexts (Jiawei, 2012). Wavelet theory could naturally play an important role in DM because it could provide data presentations that enable efficient and accurate mining process, which incorporated into the kernel for many algorithms. Standard wavelet applications are mainly powerful for

DOI: 10.4018/978-1-4666-8654-0.ch001

temporal-spatial data, which involves time-series, stream, and image data (Yu, Huang & Xia, 2012; Pimwadee, Aryya, George & Zhiyuan, 2011). It has been successfully applied to analyze large-scale image data using DM techniques. The approach is introducing a novel methodology how to reduce the amount of manual labor that usually comes with visualize and characterize big image data collections. With numeric and textual data, the techniques of extracting useful information from unstructured data have already been more or less established. However, with image-heavy datasets, processing methods such as object detection and text recognition are complex to be reliable and in most cases do not stand up to a comparison with a human doing the work.

Image mining is the process of searching and discovering valuable information and knowledge in large volumes of image data. It draws basic principles from Databases, Machine Learning (ML), Statistics, Pattern Recognition (PR) and 'soft' computing, which help to use Wavelet Transform (WT) based DM techniques enables a more efficient methods of the image data discrimination and analysis (Tao, Qi, Shenghuo & Mitsunori, 2002). However, image processing is one of those things people are still much better at than computers that use to know something new. Therefore, based on these two facts, we proposed WT based DM for visualization and characterization of the unique feature of image data. Besides DM algorithms, wavelet technique is growing importantly and having a lot of advantages that already exist numerous successful applications in image mining. The WT is syntheses of idea's computational methodologies are based orthonormal wavelet basis, which is fundamental to decompose, segments, extract and handling image data. WT based DM techniques, functions, or operators into different frequency components, the methodologies and image features' component with a resolution matched to its scale discussed in details.

The chapter is organized as first the introduction followed by section 2 about the related works, which focused on the facts and advancement of image DM in different approaches. It also includes image data managements and its attributes, segmentations, mining algorithms, distributed computing and others. In section 3, the wavelet technology, methodology and approaches are discussed. Section 4 discussed wavelet-based image annotations and measurements to visualize and characterize the detail and unique features of image data and mining techniques. In section 5, we present the summary of the chapter, which followed by the acknowledgment of the supporters of the chapter works and list of cited references.

2. A RATIONALE OF IMAGE DATA MINING

These days, image data are generated and collected in terabytes and petabytes, which are challenging to handle and analyze by traditional analytics tools. Such a huge amount of image data is generated in our daily life and each field, such as medical, satellite, all kinds of digital photographs images and others. These images involve a great number of useful and implicit information. The data types characterized by its volumes, variety, velocity … and complexity of image data that generated by the digital camera and video are unlabeled and difficult for users to discover. For example, manually annotating such a huge amount of image data is, time-consuming, laborious and prohibitively expensive (Xin, Lei, Xirong & Wei, 2007). To face the challenge, such as unlabeled online image resources, the proposed technique it is very important, which is capable and give clear insights to annotate and retrieve images based on their visual content. Therefore, WT-DM based image data synthesis is an automatic image processing and retrieval advanced techniques (Ritendra, Dhiraj, Jia & James, 2008; Mei, Shu, Min & Chengcui, 2004; Yong, Thomas & Shih, 1999).

Image mining is more than just an extension of DM to the image domain. It views as an inter-disciplinary endeavor that draws upon computer vision, image processing using ML, Artificial Intelligence (AI), database and others (Ramadass, 2011). Image mining classified into two categories. (i) The mining process involves domain-specific applications where the focus is to extract the most relevant image features into a form suitable for DM (Ruofei, Zhongfei & Sandeep, 2004). (ii) It involves general applications where the focus is to generate image patterns. The pattern helpful in the understanding of the interaction between high-level human perceptions of images and low-level image features (Matheus, Antonio, Camilo, Clement, Daniel & Marcio, 2012; Lakshmi, Sumathi & Hemalatha, 2011). In the conventional view, an image scene is more understood as a spatial configuration of objects, and its semantic recognition needs to find initially the objects and their exact locations, which represented as an object-based. In a realistic scenario, illuminate changes, dynamic backgrounds, and affine variation usually make object based image representation approach less effective. Region-based image representation approach represents image content by segmented image regions as well as their configuration relationships. However, the region based image representation also demanding reliable region segmentations (Yexi, Chang & Tao, 2011). Whereas, the context-based image representation approach is not capable, which limited as ignores most details, bypasses the traditional steps of segmentation-recognition and others.

The context-based image representation involves colors, textures, shapes, edges and other features statistics that describe the overall distribution of visual contents in images (Yong et al., 1999). The color components in RGB, HIS[1] or LUV[2] color space are used as color features; while Discrete WT (DWT) is used to extract texture features as showed Figure 1. The global image features (such as color and texture) are representing their spatial distributions as a mixture of Gaussians. However, it is also sensitive to the change of light, color and point of view (Pimwadee et al., 2011). Therefore, it cannot well represent the highly varied images in the real world. What's more, when the entire image is represented as a whole using global features, we will lose in touch with the specific characters of individual local structures in the image. The global image features suffer a significant information loss.

Figure 1. Image color characterization and visualization in terms of HIS and LUV

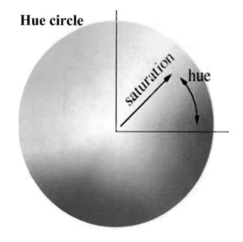
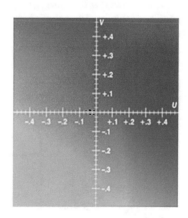

2.1. Image Data Management

The image data collection and the corresponding research work is challenging, which might be duplicated in the same object or vary in its natural scenes or other factors. Each of the images can have at least one occurrence of images contains to define object classes, such as 'person', 'animal', 'book' or others in the data sets. Such variations and heterogeneous character of image data made the data management is more complex and sensitive (Tao, Sheng & Mitsunori, 2010). As of any other data, image data can be also organized as training (training and validation data) and test data. The images of the training set manually annotated with the bounding boxes of all the occurrences of the collected object classes. In the data processing phase, noisy image data need to be amended or avoid by the human annotators. Image data preprocessing is the necessary because the real-world image data is noisy, incomplete and many times irrelevant. DM is the core components of KD processes that use various algorithms, which applies in various subject areas. Then the challenge objects will be left out while the data is preparing. The same process uses to testing data. In some case, manual Annotation of pixel-wise segmentation may be masks certain proportions of training images that need additional images as

training data for the segmentation taster competition (Adeel, Syed, Gilani, Kamran & Tahir, 2008).

Image data management concerns the specific mechanism and structures for how the data are accessed, stored and managed. It is a basic step to the implementation of DM systems that defines different structures for image mining techniques (Sanjay, Gandhe, Talel & Avinash, 2007). The process of this step is carried out for a particular keyword on the image navigations. The collection can be used to create an image database where images of a particular type can be separated (Tao et al., 2010). Then after, the KD using mining algorithms is exploring the data involving image learning, gathering and classification (Gebeyehu, He & Zhu, 2013$_a$). Image learning is a process about a particular category depending upon particular features of an image (Figure 2). The image gathering step (image acquisition) uses general search techniques used on the system that is keyword based and result in a collection of different images related to a particular search entered by the user. The image mining is needed because many time the real life scenes to classify a particular category or object classes. Image classification where some real-life scene/image provided as an input to the image mining tool. The process depends on the features of the image or the image matched with particular sets, which

Figure 2. Fundamental conceptual modeling of image processing workflow

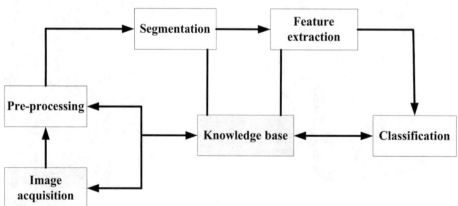

classified under a specified category for further actions (Geetha & Chitradevi, 2014; Maria, Osmar & Alexandru, 2001).

As it is shown in Figure 2 image data preprocessing is a subsequent and an important step to ensure the data quality and to improve the efficiency and ease of the mining process. The collected and generated image data tend to be incomplete, noisy, inconsistent, high, dimensional and multi-sensory, etc. and hence are not directly suitable for mining. Data preprocessing usually includes data cleaning to remove noise and outliers. Data integration is a process of multiple data/information sources fusion into a generic model to reduce the dimensionality and complexity of the data. Then after the data transformation performed to convert the data into proper forms for mining, etc., which followed by DM steps to develop data models or patterns (Adeel et al., 2008).

2.2. Image Data Objects and Attribute Types

Image objects are an entity of inline values or direct objects, and the indirect object is an object described by ID and a generation number and can be referenced by other objects. Images are stored in various formats, which includes JPEG Subset, EPS, GIF, PDF, PNG, and TIFF, and others. The data types are device-independent, and that can be used by different systems (Nishchol & Sanjay, 2012). Whereas, image attributes are features or variables of image data that representing a characteristic an entity visual qualities, which includes 'color', 'texture', or 'shape' and others. It provides understandable patterns of image segments, repeatedly sharing some characteristic properties. These can be any combination of appearance, view, or the layout of segments within the pattern. Moreover, attributes with general appearance are taken into account, such as the pattern of alternation of any two colors, which is characteristic for stripes. The unsegmented training image of the model is learned discriminate by

optimizing a likelihood ratio. Therefore, image or object's attributes described and categorized into different types. It Annotated as nominal (color, bland, red ...) or binary (1 or 0, male or female ...), ordinal (size of images -small, medium ...) and numeric (interval, ratio).

Object categories recognitions are vitally essential to computer vision and the adoption of techniques from DM, ML, AI ... and the development of better probabilistic representations (Michael, Charless, Joe Andre & Saleem, 1999). The goal has been to recognize object categories, such as car, book, tree or others. Moreover, image objects can also categorize in terms of image qualities such as color, size, and another way of descriptions. These visual attributes are important for understanding object appearance and for describing objects to other people. For example, Figure 3 shows such attributes. Automatic learning and recognition of attributes can complement category-level recognition and, therefore, improve the degree to which machines perceive visual objects. Attributes also open the door to appealing applications, such as more specific queries in image search engines (e.g. a spotted skirt, rather than just any skirt). Moreover, as different object categories often have attributes in common, modeling them explicitly allows part of the learning task, which shared among categories. It allows or learn from the past about an attribute transfer rate to a novel category, which help to reduce the total number of training images needed and improve robustness.

As it is shown on Figure 3, Object categories are visualized as diverse attributes. On the left, it showed simple attributes captured by individual image segments like color, size, and shape. Whereas on the right, more attributes in which qualified by basic image elements as binary, color, and others. The images broad range of attributes such as color (red, green, gray), complex (striped, checked), shape and pattern elements (single strip) are explicitly modeled. The pattern is along with their layout within the overall pattern (e.g. adjacent stripes are parallel). It enables our model to

Figure 3. Image objects and its attributes captured by individual image segments

cover attributes defined by appearance ('red'), by shape ('round'), or by both (the black-and-white stripes of zebras). Furthermore, the model takes into account attributes with general appearance, such as stripes, which characterized by a pattern of alternation ABAB of any two colors. 'A' and 'B' are rather than by a specific combination of colors. Since appearance, shape, and layout are modeling explicitly, the learning algorithm gains an understanding of the nature of the attribute.

2.3. Data Mining Based Image Segmentation

DM is a dynamic and ever growing field, which viewed as a result of the natural evolution of Information Technology (IT). The database and data management industry evolved in the development of several critical functionalities. Advances in image acquisition and storage technology have led to great growth in very large and detailed image databases. As Jiawei et, al. (2012) discussed "what Data Mining", it is the tool of Knowledge Discovering (KD) from large-scale data, which stored in alphanumeric relational databases. As the data growing fast, the analysis of nonstandard image data types become more challenging (Tao et al., 2002). The fundamental issue in image mining is how to preprocess image sets, so that represents to support the application of DM techniques and

algorithms. As well as knowing and identifying the image objects of interest is paramount, which is naming as to segmentation (Geetha & Chitradevi, 2014; Ramadass, 2011). Segmentation is the process of finding regions in an image that share some common attributes that require to support or enhance for many applications as the domain context and image data nature. A proper representation of an image feature is vectors, which each image vector represents some subset of feature values taken from some global set of features. A trivial example is where images are represented as primitive shape and color pairs as showed as follows:

{{blue square}, {red square}, {yellow square}, {blue circle}, {red circle}, {yellow circle}}

Subject to describe a set of images described as:

{{blue square}, {red square}, {red circle}}
{{red square}, {yellow square} {blue circle}, {yellow circle}}
{(red box}, {red circle}, {yellow circle}}

DM based image segmentation is the process of partitioning an image into homogeneous regions that are semantically meaningful with respect to some characteristic, such as intensity, texture of the image. Let the image '*I*' is segmented a cluster of 'C_j' whose union 'U' is the entire image 'I', defined as:

$$I = \bigcup_{j=1}^{n} C_j \qquad (2.1)$$

where, $C_j \cap C_k = \varnothing$ for $k \neq j$ and each C_j is connected, and 'n' is the number of clustering objects of interest. The basic of segmentation method finds those sets that correspond to distinct anatomical structures or regions that are of interest in the image. Segmentation is a process of subdividing an image into a set of homogeneous, disjointed regions. The subdivision is complete in the meaning that the process of each pixel must belong to one of the separated regions. The process approached by different techniques, and some of the methods discussed as follows (Nishchol & Sanjay, 2012).

2.3.1. Image Mining Methods and Models

Image mining method is the basic process of image analysis, which is essential to optimize performance searching or extracting valuable information from huge image data. Constrained nature and lack of the correct segmentation are the challenges of the methods, which need to dynamic and integrated techniques that proposed (Lamia & Alid, 2009; Bezdek, Hall & Klarke, 1993). Selection of one segmentation method over another depends on the type image that needs to be segmented, which lack a standard or universal method that applied to all types of images. Because of this facet's segmentation, the method can be categorized as threshold, regional, clustering or classifiers approaches and Markov random field model, artificial neural networks (Thomas & Daniel, 2010). Most of the image retrieval methods depend on the optimizations where the desired segmentation minimizes some energy or cost function, which defined by the domain contexts or applications. It is a computational maximizing of a likelihood or a posteriori probability in which a given image I, describe segmentation as:

$$\hat{X} = \arg\ \min_{x} \xi(X, Y) \qquad (2.2)$$

where ξ, the energy function depends on the observed image Y and a segmentation X. The sigmoid function ξ is challenging because of the image diverse properties that can be used, such as intensity, edges and texture as mentioned the above methods.

Modeling based image segmentation is also essential to demonstrate motivation and capability of the objects for multi-view and analysis, which representing as an object, deformable and other types of models. Model-based image mining or analysis process is dynamic and interesting for which a variety of methods have been developed. Such as the self-occlusive nature of a human body causing ambiguity from a single view. Such methods rely on a restricted dynamic model of behaviors, which can support to track an action or other features. For example, a human walking model will greatly help to predict and validate the posture estimates or elements of the body. Such as the color distribution maintained in the model is used to initialize segmentation of the object.

Deformable model based segmentation technique is a unique but also powerful approach to image analysis, which involves geometric, physic, and approximation theories. The technique is delineating region boundaries of a given image using closed parametric curves or surfaces that deform under the influence of internal and external factors. The image boundary process delineation is essential to allow for the interactive relaxation process. The internal forces are computed from the curve or surface to keep it smooth throughout the deformation. Whereas, the external forces are derived from the image towards the desired feature of interest. There are various deformable models is, which includes energy minimizing, dynamic, and probabilistic deformable model (Joanna & Joanna, 2013). Geometry serves to represent object shapes; physics imposes constraints on how the shape varied over space and time, and optimal approximation theory provides the formal mechanisms for fitting the models to measured data. According to its dynamic equations and seeks the minimum of a given energy function, which characterized as:

$$\mu(s)\frac{\partial^2 s(s,t)}{\partial^2 t} + \gamma(s)\frac{\partial x(s,t)}{\partial t} = F_{int} + F_{ext}$$

(2.3)

where, $X(s,t) = (x(s,t), y(s,t))$ is a parametric representation of the position of the model at a given time t, $\mu(s)$ and $\gamma(s)$ are parameters representing the mass density and damping density of the model, whereas F_{int} and F_{ext} are internal and external forces respectively. The deformable model is pertinent to generate closed parametric curves or surfaces from images and their inclusion of a smoothness constraint, but it also needs manual interaction to place an initial model and choose suitable parameters.

2.3.2. Image Segmentation

Image segmentation is, arguably, the most important domain of DM, which applied in the field of biomedical, astronomy, satellite, Earth science, and other fields of image data processing. Segmentation is concerned with both supervised and unsupervised techniques. The former require user interaction in which semi-automatic processing. The latter is the automated images processing into non-overlapping regions based on image's features and properties (Kelvin, Alexandre, Toga & Stott, 2014). The process is complex and needs more concerns and understanding to identify the intensity or boundary of images to diverse analyzes. Unsupervised classification technique is clustering approaches using various DM algorithms. It

includes k-means (KM), fuzzy c-means (FCM) and Expectation Maximization (EM) and others to reorganize the data based on their common behavior or similarities. The techniques are the well-known automatic tools for segmentation in many applications. Image segmentation (Ramadass, 2011; Bezdek et al., 1993) (more details in section-2.4) are capable to integrate with wavelet-based data analysis and algorithms.

Image segment extraction using wavelet-based DM algorithms are a fundamental of an attribute model. Each uniform segment's appearance detected in terms of color or shape or texture that derived from the original or typical object images. A segment is represented as a normalized graphic model over the patch types of the pixels; it contains. Based on the results, the segments can cluster that have common or similar representation of object image appearance of a subset of the segments from the training set (Figure 4). Each segment s assigned the appearance $a \in A$ with the smallest distance (Figure 4b). The appearances of various geometric properties of a segment measured from its summarized shape that curvedness, compactness, elongation (as Figure 4c), fractal dimension and area of the image. The two computed properties of pairs of segments also showed a relative orientation and area (as Figure 4d) (Gajjar1 & Chauhan, 2012).

As the Figure 4 is shown, the image with a few segments overlaid. It visualized the two pairs of adjacent segments in a striped region, and each row (b) is an entry from the appearance codebook followed by the three most frequent path types for each appearance displayed. The image segments are assigned to the white and black appearance. In (c & d) showed the geometric properties of the strips and segments in different measurement approaches. It is a generic image classification method and somewhat rudimentary, which can employ an area-based region merging approaches to constructing segments. The regions are homogeneous in terms of object's attributes such as

Figure 4. Image segmentation as visual image

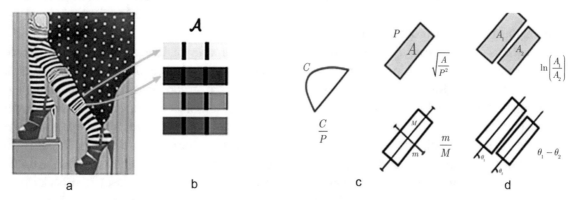

color and texture (Geetha & Chitradevi, 2014). The images in the database can be segmented by using various mining algorithms (section 2.4). The process is suitable for the analysis and understandable to users by having the intermediate segments, which considered as potential boundary box locations of each segmented image object.

2.3.3. Craquelure Approach Image Identification

Craquelure based image segmentation is the process of defining image features or characters by a similarity condition of the pattern, which is fundamental to define image formed of linear, continuous shapes, and patterns manually or automatically. Whereas, these approaches involved certain limitation. Such the manual method, the work is high, and for an automatic way, which leads to unwanted features of brush strokes, such as a canvas pattern detected (Joanna & Joanna, 2013). Therefore, if the data properly organized and annotated, query-based selection would be effective. The task of image identification consists in taking a given query image and finding out the original form. It is it possibly drives, together with any relevant metadata, such as titles, copyright information, authors, and others. Let say from a set of image I, a set of transformations T, and a

query image q, can be found the set of possible original images from which q derives $O = \{o_j\} \subseteq I$, such that:

$$\exists_t \in T: o_j = t(q) \tag{2.4}$$

In the case of multiple issues, the set of O will has exactly one element. It may be empty such as if there is no image on the set of I, which cannot originate q or if it can have many elements that need diverse transaction processes. Such as geometric transforms, photometric and colorimetric transforms that use for selection and oscillations noise, analogical/digital conversion and any other types (Tao et al., 2010). Therefore, craquelure is one of the several image segmentation techniques that focusing on image painting or intensity and image feature. It is essential to judge authenticity, artist's workshop as well as for monitoring the environmental influence on the condition of the painting (Irene, Christopher & Maricor, 2011). In this way, paintings are classified as qualitative in nature. A clear understanding of craquelure will help to build a better platform for conservators to identify the cause of damage. Thus, a proper tool for precise detection of the pattern is needed. The complex nature of the craquelure processing is a challenge to an automatic detection algorithm.

2.3.4. Retouch and Lose Segmentation

Image segmentation is a process of clustering images towards its similarity features and attributes, which involving various approaches (Sameer, Rangachar & Ramesh, 2002). The image data might be old, and noise such damaged or lost its part. In such case, a digital restoration, which refers to a set of methods of non-invasive simulation of recovering an original shape of a destroyed artwork, is paramount. The technique is divers as the situation and nature of the image data. Segmentation, inpainting, noise removal and color enhancement serve the purpose of producing a digitally restored image, which support a physical restoration process by applying retouch, craquelure or other methods. Therefore, a technique of retouch and lose image segmentation approach implemented to those images, which lost their originality (Joanna & Joanna, 2013). It is a process that is applying for images that are not clear or did not have original images. Such modification of the image in a way that is non-detectable to restore its original form or feature. It is the process of repainting old artist images for a better understanding and proper image segmentation tasks. The object of in painting is to reconstitute the missing or damaged portions of the work, to make it more legible and to restore its unity.

Retouches (fragments of the surface covered with a new paint layer) including craquelure are both secondary objects of an artwork, in the meaning; the artist didn't intend them in the original composition. Such as cracks appear as the canvas or would support the painting moves in response to changes in humidity and temperature. A precise segmentation of these objects from the background is a preliminary step and an important issue in a restoring process. Therefore, multispectral analysis of an object is a good extension allowing a better estimation of the state of preservation.

2.3.5. Segmentation by Threshold and Computational Morphology

In the process of image segmentation, a point transformation is a fundamental to intuitive and easy image group operations. The method of thresholding is, therefore, vitally essential to split pixels into subsets, defined by a single test related to the pixel value (Irene et al., 2011). In case there is only one threshold level that defines the border between two resulting classes (the background and the object) the process is called binarization. The threshold applied in many cases that might face challenges to non-uniform illumination the background as the feature of the image in which the threshold can be modified for the data types. A thresholding procedure is used to determine an intensity value, to segment the desired classes. It is the process of clustering all pixels with an intensity greater than the threshold into one class, and otherwise. Let the threshold image $g(x,y)$ of image $f(x,y)$ is defined as:

$$g(x,y) = \begin{cases} 1 & \text{iff } (x,y) \geq T \\ 0 & \text{iff } (x,y) < T \end{cases} \qquad (2.5)$$

where T is the selected threshold.

Image segmentation process is more dynamic and advanced to implement in different properties of the image. Such as segmentation method based on edge detection algorithms (Thomas & Daniel, 2010), watershed (Lamia & Alid, 2009), derivative-based filters (Yujin et al., 2012), and others. Regardless of the chosen method, pixels are classified as edge or non-edge according to the filter output. The regions do not separate by an edge allocated to the same category. The challenge of edge detection based segmentation is the discontinuity of the edges, which in worst cases implies that the entire image is flooded and annotated as one region. We may also apply region growing algorithms, which did not require any border lines defined in advance. Region growing is a segmentation technique that applied to groups' pixel or subgroup region into larger regions based on some predefined criteria for growth. The factors used for intensity information in the image based on a seed point region that can be growing by appending to each seed neighbors pixels on the predefined properties similarities. Thus, a starting point for each subset is needed and then an iterative process is run to expand the structure, according to the gradient of pixel values. As a result, the crucial factor of the method is a precise definition of the similarity condition.

The mathematical morphology is a method of image analysis based on a set theory that the topological gradient technique briefly discussed by (Lamia & Alid, 2009), which implemented to detect and restore image data. The image morphological operations are doing based on simple expanding (dilation) and shrinking (erosion) of the image. Erosion and dilation use in a variety of combinations. The methods lead to a more advanced result like skeletonization, boundary detection, and many pre- and post-processing techniques, especially edge thinning and pruning (Ramadass, 2011; Tao et al., 2002). Two very important transformations are opening (dilation of the erosion of a set A by a structuring element B) and closing (erosion over dilation). Opening removes small objects from the foreground (usually taken as the dark pixels) of an image, placing them in the background while closing removes small holes in the foreground. The primary application of morphology occurs in binary images though is also used on gray level images.

2.4. Core Image Data Mining Techniques and Algorithms

Image mining has become a vibrant research area due to speedy enhancement in the volume of digital image data sets. Advancements in image acquirement and storage technology have led to implausible growth in very large and detailed image databases, which demanding dynamic is analyzing tools to gain valuable information and knowledge implicit that can optimize decision precisions. It deals with the extracting inherent and embedded knowledge, image data relationship, or other patterns, which do not find in the images. Image mining is an interdisciplinary and challenging to reveal out how low-level pixel representation enclosed in a raw image or image sequence can be processed to recognize high-level image objects and relationship. DM algorithms are an essential to explore such a massive and complex data and image with data relationship or patterns (Xindong, Vipin, Ross, Joydeep, Qiang, Hiroshi et al., 2008). Image attributes are not directly visible to the user, which have been used to solve diverse problems, including target and object recognitions. Among various DM algorithms, few and core for image mining is discussed as follows.

DM techniques/algorithms are being applied for the analysis of data in a variety of fields. The process includes business and industries, medical imaging, bioinformatics, remote sensing, astronomy and others, which focused on the model development and pattern recognition (Yujin et al., 2012). DM algorithms are search procedures inspired by diverse techniques as the nature of the data and issue contexts. Because of these facts, DM is an agglomeration of many algorithms that can be used to optimize DM applications and performances (Xindong et al., 2008). The algorithms are implemented to solve the problem or challenge with an objective function, which is unique to each problem and must be supplied by the user. Thus, the different and core mining algorithms (which focused in this chapter) are included clustering, K-mean, EM, classification, association rules, genetic and evolutionary algorithms. DM algorithms use the same basic concepts, but differ in the way they encode the solutions, which support to search or extract the valuable outputs (pattern, information, knowledge) (Gebeyehu et al., 2013[a]).

2.4.1. Clustering Algorithm

Clustering and also segmentation algorithm is an unstructured technique, which did not need any training data that iterate between segmentation of the image and characterize the properties of each class. It is the process of partitioning a set of data objects (or observations) into subsets. It has been widely used in many applications such as image pattern recognition, Business Intelligence (BI), bioinformatics, security, etc. Suppose image data clustering based on the multi-resolution property of WT inspires the issues to consider algorithms that could identify clusters at different scales (Maya & Bhawani, 2011). Wavelet clustering of image data is a multi-resolution clustering approach for very large spatial databases. It represented in an n-dimensional feature space and the numerical attributes of a spatial object that represented by feature vector where each element of the vector corresponds to one numerical attribute (feature). Partitioning data space by a grid reduces the number of data objects while inducing only small errors. From a signal processing perspective, if the collection of objects in the feature space viewed as an n-dimensional signal, the high-frequency parts of the signal correspond to the regions of the feature space. It is a rapid change in the distribution of objects and the low-frequency of the n-dimensional signal, which has been high-amplitude corresponds to the areas of the feature space where the objects are concentrated (i.e., the clusters). Applying WT on a signal decomposes it into different frequency sub-bands. Hence to identify the clusters is then converted to find the connected components in the transformed feature space (Mei et al., 2004).

Moreover, application of wavelet transformation to feature spaces provides multi-resolution data representation and hence finding the connected components could be carried out at many resolution levels (Matheus et al., 2012). In other words, the multi-resolution property of WT enables the wavelet-based clustering algorithm could effectively identify arbitrary shape clusters at different scales with proper degrees of accuracy. A subset of a cluster, such as that objects in a cluster are similar to one another, yet dissimilar to objects in other clusters. In this context, diverse clustering algorithms generate various clustering on the same data set. Hence, clustering is useful in that it could lead to the discovery of previously unknown groups within the data. For example, the k-mean clustering algorithm is cluster unstructured data by iterative computing a mean intensity for each class and segmenting the image by classifying each pixel in the class with the closest mean. The Expectation-Maximization (EM) algorithm applies the same clustering principles with the underlying assumption, which the data follows a Gaussian Mixture Model (GMM) (Yong & Shuying, 2007). It iterates between computing the posterior probabilities and maximum likelihood estimates of the means, covariance, and mixing coefficients of the MM.

In image recognition, clustering can be used to discover groups or "subclasses" in image features or character recognition systems. Suppose we have a dataset of digits image, where each digit is labeled as 1, 2, 3, and so on. Note that there can be a large variance in the way in which people write the same digit. Take the number 2, for example. Some people may write it with a small circle at the bottom left a part, while some others may not. We can use clustering to determine subclasses for "2," each of which represents a variation on the way in which we use it. Using multiple models based on the subclasses can improve overall recognition accuracy. Clustering algorithms is a core components and pertinent to gain insight into the distribution of data, which foster to observe the characteristics of each cluster, and to focus on a particular set of clusters for further analysis. Alternatively, it may serve as a preprocessing step for other algorithms, such as characterization; attribute subset selection, and classification, which would then operate on the detected clusters.

2.4.2. K-Mean Algorithm

KM is the simplest unsupervised algorithms to generate proper classes or segments on given image data sets through iterative procedures to gain certain clusters. The algorithm is composed of the number of steps with a data set $x_i = 1, 2, ..., n$, and the iterative steps are:

Step 1: Initialize the centroids c_j, where $j = 1, 2, ..., k$

Step 2: Assign each data point to the group that has the closest centroid

Step 3: When all points assigned, calculate the positions of the k centroids

Step 4: Repeat Steps 2 and 3 until the centroids no longer move, which gain a separation of the data points into groups of the metric to minimize the computations.

This algorithm aims at minimizing an objective function, which is defined as:

$$J = \sum_{j=1}^{k} \sum_{i=1}^{n} \left\| x_1^{(j)} - c_j \right\|^2 \tag{2.6}$$

where, $\left\| x_1^{(j)} - c_j \right\|^2$ is a measure of intensity distance between a data point x_i and the cluster center c_j. The dissimilarity also measured by the Euclidean distance.

FCM utilizes the fuzzy theory, in which a fuzzy partitioning such that a data point belongs to all groups with different membership. It grades between 0 and 1 to classify into several classes at the same time but with a different degree. It is used in pattern recognition aiming to find cluster centers that minimize a dissimilarity (objective) function, and the objective function is defined as:

$$J_m = \sum_{j=1}^{k} \sum_{i=1}^{n} u_{ij}^m d_{ij} \tag{2.7}$$

where, $m \in [1, \infty]$ represents to a weighting exponent. $u_{ij} \in [1, 0]$ is the degree of membership x_i in the cluster j. x_i is the ith of d-dimensional measure data, c_j is the d-dimensional center of the cluster and d_{ij} is the Euclidean distance between i^{th} data point (x_i) and j^{th} centroid (c_j). The fuzzy partitioning is carried out through an iterative optimization of the objective function given in Equation 2.7, with the update of membership u_{ij} and the cluster centers c_j defined as:

$$u_{ij} = \frac{1}{\sum_{k=1}^{c} \left[\frac{d_{ij}}{d_{ik}} \right]^{\frac{2}{m-1}}} \tag{2.8}$$

$$c_j = \frac{\sum_{i=1}^{n} u_{ij}^m x_i}{\sum_{i=1}^{n} u_{ij}^m x_i} \tag{2.9}$$

The iteration of the algorithm will until the improvement of the objective function over previous iteration is below a threshold value, $\varepsilon \in [1, 0]$. Then after, the iteratively updating the cluster centers and the membership grades for each data point, FCM iteratively moves the cluster centers to the "right" location within a data set. The detail algorithms as (Yong & Shuying, 2007) presented:

Step 1: Randomly initialize the membership matrix $U = [u_{ij}]$, $U^{(0)}$ that has a constraint equation given by

$$\sum_{i=1}^{c} u_{ij} = 1, \forall j = 1, ..., n \tag{2.10}$$

Step 2: At k-step, calculate the centroids and objective function by using the Equations (2.9) and (2.7) respectively.

Step 3: Update U^k, U^{k+1} by using the Equation (2.8).

Step 4: If stopping criteria exist then stop; otherwise return to Step 2.

2.4.3. EM Algorithm

EM algorithm is used to find image segmentation based on modeling the image as a GMM. The algorithm is essential to model the dataset without prior knowledge of each image density and distributions. It utilizes the estimation theory (incomplete data) to estimate the missing data, which is represented as:

$$f(\mathrm{x}_i/\phi) = \sum_{k=1}^{K} p_k G(\mathrm{x}_i/\theta_k) \qquad (2.11)$$

where, k is the number of classes that need to be extracted from the image. $\theta_k \forall k = 1, 2, \ldots, K$ is a parameter vector and of its the form $[\mu_k, \sigma_k]$. Such that μ_k, σ_k are the mean and standard deviation of the distribution of k. p_k is mixing proportion of class k $(0<p_k<1, \forall k = 1\ldots K$ and $\sum_k p_k = 1)$, x_i is the intensity of the pixel i. $\phi = \{p_1\ldots p_k. \mu_1\ldots\mu_k. \sigma_1\ldots\sigma_k\}$ is the parameter vectors of a mixture of the missing data. The EM algorithm utilizes the maximum log-likelihood estimator (ϕ_{ML}) to estimate the value of ϕ, which pass to estimation and maximization algorithms steps.

1. The Expectation (E) step to compute the expected value of Z_{ik} using the current estimate of the parameter vector ϕ, which defined as:

$$Z_{ik}^{(t)} = \frac{p_k^{(t)}G(\mathrm{x}_i/\theta_k^{(t)})}{f(\mathrm{x}_i/\phi^{(t)})} \qquad (2.12)$$

where, Z_{ik} is the posterior probability that given x_i, which comes from class k. The posterior probability satisfies the constraints $(0\leq Z_{ik}\leq1$, $\sum Z_{ik}=1, \sum Z_{ik} > 0, 1\leq i\leq N, 1\leq k\leq K)$, x_i is the value of the pixel i $G(\mathrm{x}_i/\theta_k)$ is the probability of pixel i and is a member of the class k.

2. The maximization step that employ the data from the expectation step as if it were actually measured data, the computation is defined as:

$$\mu_k^{(t+1)} = \frac{\sum_{i=1}^{N} Z_{ik}^{(t)} x_i}{\sum_{i=1}^{N} Z_{ik}^{(t)}}. \qquad (2.13)$$

$$\sigma_k^{2(t+1)} = \frac{\sum_{i=1}^{N} Z_{ik}^{(t)}(\mathrm{x}_i - \mu^{(t+1)})^2}{\sum_{i=1}^{N} Z_{ik}^{(t)}} \qquad (2.14)$$

$$p_k^{(t+1)} = \frac{\sum_{i=1}^{N} Z_{ik}^{(t)}}{N} \qquad (2.15)$$

The fundamental procedure of EM computational, algorithmic equation for image segmentation represented as:

Step 1: The number of classes k and the image 'I' is provided by the system

Step 2: The initial estimation of the parameter $\phi^{(0)}$ is estimated based on the histogram of the image and the number of classes.

Step 3: Perform the E-step and M-step iteratively until convergence is reached in each iteration

14

of the E-step computes the class probability of each pixel based on the current estimation of $\phi^{(0)}$. M-step computes the new expectation of based on values computed in the previous E-step. After convergence, the maximum estimator of ϕ is produced.

Step 4: Use ML ϕ_{ML} as a classifier to generate the classification matrix C.

Step 5: Assign a label to each class based on the classification matrix C and generate the segmented image.

2.4.4. Classification Algorithms

A classification algorithm is a process to identify the characteristics that indicate the group to which each instance belongs. Classification based image pattern recognition is seeking to be a partition a feature space derived from the image using data with prior knowledge or known labels, which known as supervised methods that require training data of manually segmented. It can be used both to understand the existing data and to predict how new instances will behave. Wavelets can be very useful for image data classification tasks. The algorithms can be processed as the wavelet domain of the original data and as the multi-resolution property of wavelets. The techniques of classification used as references for automatically segmenting new data by applying various methods. Such as the (k)-Nearest Neighbor classifier where each pixel or voxel classified in the same class as a training data with the closest intensity (Bezdek et al., 1993). KNN classifier is a generalization of the nearest neighbor classifier, which support nonparametric classifier where the classification is carried out according to the majority vote within a predefined window of feature space centered at the unlabeled pixel intensity. Maximum Likelihood (ML) is the commonly used parametric classifier that the pixel intensities are independent samples from a mixture of probability distributions, and the mixture model is defined as:

$$f(\mathrm{y}_j;\theta,\pi) = \sum_{i=1}^{k} \pi_k f_k(\mathrm{y}_j;\theta_k) \qquad (2.16)$$

where, y_j is the intensity of pixel j, f_k is a component probability density function parameterized by θ_k and $\theta = (\theta_i...\theta_k)$. The variables π_k are mixing coefficients that weight the contribution of each density function and $\pi = (\pi_1...\pi_k)$. It is unlike the threshold non-iterative method, and it can be applied to many channels. Moreover, classification based image segmentation is the requirement of manual interaction for obtaining training data but long process. Other fundamental techniques of classification algorithms are rule-based systems, neural networks, and decision trees.

Rule-Based Systems representing concepts as sets of rules have long been popular in DM, which is easy to represent and humans can interpret the image segmentation properly. It is assigned a fitness value based on a reward returned by the environment. Rule based system classifier use as control systems in changing or uncertain environments, where there may not be sufficient or clear expert knowledge to produce a more conventional control. Artificial Neural Networks (ANN) vitally essential to search for the weights of the network, to identify appropriate learning parameters, or to reduce the size of the training set by selecting the most relevant features. ANN is a powerful technique to solve non-linearly separable problems by the network having at least one layer of the inputs and outputs. Therefore, the training an ANN is an optimization task with the goal of finding a set of weights that minimizes some error measure. The search space has many dimensions, and it is likely to contain multiple local optima. Decision trees are also another pertinent classifier of image data since it is easy to build and understandable to users or experts (Walid & Abdel, 2011). The internal nodes represent tests on the features that describe the data, and the leaf nodes represent the class labels. A path from the root node to one of the leaves represents a conjunction of tests. The trees are considered above used tests on a single attribute of the data. These tests are equivalent to hyperplanes that are parallel to one of the axes in the attribute space. Therefore, the resulting trees are called axis-parallel in which the trees are easy to interpret, but may be complex and inaccurate if the data is partitioned best by hyperplanes that are not axis-parallel.

2.4.5. Association Rules Algorithms

Association rule mining algorithm is a well-known DM algorithm that aims to find interesting patterns in very large-scale databases. Therefore, image mining process involves preprocessing, transformations and feature extraction, evaluation, and interpretation that demanding an association rule based searching valuable information and knowledge implicit in large image databases. However, the process is complex and challenging, which need multiple lines of code to read images. The method is capable to extract features that apply a mining algorithm, which demands a priori (Gajjar & Chauhan, 2012; Maria et al., 2001). Image association rule mining is a scripting language that allows defining a list of image source files. It is customizing association rule parameters, which the parameters include the number of terms, filters on text feature and configuration of signal features (i.e. color), support and confidence.

The computational methodology of an association rule is represented in the form A ⇒ B, which implies the presence of itemset A implies the presence of itemset B. An association rule algorithm discovers the rules that have supported and confidence larger than a specified threshold. Support of an association rule defined as the percentage of transactions that contains all items (both A and B –LHS and RHS[3]) in an association rule. The confidence of an association rule defined as the percentage of LHS items that contain RHS. LHS => RHS form with both LHS and RHS allowed containing multiple image features (color,

texture, edge …). An association rule holds if its support is greater than, minsup and confidence is greater than minconf. Both minsup and minconf are configurable that tell about the association between two or more items. The image data sets are supposed to process the raw image data into a form suitable for such analysis in three steps. (i) Image regions are labeled as perceptual synonyms using a visual thesaurus that is constructed by applying supervised and unsupervised DM techniques to low-level image features. The region labels are analogous to items in transaction databases. (ii) The orders of associations among regions with respect to a particular imagery predicate are tabulated using image features. (iii) The higher-order associations and rules are determined using an adaptation of the Apriori association rule algorithm.

An association rule tells about the association between two or more items. $U = \{u_1 \ldots U_N\}$ be set of items. A set 'A' is a K-itemset. If $A \subseteq U$ and $|A| = K.$, An association rule is an expression $A \Rightarrow B$, where A and B are itemsets that satisfy $A \cap B = \emptyset$. Let's D as a superset, i.e. $D = \{T \mid T \subseteq U\}$. Elements of database D are called transactions. Transaction $T \subseteq D$ supports an itemset A if $A \subseteq T$. Support of itemset-A overall database transaction T is defined as:

$$\text{supp}(A) = \frac{\left|\{T \in D \mid A \subseteq T\}\right|}{|D|} \qquad (2.17)$$

A priori algorithm discovers a combination of items that occur together with greater frequency than might be expected if the values or items were independent. A priori is a seminal algorithm for finding frequent itemsets of using candidate generation. The algorithm selects the most "interesting" rules based on their support and confidence. It characterized as a level-wise complete search algorithm using anti-monotonicity of itemsets, "if an itemset is not frequent, any of its superset is never frequent". Therefore, rule $A \Rightarrow B$ expresses that whenever a transaction T contains A, it probably contains B also. Thus, support and confidence measure statistical significance and strength of a rule is defined as Equations 2.18 and 2.19.

$$\text{supp}(A \Rightarrow B) = \frac{\left|\{T \in D \mid A \subseteq T \land B \subseteq T\}\right|}{|D|}$$

(2.18)

$$\text{conf}(A \Rightarrow B) = \frac{\left|\{T \in D \mid A \subseteq T \land B \subseteq T\}\right|}{\left|\{T \in D \mid A \subseteq T\}\right|}$$

(2.19)

2.4.6. Genetic or Evolutionary Algorithms

The process of extracting features that are relevant to the problem being addressed in DM is challenging and data-dependent (Manisha & Gajanan, 2014). In some types of data, the features are relatively easy to identify. For example, the features of text data the words in the text, and in the market-basket analysis are the items bought in a transaction and so on. Once the relevant features representing the data items have extracted, it is often helpful to reduce this set of features. In other cases, this task is more difficult such as in image data. In DM being applied to domains such as medical imaging, multi-media on the web, and video images, it is relevant that we have robust techniques to identify features representing an image. Since images tend to vary widely, even within a domain, the adaptive nature of evolutionary or Genetic Algorithms (GA), which exploited very effectively to address the important issues feature extraction in image data.

An image is a rectangular array of pixels, where each pixel has either a gray-scale value or a real value representing some physical quantity (Walid & Abdel, 2011). In image mining, the first task is

to identify an object in the image, which followed by extraction of features that represent the object. However, it is challenging about the conversion of the low-level representation (i.e., pixels) into a higher-level representation (i.e., objects). The two techniques that are traditionally used to identify an object in an image are segmentation, where the image is separated into several regions based on some desired criteria. The GA selects an initial set of parameters based on the statistics of an image along with the conditions under which the image was obtained such as time of day, cloud cover, etc. The performance is evaluated using multiple measures of segmentation quality that include both global characteristics of the image and local features of the object (Zobnin, Sergei & Sergei, 2011). The system is adaptive as a global population of images, their associated characteristics, and the optimal control parameters, is maintained and used to seed the population each time a new image is analyzed. This global population is also constantly updated with higher strength individuals. The method is used to identify the edge points using a filter whose parameters are optimized by a GA.

The GA approach fitness function is proportional to the degree of similarity between the contours generated by the GA and the contours identified in manually generated training examples. These filter and interpolation parameters are obtained for each new class of problems. Results on three-dimensional images show that the GA–based techniques are insensitive to significant changes in shape across a sequence of images. The inter- and intra-slice variability in the contours, thus illustrating the power of these techniques. The task of edge detection can also benefit from the use of evolutionary algorithms. Most edge detectors use simple first- and second-order derivatives to identify an edge. The methods of evolutionary algorithms to find an optimal set of parameters used for image registration, which points in one image maps to corresponding points in another image of the same scene taken under different conditions.

2.5. Distributed Image Data Mining Schema

The fundamental and advanced aspect of a new-generation DM is to be capable and scalable to handle, analyze and share the ever growing scientific and business datasets. It is the broad requirements of being able to deal with massive and distributed datasets. The integrity of services and applications is to solve the growing gap between the incremental data generation and users' understandability. It requires to know how to access, retrieve, explore, mine and integrate data from disparate sources. The Distributed Data Mining (DDM) method is a method to optimize DM application that can apply in a distributed systems. It is a technique to establish parallel and distributed applications of local model on each node and then combining these models together to form the global model (Gebeyehu, He Zhu, 2013b; Grigorios & Ioannis, 2009). Image DM takes place both locally at each distributed site, and at a global level where the local knowledge is fused to discover global knowledge. A typical

architecture of a DDM approach is depicted in Figure 5. The first phase normally involves the analysis of the local database at each distributed site. Then, the discovered knowledge is usually transmitted to a merger site, where the integration of the distributed local models is performed. The results are transmitted back to the distributed databases so that all sites become updated with the global knowledge (Nittir & Shamla, 2012).

As it is shown in Figure 5, the concept of DDM techniques pushes further and generalizes the principle as "summation form", which the data are divided into as many pieces as the system capabilities and allows to share the data. The individual results are finally aggregated to form the global result. The DM algorithms are pertinent to MapReduce modeling towards the local model that are broadcasted to all other sites so that each site can in parallel compute the global model. Distributed databases may have homogeneous or heterogeneous schemata. In the former case, the attributes describing the data are the same in each distributed database. Thus, it is is often the case when the databases belong to the same organization (e.g. local stores of a chain). In the latter case, the attributes are differed among the distributed databases. In certain applications, a key attribute might be present in the heteroge-

Figure 5. An architecture of distributed image data mining approaches

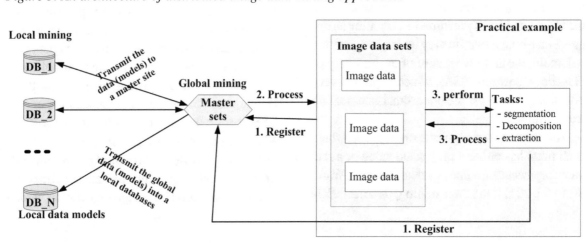

neous databases, which will allow the association between tuples. In other applications, the target attribute for prediction might be common across all distributed databases. Moreover, the orthogonal property of wavelet basis could play an important role in DDM since the orthogonally guarantees correct and independent local analysis that use as a building-block for a global model. The wavelets based distribution design and parallel algorithms are more efficient and capable, which optimize the localize processing a region of data with wavelet does not affect (Tao et al., 2002).

3. WAVELET TRANSFORM BASED IMAGE DATA MINING

The methods of image processing are dynamic and complex, which demanding advanced and scalable exploratory tools and methodologies. The technique encompasses image feature extractions, segmentations, recognitions, detections, classifications and others. Wavelet-based mining algorithms apply to all of these issues. The approach that wavelet integrated DM based data analysis provides an emerging and scalable tool for large-scale image data about a human visual system. The techniques perform a hierarchical edge detection at multiple levels of resolution processing (Maya & Bhawani, 2011; Zobnin et al., 2011) based on the continuous WT. It supports dynamic extractions from local features and training image datasets. The approach involves the process of extract useful information as a matrix of integers ranging from 0 to 255, which the values specify shades of gray with 0 being pure black and 255 pure white. The integers can be specified using 8 bits (1-byte) for each pixel (matrix element). Therefore, WT approach is a useful mathematical and computational tool for image data sets in diverse ways that are both efficient and theoretically sound (Kelvin et al., 2014; Gebeyehu et al., 2013b$_b$).

Image DM has become a significant area, including bioinformatics, astronomy, earth sci-

ence and GIS-RS spatial data, and others. It is the process of automatic extraction of the novel, useful and understandable patterns from a large collection of image data. Wavelet theory could naturally play an important role in DM since it is well founded and of very practical use. Wavelets have many favorable properties, such as vanishing moments, hierarchical and multi-resolution decomposition structure, linear time and space complexity of the transformations, décor-related coefficients, and a wide variety of basic functions. These properties could provide considerably more efficient and effective solutions to different image DM challenges. Wavelets could provide presentations of data that make the mining process more proper and accurate, which incorporated into the kernel of many image DM algorithms. Wavelets applications are mainly on data, which have temporal/spatial localities (e.g. time series, stream data, and image data). Wavelets have also been successfully applied to diverse domains in DM (Lakshmi et al., 2011). It is the dynamic process, which consists of a coarse overall approximation together with detail coefficients that influence the function at various scales of signal and image processing. WTbased mining processing is essential to gain a clear understanding and of the input relation obtaining compact data for further data segmentation and mining processes. The WT allows for concise and effective approximate representations that exploit the structure of the data. Furthermore, WT computed in linear time for very efficient algorithms.

3.1. Basics of Wavelet Transform

A wavelet for DM would have many attractable techniques. It includes the essential tasks of compact support, vanishing moments and dilating relation. The techniques support preferred properties such as smoothness and being a generator of an orthonormal basis of function spaces $L^2(R)$ (Sanjay et al., 2007). $L^2(R)$ is the space of square integral the real functions of the real line R. The compact support is the localization of wavelets or processing a region of data with wavelets, which does not affect the data out of this region. Vanishing moment is also a wavelet processing that can search the essential information, whereas, dilating relation leads fast wavelet algorithms. It is the requirements of localization, hierarchical representation and manipulation, feature selection, and efficiency in many tasks in DM that make wavelets be a very powerful tool. It is the ideas that emerged over years from various fields, such as mathematics and signal processing. WT is a tool that divides up data, functions, or operators into different frequency components and then studies each component with a resolution matched to its scale (Tao et al., 2010). Therefore, the WT is anticipated to provide economical and informative mathematical representation of many objects of interest. Wavelet approaches as a data analysis have gained popularity among scientists and engineers in various researches and applications. It has been widely applied to such computing and engineering issues involving image processing, computer vision, network management, and other DM techniques.

Furthermore, wavelets have generated a tremendous interest in both theoretical and applied areas. It has a novel approach to support large-scale image data processing. The image data processing and decomposing based on a signal into a set of "frequency bands" (scales), which projecting the signal on to an element of a set of basic functions or wavelets. The process is basis a similar approaches to each other and varying only by dilation and translation (Kelvin et al., 2014). As Tao et al. (2002) discussed, wavelets are convolution filters. It has a specific property such as Quadrature Mirror Filters (QMF) and high pass, etc. It is a function of many other factors as mentioned above (compact support …), which revealed how wavelet can be successfully applied to DM and other problem-solving matters. The wavelets can be used to create a family of time-

frequency, $\Psi_{s,u}(t) = s^{i/2}\Psi(st - u)$ via the dilation factor s and the translation u. The scaling function is defined as $\phi(t) \in L^2(R)$ where $\int_R \phi(t)dt \neq 0$. Wavelet function also defined as $\{\Psi_{j,k}(t) = 2^{j/2}\Psi(2^j t - k); j > L, k \in Z\}$ and the orthonormal basis of the wavelet is represented a signal function as $f(t) \in L^2(R)$.

$$\tilde{f}(t) = \sum_{k \in Z} c_{L,k}\phi_{L,k}(t) + \sum_{j=L}^{J}\sum_{k \in Z} d_{j,k}\psi_{j,k}(t)$$

$$(3.1)$$

where, Z denotes the set of all integers $\{0, \pm 1, \pm 2 \ldots\}$. The coefficients $c_{L,k} = \int_R f(t)\phi_{L,k}(t)dt$ are considered to be the coarser level coefficients characterizing smoother data patterns, $d_{j,k} = \int_R f(t)\psi_{j,k}(t)dt$ are viewed as the finer level coefficients describing (local) details of data patterns, $J > L$ and L corresponds to the coarsest resolution level. Consider a sequence of image data $Y = (y(t_1)\ldots y(t_N))'$ taken from $f(t)$ or obtained as a realization of $y(t) = f(t) + \in_t$ at equally spaced discrete time points $t = \in_{t_i}$'s where $\in_{t_i}$'s are random normal $N(0, \sigma^2)$ noises. The DWT of Y is defined as:

$$d = WY \qquad (3.2)$$

where, W is the orthonormal $N \times N$ DWT-matrix. From Equation (**3.1**), $d = (c_L, d_L, d_{L+1}, \ldots, d_J)$, where

$$c_L = (c_{L,0}, \ldots, c_{L,2^L-1}),$$
$$d_L = (d_{L,0}, \ldots, d_{L,2^J-1}),.$$
$$d_J = (d_{J,0}, \ldots, d_{J,2^J-1})$$

Using the inverse DWT, the N × 1 vector y from the original signal curve reconstructed as $Y = W'd$. Thus, in DM practice, the key concepts and algorithms in the use of wavelets is the Discrete Wavelet Transforms (DWT), Continuous Wavelet Transforms (CWT), multi-resolution analysis algorithms, and others.

3.1.1. Discrete Wavelet Transform Algorithm

DWT is a linear signal processing technique, which transforms a vector (v) into numerically different inverses (say $v - to - v'$) of wavelet coefficients. The two vectors are of the same length. However, it is useful for compression in the sense that wavelet transformed data are truncated (Pimwadee et al., 2011). A small compressed approximation of the data retained by storing only a small fraction of the strongest wavelet coefficient, e.g., retain all wavelet coefficients larger than some particular threshold, and the remaining coefficients set to zero. The resulting data representation is sparse. Computations that can take advantage of sparsity are very fat if performed in wavelet space. DWT is, therefore, a technique of set of coefficients of the given training or testing image data sets. The DWT algorithm is a hierarchical pyramid procedure that has the data in each iteration, which support to result in fast computational speed designed as follows:

Step 1: The length (L), of the input data vector must an integer power of 2. This condition can be met by adding the data vector with zero's as

Step 2: Each transform involves applying two functions. The first applies some data smoothing, such as sum or weighted average. The second performs a weighted difference, which acts to bring out the detailed features of the data,

Step 3: The two functions are applied to pairs of input data, resulting in two sets of data of length $L/2$, which represent a smoothed or low-frequency version so the input data and the high-frequency content of it,

Step 4: The two functions are recursively applied to sets of data obtained in the previous loop until the resulting data sets obtained are of length 2,

Step 5: A selection of values from the data sets obtained in the above iterations is designated the wavelet coefficients of the transformed data.

The Haar wavelet transform based image decomposition is pertinent to characterize image data to extract its unique features. Let the data set $x_0, x_1, ..., x_{N-1}$ contains N elements, there will be $N/2$ averages (a_i) and N/2 wavelet coefficient (c_i) values. The averages are stored in the first half of the N element array, which can be the input for the next step in the wavelet calculation. The coefficients are stored in the second half of the N element array. The computational equations are defined as:

$$a_i = \frac{x_i + x_{i+1}}{2}, \quad c_i = \frac{x_i - x_{i+1}}{2} \quad (3.3)$$

The required steps first find the average and coefficients of each pair of elements and fill the first half of the array with averages and the second half of the array with coefficients. The repeat step 5 until the image is decomposed and transformed completely. For example, color based wavelet transform would be effective for measuring similarity between images based on a color space and moment. A color space is a multidimensional space in which the different dimensions represent the many components of the color. The color moment is referring to the distribution of color in an image, which can be interpreted as a probability distribution (Roodaki, Taki, Setarehdan & avab, 2008).

The DWT is a process of determining how well a series of wavelet functions represents the signal being analyzed, which describe by the wavelet coefficients. The result is a bank of coefficients associated with two independent variables, dilation, and translation. Translation typically represents a time, while the scale is a way of viewing frequency content as the inverse proportion of the scales and frequencies. The most efficient and compact form of wavelet analysis is accomplished by decomposing a signal into a subset of translated and dilated parent wavelets. The various scales and shifts in the parent wavelet are related based on powers of two. A full representation of the signal can be achieved using a vector of wavelet coefficients the same length as the signal. Let a signal consisting of 2^M data points, where M is an integer, the DWT requires 2^M wavelet coefficients to describe the signal. DWT decomposes the signal into $M+1$ levels, where the level is denoted as j, and the levels are numbered $i=-1, 0, 1, …, M-1$. Each level i consists of $j=2^i$ translated and partially overlapping wavelets equally spaced $2^M/j$ intervals apart. The $j=2^i$ wavelets at level i are dilated such that an individual wavelet span $N=1$ of those level's intervals, where is the order of the wavelet being applied. Each of the $j=2^i$ wavelets at level i is scaled by a coefficient $a_{i,j}$ determined by the forward wavelet transform, a convolution of the signal with the wavelet. The notation is such the i corresponds to the wavelet dilation and is the wavelet translation in level i, $a_{i,j}$ is often described as vector a_{a^i+j}, where $j=0, 1, …, i-1$. The level $i=-1$ is the signal mean value.

Thus, the forward WT determines the wavelet coefficients, $a_{i,j}$, of the j wavelets at each level. i. For the signal $f(n)$, the DWT is described as:

$$a_{i,j} = a_{i^i+j} = \sum_n f(n)\psi_{i,j}(n) \qquad (3.4)$$

The wavelet decomposition of a function $f(n)$ described as:

$$f(n) = \sum_i \sum_j a_{i,j}\psi_{i,j}(n) \qquad (3.5)$$

The corresponding inverse WT is also

$$\Psi_{i,j}(n) = 2^{i/2}\Psi(2^i n - j) \qquad (3.6)$$

Subject to:

$$a = a_0^j \text{ and } b = ka_0^j b_0 \text{ for } j, k \in Z$$

where, $a_0 > 1$ is a dilated step and $b_0 \neq 0$ is a translation step. Therefore, the family of wavelets is described as:

$$\psi_{j,k}(n) = a_0^{-j/2}\psi(a_0^{-j}n - kb_0) \qquad (3.7)$$

And the wavelet decomposition of a function $f(n)$ is

$$f(n) = \sum_j \sum_k D_j(j,k)\psi_{j,k}(n) \qquad (3.8)$$

where 2-dimensions set of coefficients $D_j(j,k)$ is called DWT of a given function $f(n)$.

The most commonly used form of such discretization with $a_0=2$ and $b_0=1$ on a dyadic time-scale grid as showed Figure 6 for which the WT is described as the standard DWT.

The selection of $\Psi(n)$ is made in such a way that basis function set $\{\Psi_{j,k}\}$ constitute an orthogonal basis of $L^2(R)$ so that

$$D_j(j,k) = \langle \psi_{j,k}(n)f(n) \rangle \qquad (3.9)$$

The DWT algorithm is, therefore, a series of high and low pass filters to progressively find the wavelet coefficients, $a_{i,j}$, from the highest i level to the mean value level. In the first iteration, the upper, half of the frequency content is filtered from the original signal. The high pass signal is used to generate the 2^{M-1} wavelet coefficients that describe the high detail portion of the signal. The low pass filtered data sent to the next iteration. In the next iteration, the upper one-half of the remaining frequency content of the signal is high-pass

Figure 6. Standard DWT on dyadic time scale grid

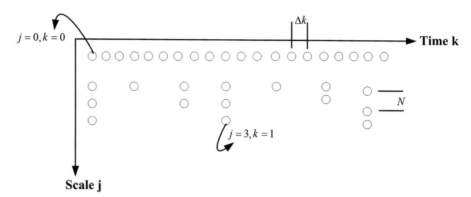

filtered once again, this time to generate the next 2^{M-2} wavelet coefficients. The iterations continue until all 2^M wavelet coefficients are determined.

3.1.2. Continuous Wavelet Transform Algorithm

A wavelet expansion uses translations and dilations of one fixed function, the wavelet $\Psi \in L^2(R)$ in which the parameters are vary continuously, and the techniques are CWT (Zobnin et al., 2011). The CWT of image data processing is a one-dimensional time signal to a two–dimensional time-scale joint representation. The time-bandwidth product of the CWT output is the square of that of the signal, which perform with a fewer signal parameters that cannot foster reducing the time-bandwidth products of the WT output. On the other hand, the WT in its CWT form provides a flexible time-frequency window narrows when observing high-frequency phenomena and widens when analyzing low-frequency behavior. Thus, time resolution becomes arbitrarily good at high frequencies while the frequency resolution becomes arbitrarily good at low frequencies. This kind of analysis is suitable for signals composed of high-frequency components with short duration and low-frequency components with a long duration, which is often the case in practical situations.

Based on the concept of wavelets as a family of functions constructed from translation and dilation of a single function Ψ, called the mother wavelet defined as follows:

$$\psi_{a,b}(\mathrm{x}) = \frac{1}{\sqrt{|a|}} \psi\left(\frac{x \Leftrightarrow b}{a}\right) \tag{3.10}$$

with $a, b \in R, a \neq 0$

where a is a scaling parameter that measures the degree of comparison or scale, and b as the translation parameter that determine the time location of the wavelet. If $|a|<1$, the wavelet Equation 3.10 is the compressed version of the mother wavelet and corresponds to higher frequencies. The wavelets have time-width adapted to their frequencies. Thus, these functions are scaled so that their $L^2(R)$ norms are independent of the parameter a. The CWT of a function $f \in L^2(R)$ is defined as:

$$w(a,b) = \langle f, \psi_{a;b} \rangle \tag{3.11}$$

The parameter a (the scaling factor) and b (the shifting factor) are the fundamentals to characterize the unique features of image data. Thus, a basis function $\Psi_{a,b}(x)$ can also be seen as a filter bank impulse response. With the increase in scale ($a>1$), the function $\Psi_{a,b}(x)$ is dilated to focus on the long-time behavior of associated signal $f(x)$ with it. It means, a large-scale reveals the global view while small-scale is a detailed view of the signal, which is a resolution feature of the image that visualizes the resolution of a signal frequency content. The scale change of continuous time signals in CWT does not alter their resolution, since the scale change can be reversed (Mei et al., 2004).

3.1.3. Multi-Resolution Analysis Algorithms

By its very nature, image data is multi-dimensional and might not have a stationary signal, which need to compute at the point of each event. The computational technique is demanding a multi-resolution analysis algorithm to determine its quality and behavior of the individual event, which decomposes a signal into a smooth version of the original set of information in a various scales (Matheus et al, 2012). A multi-resolution analysis is a technique of simultaneous image representation on different resolution via quality levels (Maya & Bhawani, 2011; Yexi et al., 2011). The resolution is determined by a threshold by which all fluctuations or details of the difference between two neighboring image features. Let us consider a one-dimensional (1-D) function $f(t)$. At the resolution level j, the approximation of the function $f(t)$ is $f_j(t)$. At the next resolution level $j+1$, the approximation of the function $f(t)$ is $f_{j+1}(t)$. The details denoted by $d_j(t)$ are included in $f_{j+1}(t)$: $f_{j+1}(t) = f_j(t) + d_j(t)$, which iterate or repeated until the function is derived as:

$$f(t) = f_j(t) + \sum_{k=j}^{n} d_k(t) \qquad (3.12)$$

Moreover, the multi-resolution analysis is based on the scaling function, which involves a continuous, square integral and, in general, real-valued function. The scaling function is vitally essential to normalized wavelet function than wavelet admission condition (since the mean value of the scaling function $\phi(t)$ is not equal to zero). The basic scaling function $\phi(t)$ is dilated by dyadic scale factors. At each scale level the scaling function is shifted by the discrete translation factors as:

$$\phi_{i,k}(t) = 2^{-i/2}\phi(2^{-i}t - k) \qquad (3.13)$$

where the coefficient $2^{-i/2}$ is normalization constant. The scaling functions of all scales 2^i with i $\in$ Z generated from the same $\phi(t)$ are all similar in shape. At each resolution level i, the set of the discrete translations of the scaling functions, $\phi_{i,k}(t)$, forms a function basis that spans a subspace, V_i. A continuous signal function may be decomposed into the scaling function basis. At each resolution level i, the decomposition is evaluated at discretely translated points. The scaling functions play a role in the average or smoothing function in the multi-resolution signal analysis. At each resolution level, the correlation between the scaling functions and the signal produces the averaged approximation of signal, which is sampled at a set of discrete points. After the averaging by the scaling functions, the signal is downsampled by a factor of two that halves the resolution. Then, the approximated signal is decomposed into the dilated scaling function basis at the next coarser resolution.

3.2. Wavelet Transforms For Image Characterization and Unique Feature Extractions

Wavelet transforms is a fundamental approach for image data characterization, which provide a clear understanding to optimal compression, classification or mining performance. In the past, it was adopted to approximate a reference signal up to a desired scale. However, currently it applied in many image features' extractions, including Content-Based Image Retrieval (CBIR) for which pertinent to extract image unique features (Lihua, Xinge, Robert, Ihsin & Yuan, 2001). The advantage is to select automatically, in a reference dataset that resembles a query image. It is advanced computer-based approaches to bridge the semantic gap between low-level image characterizations and users' perception of relevance. Considering $I=(I_{i,j})$ where $i=0…M$ and $j=0…N–1$ be an image of size $M{\times}N$ pixels. $w=(x_{k,1})$, where, $k=-K…K$ and $1=-L…L$ be a wavelet filter of support $(2K + 1) \times (2L + 1)$ (where K is the number of signal or wave, and L is the number of scaling). Thus, the wavelet filter is defined as:

$$\sum_{u=-K..K,v=-L..L} w_{u,v} = 0 \qquad (3.14)$$

Therefore, the coefficients of the wavelet transform of *I*, at any location (i,j) and analysis scale $s{\in}N$ can be defined as:

$$x_{i,j,s} = \sum_{u=-K..K,v=-L..L} w_{u,v}I_{i-su,j-sv} \qquad (3.15)$$

Thus $W_{K,L}$ denote the space of all wavelet filters in which support $(2K + 1) \times (2L + 1)$, and D denote its dimension, the central coefficient of each filter $w{\in}W_{K,L}$ redefined as:

$$D = (2K+1)(2L+1)-1 \ (i.e. \ W_{K,L} = \mathbb{R}^{D})$$

Therefore, wavelet transforms based image feature characterization is a multi-scale representation of the function. By using the wavelets, given function analyzed at various levels of resolution, which is invertible and orthogonal. Thus, wavelets seem to be effective for analysis of image features recorded with different resolution (Gw´enol´e, Mathieu, Guy, Beatrice & Christian, 2012; Roodaki et al., 2008).

In practices, wavelet transforms for image feature extraction are the technique of image pixel array detections. Let an N × N image as two-dimensional pixel array Γ with the N rows and N columns. We assume without loss of generality that the equation $N=2^{\Gamma}$ holds for some

positive integer *r*. The index starts with zero and then; the largest index is N − 1. The image pixels them self at row *i* and column *j* will be denoted by $\Gamma(i,j)$ or $\Gamma_{i,j}$, and the wavelet transformed image will be denoted by $\hat{\Gamma}$ and the coefficients are addressed with $\hat{\Gamma}(k,l)$ or $\hat{\Gamma}_{k,l}$. For the reconstructed image, we use $\tilde{\Gamma}$ and address the corresponding reconstructed $\tilde{\Gamma}(n,m)$ or $\tilde{\Gamma}_{n,m}$. The pixels and coefficients themselves are stored as signed integers in two's complementary encoding. Therefore, the range is given as:

$$\Gamma[row, col] \in [-2^{dpth-1}, 2^{dpth-1}-1]$$

Subject to $0 \leq$ row, col $<$ N is assuming a *dpth*-bit grayscale resolution. Thus, we can distinguish between the two *dpth* different values of brightness. It is the largest value $(2^{dpth-1}-1)$ correspond to black and white-gray for the other as the consequence pixels with a magnitude around zero appear as gray color.

3.3. Wavelet-Based Data Reduction Technique

The need for data reduction is to large-scale image data sets cascade into some smaller set of data with or without a loss of its originality and information. The goal of the data reduction technique is to enable effectively (compile-time) estimates of the result sizes of relational operators for the purpose of cost-based query optimization (Pimwadee et al., 2011). Thus, wavelet transformation represents the data as a sum of prototype functions, and it is shown that under certain conditions, the transformation only related to selective coefficients. In the process of reduction techniques, the data will clean and denoisy, by retaining selective coefficients, wavelets can achieve the data dimensionality reduction. Dimensionality reduction is thought as an extension of just transforms original data into a wavelet domain without discarding any coefficients (Manisha & Gajanan, 2014). The data dimensionality reduction a technique is to project the n-dimensional tuples that represent the data in a k-dimensional space, so that $k<n$ and the distances are preserved as well as possible using different approaches. Such as keep the largest k coefficients and approximate the rest with 0, keep the first k coefficients and approximate the rest with 0, and others.

Keeping the largest k coefficients achieve more accurate representation while keeping the first k coefficients is useful for indexing in. It implicitly assumes a priori the significance of all wavelet coefficients in the first k coarsest levels and that all wavelet coefficients at higher-resolution levels are negligible. Such a strong prior assumption heavily depends on a suitable choice of k and essentially denies the possibility of local singularities in the underlying function. Let, if the basis is orthonormal, in terms of L_2 loss, maintaining the largest k wavelet coefficients provides the optimal k-term Haar approximation to the original signal. Suppose the original signal is given by

$$f(x) = \sum_{i=0}^{M-1} c_i \mu_i(x),$$

where $\mu_i(x)$ is an orthonormal basis. In a discrete form, the data can then be expressed by the coefficients $c_0...c_{M-1}$. Let σ be a permutation of $0...M-1$ and $f'(x)$ be a function that uses the first M' number of coefficients of permutation σ, i.e.,

$$f'(x) = \sum_{i=0}^{M-1} c_i \mu_i(x).$$

It is then straightforward to show that the decreasing ordering of magnitude gives the best permutation as measured in L_2 norm.

3.4. Wavelet Trend Extraction and Denoising Methods

Noise is a random error or variance of a measured variable. It created in various ways, including measurement/instrumental errors during the data acquisition, human and computer errors occurring in data entry, technology limitations and natural phenomena such as atmospheric disturbances, etc. Removing noise from data considered as a process of identifying constructing optimal estimates of unknown data from available noisy data. Various smoothing techniques, such as binning methods, clustering, and outlier detection, are mentioned few. Such as, binning methods smooth a sorted data value by consulting the values around it. The DM algorithms find the anomalous as a by-product of segmentation or clustering algorithms (Mei et al., 2004), which defining outliers as points, which do not lie in clusters.

Furthermore, the post-pruning techniques by applying DM algorithms can avoid the over-all fitting problems caused by noisy data. Most of these methods, however, are not specially designed to deal with noise and noise reduction, and smoothing is only side-products of learning algorithms for other tasks. The wavelet techniques provide an effective way to denoise and have been successfully applied in various areas, especially in image research (Pimwadee et al., 2011; Tao et al., 2002). The wavelet can be used to create a family of time-frequency atoms, via the dilation and translation factors. Considering a sequence of data $y=(y_i...y_n)$ is a noisy realization of the signal $x=(x_i...x_n)$ is defined as:

$$y_i = x_i + \in_i, \text{ where } i=1...n \qquad (3.16)$$

where $\in_i$ is noise. It is commonly assumed that $\in_i$ are independent of the signal, and it is an identically distributed Gaussian random variable. A usual way to denoise is to find $\dot{x}$ such that it minimizes the Mean Square Error (MSE), which defined as:

$$MSE(\dot{x}) = \frac{1}{n} \sum_{i=1}^{n} (\dot{x}_i - x_i)^2 \qquad (3.17)$$

The discrete wavelet transform of *y* defined as:

$$d = wy \qquad (3.18)$$

where *w* is the orthonormal $N \times N$ DWT-matrix. The inverse DWT, the N × 1 vector y from the original signal curve reconstructed as $d = w^t y$. The process of applying the DWT to transform a data set closely resembles the process of computing the Fast Fourier Transformation (FFT). Therefore the DWT (d) is redefined as:

$$d = \theta + \eta \qquad (3.19)$$

where d, θ, and η represent the collections of all coefficients, parameters, and errors, transformed from the data *y*. The techniques of wavelet denoising are to transform the data into a different basis the wavelet basis, which support to reducing the errors. The large coefficients are mainly the useful information, and the smaller ones represent noise. By suitably modifying the coefficients on the new basis, noise can be directly removed from the data.

3.5. Data Transformation

A wide class of operations can be performed directly in the wavelet domain by operating on coefficients of the wavelet transforms of original data sets. Operating in the wavelet domain enables to perform these operations progressively in a coarse-to-fine fashion, to operate at different resolutions, manipulate features at various scales, and to localize the operation in both spatial and frequency domains. Performing such operations in the wavelet domain and then reconstructing the result is more efficient than performing the same operation in the standard direct fashion and reduces the memory footprint. Also, wavelet transformations have the ability to reduce temporal correlation so that the correlations of wavelet coefficients are much smaller than the correlation of a corresponding temporal process. Hence, simple models that are insufficient in the original domain may be quite accurate in the wavelet domain.

The wavelet transform is used to decompose an image into different frequency sub-bands and a mid-range frequency, which is used for PCA representation. The method reduces the computational load significantly while achieving good recognition accuracy. The technique is based on the statistics of the input image analysis order, which is used in a standard technique of pattern recognition and signal processing for data image data dimensionality reduction and feature extraction. As the pattern often image data contains redundant information, mapping it to a feature vector can get rid of this duplication and yet preserve most of the intrinsic information content of the pattern.

3.6. Similarity Search/Indexing

The image similarity is a fuzzy concept, which clarified for the user that the implicit image similarity is usually based on the human perceptual similarity. It demands dynamic and systematic approaches and understanding how to image features extractions, which is mainly based on low-level features, such as color, texture and shape (Yong & Shuying, 2007). The technique of image data similarity is given a pattern of interest for which try to find similar patterns in the data set based image features similarity measures. It is used to find similar images in a collection of the image database. Suppose, image data sets of $D = \{X_1, X_2, ..., X_i, ..., X_N\}$, where $X_i - [x_0^i, x_1^i, ..., x_n^i]$ and a given pattern is a sequence of data points $Q = [q_0, q_1, ..., q_n]$. Where a pattern Q, is the result set R from the data set

$$R = \{X_{i_1}, X_{i_2}, ..., X_{i_j}, ..., X_{i_m}\} \in_i ,$$

where that $D(X_{i_j}, Q) < d$. For the gap between the two data points (X, Y), we can be also applied the Euclidian distance measurements $D(X, Y)$ as defined:

$$D(X,Y) = \sqrt{\sum_i \left| x_j - y_j \right|^2} \qquad (3.20)$$

Wavelets are applied to similarity search by the techniques of data transformation and data dimensional reduction processes. It involves transforming the original data into wavelet domain and may also be selecting some wavelet coefficients (Tao et al., 2002). The data sets of n-dimensional space into a k-dimensional space should be considering wavelets and k-wavelet coefficients that stored for objects in the data set. Wavelet transforms based used to extract compact feature vectors and define a new similarity measure to facilitate search, which can support similarity search at different scales of adaptive and interactive ways. For example, the DWT based techniques have several advantages, which include time-frequency localization of the signal and the energy of the signal coefficients. It also has widespread applications in content-based similarity search in image/audio databases (Sameer et al., 2002).

Wavelet-Based Indexing of Images is the process region fragmentation to define a specific feature of the image. It is characterized smooth and a coarse appearance with various edges and textures. Considering the properties of in frequency domain coarseness from edges and texture in the image are mainly represented by high frequency, which has an effect of obstructing of edges and textures in the images. Moreover, using Haar wavelet transforms is powerful to extract color and texture features and applies clustering techniques to partition the image into regions. It is essential to similarity searching between matching regions (Manimala & Hemachandran, 2012). Therefore, image indexing and searching techniques are a new way of sorting and retrieval algorithm, which

provide partial sketch image searching capability for large databases. The process is comparing between high color components and low-frequency wavelet coefficients and their variance to store as feature vectors.

3.7. Principal Component Analysis

Principal component analysis (PCA) is adopted for many different tasks. Including wavelet-based image data analysis the technique of PCA can be combined to obtain proper accounting of global contributions to signal energy without loss of information on key local features (Sanjay et al., 2007). For example, PCA is vitally essential to processing multi-resolution property of wavelets at multiple scales. PCA based wavelet analysis is pertinent to recover independent sources given only sensor observations that are unknown linear mixtures of the unobserved independent source signals. The Independent Component Analysis (ICA) is, therefore, need to attempts to estimate the coefficients of an unknown mixture of n signal sources. The sources are statistically independent, the medium of transmission is deterministic, and crucially, the mixture coefficients are constant with respect to time. Moreover, ICA is a way of finding a linear non-orthogonal coordinate system in any multivariate data. The directions of the axes of this coordinate system determined by both the second and higher-order statistics of the original data. The goal is to perform a linear transform, which makes the resulting variables as statistically independent of each other as possible (SriDevi & Sunitha, 2012).

WT combines PCA utilized to a complexity problem of solve time-frequency characteristics of the mixture matrix in the source identification. ICA algorithms could also make use of the multi-scale representation of WT. Since, PCA is a statistical procedure concerned with elucidating the covariance structure of a set of variables. In particular, it allows us to identify the principal directions in which the data varies. An important issue is how to decide whether a PCA-based data or feature transformation approach is appropriate for a certain problem or not. Since the main goal of PCA is to extract new uncorrelated features, it is logical to introduce some correlation-based criterion with a possibility to define a threshold value (Manisha & Gajanan, 2014).

4. ANNOTATING THE IMAGE UNIQUE FEATURE MINING AND VISUALIZATION

The image on the storage drive or the web does not have textual descriptions or their texts do not discriminate the content for various purposes. Image data textual representation is the DM techniques to retrieve image features. The process is challenging, which demands deep understanding and computational analysis based on Automatic Image Annotation, which generates texts that describe the semantics of an image (Ruofei et al., 2004). It is a systematic representation and techniques to navigate quickly users to their interested images among massive collections. Among various types of querying methods (Nittir & Shamla, 2012) the Query-by-Keyword (QbK) image search scheme dominates commercial search engines such as Google, Bing, and others. Therefore, Annotation is a systematic representation or naming of images that would be important to access it on the web or from the given databases.

However, image Annotation is not simple, and the key challenge of Image Annotation is the semantic gap between visual features and semantic concepts (Xin et al., 2007). No semantic metrics has been successfully defined based on existing visual features such as color, texture, and local features. To minimize the gap or problem, various techniques are proposed (Zobnin et al., 2011), which includes methods of small-scale databases with limited vocabularies, learning from partially and noisily label image and others. The fundamental of developing search based Annota-

tion is essential to image access, navigation, and to avoid duplication in the databases. Therefore, an image an image can be annotated simply by propagating the texts from its duplicates. In a more realistic case of limited databases, the methods of extracting text from image discrimination result are challenging, which need salient texts to annotate the query image.

4.1. Image Feature Based Annotation

The method of features based image Annotation depend on computer-vision techniques to use visual features treating as a detection problem for each word or phrase. An image feature, which involves color, texture, shapes are pertinent to search or extract for each annotated image. Each Annotation is a set of feature primitives, which indicate suitability for image characterization or any other purposes. Image features categorized as a global or low resolution and local or high-resolution image features. The global features for image analysis constitute a singular, typically low-dimensional, feature that characterizes the entire color, edge, or texture space. The performance is extremely limited since they extract characteristics of an entire image, but they are fast to search and computing, reducing the distance complexity. Whereas, the local image feature formulate Annotation as a multiple-instance labeling problem. Each region, or "instance," is characterized by a particular feature, and an annotation applies to an image if it applies to any of its instances. The algorithms using local features collect features centered on identified key points and then perform pairwise matching to identify similar key-points. The most famous of these approaches is found in the original scale-invariant feature transform analysis (Nittir & Shamla, 2012; Lihua et al., 2001).

Image Features based Annotation is important to reduce features primitives and to play an essential role in developing an automatic annotation system. To optimize the image Annotation performance, searching keyword and Annotation modeling algorithms would be dynamic, which need to be capable of representing features from a training set. Then after it uses to compare this to the feature primitives of every image where the Annotation possibly applies (Xin, et al., 2007). Such an approach necessitates significant training information for every Annotation. The methodology of image capturing and knowing its contents are systematic descriptions and label of image based on its multiple semantic related factors, which incorporates features characteristics to form a vector for each collection. Image features $f \in R^n$ are essential to perform regularization on the feature set such that the visual data can be indexed efficiently. Such as, the color feature represents as a color histogram the image annotations. The desired property of the perceptual color difference is proportional to the numerical difference in the region space (Manimala & Hemachandran, 2012). The extraction of texture information of an image is also the important features towards image Annotation to improve image processing performances. The texture feature is represented by a vector with each elements corresponding to the energy in a specified scale and orientation of a local image in its visual descriptions (Maria et al., 2001).

Creating or having visual descriptions such as 'visual dictionary' is a fundamental preprocessing step necessary to index features, which is important to develop a valid classification tree towards similar features are grouping. The centers of the feature classes constitute the visual dictionary, without it; there is a challenge to discriminate the image feature values. For each feature attribute (color, texture, and shape), the visual dictionary is needed to use a Self-Organization Map (SOM) approach. It is a novel approach to project high-dimensional feature vectors, such as the 2-dimensional plane with mapping similar features together while separating different features apart at the same time (Ruofei et al., 2004).

4.2. Image Visualization Techniques

Image visualization technique is a fundamental process of stepwise refinement image features for an optimal image data analysis, which involves methods of verifiable, expository, and communicable concerning the domain contents. Visualization needs to be bear a clear quantitative relationship to the data, deftly expose and support some element of scientific relevance in the data, and easily facilitate a transfer of knowledge. Any images under their respective domains, image visualization techniques are generating data on the order of image features characteristics in a large scale of data sets that is predisposed to certain techniques. Wavelet-based image analysis is dynamic, and the techniques need to be scalable to adopt the changes.

The approach for visualization techniques for complex and large image data is challenging but also a prominent. The process of adapting these techniques to the changing needs of the images and its features are creating massive data sets with increasing size, complexity, and fidelity. Under this technique, we discussed more details, including different visualization techniques, namely pixel-oriented, geometric and others. For example, in a classical DM often generate huge amounts of data that could be difficult to interpret and use. Visual mining transforms raw data into visualization and makes it easier to understand the meaning of data and make suitable decisions.

4.2.1. Pixel-Oriented Visualization Technique

The technique of pixel oriented visualization is the process of image features extractions at a pixel level, which belonging to the visual components. It uses to form perceptual primitive units, by which human beings could identify the content of images (Ritendra et al., 2008). Moreover, pixels in the wavelets use to create multiscale edges. Thus, pixel-based visualization techniques have proven to be of high value in visual image data exploration. Image data points to pixels oriented visual process essential to analysis and visualization of large data sets and also allows an intuitive way to convert raw data into a graphical form. The graphical representation fosters new insights and encourages the formation and validation of new hypotheses to the end of better problem-solving and gaining deeper domain knowledge.

Pixel oriented image visualization is a dynamic and systematic visual analysis of large datasets. It includes dense pixel displays or pixel based geospatial techniques (very powerful exploration tools), which support to map each dimension value to a colored pixel and group that belonging to each adjacent area. The paradigm of pixel oriented visual technique is the process of mapping data points to certain locations on the n-dimensional map. The techniques allow the visualization of the largest amount of data possible on current huge displays (Ruofei et al., 2004). The advantage of pixel oriented visualization technique is its scalability to analysis large and complex image data sets. The approach described as two major tasks. (i) The capability of visualizations for massive datasets that constructed without losing important information. It is processing the large data points to visualize each single data point at a full detail. (ii) The technique is essential to find techniques to navigate efficiently and query such large data sets.

4.2.2. Geometric Projection Visualization Techniques

Image data analysis or decomposes demanding a high-dimensional Euclidean space. The image features extraction processes are complex and dynamic to visualize and consider each pixel, which needs deep thought of vector coordinate with a length equal to the number D of pixels in the image. The intensity of each pixel corresponds to the coordinate magnitude in that pixel's direction.

The real data points have a structure of smaller dimension d than the ambient space dimension D. In the well-studied case, when the data lie near a low-dimensional manifold 'M', which discover and characterize as the lower-dimensional structure. The methods dramatically affect the performance of tasks such as data compression, interpretation, outlier detection, classification and clustering (Gw´enol´e et al., 2012). If M is just a linear subspace, PCA can discover a dictionary of d vectors, which describe the data well at low computational cost. However, when M is nonlinear, it is usually necessary to use random dictionaries or black box optimization, which are much more complex and, in general, do not yield interpretable features of the data. Therefore, Geometric Wavelets are multi-scale dictionary elements, which are constructed directly from the data. It adapt to arbitrary nonlinear manifolds and have guarantees on the computational cost, which support number of elements in the dictionary and the sparsity of the representation.

Geometric projection techniques needed to find informative transformations of multidimensional datasets, which support a multi-scale data representation technique. It is useful for a variety of applications, namely, data compression, interpretation and anomaly detection and others. It is fundamental to image data processing for further data exploration and classification. The computational relation between data points is performed with respect to a given similarity function. At the coarsest scale, all data points are considered one group. The global PCA is yielding a d-dimensional plane fit to the data with axes in the directions of maximum variance as a parallel of scaling functions in wavelet analysis. The geometrical projection of the plane data points is the coarsest scale approximation of the data. The PCA performed the projection of the data points of the two new planes that will more accurately approximate of M. To form a compact representation of the data at this finer scale as in wavelet decomposition to visualize the differences between the original coarse projections of the data, and the points projected onto the planes. An efficient scheme is derived based on the construction of a minimal space spanning the set of differences. The axes of this difference space are geometric wavelets, whereas, the projections of the finer-scale corrections to the data points onto the plane spanned by these axes are the wavelet coefficients.

4.2.3. Icon-Based Visualization Techniques

Icon based visualization technique is also a method of mapping each multidimensional data item to an icon, which is more specific approach and the visual features vary depending on the data attribute values (Ritendra et al., 2008). Several graphical parameters are usually contained in an icon, which makes it possible to handle multidimensional data. Besides, observations of graphical features are pre-attentive that is interactive to human. Icon based visualization is dynamic and involving multiple scenarios such as Chernoff face, star and other methods of visualization of image data. It involves image features attributes (color, shape, texture …) visualizing the data point in a systematic way (Bezdek et al., 1993).

Furthermore, the icon-based technique also effective to visualize image features based on its thickness and shape, which supports image attributes to the display axes and the rotation angle. The data can be dense to display dimensionally, and the packed icons exhibit some texture's patterns that vary according to the data features, which are detected by pre-attentive perception. Moreover, the shape of the image is essential to visualize data using small arrays of pixels. Each data item is represented by one array. The pixels are mapped to a color scale according to the attribute values, which involves the arrays that contain an arbitrary number of pixels to make it possible for multidimensional data visualization. The pixels are a color based visual techniques that replaced by arrays of color fields representing the

attribute values similar to shape coding. The color or pixel produces some textures, which allow users to gain insight into the overall relationships between attributes.

4.2.4. Hierarchical Visualization Techniques

The hierarchical techniques subdivide the data space and present subspaces in a vertical fashion, which the image attributes are treated differently with diverse views of the underlying data. The techniques lay in this category concern, mainly a data in which several attributes are designed in a hierarchical architecture. The fundamental concept of hierarchical visualization technique is to compute a hierarchy of views that present the underlying data at different levels of detail. The advantage of the approach is the capability to visualize the details by navigating the hierarchy to explore regions of interest and detailed information, which support to optimize the information content of the initial visualization. Thus, the technique is not just generates a hierarchy containing different levels of detail, it rather shows important data objects at a higher detail while presenting less important data objects at a lower level of detail. It achieves by employing analytical methods in the form of objective functions in the hierarchy construction and visualization process. For example, suppose we use a clustering algorithm to detect clusters in the data. Let the objective be the detection of clusters, which contain very few data points, which may indicate outliers in the data. Therefore, our objective function gives a high importance value to data points, which belong to clusters with a small number of data points. The data points belonging to large clusters get a low importance value, which has created on the importance values of the data points; a hierarchy is created, similar to single linkage clustering.

Hierarchical visualization technique is an essential to increase scalability, which provides a compact orthogonal representation of the data with different levels of detail based on the data points to select a given number of image objects. The relevance is maximized, and each data point is contained in at least one selected data object. The relevance function allows determining the object resolution of the local screen spaces. Let $A = a\{a_0...a_{N-1}\}$. The relevance function Ψ: $A \rightarrow N$ assigns every data point $a_i \in A$, relevance values $\Psi(a_i)$. Therefore, based on the hierarchical visualization technique, the relevance function ψ depends on the application scenario and can be given by the user for computational analysis the data points.

4.3. Wavelet-Based Image Data Mining Applications

These days, wavelet-based data analysis become popular and hot issues. Such as wavelet-based image retrieval (Mei et al., 2004), decompositions (Maya & Bhawani, 2011), feature extractions and others (Lakshmi et al., 2011; Peter, 2003) mentioned. WT is a dynamically adaptable phenomenon of both mathematical and theory of science. It is a synthesis of ideas that employs in various fields and issues, which involves both computational and signal processing. Since WT is an advanced tool that implemented in the past years to divide up data functions, or operators into different frequency components, which studied accordingly with a resolution matched to its scale (Manimala & Hemachandran, 2012). Therefore, the WT is anticipated to provide economical and informative mathematical representation of many objects of interest. Currently, many computer software packages contain fast and efficient algorithms to perform WTs, which is easy, accessible and essential to wavelets have quickly gained popularity among scientists and engineers. In theoretical research and applications the method supports to optimize the performance and applications of wavelets in wide areas, which

includes computer science research areas as image processing, computer vision, network management, and DM, and others.

Wavelets have attracted much attention in the DM, which provides diverse computational data analysis and decompositions such as image data sets. Wavelet-based image mining has a variety of applications in various sectors like medical diagnosis, biology, remote sensing, space research, etc. Image data is the major one that plays a vital role in every aspect of the systems as a business for marketing, hospital for surgery, engineering for construction, the web for publication and so on. Images require large amounts of storage space and processing time, how to quickly and efficiently access and manage it, which is capable in the sense of information contents and data volume, have become challenging and important issue. Therefore, wavelet-based image decompositions such as Content-Based Image Retrieval (CBIR) research approach is paramount (Yong et al., 1999). CBIR systems perform retrieval based on the similarity defined in terms of extracted features with more objectiveness. Wavelet-based image mining applications to visualize by image retrieval, feature extractions, content-based image mining and many others. In this chapter, we discussed on these three sub-topics (Sameer et al., 2002).

4.3.1. Image Retrieval System

Image Retrieval (IR) is a fundamental and fastest growing research area in the field of multimedia technology. As far as technological advances are concerned, growth in wavelet-based image retrieval has been unquestionably rapid (Peter, 2003). In recent years, there has been significant effort put into understanding the real-world implications, applications, and constraints of the technology. The real-world application of the technology is limited. We devote this section to understanding image retrieval in the real world and discuss user expectations, system constraints, and requirements, and the research effort to make image retrieval a reality in the not-too-distant future. Therefore, designing an omnipotent real-world image search engine capable of serving all categories of users requires understanding and characterizing the user-system interaction and image search, from both user and system points-of-view.

Image retrieving is the process of getting the required content based on the user query from the available data repository or data warehouse. An Image Retrieval System (IRS) can be categorized based on the type of searches as image description and visual contents. The conventional user defined text searches based on keyword, namely size, type, date and time of capture, the identity of the owner, etc. However, such approaches did not powerful and efficient. Thus, wavelet-based searching an image as of its visual contents and features (finding the images similar to an input query image) are gained more focused (Xin et al., 2007)

4.3.2 Features Elements and Extraction

Images diverse properties are the representations or descriptions of various features elements, which will be significant to image analysis and decompositions. Image features are the measurements or properties used to classify the objects. Whereas, features extraction is a method of determining different attributes associated with a region or objects for indexing and retrieval, mainly on abstracted image information obtained through segmentation (Yong et al., 1999). The extractions of feature elements (such as color, shape, texture, edge ...) carried out by first locate the perceptual elements and then determine their main properties and give them suitable descriptions by having the following approaches.

- The features should be independent and should posses' maximum information about the image,

- Images are divided into several clusters, and for each cluster, the central value is taken as its feature elements, such as color cardinality named as different contents,
- The extracted features should be easily computable even for a large image collection (cluster) and information retrieval should be very fast,
- Involving additional attributes, such as the center coordinates and area of each cluster, are recorded to represent the position and size information of clusters.
- Image features should relate well with the human perceptual characteristics of users will finally determine the suitability of the retrieved images that perception subjectivity, there does not exist a single best representation for a feature.

The fundamental of feature extraction technique deals with image segmenting the foreground from the background. It supports to features extractions algorithms, which adapt in digital image processing for finding small parts of an image to generalize the analysis of the global image (Joanna & Joanna, 2013). The method is more effective to comper two images features or characters, which provide a clear understanding of feature element extraction with more dynamic to indicate the location of edges in images. A set of the invariant moments is used to represent the multi-scale edges in WT images, which process of image decompositions, pixel-based forms multiscale edges and computed the invariant moments at each scale of the combined feature vector of images. Color based image retrieval technique is the most popular and widely used that achieved by computing a color histogram for each image identifying its proportion of pixels within an image holding specific values. The texture as a feature extraction is the process of identification of specific textures in an image. It is achieved primarily by modeling texture as a two-dimensional gray level variation. The relative brightness of pairs of pixels is computed such that degree of contrast, regularity, coarseness, directionality, smoothness, granularity, repetitiveness, roughness, randomness and so on may be estimated.

4.3.3. Content-Based Image Mining

Image contents can be represented and described by diverse visual effects such as features, which involves features forms, vectors, shapes … are used for image identification in CBIR (Nishchol & Sanjay, 2012). These image characteristics can be extracted or retrieve as the users desires or issues like one by one or sequentially. Therefore, as a procedural searching process, first defining the image features and extracting the features from images, then retrieval is performed with these feature vectors. These feature vectors mark out an image to a point in the feature space. Detecting the point of the space feature also help to identify and search the required image type. The similarity between images that are represented by corresponding vectors is measured by distances between their representing points in the feature space. Moreover, features can be found in different levels (Lakshmi et al., 2011), such as color and textures. Hence, features like color and texture can be directly extracted from the image at pixel levels, which is a lower level of image extractions. At the middle level, features like shape are more extracted from objects in segmented images. Whereas, at the higher level. Features like space distribution (or structure relation) extracted from multiple objects in segmented images. All these levels of features can be extracted from the image and used in feature-based image retrieval.

The feature elements are defined based on these primitive units. They are discrete quantities, relatively independent of each other and have obvious, intuitive visual senses. Image features, or its contents, in general, can be considered as the sets of items based on feature element,which image classification becomes a process of counting the existence of representative image components.

In image features mining we can also use various approaches, which includes association rules between the feature elements and the class attributes of the image (Maria et al, 2001).

5. CONCLUSION

Authors discussed and introduced a novel approach and ideas on image DM, which limited the application of WT in the field of DM. The chapter provides an application-oriented overview of the WT based image DM to give a comprehensive understanding and techniques of the unique characteristics of image data sets. The purpose of this paper is to increase familiarity with fundamental techniques and applications of wavelet integrating into DM algorithms. It gives a better of image data exploration and visualizations, and also to provide reference sources and examples where the wavelets usefully applied to researchers working in data analysis. WT based DM techniques have a lot of advantages and optimal applications as discussed in section 3 &4. It goes without saying that wavelet approaches will be of growing importance in DM in which most of the current works on wavelet applications in DM is a technique of orthonormal and threshold wavelet basis approaches. It is a dynamic technique to define and considered noise data as extended categories using iterative wavelet frames.

Moreover, the chapter gives meaningful insights and inference how, WT potentially enables many other new approaches and applications. Such as multi-resolution data analysis, feature extractions, and fast approximate DM, etc. are feundamentals, which provides a clear and more detail understanding of an application-oriented of the mathematical foundations of wavelet theory, and a comprehensive wavelet-based DM techniques. The contribution of the research work is to increase familiarity with basic wavelet applications in DM towards image data analysis. It serves as a reference sources and examples where and how the wavelets apply to researchers working in image exploration. Therefore, in this chapter, under four main and more detailed sub-topics, we discussed tremendous wavelet-based DM advantages, and there already exists numerous successful applications many fields and more specifically in image data. Image DM is still a more foreland research area, and relevant theory and technology have not yet develop. To see the image DM algorithms in various aspects are an important technology that how to effectively extract the image features, which need more detail and dynamic works in the future.

REFERENCES

Antani, S., Kasturi, R., & Jain, R. (2002). A survey on the use of pattern recognition methods for abstraction, indexing and retrieval of images and video, Pergamon. *Pattern Recognition*, *35*(4), 945–965. doi:10.1016/S0031-3203(01)00086-3

Antonie, M.-L., Zaïane, O. R., & Coman, A. (2001). Application of Data Mining Techniques for Medical Image Classification. In *Proceeding of the 2nd International Workshop on Multimedia Data Mining in Conjunction with ACM SIGKDD Conference*, (pp. 94-101). ACM.

Belaid, L. J., & Mourou, A. (2009). Image Segmentation: A Watershed Transformation Algorithm. *Image Analysis & Stereology*, *28*(2), 93–102. doi:10.5566/ias.v28.p93-102

Bezdek, J. C., Hall, L. O., & Klarke, L. P. (1993). Review of MR Segmentation Techniques using Pattern Recognition. *Medical Physics*, *20*(4), 1033–1048. doi:10.1118/1.597000 PMID:8413011

Boris, Yendiyarov, & Petrushenko. (2011). Design of a Wavelet Based Data Mining Techniques. *Automatic*, 1-21,

Burl, M. C., Fowlkes, C., Roden, J., Stechert, A., & Mukhtar, S. (1999). *Diamond Eye: A Distributed Architecture for Image Data Mining*. Orlando, FL: SPIE DMKD.

Chaovalit, P., Gangopadhyay, A., Karabatis, G., & Chen, Z. (2011). Discrete Wavelet Transform-Based Time Series Analysis and Mining. *ACM Computing Surveys*, *43*(2), 1–37.

Crisologo, Monterola, & Soriano. (2011). Statistical Feature Based Craquelure Classification. *International Journal of Modern Physics*, *22*(11), 1191-1209.

Datta, Joshi, Li, & Wang. (2008). Image Retrieval: Ideas, Influences, and Trends of the New Age. *ACM Computing Surveys*, *40*(2), 1-60.

Devasena, L. C., Sumathi, T., & Hemalatha, M. (2011). An Experiential Survey on Image Mining Tools. *Techniques and Applications*, *3*(3), 1155-1167.

Gajjar, T. Y., & Chauhan, N. C. (2012). A Review of Image Mining Frameworks and Techniques. *International Journal of Computer Science and Information Technologies*, *3*(3), 4064-4066.

Gancarczyk, J., & Sobczyk, J. (2013). Data Mining Approach to Image Feature Extraction in Old Painting Restoration. *Foundation of Computing and Decision Sciences*, *38*(3), 159–174. doi:10.2478/fcds

Gebeyehu, B. G., Zhongshi, & Huazheng. (2013b). Data Mining Prospects in Mobile Social Networks. In *Data Mining in Dynamic Social Networks and Fuzzy Systems*. IGI Global.

Gebeyehu, B. G., Zhongshi, H., & Zhu, Z. H. (2013a). The Development of Invisible Data Mining, Functionality for Discovering Interesting Knowledge: In the case of Bioinformatics. *Journal of Convergence Information Technology*, *7*(4), 251–259.

Geetha, P., & Chitradevi, B. (2014). A Review of Image Processing Techniques for Synthetic Aperture Radar (SAR) Images. *International Journal of Innovative Research in Computer and Communication Engineering, 2*(4), 3823–3829.

Gw'enol'e, Q., Lamard, M., Cazuguel, G., Cochener, B., & Roux, C. (2012). Fast wavelet-based image characterization for highly adaptive image retrieval. *IEEE Transactions on Image Processing, 21*(4), 1613–1623. doi:10.1109/TIP.2011.2180915 PMID:22194244

Han, J. (2012). *Data Mining Concepts and Techniques* (3rd ed.). London, UK: Elsevier Inc.

Jiang, Perng, & Li. (2011). Natural Event Summarization. In *Proceedings of CIKM'11*. ACM.

Jin-ping, Y., Xi-mei, H., & Xiao-yun, X. (2012). Image Data Mining Technology of Multimedia. Springer-Verlag Berlin Heidelberg.

Leung, K., Cunha, A., Toga, A. W., & Parker, D. S. (2014). Developing Image Processing Meta-Algorithms with Data Mining of Multiple Metrics, Hindawi Publishing Corporation. *Computational and Mathematical Methods in Medicine, 2*, 1–8. doi:10.1155/2014/383465

Li, T., Li, Q., Zhu, S., & Ogihara, M. (2002). A Survey on Wavelet Applications in Data Mining. *SIGKDD Explorations, 4*(2), 9–68. doi:10.1145/772862.772870

Li, T., Ma, S., & Ogihara, M. (2010). Wavelet Methods for Data Mining. In O. Maimon & L. Rokach (Eds.), Data Mining and Knowledge Discovery Handbook (2nd Ed.). Springer Science+Business Media, LLC. DOI doi:10.1007/978-0-387

Mishra & Silakari. (2012). Image Mining in the Context of Content-Based Image Retrieval: A Perspective. *International Journal of Computer Science Issues, 9*(3), 69-76,

Moudani, W., & Sayed, A. R. (2011). Efficient Image Classification using Data Mining. *International Journal of Combinatorial Optimization Problems and Informatics, 2*(1), 27-44.

Mumtaz, , & Syed, , Hameed, & Jameel. (2008). Enhancing Performance of Image Retrieval Systems Using Dual Tree Complex Wavelet Transform and Support Vector Machines. *Journal of Computing and Information Technology, 16*(1), 57–68.

Nayak, M., & Panigrahi, B. S. (2011). Advanced Signal Processing Techniques for Feature Extraction in Data Mining. *International Journal of Computers and Applications, 19*(9), 30–37. doi:10.5120/2387-3160

Roodaki,, A., Taki, A., Setarehdan, S. K., & Navab, N. (2008). Modified Wavelet Transform Features for Characterizing Different Plaque Types in IVUS Images: A Feasibility Study. IEEE *Signal Processing*, 789–792.

Rui, Y., Huang, T. S., & Chang, S.-F. (1999). Image Retrieval: Current Techniques, Promising Directions, and Open Issues. *Journal of Visual Communication and Image Representation, 10*(1), 39–62. doi:10.1006/jvci.1999.0413

Sahu, N. M., & Bhopal, S. H. (2012). Image Mining: a New Approach for Data Mining Based on Text Mining. *3rd International Conference on Computer and Communication Technology.*

Sanjay, T., Gandhe, K. T., & Keskar. (2007). Image Mining Using Wavelet Transform. LNAI, 4692, 797–803.

Satone, M., & Kharate, G. (2014). Feature Selection Using Genetic Algorithm for Face Recognition Based on PCA, Wavelet and SVM. *International Journal of Electrical Engineering and Informatics, 6*(1), 39–52. doi:10.15676/ijeei.2014.6.1.3

Schoenemann, T., & Cremers, D. (2010). A Combinatorial Solution for Model-based Image Segmentation and Real-time Tracking. *IEEE Transactions on Pattern Analysis and Machine Intelligence*, *32*(7), 1153–1164. doi:10.1109/TPAMI.2009.79 PMID:20489221

Shyu, M.-L., Chen, S.-C., Chen, M., & Zhang, C. (2004). Affinity Relation Discovery in Image Database Clustering and Content-based Retrieval. ACM.

Singha, M., & Hemachandran, K. (2012). Content-Based Image Retrieval using Color and Texture, Signal & Image Processing. *International Journal (Toronto, Ont.)*, *3*(1). doi:10.5121/sipij.3104

SriDevi, N., & Sunitha, V. (2012). WT through Differential Privacy. *International Journal Of Computational Engineering Research*, *2*(5), 1344–1351.

Stanchev, P. (2003). Using Image Mining for Image Retrieval. *IASTED Conf. Computer Science and Technology*.

Sudhir, R. (2011). A Survey of Image Mining Techniques: Theory and Applications. *Computer Engineering and Intelligent Systems, 2*(6), 44-53.

Tsoumakas, G., & Vlahavas, I. (2009). Distributed Data Mining. IGI Global.

Vieira, M. A., Formaggio, A. R., Rennó, C. D., Atzberger, C., Aguiar, D. A., & Mello, M. P. (2012). Object Based Image Analysis and Data Mining applied to a remotely sensed Landsat time-series to map sugarcane over large areas, Elsevier. *Remote Sensing of Environment, 123*, 553–562. doi:10.1016/j.rse.2012.04.011

Wang, Zhang, Li, & Ma. (2007). Annotating Images by Mining Image Search Results. *IEEE Transactions on Pattern Analysis and Machine Intelligence*, 1-14.

Wu, Kumar, Quinlan, Ghosh, Yang, Motoda, et al. (2008). The top 10 Data Mining Algorithms. *Knowl Inf Syst*. DOI 10.1007/s10115

Yang, L., You, X., Haralick, R. M., Phillips, I. T., & Tang, Y. Y. (2001). Characterization of Dirac Edge with New Wavelet Transform. *LNCS*, *2251*, 129–138.

Yang, Y., & Huang, S. (2007). Image Segmentation by Fuzzy C-Means Clustering Algorithm with a Novel Penalty Term. *Computing and Informatics*, *26*, 17–31.

Zhang, Zhang, & Khanzode. (2004). *A Data Mining Approach to Modeling Relationships Among Categories in Image Collection*. ACM.

ADDITIONAL READING

Akbarpour, Sh. (2013), A Review on Content-Based Image Retrieval in Medical Diagnosis, International Journal on: Technical and Physical Problems of Engineering (IJTPE), Published by International Organization of IOTPE, ISSN 2077-3528, Issue 15, *5*(2), 148-153

Balster, E. J., Zheng, Y. F., & Ewing, R. L. (2003), Fast Feature-Based Wavelet Shrinkage Algorithm for Image Denoising, KIMAS, Boston, MA, pp. 722-2728

Berthouze, N. B. (2002). Mining Multimedia Subjective Feedback, Journal of Intelligent Information Systems, 19:1, pp, 43-59.

Blaschke, T. (2010). Object-based image analysis for remote sensing, Elsevier. *ISPRS Journal of Photogrammetry and Remote Sensing*, *65*(1), 2–16. doi:10.1016/j.isprsjprs.2009.06.004

Cannataro, M., Congiusta, A., Pugliese, A., Talia, D., & Trunfio, P. (2004). Distributed Data Mining on Grids: Services, Tools, and Applications. *IEEE Transactions on Systems, Man, and Cybernetics*, *34*(6), 2451–2465. doi:10.1109/TSMCB.2004.836890 PMID:15619945

Chelu, K. & Linyang, D. (2009). Image Processing and Image Mining using Decision Trees. *Journal of Information Science and Engineering*, *25*, 989–1003.

Dowsey, A. W., English, J. A., Lisacek, F., Morris, J. S., Yang, G.-Z., & Dunn, M. J. (2010). *Image analysis tools and emerging algorithms for expression proteomics* (pp. 4226–4257).

Embrechts, M. J., Szymanski, B., & Sternickel, K. (2005), Introduction to Scientific Data Mining: Direct Kernel Methods & Applications, Computationally Intelligent Hybrid Systems: The Fusion of Soft Computing and Hard Computing, Wiley, 317-365

Guest editorial (2007), Image fusion: Advances in the state of the art, Elsevier, Information Fusion 8, pp. 114–118,

Jeong, M. K., Lu, J.-C., Huo, X., Vidakovic, B., & Di Chen, . (2006). Wavelet-Based Data Reduction Techniques for Process Fault Detection. *Technometrics*, *48*(1), 26040. doi:10.1198/004017005000000553

Kekre, H. B., Sarode, T. K., & Ugale, M. S. (2011), An Efficient Image Classifier Using Discrete Cosine Transform, International Conference and Workshop on Emerging Trends in Technology, ACM, 978-1-4503-0449-8/11/02, pp. 330-337 doi:10.1145/1980022.1980096

Kumar, P. R. & Nagabhushan, P. (2007). Multiresolution Knowledge Mining using Wavelet Transform, Engineering Letters, 14:1, EL_14_1_30.

Kuzma, H., & Vaidya, S. (2008). *Data Mining* (pp. 48–53). Science for Security.

Rahman, A. U., & Rusthum, S. (2010). High-Resolution Data Processing for Spatial Image Data Mining, Integrated Publishing services. *International Journal of Geometric and Geosciences*, *1*(3), 327–342.

Rajendran, P., & Madheswaran, M. (2010). Novel Fuzzy Association Rule Image Mining Algorithm for Medical Decision Support System. *International Journal of Computers and Applications*, *1*(20), 87–93.

Subitha, V., & Jenicka, S. (2013). Efficient Image Fusion in Color Images Using Multiresolution Transform Techniques. *International Journal of Advanced Research in Computer and Communication Engineering*, *2*(7), 2589–2594.

Thompson, D., & Nair, J. S. (2002). Physics-Based Feature Mining For Large Data Exploration, IEEE. *Computing in Science & Engineering*, *4*(4), 22–30. doi:10.1109/MCISE.2002.1014977

Tommy (2010), Mining Object, Spatial, Multimedia, Text, and Web Data, 591-648.

Yasar, M., & Ray, A. (2008), Trend Detection and Data Mining via Wavelet and Hilbert-Huang Transforms, American Control Conference, 978-1-4244-2079-7/08/$25.00 ©2008 AACC. Pp. 4292-4297 doi:10.1109/ACC.2008.4587168

Zheng, S., Shi, W.-Z., Liu, J., Zhu, G.-X., & Tian, J.-W. (2007). Multisource Image Fusion Method Using Support Value Transform, IEEE. *Transactions on Image Processing*, *16*(7), 1831–1839. doi:10.1109/TIP.2007.896687 PMID:17605381

Zhou, X.-S., Zhan, Y., Raykar, V. C., Hermosillo, G., Bogoni, L., & Peng, Z. (2012). Mining Anatomical, Physiological and Pathological Information from Medical Images. *SIGKDD Explorations*, *14*(1), 25–34. doi:10.1145/2408736.2408741

KEY TERMS AND DEFINITIONS

Feature Extractions: Is a process of transforming a distinctive characteristic of an arbitrary data, such as text or images into numerical features that usable for machine learning. The process starts with an initial set of measured data and builds derived values (features) intended to be informative, non-redundant, which facilitating the subsequent learning and generalization steps, in some cases leading to better human interpretations that related to dimensionality reduction. It is the technique of dealing the image characterizations and segmentations of the big image into smaller windows that the features are easily extracted.

Image Characterization: Is the method present for estimating the complexity of an image based on objects or texts real contexts, which provides a means for classifying and evaluating the object features by way of their visual representations.

Image Data: Is a photographic or trace objects that represent the underlying pixel data of an area of an image element, which is created, collected and stored using image constructor devices.

Image Data Mining: Image mining is a subject-specific application of DM, which focused on extracting image features for knowledge implicit in image databases.

Image Retrieval: Is a process of searching for digital images in large image scale image data, which is computer based for browsing, searching and retrieving images from digital images.

Image Segmentation: Is the process of clustering or partitioning a digital image features into multiple sets of pixels to simplify or change the representation of an image into something, which understandable to more meaningful and easier to identify objects or other relevant information in digital formats.

Visualization: Is any technique for creating images, diagrams, or animations to communicate a message in which both abstract and concrete ideas. It means that the data must come from something that is abstract or at least not immediately visible (from the inside of the human body). This rule out photography and image processing.

Wavelet Transforms: Are a mathematical means for performing signal or wave-like oscillation with an amplitude analysis when the signal frequency varies over time. It is purposefully crafted to have specific properties that make them useful for signal processing, which provode a "reverse, shift, multiply and integrate" technique called convolution, with portions of a known signal to extract information from the unknown signal.

ENDNOTES

[1] HIS: In the HSI color space ('H' means 'hue', 'S' stands for 'saturation', while 'I' represents 'intensity'), the color information is represented in polar coordinates.

[2] The LUV color components also described as 'L' stands for 'Luminance' while 'U' 'Chrominance', and 'V' represent ''hroma', which have been proven to be more discriminative than traditional RGB color components.

[3.] LHS and RHS is implies or represent L for "Left" whereas R for "Right". HS is also "Hand Side"

Chapter 2
Total Variation Applications in Computer Vision

Vania Vieira Estrela
Universidade Federal Fluminense, Brazil

Hermes Aguiar Magalhães
Universidade Federal de Minas Gerais, Brazil

Osamu Saotome
InstitutoTecnologico de Aeronautica, Brazil

ABSTRACT

The objectives of this chapter are: (i) to introduce a concise overview of regularization; (ii) to define and to explain the role of a particular type of regularization called total variation norm (TV-norm) in computer vision tasks; (iii) to set up a brief discussion on the mathematical background of TV methods; and (iv) to establish a relationship between models and a few existing methods to solve problems cast as TV-norm. For the most part, image-processing algorithms blur the edges of the estimated images, however TV regularization preserves the edges with no prior information on the observed and the original images. The regularization scalar parameter λ controls the amount of regularization allowed and it is essential to obtain a high-quality regularized output. A wide-ranging review of several ways to put into practice TV regularization as well as its advantages and limitations are discussed.

1. INTRODUCTION

This chapter investigates robustness properties of machine learning (ML) methods based on convex risk minimization applied to computer vision. Kernel regression, support vector machines (SVMs), and least squares (LS) can be regarded as special cases of ML. The minimization of a regularized empirical risk based on convex functionals has an essential role in statistical learning theory (Vapnik, 1995), because (i) such classifiers are generally consistent under weak conditions; and (ii) robust statistics investigate the impact of data deviations on the results of estimation, testing or prediction methods.

In practice, one has to apply ML methods - which are nonparametric tools - to a data set with a finite sample size. Even so, the robustness is-

DOI: 10.4018/978-1-4666-8654-0.ch002

sue is important, because the assumption that all data points were independently generated by the same distribution can be contravened and outliers habitually occur in real data sets.

The real use of regularized learning methods depends significantly on the option to put together intelligent models fast and successfully, besides calling for efficient optimization methods. Many ML algorithms involve the ability to compare two objects by means of the similarity or distance between them. In many cases, existing distance or similarity functions such as the Euclidean distance are enough. However, some problems require more appropriate metrics. For instance, since the Euclidean distance uses of the L_2-norm, it is likely to perform scantily in the presence of outliers. The Mahalanobis distance is a straightforward and all-purpose method that subjects data to a linear transformation. Notwithstanding, Mahalanobis distances have two key problems: 1) the parameter vector to be learned increases quadratically as data grows, which poses a problem related to dimensionality; and 2) learning a linear transformation is not sufficient for data sets with nonlinear decision boundaries.

Models can also be selected by means of regularization methods, that is, they are penalizing depending on the number of parameters (Alpaydin, 2004; Fromont, 2007). Generally, Bayesian learning techniques make use of knowledge on the prior probability distributions in order to assign lower probabilities to models that are more complicated. Some popular model selection techniques are the Akaike information criterion (AIC), the Takeuchi information criterion (TIC), the Bayesian information criterion (BIC), the cross-validation technique (CV), and the minimum description length (MDL).

This chapter aims at showing how Total Variation (TV) regularization can be practically implemented in order to solve several computer vision applications although is still a subject under research. Initially, TV has been introduced in (Rudin, Osher, & Fatemi, 1992) and, since then, it has found several applications in computer vision

such as image restoration (Rudin & Osher, 1994), image denoising (Matteos, Molina & Katsaggelos, 2005; Molina, Vega & Katsaggelos, 2007), blind deconvolution (Chan & Wong, 1998), resolution enhancement (Guichard & Malgouyres, 1998), compression (Alter, Durand, & Froment, 2005), motion estimation (Drulea & Nedevschi, 2011), texture segmentation/discrimination (Roudenko, 2004). These applications involve the use of TV regularization that allows selecting the best solution from a set of several possible ones.

2. BACKGROUND

2.1. Regularization

In machine learning (ML) and inverse problems, regularization brings in extra information to solve an ill-posed problem and/or to circumvent overfitting. Representative information is taken into consideration via insertion of a penalty function based on constraints for solution smoothness or bounds on the vector space norm. Representative cases of regularization in statistical ML involve methods like ridge regression, lasso, and L_2-norm for example.

If a problem has (a) a unique solution, and (b) the solution is robust to small data perturbations, then it is called well-posed. When at least one of them is violated, it is named ill-posed and it requires special care.

Non-uniqueness is a consequence of not having enough data on the original model and it is not detrimental at all times. Depending on the desired characteristics of a good solution or some measures of goodness, then an estimate can be picked up from a set of multiple solutions. Nevertheless, if one does not know how to evaluate an estimate, then a very good way to handle non-uniqueness is to enforce some prior information about domain in order to constrain the solution set.

Instability results from an effort to undo cause-effect relations. Solving a forward problem is the most natural way of finding a solution, since cause always goes before effect. In reality, one has access to corrupted measures, which means one aims at finding the cause without a closed-form description of the system being analyzed (system model).

Regularization can be isotropic or anisotropic on the smoothness terms. Isotropic regularization schemes relax smoothness constraints at boundaries. Anisotropic formulations let smoothing occurs along the borders but not transversal to them.

The concept of regularization relies on the use of norms. This chapter will only consider expressions of this form

$$\| \mathbf{x} \|_p = \left(\sum_i | x_i |^p \right)^{\frac{1}{p}}, \tag{1}$$

where the most popular ones are described as follows:

L_2 norm: is also known as Euclidean distance. Algorithms relying on it generate smooth results, which penalize image edges.

L_1 (Manhattan) norm: is the sum of the absolute values of the distances in the original space. Algorithms using this norm preserve image edges, although they are time-consuming.

2.2. Least Squares (LS) Regularization

Given a system $\mathbf{g}=\mathbf{Hf}$, where $\mathbf{H}$ is a forward operator, the simplest form of regularizing an ill-posed problem is the linear Least Squares (LS) with Euclidean (L_2) norm that aims at minimizing the residual

$$\varepsilon^2_{LS}=J(\mathbf{f}) = \| \mathbf{Hf\text{-}g} \|_2^2. \tag{2}$$

That is,

$$\hat{\mathbf{f}}_{LS} =(\mathbf{H}^T\mathbf{H})^{-1}\mathbf{H}^T\mathbf{f}, \tag{3}$$

where $J(\mathbf{f})$ is a functional to be minimized, ε^2_{LS} is the squared of the residuals, $\hat{\mathbf{f}}$ is an estimate of $\mathbf{f}$ according to the LS squares criterion and $\| . \|_2^2 = \| . \|^2$. If $\mathbf{H}$ is ill-conditioned or singular, then (3) may not be a good estimate. A regularization term $\| \mathbf{Qf} \|^2$ (also known as regularization penalty) is included in this minimization functional, then it will lead to the Regularized Least Squares (RLS) estimate (Coelho, & Estrela, 2012a; Coelho, & Estrela, 2012b; Coelho, & Estrela, 2012c; Kang & Katsaggelos, 1995; Molina, Vega, & Katsaggelos, 2007). Hence, the new functional becomes

$$J(\mathbf{f}) = \varepsilon^2_{RLS} = \| \mathbf{Hf\text{-}g} \|^2 + \| \mathbf{Qf} \|^2 . \tag{4}$$

The most common case is $\mathbf{Q}=\lambda\mathbf{I}$, where λ is a scalar regularization parameter and $\mathbf{I}$ is the identity matrix, nevertheless other types of regularization matrix $\mathbf{Q}$ can be chosen in order to enhance problem conditioning (such as a first or a second order differentiation matrix), therefore making possible a better numerical solution given by:

$$\hat{\mathbf{f}}_{RLS} =(\mathbf{H}^T\mathbf{H}+\mathbf{Q}^T\mathbf{Q})^{-1}\mathbf{H}^T\mathbf{f}. \tag{5}$$

From a Bayesian point of view, this is equivalent to adding some additional assumptions with in order to obtain a stable estimate. Statistically, $\mathbf{f}$ prior is frequently assumed to be zero-mean Gaussian with independent and identically distributed (iid) components with identical standard deviation σ_f. The data $\mathbf{g}$ are also erroneous, and iid with zero mean and standard deviation σ_g. When $\mathbf{Q}=\lambda\mathbf{I}$, $\hat{\mathbf{f}}_{RLS}$ has $\lambda = \sigma_g / \sigma_f$ according to the previous expression.

2.3. Generalized Tikhonov regularization (GTR)

A more general functional is

$$J(\mathbf{f}) = \| \mathbf{Hf\text{-}g} \|_P^2 + \| \mathbf{f\text{-}f_0} \|_Q^2 . \tag{6}$$

where $\| \mathbf{f} \|_Q^2 =\mathbf{f}^T\mathbf{Qf}$ is a weighted norm. A Bayesian analysis shows that $\mathbf{P}$ is the inverse covariance matrix of $\mathbf{g}$, $\mathbf{f}_0 = E\{\mathbf{f}\}$, and $\mathbf{Q}$ the inverse covariance matrix of $\mathbf{f}$. The Tikhonov matrix Λ is obtained from $\mathbf{Q} = \Lambda^T \Lambda$ (the Cholesky factorization), and it can be regarded as a whitening filter.

The resulting estimate is $\hat{\mathbf{f}}_{GTR} = \mathbf{f}_0 + (\mathbf{H}^T\mathbf{P}\mathbf{H}+\mathbf{Q})^{-1} \mathbf{H}^T\mathbf{P}(\mathbf{g}-\mathbf{H}\mathbf{f}_0)$. The LS and RLS estimates are special cases of the GTR solution (Blomgren & Chan, 1998; Chan & Wong, 1998; Coelho, & Estrela, 2012c).

Usually, the discretization of integral equations lead to discrete ill-conditioned problems, and Tikhonov regularization can be applied in the original infinite dimensional space. The previous expression can be interpreted as follows: $\mathbf{H}$ is a Hilbert space compact operator, plus $\mathbf{f}$ and $\mathbf{g}$ are elements in the domain and range of $\mathbf{H}$ respectively. This implies that the operator $(\mathbf{H}^*\mathbf{H}+\mathbf{Q}^T\mathbf{Q})$ is a self-adjoint as well as a bounded invertible operator.

2.4. Total Variation Regularization

Total Variation (TV) regularization is a deterministic technique that safeguards discontinuities in image processing tasks. For a known kernel $\mathbf{H}$, the true image $\mathbf{f}$ satisfies the relationship $\mathbf{g} \approx \mathbf{H}\mathbf{f}$. The approximation symbol accounts for noise. With the purpose of imposing uniqueness and circumvent distortions, the predicted image $\hat{\mathbf{f}}$ can be described as the minimizer of

A new functional can be stated as,

$$J_{TV}(\mathbf{f}) = \frac{1}{2}\|\mathbf{Hu\text{-}g}\|_2^2 + \lambda TV(\mathbf{f}), \qquad (7)$$

where $\mathbf{r}=(x,y)$ is a pixel location, $\nabla \mathbf{f}$ is the gradient of $\mathbf{f}$, Ω is the corresponding Hilbert space and $\lambda \geq 0$ is a hyperparameter whose value depends on the amount of noise. The TV norm is defined by

$$TV(\mathbf{f}) = \int_\Omega \sqrt{|\nabla \mathbf{f}|^2}\,dxdy . \qquad (8)$$

In the previous expression, $\nabla \mathbf{f}$ is the Laplacian of $\mathbf{f}$, the term $\|\mathbf{Hf\text{-}g}\|^2$ is a fidelity (penalty) term.

Recently, various efficient implementation of the TV norm have been proposed. Nevertheless, finding the exact value of λ is computationally demanding. Despite some difficulties concerning the discretization of the previous equation because it introduces high frequency artifacts in the estimated solution, it can be proven that they can be avoided by different TV discretization strategies (Sfikas, Nikou, Galatsanos, & Heinrich, 2011). The main advantage of TV regularization is the fact that this variational approach has edge-preserving properties, but textures and fine-scale details are still removed. Given that it is not possible to differentiate TV($\mathbf{f}$) at zero, a small constant $\alpha > 0$ is placed in the preceding expression in this fashion:

$$TV(\mathbf{f}) = \int_\Omega \sqrt{|\nabla \mathbf{f}|^2 + \alpha^2}\,dxdy . \qquad (9)$$

The TV regularization term allows selecting amid numerous potential estimates the optimal one. With the intention of enforcing uniqueness and evade serious ringing artifacts, the estimated image $\hat{\mathbf{f}}$ will be the value of $\mathbf{f}$ that minimizes the following functional:

$$J_{TV}(\mathbf{f}) = \frac{1}{2}\|\mathbf{Hu\text{-}g}\|_2^2 + \lambda\int_\Omega \sqrt{|\nabla \mathbf{f}|^2 + \alpha^2}\,dxdy .$$
$$(10)$$

Knowledge on the image discontinuities accounts for the gradient magnitude $\sqrt{|\nabla \mathbf{f}|^2 + \alpha^2}\,dxdy$. To find $\hat{\mathbf{f}}$ involves two steps: to define a discrete version of $J_{TV}(\mathbf{f})$ for images and to find an algorithm to minimize the discrete problem. Provided the chosen algorithm converges, the solution will depend only on the discretization selected, which is a modeling concern.

Analogously to what happens in RLS (Galatsanos & Katsaggelos, 1992), λ is very important when it comes to controlling the amount of noise allowed in the process. If $\lambda=0$, then no denoising is applied and the outcome is equal to the original image. On the other hand, as $\lambda \longrightarrow \infty$, the TV term becomes progressively stronger, then the output image becomes more different from the original one that is corresponding to having smaller TV. Consequently, the selection of regularization parameter is vital to attain the adequate amount of noise elimination.

Practically speaking, the gradient can be approximated by means of different norms. The TV norm introduced by (Rudin, Osher, & Fatemi, 1992) is named TV_{fro} in this text. It is isotropic, L_2-based, and non-differentiable. If the gradient of **f** is $\nabla \mathbf{f} = (D^x_{i,j}, D^y_{i,j})$ where,

$$D^y_{i,j}\mathbf{f} = \frac{f_{i,j} - f_{i,j-1}}{\Delta y},$$

and

$$\Delta x = \Delta y = 1,$$

then (9) can be rewritten as

$$TV_{fro}(\mathbf{f}) = \sum_{i,j} \sqrt{|f_{i+1,j} - f_{i,j}|^2 + |f_{i,j+1} - f_{i,j}|^2 + \alpha^2}.$$

(11)

Since other choices of discretization are possible for the gradient, then an alternative to TV_{fro} relying on the L_1-norm for an $M \times N$ image can be obtained by taking into consideration the following relationships and approximations:

$$TV_{L_1\text{-}fro}(\mathbf{f}) = \sum_{i,j}\left\{\sqrt{|f_{i+1,j} - f_{i,j}|^2} + \sqrt{|f_{i,j+1} - f_{i,j}|^2} + \alpha\right\}$$
$$= \sum_{i,j}\left\{|f_{i+1,j} - f_{i,j}| + |f_{i,j+1} - f_{i,j}| + \alpha\right\}$$
$$= MN\alpha + \sum_{i,j}\left\{|f_{i+1,j} - f_{i,j}| + |f_{i,j+1} - f_{i,j}|\right\}.$$

$TV_{L1\text{-}fro}$ is easier to minimize, it is also anisotropic and less time-consuming. Because unraveling this denoising problem is far from trivial, modern investigation on compressed sensing algorithms

such as (Chambolle, 2004; Donoho, 2008; Friedman, Hastie, & Tibshirani, 2010; Afonso, Bioucas-Dias, & Figueiredo, 2011) solve variants of the original TV-norm problem.

The modification to the L_p-norm has a remarkable effect on the calculation of $\hat{\mathbf{f}}$. The solution consists of polynomial pieces, and the degree of polynomials is p-l.

The problem can be better stated by defining a function $\Psi(t) = 2\sqrt{t + \alpha^2}$ and rewriting (9), (10), and (12) as follows:

$$TV(\mathbf{f}) = \frac{1}{2}\sum_{i=1}^{M}\sum_{j=1}^{N}\Psi\left(\left(D^x_{i,j}\mathbf{f}\right)^2 + \left(D^y_{i,j}\mathbf{f}\right)^2 + \alpha^2\right)$$
$$\Rightarrow TV(\mathbf{f}) =$$
$$\frac{1}{2}\sum_{i=1}^{M}\sum_{j=1}^{N}\Psi\left\{|f_{i+1,j} - f_{i,j}| + |f_{i,j+1} - f_{i,j}| + \alpha^2\right\}$$

(12)

Gradient of Total Variation from (14) is given by

$$\Rightarrow \nabla TV(\mathbf{f}) =$$
$$\frac{1}{2}\sum_{i=1}^{M}\sum_{j=1}^{N}\Psi'\left\{|f_{i+1,j} - f_{i,j}| + |f_{i,j+1} - f_{i,j}| + \alpha^2\right\}.$$

(13)

A new estimate of $\mathbf{f}_{k+1}$ can be stated as a function of $\mathbf{f}_k$ with the help of this relationship:

$$\mathbf{f}^{k+1} = \left[\mathbf{H}^T\mathbf{H} + \lambda\mathbf{L}(\mathbf{f}^k)\right]^{-1}\mathbf{H}^T\mathbf{g}$$
$$\Rightarrow \mathbf{f}^{k+1} = \mathbf{f}^k - \left[\mathbf{H}^T\mathbf{H} + \text{»}\mathbf{L}(\mathbf{f}^k)\right]^{-1}\nabla\mathbf{T}(\mathbf{f}^k)$$

(14)

The regularization operator $\mathbf{L}(\mathbf{f}^k)$ can be computed using the expression

$$L(\mathbf{f}) = D^T_x \, diag\left(\Psi'(\mathbf{f})\right) D_x + D^T_y \, diag\left(\Psi'(\mathbf{f})\right) D_y$$
$$= \begin{bmatrix} D^T_x & D^T_Y \end{bmatrix} \begin{bmatrix} diag(\Psi'(\mathbf{f})) & 0 \\ 0 & diag(\Psi'(\mathbf{f})) \end{bmatrix} \begin{bmatrix} D_x \\ D_y \end{bmatrix}$$

where

$$\Psi'_{i,j}(\mathbf{f}) = \Psi'\left(\left(D^x_{i,j}\mathbf{f}\right)^2 + \left(D^y_{i,j}\mathbf{f}\right)^2\right).$$

The desired value of **f** can be computed by means of several numerical algorithms. The Conjugate Gradient (CG) algorithm is the simplest one, and we will need the initial values of α, $\mathbf{f_0}$, ϵ, and K, where ϵ is the error tolerance between estimates and K is the maximum number of iterations. $\mathbf{f_0}$ can be an even image (one color rectangle where all intensities have the value of the mean of the intensities). CG just computes the initial gradients and search for new direction to proceed. However, CG will converge slowly and linearly to the best solution. The above-mentioned procedure computes the conjugate gradient of (13) and gradually converges in a linear manner.

2.5. State of the Art on TV Norm

LS (Galatsanos & Katsaggelos, 1992. Coelho, & Estrela, 2012a) and TLS (VanHuffel, & Vandewalle, 1991; Markovsky et al., 2010) regularization functionals are based, respectively on the L_2 and Frobenius norms. The first is very simple and works fine for signals with light iid noise. The second cannot be used in its classical form, since it is more sensitive to ill-conditioning. To solve problems related to TLS, several improvements have been proposed (VanHuffel, & Vandewalle, 1991; Markovsky et al., 2010).

This chapter, focuses exclusively on L_1-minimization decoding models, that is TV norm models, because they have the following advantages: (a) flexibility to incorporate prior information into decoding models, (b) stability, and (c) uniform recoverability. Stability addresses the recovery robustness issues when measurements are noisy and/or sparsity is inexact.

TV regularization is a broadly applied method because it keeps image edges. Developments on

this technique are centered mostly on the application of higher order derivatives (Chan, Esedoglu, Park, & Yip, 2005; Stefan, Renaut, & Gelb, 2010; Chambolle & Lions, 1997; Yuan, Schnörr, & Steidl, 2009; Chan, Marquina, & Mulet, 2000) and on nonlocal simplifications too. The fundamental idea behind TV regularization can benefit from the use of a more general differential operator. This increases flexibility because it accounts for the occurrence of a linear system and assorted inputs.

Compressive Sensing (CS) is a technology that acquires data in a compressed format. Next, these compressed measurements are inputted to an inversion algorithm (non-linear optimization algorithm) to generate the complete signal. One goal of a CS system is to find a matrix **A** whose worst-case coherence is as close to the minimum value as possible. That is, given a vector $\mathbf{y}=\mathbf{\Phi\Psi\Phi}+\mathbf{\nu}=\mathbf{A\theta}+\mathbf{\nu}$ of noisy observations of a basic K-sparse vector $\mathbf{\theta}\in R^N$, where $\mathbf{\Phi}$ is the poorly correlated (incoherent) measurement matrix, $\mathbf{\Psi}$ is a sparse representation (signal basis matrix)), **y** $\in R^n$, and $n<N$. According to CS, $\mathbf{\Psi}$ and $\mathbf{\Phi}$ should be incoherent to each other.

TV is convex, hence permitting the design of efficient optimization methods. Despite the popularity that TV regularization enjoys, it has been widely reported (cf. (Lysaker & Tai, 2006) for instance) that, if it is applied in the presence of noise to signals not essentially piecewise constant, then it leads to the staircase effect. In fact, TV allows for vanishing first-order derivatives and, thus, it yields solutions belonging to the class of piecewise-constant functions. This result can be extremely undesirable particularly in applications like biomedical imaging, where image understanding can be brutally obstructed.

To overcome this occasional undesirable effect induced by the TV norm, there is a growing awareness in recent writing for regularization methods involving higher-order differential operators (Lysaker, & Tai, 2006; Steidl, 2006; Bredies et al., 2010). The inspiration behind this effort is to potentially restore a wider set of images evading staircase effects, while conserving image sharpness. These regularizers frequently involve second-order operators, since vanishing second-order derivatives cause piecewise-linear results that better fit smooth intensity alteration.

In (Lefkimmiatis et al., 2012) there is a brief review the class of second order regularizers recently introduced in as an extension of TV. It proposes a projected-gradient method for their efficient minimization under additional convex constraints is well-suited for restoring a larger category of images than simply piecewise-constant. Recently, (Lefkimmiatis et al., 2012) introduced a class of non-quadratic Hessian-based regularizers as a higher-order extension of the TV functional. These regularizers keep some of the most positive properties of TV, at the same time as they can effectively deal with the staircase effect that is commonly met in TV-based reconstructions.

3. APPLICATIONS OF TV-NORM IN COMPUTER VISION

3.1. Computation Challenges

In order to minimize $J_{TV}(\mathbf{f})$, the gradient has to be computed. Differentiating $J_{TV}(\mathbf{f})$ with respect to $\mathbf{f}$ yields to the following nonlinear equation:

$$\mathbf{T}(\mathbf{f}) = \nabla J_{TV}(\mathbf{f}) = -\lambda \nabla \cdot \left(\frac{\nabla \mathbf{f}}{|\nabla \mathbf{f}|}\right) + \mathbf{H}^* (\mathbf{Hf} - \mathbf{g}) = 0. \tag{15}$$

The preceding minimization has the following computational challenges:

- The operator $\nabla \cdot \left(\frac{\nabla \mathbf{f}}{|\nabla \mathbf{f}|}\right) \nabla \cdot \left(\frac{\nabla \mathbf{x}}{|\nabla \mathbf{x}|}\right)$ is extremely nonlinear; and

- $\nabla \cdot \left(\frac{\nabla \mathbf{f}}{|\nabla \mathbf{f}|}\right) \nabla \cdot \left(\frac{\nabla \mathbf{x}}{|\nabla \mathbf{x}|}\right)$ and $\mathbf{H}^*\mathbf{H}$ can be ill-conditioned which leads to numerical difficulties.

The conjugate gradient (CG) method can be used to solve (13). This procedure generates consecutive approximations of the estimation, the errors associated to the iterations, and the acceptable search directions used to revise all the required variables.

Although several schemes (Vogel & Oman, 1996; Chambolle, 2004) have been devised to minimize $J_{TV}(\mathbf{f})$, it continues to be a time-consuming enterprise because it poses severe computational loads to problems with large $\mathbf{H}$ that lack some high-speed realization trick and/or suitable matrix representation.

3.1.1. TV Denoising or Deconvolution

The application of Bayesian models to blind deconvolution is complicated when there is a difficult to handle probability density function (pdf) involving hidden variables $\mathbf{f}$ and $\mathbf{H}$ and the given observations $\mathbf{g}$ (Mateos, Molina, & Katsaggelos, 2005). This fact makes impossible the use simpler and less computationally demanding algorithms such as the EM technique (Coelho, & Estrela, 2012b). On the other hand, with variational approaches it is feasible to circumvent this problem.

The standard TV denoising problem has the form of (6) and it is a way of removing noise from images. It relies on the principle that signals with too much and perhaps spurious elements have high TV (the integral of the absolute gradient of the image has an elevated value). Hence, reducing the TV-norm of the image while keeping it very close to the original image, takes out unnecessary detail whereas conserving significant features such as boundaries (Rudin, Osher, & Fatemi, 1992).

This noise elimination procedure is better than simpler practices, which diminish noise though at the same time wipe out edges to a greater or less important extent. Moreover, TV-norm denoising is extremely successful at preserving boundaries while concomitantly eliminating noise in regions, regardless of the signal-to-noise ratio (SNR) (Strong & Chan, 2003; Caselles, Chambolle, & Novaga, 2011).

Figure 1 shows an example of image denoising when white Gaussian noise is added to the original image with *a-priori* known noise.

3.1.2. TV Minimizing Blind Deconvolution

In the previous case, deconvolution was performed with the help of a known point spread function (PSF). Blind deconvolution (BD) allows the recuperation of an image from a defectively observed or unknown PSF of one or a set of several blurred images. BD estimates the PSF from an image or image set. Hence, there are no assumptions made about **H**. BD betters the PSF estimations and the true image **f** at each iteration. Popular BD methods comprise maximum a posteriori estimation (MAP) and expectation-maximization (EM) algorithms.

Figure 1. The left column shows noisy images and the right side illustrate TV denoising by means of the TV algorithm

A good initial PSF guess facilitates a faster convergence, although it is not indispensable.

(Money, 2006) broadened the minimizing functional proposed by (Chan & Wong, 1998) by adding a reference image to improve the quality of the estimated image and to reduce the computational load for the BD as follows:

$$T(\mathbf{f}) = \|\mathbf{Hf\text{-}g}\|^2 /2 + \lambda_1 TV(\mathbf{f}) + \lambda_1 TV(\mathbf{f}). \quad (16)$$

Then, the problem can be recast as solving the equivalent Euler-Lagrange forms

$$\mathbf{H}^* (\mathbf{Hf\text{-}g}) - \lambda 1 \nabla \cdot \left(\frac{\nabla \mathbf{f}}{|\nabla \mathbf{f}|} \right) = \mathbf{0}, \text{ solve for } \mathbf{H}.$$
$$(17a)$$

$$\mathbf{H}^* (\mathbf{Hf\text{-}g}) - \lambda 2 \nabla \cdot \left(\frac{\nabla \mathbf{f}}{|\nabla \mathbf{f}|} \right) = \mathbf{0}, \text{ solve for } \mathbf{f}.$$
$$(17b)$$

The subsequent algorithm was proposed by (Chan & Wong, 1998) and it is called the Alternating Minimization(AM) method.

AM Algorithm
1.   Initial conditions: α, $\mathbf{f}_0$, ϵ, $\mathbf{H}_0$ and K, where ϵ is the error tolerance between estimates, $\mathbf{H}_0$ is the initial estimate of $\mathbf{H}$ and K is the maximum number of iterations.
2.   while (k < K) or (($\mathbf{f}_k\text{-}\mathbf{f}_{k-1}$)< ϵ do
Solve (15a) for $\mathbf{H}_k$.
Solve (15b) for $\mathbf{f}_k$.
end

3.1.3. Image Restoration

The restoration obtained with regularization methods like RLS smoothes out the edges in the restored image. This can be alleviated by methods relying on L_1-norm regularization like TV regularization keeps the edges in the estimated image. The purpose is to recuperate a real image from an image distorted by several simultaneous phenomena such as blur and noise using the TV norm.

The image formation (forward process) is modeled mathematically using the expression

$$\mathbf{g}=\mathbf{Hf}+\mathbf{n},$$

where, $\mathbf{g}$ is the observed distorted and noisy image, $\mathbf{H}$ represents some Point Spread Function (PSF) or blurring function, $\mathbf{f}$ is the original image, $\mathbf{n}$ is white Gaussian noise.

The Least Absolute Shrinkage and Selection Operator (LASSO) estimator is a shrinkage and selection procedure relying on the L_1 norm for linear regression created by (Tibshirani, 1996). The LASSO estimate is calculated by means of the minimization of a quadratic problem consisting of the customary sum of squared errors, with a bound on the summation of the absolute values of the coefficients f_i and it is defined by

$$\sum_i \left(g_i - \sum_j H_{ij} f_j \right)^2$$

subjected to

$$\sum_j | f_j | \leq c,$$

where c is a parameter controlling the amount of regularization.

TV techniques conserve edge information in computer vision algorithms at the expense of a high computational load. Restoration time in L_1-based TV regularization, for instance, is higher than when LASSO is used. Restoration time using and image quality are respectively lower and better with LASSO than with L_1-based TV regularization. Hence, for some settings, LASSO provides an noteworthy alternative to the L_1-TV norm. Studies illustrate that an augment in the amount

Figure 2. Original blurred and noisy image (top). Reconstruction using Total Variation regularization (left) and LASSO regularization (right)

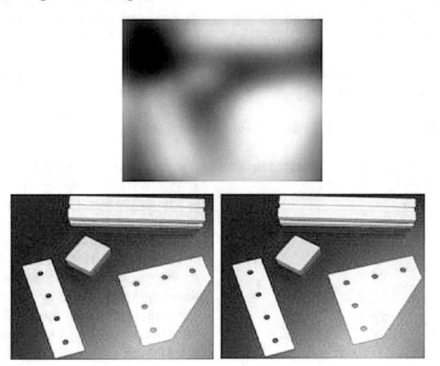

of blur amplifies the restoration error when the L_1 is employed. An increase in the noise level exerts a significant influence on the residual error (Agarwal, Gribok, & Abidi, 2007). Nevertheless, since there are other ways of calculating the TV norm, the computation time and the estimation quality can be further improved and outdo LASSO. Figure 2, shows restored images obtained from an observed one subjected to blurring and noise.

3.1.4. Optical Flow Estimation

In computer vision, the existent motion estimation problem in a video sequence was first studied by (Hom & Schunck, 1981) and it can bring in lots of information to help understanding a given system, scenario and/or problem. Characteristically, the goal is to identify the displacement vector field (DVF) involving successive frames also known as optical flow (OF). On the other hand, variational techniques are very important, and allow for ac-

curate estimation of the DVFs while rooted in the minimization of functionals.

Consider an image sequence $f(x, y, t)$, where (x, y) stands for the location within a frame domain Ω, and $t \in [0, T]$ indicates time. After that, the postulation of unchanging brightness along time (invariance of the displaced frame difference, also known as DFD) can be stated as

$$DFD(\mathbf{f}, u, v) = \mathbf{f}(x + u, y + v, t + 1) - \mathbf{f}(x, y, t) = 0. \tag{18}$$

With the help of a Taylor expansion and after dropping all higher order terms, one obtains its linearized form, the so-called optic flow constraint (OFC)

$$f_x u + f_y v + f_t = 0. \tag{19}$$

Here, the function $\mathbf{u}(x, y, t) = (u, v)$ is the wanted DVF and subscripts denote partial derivatives.

There are different types of regularization for the non-unique solution of the OF problem:

1. Uniform regularization takes for granted an overall smoothness constraint and it does not adjust itself to semantically noteworthy image and/or OF arrangements;

2. Image-driven regularization that assumes piecewise smoothness and respects discontinuities in the image (Nagel & Enkelmann, 1986); and

3. OF regularization assumes piecewise smoothness and respects borders in the DVF as in (Cohen, 1993; Weickert & Schnörr, 2001).

Variational methods are among the finest techniques for estimating the OF by means of error evaluation procedures, however they are frequently slow for real-time applications (Slesareva, Bruhn, & Weickert, 2005; Brox, Bruhn, & Weickert, 2006). For the most part, the computational costs for solving the nonlinear system of equations via typical numerical methods are considered significantly elevated. Variational schemes relying on bidirectional multigrids generate a refined hierarchy of equation systems with first-rate error decrease.

OF algorithms based on variational approaches have been gaining lots of popularity, because they handle dense flow fields and their performance can be good if spatial and temporal discontinuities are retained in the video. Regrettably, this flexibility implies elevated computational load, but this does not preclude real-time performance if methods such as multigrid are employed (Bruhn, Weickert, Kohlberger, & Schnörr, 2005).

Variational computer vision algorithms belong to one of the following classes: i) anisotropic image-driven techniques as proposed by (Nagel & Enkelmann, 1986) which results in a linear system of equations; and ii) isotropic OF-driven schemes with TV regularization that involve solving a nonlinear system of equations.

$$J(u,v) = \int_{\Omega} ((f_x u + f_y v + f_t)^2 + \lambda (\nabla u^T D(\nabla f) \nabla u + \nabla v^T D(\nabla f) \nabla v)) dx dy \tag{20}$$

where $\nabla = (\delta x, \delta y)^T$ denotes the spatial gradient and $D(\nabla f)$ is a projection matrix perpendicular to ∇f that is defined as

$$D(\nabla f) = \frac{1}{|\nabla f| + 2\varepsilon^2} \begin{bmatrix} f_y^2 + \varepsilon^2 & -f_x f_y \\ -f_x f_y & f_x^2 + \varepsilon^2 \end{bmatrix} = \begin{pmatrix} a & b \\ b & c \end{pmatrix}. \tag{21}$$

ε serves as a parameter that prevents matrix $D(\nabla f)$ from being singular. The minimization of this convex functional comes down to solving the following equations

$$f_x^2 u + f_x f_y v + f_x f_t - \frac{\lambda}{2} L_{AN}(u,v) = 0, \tag{22}$$

and

$$f_x f_y u + f_y^2 v + f_y f_t - \frac{\lambda}{2} L_{AN}(v,u) = 0, \tag{23}$$

with

$$L_{AN}(z(x,y), \ \tilde{z}(x,y)) = div(D(\nabla z(x,y), \ \nabla \tilde{z}(x,y)) \nabla z(x,y)) \tag{24}$$

In contrast to image-driven regularization methods, OF-driven techniques trim down smoothing where edges in the flow field occur during computation. (Drulea & Nedevschi, 2011) proposed for this class of variational OF techniques an isotropic method that penalizes deviations from the smoothness constrain with the $\mathbf{L}_1 L_1$-norm of the flow gradient magnitude. This strategy matches TV regularization and it can be linked to norms that are statistically robust to error. In that way, large variations are penalized more mildly than what happens when the popular L_2-norm is used. Therefore, regions with large gradients as it is the case with edges are better handled. Rewriting (18) yields

$$J(u,v) = \int_{\Omega} ((f_x u + f_y v + f_t)^2$$
$$+ \lambda \sqrt{|\nabla u|^2 + |\nabla v|^2 + \varepsilon^2})dxdy$$

where ε serves as small control parameter to avoid having a zero denominator in (19). Another functional that also provides a TV regularization estimate is proposed in (Drulea & Nedevschi, 2011). Apparently, the consequent Euler-Lagrange equations given by

$$f_x^2 u + f_x f_y v + f_x f_t - \frac{\lambda}{2} L_{TV}(u,v) = 0,$$

and

$$f_x f_y u + f_y^2 v + f_y f_t - \frac{\lambda}{2} L_{TV}(v,u) = 0$$

are very similar in structure to (22)-(23). However,

$$L_{TV}(z(x,y), \ \tilde{z}(x,y)) =$$
$$div(D(\nabla z(x,y), \ \nabla \tilde{z}(x,y))\nabla z(x,y))$$

is clearly a nonlinear differential operator in z and z̃, since

$$D(\nabla z, \nabla \tilde{z}) = \frac{1}{\sqrt{|\nabla z|^2 + |\nabla \tilde{z}|^2 + \varepsilon^2}} I,$$

with **I** is the identity matrix, $b=0$ and $c=a$. Soon, it will become clear that the differential operator

L_{TV} is nonlinear and that it impacts seriously the resultant discrete system of equations.

A suitable discretization for the previous Euler-Lagrange equations can be obtained via unknown functions $u(x, y, t)$ and $v(x, y, t)$ on a grid with pixel size $\mathbf{h}=(h_x, h_y)^T$, where $u_{i,j}{}^h$ stands for the approximation to **u** at some pixel located at (i,j) with $i=1, ...,N_x$ and $j=1, ...,N_y$. Spatial and temporal derivatives of the image data and discretized versions of the operators L_{AN}, L_{NE} and L_{TV} are approximated using finite differences as follows:

$$f_{xi,j}^{2,h} u_{i,j}^h + f_{xi,j}^h f_{yi,j}^h v_{i,j}^h + f_{xi,j}^h f_{ti,j}^h - \lambda L_{ANi,j}^h u_{i,j}^h = 0$$

$$f_{(xi,j)}^h f_{(yi,j)}^h u_{(i,j)}^h + f_{(yi,j)}^{(2,h)} v_{(i,j)}^h$$
$$+ f_{(yi,j)}^h f_{(ti,j)}^h - \lambda L_{ANi,j}{}^h v_{i,j}^h = 0$$

where the operator $L_{NEi,j}^h$ indicates L_{AN} discretized at some pixel located at (i,j). The previous expressions amount to a linear system of $2N_x N_y$ equations in $u_{i,j}^h$ and $v_{i,j}^h$. Discretizing the Euler-Lagrange equations for the corresponding TV-based method leads to the nonlinear system of equations shown underneath

$$f_{xi,j}^{2,h} u_{i,j}^h + f_{xi,j}^h f_{yi,j}^h v_{i,j}^h + f_{xi,j}^h f_{ti,j}^h - \lambda L_{TVi,j}^h u_{i,j}^h = 0$$

$$f_{(xi,j)}^h f_{(yi,j)}^h u_{(i,j)}^h + f_{(yi,j)}^{(2,h)} v_{(i,j)}^h$$
$$+ f_{(yi,j)}^h f_{(ti,j)}^h - \lambda L_{TVi,j}^h v_{i,j}^h = 0$$

Here the finite difference approximation of $L_{TV}(u, v)$ and $L_{TV}(v, u)$ yields the product of a common nonlinear operator $L_{TVi,j}^h \left(u_{i,j}^h, v_{i,j}^h \right)$ and the pixels $u_{i,j}^h$ and $v_{i,j}^h$, respectively.

3.2. Solutions and Recommendations

TV norms can be discretized differently from what was shown in previous sections if finite differences, with atypical geometric arrangements of close pixels involving 3, 4 or 8 neighbors, and/ or special norms are used. In Section 2, the TV norm regularization was stated so that it could benefit from the fast algorithm proposed by (Chambolle, 2004).

A discretization procedure is an approximated representation of real continuous signals. Since the pixel dimension cannot usually be selected in computer vision, presupposing it is small enough may not be appropriate. TV-norms founded on finite differences are also arguable due to the need of having sub-pixel accuracy in algorithms that require, for example, sub-pixel interpolation. According to the sampling theory, the discretization procedure shown in Section 2 is not good, because notwithstanding the fact that $\mathbf{f}$ was sampled consistently with Shannon's theorem, the squares in $|\nabla \mathbf{f}|$ bring in high frequencies that require smaller sampling intervals to be attenuated. Therefore, the estimation of $|\nabla \mathbf{f}|$ has problems due to alias and the resulting TV norm estimate of $\mathbf{f}$ will carry artifacts.

Despite the fact that using TV-norm can decrease fluctuations and improve regularization of inverse problems in computer vision without compromising edges, it has some undesirable side effects:

1. The solution to the (Rudin, Osher, & Fatemi, 1992) model is prone to contrast loss due to scaling of the regularization and fidelity terms because it decreases the bounded TV norm of a function, in the vicinity of its mean. In general, a reduction of the contrast decreases the regularization term of the (Rudin, Osher, & Fatemi, 1992) model and boosts the fidelity term.

2. Geometric alterations may perhaps appear since the TV norm of a function is reduced once the length of all level sets is decreased. Sometimes, this distorts silhouettes that are not part of the shape-invariant set when the (Rudin, Osher, & Fatemi, 1992) model is employed. Still, for circular parts, (Strong & Chan, 2003) have demonstrated that shape is kept for a small variation in λ as well as location albeit in the presence of moderate noise. Corners may suffer deformation as well.

3. Staircasing refers to the case when the estimated image may appear blocky outside corners due to the high values of the level sets curvature. TV norm amendments, which include higher-order derivatives, are an alternative to this problem when there is sensible parameter selection.

4. Even though extremely valuable, the TV norm cannot always keep textures because the model from (Rudin, Osher, & Fatemi, 1992) has the propensity to affect small features present in images and it can suffer because of scaling. Hence, the net effect is texture loss.

The NUMIPAD library has a collection of techniques to solve inverse problems such as Tikhonov regularization, Total Variation, Basis Pursuit, etc. (Rodrıguez & Wohlberg). Other very good package written in MATLAB is the L_1-magic (Candes, Romberg, & Tao).

4. FUTURE RESEARCH DIRECTIONS

For models such as $\mathbf{g} = \mathbf{Hf} + \mathbf{n}$, it is not viable to state unambiguously the probabilistic relationship associated to the convolving functions when $\mathbf{g}$ is known and Bayesian inference is used (Likas & Galatsanos, 2004; Mateos, Molina, & Katsaggelos, 2005). A variational scheme can help to overcome this hindrance with higher performance than conventional techniques. The principal deficiency of the variational line of reasoning is the lack of systematic evaluation procedures to appraise the variational bound stiffness. Evidently, more studies on this topic and optimization procedures are required. Still, the suggestd method is rather extensive, so that it can be combined with other Bayesian models for several imaging applications.

It is a well-known fact that LS estimate is not robust to outliers. There are some recent efforts in compressed sensing (Candes. E.J. & Wakin, 2008; Candes, Romberg, & Tao, 2006) that focus on the L_0-L_1 equivalence to determine the gradient which best replaces the degraded gradient field. These works investigate robust strategies to estimate gradient by taking into consideration error corrections along with concepts from research on sparse signal retrieval. Among other things, they confirm that the location of errors is as important as the number of errors when it comes to the gradient integration required by the TV norm.

To reconcile TV with Shannon Theory (Shannon, 1948), the TV of a discrete image **f** u can be defined as being the exact (continuous) TV of its Shannon interpolate **F** which is equal to the Fourier transform of **f**. However, since TV(**F**), TV(U) cannot be computed exactly, (Moisan, 2007*)* uses a Riemann sum with an oversampling factor n, and define the Spectral Total Variation (STV) of **f** u (of order $n \geq 1$) in this manner:

$$STV_n\left(\mathbf{f}\right) = \left(1/n^2\right)\Sigma_{0 \leq k,l < nN}\left[\left|D\mathbf{F}\right|\left(k/n,l/n\right)\right].$$

$STV_n(\mathbf{f})$, $STV_n(u)$ is supposed to yield a fine estimate of TV(U), $TV(\mathbf{F})$ for any **f** u, given that this measure is a regularization term. $n=1$ is not a good option, because controlling the gradient norm of **F** only at grid points does not permit its control between grid points. When $n=2$, a new TV discretization is obtained along with several improvements: grid independence, compatibility

with Shannon theory and the possibility of achieving sub-pixel precision, at the expense of applying Fourier Transforms, which is a widespread necessity in deconvolution problems, for instance.

Adaptive TV norm calculations are needed in order to better care for texture along with fine-scale details. Afterwards, the adaptive procedure enforces local constraints depending on local metrics (Gilboa, Sochen, & Zeevi, 2003).

Despite the fact that most works concentrate on scalar functions, the extension of the reasoning used in this chapter to color or multi-channel images remains an important challenge because it requires vector valued parameters and/or functions. This generalization is not trouble-free, but it can result from geometric measure theory.

The improvement of proper multigrid approaches becomes more complicated thanks to the anisotropy and/or nonlinearity of the basic regularization strategies, but they can lead to real-time performance.

5. CONCLUSION

This chapter focuses on: (i) a brief overview of regularization; (ii) the definition and explanation of the purpose of a regularization procedure called total variation norm (TV-norm) in image processing; (iii) a concise discussion of the mathematical conditions of TV methods; and (iv) setting up a relations connecting models and a few present techniques to solve problems cast as TV-norm.

The TV norm examined in this text rely exclusively on L_1-minimization decoding models. They have the subsequent advantages: (a) it is easy to include prior data into decoding models, (b) stability, and (c) uniform recoverability.

Predominantly, computer vision algorithms blur the borders of predicted images, nevertheless TV regularization preserves the boundaries without prior information on the original images. The regularization parameter λ directs the quantity of regularization permissible and it is essential to attain a high-quality regularized output.

LS and TLS regularization functionals are based, respectively on the L_2 and Frobenius norms. The first is very simple and works fine for signals with light iid noise. The second cannot be used in its classical form, since it is more sensitive to ill-conditioning. To solve problems related to TLS, several improvements have been proposed.

In view of the fact that there exist further ways of estimating the divergence operator required by the TV norm, the totaling time and image quality can be made superior.

To augment the efficiency of the regularization procedure, alternative algorithms relying on dual forms of the TV norm call for further research on topics such as exponential spline wavelets (Khalidov & Unser, 2006) or generalized Daubechies wavelets (Schwamberger, Le, Schölkopf, & Franz, 2010; Vonesch, Blu, & Unser, 2007). Undeniably, these wavelet improvements can be tuned to a given differential operator and their use for regularized computer vision purposes corresponds to a synthesis prior (Franz & Schölkopf, 2006). Prospective research is also wanted to strengthen a more precise relationship involving discrete domain approaches and suitable forms of TV regularization in the continuous domain. Current work (Vonesch, Blu, & Unser, 2007) has shown that the usual TV norm calculation via the L_1-norm with finite differences can be associated to appropriate representations of stochastic processes.

Compressed sensing (CS) enables recovery of compressed images from a small number of linear measurements (Kienzle, Bakir, Franz, & Schölkopf, 2005; Candes, & Wakin, 2008). It can be an alternative to methods that try to handle missing information, but it involve larger image representations. It had been well known that without noise contamination, images with completely sparse gradients can be recovered with a high degree of accuracy through TV-norm. Hence, there are several CS algorithms relying on TV regularization because according to (Candes,

Romberg, & Tao, 2006) they have outstanding outputs in the presence of images with sparse discrete gradients. TV methods also work well with piecewise constant images. Furthermore, since images are easier to compress when the discrete gradient representation is used, the TV-norm has advantages over wavelets in the presence of additive and/or quantization noise (Jiang, Li, Haimi-Cohen, Wilford, & Zhang, 2012).

Noise can obliterate image analysis. Images with unknown noise can be handled with no priors if a wavelet decomposition technique is used with a non-isotropic TV filtering in a way that there is gain from both the multiresolution capacity of the wavelet as well as the edge-preserving properties of the TV-norm (Zhang, 2009).

REFERENCES

Acar, R., & Vogel, C. R. (1994). Analysis of bounded variation penalty methods for ill-posed problems. *Inverse Problems*, 10(6), 1217–1229. doi:10.1088/0266-5611/10/6/003

Afonso, M. V., Bioucas-Dias, J. M., & Figueiredo, M. A. (2010). An augmented Lagrangian approach to linear inverse problems with compound regularization. *ICIP 2010 17th IEEE International Conference on Image Processing* (pp. 4169–4172). IEEE.

Afonso, M. V., Bioucas-Dias, J. M., & Figueiredo, M. A. (2011). An augmented Lagrangian approach to the constrained optimization formulation of imaging inverse problems. *IEEE Transactions on Image Processing*, 20(3), 681–695. doi:10.1109/TIP.2010.2076294 PMID:20840899

Agarwal, V., Gribok, A., & Abidi, M. (2007). Image restoration using l1 norm penalty function. *Inverse Problems in Science and Engineering*, 15(8), 785–809. doi:10.1080/17415970600971987

Alpaydin, E. (2004). *Introduction to Machine Learning*. Cambridge, MA: MIT Press.

Alter, F., Durand, S., & Froment, J. (2005). Adapted total variation for artifact free decompression of JPEG images. *J. Math. Imaging and Vision, 23*(2), 199–211.

Blomgren, P., & Chan, T. F. (1998). Color TV: total variation methods for restoration of vector-valued images. *IEEE Transactions on Image Processing, 7*(3), 304-309. Retrieved from http://www.ncbi.nlm.nih.gov/pubmed/18276250

Bredies, K., Kunisch, K., & Pock, T. (2010). Total generalized variation. *SIAM Journal on Imaging Sciences, 3*(3), 492–526. doi:10.1137/090769521

Brox, T., Bruhn, A., & Weickert, J. (2006). Variational motion segmentation with level sets. *European Conference on Computer Vision (ECCV), 1,* 471-483.

Bruhn, A., Weickert, J., Kohlberger, T., & Schnörr, C. (2005). Discontinuity-preserving computation of variational optic flow in real-time. *Scale Space and PDE Methods in Computer Vision, 3459,* 279-290. Retrieved on August 29, 2014 from http://www.springerlink.com/index/jbevcvnfeg-kdrw0k.pdf

Candes, E., Romberg, J., & Tao, T. (2006). Robust uncertainty principles: Exact signal reconstruction from highly incomplete frequency information. *IEEE Transactions on Information Theory, 52*(2), 489–509. doi:10.1109/TIT.2005.862083

Candes, E. J., Romberg, J., & Tao, T. (n.d.). Retrieved from http://users.ece.gatech.edu/~justin/l1magic/

Candes, E.J. & Wakin, M. (2008). An introduction to compressive sampling. *IEEE Signal Processing Magazine, 25*(2), 21-30.

Caselles, V., Chambolle, A., & Novaga, M. (2011). Total variation in imaging. Media, *1*(1), 1015-1057.

Chambolle, A. (2004). An algorithm for total variation minimization and applications. *Journal of Mathematical Imaging and Vision, 20*(1/2), 89-97. doi:10.1023/B:JMIV.0000011321.19549.88

Chambolle, A., & Lions, P. L. (1997). Image recovery via total variation minimization and related problems. *Numerische Mathematik, 76*(2), 167-188. doi:10.1007/s002110050258

Chan, T., Esedoglu, S., Park, F., & Yip, A. (2005). *Recent developments in total variation image restoration. In Handbook of Mathematical Models in Computer Vision* (pp. 17–30). New York: Springer.

Chan, T. F., Marquina, A., & Mulet, P. (2000). High-order total variation-based image restoration. *SIAM Journal on Scientific Computing, 22*(2), 503–516. doi:10.1137/S1064827598344169

Chan, T. F., & Shen, J. (2005). *Image Processing and Analysis - Variational, PDE, Wavelet, and Stochastic Methods.* SIAM. doi:10.1137/1.9780898717877

Chan, T. F., & Wong, C. K. (1998). Total variation blind deconvolution. *IEEE Transactions on Image Processing, 7*(3), 370–375. doi:10.1109/83.661187 PMID:18276257

Cheng-wu, L. (2009). A fast algorithm for variational image inpainting. *2009 AICI International Conference on Artificial Intelligence and Computational Intelligence, 3,* 439-443.

Coelho, A. M., & Estrela, V. V. (2012a). Data-driven motion estimation with spatial adaptation. [IJIP]. *International Journal of Image Processing, 6*(1). Retrieved from http://www.cscjournals.org/csc/manuscript/Journals/IJIP/volume6/Issue1/IJIP-513.pdf

Coelho, A. M., & Estrela, V. V. (2012b). EM-based mixture models applied to video event detection. In P. Sanguansat (Ed.), *Intech.* doi:10.5772/2693

Coelho, A. M., & Estrela, V. V. (2012c). A study on the effect of regularization matrices in motion estimation. *IJCA*, 2012.

Cohen, I. (1993). Nonlinear variational method for optical flow computation. *Proc. Eighth Scandinavian Conference on Image Analysis*, *1*, 523-530.

Donoho, D., & Tsaig, Y. (2008). Fast solution of l1-norm minimization problems when the solution may be sparse. *IEEE Transactions on Information Theory*, *54*(11), 4789–4812. doi:10.1109/TIT.2008.929958

Drulea, M., & Nedevschi, S. (2011). Total variation regularization of local-global optical flow. *Proc. 14th International IEEE Conference on Intelligent Transportation Systems (ITSC)*, (pp. 318 - 323). doi:10.1109/ITSC.2011.6082986

Efron, B., Hastie, T., Johnstone, I., & Tibshirani, R. (2004). Least angle regression. *Annals of Statistics*, *32*(2), 407–499. doi:10.1214/009053604000000067

Fontana, R. (2004). Recent system applications of short-pulse ultra-wideband (uwb) technology. *IEEE Transactions on Microwave Theory and Techniques*, *52*(9), 2087–2104. doi:10.1109/TMTT.2004.834186

Franz, M., & Schölkopf, B. (2006). A unifying view of Wiener and Volterra theory and polynomial kernel regression. *Neural Computation*, *18*(12), 3097–3118. doi:10.1162/neco.2006.18.12.3097 PMID:17052160

Friedman, J., Hastie, T., & Tibshirani, R. (2010). Regularization paths for generalized linear models via coordinate descent. *Journal of Statistical Software*, *33*(1), 1. doi:10.18637/jss.v033.i01 PMID:20808728

Fromont, M. (2007). Model selection by bootstrap penalization for classification. *Machine Learning*, *66*(2-3), 165–207. doi:10.1007/s10994-006-7679-y

Galatsanos, N. P., & Katsaggelos, A. K. (1992). Methods for choosing the regularization parameter and estimating the noise variance in image restoration and their relation. *IEEE Transactions on Image Processing*, *1*(3), 322–336. doi:10.1109/83.148606 PMID:18296166

Gilboa, G., Sochen, N., & Zeevi, Y. Y. (2003). Texture preserving variational denoising using an adaptive fidelity term. *Proc. VLSM 2003*. Nice, France.

Guichard, F., & Malgouyres, F. (1998). Total variation based interpolation. *Proc. European Signal Processing Conf.*, *3*, 1741-1744.

Hom, B., & Schunck, B. (1981). Determining optical flow. *Artificial Intelligence*, *17*(1-3), 185–203. doi:10.1016/0004-3702(81)90024-2

Jiang, H., Li, C., Haimi-Cohen, R., Wilford, P., & Zhang, Y. (2012). Scalable video coding using compressive sensing. *Bell Labs Technical Journal*, *16*(4), 149–169. doi:10.1002/bltj.20539

Kang, M. G., & Katsaggelos, A. K. (1995). General choice of the regularization functional in regularized image restoration. *IEEE Transactions on Image Processing*, *4*(5), 594–602. doi:10.1109/83.382494 PMID:18290009

Khalidov, I., & Unser, M. (2006). From differential equations to the construction of new wavelet-like bases. *IEEE Transactions on Signal Processing*, *54*(4), 1256–1267. doi:10.1109/TSP.2006.870544

Kienzle, W., Bakir, G., Franz, M., & Schölkopf, B. (2005). Face detection - efficient and rank deficient. Academic Press.

Lefkimmiatis, S., Bourquard, A., & Unser, M. (2012). Hessian-based norm regularization for image restoration with biomedical applications. *IEEE Transactions on Image Processing*, *21*(3), 983–995. doi:10.1109/TIP.2011.2168232 PMID:21937351

Likas, A., & Galatsanos, N. (2004). A variational approach for bayesian blind image deconvolution. *IEEE Transactions on Signal Processing, 52*(8), 2222–2233. doi:10.1109/TSP.2004.831119

Lysaker, M., & Tai, X.-C. (2006). Iterative image restoration combining total variation minimization and a second-order functional. *International Journal of Computer Vision, 66*(1), 5–18. doi:10.1007/s11263-005-3219-7

Markovsky, I., Sima, D., & Van Huffel, S. (2010). Total least squares methods. *WIREs Computational Statistics, 2*(2), 212–217. doi:10.1002/wics.65

Mateos, J., Molina, R., & Katsaggelos, A. (2005). Approximations of posterior distributions in blind deconvolution using variational methods. *Proceedings of the IEEE International Conference on Image Processing (ICIP 2005), 2*, 770-773. doi:10.1109/ICIP.2005.1530169

Moisan, L. (2007) How to discretize the total variation of an image? *PAMM · Proc. Appl. Math. Mech.* 7. DOI 10.1002/pamm.200700424

Molina, R., Vega, M., & Katsaggelos, A. K. (2007). From global to local Bayesian parameter estimation in image restoration using variational distribution approximations. *2007 IEEE International Conference on Image Processing* (Vol. 1). doi:10.1109/ICIP.2007.4378906

Money, J. H. (2006). *Variational methods for image deblurring and discretized Picard's method.* University of Kentucky Doctoral Dissertations. Paper 381. Retrieved from http://uknowledge.uky.edu/gradschool_diss/381

Nagel, H. H., & Enkelmann, W. (1986). An investigation of smoothness constraints for the estimation of displacement vector fields from image sequences. *IEEE Transactions on Pattern Analysis and Machine Intelligence, 8*(5), 565–593. doi:10.1109/TPAMI.1986.4767833 PMID:21869357

Reddy, D., Agrawal, A., & Chellappa, R. (2009). Enforcing integrability by error correction using L1-minimization. *Proceedings of the IEEE Conference on Computer Vision and Pattern Recognition CVPR09,* (pp. 2350-2357). doi:10.1109/CVPR.2009.5206603

Rodrıguez, P., & Wohlberg, B. (n.d.). *Numerical methods for inverse problems and adaptive decomposition (NUMIPAD).* Retrieved from http://sourceforge.net/projects/numipad/

Roudenko, S. (2004). *Noise and texture detection in image processing.* LANL report: W-7405-ENG-36.

Rudin, L., Osher, S., & Fatemi, E. (1992). Nonlinear total variation based noise removal algorithms. *Physica D. Nonlinear Phenomena, 60*(1-4), 259–268. doi:10.1016/0167-2789(92)90242-F

Rudin, L. I., & Osher, S. (1994). Total variation based image restoration with free local constraints. *Proc. IEEE Int. Conf. Image Processing, 1*, 31–35. doi:10.1109/ICIP.1994.413269

Schwamberger, V., Le, P. H., Schölkopf, B., & Franz, M. O. (2010). The influence of the image basis on modeling and steganalysis performance. In: R. Böhme, & P. Fong (Ed.), *Proc. of the 12th Intl. Conf. on Information Hiding,* (pp. 133-144). Calgary. doi:10.1007/978-3-642-16435-4_11

Sfikas, G., Nikou, C., Galatsanos, N., & Heinrich, C. (2011). Majorization-minimization mixture model determination in image segmentation. *CVPR, 2011,* 2169–2176.

Shannon, C. (1948). A mathematical theory of communication. Bell System Technical Journal, 27, 379–423, 623–656.

Stefan, W., Renaut, R., & Gelb, A. (2010). Improved total variation-type regularization using higher order edge detectors. *SIAM J. Imag. Sci.,* 232–251.

Steidl, G. (2006). A note on the dual treatment of higher-order regularization functionals. *Computing*, *76*(1-2), 135–148. doi:10.1007/s00607-005-0129-z

Strong, D., & Chan, T. (2003). Edge-preserving and scale-dependent properties of total variation regularization. *Inverse Problems*, *19*(6), S165–S187. doi:10.1088/0266-5611/19/6/059

Tibshirani, R. (1996). Regression shrinkage and selection via the lasso. *Journal of the Royal Statistical Society. Series B. Methodological*, *58*, 267–288.

VanHuffel, S., & Vandewalle, J. (1991). *The total least squares problem: computational aspects and analysis*. SIAM. doi:10.1137/1.9781611971002

Vapnik, V. (1995). *The nature of statistical learning theory*. New York: Springer Verlag. doi:10.1007/978-1-4757-2440-0

Vogel, C. R., & Oman, M. E. (1996). Iterative methods for total variation denoising. *SIAM J. on Scientiffic Computing*, *17*(1-4), 227–238. doi:10.1137/0917016

Vonesch, C., Blu, T., & Unser, M. (2007). Generalized Daubechies wavelet families. *IEEE Transactions on Signal Processing*, *55-9*(9), 4415–4429. doi:10.1109/TSP.2007.896255

Wang, L., Gordo, M. D., & Ji Zhu, J. (2006). Regularized least absolute deviations regression and an efficient algorithm for parameter tuning. *Sixth International Conference on Data Mining*, (pp. 690–700). doi:10.1109/ICDM.2006.134

Wang, Y., Yang, J., Yin, W., & Zhang, Y. (2008). A new alternating minimization algorithm for total variation image reconstruction. *Journal SIAM Journal on Imaging Sciences*, *1*(3), 248–272. doi:10.1137/080724265

Weickert, J., & Schnörr, C. (2001). A theoretical framework for convex regularizers in PDE-based computation of image motion. *International Journal of Computer Vision*, *45*(3), 245–264. doi:10.1023/A:1013614317973

Yuan, J., Schnörr, C., & Steidl, G. (2009). Total-variation based piecewise affine regularization. *Proc. of the 2nd Int. Conf. Scale Space Variation. Methods in Comput. Vis. (SSVM)*, (pp. 552–564). doi:10.1007/978-3-642-02256-2_46

Zeng, T., & Ng, M. K. (2010). On the total variation dictionary model. *IEEE Transactions on Image Processing*, *19*(3), 821–825. doi:10.1109/TIP.2009.2034701 PMID:19840910

Zhang, Y. (2009). *User's Guide for YALL1: Your Algorithms for L1 Optimization*. Technical Report TR09-17, Department of Computational and Applied Mathematics, Rice University.

Zuo, W. (2011). A generalized accelerated proximal gradient approach for total-variation-based image restoration. *IEEE Transactions on Image Processing*, *20*(10), 2748–2759. doi:10.1109/TIP.2011.2131665 PMID:21435979

ADDITIONAL READING

Charbonnier, P., Blanc-Feraud, L., Aubert, G., & Barlaud, M. (1997). Deterministic edge-preserving regularization in computed imaging. *IEEE Transactions on Image Processing*, *6*(2), 298–311. http://www.ncbi.nlm.nih.gov/pubmed/18282924 doi:10.1109/83.551699 PMID:18282924

Christiansen, O., Lee, T.-M., Lie, J., Sinha, U., & Chan, T. F. (2007). Total variation regularization of matrix-valued images. *International Journal of Biomedical Imaging*, *2007*(2007), 27432. Hindawi Publishing Corporation. Retrieved from http://www.pubmedcentral.nih.gov/articlerender.fcgi?artid=1994779&tool=pmcentrez&rendertype=abstract

Coelho, A. M., Estrela, V. V., do Carmo, F. P., & Fernandes, S. R. (2012). Error concealment by means of motion refinement and regularized Bregman divergence. *Proceedings of the Intelligent Data Engineering and Automated Learning -IDEAL 2012*, (Eds.): Yin, H., Costa, J. A. F., Barreto, G. A., 13th International Conference, Natal, Brazil, 650-657 doi:10.1007/978-3-642-32639-4_78

Combettes, Patrick L., & Pesquet, J.-C. (2004). Image restoration subject to a total variation constraint. *IEEE Transactions on Image Processing, 13*(9), 1213-1222. IEEE. doi:10.1109/TIP.2004.832922

Combettes, P. L., & Pesquet, J. C. (2003a). Total variation information in image recovery. *Proceedings 2003 International Conference on Image Processing Cat No03CH37429, 3.* doi:10.1109/ICIP.2003.1247259

Combettes, P. L., & Pesquet, J. C. (2003b). Image deconvolution with total variation bounds. *Seventh International Symposium on Signal Processing and Its Applications 2003 Proceedings 1*, 441-444. Ieee. doi:10.1109/ISSPA.2003.1224735

Drapaca, C. S. (2009). A nonlinear total variation-based denoising method with two regularization parameters. *IEEE Transactions on Bio-Medical Engineering, 56*(3), 582–586. doi:10.1109/TBME.2008.2011561 PMID:19174344

Estrela, V. V., Rivera, L. A., Beggio, P. C., & Lopes, R. T. (2003). Regularized pel-recursive motion estimation using generalized cross-validation and spatial adaptation (pp. 331–338). SIBGRAPI; Retrieved from http://dblp.uni-trier.de/db/conf/sibgrapi/sibgrapi2003.html#EstrelaRBL03 doi:10.1109/SIBGRA.2003.1241027

Farcomeni, A. (2010). Bayesian constrained variable selection. *Statistica Sinica, 20*(1), 1043–1062. doi:10.1007/s00439-008-0582-9

Figueiredo, M., Dias, J., Oliveira, J., & Nowak, R. (2006). On total variation denoising: a new majorization-minimization algorithm and an experimental comparison with wavalet denoising. *IEEE International Conference on Image Processing 2006*(5), 2633-2636. doi:10.1109/ICIP.2006.313050

Figueiredo, M. A. T., Bioucas-Dias, J. M., & Nowak, R. D. (2007). Majorization-minimization algorithms for wavelet-based image restoration. *IEEE Transactions on Image Processing, 16*(12), 2980–2991. http://www.ncbi.nlm.nih.gov/pubmed/18092597 doi:10.1109/TIP.2007.909318 PMID:18092597

Fornasier, M. Langer, A., & Schönlieb, C.-B. (2009). A convergent overlapping domain decomposition method for total variation minimization. *Numerische Mathematik, 116*(4), 645-685. Springer. Retrieved from http://arxiv.org/abs/0905.2404

Fornasier, Massimo, & Schönlieb, C.-B. (2007). Subspace correction methods for total variation and -minimization. *Physics, 47*(5), 33. SIAM. Retrieved from http://arxiv.org/abs/0712.2258

Galatsanos, N. (2008). A majorization-minimization approach to total variation reconstruction of super-resolved images. *Stat*, (30): 2–6.

Hnetynkova, I., Plesinger, M., Sima, D., Strakos, Z., & Van Huffel, S. (2011). The total least squares problem in B. A new classification with the relationship to the classical works. *SIAM Journal on Matrix Analysis and Applications, 32*(3), 748–770. doi:10.1137/100813348

Hu, Y., & Jacob, M. (2012). Higher degree total variation (HDTV) regularization for image recovery. *IEEE Transactions on Image Processing, 21*(5), 2559–2571. doi:10.1109/TIP.2012.2183143 PMID:22249711

Hutter, M. (2009). Discrete MDL predicts in total variation. (Y. Bengio, D. Schuurmans, J. Lafferty, C. K. I. Williams, & A. Culotta, Eds.) *Advances in Neural Information Processing Systems*, (x), 1-9. Curran Associates. Retrieved from http://eprints.pascal-network.org/archive/00005838/

Jaggi, M. (2010). A simple algorithm for nuclear norm regularized problems. *In Practice*, (X), 471-478. Citeseer. Retrieved from http://citeseerx.ist.psu.edu/viewdoc/download?doi=10.1.1.167.4776&rep=rep1&type=pdf

Jin, B., & Lorenz, D. (2010). Heuristic parameter-choice rules for convex variational regularization based on error estimates. *Program, 48*(3), 1-24. SIAM. Retrieved from http://arxiv.org/abs/1001.5346

Kang, M. G., & Katsaggelos, A. K. (1995). General choice of the regularization functional in regularized image restoration. *IEEE Transactions on Image Processing*, 4(5), 594–602. http://www.ncbi.nlm.nih.gov/pubmed/18290009 doi:10.1109/83.382494 PMID:18290009

Knoll, F., Bredies, K., Pock, T., & Stollberger, R. (2011). Second order total generalized variation (TGV) for MRI. *Magnetic Resonance in Medicine, 65*(2), 480-491. Wiley Online Library. doi:10.1002/mrm.22595

Koko, J., & Jehan-Besson, S. (2010). An augmented Lagrangian method for TVG +L 1-norm minimization. *Journal of Mathematical Imaging and Vision, 38*(3), 182-196. Springer Netherlands. doi:10.1007/s10851-010-0219-1

Lasenby, A. N., Barreiro, R. B., & Hobson, M. P. (2001). Regularization and inverse problems. (J. Skilling, Ed.) *Inverse Problems, 375*, 15. Kluwer. Retrieved from http://arxiv.org/abs/astro-ph/0104306

Lee, S.-H. L. S.-H., & Kang, M. G. K. M. G. (2007). Total variation-based image noise reduction with generalized fidelity function. *IEEE Signal Processing Letters* (Vol. 14, pp. 832–835). IEEE. doi:10.1109/LSP.2007.901697

Li, Y., & Santosa, F. (1996). A computational algorithm for minimizing total variation in image restoration. *IEEE Transactions on Image Processing*, 5(6), 987–995. http://www.ncbi.nlm.nih.gov/pubmed/18285186 doi:10.1109/83.503914 PMID:18285186

Lv, J., & Fan, Y. (2009). A unified approach to model selection and sparse recovery using regularized least squares. *Annals of Statistics, 37*(6A), 3498–3528. http://arxiv.org/abs/0905.3573 doi:10.1214/09-AOS683

Marquina, A., & Osher, S. J. (2008). Image super-resolution by TV-regularization and Bregman iteration. *Journal of Scientific Computing*, 37(3), 367–382. doi:10.1007/s10915-008-9214-8

Michailovich, O. V. (2011). An iterative shrinkage approach to total-variation image restoration. *IEEE Transactions on Image Processing, 20*(5), 1281-1299. IEEE. Retrieved from http://arxiv.org/abs/0910.5002

Mohammad-Djafari, A. (2001). Bayesian inference for inverse problems. (R. L. Fry, Ed.) *AIP Conference Proceedings, 617*, 477-496. AIP. Retrieved from http://arxiv.org/abs/physics/0110093

Molina, R., Vega, M., & Katsaggelos, A. K. (2007). From global to local Bayesian parameter estimation in image restoration using variational distribution approximations. *2007 IEEE International Conference on Image Processing* (Vol. 1). doi:10.1109/ICIP.2007.4378906

Morgan, S. P., & Vixie, K. R. (2006). L1-TV computes the flat norm for boundaries. *Abstract and Applied Analysis, 2007*, 1–19. http://arxiv.org/abs/math/0612287 doi:10.1155/2007/45153

Ng, M. K., Shen, H., Lam, E. Y., & Zhang, L. (2007). A total variation regularization based super-resolution reconstruction algorithm for digital video. *EURASIP Journal on Advances in Signal Processing, 2007*, 1–17. doi:10.1155/2007/74585

Oliveira, J. P., Bioucas-Dias, J. M., & Figueiredo, M. A. T. (2009). Adaptive total variation image deblurring: A majorization–minimization approach. *Signal Processing, 89*(9), 1683–1693. doi:10.1016/j.sigpro.2009.03.018

Osher, Stanley, Solé, A., & Vese, L. (2003). Image decomposition and restoration using total variation minimization and the H1. *Multiscale Modeling Simulation, 1*(3), 349. Citeseer. doi:10.1137/S1540345902416247

Osher, S. Burger, M., Goldfarb, D., Xu, J., & Yin, W. (2005). An iterative regularization method for total variation-based image restoration. (W. G. Lehnert & M. H. Ringle, Eds.)Multiscale Modeling Simulation, 4(2), 460. SIAM. doi:10.1137/040605412

Osher, S., Sole, A., & Vese, L. (2003). Image decomposition, image restoration, and texture modeling using total variation minimization and the H-1 norm. *Proceedings 2003 International Conference on Image Processing Cat No03CH37429* (Vol. 1, p. 3). Ieee. doi:10.1109/ICIP.2003.1247055

Press, W. H., Teukolsky, S. A., Vetterling, W. T., & Flannery, B. P. (2007). Numerical Recipes Source Code CD-ROM 3rd Edition: The Art of Scientific Computing. Retrieved from http://dl.acm.org/citation.cfm?id=1388393

Rodríguez, P., & Wohlberg, B. (2009). Efficient minimization method for a generalized total variation functional. *IEEE Transactions on Image Processing, 18*(2), 322–332. doi:10.1109/TIP.2008.2008420 PMID:19116200

Rosasco, L., Santoro, M., Mosci, S., Verri, A., & Villa, S. (2010). A regularization approach to nonlinear variable selection. *Proceedings of the International Conference on Artificial Intelligence and Statistics, 9*, 653-660. Retrieved from http://jmlr.csail.mit.edu/proceedings/papers/v9/rosasco10a/rosasco10a.pdf

Sakurai, M., Kiriyama, S., Goto, T., & Hirano, S. (2011). Fast algorithm for total variation minimization. 2011 18th IEEE International Conference on Image Processing (pp. 1461–1464). IEEE; Retrieved from http://ieeexplore.ieee.org/lpdocs/epic03/wrapper.htm?arnumber=6115718

Scales, J. A., & Gersztenkorn, A. (1988). Robust methods in inverse theory. (J. A. Scales, Ed.) Inverse Problems, 4(4), 1071-1091. Soc. of Expl. Geophys. doi:10.1088/0266-5611/4/4/010

Sidky, E. Y., Chartrand, R., Duchin, Y., Ullberg, C., & Pan, X. (2010). High resolution image reconstruction with constrained, total-variation minimization. *IEEE Nuclear Science Symposuim Medical Imaging Conference, 2*, 2617-2620. IEEE. Retrieved from http://arxiv.org/abs/1104.0909

Sidky, E. Y., Duchin, Y., Ullberg, C., & Pan, X. (2010). A constrained, total-variation minimization algorithm for low-intensity X-ray CT. *Medical Physics, 38*(S1), S117. http://arxiv.org/abs/1011.4630 doi:10.1118/1.3560887 PMID:21978112

Slesareva, N., Bruhn, A., & Weickert, J. (2005). Optic flow goes stereo: a variational method for estimating discontinuity-preserving dense disparity maps. *German Conference on Pattern Recognition (DAGM)*, Vol. 1 (pp. 33-40). doi:10.1007/11550518_5

Strong, D. M., Chan, T. F., & R. (1996). *Exact Solutions to Total Variation Regularization Problems. UCLA CAM Report*. Retrieved from http://citeseerx.ist.psu.edu/viewdoc/summary?doi=10.1.1.51.798

Stuart, A. M. (2010). Inverse problems: A Bayesian perspective. Acta Numerica, 19(1), 451-559. Cambridge University Press. doi:10.1017/S0962492910000061

Tao, M. I. N., & Yang, J. (2009). Alternating direction algorithms for total variation deconvolution in image reconstruction. *TR0918 Department of Mathmatics*, (x), 1-17. Retrieved from http://www.optimization-online.org/DB_FILE/2009/11/2463.pdf

Tarantola, A. (2005). Inverse problem theory. (Siam, Ed.)Physica B: Condensed Matter (Vol. 130, pp. 77-78). SIAM. doi:10.1137/1.9780898717921

Tsai, C.-L., & Chien, S.-Y. (2011). New optimization scheme for L2-norm total variation semi-supervised image soft labeling. *2011 18th IEEE International Conference on Image Processing* (pp. 3369-3372). IEEE.

Wang, Yang, & Zhou, H. (2006). Total variation wavelet-based medical image denoising. *International Journal of Biomedical Imaging, 2006*, 1-6. Hindawi Publishing Corporation. Retrieved from http://www.hindawi.com/journals/ijbi/2006/089095/abs/

Wedel, A., Pock, T., Zach, C., Bischof, H., & Cremers, D. (2009). An improved algorithm for TV-L1 Optical Flow. (D. Cremers, B. Rosenhahn, A. L. Yuille, & F. R. Schmidt, Eds.) Statistical and Geometrical Approaches to Visual Motion Analysis, 1(x), 23-45. Springer. doi:10.1007/978-3-642-03061-1_2

Weiss, P., Blanc-Feraud, L., & Aubert, G. (2009). Efficient schemes for total variation minimization under constraints in image processing. *SIAM Journal on Scientific Computing, 31*(3), 2047–2080. doi:10.1137/070696143

Wen, Y., & Chan, R. (2011). Parameter selection for total variation based image restoration using discrepancy principle. *IEEE Transactions on Image Processing*, 2, 1–12. doi:10.1109/TIP.2011.2181401 PMID:22203711

Wen, Y.-W. W. Y.-W., Ng, M. K., & Huang, Y.-M. H. Y.-M. (2008). Efficient total variation minimization methods for color image restoration. *IEEE Transactions on Image Processing, 17*(11), 2081–2088. doi:10.1109/TIP.2008.2003406 PMID:18972651

Wohlberg, B., & Rodriguez, P. (2007). An iteratively reweighted norm algorithm for minimization of total variation functionals. *IEEE Signal Processing Letters, 14*(12), 948–951. doi:10.1109/LSP.2007.906221

Yin, W., Goldfarb, D., & Osher, S. (2005). Image cartoon-texture decomposition and feature selection using the total variation regularized L1 functional. *Variational Geometric and Level Set Methods in Computer Vision, 3752*(05-47), 73-84. Springer. Retrieved August 29, 2014, from http://www.springerlink.com/index/D3JNF25VRHPXLUN1.pdf

Zach, C., Pock, T., & Bischof, H. (2007). A duality based approach for realtime TV-L1 optical flow. (F. A. Hamprecht, C. Schnörr, & B. Jähne, Eds.)Computer, 1(1), 214–223. Springer-Verlag. doi:10.1007/978-3-540-74936-3_22

Zeng, T., & Ng, M. K. (2010). On the total variation dictionary model. *IEEE Transactions on Image Processing, 19*(3), 821–825. doi:10.1109/TIP.2009.2034701 PMID:19840910

KEY TERMS AND DEFINITIONS

Blind Deconvolution: It refers to the implementation of a deconvolution with no explicit information on the impulse response function employed by the related convolution.

Machine Learning: It is concerned with the study of pattern recognition as well as computational learning in artificial intelligence, exploring the structure and studying algorithms that can infer knowledge from and formulate predictions about data. Such algorithms work by building a model from known inputs so as to craft data-driven predictions or decisions, instead of pursuing a predetermined program.

Regularization: It refers to the procedure of bringing in additional knowledge to solve an ill-posed problem or to avoid overfitting. This information appears habitually as a penalty term for complexity, such as constraints for smoothness or bounds on the norm.

Support Vector Machine: It is concerned with supervised learning models that rely on associated learning algorithms to examine data and to identify patterns, intended for classification, clustering and regression analysis.

Total Least Squares: It is a type of errors-in-variables regression, that is, a least-squares data modeling method in which observational errors on both dependent and independent variables are taken into account. It is basically identical to the best, in the Frobenius norm sense, low-rank approximation of a data matrix.

Total Variation: It is a norm characterized on the space of measures of bounded variation.

Variational Method: It is a field of mathematical analysis that works with the maximization or minimization of functionals.

Chapter 3
Vision Enhancement in Bad Weather

Md. Imtiyaz Anwar
Dr. B. R. Ambedkar NIT Jalandhar, India

Arun Khosla
Dr. B. R. Ambedkar NIT Jalandhar, India

ABSTRACT

Road accident is a serious issue in most of the countries due to degraded visibility in bad weather such as fog, haze and rain. A better visibility is a key requirement for passenger's safety while maintaining the speed of the vehicle. Researchers throughout the world are focusing to enhance the visibility through bad weather mainly due to fog or haze to minimize accidents. Many efforts are being put up to clearly visualize the scene using computer vision. Classifications of fog and analysis of de-weathering techniques are prime motive of research. This book chapter addresses and summarizes the progress in the development of vision enhancement techniques for road safety in turbid medium, particularly with fog which greatly affects the vision. This chapter also presents a brief comparative analysis on different weather conditions and classification of fog which is important for application point of view.

INTRODUCTION

Visibility is necessary to drive either naturally or through an image acquisition device (camera). Current vision systems are designed to perform in normal weather conditions. However, no one can escape from adverse weather conditions in any outdoor application (Nayar & Narashimhan, 1999). Fatal crashes related to bad weather occur frequently in the north India and other countries like Florida and Spain. Traffic death rates are higher at night than during the day because vis-

ibility distance in the day time is approximately six times more than in night in a clear weather. A major cause of vehicle accidents is degraded visibility due to bad weather such as fog, haze and rain that presents noisy visual effects. When the weather is poor due to haze, fog, darkness, rain etc., the driver can't get a clear view of the road, road signs or traffic signals and can meets with an accident. Road signs or traffic signs are designed to assist the driver to reach the destination safely. Development of Road Sign Recognition (RSR) system in real time can be used in vision based

DOI: 10.4018/978-1-4666-8654-0.ch003

Driver Assistance System (DAS) that assist the driver to navigate vehicle by providing road signs information (Hautière, Tarel, & Aubert, 2010). A real time bad weather removal algorithm has a contribution in RSR system (Siogkas & Dermatas, 2006). The intensity of an image is a function as a product of illumination and reflectance components (Gonzalez & Woods, 1993). The study of the interaction of light with the atmosphere (and hence weather) is widely known as atmospheric optics. Atmospheric optics lies at the heart of the most magnificent visual experiences known to man, including, the colors of sunrise and sunset, the blueness of the clear sky, and the rainbow. The key characteristics of light, such as intensity and color, are altered by its interaction with the atmosphere. These interactions can be broadly classified into three categories, viz. scattering, absorption and emission. Of these, scattering and absorption due to suspended particles are more dominant that leads to complex visual effects (Narashimhan & Nayar, 2002). Due to the absorption and scattering of light, the visibility becomes poor in bad weather and can be treated as noisy visual effects. Under bad weather conditions, the contrast and color of images are drastically altered or degraded. It degrades the image quality and performance of computer vision algorithms such as object tracking, surveillance, segmentation, navigation and recognition (Srinivasa, Narasimhan & Nayar, 2003). Hence, it is imperative to study the weather effects removal mechanism from images in order to make vision systems more reliable. A better visibility is a key requirement for passenger's safety while maintaining the speed of the vehicle.

BAD WEATHER: PARTICLES AROUND US

From atmospheric point of view, weather conditions differ mainly in the types and sizes of the particles present and their concentrations in space around us. In general, the exact nature of scattering is highly complex and depends on the types, orientations, sizes, and distributions of particles constituting the media, as well as wavelengths, polarization states, and directions of the incident light (Mahadev & Henry, 2000). A great deal of effort has gone into measuring the size of these particles and concentrations for a variety of conditions with visibility (see Table 1). Given the small size of air molecules, relative to the wavelength of visible light, scattering due to air is rather minimal.

Based on the type of visual effects, bad weather conditions are broadly classified into two categories: Steady and dynamic. Fog, mist and haze come under steady weather whereas rain, snow and hail are dynamic in nature (Garg & Nayar, 2007). In a steady bad weather, constituent droplets are very small (10^{-4}- 10μm) which steadily float in the air. In dynamic bad weather, constituent droplets are thousand times larger (0.1-10 mm) than those of the steady weather. The authors introduce these weather conditions briefly.

Table 1. Weather conditions and associated particle types, sizes and concentrations

Weather Condition	Visibility Condition	Particle Type	Radius (μm)	Concentration (cm^{-3})
Air	Normal	Molecule	10^{-4}	10^{19}
Haze	Poor	Aerosol	10^{-2}-1	10^{3}-10
Fog		Water droplet	1-10	100-10
Cloud		Water droplet	1-10	300-10
Rain		Water drop	10^{2}-10^{4}	10^{-2}-10^{-5}

Haze: Haze is constituted of aerosol which is a dispersed system of small particles suspended in gas. It has a diverse set of sources including volcanic ashes, foliage exudation, combustion products and sea salt (Hidy, 1972). The particles produced by these sources respond quickly to changes in relative humidity and act as nuclei (centers) of small water droplets when the humidity is high. It gives a cloudy sky appearance when occurs with dust and smoke particles. Haze particles are larger than air molecules but smaller than fog droplets. Haze tends to produce a distinctive gray or bluish hue and affect visibility.

Fog: Fog evolves when the relative humidity of an air parcel reaches saturation and consequently some of the nuclei grow by condensation into water droplets. Hence, fog and certain types of haze have similar origins and an increase in humidity is sufficient to turn haze into fog (Narashimhan & Nayar, 2002). This transition is quite gradual and an intermediate state is referred to as mist. While perceptible haze extends to an altitude of several kilometers, fog is typically just a few hundred feet thick. The visibility is greatly reduced by fog as compared to haze that is caused by attenuation and airlight. Foggy condition affects the perceptual judgments of speed and the distance between the scene point and camera or viewer.

Cloud: A cloud differs from fog only existing at higher altitudes rather than sitting at ground level. While most clouds are made of water droplets like fog, some are composed of long ice crystals and ice coated dust grains (Mason, 1975). Considering the scope of the chapter, clouds are of less relevance to us as we restrict ourselves to vision at ground level rather than high altitudes.

Rain and Snow: The process by which cloud droplets turn to rain is a complex one, (Mason, 1975). Rain causes random spatial and temporal variations in images and hence must be dealt differently from the more static weather conditions mentioned above. Rain affects visibility by changing the light reflected from the road back to the driver's eye. Water drop acts as a lens which disperses the lights, so that much of it is reflected in different directions. When light strikes the raindrops, only a part of it passes through while the rest scatters. The raindrop therefore obstructs some of the light reflected by objects. Similar arguments apply to snow, where the flakes are rough and have more complex shapes and optical properties (Koenderink & Richards, 1992, Ohtake, 1970). The origin of snowflakes is hidden in the clouds. The water vapors go up into the air and gets cold and whenever it gets a dust particle, the water vapor freezes. Snow may be viewed as frozen rain. This is how snowflakes are formed and fall into the surface of the earth. The adverse visual appearance of the bad weather conditions are shown in Figure 1. Apart from above bad weather conditions, smoke has very different nature and variable particle sizes depending upon the source of release.

Figure 1. Visual appearance of bad weather conditions (a) rain, (b) haze (c) snow, and (d) fog

(a)　　　　　(b)　　　　　(c)　　　　　(d)

CHALLENGES AND FRAMEWORK FOR VISION ENHANCEMENT

Images of outdoor scenes often contain haze, fog, or other types of atmospheric particles. Light reflected from the object surface is attenuated due to the scattering by molecule, aerosol, water droplet and water drop. Scattering of the light towards eye or camera is the result of refraction. When light passes from one medium to another, speed gets changed and deflection occurs. The visibility degradation level is increased with the distance from camera to scene. Contrast and the color characteristics of images are drastically changed. The attenuation of luminance through the atmosphere was studied by Koschmieder (Middleton, 1952) who derived an equation relating to apparent luminance under adverse weather conditions. Visible light (wavelength between 400-700nm) coming from the source is scattered by fog and part of it travels toward camera and leads to shift in color. This phenomenon is called airlight and adds whiteness into the scene. Therefore, attenuation and depth map must be calculated for analyzing the scene. Airlight map is the function of the distance between the object and camera. Normal weather images have more contrast than foggy and hazy images.

Fog and Haze Imaging Model

Both fog and haze constituted of water droplets and the only difference is the size. So, a single model is valid for both fog and haze whereas the values for attenuation and airlight may differ. Physics behind fog and haze imaging model is shown in Figure 2.

In image processing and computer vision, widely used model for the generation of a foggy image is mainly caused by two scattering phenomenon: attenuation and airlight which described as fog or haze imaging equation (Schechner, Narasimhan, & Nayar, 2001):

$$I(x) = J(x)t(x) + A(1 - t(x)) \qquad (1)$$

where x is 2D vector representation of a pixel's location in the image, $I(x)$ is the observed degraded image, $J(x)$ is the scene radiance and it would be the light seen by the observer in the absence of haze or fog, A is the global atmospheric or sky light usually assumed to be spatially constant and $t(x)$ is the transmission parameter or transparency, the portion of light which directly goes towards observer without scattering in the medium. The values of $t(x)$ varies from 0 to1, where $t(x) = 0$ means completely foggy or opaque and $t(x) =1$

Figure 2. Fog and Haze imaging model

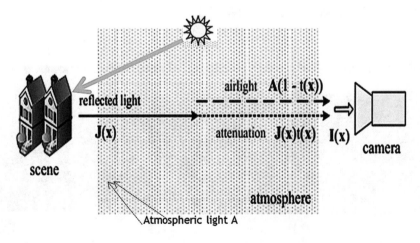

means completely clear or fog free and other intermediate values are responsible for semi-transparency. The product of *J(x)* and *t(x)* is called as direct attenuation (Hautiere, 2006) and the product of sky light (*A*) and *(1-t(x))* is called as atmospheric light or airlight. Due to direct attenuation, scene radiance decays exponentially in the medium while airlight leads to shift in the scene color.

Transmission *t(x)* exponentially decays with scene depth, *d* in a medium. Equation (1) can be illustrated below as Equation (2) by assuming the intrinsic luminance $L_0(x, y)$ of an object in the absence of fog and its apparent luminance *L(x, y)* due to fog having scattering coefficient *k*:

$$L(x,y) = L_0(x,y)e^{-kd(x,y)} + L_\infty(1 - e^{-kd(x,y)}) \qquad (2)$$

where, *d(x, y)* is the distance of the object from the observer or camera or scene depth, L_∞ is the global atmospheric constant or luminance of the sky at infinite distance from the observer. Vision enhancement in bad weather is a challenging task due to complexity in recovering luminance and chrominance while maintaining the color fidelity.

Figure 3. Generic block diagram for restoration based approach for vision enhancement

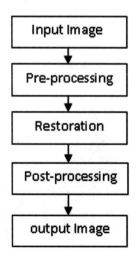

Framework

For single image, estimation of image depth information is required. The estimation of depth information can be treated in terms of airlight map, transmission parameter or depth map. This information has estimated using scene properties in many previous reported vision enhancement techniques. After estimation of depth map, images can be restored easily. A generic block diagram as shown in Figure 3 represents a framework to enhance vision in bad weather using restoration based approach which is widely used. Weather degraded image is taken as input image to produce finally an enhanced image.

RESEARCH AND IMPROVEMENTS ON DE-WEATHERING TECHNIQUES

In modern era, people frequently use CMOS digital cameras to capture images. Computer vision systems employing CCD and CMOS cameras also fail to produce desirable results in the presence of fog, rain, haze, snow and low lightning with graininess and blurriness in the captured images or videos (Malik & Goel, 2012). Small lux rating (see Table 2) low light cameras may be able to capture images in low visibility conditions from a distance but the resulting image may be of very poor quality.

Initial research works on fog and haze removal were based on contrast enhancement. Later on,

Table 2. Comparison of imaging sensors

Camera Type	Visibility Range (meters)	LUX Rating (lux)
CMOS	2-3	>10
CCD	4-5	1.5-5
Low Light	6-8	0.1-1
Infrared	3-4	0.0

restoration based approaches are using. Contrast enhancement techniques are divided in to two classes (John & Wilscy, 2008):

- Non model based, and
- Model based

Different filtering (median, average smoothing, homomorphic etc.) approaches can be used to enhancement images for a specific purpose. Non-linear filters give better results as compared to linear filters in fog or haze.

Non-Model Based Approach

Non-model based methods for de-weathering utilize image information for processing. Histogram approach is one of the oldest and simplest techniques that also used for segmentation of images (Anwar & Khosla, 2013). Histogram of an image is a graphical representation of the pixel intensity distribution in a digital image as shown below in Figure 4. The most common used methods are histogram equalization that is categorized into adaptive histogram equalization (Pizer, 1987) and global histogram equalization.

Histogram equalization methods do not take the distance of scene point into account. Global histogram equalization is simple, effective and the most popular but some contrast loss occurs as it does not take the local image information into account. In contrast, local histogram equalization has given better results but Xu, Liu and Chen (Xu, Liu, & Chen, 2009) have identified few problems such as slow speed and enhancement of noise. Contrast Limited Adaptive Histogram Equalization (CLAHE) is used to overcome such problems. CLAHE method can operate on entire image and sub regions of an image by assuming a window size of $n \times n$ depending upon desired contrast of an image. CLAHE using sub region histogram technique induce artificially generated boundaries that can be eliminated using bilinear interpolation. There are other approaches like retinex theory (Jobson, Rahman, & Woodell, 1997), and wavelet based (Enjun, Qing, Xiumin, & Lie, 2008). Retinex algorithm maintains the balance between the human vision and the machine vision. The retinex algorithm is divided into Single Scale Retinex (SSR) and Multi Scale Retinex (MSR) and MSR with color restoration (MSRCR). The MSR is a non-linear image enhancement technique and simply the weighted sum of several SSR outputs. MSR also brighten up the poor contrast areas but not at the expense of good contrast saturated areas. According to Hines (Hines, Rahman, Jobson, &

Figure 4. (a) Digital image with its (b) histogram

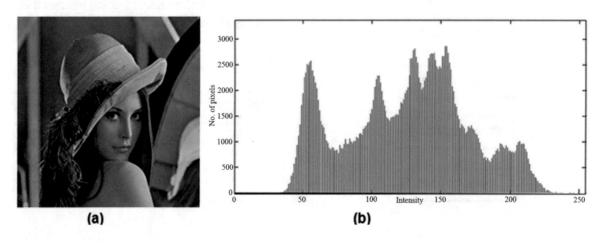

(a)　　　　　　　　　　(b)

Woodell, 2004), SSR algorithm can produce a maximum performance of 34.1fps (frames per second). This is higher than the real time requirement of 30fps and can be used for real time vision based driver assistance system because of the performance. Depending on the different spatial frequency character of the details components between the different decompositions, a choice fusion operator based on regional characteristic measure is adopted to enhance the images of low visibility road using wavelet transform (Enjun, Qing, Xiumin, & Lie, 2008). The problem with the non model based methods is to preserve the color fidelity. It is observed as the main reason for not getting an effective output. Thus, a considerable amount of research has been directed towards physics based model.

Model Based Approach

Physics based or simply model based methods mainly include restoration principle to de-fog, de-haze, and de-rain the images. These methods require extra information about the imaging environment and then provide better results. The depth map, transmission function estimations are the extra information. Restoration based algorithms use models for de-weathering that can be divided into single image restoration and multiple image restoration approach. Single image restoration can be further classified as interactive or automatic de-weathering related to estimation of prior information. Prior information or assumption can be estimated automatically or given by the user. Degradation in image quality is due to attenuation and airlight as represented by Equation (3) that are function of distance from scene to observer as stated above in Equation (2). Simply according to Koschmieder's law:

Degraded image,

$$I(x,y) = I_{attenuate}(x,y) + A_{irlight}(x,y) \qquad (3)$$

Now the authors are going towards rain removal techniques and observed that the effects of rain are very complex. It is a common practice to detect the rain pixels, i.e. pixels affected by rain for inpainting (Patwardhan & Sapiro, 2003). For refinement, some rain properties or rain models were used which vary from algorithm to algorithm. Once potential rain candidates found, these rain pixels inpainted. For most of the algorithms, the rain detection stage remains same except for the number of frames. Rain removal algorithms first detect all possible rain candidates and refine these candidates to reduce the false candidates. For rain removal during acquisition, Garg and Nayar proposed a method by adjusting the camera parameters (Garg & Nayar, 2005). It is shown that properties of rain (drop size, high velocity, and low density) make the visibility of rain strongly dependent on camera parameters such as exposure time and depth of field. These parameters can be selected so as to reduce the effects of rain without altering the appearance of the scene. However, this method fails to handle heavy rain and fast moving objects which are close to the camera. Barnum et al., (Barnum, Narasimhan, & Kanade, 2010) presented a method to detect rain or snow streaks and reduce or increase the effect of it. With the use of statistical properties of rain and snow this methods provides better results. Requirement of high computational power is the disadvantage. Zhao et al. (Zhao, P. Liu, J. Liu, & Tang, 2013) proposed a pixel-wise framework combining a detection method with a removal approach. Dynamic weather conditions are detected by strategy driven state transition which integrates using K-means clustering with Gaussian Mixture Model (GMM) and a variable time window is present for removal of rain and snow. A list of various rain removal algorithms are shown in Table 3.

Now the authors discuss fog and haze removal techniques. A brief comparison of various restoration based vision enhancement techniques in foggy and hazy conditions are presented (see

Table 4). When prior information of the about the scene is known, Oakley and Satherlay (Oakley & Satherley, 1998) proposed a model based method but it requires multiple images of the same scene to satisfy the prior information. Schechner *et al.* (Schechner, Narasimhan, & Nayar, 2001) proposed a method to remove the hazy effects easily from color and gray images by assuming the airlight scattered by atmospheric particles is partially polarized. The method also used multiple images taken through a polarizer at different orientations. It gives a great improvement of scene contrast and correction of color and information about atmospheric particles properties. In 2002, Narasimhan and Nayar (Narasimhan & Nayar, 2002) proposed a method which also requires multiple images of the same scene taken at different weather conditions. This method is valid for both gray and color images. Changes in intensity from different weather conditions provide simple constraints and detect depth discontinuities. Narasimhan and Nayar in 2003, (Narasimhan & Nayar, 2003) presented a de-weathering technique using simple additional information provided interactively by the user. Single color or gray image is sufficient for this method. Oakley and Bu (Oakley & Bu, 2007) proposed a method which removes fog from single image automatically by determining the constant airlight level through the image. This method involves the minimization of scalar global

cost function without region segmentation. It is applicable to both gray and color images. This method fails in the presence of non-uniform airlight. Kim et al. (Kim, Jeon, Kang, & Ko, 2008) improves the method and make it suitable for even for non-uniform airlight with the use of region segmentation. Uniformly segmented regions help to estimate airlight. It gives better results but only for narrow range of scene depth. Tan (Tan, 2008) proposed a method based on spatial regularization from a single color or gray scale image. Fog removal was possible by maximizing the contrast of the direct transmission while assuming a smooth layer of airlight. Further Markov random field (MRF) model is used to regularize the result but produce some halos near depth discontinuities in the scene. In 2008, Fatttal (Fattal, 2008) proposed a method based on Independent Component Analysis (ICA). He considered the shading and transmission signals are uncorrelated and used ICA to estimate transmission and then inferred the color of whole image by MRF. Restoration was based on color information, hence can't apply for gray image and dense fog because dense fog is often colorless, whereas (Koef et al., 2008) in the same year, a 3-D model based method of a scene comes into picture. This method requires the interaction with an expert user for the estimation of sky intensity and other functions. It can't prefer to use for driver assistance system. Tarel

Table 3. List of rain removal algorithms

Method	Properties Used (Model)
Starik and Werman (2003)	Temporal properties
Garg and Nayar (2005)	Adjustment of camera parameter
Zhang et al. (2006)	Chromatic properties for detection and temporal properties for refinement
Barnum, Narasimhan, and Kanade (2010)	Blurred Gaussian model
Park and Lee (2008)	Temporal properties for detection and Kalman filter for removal
Zhao et al. (2013)	Histogram model for the detection
Liu et al. (2009)	Chromatic properties for detection and refinement
Bossu et al. (2011)	Gaussian mixture model for detection and orientation of histogram for refinement

and Hautiere simulated a fast visibility restoration algorithm. This method assumes the airlight as a percentage between the local standard deviation and the local mean of the whiteness and based on linear operations but requires many parameters for adjustment. They maximized the contrast of the resulting image, assuming that the depth map must be smooth except along the edges (Tarel & Hautiere, 2009, 2011). So, it was a fast algorithm and paves the way for real time implementation. The restored image quality was not so good in the presence of discontinuities in the scene depth. Best paper warded researchers, He *et al.* (He, sun, & Tang, 2009) proposed a very simple but effective single image haze removal method using dark channel prior (DCP) generated after testing on 5000 images. DCP is a kind of statistics of outdoor haze free images that contain some pixels whose intensity is very low in at least one colour channel. Using this prior with haze imaging model, direct estimation of haze thickness is possible and a high quality haze free image is recovered. Zhu *et al.* (Zhu, Fang, & Zhang, 2009) proposed a new method to remove weather effects from a single image of road. Based on physical model, Hough transform is used for extracting vanishing point and maximum entropy theory to acquire the optimal parameter. This method has no longer required precise information about the scene depth and weather conditions. So, it can be used in real time. Tripathi and Mukhopadhyay (Tripathi & Mukhopadhyay, 2012) proposed a novel, efficient fog removal algorithm that uses anisotropic diffusion for estimation of airlight to recover scene contrast. Histogram equalisation and histogram stretching are used as a pre- processing and post processing steps for the proposed algorithm. For colour image, RGB (red, green and blue) and HSI (hue, saturation, & intensity) model can be used. Proposed algorithm has few parameters and constant and doesn't require any user intervention and independent of fog density. It shows HSI model is faster than RGB model. Ancuti

and Ancuti demonstrated the first fusion based approach for dehazing by applying a white balance and contrast enhancing procedure using single degraded image. This technique has been tested on a large data set of natural hazy images. They filter their important features by computing three measures: luminance, chromaticity and saliency. To minimize artifacts introduced by measures, the approach was in a multiscale fashion using a Laplacian pyramid representation. Technique is limited to homogeneous hazy images. This is the first method based on fusion (O. Ancuti & C. Ancuti, 2013). Unlike previous work, currently Lai et al. (Lai et al., 2014) used theoretic and heuristic bounds of scene transmission to find the optimum solution including two scene priors. This method basically improved the transmission map rather than to maximize the visibility.

CLASSIFICATION OF FOG

For vision enhancement and minimization of road accidents in bad weather, modern vehicles are often equipped with a camera connected to Head-Up Display (HUD), which captures and displays the scene in front of a vehicle. Classification is a methodology to identify the type of fog and their optical characteristics for vision enhancement algorithms to make them more efficient. Fog with varying density of atmospheric particles (water droplets) within an image are classified as homogeneous and heterogeneous (Tarel et al., 2012). Generation of synthetic foggy images is possible using SiVIC™ software. In previous reported works don't show the classification of camera images directly with reference to synthetic images with the help of any classification or performance metric but several vision enhancement techniques on synthetically generated foggy images are given by the researchers.

As natural fog is not always homogeneous, it can be classified as homogeneous and hetero-

Table 4. A brief comparison of various fog and haze removal algorithms

Method	Input Image(s)	Image Type	Assumption
Oakley and Satherley (1998)	Multiple	Gray	Prior knowledge of scene depth
Schechner et al. (2001)		Gray & Color	Airlight scattered by atmospheric particles is partially polarized
Narasimhan and Nayar (2002)			Uniform condition of bad weather
Narasimhan & Nayar (2003)	Single	-do-	Additional information provided by the user (Interactive)
Oakley and Bu (2007)		-do-	Constant airlight
Kim et al. (2008)		Color	Cost function based on human visual model
Tan (2008)		Gray & Color	Based on spatial regularization and contrast maximization
Fattal (2008)		Color	Independent component analysis (ICA)
Koef et al. (2008)		Gray & Color	Based on 3-D image model (Interactive)
Tarrel and Hautiere (2009)			Airlight as a percentage between the local standard deviation and the local mean of the whiteness and linear operations
He, Sun, and Tang (2011)			Dark channel prior (DCP)
Zhu, Fang, and Zhang (2009)			Hough transform for extracting vanishing point and maximum entropy theory
Tripathi and Mukhopadhyay (2012)			Anisotropic diffusion
Ancuti and Ancuti (2013)		Color	Fusion based
Lai et al. (2014)		Color	Use of theoretic and heuristic bounds

geneous similar to synthetic fog. In this chapter, synthetic images are chosen and classified in four different types of fog, one is uniform (homogeneous) and the others are treated as heterogeneous (see Table 5). As the intrinsic luminance for any kind of fog is assumed to be constant but the variability in fog due to other two parameters is described by Equation (2) except average visibility distance, $d(x,y)$ in an image.

Dynamic range of image pixels is also used previously as a classification parameter (Anwar & Khosla, 2014) and found that homogeneous foggy images have lesser distribution range of pixel intensities than heterogeneous. Mean intensity and color entropy of image is proposed here to classify camera images with homogeneous or heterogeneous fog. Mean intensity of an image is the average of all pixels with different gray levels.

Table 5. Classification of fog [45, 48]

Homogeneous Fog	Heterogeneous Fog		
	k- fog	*L_∞- fog*	*k and L_∞ -fog*
Koschmieder's law is applied with the all constant parametric values (k and L_∞).	Image with different weights of scattering coefficient k with respect to pixel position and all other parameters are constant. These spatial weights are obtained by means of Perlin's noise between 0–1 (Perlin, 1985).	k is constant and L_∞ is heterogeneous. It produces fog with cloudy sky.	Both k and L_∞ are varying. To challenge vision enhancement algorithms, consider fog with both k and L_∞ heterogeneous.

For image $I(x,y)$ of size $M{\times}N$, mean intensity is defined as:

$$Mean = \frac{1}{MN}\sum_{x=1}^{M}\sum_{y=1}^{N}I\left(x,y\right) \qquad (4)$$

Entropy is a statistical measure of randomness that can be used to characterize the texture of the input image and mathematically defined as:

$$Entropy = \sum_{k=0}^{L-1}p_k \log_2 p_k \qquad (5)$$

where, L is the number of gray levels and p_k is the probability associated with gray level k or histogram count. Minimum entropy of an image indicates that all of the pixels have the same gray levels and image itself is constant with little contrast whereas maximum entropy is achieved for a uniformly distributed probability.

SIMULATION ANALYSIS AND DISCUSSION

In this chapter, first analyze the results of 18 synthetic images with fog after calculating their mean intensity and color entropy and then computed the same with 66 synthetic images of size 640 x 480 that having different fog conditions for different road scenes. A subset of 4 images is shown in the first column and their respective synthetic fog added images in subsequent columns of Figure 5. Finally second database contains 4 set of 66 foggy images, i.e., a total of 264 foggy images associated with 66 original images. Color entropy variation of homogeneous (Image_U) and heterogeneous (Image_K, Image_L and Image_M) fog added 18 synthetic images are shown in Figure 6. From the analysis of mean intensity variation (see Table 6) of 18 images from first database it is clearly

observed that minimum and maximum intensity values of homogeneous foggy images (Image_U) are always greater than minimum and maximum intensity values of all other heterogeneous foggy images (Image_K, Image_L and Image_M) respectively. The average value of mean intensity of 18 images shows that the greater value 192 is achieved by homogeneous foggy images with respect to heterogeneous foggy images having values 172, 178 and 161. In three heterogeneous fog conditions, Image_M contains lower and Image_L have higher mean intensity value. It shows from the bar graphs in figure 6, entropy of homogeneous foggy images have always less than the entropy of any kind of heterogeneous foggy images. Minimum entropy shows the uniform distribution of fog over the entire single image as compared to the same image with heterogeneous fog. Analysis of mean intensity and color entropy variation with uniform and non-uniform fog conditions for 66 synthetic images are shown (see Table 7 and Table 8). Again homogeneous images have higher average of mean intensity of value and varies from 173.78-207.90, which is very close to the result obtained from first data set. Within heterogeneous fog, Image_M have lower intensity than Image_L and Image_K as stated previously for first data set.

So, single images at different fog conditions have always higher mean intensity with homogeneous and comparatively lower with heterogeneous fog. Entropy analysis of 66 images (see Table 8) exhibit that images with uniform fog (Image_U) have less entropy than non-uniform foggy images (Image_K, Image_L and Image_M).

Mean intensity and color entropy of few camera images with unknown fog of size 640 x 480 shown in Figure 7 to classify as homogeneous and heterogeneous. Computed mean intensity and color entropy indicated that none of the camera images have mean intensity greater than 172. Except the first image (a)in Figure 7, which is very close to

Figure 5. Synthetic images database. (a) Original synthetic image, image added with (b) heterogeneous k-fog (Image_K), (c) heterogeneous L_∞ -fog (Image_L), (d) heterogeneous k and L_∞ -fog (Image_M) and (d) homogeneous fog (Image_U)

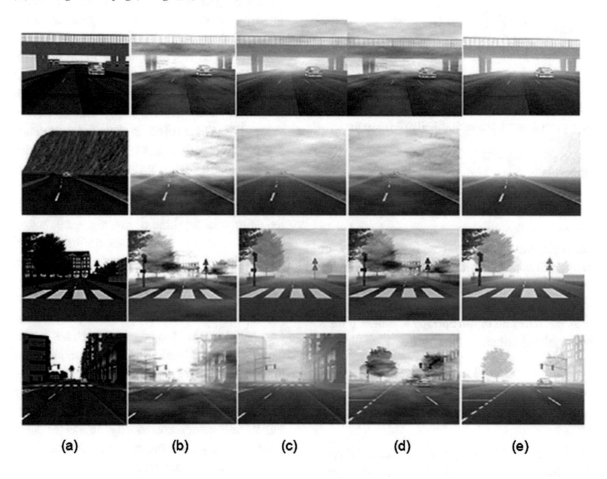

(a) (b) (c) (d) (e)

Table 6. Analysis of mean intensity variation of 18 synthetic foggy image data set

Type of Image		Average of Mean Intensity of 18 Images	Minimum Intensity	Maximum Intensity
Heterogeneous foggy	Image_K	172	149.96	192.54
	Image_L	178	156.51	196.23
	Image_M	161	138.29	183.23
Homogeneous foggy	Image_U	192	172.07	208.72

consider as homogeneous foggy image, all other images have greater entropy. Therefore, it can say that the most of the camera images with fog are heterogeneous in nature but the algorithms for fog removal assume uniform fog in nature.

As the classification of foggy images using mean intensity and color entropy is useful to differentiate the fog into homogeneous and heterogeneous but still have few limitations. This method requires a number of images as reference

Figure 6. Entropy of 18 heterogeneous and homogeneous synthetic foggy images

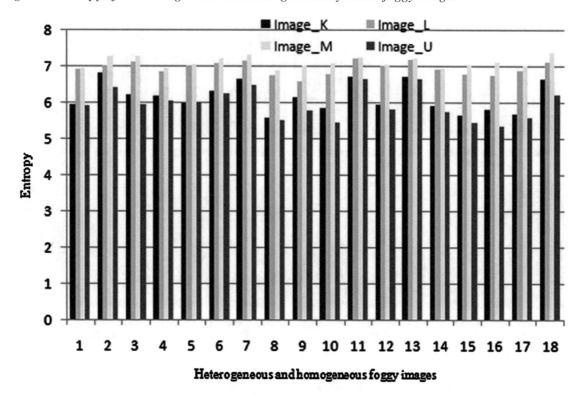

Table 7. Analysis of mean intensity variation of 66 synthetic foggy image data set

Type of Image		Average of Mean Intensity of 66 Images	Minimum Intensity	Maximum Intensity
Heterogeneous foggy	Image_K	189	166.86	208.52
	Image_L	176	157.96	191.08
	Image_M	174	152.38	187.88
Homogeneous foggy	Image_U	192	173.78	207.90

Table 8. Analysis of color entropy variation of 66 synthetic foggy image data set

Type of Image		Average Entropy of 66 Images	Minimum Entropy	Maximum Entropy
Heterogeneous foggy	Image_K	5.76	4.12	6.85
	Image_L	6.87	6.46	7.42
	Image_M	6.96	6.53	7.50
Homogeneous foggy	Image_U	5.59	3.94	6.65

Figure 7. Camera images in bad weather with their mean intensity and entropy

(a) Mean intensity = 145.58, Entropy=6.43

(b) Mean intensity=146.12, Entropy= 7.10

(c) Mean intensity=118.13, Entropy=7.47

(d) Mean intensity=167.11, Entropy=7.33

(e) Mean intensity=135.99, Entropy=6.73

(f) Mean intensity=128.21, Entropy=7.42

(g) Mean intensity=136.33, Entropy=7.60

(h) Mean intensity=127.46, Entropy=7.34

for much accurate threshold value for classification. Sometimes, for foggy images, it is difficult to identify whether the images have homogeneous fog or heterogeneous fog as the entropy and mean intensity values are very close to their threshold values respectively. This method of classification is only applicable to classify fog but heavy smoke may be considered as fog.

CONCLUSION AND FUTURE DIRECTION

The problem of visibility degradation due to bad weather is a major challenging problem for transportation, surveillance, tracking system and in many other vision based applications. Multiple image and interactive de-weathering technique is not suitable for driver assistance system where cost, interaction of user and processing time has

a significant role. Classification of fog is a prior task that helps to develop algorithms for vision enhancement. The use of mean intensity and color entropy as classification parameters are very helpful to classify camera images with fog. This chapter shows that several other techniques can be added with new constraints for classification purpose and then design an efficient fog removal algorithm. The image acquisition of image is usually noisy and blur. So, it is important to apply de-noising and de-blurring algorithms prior to the vision enhancement algorithms. A fast and accurate method always increases the speed and improved image quality. Data sets and vision enhancement algorithms for road images are available but visibility degradation problem also effect railways and airways where the travelling time with safety is very important for the passengers. It also found that visibility degradation is more in night time as compared to day time. Therefore, it is also a challenging task for the drivers to drive in night but somewhere the use of thermal or infrared cameras make it easier. For future research, railways and airways images and short time videos can be taken as reference to implement an algorithm. While capturing images or videos, blurring always occurs. So, de-blurring algorithms can be useful in addition with de-weathering techniques. New hybrid model with colour transformation from RGB to HSI, CMYK and Lab colour space can be used in future for better improvement with less simulation time for colour images or videos. Railways can adopt a robust system to overcome the delay and for smooth running of trains mostly for winter in India. Classification of fog to identify the type of fog and then create a suitable fog removal algorithm using a model may be useful in future to build a robust system.

REFERENCES

Ancuti, C. O., & Ancuti, C. (2013). Single image dehazing by multi-scale fusion. *Image Processing. IEEE Transactions on*, 22(8), 3271–3282.

Anwar, M. I., & Khosla, A. (2013). Segmentation Methods for Images: A Systematic Review, Journal of Remote Sensing & GIS. *STM Journals*, 4(3), 61–67.

Anwar, M. I., & Khosla, A. (2014). Classification of Homogeneous and Heterogeneous Fog for Vision Enhancement. *Current Trends in Signal Processing*, 4(2), 7–10.

Barnum, P. C., Narasimhan, S., & Kanade, T. (2010). Analysis of rain and snow in frequency space. *International Journal of Computer Vision*, 86(2-3), 256–274. doi:10.1007/s11263-008-0200-2

Bossu, J., Hautière, N., & Tarel, J. P. (2011). Rain or snow detection in image sequences through use of a histogram of orientation of streaks. *International Journal of Computer Vision*, 93(3), 348–367. doi:10.1007/s11263-011-0421-7

Enjun, W., Qing, W., Xiumin, C., & Lei, X. (2008, September). Research on road image fusion enhancement technique based on wavelet transform. In *Vehicle Power and Propulsion Conference, 2008. VPPC'08. IEEE* (pp. 1-5). IEEE. doi:10.1109/VPPC.2008.4677691

Fattal, R. (2008, August). Single image dehazing. *ACM Transactions on Graphics*, 27(3), 72. doi:10.1145/1360612.1360671

Garg, K., & Nayar, S. K. (2005, October). When does a camera see rain? In *Computer Vision, 2005. ICCV 2005. Tenth IEEE International Conference on*. IEEE. doi:10.1109/ICCV.2005.253

Garg, K., & Nayar, S. K. (2007). Vision and rain. *International Journal of Computer Vision*, 75(1), 3–27. doi:10.1007/s11263-006-0028-6

Gonzales, R. C., & Woods, R. E. (1993). *Digital image processing*. Academic Press.

Hautière, N., Tarel, J. P., & Aubert, D. (2010). Mitigation of visibility loss for advanced camera-based driver assistance. *Intelligent Transportation Systems. IEEE Transactions on*, 11(2), 474–484.

Hautiere, N., Tarel, J. P., Lavenant, J., & Aubert, D. (2006). Automatic fog detection and estimation of visibility distance through use of an onboard camera. *Machine Vision and Applications*, 17(1), 8–20. doi:10.1007/s00138-005-0011-1

He, K., Sun, J., & Tang, X. (2011). Single image haze removal using dark channel prior. *Pattern Analysis and Machine Intelligence. IEEE Transactions on*, 33(12), 2341–2353.

Henry, R. C., Mahadev, S., Urquijo, S., & Chitwood, D. (2000). Color perception through atmospheric haze. *JOSA A, 17*(5), 831–835. doi:10.1364/JOSAA.17.000831 PMID:10795630

Hidy, G. M. (1972). *Aerosols and Atmospheric Chemistry*. New York: Academic Press.

Hines, G. D., Rahman, Z. U., Jobson, D. J., & Woodell, G. A. (2004, September). Single-scale retinex using digital signal processors. In *Global Signal Processing Conference*.

Jobson, D. J., Rahman, Z. U., & Woodell, G. A. (1997). A multiscale retinex for bridging the gap between color images and the human observation of scenes. *Image Processing. IEEE Transactions on, 6*(7), 965–976.

John, J., & Wilscy, M. (2008, September). Enhancement of weather degraded video sequences using wavelet fusion. In *Cybernetic Intelligent Systems, 2008. CIS 2008. 7th IEEE International Conference on* (pp. 1-6). IEEE. doi:10.1109/UKRICIS.2008.4798926

Kim, D., Jeon, C., Kang, B., & Ko, H. (2008, August). Enhancement of image degraded by fog using cost function based on human visual model. In *Multisensor Fusion and Integration for Intelligent Systems, 2008. MFI 2008. IEEE International Conference on* (pp. 64-67). IEEE. doi:10.1007/978-3-540-89859-7_12

Koenderink, J. J., & Richards, W. A. (1992). Why is snow so bright? *JOSA A, 9*(5), 643–648. doi:10.1364/JOSAA.9.000643

Kopf, J., Neubert, B., Chen, B., Cohen, M., Cohen-Or, D., Deussen, O., & Lischinski, D. et al. (2008, December). Deep photo: Model-based photograph enhancement and viewing. *ACM Transactions on Graphics, 27*(5), 116. doi:10.1145/1409060.1409069

Lai, Y. H., Chen, Y. L., Chiou, C. J., & Hsu, C. T. (2014). *Single Image Dehazing Via Optimal Transmission Map Under Scene Priors*. Academic Press.

Liu, P., Xu, J., Liu, J., & Tang, X. (2009). Pixel based temporal analysis using chromatic property for removing rain from videos. *Computer and Information Science, 2*(1), P53.

Malik, M., & Goel, V. (2012). *Vision in Bad Weather using IR Cameras- Challenges & Opportunities, Advance Signal processing and Integrated circuits*. IJERA.

Mason, B. J. (1975). *Clouds, rain, and rainmaking*. Cambridge University Press.

Middletoneton, W. E. (1952). *Vision through the Atmosphere*. Toronto, Canada: Univ. Toronto Press.

Narasimhan, S. G., & Nayar, S. K. (2002). Vision and the atmosphere. *International Journal of Computer Vision, 48*(3), 233–254. doi:10.1023/A:1016328200723

Narasimhan, S. G., & Nayar, S. K. (2003). Contrast restoration of weather degraded images. *Pattern Analysis and Machine Intelligence. IEEE Transactions on, 25*(6), 713–724.

Narasimhan, S. G., & Nayar, S. K. (2003, October). Interactive (de) weathering of an image using physical models. In *IEEE Workshop on Color and Photometric Methods in Computer Vision 6*. IEEE.

Nayar, S. K., & Narasimhan, S. G. (1999). Vision in bad weather. In *Computer Vision, 1999. The Proceedings of the Seventh IEEE International Conference on*. IEEE. doi:10.1109/ICCV.1999.790306

Oakley, J. P., & Bu, H. (2007). Correction of simple contrast loss in color images. *Image Processing. IEEE Transactions on, 16*(2), 511–522.

Oakley, J. P., & Satherley, B. L. (1998). Improving image quality in poor visibility conditions using a physical model for contrast degradation. *Image Processing. IEEE Transactions on, 7*(2), 167–179.

Ohtake, T. (1970). Factors affecting the size distribution of raindrops and snowflakes. *Journal of the Atmospheric Sciences, 27*(5), 804–813. doi:10.1175/1520-0469(1970)027<0804:FATSDO>2.0.CO;2

Park, W. J., & Lee, K. H. (2008, April). Rain removal using Kalman filter in video. In *Smart Manufacturing Application, 2008. ICSMA 2008. International Conference on* (pp. 494-497). IEEE. doi:10.1109/ICSMA.2008.4505573

Patwardhan, K. A., & Sapiro, G. (2003, September). Projection based image and video inpainting using wavelets. In *Image Processing, 2003. ICIP 2003. Proceedings. 2003 International Conference on*. IEEE. doi:10.1109/ICIP.2003.1247098

Perlin, K. (1985). An image synthesizer. *Computer Graphics, 19*(3), 287–296. doi:10.1145/325165.325247

Pizer, S. M., Amburn, E. P., Austin, J. D., Cromartie, R., Geselowitz, A., Greer, T., & Zuiderveld, K. et al. (1987). Adaptive histogram equalization and its variations. *Computer Vision Graphics and Image Processing, 39*(3), 355–368. doi:10.1016/S0734-189X(87)80186-X

Schechner, Y. Y., Narasimhan, S. G., & Nayar, S. K. (2001). Instant dehazing of images using polarization. In *Computer Vision and Pattern Recognition, 2001. CVPR 2001. Proceedings of the 2001 IEEE Computer Society Conference on*. IEEE. doi:10.1109/CVPR.2001.990493

Siogkas, G. K., & Dermatas, E. S. (2006, May). Detection, tracking and classification of road signs in adverse conditions. In *Electrotechnical Conference, 2006. MELECON 2006. IEEE Mediterranean* (pp. 537-540). IEEE. doi:10.1109/MELCON.2006.1653157

Starik, S., & Werman, M. (2003, October). Simulation of rain in videos. In *Texture Workshop, ICCV*.

Tan, R. T. (2008, June). Visibility in bad weather from a single image. In *Computer Vision and Pattern Recognition, 2008. CVPR 2008. IEEE Conference on* (pp. 1-8). IEEE. doi:10.1109/CVPR.2008.4587643

Tarel, J. P., & Hautiere, N. (2009, September). Fast visibility restoration from a single color or gray level image. In *Computer Vision, 2009 IEEE 12th International Conference on* (pp. 2201-2208). IEEE. doi:10.1109/ICCV.2009.5459251

Tarel, J. P., Hautière, N., Caraffa, L., Cord, A., Halmaoui, H., & Gruyer, D. (2012). Vision enhancement in homogeneous and heterogeneous fog. *Intelligent Transportation Systems Magazine, IEEE, 4*(2), 6–20. doi:10.1109/MITS.2012.2189969

Tripathi, A. K., & Mukhopadhyay, S. (2012). Single image fog removal using anisotropic diffusion. *Image Processing, IET, 6*(7), 966–975. doi:10.1049/iet-ipr.2011.0472

Xu, Z., Liu, X., & Chen, X. (2009, December). Fog removal from video sequences using contrast limited adaptive histogram equalization. In *Computational Intelligence and Software Engineering, 2009. CiSE 2009. International Conference on* (pp. 1-4). IEEE. doi:10.1109/CISE.2009.5366207

Zhang, X., Li, H., Qi, Y., Leow, W. K., & Ng, T. K. (2006, July). Rain removal in video by combining temporal and chromatic properties. In *Multimedia and Expo, 2006 IEEE International Conference on* (pp. 461-464). IEEE. doi:10.1109/ICME.2006.262572

Zhao, X., Liu, P., Liu, J., & Tang, X. (2013). Removal of dynamic weather conditions based on variable time window. Computer Vision, IET, 7(4).

Zhu, Y., Fang, B., & Zhang, H. (2009, December). Image de-weathering for road based on physical model. In *Information Engineering and Computer Science, 2009. ICIECS 2009. International Conference on* (pp. 1-4). IEEE. doi:10.1109/ICIECS.2009.5365298

Chapter 4
Collective Event Detection by a Distributed Low-Cost Smart Camera Network

Jhih-Yuan Hwang
National Sun Yat-sen University, Taiwan

Wei-Po Lee
National Sun Yat-sen University, Taiwan

ABSTRACT

The current surveillance systems must identify the continuous human behaviors to detect various events from video streams. To enhance the performance of event recognition, in this chapter, we propose a distributed low-cost smart cameras system, together with a machine learning technique to detect abnormal events through analyzing the sequential behaviors of a group of people. Our system mainly includes a simple but efficient strategy to organize the behavior sequence, a new indirect encoding scheme to represent a group of people with relatively few features, and a multi-camera collaboration strategy to perform collective decision making for event recognition. Experiments have been conducted and the results confirm the reliability and stability of the proposed system in event recognition.

INTRODUCTION

Using cameras to guard the security of our society has become a more popular method of public area surveillance. With the aid of video streams recorded by the surveillance equipment, security staffs can detect sudden unusual events and respond promptly to the emergent situations rapidly to reduce the risks. To reach an even higher safety level, more and more surveillance devices are now required to increase sensing coverage and to capture images from different visual angels. Yet, monitoring video steams manually is indeed a tedious and costly work. To reduce the load of security staffs and cost, many advanced vision-based techniques for automatic video content analysis have been developed. Based on the results, the surveillance system can only inform security staffs whenever necessary.

To detect various events from video streams, it is a trend for today's surveillance systems to develop from analysis of individual images to

DOI: 10.4018/978-1-4666-8654-0.ch004

that of continuous human behaviors (Krishnan & Cook, 2014; Popoola & Wang, 2012; Kamal, Ding, Morye, Farrell, & Roy-Chowdhury, 2014). Consequently, more powerful computational equipment is in demand in order to process the largely increasing amount of data. Also, in many cases a single view is not sufficient enough to cover a targeted region, and a network of cameras is thus required to cope with an open area in which many people move arbitrarily. At present, most of the camera networks follow a centralized architecture, which often suffers the problems of high communication cost and scalability (Munishwar & Abu-Ghazaleh, 2010; Rinner & Wolf, 2008). Therefore, an efficient surveillance system not only has to perform behavior recognition, but also to overcome the problem of bandwidth limitation. A promising solution is to adopt a distributed smart camera sensor network (Rinner & Wolf, 2008, Song, et al., 2010), in which a smart camera is an embedded system with reasonable computing ability and storage. The camera nodes can process locally available images, perform data compression, and transmit the results to the neighborhood nodes in the same network for information sharing. The nodes communicate in a peer-to-peer-manner, while only abstract information is exchanged between nodes. In this way, the overall computation can be achieved in a distributed way by a set of inexpensive devices.

The main goal of developing a distributed smart camera system in public area is to detect abnormal human behaviors or unusual events. Abnormal events mean observable events that occur unexpectedly, abruptly and unintentionally, and they invoke an emergency situation that requires fast responses (Roshtkhari & Levine, 2013). To achieve the above goal, some important issues need to be addressed. One is to extract pedestrian features from the video streams recorded by the cameras. With a set of properly defined features to represent target data, a computational method (specifically a machine learning method) can be employed to construct robust and reliable classi-

fiers for event recognition. The other issue is to build behavior sequences with the selected feature. Though there have been many works focusing on how to precisely construct behavior sequences for the pedestrians from different image frames, most of such approaches are expensive in computation. To deploy the distributed camera network approach to a real life environment, more simple and efficient strategies are needed. Since the goal here is to train a classifier to detect an abnormal event occurring to a group of people acting in the public space, the data representation for these persons must be as concise as possible to ensure the efficiency and effectiveness of the learning method. The traditional encoding scheme of combining all personal features from the group is computationally expensive and the streaming nature of video data will result in high dimensional data that involve more resource requests. A new encoding scheme is thus needed. In addition, individual cameras are often not able to capture complete behavior sequences perfectly, due to some environmental factors in the real world, such as the blind angles of the camera network, the light reflection and the obstruction between objects. An efficient strategy with a relatively low resource need (in terms of computing and communicating) is required to exploit the device collaboration within a smart camera network.

To overcome the difficulties associated with the above issues, in this work we develop a distributed smart camera network system with several unique properties. These mainly include a simple but efficient strategy to organize the behavior sequence, a new indirect encoding scheme to represent a group of people with relatively few features (and thus reduce the dimensionality of the data), a machine learning approach to train robust event classifiers, and a collaborative strategy to detect abnormal events by making collective decision. With these properties, our approach has several computational advantages. It can thus be realized by a set of networked low-cost smart cameras. To evaluate the performance of the proposed approach and to compare different strategies coupled within the camera network, a series of experiments has been conducted. The results confirm the efficiency and effectiveness of the proposed approach.

BACKGROUND

Provide broad definitions and discussions of the topic and incorporate views of others (literature review) into the discussion to support, Video-based human activity recognition is becoming more and more popular in recent years. Video sensing techniques have now been applied to different surveillance systems that play many positive roles in our everyday life. In addition to the monitoring purpose, some works further included the function of pedestrian recognition into video surveillance systems to develop new video sensing applications. For example, to enhance the car safety system, industries start to apply the pedestrian detection technique to collision prevention (Geronimo, Lopez, Sappa, & Graf, 2010; Ryoo, Choi, Joung, Lee, & Yu, 2013). Video-based activity recognition has been well-researched, and different approaches have been proposed to tackle this problem. They differ mainly in their underlying image sensing and processing techniques (i.e., motion detection and feature extraction), and in the machine learning methods (i.e., naive Bayes classifiers, hidden Markov models) adopted to build the recognition models (Krishnan & Cook, 2014; Truong, Lin, & Chen, 2007).

According to Venu (2011), in the video-based recognition studies, Govindaraju *et al.* defined a three levels semantic hierarchy to describe the happenings in a video, including "action", "activity" and "event". "Action" is an atomic motion-pattern that is often gesture-like and has a single-cut trajectory, whereas "activity" is a series of actions in an ordered sequence depending on motion patterns, and "event" is on the top level of the hierarchy and constituted by a sequence of activities. Considering the hierarchical relation-

ship between "action", "activity", and "event", the main focus of such a surveillance system now moves towards the event detection and recognition, after the goals of recognizing simple body movements and human activities are achieved.

A video event can only be understood through a sequence of images. Therefore, analyzing video data for event recognition is a time consuming task, due to the streaming nature of the data. To successfully recognize a target event from a video, the system has to combine temporal activities, spatial locations, and context information. Some approaches have been proposed to extract representative features from image frames in order to reduce the data amount in the recognition procedure. For example, in (Zulkifley, Moran, & Rawlinson, 2012; Cosar & Cetin, 2014), the authors analyzed motion of a sequence of images and deduced a set of features such as optical flow with a differential approach. In addition, there have been some works utilizing the action and location information captured by specific equipment to understand indoor events (Brdiczka, Langet, Maisonnasse, & Crowley, 2009; Chaaraoui, Climent-Pérez, & Flórez-Revuelta, 2012). For example, in the work by Lymberopoulos (2008), the authors have used the successive locations of a person to infer the daily events he was engaged. To obtain even more accurate recognition results, some researchers have exploited the advantages of multiple cameras to infer human activities: the authors in (Mosabbeb, Raahemifar, & Fathy, 2013) deployed distributed cameras to improve their accuracy, and the authors in (Holte, Tran, Trivedi, & Moeslund, 2012) used multiple cameras to build a system for human 3D activity recognition. More detailed works on event recognition are referred to (Fleck & Strasser, 2008; Suriani, Hussain, & Zulkifley, 2013).

Differentiating abnormal events from normal ones is especially important in the study of event recognition. It can be applied to various real life surveillance applications (Chiu & Tsai, 2010; Lymberopoulos, Teixeira, & Savvides, 2008;

Singla, Cook, & Schmitter-Edgecombe, 2010). For example, in the work by Bamis (2010), the authors developed an event detection framework for elderly healthcare, and the smart cameras and SVM classification have been used in (Fleck & Strasser, 2008) to detect a human falling in a home environment. In the application for public safety monitoring, a video surveillance system with the ability of abnormal event recognition can provide timely alarms to the security staffs, start safety measurement, and display the escape paths for the group of people. However, previous studies tended to infer events from the single person's behavior, but hardly extracted and analyzed behavior data of a group of people. The analysis of several people needs more advanced cameras and introduces higher error rates, due to the behavior discrepancy of the people being observed. As mentioned above, our approach involves a set of low cost smart cameras to make the recognition decision in a collective way. Further details are described in the sections below.

A Collective Smart Camera System for Event Recognition

To detect abnormal events with low cost cameras, we develop a distributed smart camera network for making collective decision. This strategy is to take the advantages of collective intelligence: a high-level phenomenon that emerges naturally from the interplay of collaboration and competition of many individuals of a population (Król & Lopes, 2012; Woolley, Chabris, Pentland, Hashmi, & Malone, 2010), and is usually defined as the ability of a group to solve problems which cannot be solved by the members individually.

Figure 1 depicts the system architecture and illustrates how the system operates. As shown, the system flow includes the following steps: (1) the raw image data are captured by the video sensor; (2) the regions of interest are marked and the pedestrians are detected; (3) the pre-defined features are extracted from the marked regions

and the successive features for each pedestrian are recorded; (4) features are reduced and encoded, and feature data from different persons in the same region are combined to be a data vector (for training); (5) classifiers are built from the training data and used to detect patterns of abnormal events; and (6) each camera goes through the communication unit to transmit its processed data to the neighbor cameras, and to pass the result of event recognition to the management center. Each camera performs the steps described above and they work together to achieve the overall task of event detection in a surveillance area. The details of the major parts illustrated in Figure 1 are described in the following subsections.

Feature Extraction and Behavior Sequence Collection

The first phase in event detection is to extract specific target features from the video stream and then the system can infer what event is happening accordingly. To reduce the computational load of the cameras, our system does not deal with all image frames in real time, but instead simply sample some frames within a specific time interval. In this work, we adopt the OpenCV (an open source computer vision library, http://opencv.org/) that supports pedestrian detection by analyzing Histogram of Oriented Gradients (HOG) to determine if there is any person existing in an image. The HOG descriptor has several advantages: it captures local shape characteristics (i.e., edge or gradient structure) and upholds invariance to geometric and photometric transformations (i.e., translations or rotations make little difference if the pedestrian's body movement maintains a roughly upright position) (Dalal & Triggs, 2005). As shown in Figure 1, the system marks a region of interest (ROI, the rectangle in the feature extraction block) for each person detected. Here, we take the height of ROI, meaning the current height of a person in the image, as the feature data to represent a person. Although using more complicated features may

Figure 1. The operational flow of our collective recognition system

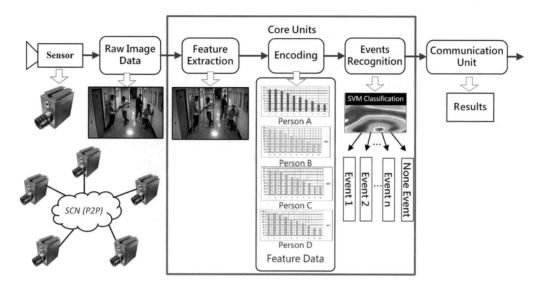

improve the recognition performance, more computational resources are required correspondingly. It is notable that the goal here is to develop a low-cost smart camera network for event recognition. With the cost constraint, it is essential to select a proper feature to achieve a reasonable system performance in real time. Therefore, we develop a mechanism to use the changes of ROI (i.e., the height discrepancy) recorded within a specific time interval to constitute a feature vector for event recognition.

To detect a specific event, the system needs to continuously detect and mark the pedestrians, and then extract the feature data described above from their behavior sequences. Because several people may move within the surveillance area a smart camera can cover, the system has to make distinctions among them to construct a correct data sequence for each person. One plausible way is to compare the HOG of two consecutive images at each time step to ensure the consistency of the targets in the two images (i.e., belonging to the same behavior sequence). However, this is more computationally expensive than a single smart camera can afford. Therefore, we develop a simple but efficient strategy that can reduce the number

of the comparisons to save the computational cost. Here, we assume that human behaviors are harmonious and inertial, so the directions of a person's body parts are often consistent (without sudden change in a very short period of time) in motion. With this assumption, the system only performs the HOG comparison for the images to build a forward vector for a person when he first appears in the space where a smart camera is monitoring. After that, it calculates the cosine value of two consecutive motion vectors (see Figure 2) but not the complete HOG computation to confirm the moving trajectory of a single person (by taking the image with minimal cosine value).

In the real world situations, the image frames included in a behavior sequence are not always reliable, due to the unexpected environmental effects (such as the clutter and occlusion problems). In this work, we use the OpenCV to acquire ROI and choose not to deal with these problems particularly at the image-processing level. Instead, we develop a collective decision method at the strategic level to enhance the robustness of event recognition.

In addition to identifying the behavior sequence for each person in the same surveillance area, the

Figure 2. The forward vectors in the consecutive time and the resulting moving trajectory

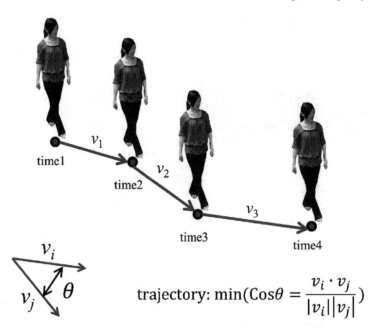

$$\text{trajectory: } \min\left(\text{Cos}\theta = \frac{v_i \cdot v_j}{|v_i||v_j|}\right)$$

system has to convert the height of each ROI to its original size (the discrepancy is caused by the distance between the target and the camera in each image: a larger size ROI is obtained when a person moves towards the camera), in order to construct a complete feature vector for each person. To recover a person's real height from the ROI, the distance between the person and the camera (i.e., the depth) needs to be calculated. This distance can be estimated by different methods, such as using multiple views methods (Colonnese, Rinauro, & Scarano, 2014; Zhang, Jia, Wong, & Bao, 2009) or making some geometric hypotheses. For simplicity, this work assumes that the person's position on the ground plane is known and which can then be used to calculate the depth of the person in the scene. With the depth estimation, we can then convert the feature values to its original form for the series of image frames collected.

Feature Data Encoding for a Group of People

As is mentioned, once a person's behavior sequence is identified and the ROI sizes are con-

verted, a feature vector for a single pedestrian can be built. Figure 3 illustrates an example of a behavior sequence recorded by the camera within a specific time interval (i.e., 10 time steps) and the corresponding feature vector. In this example, the feature value below each time step represents the height of ROI measured.

To detect a specific event in a public space, the system observes the behaviors of a group of people in the same region (rather than that of any individual), and infer what event is happening accordingly. A direct way is to append the feature vectors built for different persons to form a new vector for the group. But it should be noted that the dimension of this combined vector will increase dramatically along with the number of people in the surveillance area. The high dimensional feature data thus become a burden for a smart camera network: though with limited computational power, it is expected to respond to an abnormal event in real time. Under such circumstances, the dimension of the combined feature vector has to be further reduced.

In this work, we develop an indirect encoding scheme that derives a concise and compact

Figure 3. An example of transferring a behavior sequence to a set of ROI heights, which are used to derive three feature to represent a person. Features for ten persons constitute an input data

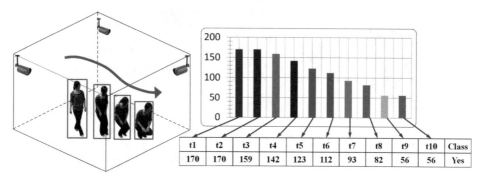

t1	t2	t3	t4	t5	t6	t7	t8	t9	t10	Class
170	170	159	142	123	112	93	82	56	56	Yes

representation from the feature vectors described above to represent the behavior sequences of a set of people. In this representation, the vector for each person is reduced to include three new features f_1, f_2, and f_3, which are the maximal change of the ROI height, the number of image frames within which the maximal change happens, and the frequency of the considerable ROI change. The first feature f_1 is to measure the maximal behavior variation (i.e., the difference of the maximal and minimal ROI heights; the value could be positive or negative) of a person within a pre-defined time interval (i.e., ten time steps in our experiment). This value is normalized, subject to the maximal height. The second feature f_2 means to describe the changing rate from the maximal/minimal to minimal/maximal heights in terms of the number of image frames. The third feature f_3 indicates how often a person changes his behaviors, and this is obtained by measuring the variation between two consecutive ROI heights (i.e., the slope value changes from positive/negative to negative/positive) and checking if the variation exceeds a pre-defined threshold (20% of the first ROI height, determined by a preliminary test). For example, the behavior sequence shown in Figure 3 is represented as <0.67, 9, 0>, in which 0.67 is the normalized change rate (from 170 to 56), 9 is the number of frames corresponding to the interval of the above change, and 0 means no slope change in this interval.. In this way, the

dimension of the combined feature vector can be largely reduced and the system performance can thus be improved. Here, each data vector means a group of ten people and includes thirty features in total, and it can be represented as <$f_1^1, f_2^1, f_3^1, f_1^2, f_2^2, f_3^2, ..., f_1^{10}, f_2^{10}, f_3^{10}$>, in which the superscripts are the identifiers of the people detected.

Collective Event Recognition

After encoding the behavior sequences of a group of people as feature data, we adopt a machine learning method to classify the target events occurring in a surveillance area. Many popular classification methods can be used to build up classifiers for event recognition, for example the *k*-nearest neighbor method (*k*-NN), decision tree, artificial neural network (ANN), and support vector machine (SVM). According to previous studies (Brdiczka, Langet, Maisonnasse, & Crowley, 2009; Geronimo, Lopez, Sappa, & Graf, 2010; Lavee, Rivlin, & Rudzsky, 2009), SVM is the method most suitable for our classification task here, due to its good performance in dealing with multi-class and high-dimensional data (thirty features for each data in this work) constituted by real numbers. Therefore, we choose to use SVM classifiers for event detection. In this work, the classifiers are used for both single event recognition (with two classes of target and non-target events) and multiple event recognition (with four

Figure 4. The training and operating phases of building a classifier for event recognition

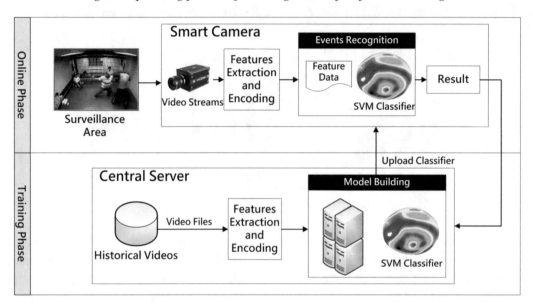

classes of events: earthquake, gun shooting, fighting, and normal). For the multi-event recognition, the output of the classifier needs to indicate which event is happening.

To train a SVM classifier, the system includes the offline training and online operating phases, as illustrated in Figure 4. The training phase involves collecting historical video files and analyzing of video streams for features data extraction. The data can be processed on a workstation or a server level computer (rather than on a smart camera) of which its computation is more powerful to build a classifier. The classifier built can then dispatched to all smart cameras in the same network. In this work, we use the online available software LISVM (Chang & Lin, 2011) and chose the SVM type C-SVC (regularized support vector classification) with a kernel type of linear to construct the SVM classifiers. This configuration is selected as it achieves a good balance of the processing speed and the recognition accuracy.

Once the classifier is constructed, it is then used for event recognition in an online manner. The recognition phase operates on each single smart camera. When a smart camera is monitor-

ing the environment, it adopts sliding window in the way of "first in first out" to process the video frames. It accumulates a certain number of time-series data, and then inputs the feature data to the classifier to perform real-time event recognition.

As mentioned above, a smart camera has an embedded system structure with very limited computational power and storage (compared to the traditional personal computers or central servers). Therefore it only functions for feature extraction, encoding, and event recognition. In addition, each camera can duplicate the HOG data it has identified and transmit them to the neighborhood sensor nodes (or any nodes in the same network, depending on the pre-defined strategy) to ensure the completeness of each feature vector (i.e., to mend any incomplete data). Though the high level computer vision algorithms can be divided so that intermediate results can be exchanged with other cameras, we do not perform such partition because our goal here is to use relative small amount of shared information to achieve event recognition through the strategy of making collective decision. Therefore, during the monitoring process, a smart camera just transmits the processed information (i.e., the HOG data) to other camera nodes (the destination nodes can be determined by a pre-defined configuration) for mending incomplete data. A camera can mend an incomplete behavior sequence by comparing the features of the HOG data it collected to that of transmitted by other cameras to perform person-matching, and then combining the features of the matched persons (Fleck, Busch, & Straßer, 2007; Kuo, Huang, & Nevatia, 2010). The data transmission interval can be determined in advance, depending on the system planning. . In this way, the transmission load of the system can be largely reduced and the system can thus be scaled up to include more sensor nodes to monitor a huge surveillance area. With the above design, each camera performs the recognition task independently (through the data it collected and the data shared by others) and then all cameras vote for the final result. The collective event recognition is thus achieved.

EXPERIMENTS AND RESULTS

Experimental Environment and Data Sets

To evaluate the proposed approach for event de-tection, we conducted a series of experiments, in which three target events were recognized, includ-ing earthquake, gun shooting, and fighting. Since it is difficult to obtain a large number of video data for training and testing the three events in reality, for practical reason, we took a simulation-based strategy for data collection. Three scenarios were designed for the events mentioned above and some participants were asked to demonstrate their responses (i.e., the behavior sequences, as shown in Figure 5) to the different events. The collected data samples were then extended to generate data sets through a statistic-based approach. With the simulated data sets, the popular data mining ap-

Figure 5. The three target events: (A) earthquake; (B) gun shooting; (C) fighting

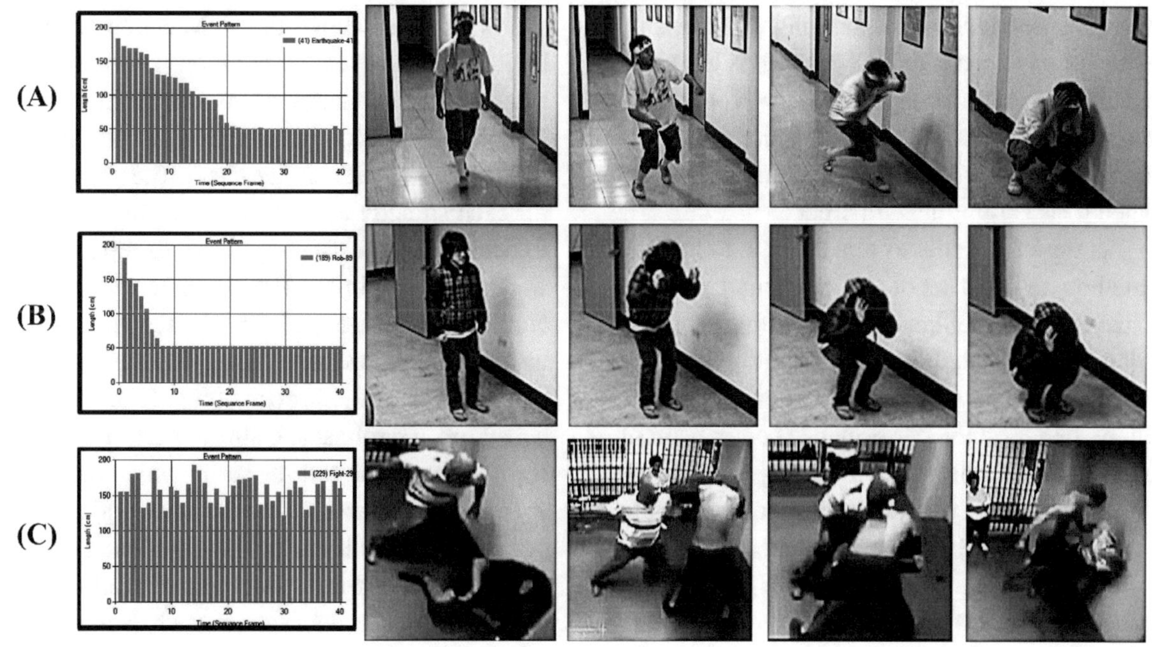

plication software "WEKA" (Hall, et al., 2009) was used to build the event classifiers to verify the feasibility and reliability of our approach.

The creation of simulated data for the earthquake event was based on the observation that when the earthquake was happening in a public area, there would be a certain proportion of the group of people taking emergence evacuation actions, such as to hide under a desk or to crouch near a pillar. The possible behaviors have a common feature: the height of a person is decreasing, though the moving speed and distance of different persons may differ from one to another. Thus, to create a data set to train classifiers for this event, we collected the sample behaviors from the demonstration procedure and used these samples to build a normal distribution to randomly generate a height variation for each person at each time step. That is, in simulation the height of a person varied according to the rule $H_{t+1} = H_t - N(\mu, \sigma)$, where H represented the height and N was a normal distribution with mean μ and standard deviation σ. Similarly, two datasets were generated for the events of gun shooting and fighting respectively. The rule used for the gun shooting was the same as the one for earthquake, while the rule for the fighting event was changed to $H_{t+1} = H_t + N(0, \sigma)$. This distribution has a mean 0 in order to produce positive and negative height variations for a person when he was fighting with others.

As the major goal of this study is to investigate how to use a set of low-cost smart cameras to develop a surveillance system with reasonably good performance. Therefore, in the experiments, we focus on the evaluation of the design methodology, rather on the performance comparison of different approaches. In the following, we describe the experimental runs with different settings to evaluate the developed framework.

Event Recognition

With the above data sets, different series of experiments were conducted to verify the feasibil-

ity and reliability of our approach. As described previously, our goal is to detect a specific event through the recognition of the behaviors of a group of people. Therefore, each data record is constituted by the features collected from several persons (ten in this work and each data thus includes thirty features as described above). It is notable that people may have different responses to the same event. To investigate the effect of inconsistent human behaviors, in the first series of experiments, we designed several strategies with different ratios (ranging from 0.0 to 1.0) of two types of behaviors (i.e., target or non-target) to train and test the classifiers. For example, in the case of earthquake, a ratio of 0.1 means that there were 10% of people in the group with non-target behaviors (which were randomly selected from the other two distributions, gun shooting and fighting, generated in the experiment section), and 90% of people with target behavior (selected from the distribution of earthquake). For each strategy (i.e., ratio), 1000 data records (each record included ten people and each person was represented by three features) were created.

As indicated above, the SVM classifiers were built for single event recognition (i.e., to predict a data record is a target event or not), in which a 10-fold cross validation method was used to train and test the classifiers. The results (i.e., accuracy) for each strategy are presented in Figure 6 (up). In addition to the training phase, different ratios were also used in the test phase to observe the corresponding effects. As can be seen in this figure, the classifiers trained from feature data with certain levels (i.e., 0% up to 60%) of non-relevant behaviors, are robust and able to perform precise recognition in the test phase (in which data also contained target and non-target behaviors). But the performance declines (i.e., the right hand side of the figure) when the test data contained more than 50% of non-target behaviors in each data (i.e., ten people) data. On the contrary, the classifier built from data with a high ratio of non-target behaviors (i.e. 80%) could not deliver a high recognition accuracy as others for the test cases with low ratios of non-target behaviors, while better results were obtained for the test cases with high impurity (in which the test data became more and more similar to the training data that had a high rate of non-target behaviors). In addition, the false positive rates correspond to the above strategies are presented in Figure 6 (down). It shows that due to the two-class (target and non-target) effect (meaning that most of the recognition faults belong to the type of false positive), the false positive rates are complement to the accuracy rates illustrated in Figure 6 (up). This is mainly due to the situation of class imbalance (Japkowicz & Stephen, 2002; Yang & Lee, 2011) (meaning that in a classification task, when the numbers of examples within each class are quite different), the classification performance of the standard classifier may be damaged. Therefore, to obtain a higher accuracy, the amount of different classes of training data needs to be arranged carefully.

After the series of experiments of building SVM classifiers for single event detection, we employed the same approach to train classifiers for multiple event recognition. In this experiment, the output of the classifier needed to indicate which event among the four (earthquake, gun shooting, fighting, and normal) was happening. The class of normal events here represents the features of the behavior sequences remain more or less the same. The event was simulated by a stable behavior sequence with a small random variation on each ROI included in the sequence. The same training and test procedures as above were performed and the results are shown in Figure 7 (up). As can be observed, the effects caused by different ratios are similar to those obtained from the single event recognition presented in Figure 6 (up), though the classifiers for multiple event recognition are not as precise as those for single event recognition. It is worth noting that classifiers trained from the data with lower levels impurity (i.e. 0~20%) did not have results with high accuracy in the test cases with high rations of data impurity, because

the classifiers have overly fitted the training data. The false positive rates are also shown in Figure 7 (down). It can be observed that similar to the above results for the single event recognition, the false positive rates in this case also complement the accuracy rates. However, in this case there are four different classes of sample events included in the dataset, and the importance of each data class thus decreases. Therefore, the false positive rates for multi-event recognition become lower, if compared to the case of single event (two classes) recognition.

Effect of the Number of Persons Considered

To investigate the effect of considering different numbers of people in the group for event detection, we adopted the encoding scheme described previously and conducted a series of experiments to evaluate the corresponding performance of including different numbers of persons in each data record. The numbers ranged from 3 to 12, and for each number three different ratios of impurity (i.e., 0.0, 0.2 and 0.4 that provided better results in the previous experiments) were arranged as in the last section. Figure 8 illustrates the results. As shown in this figure, though taking into account more persons' behaviors (i.e., 10-12 in our experiments) for event recognition can give better performance, it requires higher computational cost. Accounting for both recognition accuracy and computational cost, ten people for each data record is a suitable choice for our work here.

In a surveillances task, the number of people within the region monitored by a smart camera may be more or less than the expected number (i.e., ten in this work) in practice. The system needs an efficient strategy to re-organize the data records to obtain best performance. For the case of more than the expected number of persons being identified, the system can simply choose the amount it needs based on a first-detected-first-chosen strategy; but for the case without enough number of persons

Figure 6. The experimental results for strategies with different levels of data impurity (up); and the false positive rates correspond to the results of single event recognition (down)

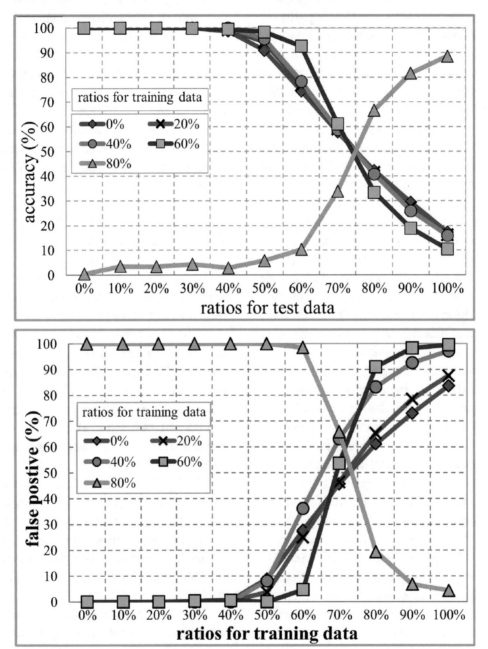

is not sufficient, the system needs to supplement some features to make a complete data record (for example, a record of ten people in this study). Two simple strategies were used: to fill either a value of null or a value averaged from the avail- able features in each empty feature in the record. In the experiments, different ratios (percentages) of missing frames were used, and the above two strategies were employed to re-form a complete data record of ten persons for training. Then, the

Figure 7. Results for multi-event recognition (up); and the false positive rates correspond to the results of multi-event recognition (down)

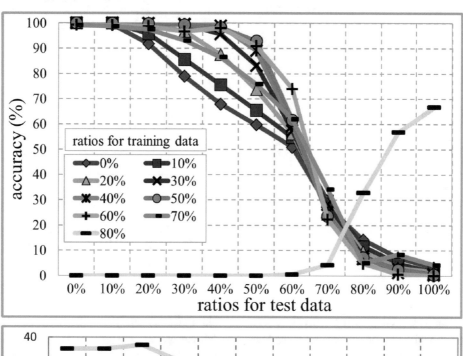

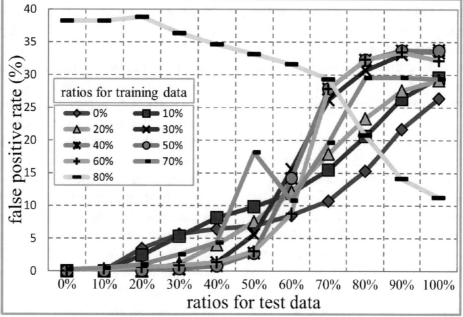

trained classifies were tested on eleven types of data (with different ratios of missing persons, ranging from 0 to 100%). Figures 9 present the recognition results for the above two strategies, respectively, in which the *x*-axis indicates the ratio of missing persons in test data, and *y*-axis, the recognition performance. They show that similar results can be obtained for both strategies. For the training cases with less missing data (e.g., 0~20%), the performance declined in a more natural way.

Figure 8. The effects of considering different numbers of persons for event detection

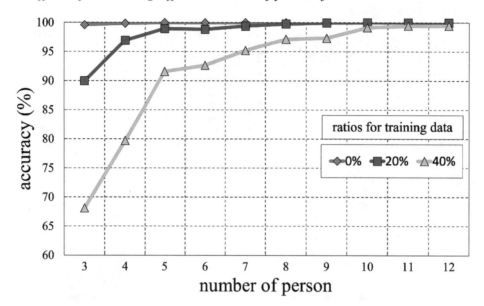

Collective Event Recognition

In the real world, it is in fact difficult for the collective smart cameras to capture all behavior changes among a group of people, due to some undesired environmental effects (such as the blind angles of mounted sensors, coverage rates of the sensors, noisy, and people obstructed). That is, the data (image frames) collected from the cameras may be incomplete (not enough to form a behavior sequence for each single person). To overcome such as a problem, the system needs some strategies amended and to achieve precise event recognition in the real life environment. One possible way is to distribute the images collected by a camera to its neighbors to repair the behavior sequence, and many algorithms have been proposed to construct complete data. However, as mentioned in the background section, this method has to exchange

In contrast, for the cases with relatively more missing data in training, the classifiers were less accurate in general. In both situations, the classifiers performed better when the ratios of missing data in the training and testing phases came close.

data continuously. It thus increases the network transmission load largely. Therefore, we proposed to recognize the event through making collective decision, in which each camera performed the recognition task independently and all cameras voted for the final decision.

To evaluate the collective decision method, a series of experiments was conducted. In the experiments, the behavior sequence for each single person (including 15 consecutive image frames as described in the section for feature extraction) was randomly impaired up to 20% (i.e., 1~3 frames were removed from the original data) to simulate the effect of incomplete data. In addition, a ratio of 0.3 was used to train SVM classifiers (as it was reported previously to derive a robust classifier). Four different numbers of smart cameras were tested for the collective surveillance, and the results are presented in Figure 10. They show that incomplete data caused different degrees of damage in recognizing different types of event. As can be seen in the figure, when more cameras were deployed in the environment with a collective decision, the performance can be improved effectively.

Figure 9. Test results for the first strategy (up); and test results for the second strategy (down)

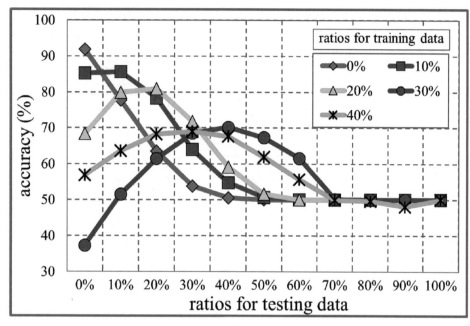

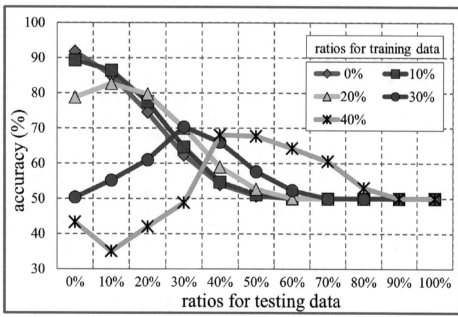

CONCLUSION

Smart camera networks are now popular for the surveillance of public areas. To deploy a surveillance system in a cost efficient manner, in this study we presented a simple but efficient strategy to organize human behavior sequence and a new encoding scheme to represent a group of people. Most importantly, we developed a collective approach to detect abnormal events. In our approach, the smart cameras can cooperate with each other to make group decision when lacking some data due

Figure 10. Results of collective surveillance

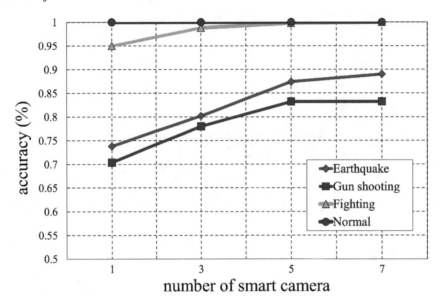

to unpredictable environmental factors. Because the proposed encoding scheme can represent a group of people with relatively few features, the dimensionality of the data can thus be reduced, and the task of training a classifier for event recognition becomes more achievable. With these advantages, a machine learning approach can be used to train robust event classifiers, and a collaborative strategy can be adopted to detect abnormal events by making collective decision. Different series of experiments have been conducted to evaluate the developed approach, and the results show that our system can provide a certain degree of stability and reliability with a low cost.

Though the proposed approach provides an inexpensive and efficient way for surveillance, it has some limits. For example, the low-cost smart cameras are not as precise as the more expensive ones with advanced capabilities when dealing with image frames. Our approach is thus not designed for sensitive events that involve differentiating small variations between behavior sequences. Moreover, to reduce the computational load, the proposed approach does not frequently exchange data between sensor nodes to mend the incomplete behavior sequence. This may produce negative influences in event recognition.

Based on the work presented here, we are currently extending our system to recognize more events and investigating new ways to address the scalability issue of the camera network. In addition, we plan to develop an adaptive mechanism that can detect the technical faults of the cameras, and automatically adjust the visual angles of some neighborhood cameras to watch the area where faulty cameras could not execute their functions. This new approach can greatly help guarding the security of the public space.

REFERENCES

Bamis, A., Lymberopoulos, D., Teixeira, T., & Savvides, A. (2010). The BehaviorScope framework for enabling ambient assisted living. *Personal and Ubiquitous Computing, 14*(6), 473–487. doi:10.1007/s00779-010-0282-z

Brdiczka, O., Langet, M., Maisonnasse, J., & Crowley, J. L. (2009). Detecting human behavior models from multimodal observation in a smart home. *IEEE Transactions on Automation Science and Engineering*, *6*(4), 588–597. doi:10.1109/TASE.2008.2004965

Chaaraoui, A. A., Climent-Pérez, P., & Flórez-Revuelta, F. (2012). A review on vision techniques applied to human behaviour analysis for ambient-assisted living. *Expert Systems with Applications*, *39*(12), 10873–10888. doi:10.1016/j.eswa.2012.03.005

Chang, C.-C., & Lin, C. J. (2011). LIBSVM: A library for support vector machines. *ACM Transactions on Intelligent Systems and Technology*, *2*(3), 1–27. doi:10.1145/1961189.1961199

Chiu, W.-Y., & Tsai, D.-W. (2010). A macro-observation scheme for abnormal event detection in daily-life video sequences. *EURASIP Journal on Advances in Signal Processing*, *2010*(1), 525026. doi:10.1155/2010/525026

Colonnese, S., Rinauro, S., & Scarano, G. (2014). Current research results on depth map interpolation techniques. In P. D. Giamberardino, D. Iacoviello, R. N. Jorge & J. M. R. S. Tavares (Eds.), Computational Modeling of Objects Presented in Images (LNCVB) (vol. 15, pp. 187-200). Berlin, Germany: Springer. doi:10.1007/978-3-319-04039-4_11

Dalal, N., & Triggs, B. (2005). Histograms of oriented gradients for human detection. In *Proceedings of IEEE International Conference on Computer Vision and Pattern Recognition* (pp. 886-893). IEEE Press. doi:10.1109/CVPR.2005.177

Fleck, S., Busch, F., & Straßer, W. (2007). Adaptive probabilistic tracking embedded in smart cameras for distributed surveillance in a 3D model. *EURASIP Journal on Embedded Systems*, *2007*(1), 29858. doi:10.1186/1687-3963-2007-029858

Fleck, S., & Strasser, W. (2008). Smart camera based monitoring system and its application to assisted living. *Proceedings of the IEEE*, *96*(10), 1698–1714. doi:10.1109/JPROC.2008.928765

Geronimo, D., Lopez, A. M., Sappa, A. D., & Graf, T. (2010). Survey of pedestrian detection for advanced driver assistance systems. *IEEE Transactions on Pattern Analysis and Machine Intelligence*, *32*(7), 1239–1258. doi:10.1109/TPAMI.2009.122 PMID:20489227

Hall, M., Frank, E., Holmes, G., Pfahringer, B., Reutemann, P., & Witten, I. H. (2009). The WEKA data mining software: An update. *SIGKDD Explorations*, *11*(1), 10–19. doi:10.1145/1656274.1656278

Holte, M. B., Tran, C., Trivedi, M. M., & Moeslund, T. B. (2012). Human pose estimation and activity recognition from multi-view videos: Comparative explorations of recent developments. *IEEE Journal of Selected Topics in Signal Processing*, *6*(5), 538–552. doi:10.1109/JSTSP.2012.2196975

Japkowicz, N., & Stephen, S. (2002). The class imbalance problem: A systematic study. *Intelligent Data Analysis*, *6*(5), 429–450.

Kamal, A. T., Ding, C., Morye, A. A., Farrell, J. A., & Roy-Chowdhury, A. K. (2014). An overview of distributed tracking and control in camera networks. In V. K. Asari (Ed.), *Wide Area Surveillance: Augmented Vision and Reality* (pp. 207–234). Berlin, Germany: Springer. doi:10.1007/8612_2012_10

Krishnan, N. C., & Cook, D. J. (2014). Activity recognition on streaming sensor data. *Pervasive and Mobile Computing*, *10*, 138–154. doi:10.1016/j.pmcj.2012.07.003 PMID:24729780

Król, D., & Lopes, H. S. (2012). Nature-inspired collective intelligence in theory and practice. *Information Sciences*, *182*(1), 1–2. doi:10.1016/j.ins.2011.10.001

Kuo, C.-H., Huang, C., & Nevatia, R. (2010). Inter-camera association of multi-target tracks by on-line learned appearance affinity models. In K. Daniilidis, P. Maragos & N. Paragios (Eds.), *Computer Vision: Proceedings of European Conference on Computer Vision* (*LNCS*) *6331*, 381-396). Berlin, Germany: Springer. doi:10.1007/978-3-642-15549-9_28

Lavee, G., Rivlin, E., & Rudzsky, M. (2009). Understanding video events: A survey of methods for automatic interpretation of semantic occurrences in video. *IEEE Trans. on Systems, Man, and Cybernetics, Part C: Applications and Reviews*, *39*(5), 489–504. doi:10.1109/TSMCC.2009.2023380

Lymberopoulos, D., Teixeira, T., & Savvides, A. (2008). Macroscopic human behavior interpretation using distributed imager and other sensors. *Proceedings of the IEEE*, *96*(10), 1657–1677. doi:10.1109/JPROC.2008.928761

Mosabbeb, E. A., Raahemifar, K., & Fathy, M. (2013). Multi-view human activity recognition in distributed camera sensor networks. *Sensors (Basel, Switzerland)*, *13*(7), 8750–8770. doi:10.3390/s130708750 PMID:23881136

Munishwar, V. P., & Abu-Ghazaleh, N. B. (2010). Scalable target coverage in smart camera networks. In *Proceedings of the Fourth ACM/IEEE International Conference on Distributed Smart Cameras* (pp. 206-213). ACM Press. doi:10.1145/1865987.1866020

Popoola, K., & Wang, O. P. (2012). Video-based abnormal human behavior recognition-a review. *IEEE Trans. Systems, Man, and Cybernetics. Part C*, *42*(6), 865–878.

Rinner, B., & Wolf, W. (2008). An introduction to distributed smart cameras. *Proceedings of the IEEE*, *96*(10), 1565–1575. doi:10.1109/JPROC.2008.928742

Roshtkhari, M. J., & Levine, M. D. (2013). Online dominant and anomalous behavior detection in videos. In *Proceedings of IEEE Conference on Computer Vision and Pattern Recognition*. IEEE Press doi:10.1109/CVPR.2013.337

Ryoo, M. S., Choi, S., Joung, J.-H., Lee, J.-Y., & Yu, W. (2013). Personal driving diary: Automated recognition of driving events from first-person videos. *Computer Vision and Image Understanding*, *117*(10), 1299–1312. doi:10.1016/j.cviu.2013.01.004

Singla, G., Cook, D. J., & Schmitter-Edgecombe, M. (2010). Recognizing independent and joint activities among multiple residents in smart environments. *Journal of Ambient Intelligence and Humanized Computing*, *1*(1), 57–63. doi:10.1007/s12652-009-0007-1 PMID:20975986

Song, B., Kamal, A. T., Soto, C., Ding, C., Farrell, J. A., & Roy-Chowdhury, A. K. (2010). Tracking and activity recognition through consensus in distributed camera networks. *IEEE Transactions on Image Processing*, *19*(10), 2564–2579. doi:10.1109/TIP.2010.2052823 PMID:20550994

Suriani, N. S., Hussain, A., & Zulkifley, M. A. (2013). Sudden event recognition: A survey. *Sensors (Basel, Switzerland)*, *13*(8), 9966–9998. doi:10.3390/s130809966 PMID:23921828

Truong, T.-K., Lin, C.-C., & Chen, S.-H. (2007). Segmentation of specific speech signals from multi-dialog environment using SVM and wavelet. *Pattern Recognition Letters*, *28*(11), 1307–1313. doi:10.1016/j.patrec.2006.11.020

Venu, G. A. (2011). Generative framework to investigate the underlying patterns in human activities. In *Proceedings of IEEE International Conference on Computer Vision Workshops* (pp. 1472–1479). IEEE Press.

Woolley, A. W., Chabris, C. F., Pentland, A., Hashmi, N., & Malone, T. W. (2010). Evidence for a collective intelligence factor in the performance of human groups. *Science*, *330*(6004), 686–688. doi:10.1126/science.1193147 PMID:20929725

Yang, T.-H., & Lee, W.-P. (2011). Combining GRN modeling and demonstration-based programming for robot control. *Neural Computing & Applications*, *20*(6), 909–921. doi:10.1007/s00521-010-0496-z

Zhang, G., Jia, J., Wong, T.-T., & Bao, H. (2009). Consistent depth maps recovery from a video sequence. *IEEE Transactions on Pattern Analysis and Machine Intelligence*, *31*(6), 974–988. doi:10.1109/TPAMI.2009.52 PMID:19372604

Zulkifley, M. A., Moran, B., & Rawlinson, D. (2012). Robust foreground detection: A fusion of masked grey world, probabilistic gradient information and extended conditional random field approach. *Sensors (Basel, Switzerland)*, *12*(5), 5623–5649. doi:10.3390/s120505623 PMID:22778605

KEY TERMS AND DEFINITIONS

Collective Intelligence: A form of distributed intelligence that emerges from the collaboration, collective efforts, and competition of many individuals and appears in consensus decision making.

Feature Extraction: When the data is too large to be processed, the data will be transformed into a reduced representation set of features. The process of transforming the input data into the set of features is called feature extraction.

Histogram of Oriented Gradient (HOG): HOG counts occurrences of gradient orientation in localized portions of an image. HOG can be used to describe feature descriptors in computer vision and image processing for the purpose of object detection.

Region of Interest (ROI): A selected subset of samples within a dataset identified for a particular purpose. In computer vision, the ROI defines the borders of an object under consideration to perform some operation on it.

Smart Camera: A self-contained vision system with built-in image sensor, capable of capturing images, extracting application-specific information from the images, generating event descriptions, and making decisions.

Support Vector Machine (SVM): A supervised machine learning method that constructs classification models with associated learning algorithms that analyze data and recognize patterns.

Video Surveillance Systems: A video system for monitoring the behavior, activities, or other changing information of the targets. It is for the purpose of influencing, managing, directing, or protecting the targets.

Chapter 5
Impulse Noise Filtering:
Review of the State-of-the-Art Algorithms for Impulse Noise Filtering

Abhijit Chandra
Jadavpur University, India

Srideep Maity
Indian Institute of Technology, Kharagpur, India

ABSTRACT

Digital images are often corrupted by various types of noises amongst which impulse noise is most prevalent. Impulse noise appears during transmission and/or acquisition of images. Intrusion of impulse noise degrades the quality of the image and causes the loss of fine image details. Reducing the effect of impulse noise from corrupted images is therefore considered as an essential task to be performed before letting the image for further processing. However, the process of noise reduction from an image should also take proper care towards the preservation of edges and fine details of an image. A number of efficient noise reduction algorithms have already been proposed in the literature over the last few decades which have nurtured this issue with utmost importance. Design and development of new two dimensional (2D) filters has grown sufficient interest amongst the researchers. This chapter attempts to throw enough light on the advancement in this field by illustratively describing existing state-of-the-art filtering techniques along with their capability of denoising impulse noises.

1. INTRODUCTION

Digital images are often corrupted by various types of noises amongst which impulse noise is most prevalent. Impulse noise appears during transmission and/or acquisition of images. Intrusion of impulse noise degrades the quality of the image and causes the loss of fine image details. Reduc-

ing the effect of impulse noise from corrupted images is therefore considered as an essential task to be performed before letting the image for further processing. However, the process of noise reduction from an image should also take proper care towards the preservation of edges and fine details of an image.

DOI: 10.4018/978-1-4666-8654-0.ch005

A number of efficient noise reduction algorithms have already been proposed in the literature over the last few decades which have nurtured this issue with utmost importance. In regard to this, algorithms like standard median filter (SMF) (Huang et al., 1979), center weighted median (CWM) filter (Ko & Lee, 1991), adaptive median filter (AMF) (Hwang & Haddad, 1995), progressive switching median filter (PSMF) (Wang and Zhang, 1999), multi-state median (MSM) filter (Chen and Wu, 2000), modified decision based un-symmetric trimmed median filter (MDBUTMF) (Esakkirajan et. al., 2011) and decision-based coupled window median filter (DBCWMF) (Bhadouria, Ghoshal, & Siddiqi, 2014) have been proposed in subsequent times. These algorithms have judiciously pointed out the limitations of the preceding algorithms and come up with solutions to mitigate those shortcomings. As a matter of fact, design and development of new two dimensional (2D) filters has grown sufficient interest amongst the researchers.

This chapter aims to throw sufficient light on the advancement in this field by illustratively describing existing state-of-the-art filtering techniques towards the elimination of impulse noises from the two-dimensional image. Each of these algorithms has been described with the help of mathematical backbone and the capability of noise elimination has been explained analytically. Numerical results have been included in order to substantiate the claims of the authors and to make a comparative study amongst various algorithms.

The entire chapter has been organized as follows: section II provides a brief description about various types of impulse noises available in practice and section III projects median filter as an efficient tool to eliminate the effect of impulse noise while section IV highlights some of the recent trends employed for this specific application. Section V makes a comparative analysis amongst various methods with the avenues of

future research have been indicated in section VI. Finally, the chapter is concluded in section VII.

2. VARIANTS OF IMPULSE NOISE

Images are often corrupted by impulse noise during the process of acquisition and transmission. Impulse noise may be of type unipolar or bipolar. Bipolar impulse noise is commonly known as salt-and-pepper noise (SPN) (Gonzalez & Woods, 2002; Huang, Yang, & Tang, 1979). The main property of salt-and-pepper noise is that the pixel corrupted by this noise gets the maximum or minimum value present in the dynamic range of available values, such as 0 and 255 in case of 8-bit gray-scale image. The SPN is commonly modeled in accordance with

$$Y_{i,j} = \begin{cases} \{0, \ 255\} & \text{with probability } p \\ X_{i,j} & \text{with probability } 1-p \end{cases}$$

(1)

where $X_{i,j}$ and $Y_{i,j}$ denote the intensity value of the original and corrupted images at coordinate (i,j) respectively and p is the noise density.

Various methods have been proposed in the literature for estimating the intensity values of noisy pixels. Some of the best existing methods are opening-closing sequence (OCS) filter (Ze-Feng Zhou-Ping, & You-Lun, 2007), edge-preserving algorithm (EPA) (Chen & Lien, 2008), switching-based adaptive weighted mean (SAWM) filter (Zhang & Xiong, 2009), decision-based average or median filter (DAM) (Jourabloo, Feghahati, & Jamzad, 2012) and so on. In connection to this, boundary discriminative noise detection (BDND) method (Ng & Ma, 2006) classifies the pixels according to their intensities and image restoration is done by using the switching median filter (SMF). Instead of two fixed values, impulse noise can be more realistically modeled by two fixed ranges appearing at both ends (Ng & Ma, 2006; Xia, Xiong, Xu, & Zhang, 2010). This model is known as fixed-range impulse noise (FRIN) (Hosseini & Marvasti, 2013) which has been described as:

$$Y_{i,j} = \begin{cases} 0, \ m & \text{with probability } p_1 \\ X_{i,j} & \text{with probability } 1-p \\ 255-m, \ 255 & \text{with probability } p_2 \end{cases} \quad (2)$$

where $X_{i,j}$ and $Y_{i,j}$ denote the intensity value of the original and corrupted images at coordinate (i,j) respectively and $p=p_1+p_2$.

Another realistic description about impulse noise is obtained in general fixed-valued impulse noise (GFN) model (Hosseini & Marvasti, 2013) which implies that, instead of fixed values or ranges, impulses can take any subset of the entire dynamic range. GFN is modeled as:

$$Y_{i,j} = \begin{cases} S & \text{with probability } p \\ X_{i,j} & \text{with probability } 1-p \end{cases} \quad (3)$$

where $X_{i,j}$ and $Y_{i,j}$ denote the intensity value of the original and corrupted pixels at location (i,j) respectively and S is the set of impulse noise values with k elements chosen from the set $[0, 255]$.

Models of these types require a more complex impulse detector because the noise values are not necessarily located at low and high intensities. In this context, impulse noise detection is based on image entropy measurement and image restoration is done by adaptive iterative mean (AIM) filter (Hosseini & Marvasti, 2013). AIM filter restores the noisy pixel by computing the distance transform of the image where each element of transformed image indicates the Euclidean distance between the corresponding image pixels and the nearest uncorrupted pixel (Maurer, Qi & Raghavan, 2003).

There exist several methodologies to eliminate or at least reduce the effect of different types of impulse noises from the digital images. Mean or average filter is considered to be the simplest technique for this purpose. However, it results in a number of shortcomings including the blurring of image details which has essentially imposed serious limitations on eliminating impulse noise. On the other hand, different types of median filter have invariably been used as an efficient tool of impulse noise removal with their own advantages and deficiencies. This issue has been explicitly described in the subsequent section.

3. MEDIAN FILTER AS A TOOL OF IMPULSE NOISE REMOVAL

Intrusion of noise inevitably alters gray values of some pixels while gray values of other pixels remain unaffected and thus, degrades image quality and causes loss of some information details. As a matter of fact, an efficient noise suppression technique is essentially required prior to subsequent image processing operations (Bovik, 2010). Impulse noise reduction has traditionally been done by using linear spatial filter. The output of such a filter is obtained by calculating the average of the pixels contained in the neighborhood defined by the filter mask. This filter is also called averaging filters or low-pass filters (Gonzalez & Woods, 2002) as it removes high frequency components from an image while preserving low frequency components. This type of filter is called as linear filter as it obeys the principle of superposition. For any two images A and B and for linear filter $\mathbb{LF}$,

$$\mathbb{LF}(fA + gB) = f\mathbb{LF}(A) + g\mathbb{LF}(B) \quad (4)$$

where f and g are scalars.

Several nonlinear filters have subsequently been proposed for the restoration of images corrupted by impulse noise so as to overcome the drawback of linear spatial filter. Out of them, a class of nonlinear digital filter known as median filter (Gonzalez & Woods, 2002; Huang et al., 1979) is widely used for removing impulse noise by preserving image boundaries. Median filter is a non-linear filter because it does not satisfy linearity condition. Therefore, for a non-linear filter $\mathbb{NLF}$,

$$\mathbb{NLF}\left(fA + gB\right) \neq f\mathbb{NLF}\left(A\right) + g\mathbb{NLF}\left(B\right) \tag{5}$$

where f and g are scalars.

One of the most popular and robust nonlinear filter is the standard median filter (SMF) (Gonzalez & Woods, 2002) that replaces the value of a pixel by the median of the gray levels in the neighborhood of that pixel in which case the gray value of that pixel is included during computation of the median. For an image X corrupted by impulse noise, output of standard median filter can be mathematically written as:

$$Y_{i,j} = \underset{W}{\text{median}}\left\{X_{i,j}\right\} \forall i,j \tag{6}$$

where $Y_{i,j}$ is the restored image and W represents a spatial window around a pixel, centered at location (i,j).

Median filtering, being a nonlinear filtering technique is usually superior to linear filtering in terms of impulse noise suppression but it tends to blur fine details or destroy edges while filtering out impulses. In order to make tradeoff between preservation of image details and reduction of impulse noise, center weighted median (CWM) filter was proposed by Ko and Lee in the year 1991 (Ko & Lee, 1991), where a weight adjustment is applied to the central pixel within the sliding window. For any pixel $X_{i,j}$, the corresponding output resulting from CWM filter may be defined as:

$$Y_{i,j} = \underset{W}{\text{median}}\left\{X_{i-s,j-t}, \; w \circ X_{i,j}\right\} \forall i,j \tag{7}$$

where $(s,t) \in W$ and $(s,t) \neq (0,0)$.

In the above equation, w is the center weight, W signifies the window and the operator $\circ$ denotes repetition operation. As for example, a 3 X 3 window is identified by $W = \{(s,t), -1 \leq s \leq 1$ and $-1 \leq t \leq 1\}$ and the median is computed based on those $8+w$ pixel values. CWM filter becomes SMF with $w=1$. On the other hand, when w is equal to or larger than the sliding window size (i.e. with $w \geq 9$ for a 3 X 3 window); CWM filter becomes an identity filter causing no change to its input pixel.

In general, median filters operate uniformly across the image and therefore modify both noisy and noise-free pixels. As a matter of fact, a noise detection procedure for discriminating noisy and noise-free pixels became necessary before nonlinear filtering operation (Eng & Ma, 2001; Zhang & Karim, 2002; Pok & Liu, 1999). In connection to this, various types of median filters viz. adaptive median filter (AMF), decision-based or switching median filters have been recently proposed (Bhadouria, Ghoshal, & Siddiqi, 2014). These algorithms have identified possible noisy pixels and replaced them using the median value or its variants while uncorrupted pixels are kept unmodified. However, with an increase in the intensity of impulse noise in a given image, variants of median filter would yield better noise removal but simultaneously blur the appearance of the overall image as well. AMF may have variable window sizes for removal of impulses while preserving sharpness. Although AMF performs well at low noise densities, it may result in serious blurring effect because of the use of larger window size in case of high noise density (Bhadouria et al., 2014).

Switching median filters like tri-state median (TSM) filter, multi-state median (MSM) filter and progressive switching median filter (PSMF) fulfill the abovementioned objective. These filters first identify possible noisy pixels and then replace them by the median value or its variants, while leaving all other pixels unchanged; thus providing better result in detecting noise even at high noise level. Chen, Ma and Chen (Chen et. al. 1999) have proposed tri-state median (TSM) filter in which standard median (SM) filter and center weighted median (CWM) filter are incorporated into a noise detection framework, which determines whether a pixel is corrupted or not before applying the filtering operation. For a given pixel X_{ij}, output of a tri-state median (TSM) filter can be represented as:

$$Y_{ij}^{TSM} = \begin{cases} X_{ij} & T \geq d_1; \\ Y_{ij}^{CWM} & d_2 \leq T < d_1; \\ Y_{ij}^{SM} & T < d_2; \end{cases} \quad (8)$$

where Y_{ij}^{CWM} and Y_{ij}^{SM} are the outputs of CWM filter and SM filter respectively, $d_1 = |X_{ij} - Y_{ij}^{SM}|$, $d_2 = |X_{ij} - Y_{ij}^{CWM}|$ and T is the predefined threshold used for the switching operation.

In multi-state median (MSM) filter, as proposed by Chen and Wu (Chen and Wu, 2000), output of the filter is adaptively switched among a group of CWM filters with varying center weights depending on the result of a thresholding operation. For any pixel X_{ij}, output of multi-state median (MSM) filter can be illustrated as follows:

$$Y_{ij}^{MSM} = \begin{cases} X_{ij} & d_1 < T; \\ Y_{ij}^{N+1-w} & d_w < T < d_{w-2} \text{ for } 3 \leq w \leq N-2; \\ Y_{ij}^1 & d_{N-2} \geq T > d_N; \end{cases} \quad (9)$$

where $T (>0)$ is the pre-specified threshold used for the above switching operation, and $d_w = |Y_{ij}^w - X_{ij}| (w = 1, 3, ..., N-2)$ and $d_N = |Y_{ij}^N - X_{ij}| = 0$.

Progressive switching median filter (PSMF), on the other hand, works in two stages (Wang and Zhang, 1999). In the first stage, an impulse detection algorithm is used before filtering in

order to filter out only noisy pixel whereas the second stage progressively applies noise filtering through several iterations.

The main problem associated with switching median filters is that they cannot be used due to difficulty in defining a robust decisive measure arising out of proper thresholding during decision making operation. Moreover, the noisy pixels are replaced by some median value in their neighborhood without caring about local features of the image like probable presence of edges, contours etc. As a matter of fact, details and edges are not completely restored especially at high noise density (Chan, Ho & Nikolava, 2005, Bhadouria et. al., 2014).

As an attempt to conquer this problem, a two-phase algorithm was proposed by Chan, Ho and Nikolava (Chan et. al., 2005). In the first phase, an adaptive median filter is used to identify pixels which are likely to be contaminated by noise and in the next phase, image is restored using a specialized regularization method that applies only to those selected pixels. As this scheme incorporates both adaptive median filter and edge preserving regularization method so it gives good results in terms of noise reduction and edge preservation. It uses a very large window size of 39×39 resulting in a larger processing time. This has led to the proposition of decision-based algorithm (DBA) by Srinivasan and Ebnezer (2007) in which denoising is performed using fixed window dimension of 3×3. Resultant gray value as obtained from this algorithm may be noisy itself at a high noise density in which case DBA considers neighboring pixels for replacement. However, repeated placement of neighboring pixels causes the problem of streaking which causes streaks (linear patches) or amorphous blotches to appear in the image.

The concept of DBA was subsequently improved by modified decision-based algorithm (MDBA) (Aiswarya et. al., 2010). Further improvement was carried out by modified decision based un-symmetric trimmed median filter (MDBUTMF) (Esakkirajan et. al., 2011). This algorithm considers fixed window dimension of 3×3 for denoising purpose. At higher noise density, MDBUTMF calculates the mean of the window under processing in which case the probability of the event that all the pixels in the local window are noisy is high. Therefore, this replacement produces dark patch-like surface in the restored image. Drawbacks of these algorithms have recently been overcome in decision-based coupled window median filter (DBCWMF) (Bhadouria et al., 2014). Proposed algorithm considers coupled window of increasing dimension to surmount the above problem.

Apart from the conventional approaches pertaining to median filter design, researchers in recent times have also employed a number of emerging and promising technologies like artificial intelligence, soft computing, and evolutionary computation towards the elimination of impulse noise. It is to be anticipated that the application of these upcoming technologies will enrich this area of image processing in near future.

4. RECENT TRENDS TOWARDS THE ELIMINATION OF IMPULSE NOISE

Randomness and fuzziness are two most important features among the uncertainties involved in impulse noise. Idea behind the randomness is mainly reflected in two aspects, i.e., the pixels are randomly corrupted by noise and noisy pixels are randomly set to maximum or minimum value. Alternatively, fuzziness focuses on pixels with extreme values to determine whether they are noisy or not (Zhou, 2012).

In early denoising techniques, median filter and its variants (Gonzalez & Woods, 2002; Chen, Ma, & Chen, 1999; Chen & Wu, 2000) have considered randomness as the only feature of impulse noise. They processed each and every pixel without considering whether the pixel is noisy or not. Consequently, uncorrupted pixels

were altered and many image details were lost at high noise density.

As an attempt to represent the uncertainties in a better way and to resolve the abovementioned problems, an effective filter based on the cloud model (CM) has been proposed by Zhou (Zhou, 2012) for impulse noise removal. As compared with conventional switching filters, the cloud model (CM) filter yields better performance in image denoising across a wide range of noise levels. Besides CM filter, there exists other techniques based on fuzzy logic which are quite useful for filtering impulse noise of various intensities (Russo & Ramponi, 1996). Fuzzy filters are basically non-linear filters that employ two stages for filtering operation. Process of noise detection is carried out in first stage in which the pixels are classified as noisy or noise-free pixels. Detected noisy pixels are filtered in the next stage and subsequently replaced by a new pixel value depending upon the information obtained from neighboring pixels (Goel & Mittal, 2012).

Several other approaches inspired by the fuzzy logic like fuzzy inference rule by else-action (FIRE) (Pillai, Riji, Nair, & Wilscy, 2012) filters, directional weighted median-based fuzzy impulse-noise detection and reduction method (DWMFI-DRM) (Pillai et al., 2012) are being developed for denoising all categories of impulse noise. Contribution of this novel impulse noise reduction technique lies in combining three different methods namely the impulse noise detection phase utilizing the concept of fuzzy gradient values, the edge-preserving noise reduction phase based on the directional weighted median of the neighboring pixels and the final filtering step dealing with noisy pixels of non-zero degree.

Apart from the fuzzy logic, genetic programming and neural network-based techniques have also been developed for impulse noise reduction. Genetic programming is employed for the construction of impulse noise detector in universal impulse noise filter (Petrovic & Crnojevic, 2008).

Impulse detector has been implemented using feed forward neural network (FFNN) in predictive-based adaptive switching median filter (PASMF) (Nair & Shankar, 2013).

5. COMPARATIVE ANALYSIS AMONGST DIFFERENT APPROACHES

In order to compare the performances of various algorithms towards the reduction of impulse noise from the digital images, a number of performance parameters have been introduced in this section and accordingly the impact of the algorithms over these parameters has been extensively studied. This article considers four such parameters, namely peak signal-to-noise ratio (PSNR) (Wang & Bovik, 2009), structural similarity index measure (SSIM) (Wang et al., 2004), image enhancement factor (IEF) (Jayaraj & Ebenezer, 2010) and image quality index (IQI) (Wang & Bovik, 2002; Bhadouria et. al., 2014) which are defined as follows:

$$PSNR = 20\log_{10}\left(\frac{I_{max}}{\sqrt{\frac{1}{AB}\sum_{i=1}^{A}\sum_{j=1}^{B}\left\{I_{ij}-K_{ij}\right\}^2}}\right) \quad (10)$$

$$SSIM = \frac{\left(2\mu_I\mu_K+C_1\right)\left(2\sigma_{IK}+C_2\right)}{\left(\mu_I^2+\mu_K^2+C_1\right)\left(\sigma_I^2+\sigma_K^2+C_2\right)} \quad (11)$$

$$IEF = \frac{\sum_{i=1}^{A}\sum_{j=1}^{B}\left\{X_{ij}-I_{ij}\right\}^2}{\sum_{i=1}^{A}\sum_{j=1}^{B}\left\{K_{ij}-I_{ij}\right\}^2} \quad (12)$$

$$IQI = corr(I,K).lum(I,K).cont(I,K)$$

with

$$corr(I,K) = \frac{\sigma_{IK}}{\sigma_I.\sigma_K}$$

$$lum(I,K) = \frac{2\mu_I\mu_K}{\left(\mu_I^2+\mu_K^2\right)}$$

$$cont(I,K) = \frac{2\sigma_I\sigma_K}{\left(\sigma_I^2+\sigma_K^2\right)} \quad (13)$$

where the original, noisy and restored images are represented by *I, X,* and *K* respectively and the rest of the variables are self-explanatory.

Impact of different median filters in minimizing the effect of impulse noise from a particular test image (Lena) has been summarized and compared in Table 1 to 4 below with respect to four different performance parameters, namely PSNR, SSIM, IEF and IQI and at five distinct noise densities. Different types of median filters like SMF, AMF, PSMF, MDBA, MDBUTMF and DBCWMF have been included for the purpose of comparison. It has been established that DBCWMF outperforms almost all of the algorithms or performs comparably irrespective of the noise densities and performance metrics under consideration. In regard to this, percentage improvement as achieved with DBCWMF over other algorithms has been shown in Figure 1 through 4 in terms of PSNR, SSIM, IEF and IQI respectively.

Supremacy of DBCWMF algorithm over the other techniques has been firmly established from the numerical entries as available in tables 1 to 4. In connection to this, DBCWMF has always produced better results than its predecessors irrespective of the value of noise density. Moreover, it can also be seen from the available results that while the performance of few algorithms like SMF and PSMF significantly degrade at higher noise den-

Table 1. Performance comparison among different median filters in terms of PSNR

Type of the filter	Noise density (%)				
	10	**30**	**50**	**70**	**90**
SMF: (Gonzalez & Woods, 2002)	33.16	23.41	15.23	10.02	6.63
AMF: (Hwang & Haddad,1995)	40.34	28.72	19.78	14.39	10.91
PSMF: (Wang and Zhang, 1999)	36.84	28.76	20.88	9.96	6.62
MDBA: (Aiswarya et. al., 2010)	41.51	34.67	30.33	25.57	19.8
MDBUTMF: (Esakkirajan et. al., 2011)	41.75	35.77	31.27	23.6	14.86
DBCWMF: (Bhadouria et. al., 2014)	41.76	35.84	32.49	29.72	25.85

Table 2. Performance comparison among different median filters in terms of SSIM

Type of the filter	Noise density (%)				
	10	**30**	**50**	**70**	**90**
SMF: (Gonzalez & Woods, 2002)	0.91	0.7	0.23	0.05	0.01
AMF: (Hwang & Haddad,1995)	0.97	0.79	0.31	0.09	0.02
PSMF: (Wang and Zhang, 1999)	0.98	0.9	0.57	0.05	0.01
MDBA: (Aiswarya et. al., 2010)	0.98	0.95	0.89	0.79	0.58
MDBUTMF: (Esakkirajan et. al., 2011)	0.99	0.97	0.93	0.69	0.17
DBCWMF: (Bhadouria et. al., 2014)	0.99	0.97	0.93	0.9	0.81

Table 3. Performance comparison among different median filters in terms of IEF

Type of the filter	Noise density (%)				
	10	**30**	**50**	**70**	**90**
SMF: (Gonzalez & Woods, 2002)	59.23	18.86	4.77	2	1.18
AMF:(Hwang & Haddad,1995)	110.99	23.28	5.01	2.05	1.19
PSMF: (Wang and Zhang, 1999)	138.02	64.72	17.54	1.98	1.18
MDBA: (Aiswarya et. al., 2010)	404.65	252.41	154.37	72.07	24.56
MDBUTMF: (Esakkirajan et. al., 2011)	456.74	344.38	203.48	48.75	8.38
DBCWMF: (Bhadouria et. al., 2014)	458.75	349.7	269.58	199.34	105.23

Table 4. Performance comparison among different median filters in terms of IQI

Type of the filter	Noise density (%)				
	10	**30**	**50**	**70**	**90**
SMF: (Gonzalez & Woods, 2002)	0.999	0.998	0.986	0.943	0.864
AMF: (Hwang & Haddad,1995)	1	0.999	0.987	0.943	0.864
PSMF: (Wang and Zhang, 1999)	0.999	0.999	0.995	0.951	0.87
MDBA: (Aiswarya et. al., 2010)	1	0.999	0.999	0.997	0.978
MDBUTMF: (Esakkirajan et. al., 2011)	1	0.999	0.999	0.998	0.959
DBCWMF: (Bhadouria et. al., 2014)	1	1	0.999	0.999	0.993

Figure 1. Percentage improvement of DBCWMF over other algorithms in terms of PSNR

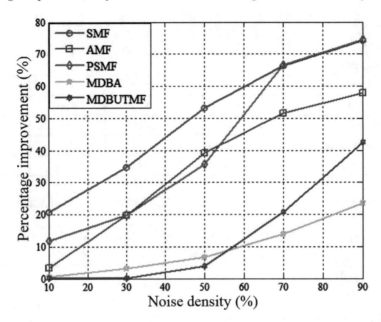

Figure 2. Percentage improvement of DBCWMF over other algorithms in terms of SSIM

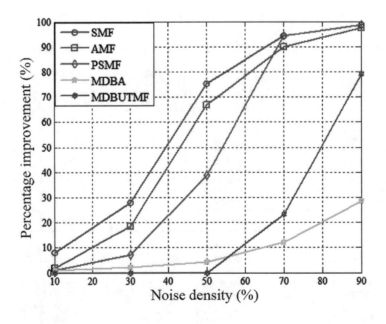

sity; DBCWMF continues to provide acceptable result. It can also be inferred from Figure 1 to 3 that while the performance of MDBUTMF closely matches with that of DBCWMF at low noise density, it degrades significantly at higher noise density when measured with respect to PSNR, SSIM and IEF. However, MDBA, MDBUTMF and DBCWMF perform almost comparably even at higher noise density with respect to IQI and the percentage improvement is limited to 15% only.

Figure 3. Percentage improvement of DBCWMF over other algorithms in terms of IEF

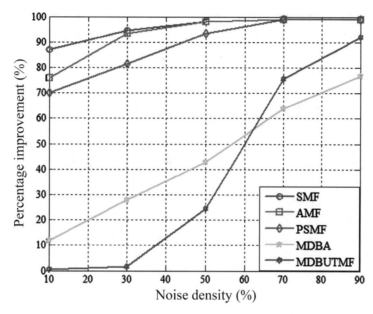

Figure 4. Percentage improvement of DBCWMF over other algorithms in terms of IQI

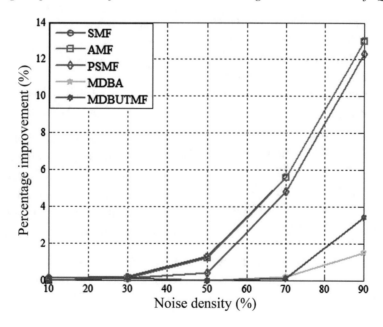

6. FUTURE RESEARCH DIRECTIONS

Among the various uncertainties embedded within the impulse noise, randomness and fuzziness are considered to be the two most important aspects. Median filter and its different variants have primar-

ily focused on the randomness while eliminating impulse noise from the digital images. However, design and development of filters focusing on the concept of fuzziness for better understanding the uncertainties of impulse noise is an emerging field of impulse noise filtering of late (Schulte,

Nachtegael, De Witte, Van der Weken, & Kerre, 2006). Fuzzy logic along with genetic programming and neural network has opened a new door in this field of image processing by developing powerful yet flexible algorithms.

Detection of impulse noise and its subsequent removal with a view to restore the original image by incorporating the concept of artificial intelligence in a large scale is emerging as a future trend in this field of image processing (Konar, 2005). Moreover, combination of two or more paradigms such as fuzzy logic and neural network for better performance in noise reduction and image restoration may also be explored in an extensive way (Russo, 2000). It is anticipated that integration of artificial intelligent techniques encompassing fuzzy, neural, and genetic paradigms will provide a powerful resource to address new challenges of impulse noise cancellation and image restoration (Russo, 1998).

However, several algorithms employ too many fuzzy rules to improve the quality of the restored images which in turn makes the filtering operation computationally a little expensive. Moreover, achievable results are also excessively dependent on the number of membership functions and the control parameters associated with them. This imposes a practical constraint on applying such methods for real-time processing. As a matter of fact, design and development of computationally efficient fuzzy filters is regarded as a promising area for carrying out future research. Attempts may also be made for filtering out impulse noises from the color images as most of the fuzzy filters are especially developed for grayscale images (Schulte et al., 2006).

7. CONCLUSION

This chapter aims to focus on the impact of different two dimensional (2D) non-linear median filters for reducing the influence of impulse noise from digital images. Denoising performances of filtering techniques have been evaluated on the basis of quantitative performance parameters like PSNR, SSIM, IEF, and IQI. Role of artificial intelligence in connection to this filtering technique has been briefly summarized. Possible advancement over the present achievement has also been suggested.

REFERENCES

Aiswarya, K., Jayaraj, V., & Ebenezer, D. (2010). A new and efficient algorithm for the removal of high density salt and pepper noise in images and videos. In *Proceedings of Second International Conference on Computer Modeling and Simulation*. IEEE. doi:10.1109/ICCMS.2010.310

Bhadouria, V. S., Ghoshal, D., & Siddiqi, A. H. (2014). A new approach for high density saturated impulse noise removal using decision-based coupled window median filter. *Signal. Image and Video Processing*, *8*(1), 71–84. doi:10.1007/s11760-013-0487-5

Bovik, A. C. (2010). *Handbook of image and video processing*. Academic Press.

Chan, R. H., Ho, C. W., & Nikolova, M. (2005). Salt-and-pepper noise removal by median-type noise detectors and detail-preserving regularization. *IEEE Transactions on Image Processing*, *14*(10), 1479–1485. doi:10.1109/TIP.2005.852196 PMID:16238054

Chen, P. Y., & Lien, C. Y. (2008). An efficient edge-preserving algorithm for removal of salt-and-pepper noise. *IEEE Signal Processing Letters*, *15*, 833–836. doi:10.1109/LSP.2008.2005047

Chen, T., Ma, K. K., & Chen, L. H. (1999). Tri-state median filter for image denoising. *IEEE Transactions on Image Processing*, *8*(12), 1834–1838. doi:10.1109/83.806630 PMID:18267461

Chen, T., & Wu, H. R. (2000). Impulse noise removal by multi-state median filtering. In *Proceedings of IEEE International Conference on Acoustics, Speech, and Signal Processing*. IEEE.

Eng, H. L., & Ma, K. K. (2001). Noise adaptive soft-switching median filter. *IEEE Transactions on Image Processing, 10*(2), 242–251. doi:10.1109/83.902289 PMID:18249615

Esakkirajan, S., Veerakumar, T., Subramanyam, A. N., & PremChand, C. H. (2011). Removal of high density salt and pepper noise through modified decision based unsymmetric trimmed median filter. *IEEE Signal Processing Letters, 18*(5), 287–290. doi:10.1109/LSP.2011.2122333

Gonzalez, R. C., & Woods, R. E. (2002). *Digital Image Processing*. Pearson Education.

Hosseini, H., & Marvasti, F. (2013). Fast restoration of natural images corrupted by high-density impulse noise. *EURASIP Journal on Image and Video Processing, 15*, 1–7.

Huang, T., Yang, G., & Tang, G. (1979). A fast two-dimensional median filtering algorithm. *IEEE Transactions on Acoustics, Speech, and Signal Processing, 27*(1), 13–18. doi:10.1109/TASSP.1979.1163188

Hwang, H., & Haddad, R. (1995). Adaptive median filters: New algorithms and results. *IEEE Transactions on Image Processing, 4*(4), 499–502. doi:10.1109/83.370679 PMID:18289998

Jourabloo, A., Feghahati, A. H., & Jamzad, M. (2012). New algorithms for recovering highly corrupted images with impulse noise. *Scientia Iranica, 19*(6), 1738–1745. doi:10.1016/j.scient.2012.07.016

Ko, S. J., & Lee, Y. H. (1991). Center weighted median filters and their applications to image enhancement. *IEEE Transactions on Circuits and Systems, 38*(9), 984–993. doi:10.1109/31.83870

Koli, M., & Balaji, S. (2013). Literature survey on impulse noise reduction. *Signal & Image Processing: An International Journal, 4*(5), 75–95.

Nair, M. S., & Shankar, V. (2013). Predictive-based adaptive switching median filter for impulse noise removal using neural network-based noise detector. *Signal. Image and Video Processing, 7*(6), 1041–1070. doi:10.1007/s11760-012-0310-8

Ng, P. E., & Ma, K. K. (2006). A switching median filter with boundary discriminative noise detection for extremely corrupted images. *IEEE Transactions on Image Processing, 15*(6), 1506–1516. doi:10.1109/TIP.2005.871129 PMID:16764275

Petrovic, N. I., & Crnojevic, V. (2008). Universal impulse noise filter based on genetic programming. *IEEE Transactions on Image Processing, 17*(7), 1109–1120. doi:10.1109/TIP.2008.924388 PMID:18586619

Pillai, K. A. S., Riji, R., Nair, M. S., & Wilscy, M. (2012). Fuzzy based directional weighted median filter for impulse noise detection and reduction. *Fuzzy Information and Engineering, 4*(4), 351–369. doi:10.1007/s12543-012-0120-2

Pok, G., & Liu, J. C. (1999). Decision-based median filter improved by predictions. In *Proceedings of 1999 International Conference on Image Processing*. IEEE.

Schulte, S., Nachtegael, M., De Witte, V., Van der Weken, D., & Kerre, E. E. (2006). A fuzzy impulse noise detection and reduction method. *IEEE Transactions on Image Processing, 15*(5), 1153–1162. doi:10.1109/TIP.2005.864179 PMID:16671296

Srinivasan, K. S., & Ebenezer, D. (2007). A new fast and efficient decision-based algorithm for removal of high-density impulse noises. *IEEE Signal Processing Letters, 14*(3), 189–192. doi:10.1109/LSP.2006.884018

Wang, Z., & Zhang, D. (1999). Progressive switching median filter for the removal of impulse noise from highly corrupted images. *IEEE Transactions on Circuits and Systems II: Analog and Digital Signal Processing, 46*(1), 78–80. doi:10.1109/82.749102

Xia, J., Xiong, J., Xu, X., & Zhang, Q. (2010). An efficient two-state switching median filter for the reduction of impulse noises with different distributions. In *Proceedings of 3rd International Congress on Image and Signal Processing*. IEEE. doi:10.1109/CISP.2010.5647235

Ze-Feng, D., Zhou-Ping, Y., & You-Lun, X. (2007). High probability impulse noise-removing algorithm based on mathematical morphology. *IEEE Signal Processing Letters, 14*(1), 31–34. doi:10.1109/LSP.2006.881524

Zhang, S., & Karim, M. A. (2002). A new impulse detector for switching median filters. *IEEE Signal Processing Letters, 9*(11), 360–363. doi:10.1109/LSP.2002.805310

Zhang, X., & Xiong, Y. (2009). Impulse noise removal using directional difference based noise detector and adaptive weighted mean filter. *IEEE Signal Processing Letters, 16*(4), 295–298. doi:10.1109/LSP.2009.2014293

Zhou, Z. (2012). Cognition and removal of impulse noise with uncertainty. *IEEE Transactions on Image Processing, 21*(7), 3157–3167. doi:10.1109/TIP.2012.2189577 PMID:22389145

ADDITIONAL READING

Goel, A., & Mittal, V. (2012). Removal of Impulse Noise Using Fuzzy Techniques: A Survey. *International Journal of Applied Engineering Research, 7*(11).

Jayaraj, V., & Ebenezer, D. (2010). *A new switching-based median filtering scheme and algorithm for removal of high-density salt and pepper noise in images. EURASIP Journal on Advances in Signal Processing,* Konar, A. (2005). *Computational Intelligence: Principles, Techniques and Applications.* Springer.

Maurer, C. R. Jr, Qi, R., & Raghavan, V. (2003). A linear time algorithm for computing exact Euclidean distance transforms of binary images in arbitrary dimensions. *IEEE Transactions on Pattern Analysis and Machine Intelligence, 25*(2), 265–270. doi:10.1109/TPAMI.2003.1177156

Russo, F. (1998). Recent advances in fuzzy techniques for image enhancement. *IEEE Transactions on Instrumentation and Measurement, 47*(6), 1428–1434. doi:10.1109/19.746707

Russo, F. (2000). Image filtering using evolutionary neural fuzzy systems. In *Soft computing for image processing* (pp. 23–43). Physica-Verlag HD. doi:10.1007/978-3-7908-1858-1_2

Russo, F., & Ramponi, G. (1996). A fuzzy filter for images corrupted by impulse noise. *IEEE Signal Processing Letters, 3*(6), 168–170. doi:10.1109/97.503279

Wang, Z., & Bovik, A. C. (2002). A universal image quality index. *IEEE Signal Processing Letters, 9*(3), 81–84. doi:10.1109/97.995823

Wang, Z., & Bovik, A. C. (2009). Mean squared error: Love it or leave it? A new look at signal fidelity measures. *IEEE Signal Processing Magazine, 26*(1), 98–117. doi:10.1109/MSP.2008.930649

Wang, Z., Bovik, A. C., Sheikh, H. R., & Simoncelli, E. P. (2004). Image quality assessment: From error visibility to structural similarity. *IEEE Transactions on Image Processing, 13*(4), 600–612. doi:10.1109/TIP.2003.819861 PMID:15376593

KEY TERMS AND DEFINITIONS

Fuzzy Logic: Fuzzy logic is a problem solving tool of artificial intelligence which deals with approximate reasoning rather than fixed and exact reasoning.

Genetic Programming: Genetic programming is a model of programming influenced by the concepts of biological evolution.

Image Denoising: Image denoising is the process of removing noise from an image.

Image Restoration: Image restoration is the process of recovering original pixel information from degraded or noisy image.

Local Features: The features of an image which have a limited spatial extent i.e. cover only a small portion of the image such as contours, probable presence of edges etc.

Neural Network: Neural network is a computational model built in accordance with the central nervous system of human being.

Sharpness: Sharpness is an important image quality factor. It determines the amount of detail an image can convey.

Chapter 6
Utilizing Image Color Channels for High Payload Embedding

Ankit Chaudhary
Truman State University, USA

Sandeep Kumar
Government College of Engineering & Technology, Bikaner, India

ABSTRACT

Steganography is the technique which has been used in many fields for hiding information and many different versions for each application are available in the literature. This chapter demonstrates how to increase the security level and to improve the storage capacity of hidden data, with compression techniques. The security level is increased by randomly distributing the text message over the entire image instead of clustering within specific image portions. The degradation of the images can be minimized by changing only one least significant bit per color channel for hiding the message. Using steganography alone with simple LSB has a potential problem that the secret message is easily detectable from the histogram analysis method. To improve the security as well as the image embedding capacity indirectly, a compression based scheme is introduced. Various tests have been done to check the storage capacity and message distribution.

INTRODUCTION

Since the starting of civilization, hiding secrets and sending them to other places securely has been a challenging problem. Steganography is a technique used to transfer a secret message from a sender to a receiver in a way such that a potential intruder does not suspect the existence of the message. It has been used since BC 400 to send messages in different forms. These days, this is done by embedding the secret message within another digital medium such as text, image, audio or video. The terms cryptography and steganography are often used synonymously although they are essentially distinct. In cryptography, a plain message is encrypted into cipher text and might look like a meaningless jumble of characters. Whereas in case of steganography, the plain message is hidden inside a medium that looks quite normal and does not provide any reason for suspecting the existence of a hidden message. When we encrypt a message, the form of the message is changed.

DOI: 10.4018/978-1-4666-8654-0.ch006

If the message is sent in encrypted form over the wireless medium, the attacker can suspect the secret message. This would be one of the best advantages of using steganography over cryptography. The message embedded in an image or any digital medium would not create suspicion among attackers about the secret message.

Electronic steganography approaches use digital processing techniques for hiding and detecting embedded information. In case of image steganography, the secret message is transmitted embedded within a digital image called a *cover* image. Once the message is embedded within the image, it is referred to as a *stego* image. In a keyless steganography approach the sender includes only the information and does not include any cryptography algorithm. Therefore, the reliability and the security are totally dependent on the efficiency of the steganography algorithm itself. Now a days military to militants, all use some kind of data hiding technique for sending messages. This chapter proposes a secure lossless data hiding steganographic technique in RGB images using steganography. For this we need to take care about the resource utilization, the space requirements and the level of security. In addition, the quality of the cover object i.e. digital medium is important after using it for steganography. A keyless steganography algorithm applicable for lossless image formats like BMP, PNG or TIF is proposed. Attempts are made to improve the storage capacity while incurring minimal quality

degradation of the image. Security is enhanced by distributing the message throughout the image.

RELATED WORK

Traditional and novel techniques for addressing the data-hiding process and evaluated these techniques with various perspectives are discussed in (Bender, 1996). A state of the art can be seen in (Rabah, 2004; Kipper, 2005). The theoretical model of steganography with respect to images as digital medium is well discussed in (Johnson, 1998; Eggers, 2002; Cachin, 1998). We preferred using images over audio files as they lack in embedding capacity, which is one of the most important criteria for implementing steganography.

The most widely used technique to hide data is the use of the LSB. Figure 1 shows storage pattern in LSB. Although there are several disadvantages to this approach, it is relatively one of the easiest to implement. This method uses bits of each pixel in the image, it is necessary to use a lossless compression format otherwise the hidden information will get lost in the transformations of a lossy compression algorithm. Least Significant Bit replacement embeds fixed-length secret bits into the least significant bits of pixels by directly replacing the Least Significant Bits of each byte of the cover image with the secret message bits. Some stegno analysis methods will identify the pixel difference in the host image very easily (Johnson,

Figure 1. Storage in LSB

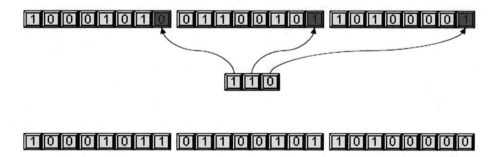

1998). For a 24 bit image, 3 bits can be stored in each pixel. To the human eye, the resulting stego image looks almost identical to the cover image. A random LSB insertion method in which secret message is spread out among the image data in a seemingly random manner (Sutaone, 2008). This is an efficient approach but changes to the MSB bits can degrade the image quality substantially.

In the past two decades, there are numerous LSB-based data hiding techniques, which find some pixels based on specialty and suitability of those pixels to act as substitute hosts in the host media, then embed data into the LSB of those pixels. Typical approaches include Adelson (1990), Turner (1989) and van Schyndel (1994). Wang (2001) proposed to embed secret messages in the moderately significant bit of the cover-image. Optimal substitution matrix using a genetic algorithm is developed to find an for the embedding of the secret messages. Use of local pixel adjustment process (LPAP) was also proposed by them, to improve the image quality of the stego-image. Traditionally, like Wang (2001) proposed a method to hide data inside the host image, based on simple LSB substitution. They also developed the optimal k-LSB substitution method to solve the problem when k is large. Li (2007) proposed a steganographic method based on JPEG and Partical Swarm Optimization algorithm. His method could have been inspired from the optimal LSB substitution approach used by (Wang, 2001). This strategy could be used in spatial domain and thus applied to transform domain.

Upreti (2010) proposes a variable length bits embedding in RGB images. She used IDEA and RSA to encrypt the message to hide in the image. Youssef (2012) proposes lossless data hiding in gray and RGB images using frequency domain steganography for large data. Bandyopadhyay (2010) use palette approach where he takes advantage of compiler padding option. RGB data would take four byte to store, three for RGB and fourth one for the steganography. The result image had distortion than the original image and easily known

to the intruder about the image compromization. Yang (2011) presents a block difference histogram algorithm for BMP color images. He used PSNR till 30db and 'bpp' to store capacity in the image. Li (2010) presents a color clustering based information hiding algorithm. He assembles the pixels of same color in one cluster and other color in other cluster based on NBS distance in HVC color space. He proposed IHPCC algorithm based on LSB and shows less distortion in difference image than LSB. Liu (2007) address a different issue, he talks about the security of hidden data in JPEG images. Bahi (2011) presents chaos based non-blind algorithm for information hiding. He proposed formal proof based on Boolean discrete Dynamical Systems but no implementation details are provided. Levicky (2012) shows histogram preserving technique for JPEG images in DCT domain. He proposes MWF algorithm similar to JPEG-LSB but on gray images.

One of the best keyless steganography approaches is the Pixel Indicator Technique (PIT) algorithm proposed by Gutub (2010) where a color channel is used as a pixel indicator and the other two channels are used as for message embedding. The main drawback is that one of the channels cannot be used to store the actual message. To increase the capacity, usage of 2, 3 or 4 are proposed in (Neeta, 2006). A heuristic based approach for information embedding in the form of multimedia objects or text using steganography is proposed in (Bandyopadhyay, 2008). In (Singh, 2007), the least significant bit (LSB) of each pixel is modified sequentially. In (Chaudhary, 2012) the authors have proposed a steganographic technique by mixing with it cryptography to increase the security layer. There are other approaches available using Discrete Cosine Transformation (DCT) and Wavelet Transform (WT) (Khare 2010). Gupta (2014) has introduced a nature inspired method to hide a sound file in the image, while the size of the host image was increased substancialy.

In the next section, details of proposed method are discussed.

Figure 2. MSB to LSB

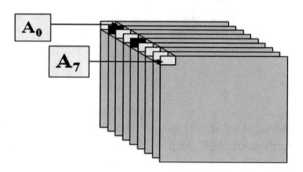

STEGO METHOD

The main motivation of the proposed work is to overcome the shortcomings of the techniques suggested in (Roy, 2011), which is an improvement of Pixel Indicator Technique (PIT) proposed in (Gutub, 2010). The process can be made efficient by considering only a single function i.e. randomization, instead of calculating K1 and K2. There is another shortcoming with the approach suggested in (Roy, 2011) that K1 and K2 calculations are dependent upon image size and message length. Our approach also takes care of distribution of the message over the cover image, as an improvement of not storing the message bits within the cover image in contiguous pixels only in the upper portion of the image (Gutub, 2010). Additionally the proposed work also attempts to increase the security level by introducing a text message compression at the first level, which indirectly increases the embedding capacity of the image.

Indicator Values

The first step towards the random distribution of the message in image is using indicator values. In the current work, we use MSB bits of Red, Green and Blue channel as pixel indicator values instead of utilizing an entire channel as in (Gutub, 2010), which is suggested in (Roy, 2011). The MSBs indicate in what sequence the message is hidden using the LSBs as shown in Figure 2. In addition to this, this scheme is applied after applying compression to the original message. Therefore it would be make it extremely difficult to break, even after suspicion of the message within an image.

In this scheme the MSB remains unchanged when an LSB of a byte is utilized for storing a message. The sequences of LSB bits containing the message are indicated in Table 1. For example if the MSB code of channels is 001, then the message hiding LSB sequence is RGB, but if the MSB is 100, then the message hiding sequence becomes BGR. This scheme enables us to fully utilize all the LSBs of every channel of the cover image to store the hidden message and hence improve its capacity. Moreover the varying indicator values introduce a security aspect as it becomes increasingly difficult to decode the message even if its

Table 1. Indicator Values

MSB bits of Red, Green and Blue channel sequentially	Sequence of channel's LSB bits where the message bits needs to be Hidden
000	Red, Green and Blue (RGB)
001	Red, Green and Blue (RGB)
010	Red, Blue and Green (RBG)
011	Blue, Red and Green (BRG)
100	Blue, Green and Red (BGR)
101	Green, Red and Blue (GRB)
110	Green, Blue and Red (GBR)
111	Green, Blue and Red (GBR)

presence is suspected. We are not changing the scheme suggested for Indicator values in (Roy, 2011). The image degradation results from 9 are shown in Figure 3.

Message Distribution

Here, we are not storing the message only in the upper portion of the image in contiguous pixels as in (Gutub, 2010). There is also a technique proposed to distribute the message over the entire image. There is a key-number generated which indicate the gap value between two pixels containing the message to be hidden. This key-number K2 is computed based on *MessageLength* and image dimension i.e. *ImageWidth* and *ImageHeight* of the cover image. K2 is an integer which indicates the gap between pixels which contain the actual hidden information i.e. the information is inserted after every K2 pixels. The potential drawback with this is that the message distribution within the image is fixed in order. i.e. information is inserted after every K2 number of pixels.

This proposed approach is based on randomization and hashing with respect to the MSBs of

the channels to skip R numbers of bytes. Here R is a generated random numbers based on the seed value S given to a random numbers algorithm. To illustrate the procedure where a XOR operation between the LSB bits of the cover image and the stego image indicate the pixels which have changed. The message is seen clustered towards the upper portion of the stego image. As result of the proposed approach, the message is seen to be distributed with skipping K2 bytes after storing information once. The result of proposed approach is better than the above two approaches where the message is distributed randomly after storing information once.

Image Quality

In steganography, image quality can degrade during the data embedding. This is one of the most important issues because degradation in image quality suggests directly towards 'something embedded in the image'. The quality of an image is degraded by changing the bits of an image to store information. As the number of LSB bits used to store the message increases, the quality of the

Figure 3. Less Image degradations results (Roy, 2011)

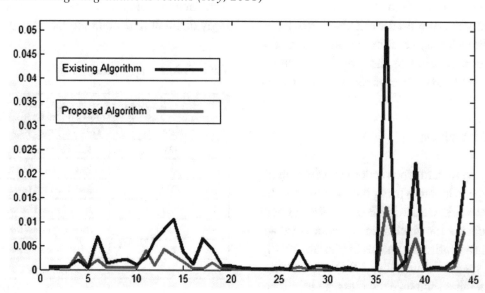

stego image correspondingly degrades more. To limit this degradation the proposed approach uses stego-1 bit LSB (Neeta, 2006) which implies that we are storing 1 message bit per channel. However we can use maximum of four Least Significant bits of each channel from an image. This improves the quality compared to the algorithm proposed in (Gutub, 2010) where two LSB bits are used for the purpose. The other improvement in the image quality is due to randomization, i.e. not all the image bytes are used for the embedding purpose.

Message Encoding Process

The message encoding process is summarized below:

Input: Cover Image, Secret Message File.
Step1: Take as input the cover image, message/file to be hidden.
Step2: Compress the original secret file. (Output: .zip file)
Step3: Store the compressed file within the cover image (using the indicator values specified in Table 1).
Step4: Calculate the random number R and skip R no. of bytes.
Step5: Repeat steps 3 and 4 till the message embedding is not over.
Output: Stego Image.

Message Retrieving Process

The message retrieving process is summarized below:

Input: Stego Image.
Step1: Take the stego image as an input.
Step2: Retrieve the message from the image by generating random number R and skipping R bytes every time, using the table indicator values.
Step3: The output would be a compressed text file (.zip). By uncompressing the file, we would get the original text message file.
Output: Secret Message.

EXPERIMENTAL RESULTS

A number of validations were done to test this approach. Many types of images with different resolution were used to embed data. Different sizes of messages inserted to different cover images. Table 2 shows the analysis with respect to embedding capacities of different algorithms. Figure 4a, 5a and 6a shows the original image while Figure 4b, 5b and 6b shows the stego image with embed data. The sample image contains more than 1 KB data. It is clear that, the change in image after embedding the data is not visible in the image, by bared eyes.

Table 2. Embedding capacity

Algo \ MsgSize	10 B	1 KB	100 KB	1 MB	3 MB	5 MB	7 MB
Simple LSB	Y	Y	Y	Y	Y	Y	N
Padding Based Approach#	Y	Y	Y	Y	Y	Y	Y
PIT	Y	Y	Y	N	N	N	N
Ref-10 (max = 2.2MB)	Y	Y	Y	Y	N	N	N
Suggested Approach (max = 3.8MB)	Y	Y	Y	Y	Y	N	N

*considering imagesize = 800*600

Figure 4a. Original Image

Figure 4b. Stego Image

Figure 5a. Original Image

Figure 5b. Stego Image

Figure 6a. Original Image

Here, '*Y*' in Table 2 represents the possibility of data embedding and '*N*' represents that embedding is not possible. It can be seen from the Table 2 that the embedding capacity of the suggested approach is comparable to the approach suggested in (Roy, 2011). In our approach, although randomization tries to distribute message more, compression in the first step would compress the original message,

increasing the embedding capacity of the image indirectly. One important thing to note here is, the cover image size should not be affected after embedding. That makes the whole difference in our approach than others. However, padding based approach increases the image size by message size after embedding.

Figure 6b. Stego Image

CONCLUSION

Optimizing usage of avalilable space could give maximum performance in minimum resourses. An improved steganography approach for hiding text messages within lossless RGB images has been proposed here. The goal is to increase the security level and improve the storage capacity while incurring minimal quality degradation. The size of the image is not changed after embedding the data, this is one major achievement of this approach. This is very hard to find that image is hiding something as the size of image from original image would not be changed. We hope that this will lead to a new era where unidentifiable stego can be produced without changing any parameter in host image.

In future, we would like to compress the message and then store the data to increase the capacity further. We also want to insert any message both text and image at the same time (might be in PDF or WORD format). We would also like to improve our algorithm by keeping in mind the robustness issue.

REFERENCES

Adelson, E. (1990). *Digital signal encoding and decoding apparatus*. U.S. Patent, (4), 939, 515.

Bahi, J. M., Couchot, J.-F., & Guyeux, C. (2011). Steganography: A Class of Algorithms having Secure Properties. In *Intelligent Information Hiding and Multimedia Signal Processing (IIH-MSP), 2011 Seventh International Conference on.* doi:10.1109/IIHMSP.2011.87

Bandyopadhyay, S. K., Bhattacharyya, D., Das, P., Mukherjee, S., & Ganguly, D. (2008). A secure scheme for image transformation. In *Proceedings of 9th ACIS International Conference on Software Engineering, Artificial Intelligence, Networking, and Parallel/Distributed Computing*.

Bandyopadhyay, S. K., Maitra, I. K., Bhattacharyya, D., & Tai-Hoon, K. (2010). Reserved Fields of Palette for Data Hiding in Steganography. In *Computational Intelligence and Communication Networks (CICN), 2010 International Conference on.* doi:10.1109/CICN.2010.82

Bender, W., Gruhl, D., Morimoto, M., & Lu, A. (1996). Techniques for Data Hiding. *IBM Systems Journal*, *35*(3&4), 313–336. doi:10.1147/sj.353.0313

Bhattacharyya, D., Das, P., Bandyopadhyay, S. K., & Kim, T. (2009). Text steganography: A novel approach. *International Journal of Advanced Science and Technology*, *3*, 79–86.

Cachin, C. (1998). An information-theoretic model for steganography. In *Proceedings of 2nd Workshop on Information Hiding*. Springer.

Chaudhary, A., Raheja, J. L., & Verma, B. K. (2010). An Algorithmic Approach to Intrusion Detection. In *Proceedings of 4th IEEE International Conference on Advanced Computing and Communication Technologies*.

Chaudhary, A., Vasavada, J., Raheja, J. L., Kumar, S., & Sharma, M. A. (2012). Hash based Approach for Secure Keyless Steganography in Lossless RGB Images. In Proceedings of 22nd Graphicon. doi:10.1109/ICUMT.2012.6459795

Eggers, J.J., Bauml, R. Girod, B. (2002). A communication approach to image steganography. *Security and Watermarking of Multimedia Contents V of SPIE Proceedings, 4675*, 26-37.

Gregory, K. (2005). Investigator's Guide to Steganography (2nd ed.). Academic Press.

Gupta, A., & Chaudhary, A. (2014). Hiding Sound in Image by k-LSB Mutation using Cuckoo Search. In Proceedings of 2nd IEEE-INNS ISCBI. doi:10.1109/ISCBI.2014.12

Gutub, A. A. (2010). Pixel indicator technique for RGB image steganography. *Journal of Emerging Technologies in Web Intelligence*, *2*(1), 56–64. doi:10.4304/jetwi.2.1.56-64

Hsien-Wei, Y., & Kuo, F. H. (2011). Reversible Data Hiding for Color BMP Image Based on Block Difference Histogram. In *Ubi-Media Computing (U-Media), 2011 4th International Conference on.*

Jiang, L., & Zheng-quan, X. (2010). Color Image Information Hiding Based on Perceptual Color Clustering. In *Wireless Communications Networking and Mobile Computing (WiCOM), 2010 6th International Conference on.* doi:10.1109/WICOM.2010.5601277

Johnson, N. F., & Jajodia, S. (1998). Exploring steganography: Seeing the unseen. *IEEE Computer Magazine*, *31*(2), 26–34. doi:10.1109/MC.1998.4655281

Khare, A., Kunari, M, Khare P. (2010). Efficient Algorithm For Digital Image Steganography. *Journal of Information Science, Knowledge and Research in Computer Science and Application*, 1-5.

Levicky, D., Bugar, G., Banoci, V. (2012). A novel JPEG steganography method secure against histogram steganalysis. In *ELMAR, 2012 Proceedings.*

Li, X., & Wang, J. (2007). A steganographic method based upon JPEG and particle swarm optimization algorithm. *Information Sciences*, *177*(15), 3099–3109. doi:10.1016/j.ins.2007.02.008

Liu, N., Amin, P., & Subbalakshmi, K. P. (2007). Security and Robustness Enhancement for Image Data Hiding. *Multimedia, IEEE Transactions on*, *9*(3), 466–474. doi:10.1109/TMM.2006.888005

Neeta, D., Snehal, K., & Jacobs, D. (2006). Implementation of LSB steganography and its evaluation for various bits. In *Proceedings of 1st International Conference on Digital Information Management.*

Rabah, K. (2004). Steganography- the Art of Hiding Data. *Information Technology of Journal*, *3*(3), 245–269. doi:10.3923/itj.2004.245.269

Raheja, J. L., Manasa, M. B. L., Chaudhary, A., & Raheja, S. (2011). ABHIVYAKTI: Hand Gesture Recognition using Orientation Histogram in different light conditions. In *Proceedings of the 5th Indian International Conference on Artificial Intelligence*.

Roy, S., & Parekh, R. (2011). A Secure Keyless Image Steganography Approach for Lossless RGB Images. In *Proceedings of ACM ICCCS, Rourkela*. doi:10.1145/1947940.1948059

Schyndel, V., Ron, G., Andrew, Z. T., & Charles, F. O. (1994). A digital watermark. *Image Processing, 1994. Proceedings. ICIP-94., IEEE International Conference*. IEEE.

Singh, M., Singh, S. B., & Singh, L. S. S. (2007). Hiding encrypted message in the features of images. *International Journal of Computer Science and Network Security*, *7*(4), 302–307.

Sutaone, M. S., & Khandare, M. V. (2008). Image based steganography using LSB insertion technique. In *Proceedings of International Conference on Wireless, Mobile and Multimedia Networks*.

Turner, L. F. (1989). *Digital data security system*. Patent IPN wo 89: 08915.

Upreti, K., Verma, K., & Sahoo, A. (2010). Variable Bits Secure System for Color Images. *Advances in Computing, Control and Telecommunication Technologies (ACT), 2010 Second International Conference on*. doi:10.1109/ACT.2010.58

Wang, R., Chi-Fang, L., & Ja-Chen, L. (2001). Image hiding by optimal LSB substitution and genetic algorithm. *Pattern Recognition*, *34*(3), 671–683. doi:10.1016/S0031-3203(00)00015-7

Youssef, S. M., Elfarag, A. A., & Raouf, R. (2012). C7. A multi-level information hiding integrating wavelet-based texture analysis of block partition difference images. *Radio Science Conference (NRSC), 2012 29th National*. doi:10.1109/NRSC.2012.6208525

KEY TERMS AND DEFINITIONS

Degradation: if the color quality of image as host signal OR any attribute of host signal changes after hiding another signal, this change in attribute quality deragrade host signal. This process is called degradation.

Host Signal: This is a signal which may be image, audio, video or something else, which would be used to hide a signal inside.

LSB: Least Significate Bit is generally used for data storage because by changing this, it give minimum or say none effect on color quality in the image.

Pixel: This is the smallest element in the image. Pixel is picture element. It may be circular or square. Its size depends on hardware.

Random Distribution: This is a way to distribute a series or pattern or something in random way. This can be purely random or pseudo-random, so that it can be somehow predictable.

Resolution: The width and height of an image is counted in terms of pixels. The resolution is shown in terms of width*height, like 640*480.

Steganography: This is an area where a signal (any kind of data) can be inserted into host signal (generally Image) to hide. Only host signal is visible after the process.

Chapter 7
Anomaly Detection in Hyperspectral Imagery:
An Overview

Karim Saheb Ettabaa
Ensi University, Tunisia

Manel Ben Salem
IsitCom, Tunisia

ABSTRACT

In this chapter we are presenting the literature and proposed approaches for anomaly detection in hyperspectral images. These approaches are grouped into four categories based on the underlying techniques used to achieve the detection: 1) the statistical based methods, 2) the kernel based methods, 3) the feature selection based methods and 4) the segmentation based methods. Since the first approaches are mostly based on statistics, the recent works tend to be more geometrical or topological especially with high resolution images where the high resolution implies the presence of many materials in the same geographic area that cannot be easily distinguished by usual statistical methods.

INTRODUCTION

Anomaly detection is an important research topic for diverse domains. For the Cyber-Intrusion detection (Yu & Wu, 2012) and Fraud detection (Eberle & Holder, 2013; Lee, Yeh & Wang, 2013), the aim of anomaly detection is to avoid malicious attacks in critical systems. In the medical field, anomaly detection can be of a great importance for preventing attacks (Zhang, Raghunathan & Jha, 2013) or detecting patient anomalies (SA-LEM, Guerassimov, Mehaoua, Marcus & Furht, 2013) in personal healthcare systems or for diagnosing tumor in medical images (Goswami & Bhaiya, 2013). In sensor networks (OReilly, Gluhak, Imran, & Rajasegarar, 2014), anomaly detection can provide an idea about sensors data quality and integrity. In the industrial word, the damage detection aims to detect different faults and failures in complex industrial systems (Hu, Subbu, Bonissone, Qiu, & Iyer, 2008). Another anomaly detection field concerns the detection of

DOI: 10.4018/978-1-4666-8654-0.ch007

anomalies in documents such as texts (Srivastava & Zane-Ulman, 2005) and images (Kim, 2013). More details about these anomaly detection applications are addressed in this survey (Chandola, Banerjee & Kumar, 2009).

In remote sensing, the anomaly detection aims to detect anomalous pixels in multispectral and hyperspectral images. Anomalies are pixels that deviate from the expected behavior and can hold interesting information. For instance, anomaly can be rare vegetation species, anomaly in vegetation growth, illegal plants associated to drug commerce, polluted area in coastal waters, adventurers lost in the dessert, buried archaeological structures, illegal border crossing or military vehicle under vegetative cover.

The remainder of this chapter is organized as follows; the second section gives a survey of anomaly detection, including problems faced and proposed statistical based, kernel based, feature selection based and segmentation based approaches. The third section enumerates the different criterion used for the evaluation of anomaly detectors. The fourth section discusses the advantages and inconvenient of these presented solutions and gives an idea about the future direction in anomaly detection. And the last section will conclude this overview.

ANOMALY DETECTION IN HYPERSPECTRAL IMAGERY

Problems

The magnitude of anomalies motivated researches in anomaly detection and interpretation for hyperspectral images. Since the beginning, researchers had to cope with the problem of the absence of any prior knowledge about the treated data. Therefore, they try to use statistical methods to compare between the Pixel Under Test (PUT) and the background. For statistical methods the background is modeled with a linear distribution of the Probability Density Function (PDF) that supposes its homogeneity. This supposition accentuates the False Alarm Rate (FAR) especially for high resolution images where the supposition of homogeneity seems to be inappropriate since the big diversity of existing materials. To decrease this fact, non linear models of the background have been proposed with the kernel based anomaly detectors. Other researches try to solve the anomaly detection problem with different techniques as feature selection and the segmentation.

Whatsoever the underlying techniques are, there are three principal challenges to overcome. The first challenge concerns increasing the detection rate while decreasing the false alarm rate which is related to the fact that the presence of noise, the contamination of the background statistics with the signature of the anomaly and the supposition of background homogeneity increase considerably the false alarm rate. The second challenge is related to the detection of anomaly with different shapes and sizes. In fact the size of anomalies can range from sub-pixel level to few pixels and the detection of these different sizes anomalies with the same detector steels a big challenge. The third challenge aims to achieve the nearest computational cost to real-time processing to perform anomaly detection on board as pixels are received.

Solutions

To achieve anomaly detection, researchers adopt several techniques relevant to diverse disciplines such as statistic, information theory, graph theory, and so on. Figure 1 shows that these approaches can be grouped into four families based on the underling techniques.

Figure 1. Anomaly detection approaches

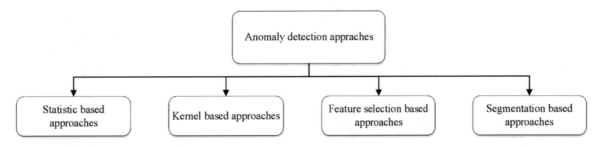

Statistic Based Anomaly Detectors

First and Second Order Statistics Anomaly Detectors

The real genesis of the anomaly detection for multi/hyperspectral images was marked by the proposition of the RX detector (RXD) (Reed, Ye, 1990), which is considered now as the benchmark anomaly detector for hyperspectral imagery. This approach proposed by Reed and Ye, presents a generalization of the constant false alarm rate (CFAR) algorithm proposed in (Chen and Reed 1987).

The background is modeled as a zero mean normal distribution under the first hypothesis and as a linear combination of the target signal and the distribution of the residual background plus noise, under the second hypothesis.

$$\mathbf{H_0}: x(n) = x^0(n)$$
$$\mathbf{H_1}: x(n) = x^0(n) + bs(n) \tag{1}$$

In order to ensure the Gaussian distribution of the PDF of the background, minimizing the third moment of the image minus his non stationary local mean tends to create a distribution $\overline{X}$ which is close to Gaussian.

$$\overline{X} = \frac{1}{L^2}\left[X * W\right] \tag{2}$$

where W is an L by L all-ones matrix and the saterisk (*) denotes convolution. As adaptation of the binary hypothesis of Neyman-Pearson (Lehmann, 1993) to the generalized maximum likelihood ratio test (GLRT), the RXD try to maximize the detection probability with constraint of maintaining a constant false alarm probability at a desired value.

Since this approach has proved its performance, it suffers from many problems like: 1) high computational cost, 2) non ability of small size anomalies' detection, 3) high false alarm rate

Figure 2. First and second order statistic based approaches

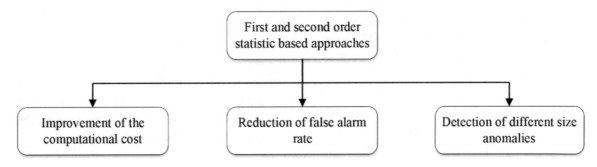

due to the assumption of the background homogeneity especially with high resolution images and 4) background contamination with the signal of the anomaly (Matteoli, Diani, & Corsini, 2014) for local anomaly detectors. Therefore many approaches, like shows figure 2, are proposed to improve the RXD capabilities.

To reduce the false alarm rate Chang and Chiang in (Chang, & Chiang, 2002) presented four modified variants of the RXD based on the replacement of the covariance matrix in the Mahalanobis distance by the correlation matrix and the removal of the subtraction of the mean of the data, in order to account for both the first and second order statistics what have improved the detection results over the RXD.

$$\bar{\delta}_{RXD}(r) = r^T R_{LxL}^{-1} r \tag{3}$$

Equation 3 presents the new detector where R is an L by L sample correlation matrix, L is the number of spectral bands and r is the spectra of the tested pixel.

The first two proposed variants are the Normalized RXD (NRXD) and the Modified RXD (MRXD) which can be interpreted as matched-filters. The third approach is an adaption of the Uniform Target Detector (Harsanyi, 1993) to the RXD. And the fourth one is a causal RXD (3) (CRXD) which is preserved for the proposed real-time processing approach. Detected anomalies are then classified using the histogram of the correlation matched filter measure (RMFM) and for the real-time processing; the classification is performed by the Linearly Constrained Minimum Variance LCMV (Chang, Ren, & Chiang, 2001). This approach proposed an automatic thresholding method using the histogram of the image to determine the rejection probability.

For the same aim as above, (Guo et al., 2014) proposed two variants of the RXD that try to improve the background characterization for better detection results: 1) the Weighted-RXD (W-RXD)

that performs a reduction of the weight of the anomalous pixels or noise signals and a rising of the weight of the background samples and 2) the Linear Filter-based RXD (LF-RXD) that uses the probability of each pixel of the background to filter wrong anomalous or noisy instances. This approach improved the performance with regards to the RXD (particularly, in terms of reducing FAR) without significantly increasing the computational complexity.

To speed up the detection, (Du & Zhang, 2011) proposed an RXD version consisting of an arbitrary choice of the background representative pixels for each data block instead of using the whole image (RSAD). The traditional Malanahobis distance is calculated then, between the PUT and representatives pixels of the each block and results are merged by a majority voting rule. This approach is less sensitive to contamination by the signal of the anomaly and presents a better separability between anomalies and the background since there is a low probability to choose an anomalous pixel in the randomly choice of samples to represent the image clutter. A real-time processing version is proposed for this approach.

A parallel implementation of an anomaly detector can be a useful tool to reach a real-time processing detection, for that (Molero, Garzon, Garcia & Plaza, 2013) proposed a parallel implementation of the Global RX (PGRX) and the Local RX (PLRX) detectors based on multi-core platforms. This approach is mainly based on the Chang and Chiang approach discussed in (Chang, Chiang, 2002), but offers in addition several optimizations in order to achieve a real-time processing detection. The first optimization involves the use of the linear algebra that performs a resolution of a matrical equations system to escape the inversion of the correlation matrix. And the second one takes benefit of the symmetry property of the correlation matrix to compute only the half. For the LRX the recurrence relation among to the matrices associated to neighboring pixels is well exploited.

Another challenge with the anomaly detection is the detection of different size anomalies, for that in (Liu & Chang, 2013) authors proposed a multiple window based approach which performs a background subtraction using different sizes windows around the pixel under test. The approach is proposed to suit three types of detectors: 1) the RXD (MW-RXD), 2) the Nested Spatial Window-based approach to Target Detection (NSWTD) (Liu & Chang, 2004) (MW-NSWTD) and 3) the Dual Window-based Eigen Separation Transform (DWEST) (Kwon, Der, & Nasrabadi, 2003) (MW-DWEST) and succeed to detect 1 by 1 pixel panels for the three detectors. This approach offers a real-time processing per pixel.

Some other detectors are interested in detecting subpixels anomalies. For instance, in (Khazai, Safari, Mojaradi & Homayouni, 2013), authors proposed a single band anomaly detection method that performs an evaluation of all spectral bands searching for the most discriminative band for anomaly detection (i.e. search for the feature for which the anomaly value is the maximum). The median absolute deviation measure, as a robust measure of deviation, is used to compute the absolute deviation from the data's median. Experiments conducted in state-of-the-art anomaly detection methods show that the use of one discriminative band for subpixel anomaly detection is more efficient than the use of all band and that this approach is computationally expedient. (Jiayi, Hongyan, & Liangpei, 2014) proposed to represent the local background pixels by a joint sparsity model, and then an unconstrained linear unmixing approach is used to decompose the abundance of the pixel under test. Unmixing results are then compared to the joint sparse representation using the energy disparity. This approach gives a good performance stability compared to the RXD and orthogonal subspace projection based detector.

High Order Statistics Anomaly Detectors

A new approach was proposed by Xun and Fang in (Xun, & Fang, 2006) that introduces the use of the high order statistics for anomaly detection. This approach uses an augmented Lagrange multiplier to search for a projection that maximizes the skewness and the kurtosis as the normalized third and fourth central moments. Experiments show the effectiveness of these measures for detection of outliers.

Later, in (Ren et al., 2006) it is shown by experiments that using the second order statistics to detect target occurring with low probability and small population is less effective than using high order statistics. In fact, the contribution of anomalies to high order statistic is more effective than its contribution to the second order statistics.

Therefore, Ren et al. in (Ren et al., 2006) proposed the use of high order statistics like the skewness, the kurtosis and the fifth order central moment for target detection, and then in (Chang, Xiong & Wen, 2014) authors give an evolution of this solution for anomaly detection. (Chang, Xiong & Wen, 2014) proposed the computation of the virtual dimensionality to detect automatically the number of the spectrally distinct signatures present in the data. The problem is then formulated with a binary hypothesis and two detectors have been proposed: 1) a Byes detector for the Maximal Orthogonal Complement Algorithm (Kuybeda, Malah & Barzohar, 2007) (HOS-MOCA), and 2) (HOS-HFC) a NP problem formulation. For this approach the projection is performed by a fast independent component analysis (Hyvärinen & Oja, 2000) with the negentropy criterion to approximate the mutual information, instead of the Orthogonal Subspace Projection (OSP), in (Ren et al., 2006), to speed up the progression of the detection. The results show the significance of the virtual dimensionality and the high order statistics over the second order statistics.

(Gu, Liu & Zhang, 2008) (HOS-SKPCA) proposed to start with a Selective Kernel Principal Component Analysis for a better exploitation of the high order spectral bands correlation, and then to calculate the Average Local Singularity (ALS) based on high order statistics, the component with the maximal ALS is considered as the anomaly.

One of the problems of all this approaches returns to the fact that they require step-by-step iterations to reach the optimal solution, so they produce multiple detection maps rather than a single anomaly distribution image. Therefore, (Geng, Sun, Ji, & Zhao, 2014) proposed a new approach based on the use of a coskewness tensor which combines the concept of third order statistic tensor and the idea of the RXD. Results conducted by this approach overcome the RXD results and give similar results as the fast ICA in the ROC curve.

Another drawback of high order statistics is the computational cost of the proposed approach, which still an open research topic.

Kernel Based Anomaly Detectors

The major problem with statistics based anomaly detectors is the assumption of the linearity of the background. In fact, in reality the distribution of the probability density function of hyperspectral images is far away from the normal distribution. Therefore, nonlinear anomaly detectors were proposed using kernel strategies like shows figure 3.

One idea was the kernelization of the RXD in the feature space in terms of kernels that implicitly compute dot products in the feature space. This approach was proposed by Heesung and Nasrabadi in (Heesung, & Nasrabadi, 2005) and was known as the Kernel RX detector (KRX). To estimate the kernel matrix, which is a Gram matrix; proprieties of the kernel principal component analysis are used. For the experimentation, the Gaussian RBF kernel is used to represent the RX kernel. The problem with this method is related to the fact that the efficiency of the approach is strongly related to the bandwidth parameter choice, therefore Kwon and Gurram in (Kwon, & Gurram, 2010) proposed new method to decide the optimal full diagonal bandwidth parameters of the Gaussian RBF kernel. This approach is based on the estimation of the full diagonal parameters from the cross-validation optimal single bandwidth parameter using the variance of spectral bandwidth which results an improvement of the detection probability at a given false alarm rate compared with the original KRX.

Another idea for the adaptation of the RX detector to kernel trick was proposed by (Matteoli, Veracini, Diani & Corsini, 2013). This approach tries to benefit of the ability of nonparametric approaches at modeling complex backgrounds and to address the issue of bandwidth parameter selection by proposing a solution based on the locally adaptive Kernel Density Estimator (Veracini, Matteoli, Diani & Corsini, 2011) which is employed within the likelihood ratio test rule to model the

Figure 3. Kernel based approaches

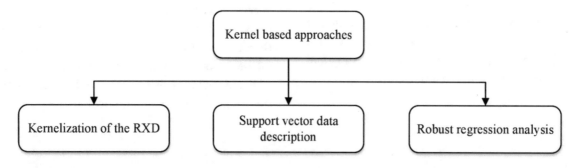

local background. In fact, information extracted from the image is injected into the bandwidth selection process using the k nearest neighbor to compute the adaptive local background distribution. Results proved that this approach overcomes the traditional RX detector and the KRX detector in term of performance and computational cost, but its computational cost still far away from the real-time processing.

Kwon and Nasrabadi in (Kwon & Nasrabadi, 2005) proposed (KASD) a nonlinear version of the Adaptive Subspace Detector (ASD) (Kraut & Scharf, 1999). This approach represents data with a nonlinear function using the Gaussian RBF kernel, which ensures the translation invariance propriety. Results overcome the conventional ASD (Kraut & Scharf, 1999).

The support vector data description is widely used for anomaly detection. The basic idea is to find a hypersphere with the minimum volume that enclose all the normal training samples of the target class. For instance in (Banerjee, Burlina & Diehl, 2006), authors proposed the detection of pixels out of the support region of the Support Vector Data Description (SVDD) as anomalies. For the determination of the scale parameter sigma; this approach proposes a minimax method that takes the value of sigma that produces the smallest average fraction of support vectors from large sets of training data. Another problem with this method consists in the difficulty to determine the detection threshold automatically, so the threshold is fixed by the experience on a large number of

images with different background sets and different atmospheric conditions. This approach presented a significant improvement over the RXD for the lower SNIR levels and a better detection for scenes that contain multiple types of landscape. The improvement was remarkable also in the computation cost of the detector. In order to suppress the contamination of the detection statistics by anomalies targets, (Zhao, Du & Zhang, 2014) used the robust regression analysis in the kernel feature space where the input data are implicitly mapped into an appropriate high-dimensional kernel feature space by nonlinear mapping.

The kernel based approaches efficiency is strongly related to the good choice of the kernel parameters. Many researches (Khazai, Homayouni, Safari & Mojaradi, 2011; Kwon& Gurram, 2010; Gurram & Kwon, 2011, 2011; Gurram, Kwon & Han, 2012) target this subject but it is still an open research subject.

Feature Selection Based Anomaly Detectors

Feature selection based anomaly detectors try to minimize the amount of treated data and focus on the interesting features for anomaly detection, different feature methods are proposed, like shows figure 4.

Independent Component Analysis (ICA) was investigated for anomaly detection by (Johnson, Williams & Bauer, 2013). This approach is based on the statistical approach proposed by Robila

Figure 4. Feature selection based approaches

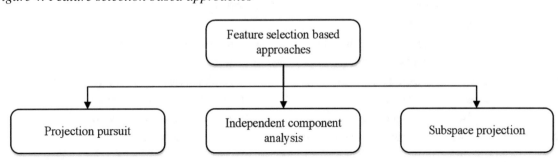

and Varshney in (Robila & Varshney, 2002) for target detection. To avoid the calculation of the kurtosis proposed in (Robila & Varshney, 2002), the zero detection histogram is used for feature selection and potential anomalies determination, and then the noise is smoothed by the use of the adaptive Winer filter that recurrently reduces the power of the background while maintaining the power of anomalies. This approach proposes to determinate the number of principal component automatically. Results show that this approach overcomes the RXD and the approach described in (Banerjee, Burlina & Diehl, 2006) mainly in term of computational cost.

A selective kernel principal component analysis was proposed for anomaly detection in (Gu, Liu & Zhang, 2006). The singularity of each nonlinear principal component transformed is measured using high-order statistics in local background to define the local average singularity. Depending in this measure, the component with the maximum singularity is selected and the RX detector is performed on this selected component which leads to better performance than the RXD. A comparative study of some feature extraction methods with different rules applied to the RX detector was conducted in (Liu, Gu & Zhang, 2010). This study evince that the use of KPCA with local singularity improves the detection performance of the RXD.

The projection pursuit as well was employed for target and anomaly detection. Therefore, in (Chiang, Chang & Ginsberg, 2001), authors proposed the use of the projection pursuit for target detection (PPTD). This approach looks for the optimal projection index by an evolutionary algorithm. It proposes the use of a zero detection thresholding method. Non detected pixel will be considered for the next projection process till convergence. To achieve anomaly detection Huck and Guillaume in (Huck, & Guillaume, 2010) proposed to establish a link between the projection pursuit and the binary testing hypothesis that leads to an

asymptotically constant false-alarm rate resulting approach (BHPP) that benefit of the spectral discrimination rate of the projection pursuit.

The subspace projection was also exploited for anomaly detection in (Wang, Zhao & Wang, 2011), where authors proposed a subspace band selection based RX algorithm for anomaly detection in hyperspectral imagery. The approach starts with an adaptive subspace decomposition to divide the high dimensional hyperspectral image into subsets of low dimensions according to the correlation between spectral bands. In each subset the principal component analysis is used for selecting the principal components for the RX detector and then results of each subset are fused and thresholded to detect anomalies. Chang et al. in (Chang, Zhao, Mark & Pan, 1998) proposed three unconstrained least squares subspace projections that can be considered as a posteriori orthogonal subspace projection (OSP), these approaches can be used to estimate the target signature abundance or to detect sub-pixels. Later Chang in (Chang, 2005) presented an approach based on the adaptation of the RXD to the OSP (OSP-RXD) and proved that the new approach outperforms the classical RXD. A parallel implementation of an OSP target detection method was proposed by Paz and Plaza in (Paz & Plaza, 2010); in which authors tried to have an evaluation of cluster based and GPU implementations. Liu and Chang in (Liu & Chang, 2013) used also the OSP for detection of anomalies based on multiple windows for the two approaches MW-NSWTD and MW-DWEST.

Segmentation Based Anomaly Detectors

To cope with the effect of the hypothesis of homogeneity of the background on the increasing of the false alarm rate, segmentation based anomaly detectors were proposed. The segmentation can be performed either with respect to spectral features or to spectral and spatial features.

Spectral Segmentation Based Anomaly Detectors

Spectral segmentation allows the segmentation of the hyperspetral image into homogeneous regions representing the distribution of different materials of the image scene, and then yields an additional knowledge for anomaly detection. Carlotto in (Carlotto, 2005) proposed the Cluster Based Anomaly Detector (CBAD) which is considered later as the benchmark anomaly detector for the segmentation based approaches. For this approach pixels are grouped in clusters according to the histogram quantization of image's principal components and inside each cluster, a Gaussian mixture model (GMM) is supposed. The Mahalanobis distance is calculated then, between the PUT and the center of each cluster. Pixels that exceed the threshold are considered as anomalies. This approach is capable of detecting objects of different sizes and is computationally more efficient than other cluster based approach seeing the use of quantization. The effectiveness of this approach had been proved in (Hytla, Hardie, Eismann & Meola, 2007) where a comparative study of Gaussian mixture models had been achieved between the CBAD and two other approaches.

In (Borghys, Truyen, Shimoni & Perneel, 2009), authors proposed two approaches (TLSAD) consisting of dividing the image into windows of the same size and for each window the mean clusters are derived by the k-means clustering for the first approach, and the N-Finder endmembers selection for the second approach. Spectra of the background clusters are then compared to the pixels of the image to find out pixels with the minimum spectral distance to the centers of the clusters using the spectral distance and a binary coding for the clustering method, and the residue of the estimated mixture in each pixel for the endmember selection method. These approaches are more robust than the RXD for complex scenes.

Ma et al. in (Ma, Crawford & Tian, 2010) proposed a new approach based on the local tangent space alignment which is dimensionality reduction method coupled with a minimum distance detector. The local tangent space alignment can learn a nonlinear embedding into low dimensional coordinates from high dimensional data, the training data that should represent all the background types are generated by the recursive hierarchical segmentation algorithm with the elimination of very small segments that may represent anomalies. The rest of data is employed for test. As results, anomalies can be detected using small number of features in the embedded space which result superior performance compared to the RXD.

The computation time of segmentation based approaches is delayed due to the additional cost added in the segmentation step, so Duran and Petrou in (Duran & Petrou, 2007) proposed a time efficient approach (TEAD) based on the arbitrary choice of a small percentage of the background for the construction of clusters. Many clustering approaches are tested and the auto-organizing maps were selected; this approach is based on the local mean of the Unified Distance Matrix. Anomalies are pixels of the greatest distance to the clusters centers.

Spatial Spectral Segmentation Based Anomaly Detectors

Spatial spectral segmentation based anomaly detectors adds the contextual information to the spectral one in the segmentation process. For this purpose, in (Goovaerts, Jacquez & Marcus, 2005) authors proposed a geostatistical filtering of noise and regional background using the factorial kriging followed by a local indicator of spatial autocorrelation (GLCAAD). Anomalies are guided by the sign and the magnitude of the local indicator of spatial autocorrelation for all images of principal components. This approach presents a lower FAR than the RXD mainly in presence of noise.

Another idea was proposed by Kim and Finkel in (Kim & Finkel, 2003) which starts by grouping pixels of the image by the k-means clustering method, and then representative pixels of each cluster are chosen for the Locally Linear Embedding (LLE) algorithm (LLEAD). This method decreases the dimensionality while preserving the spatial spectral relationship between pixels and succeeds to detect anomalies.

The Gauss-Markov Random Field (GMRF), are also used for the segmentation of the image clutter before anomaly detection, therefore Schweizer and Moura in (Schweizer & Moura, 2000) supposed that the background clutter can be seen as a three dimensional Gauss-Markov Random Field (GMRF). This model enables the cutting of the image into colored Gauss-Markov zones representing different materials. Three approaches are proposed to estimate the parameters of GMRF: the maximum likelihood, the least square and the approximate maximum likelihood. Compared to the RXD, this approach escapes the inversion of the covariance matrix by the direct parameterization of its inverse which results on a lower computational cost. Hazel in (Hazel, 2000) proposed to join the Gauss Markov random field texture models, to represent joint spatial-spectral modeling of multispectral imagery, and a multivariate parametric clustering algorithm for anomaly detection. Results proved that this model improved the detection over spectral clustering. Authors in (Liu, Guojing & Zhang, 2008) reuse the Gauss Markov random field texture model in the segmentation step of the image to model the distribution of background pixel values. The RX detector is applied on each segmented textures and gives better result over the conventional RX detector.

In (Li, Prasad & Fowler, 2013) Li et al. proposed a block-based modulo partitioning of the image using the compressive-projection principal component analysis which preserves the local spatial coherence (CPPCAAD). Spatial segmentation results are combined to the classification of pixels with a majority voting rule. Results proved that using the RX detector operating with the block-based modulo portioning followed by

the random projection-projected subspace outperforms the detector operating with pixel-based modulo portioning.

Yuan et al. in (Yuan, Sun, Ji, Li & Zou, 2014) proposed a novel anomaly detector based on the local sparsity divergence. The proposed approach starts by the construction of the local spectral and spatial dictionaries using a dual-window which enable the extraction of the sparse coefficients of each pixel. The next step is about the computation of the local sparsity divergence map at each spectral band separately and then a joint segmentation of the local sparsity divergence maps over different bands is performed for anomaly detection which results on a better performance over a state of the art anomaly detector.

Another spatial spectral method for image segmentation refers to the use of graphs. In (Doster, Ross, Messinger & Basener, 2009) authors proposed the transformation of the image into a graph where components of the graph present different materials (TAD). If the population of a graph component is less than the threshold it will be considered as potential anomaly. The rank of each potential anomaly pixel determines if it will be considered for the process of classification. Anomalies' clustering is performed by the calculation of paths between anomalous nodes. This approach gives a good classification results even for distant pixels that are spectrally similar. Messinger and Albano in (Messinger & Albano, 2011) proposed to cut the image into windows and for each window a connected graph is designed in relation with spectral characteristics (GTAD). The connectivity of each pixel to the graph is estimated by the vertex weighted volume in this pixel. Anomalous pixels are isolated pixels and far from the background components.

Criterion of Evaluation of Anomaly Detectors

To evaluate the anomaly detectors many process have been adopted. The first way is to calculate accuracy measures like the False Positive Fraction

FPF and the False Negative Fraction FNF adopted in (Johnson, Williams & Bauer, 2013) and which can refer respectively to 1 - (specificity) and 1 - (sensitivity) where the specificity represents the true negative fraction and the sensitivity represents the true positive fraction. Such measures give an idea about the accuracy of the detected anomaly, but to have more relevant decision on the ability of the detector to pick out anomalies other process have been adopted. The detection maps, the ROC curves and the area under the ROC curves are often used for constructing a decision about the capability of an anomaly detector.

The Detection Maps

The detection maps represent the different detected anomalies of the image. For most statistical detectors, these maps are binary images representing the detected pixels or objects over different thresholds. The detection can be derived also in different bands or window sizes depending on the detectors. For each of this type of detector a detection binary map is calculated and from the detected pixels or object a comparative study is derived between the detection maps and the ground truth reality map for extracting true detected pixels or object and false alarms. The resulting number of detected pixels and false alarm will be useful for the construction of the ROC curve discussed in the next subsection.

The ROC Curve

The receiver operating characteristic (ROC) curve is curve that plots the false alarm rate and the detection rate as the "x" and "y" axis of the curve. With the detection rate and the false alarm rate are given by Equations (4) and (5).

Detection Rate=

$$\frac{\text{Number of correctly detected anomalies}}{\text{Total number of anomalies}} \quad (4)$$

False Alarm Rate=

$$\frac{\text{False detected anomalies}}{\text{Total number of data}} \quad (5)$$

It is used for the first time during the World war two for the analysis of radar images and indicates all possible combinations of detection when varying the false alarm threshold. In fact, these ratios are computed by varying the detection threshold and calculating the produced false alarms. It is a useful tool for comparing different detector especially when they are plotted in the same figure but it cannot be represented itself as a quantifiable quantity, there for many researcher use the area under the curve as measure of accuracy between two detectors.

The Area under the Curve

The area under the curve represents an accuracy measure that summaries the ROC curve. In fact this measure calculates area under a ROC curve. An area of 1 represents a perfect test; an area of 0.5 represents a worthless test. Between these two quantities the value of the area is acceptable and the greatest it is, the best the results.

Two methods are commonly used for calculating the area under the curve: a non-parametric method based on constructing trapezoids under the curve as an approximation of area and a parametric method using a maximum likelihood estimator to fit a smooth curve to the data points. For the first method, many samples are picked from the curve and a trapezoidal area under each vertical slice relating two points is calculated, these areas are then summed to have the total area. The second method is used only if the statistical distribution of anomalies is known in advance and follows a usual statistical distribution like the normal distribution.

DISCUSSION AND FUTURE RESEARCH DIRECTIONS

In this overview we are investigating different methods of anomaly detection in hyperspectral imagery. The table 1 summarizes characteristics of a number of anomaly detectors described above and many remarks can be picked out.

It is clear that the first anomaly detectors proposed rely on statistical methods, although this methods are powerful for anomaly detection, they suffer from many problems like the high compu-

Table 1. Characteristics of some anomaly detectors

Approach	Nature	Data Description	Size of Detected Anomaly	Notes on Complexity	Contribution
RXD [12]	Statistical	Spectral	Large size anomalies only	$O(B^3)$*	Detection of unknown signal in many spectral bands
CRXD	Statistical	Spectral	Large size anomalies	Real-time	Automatic threshold Anomaly classification Real-time processing
RSAD	Statistic	Spectral	Large size anomalies	Real time	Less sensitive to signal contamination Less false alarm in transitory zones Real-time processing
PGRX	Statistic	Spectral	Large size anomalies	Real-time	Performance in presence of noise Faster than the standard version
PLRX	Statistic	Spectral	Small size and sub-pixels	$O((2/3)B^3)$*	
MW-RXD	Statistic	Spectral	Different size of anomalies	Real-time per pixel	Better detection with less false alarms than the standard versions Real-time processing Detection of anomalies of different sizes
MW-NSWTD	Statistic and projection				
MW-DWEST					
HOS-MOCA	Statistic and projection	Spectral	Target of different sizes and endmembers	—	Estimation of the virtual dimensionality for HOS characterized data Detection of rare targets characterized by the HOS
HOS-HCF					
CBAD	Segmentation and statistic	Spectral	Different size anomalies	Nearly RXD	Anomaly and change detection Reduced segmentation time due to the quantization
GMRF	Segmentation and statistics	Spectral and spatial	Large size anomalies	Less than the RXD	Parameterization of the inverse of the covariance matrix to avoid the inversion Exploitation of the spatial spectral correlation Improvement of the computational coast over RXD
TAD	Segmentation	Spectral and spatial	Different size anomalies	$O(B)$*	Detection and classification of anomalies Use of a topological approach Detection of different size anomalies
PPTD	Projection	Spectral	Different size anomalies	Expensive	Good detection of targets of different sizes Extraction of the abundance maps of each class
AutoGAD	Projection	Spectral	—	Real-time	A simple and automatic detection of the dimensionality of the image Selection of the IC without using the kurtosis Less of false alarm due to the adaptive filter
KRX	Kernel and statistic	Spectral	Large size anomalies	$O(P^3)$ **	Better performance in the detection than the RXD
SVDD	Kernel	Spectral	—	$O(P^3)$**	Better detection for lower SNIR levels than RXD Better detection for multiple types of terrains scenes since it model a non parametric background Computational coast lower than the RXD

* complexity of every pixel is proportional to the number b of spectral bands
** complexity of every pixel is proportional to the number p of pixel in the local background

tational cost, the luck of ability of detecting small sizes anomalies, the big amount of FAR and the contamination of the background by the signal of the anomaly. Therefore many approaches are proposed as a solution of one or more of these problems.

Approaches described in (Chang & Chiang, 2002; Du & Zhang, 2011; Molero, Garzon, Garcia & Plaza, 2013) succeed to offer a real-time processing however they ignore anomalies of small sizes. Small sizes anomalies can be detectable by the LRXD, however the challenge is to detect anomalies of different sizes with the same approach, therefore Liu and Chang in (Liu & Chang, 2013) proposed an approach based on the use of multiple windows; this approach offer a nearly real-time processing solution for each pixel.

For the improvement of detection rate with constraint of minimizing the false alarm rate, high order statistics methods (Xun & Fang, 2006; Ren et al., 2006; Gu, Liu & Zhang, 2008; Chang, Xiong & Wen, 2014; Geng, Sun, Ji, & Zhao, 2014) have been proposed. These approaches benefit from the fact that the contribution of anomalies to the high order statistics is more significant than its contribution to the second order statistics. They are capable of detecting anomalies of different sizes but they are time consuming. Another solution to reduce the false alarm rate is the use of kernel based anomaly detectors that can model the background with a nonlinear distribution. They give a better detection results than the RXD mainly for high resolution images but the determination of optimal parameters of the kernels steel an open research domain.

The segmentation based anomaly detectors are also proposed to cope with the problem of the great false alarm rate. In fact, the segmentation allows an additional knowledge about the image existing materials and their distribution that facilitates the detection process. These approaches avoid false alarms resulting of material in other windows reported with local anomaly detectors. Segmentation based anomaly detectors give better results than statistical based anomaly detectors for high resolution scenes and are able of detecting anomalies of different sizes. The spatial spectral segmentation based approaches offer a better segmentation of the image than spatial ones.

With the scientific progress of spectrometers the segmentation based approaches will be the future of the anomaly detector because of their ability of detection even in high resolution scenes especially when using the spatial spectral characterization of the data. For segmentation based anomaly detector the real-time processing is an open research topic because of the additional time produced by the segmentation. The feature selection based anomaly detectors like the segmentation based ones, try to construct knowledge about the image before the detection of anomalies by the projection of pixels of the image in different spaces.

CONCLUSION

This overview studied different aspects of the anomaly detection in hyperspectral images. In fact, we had started with the enumeration of different problems related to anomaly detection and then we had detailed different proposed approaches. These approaches are grouped into four categories based on the underlying techniques used for the detection. In first group, statistic based approaches tried to solve anomaly detection problems by the calculation of statistical distances between pixels of the image and succeeded to have a good detection rate except that the assumption of homogeneity of the background creates other problems like the high false alarm rate, the high computational cost and the contamination of the background by the signal of the anomaly. So other approaches had been proposed based on kernel, projection and segmentation techniques. These approaches tried to improve the detection with constraint of minimizing false alarms and gave better results than statistical one especially for high resolution images which presents big diversity of materials that cannot be detected by usual statistical methods. As a conclusion we can say that the research in anomaly detection steel a promoting field view the importance of applications based on anomaly detection and that the different proposed approaches steel need more works mainly for high resolution images.

REFERENCES

Banerjee, A., Burlina, P., & Diehl, C. (2006). A support vector method for anomaly detection in hyperspectral imagery. *IEEE Transactions on Geoscience and Remote Sensing, 44*(8), 2282–2291. doi:10.1109/TGRS.2006.873019

Borghys, D., Truyen, E., Shimoni, M., & Perneel, C. (2009). Anomaly detection in hyperspectral images of complex scenes. In *Proceedings of 29th Earsel Symposium.*

Carlotto, M. J. (2005). A Cluster-Based Approach for Detecting Man-Made Objects and Changes in Imagery. *IEEE Transactions on Geoscience and Remote Sensing, 43*(2), 374–387. doi:10.1109/TGRS.2004.841481

Chandola, V., Banerjee, A., & Kumar, V. (2009). Anomaly Detection: A Survey. *ACM Computing Surveys, 41*(3), 1–72. doi:10.1145/1541880.1541882

Chang, Ch.-I. (2005). Orthogonal subspace projection (OSP) revisited: A comprehensive study and analysis. *IEEE Transactions on Geoscience and Remote Sensing, 43*(3), 502–518. doi:10.1109/TGRS.2004.839543

Chang, Ch.-I., & Chiang, Sh.-Sh. (2002). Anomaly detection and classification for hyperspectral imagery. *IEEE Transactions on Geoscience and Remote Sensing, 40*(6), 1314–1325. doi:10.1109/TGRS.2002.800280

Chang, Ch.-I., Ren, H., & Chiang, Sh. (2001). Real-Time Processing Algorithms for Target Detection and Classification in Hyperspectral Imagery. *IEEE Transactions on Geoscience and Remote Sensing, 39*(4), 760–768. doi:10.1109/36.917889

Chang, Ch.-I., Xiong, W., & Wen, C.-H. (2014). A Theory of High-Order Statistics-Based Virtual Dimensionality for Hyperspectral Imagery. *IEEE Transactions on Geoscience and Remote Sensing, 52*(1), 188–208. doi:10.1109/TGRS.2012.2237554

Chang, C. I., Zhao, X. L., Mark, L. G., & Pan, J. J. (1998). Least Squares Subspace Projection Approach to Mixed Pixel Classification for Hyperspectral Images. *IEEE Transactions on Geoscience and Remote Sensing, 36*(3), 898–912. doi:10.1109/36.673681

Chen, J. Y., & Reed, I. S. (1987). A Detection Algorithm for Optical Targets in Clutter. *IEEE Transactions on Aerospace and Electronic Systems, AES-23*(1), 46–59. doi:10.1109/TAES.1987.313335

Chiang, S. S., Chang, Ch. I., & Ginsberg, I. W. (2001). Unsupervised Target Detection in Hyperspectral Images Using Projection Pursuit. *IEEE Transactions on Geoscience and Remote Sensing, 39*(7), 1380–1391. doi:10.1109/36.934071

Doster, T. J., Ross, D. S., Messinger, D. W., & Basener, W. F. (2009). Anomaly Clustering in Hyperspectral Images. In *Proceedings of SPIE 7334, Algorithms and Technologies for Multispectral, Hyperspectral, and Ultraspectral Imagery XV.* Orlando, FL: SPIE. doi:10.1117/12.818407

Du, B., & Zhang, L. (2011). Random-Selection-Based Anomaly Detector for Hyperspectral Imagery. *IEEE Transactions on Geoscience and Remote Sensing, 49*(5), 1578–1589. doi:10.1109/TGRS.2010.2081677

Duran, O., & Petrou, M. (2007). A Time-Efficient Method for Anomaly Detection in Hyperspectral Images. *IEEE Transactions on Geoscience and Remote Sensing, 45*(12), 3894–3904. doi:10.1109/TGRS.2007.909205

Eberle, W., & Holder, L. (2013). Incremental Anomaly Detection in Graphs. In *Proceedings of the IEEE 13th International Conference on Data Mining Workshops (ICDMW)*. Dallas, TX: IEEE.

Geng, X., Sun, K., Ji, L., & Zhao, Y. (2014). A High-Order Statistical Tensor Based Algorithm for Anomaly Detection in Hyperspectral Imagery. *Scientific Reports, 4*(6869), 1–7. PMID:25366706

Goovaerts, P., Jacquez, G. M., & Marcus, A. (2005). Geostatistical and local cluster analysis of high resolution hyperspectral imagery for detection of anomalies. *Remote Sensing of Environment, 95*(3), 351–367. doi:10.1016/j.rse.2004.12.021

Goswami, S., & Bhaiya, L. K. P. (2013). A hybrid neuro-fuzzy approach for brain abnormality detection using GLCM based feature extraction. In *Proceedings of the International Conference on Emerging Trends in Communication, Control, Signal Processing & Computing Applications (C2SPCA)*. Bangalore: IEEE. doi:10.1109/C2SPCA.2013.6749454

Gu, Y., Liu, Y., & Zhang, Y. (2006). A Selective Kernel PCA Algorithm for Anomaly Detection in Hyperspectral Imagery. In *Proceedings of the IEEE International Conference on Acoustics, Speech and Signal Processing*. Toulouse: IEEE.

Gu, Y., Liu, Y., & Zhang, Y. (2008). A Selective KPCA Algorithm Based on High-Order Statistics for Anomaly Detection in Hyperspectral Imager. *IEEE Geoscience and Remote Sensing Letters, 5*(1), 43–47. doi:10.1109/LGRS.2007.907304

Guo, Q., Zhang, B., Ran, Q., Gao, L., Li, J., & Plaza, A. (2014). Weighted-RXD and Linear Filter-Based RXD: Improving Background Statistics Estimation for Anomaly Detection in Hyperspectral Imagery. *IEEE Journal of Selected Topics in Applied Earth Observations and Remote Sensing, 7*(6), 2351–2366. doi:10.1109/JSTARS.2014.2302446

Gurram, P., & Kwon, H. (2011). Support-Vector-Based Hyperspectral Anomaly Detection Using Optimized Kernel Parameters. *IEEE Geoscience and Remote Sensing Letters, 8*(6), 1060–1064. doi:10.1109/LGRS.2011.2155030

Gurram, P., & Kwon, H. (2011). Hyperspectral anomaly detection using an optimized support vector data description method. In *Proceedings of 2011 3rd Workshop on Hyperspectral Image and Signal Processing: Evolution in Remote Sensing (WHISPERS)*. Lisbon: IEEE. doi:10.1109/WHISPERS.2011.6080965

Gurram, P., Kwon, H., & Han, T. (2012). Sparse Kernel-Based Hyperspectral Anomaly Detection. *IEEE Geoscience and Remote Sensing Letters, 9*(5), 943–947. doi:10.1109/LGRS.2012.2187040

Harsanyi, J. C. (1993). *Detection and Classification of Subpixel Spectral Signatures in Hyperspectral Image Sequences*. (Doctoral dissertation). Université de Maryland Baltimore County.

Hazel, G. G. (2000). Multivariate Gaussian MRF for multispectral scene segmentation and anomaly detection. *IEEE Transactions on Geoscience and Remote Sensing, 38*(3), 1199–1211. doi:10.1109/36.843012

Heesung, K., & Nasrabadi, N. M. (2005). Kernel RX-algorithm: A nonlinear anomaly detector for hyperspectral imagery. *IEEE Transactions on Geoscience and Remote Sensing, 43*(2), 388–397. doi:10.1109/TGRS.2004.841487

Hu, X., Subbu, R., Bonissone, P., Qiu, H., & Iyer, N. (2008). Multivariate anomaly detection in real-world industrial systems. In *Proceedings of IEEE International Joint Conference on Neural Networks*. Hong Kong: IEEE.

Huck, A., & Guillaume, M. (2010). Asymptotically CFAR-Unsupervised Target Detection and Discrimination in Hyperspectral Images With Anomalous-Component Pursuit. *IEEE Transactions on Geoscience and Remote Sensing, 48*(11), 3980–3991.

Hytla, P., Hardie, R. C., Eismann, M. T., & Meola, J. (2007). Anomaly detection in hyperspectral imagery: a comparison of methods using seasonal data. In *Proceedings of SPIE 6565, Algorithms and Technologies for Multispectral, Hyperspectral, and Ultraspectral Imagery XIII*. Orlando, FL: SPIE. doi:10.1117/12.718381

Hyvärinen, A., & Oja, E. (2000). Independent component analysis: Algorithms and applications. *Neural Networks, Elsevier Science Ltd, 13*(4-5), 411–430. doi:10.1016/S0893-6080(00)00026-5 PMID:10946390

Jiayi, L., Hongyan, Z., & Liangpei, Z. (2014). Background joint sparse representation for hyperspectral image subpixel anomaly detection. In *Proceeding of 2014 IEEE International Geoscience and Remote Sensing Symposium (IGARSS)*. Quebec City, Canada: IEEE. doi:10.1109/IGARSS.2014.6946729

Johnson, R. J., Williams, J. P., & Bauer, K. W. (2013). AutoGAD: An Improved ICA-Based Hyperspectral Anomaly Detection Algorithm. *IEEE Transactions on Geoscience and Remote Sensing, 51*(6), 3492–3503. doi:10.1109/TGRS.2012.2222418

Khazai, S., Homayouni, S., Safari, A., & Mojaradi, B. (2011). Anomaly Detection in Hyperspectral Images Based on an Adaptive Support Vector Method. *IEEE Geoscience and Remote Sensing Letters, 8*(4), 646–650. doi:10.1109/LGRS.2010.2098842

Khazai, S., Safari, A., Mojaradi, B., & Homayouni, S. (2013). An Approach for Subpixel Anomaly Detection in Hyperspectral Images. *IEEE Journal of Selected Topics in Applied Earth Observations and Remote Sensing, 6*(2), 769–778. doi:10.1109/JSTARS.2012.2210277

Kim, D. H., & Finkel, L. H. (2003). Hyperspectral Image Processing Using Locally Linear Embedding. In *Proceedings of the 1st International IEEE EMBS Conference on Neural Engineering*. IEEE. doi:10.1109/CNE.2003.1196824

Kim, M. S. (2013). Robust, Scalable Anomaly Detection for Large Collections of Images. In *proceeding of International Conference on Social Computing (SocialCom)*. Alexandria, VA: IEEE. doi:10.1109/SocialCom.2013.170

Kraut, S., & Scharf, L. L. (1999). The CFAR adaptive subspace detector is a scale-invariant GLRT. *IEEE Transactions on Signal Processing, 47*(9), 2538–2541. doi:10.1109/78.782198

Kuybeda, O., Malah, D., & Barzohar, M. (2007). Rank Estimation and Redundancy Reduction of High-Dimensional Noisy Signals With Preservation of Rare Vectors. *IEEE Transactions on Signal Processing, 55*(12), 5579–5592. doi:10.1109/TSP.2007.901645

Kwon, H., Der, S. Z., & Nasrabadi, N. M. (2003). Adaptive anomaly detection using subspace separation for hyperspectral imagery. *Optical Engineering (Redondo Beach, Calif.), 42*(11), 3342–3351. doi:10.1117/1.1614265

Kwon, H., & Gurram, P. (2010). Optimal kernel bandwidth estimation for hyperspectral kernel-based anomaly detection. In *Proceedings of 2010 IEEE International Geoscience and Remote Sensing Symposium (IGARSS)*. Honolulu, HI: IEEE. doi:10.1109/IGARSS.2010.5649775

Kwon, H., & Gurram, P. (2010). Optimal kernel bandwidth estimation for hyperspectral kernel-based anomaly detection. In *Proceedings of the IEEE International Geoscience and Remote Sensing Symposium (IGARSS)*. Honolulu, HI: IEEE. doi:10.1109/IGARSS.2010.5649775

Kwon, H., & Nasrabadi, N. M. (2005). Kernel adaptive subspace detector for hyperspectral target detection. In *Proceedings of the IEEE International Conference on Acoustics, Speech, and Signal Processing, (ICASSP '05)*. IEEE.

Lee, Y., Yeh, Y.-R., & Wang, Y.-C. (2013). Anomaly Detection via Online Oversampling Principal Component Analysis. *IEEE Transactions on Knowledge and Data Engineering*, *25*(7), 1460–1470. doi:10.1109/TKDE.2012.99

Lehmann, E. L. (1993). The Fisher, Neyman-Pearson theories of testing hypotheses: One theory or two? *Journal of the American Statistical Association*, *88*(424), 1242–1249. doi:10.1080/01621459.1993.10476404

Li, W., Prasad, S., & Fowler, J. E. (2013). Integration of Spectral–Spatial Information for Hyperspectral Image Reconstruction From Compressive Random Projections. *IEEE Geoscience and Remote Sensing Letters*, *10*(6), 1379–1383. doi:10.1109/LGRS.2013.2242043

Liu, D., Guojing, H., & Zhang, J. (2008). Texture segmentation based anomaly detection in remote sensing images. *33rd International Conference on Infrared, Millimeter and Terahertz Waves, IRMMW-THz 2008*. Pasadena, CA: IEEE.

Liu, W., & Chang, Ch.-I. (2004). A nested spatial window-based approach to target detection for hyperspectral imagery. In *Proceedings of IEEE International Geoscience and Remote Sensing Symposium, IGARSS '04*. IEEE.

Liu, W.-M., & Chang, Ch.-I. (2013). Multiple-Window Anomaly Detection for Hyperspectral Imagery. *Selected Topics in IEEE Journal of Applied Earth Observations and Remote Sensing*, *6*(2), 644–658. doi:10.1109/JSTARS.2013.2239959

Liu, Z., Gu, Y., & Zhang, Y. (2010). Comparative Analysis of Feature Extraction Algorithms with Different Rules for Hyperspectral Anomaly Detection. In *Proceedings of 2010 First International Conference on Pervasive Computing Signal Processing and Applications (PCSPA)*. Harbin: IEEE. doi:10.1109/PCSPA.2010.78

Ma, L., Crawford, M. M., & Tian, J. (2010). Anomaly detection for hyperspectral images using local tangent space alignment. In *Proceedings of 2010 IEEE International Geoscience and Remote Sensing Symposium (IGARSS)*. Honolulu, HI: IEEE. doi:10.1109/IGARSS.2010.5652183

Matteoli, S., Diani, M., & Corsini, G. (2014). Impact of Signal Contamination on the Adaptive Detection Performance of Local Hyperspectral Anomalies. *IEEE Transactions on Geoscience and Remote Sensing*, *52*(4), 1948–1968. doi:10.1109/TGRS.2013.2256915

Matteoli, S., Veracini, T., Diani, M., & Corsini, G. (2013). A Locally Adaptive Background Density Estimator: An Evolution for RX-Based Anomaly Detectors. *IEEE Geoscience and Remote Sensing Letters*, *11*(1), 323–327. doi:10.1109/LGRS.2013.2257670

Messinger, D. W., & Albano, J. (2011). A graph theoretic approach to anomaly detection in hyperspectral imagery. In *Proceedings of 3rd Workshop on Hyperspectral Image and Signal Processing: Evolution in Remote Sensing (WHISPERS)*. Lisbon: IEEE. doi:10.1109/WHISPERS.2011.6080899

Molero, J. M., Garzon, E. M., Garcia, I., & Plaza, A. (2013). Analysis and Optimizations of Global and Local Versions of the RX Algorithm for Anomaly Detection in Hyperspectral Data. *Selected Topics in IEEE Journal of Applied Earth Observations and Remote Sensing, 6*(2), 801–814. doi:10.1109/JSTARS.2013.2238609

OReilly, C., Gluhak, A., Imran, M. A., & Rajasegarar, S.OReilly. (2014). Anomaly Detection in Wireless Sensor Networks in a Non-Stationary Environment. *IEEE Communications Surveys and Tutorials, 16*(3), 1413–1432. doi:10.1109/SURV.2013.112813.00168

Paz, A., & Plaza, A. (2010). Cluster versus GPU implementation of an Orthogonal Target Detection Algorithm for Remotely Sensed Hyperspectral Images. In *Proceedings of the IEEE International Conference on Cluster Computing (CLUSTER)*. Heraklion, Crete: IEEE. doi:10.1109/CLUSTER.2010.28

Reed, I. S., & Yu, X. (1990). Adaptive multiple-band CFAR detection of an optical pattern with unknown spectral distribution. *IEEE Transactions on Acoustics, Speech, and Signal Processing, 38*(10), 1760–1770. doi:10.1109/29.60107

Ren, H., Du, Q., Wang, J., Chang, Ch.-I., Jensen, J. O., & Jensen, J. L. (2006). Automatic target recognition for hyperspectral imagery using high-order statistics. *IEEE Transactions on Aerospace and Electronic Systems, 42*(4), 1372–1385. doi:10.1109/TAES.2006.314578

Robila, S. A., & Varshney, P. K. (2002). Target detection in hyperspectral images based on independent component analysis. In *Proceedings of the 12th SPIE* 4726, *Automatic Target Recognition*. Orlando, FL: SPIE. doi:10.1117/12.477024

Salem, O., Guerassimov, A., Mehaoua, A., Marcus, A., & Furht, B. (2013). Sensor fault and patient anomaly detection and classification in medical wireless sensor networks. In *Proceedings of the IEEE International Conference on Communications (ICC)*. Budapest: IEEE.

Schweizer, S. M., & Moura, J. M. F. (2000). Hyperspectral imagery: Clutter adaptation in anomaly detection. *IEEE Transactions on Information Theory, 46*(5), 1855–1871. doi:10.1109/18.857796

Srivastava, A. N., & Zane-Ulman, B. (2005). Discovering recurring anomalies in text reports regarding complex space systems. In *Proceedings of the IEEE Aerospace Conference*. Big Sky, MT: IEEE. doi:10.1109/AERO.2005.1559692

Veracini, T., Matteoli, S., Diani, M., & Corsini, G. (2011). An anomaly detection architecture based on a data-adaptive density estimation. In *Proceedings of 2011 3rd Workshop on Hyperspectral Image and Signal Processing: Evolution in Remote Sensing (WHISPERS)*. Lisbon: IEEE. doi:10.1109/WHISPERS.2011.6080919

Wang, Y.-L., Zhao, Ch.-H., & Wang, Y. (2011). Anomaly detection using subspace band section based RX algorithm. In *Proceedings of 2011 International Conference on Multimedia Technology (ICMT)*. Hangzhou: IEEE.

Xun, L., & Fang, Y. (2006). Anomaly Detection Based on High-order Statistics in Hyperspectral Imagery. In *Proceedings of the Sixth World Congress on Intelligent Control and Automation*. Dalia: IEEE.

Yu, Y., & Wu, H. (2012). Anomaly intrusion detection based upon data mining techniques and fuzzy logic. In *Proceedings of the IEEE International Conference on Systems, Man, and Cybernetics (SMC)*. Seoul: IEEE. doi:10.1109/ICSMC.2012.6377776

Yuan, Z., Sun, H., Ji, K., Li, Zh., & Zou, H. (2014). Local Sparsity Divergence for Hyperspectral Anomaly Detection. *IEEE Geoscience and Remote Sensing Letters*, *11*(10), 1697–1701. doi:10.1109/LGRS.2014.2306209

Zhang, M., Raghunathan, A., & Jha, N. K. (2013). MedMon: Securing Medical Devices Through Wireless Monitoring and Anomaly Detection. *IEEE Transactions on Biomedical Circuits and Systems*, *7*(6), 871–881. doi:10.1109/TB-CAS.2013.2245664 PMID:24473551

Zhao, R., Du, B., & Zhang, L. (2014). A Robust Nonlinear Hyperspectral Anomaly Detection Approach. *IEEE Journal of Selected Topics in Applied Earth Observations and Remote Sensing*, *7*(4), 1227–1234. doi:10.1109/JSTARS.2014.2311995

KEY TERMS AND DEFINITIONS

Anomaly Detection: A blind detection of objects from hyperspectral images that deviate from the rest of the image.

Feature Selection Based Anomaly Detectors: Detectors that start by selecting features from the image, before anomaly detection, and use these features for the differentiation between anomalies and the background.

Hyperspectral Images: A satellite image collected over hundreds of spectral bands that are narrow over a continuous spectral range. Every pixel illustrates the behavior of objects sun light reflection.

Kernel Based Anomaly Detectors: Detectors that use kernel strategies to separate the few pixels of the image that diverge from the background.

RX Detector: An anomaly detection approach that took the name of its founders Reed and Xioli. It consists in calculating the statistical difference between the image pixels to look for anomalies.

Segmentation Based Anomaly Detectors: Anomaly detection approaches that are based on the segmentation of the hyperspectral image for the discrimination of the background pixels and then the deduction of anomalies.

Statistic Based Anomaly Detectors: Anomaly detectors that use statistical metrics to calculate the difference between pixels of the background and anomalies.

Chapter 8
Cloud–Based Image Fusion Using Guided Filtering

Piyush Kumar Shukla
UIT RGPV, India

Madhuvan Dixit
Millennium Institute of Technology and Science, India

ABSTRACT

Current image coding with image fusion schemes make it hard to utilize external images for transform even if highly correlated images can be found in the cloud. To solve this problem, we explain an approach of cloud-based image transform coding with image fusion methodwhich is distinguish from exists image fusion method. A fast and efficient image fusion technique is proposed for creating a highly generated fused image through merging multiple corresponding images. The proposed technique is based on a two-scale decomposition of an image into a low layer containing large scale variations, and a detail layer acquiring small scale details. A novel approach of guided filtering-based weighted average method is proposed to make full use of spatial consistency for merge of the base and detail layers. Analytical results represent that the proposed technique can obtain state-of-the-art performance for image fusion of multispectral, multifocus, multimodal, and multiexposure images.

INTRODUCTION

Image fusion is an important technique for various image processing and computer vision applications such as feature extraction and target recognition. Through image fusion, different images of the same scene can be combined into a single fused image (A. A. Goshtasby, 2007). The fused image can provide more comprehensive information about the scene which is more useful for human and machine perception. For instance, the performance of feature extraction algorithms can be improved by fusing multi-spectral remote sensing images (Socolinsky, 2002). The fusion of multi-exposure images can be used for digital photography (Shen 2011). In these applications, a good image fusion method has the following properties. First, it can preserve most of the useful information of differ-

DOI: 10.4018/978-1-4666-8654-0.ch008

ent images. Second, it does not produce artifacts. Third, it is robust to imperfect conditions such as mis-registration and noise.

Image search has been demonstrated as a successful application on the Internet (Mandic, 2009). By submitting the description of one image,including semantic content (Mandic, 2009), outline (Crow,1984), (Rockinger, 1997), and local feature descriptors (Zeng, 2012), (Varshney, 2011), one can easily retrieve many similar images. Near and partial duplicate image detection is a hot research topic in this field (Zeng, 2012), (Tang, 2010), (Szeliski, 2008). However, the purpose of image search is not to generate an image from search results. In fact, reconstructing a given image from similar images is tougher than the image search itself.

LITERATURE REVIEW

A large number of image fusion methods (Wang, 2004)– (Mandic, 2009) have been proposed in literature. Among these methods, multi-scale image fusion (Cruz, 2004) and data-driven image fusion (Mandic, 2009) are very successful methods. They focus on different data representations, e.g., multi-scale co-efficient Crow, (Jan. 1984), (Rockinger, 1997), or data driven decomposition co-efficient (Mandic, 2009), (Zeng, 2012) and different image fusion rules to guide the fusion of co-efficient. The major advantage of these methods is that they can well preserve the details of different source images. However, these kinds of methods may produce brightness and color distortions since spatial consistency is not well considered in the fusion process. To make full use of spatial context, optimization based image fusion approaches, e.g., generalized random walks (Shen 2011), and Markov random fields (Rockinger, 1997) based methods have been proposed. These methods focus on estimating spatially smooth and edge-aligned weights by solving an energy function and then fusing the source images by weighted average of

pixel values. However, optimization based methods have a common limitation, i.e., inefficiency, since they require multiple iterations to find the global optimal solution. Moreover, another drawback is that global optimization based methods may over-smooth the resulting weights, which is not good for fusion(Varshney, 2011).

SIFT descriptors, proposed by Lowe in Tang, (Sep. 2010), present distinctive invariant features of images that consist of location, scale, orientation, and feature vector. The scale and location of SIFT descriptors are determined by maxima and minima of difference-of-Gaussian images. One orientation is assigned to each SIFT descriptor according to the dominant direction of the local gradient histogram. The feature vector is a 128-dimension vector that characterizes a local region by gradient histogram in different directions. Since SIFT descriptors have a good interpretation of the response properties of complex neurons in the visual cortex (Smith, 1981) and an excellent practical performance, they have been extensively applied to object recognition, image retrieval, 3D reconstruction, annotation, watermarking, and so on.

IMAGE IN CLOUD RESOURCES

The cloud is characterized by a large amount of computing resources, storage, and data(A. A. Goshtasby, 2007). Imagining a cloud that collects a huge number of images, e.g., Google street view images (Socolinsky, 2002), when you randomly take a picture with your phone on the street, you can often find some highly correlated images in the cloud that were taken at the same location at different view- points and angles, focal lengths, and illuminations. If you try to share the photo with friends through the cloud, it is problematic to use conventional image coding (e.g., JPEG) that usually provides only 8:1 compression ratio (Shen 2011). It will consume a lot of precious power and network bandwidth to transmit such a high-resolution and high-quality JPEG image. It would be more convenient to take advantage of the cloud for compression and transmission if there is a high probability of finding very similar images in the cloud.

Image inpainting is the task of filling in or replacing a region of an image (Liu, 2008). Many approaches have been proposed to learn from known regions of an image and then recover an unknown region from what has been learned. Hays et al. are the first to propose image completion from a large-scale image database (Dorsey, 2002). The proposed approach uses GIST descriptors to retrieve images of similar scenes that are applied to recover unknown region of an image. Later propose retrieving images of the same scene from the Internet via viewpoint invariant search and replacing a user specified region (Smith, 1981).

Image composition can be viewed as the recovery of all objects in an image. The objects are only represented by input sketch. It is a much tougher problem than image inpainting and completion. Human interactions are required in current sketch-to-photo schemes. Although it requires only a small number of bits to represent a sketch and text labels, it is unacceptable to compress an image using interactions. From the compression viewpoint, composed images must look like input images in detail. But for an input sketch, image composition may generate quite different results in color and texture. Taking CG (Computer Graphics) images as input is an improvement over sketch (Philips, 2007).

CLOUD BASED IMAGE TRANSFORMATION

The block diagram of the proposed cloud-based image encoder is shown in figure 1. For the input image, a down-sampled image is first generated and compressed. SIFT descriptors are also extracted from the original image. The location, scale, and orientation of every extracted SIFT descriptor guide to extract a feature vector as prediction from the decompressed image after up-sampling. Finally, the prediction is subtracted from the feature vector. All components of SIFT

Figure 1. The block diagram of the proposed cloud-based image encoder

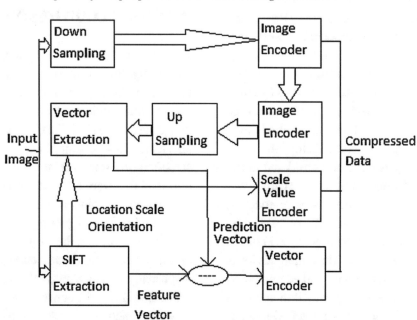

descriptors are compressed and transmitted to the cloud with the compressed down-sampled image.

The block diagram of the proposed cloud-based image de- coder is depicted in figure 2. In the cloud, a server first decompresses the down-sampled image and SIFT data. By using the decompressed location, scale, and orientation of every SIFT descriptor again, one prediction vector, exactly the same as that in figure 1, is extracted from the decompressed image after up-sampling. Then, the SIFT feature vector is reconstructed by adding the prediction. To reconstruct the input image, decompressed SIFT descriptors are used to retrieve highly correlated image patches.For everyretrieved image patch,we estimatethe transformation and then stitch it to the up-sampled decompressed image. Finally, a high-resolution and high-quality image is obtained.

IMAGE FUSION

A large number of image fusion methods (Wang, 2004)– (Mandic, 2009) have been proposed in literature. Among these methods, multi-scale

image fusion (Cruz, 2004) and data-driven image fusion (Mandic, 2009) are very successful methods. They focus on different data representations, e.g., multi-scale coefficients Crow, (Jan. 1984), (Rockinger, 1997), or data driven decomposition coefficients (Mandic, 2009), (Zeng, 2012) and different image fusion rules to guide the fusion of coefficients. The major advantage of these methods is that they can well preserve the details of different source images. However, these kinds of methods may produce brightness and color distortions sincespatial consistency is not well considered in the fusion process. To make full use of spatial context, optimization based image fusion approaches, e.g., generalized random walks (Shen 2011), and Markov random fields (Varshney, 2011) based methods have been proposed. These methods focus on estimating spatially smooth and edge- aligned weights by solving an energy function and then fusing the source images by weighted average of pixel values. However, optimization based methods have a common limitation, i.e., inefficiency, since they require multiple iterations to find the global optimal solution. Moreover, another drawback is that global optimization

Figure 2. The block diagram of the proposed cloud-based image decoder

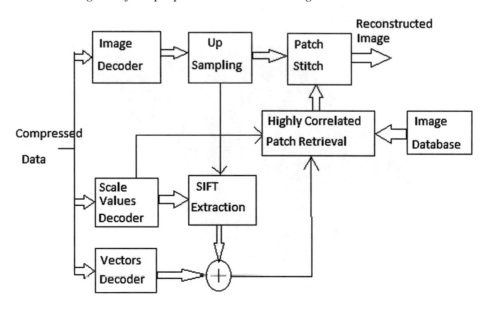

based methods may over-smooth the resulting weights, which is not good for fusion. To solve the problems mentioned above, a novel image fusion method with guided filtering is proposed in this paper. Experimental results show that the proposed method gives a performance comparable with state-of-the-art fusion approaches. Several advantages of the proposed image fusion approach are highlighted in the following. 1) Traditional multi-scale image fusion methods require more than two scales to obtain satisfactory fusion results. The key contribution of this paper is to present a fast two-scale fusion method which does not rely heavily on a specific image decomposition method. A simple average filter is qualified for the proposed fusion framework. 2) A novel weight construction method is proposed to combine pixel saliency and spatial context for image fusion. Instead of using optimization based methods, guided filtering is adopted as a local filtering method for image fusion. 3) An important observation of this paper is that the roles of two measures, i.e., pixel saliency and spatial consistency are quite different when fusing different layers. In this paper, the roles of pixel saliency and spatial consistency are controlled through adjusting the parameters of the guided filter.

GUIDED FILTERING: A METHOD OF IMAGE FUSION

Recently, edge-preserving filters (Tang, 2010), (Szeliski, 2008) have been an active research topic in image processing. Edge-preserving smoothing filters such as guided filter (Tang, 2010), weighted least squares (Szeliski, 2008), and bilateral filter (Dorsey, 2002) can avoid ringing artifacts since they will not blur strong edges in the decomposition process. Among them, the guided filter is a recently proposed edge-preserving filter, and the computing time of which is independent of the filter size. Furthermore, the guided filter is based on a local linear model, making it qualified for other applications such as image matting, up-sampling and colorization (Tang, 2010). In this paper, the guided filter is first applied for image fusion. In theory, the guided filter assumes that the filtering output O is a linear transformation of the guidance image I in a local window ω_k centered at pixel k (see Figure 3).

$$O_i = a_k I_i + b_k \forall i \in \omega_k \tag{1}$$

where, ω_k is a tile window of size $(2r+1)\times(2r+1)$. The linear value coefficients a_k and b_k are constant

Figure 3. Illustration of window choice

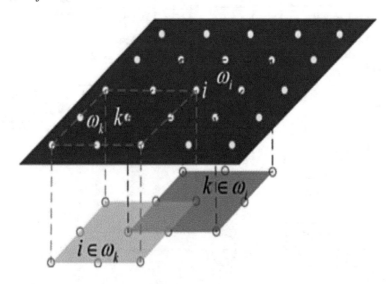

value in ω_k and can be calculated by reducing the squared difference between the output picture O and the input picture P.

$$E(a_k, b_k) = \sum_{i \in \omega_k} ((a_k I_i + b_k - P_i)^2 + ea_k^2)$$

(2)

where e is a regularization argumentsupply by the user. The coefficients value a_k and b_k can be directly solved by linear regression value (Smith, 1981) as follows:

$$a_k = \frac{\frac{1}{|\omega|} \sum_{i \in \omega_k} I_i P_i - \mu_k \overline{P_k}}{\delta_k + e}$$

(3)

$$b_k = \overline{P_k} - a_k \mu_k$$

(4)

whereμ_k and δ_k are the mean and variance value of I in ω_k respectively, $|\omega|$ is the no. of pixels in ω_k, and P_k is the mean of P in ω_k. Next, the result image can be calculated as per equation to (1). As shown in Fig. 1, all local value windows centered at pixel k in the window $\omega_i$that will contain pixel i. So, the cost of O_i in (1) will change when it is computed in different windows ω_k. To solve this question, all the possible costs of coefficients a_k and b_k are first averaged. Then, the filtering output is estimated as follows:

$$O_i = \overline{a_i} I_i + \overline{b_i}$$

(5)

where

$$\overline{a_i} = \frac{1}{|\omega|} \sum_{k \in \omega_i} a_k, \overline{b_i} = \frac{1}{|\omega|} \sum_{k \in \omega_i} b_k.$$

In this chapter $G_{r,e}(P,I)$ is used to represent the guided filtering operation, where r and e are the parameters which decide the filter size and blur degree of the guided filter, respectively. Moreover, P and I refer to the input image and guidance image,respectively. Furthermore, when the input is a color image, the filtering output can be obtained by conducting the guided filteringon the red, green, and blue channels of the input image, respectively. And when the guidance image I is a color image, the guided filter should be extended by the following steps. First, Equation (1) is rewritten as follows:

$$O_i = a_k^T I_i + b_k, \forall i \in \omega_k$$

(6)

wherea_k is a 3×1 coefficient vector and I_i is a 3×1 color vector. Then, similar to (3)–(5), the output of guided filtering can be calculated as follows:

$$a_k = (\sum_k + eU)(\frac{1}{|\omega|}) \sum_{i \in \omega_k} I_i p_i - \mu_k \overline{P_k}$$

(7)

$$b_k = \overline{p_k} - a_k^T \mu_k$$

(8)

$$O_i = \overline{a_i}^T I_i + \overline{b_i}$$

(9)

whereΣ_k is the 3×3 covariance matrix of I in ω_k, andU is the 3×3 identity matrix.

CLOUD BASED IMAGE FUSION

Some of the techniques from existing research work being used in my chapter work. These technique are listed below

SCALE INVARIENT FEATURE DESCRIPTOR (SIFT)

Images of one scene may be taken from different viewpoints or may suffer transformations such as rotation, noise etc (Socolinsky, 2002;Wolff, 2002)- (Mandic, 2009). So it is likely that two images of the same scene will be different. The task of finding similarity correspondences between two images of the same scene or object has thus become a challenging problem in a number of vision applications. Such applications range from image registration, camera calibration, object recognition, scene localization in navigation systems, image retrieval based search engines etc. For image matching, extraction of such information (i.e. features) is required from the images which can provide reliable matching between different viewpoints of the same image. Feature detection occurs within an image and seeks to describe only those parts of that image where we can get unique information or signatures (i.e. feature descriptors). During training, feature descriptors are extracted

from sample images and stored. In classification, feature descriptors of a query image are then matched with all trained image features and the trained image giving maximum correspondence is considered the best match. Feature descriptor matching can be based on distances such as Euclidean, Mahalanobis or distance ratios. For detect feature descriptors, we use SIFT method (Rockinger, 1997). SIFT Feature Descriptor detector has four main stages namely as

- Scale-space extrema detection.
- Keypoint localization.
- Orientation computation.
- Key point descriptor extraction.

In SIFT, we have to perform following process Assume that, Take a 16 x16 window area that around interest node.Separate into a 4x4 grid of rectangular cells.Compute histogram of image gradient directions in each rectangular cell (8 bins each). 16 histograms x 8 orientations = 128 feature descriptors (see Figures 4 through 6).

Figure 4. Computing process of keypoint descriptor

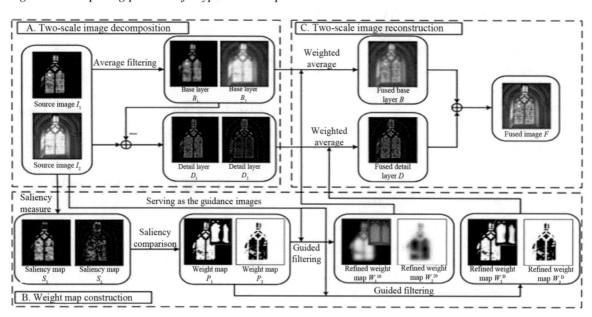

Figure 5. Evaluate scale space with its octave

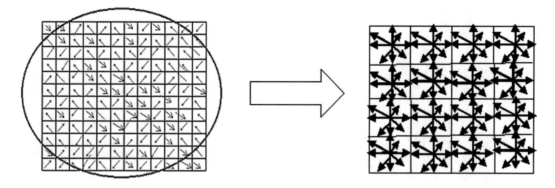

Figure 6. Finding DoG from different scales

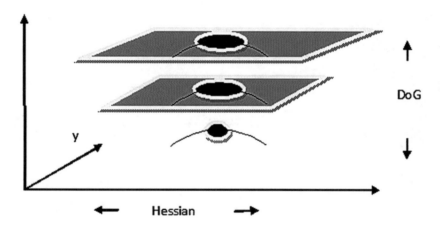

SCALE SPACE EXTREMA DETECTION

In this stage, we can extract scale-space and rotation invariant interest points. BFind local maximum of region of interest (ROI) of image dataset, Hessian mapping in scale-space DoG (Difference of Gaussian) in scale (see Figure 5).

DoG image dataset nodes are grouped by octaves (for example doubling of σ_0)Constant number of levels per octave (see Figure 6).

$$D(x, y, \sigma) = L(x, y, k\sigma) - L(x, y, \sigma)$$

- Here $L(x, y, \sigma) = G(x, y, \sigma) * I(x, y)$
- Image dataset within each given octave are divided by a fixed factor k

- If each given octave is separated in s-1 intervals:

$$k^s = 2 \text{ or } k = 2^{1/s}$$

The Gaussian Scale-space of first given octave can be represented as follows. This scale-space is generated from every region of interest of image datasets (see Figure 7)

Parameters were chosen practically based on set of key point

1. Iteratively
2. Localization
3. Dataset Matching Accuracy

From Lowe's reference paper:

Figure 7. Gaussian scale space

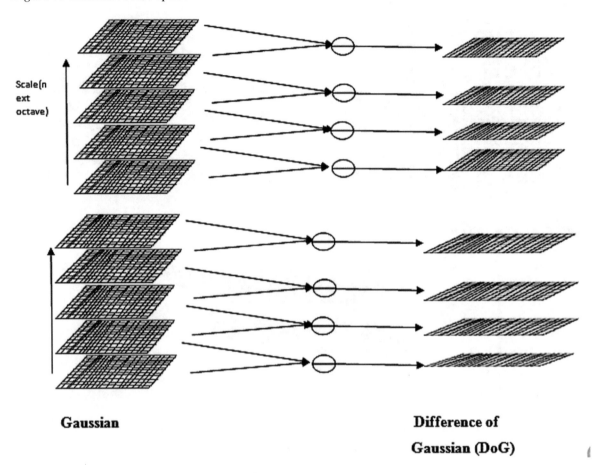

Gaussian

Difference of Gaussian (DoG)

Number of scale-spaces per octave: 3

$\sigma_0 = 1.6$

Extract local level extreme in DoG scale-space. Comparison of each node to its 8 nearest nodes at the same level of image dataset nodes, nine nearest nodes in the level mentioned above, and 9 nearest nodes in the level below. In following layout, represent three different scale-spaces, in this situation every feature descriptors is covered from nearest feature descriptors. These feature descriptors are represented from the SIFT approach. The feature descriptors of an image dataset reflect the different feature descriptor of image dataset like shape, texture, color features (see Figure 8).

KEYPOINTS LOCALIZATION

Examine the place and scale-space of key points to sub-pixel and sub-scale spaces accuracy by up to date fitting a 3D quadratic polynomial form

Keypoint place

$$X_i = (x_i, y_i, \sigma_i)$$

Offset value

$$\Delta X = (x - x_i, y - y_i, \sigma - \sigma_i)$$

Sub-pixel, sub-scale space calculated place

$$X_i \leftarrow X_i + \Delta X$$

Figure 8. Scale space with its neighbors

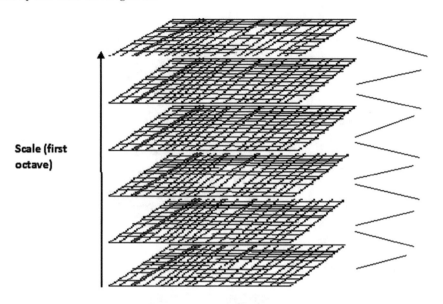

Scale (first octave)

Substantial performance to matching and stability neglect key points have low contrast ratio. Sensitive to noise ratio If $|D(X_i + \Delta X)| < 0.03$ neglect key points for example, consider that image dataset values have been normalized range in [0,1].Neglect nodes lying on sides (or being close to edges) Harris uses the auto-correlation two dimensional array

$$A_W(x, y) = \sum_{x \in W, y \in W} \begin{bmatrix} f_x^2 & f_x f_y \\ f_x f_y & f_y^2 \end{bmatrix}$$

$R(A_W) = \det(A_W) - \alpha \operatorname{trace}^2(A_W)$ or $R(A_W) = \lambda_1 \lambda_2 - \alpha (\lambda_1 + \lambda_2)^2$

SIFT approach uses the Hessian 2d array. For example, Hessian encodes the principal curvatures.

α=largest eigen cost (λ_{max}),
β= smallest eigen cost (λ_{min}),

(Proportional to standard curvatures) (see Figure 9)

$$T_r(H) = D_{xx} + D_{yy} = \alpha + \beta$$
$$Det(H) = D_{xx} D_{yy} - (D_{xy})^2$$
$$\frac{T_r(H)^2}{Det(H)} = \frac{(\alpha + \beta)^2}{\alpha\beta} = \frac{(r\beta + \beta)^2}{r\beta^2} = \frac{(r+1)^2}{r}$$

where, $r = \alpha/\beta$. Neglect key point if:

$$\frac{Tr(H)^2}{Det(H)} < \frac{(r+1)^2}{r} \text{ (SIFT uses r = 10).}$$

ORIENTATION ASSIGNMENT

Construct histogram of gradient (HoG) directions, within a domain around the given key point, at choose scale-space (see Figure 10).

Figure 9. (a) 233x189 image (b) 832 DoG extrema (c) 729 left after low contrast threshold (d) 536 left after testing ratio based on Hessian

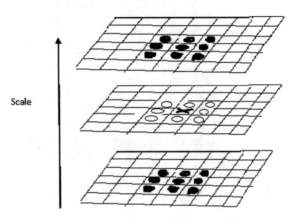

Figure 10. Histogram form of orientation

(a)   (b)

(c)   (d)

$$L(x, y, \sigma) = G(x, y, \sigma) * I(x, y)$$

$$m(x,y) = \sqrt{\begin{array}{l}(L(x+1,y)-L(x-1,y))^2 \\ +(L(x,y+1)-L(x,y-1))^2\end{array}}$$

$$\theta(x, y) = a\tan2((L(x, y+1) - L(x, y-1))/(L(x+1, y) - L(x-1, y)))$$

36 bins histogram entries are weighted cost by (i) gradient magnitude value and (ii) a Gaussian

mapping with σ equal to 2.5 times the scale-space of the key point assign a principal orientation at peak of smoothed histogram (exact oval tobetter localize peak).For calculating the effectiveness of low bitrates feature descriptors, we can use two different data sets provided by Scientists Winder and Brown in their most recent task (Dorsey, 2002).From the ranges between matching and non-matching pairs of feature descriptors, we achieve a Receiver Operating Characteristic (ROC) curve which draws correct match value against incor-

Figure 11. Processing of orientation

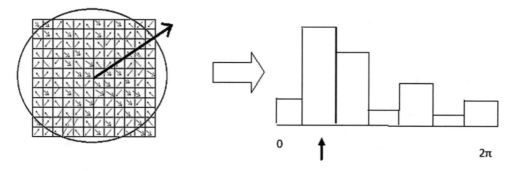

rect match value. For a legal comparison at the authentic same bitrates, we assume that the Equal Error Rate (EER) node on the distinguish ROC plotsfor each scheme (see Figure 11).

In the case of highest within 80% of max peak, multiple principal orientations applied to key points. About 25% of key points have been multiple principal orientations applied. Significantly increase performance stability of desired matching.

KEYPOINTS DESCRIPTOR EXTRACTION

We consider that a 16x16 window around detected interest key point. Separate into a 4x4 grid of rectangular cells. Estimate the histogram in each cell grid. Local image features descriptors have been protected in the areas of computer vision technique and image retrieval. Feature descriptors compression approach is play for decrement in storage and distribution in mobile visual find applications.

Each histogram entry is cost by (i) gradient absolute value and (ii) a Gaussian level mapping with σ equal to 1.5 times the width of the image feature descriptors of area window (see Figure 12).

Distribution node histogram entries into adjacent dataset bin. Each level entry is added to all existing bins, and multiplication is perform, by a value of 1-d, where d is the express as limited distance from the bin whichit belongs to aimage dataset.

Figure 12. Process for finding key point descriptors

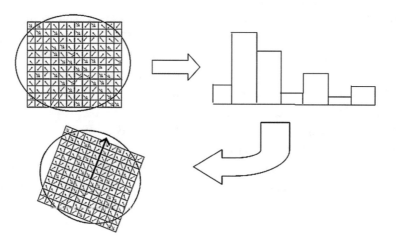

Figure 13. Schematic diagram of the proposed image fusion method based on guided filtering

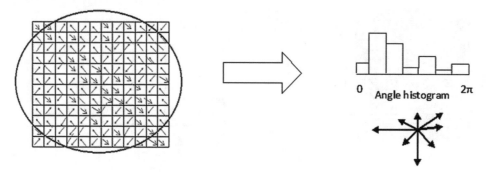

Descriptor based on two main parameters:

1. Number of orientations scale s
2. m x m matrix of orientation histograms levels

The no. of feature descriptor is sm^2, SIFT: s=8, m=4

Features Descriptor = 128

Normalization to unit distance is sufficient 128 features descriptor non-linear illumination changes in dataset. Consequently, the feature descriptor is modified to reduce the effects of light illumination change. First, the descriptor is normalized to unit distance. A modification in image contrast in which each pixel value of ROI is multiplied by a fixed value will multiply gradients by the same fixed value, since this contrast modification will be rejected by vector normalization procedure. A illumination changes that a fixed value is added to each image pixel ROI will not affect the gradient data values, as they are calculated from pixel differences. Hence, the descriptors is invariant scale to desired affine changes in illumination levels. Therefore, linear or non-linear illumination changes can also be occur due to camera light saturation or due to illumination modification that affect 3D surfaces with differing orientations by different amounts.

IMAGE FUSION WITH GUIDED FILTERING

In following figure the main processes of the proposed guided filtering based fusion method (GFF). First, an average filter is utilized to get the two-scale representations. Then, the base and detail layers are fused through using a guided filtering based weighted average method.

A. Two-Scale Image Decomposition

As shown in following figure, the source images are first decomposed into two-scale representations by average filtering. The lower layer of each given image is obtained in following way (see Figure 13):

$$B_n = I_n * Z \qquad (10)$$

where I_n is the nth source image, Z is the average value of filter, and the size of the filter is conventionally fixed. Once the lower layer is found, the detail layer can be found by subtracting the lower layer from the source image.

$$D_n = I_n - B_n. \qquad (11)$$

The two-scale decomposition step concerns at separating each source image into a lower layer consisting the large-scale variations in intensity level and an another layer containing the small-scale details.

B. Weight Map Construction With Guided Filtering

The weight map is constructed as follows as per above figure. First, Laplacian filtering is applied to each given image to obtain the high-pass image H_n.

$$H_n = I_n * L \tag{12}$$

where L is a 3×3 Laplacian filter matrix. Then, the local average of the value of H_n is used to design the saliency maps S_n.

$$S_n = |H_n| * g_{rg,\sigma g} \tag{13}$$

g is a Gaussian low-pass filter, and the parameters rg and σg are set to 5. The measured saliency maps support good characterization level of the saliency of detail information. Next, the saliency value are compared to determine the weight maps as follows:

$$P_n^k = \begin{cases} 1 \\ 0 \end{cases} \tag{14}$$

1 if $S_n^k = \max(S_1^k, S_2^k, ..., S_N^k)$, 0 otherwise

where N is number of given images, S_n^k is the saliency value of the pixel k in the nth image. However, the weight value obtained above are usually noisy and not aligned with object boundaries, which may produce artifacts to the fused image. Using spatial consistency is an effective way to solve this problem. Spatial consistency means that if two adjacent pixels have similar brightness or color, they will tend to have similar weights. A popular spatial consistency based fusion approach is formulating an energy function, where the pixel saliencies are encoded in the

function and edge aligned weights are enforced by regularization terms, e.g., a smoothness term. This energy function can be then minimized globally to obtain the desired weight maps. However, the optimization based methods are often relatively inefficient.an interesting alternative to optimization based methods is proposed. Guided image filtering is performed on each weight map P_n with the corresponding source image I_n serving as the guidance image.

$$W_n^B = G_{r1,e1}(P_n, I_n) \tag{15}$$

$$W_n^D = G_{r2,e2}(P_n, I_n) \tag{16}$$

where r_1, e_1, r_2, and r_2 are the parameters of the guided filter, W_n^B and W_n^D are the resulting weight maps of the base and detail layers. Finally, the values of the N weight maps are normalized such that they sum to one at each pixel k.

The motivation of the proposed weight construction method is as follows. According to (1), (3) and (4), it can be seen that if the local variance at a position i is very small which means that the pixel is in a flat area of the guidance image, then a_k will become close to 0 and the filtering output O will equal to $\overline{P_k}$ i.e., the average of adjacent input pixels. In contrast, if the local variance of pixel i is very large which means that the pixel i is in an edge area, then a_k will become far from zero. As demonstrated in (Tang, 2010), $\nabla O \approx \overline{a} \nabla I$ will become true, which means that only the weights in one side of the edge will be averaged. In both situations, those pixels with similar color or brightness tend to have similar weights. This is exactly the principle of spatial consistency.

Furthermore, as shown in above figure, the base layers look spatially smooth and thus the corresponding weights also should be spatially smooth. Otherwise, artificial edges may be produced. In contrast, sharp and edge-aligned weights are preferred for fusing the detail layers since details may be lost when the weights are over-smoothed. Therefore, a large filter size and a large blur degree are preferred for fusing the base layers, while a small filter size and a small blur degree are preferred for the detail layers.

C. Two-Scale Image Reconstruction

Two-scale image reconstruction consists of the following two steps. First, the base and detail layers of different source images are fused together by weighted averaging

$$\overline{B} = \sum_{n=1}^{N} W_n^B B_n \qquad (17)$$

$$\overline{D} = \sum_{n=1}^{N} W_n^D D_n \qquad (18)$$

Then, the fused image F is obtained by combining the fused base layer $\overline{B}$ and the fused detail layer $\overline{D}$

$$F = \overline{B} + \overline{D} \qquad (19)$$

FRAMEWORK

The proposed method of my chapter work is CBIF-Guided Filtering (Cloud Based Image Fusion Using Guided Filtering. CBIF technique is based on generic SIFT method, which is used for finding the keypoint descriptor. Guided Filtering is used for find fused image from image descriptor. This method increases the accuracy of pixel ratio of fused image. Hence, we are explain the proposed CBIF (Content Based Image Fusion) based on Guided Filtering method.The potential of the CBIF-Guided Filtering is illustrated on a 3D object recognition task using the Coil database.

The images are either represented by a matrix of their pixel values (bitmap representation) or by a color histogram. In both cases, the proposed system requires feature extraction and performs recognition on images regarded as points of a space of high dimension. The feature extraction is perform by SIFT scheme. We also purpose an extension of the basic color histogram which keeps more about the information contained in the images.

The Algorithm of proposed method is explained below:

Algorithm: [retimageArray] = CBIF_ GuidedFilter(imagedataset)

Step 1: Consider the image dataset are resize into 200x300 size.

Step 2: Given all the images of image dataset is partitioned into 2x3 array.

Step 3: Now we find out the SIFT descriptors of each image patch of cell array for image of image dataset. SIFT method perform the following sequence of steps for find the keypoint descriptors for texture feature.

  ○ **Scale-Space Extreme Detection in Image:**The initial step of evaluation finds total all scale-space and different image area in image dataset nodes (Wang, 2004). It is completely apply effectively by using a Difference-of-Gaussian (DoG) mapping to represents potential interest keypoints of feature descriptors whichare scale invariant and orientation in image dataset nodes (Mandic, 2009).

  ○ **Keypoints Localization:**All candidate area of image in selected ROI (Region of Interest), a detailed prototype is fit to analyze keypoints area and its scale-space (Cruz, 2004). Keypoints of image area in image ROI are chooses basis on calculate ofexisting stability (Mandic, 2009).

- ○ **OrientationAssignment:** One or more orientations task are applied to each keypoints area based on local image data nodes gradient directions (Socolinsky, 2002;Wolff, 2002). Each and every future image operations are implemented on image keypoint dataset which has been transformed relative to the applied orientation, scale, and location for each feature descriptor, hence providing in variance to these transformations in image data nodes (Mandic, 2009).
- ○ **Keypoints Descriptor:** The local image gradients value are measured at the choose scale-space in the Region of Interest(ROI) around all keypoints in image dataset points (Wang, 2004). These are transformed in to a presentation that permits for significant levels of local shape, location and orientation andchanges inillumination of image dataset points (Mandic, 2009).

Step 4: Above step are perform in repeated form, then all the descriptor of images are store, now apply Guided Filtering method for retrieving fused images.

Step 5: In Guided Filtering, apply two-scale image decomposition for finding the base layer of each source image from image database.

Step 6: Now apply weight map construction with guided filtering for finding detail layer of each source image from image database.

Step 7: Now image reconstruction on the base layer and detail layer of each source image. Hence, the reconstruct image is taken as fused image.

IMPLEMENTATION

Experiments are performed on three image databases, i.e., the Petrovic´ database (Petrovic´, 2007)

which contains 50 pairs of images including aerial images, outdoor images (natural, industrial) and indoor images (with different focus points and exposure settings), the multi-focus image database which contains 10 pairs of multi-focus images, and the multi-exposure and multi-modal image database which contains 2 pairs of color multi-exposure images and 8 pairs of multi-modal images. The testing images have been used in many related papers (Shen 2011)–(Zeng, 2012),(Piella, 2009). The proposed guided filtering based fusion method (GFF) is compared with seven image fusion algorithms based on Laplacian pyramid (LAP) Crow, (Jan. 1984), stationary wavelet transform (SWT) (Rockinger, 1997), curvelet transform (CVT), nonsubsampled contourlet transform (NSCT) (Philips, 2007), generalized random walks (GRW) (Shen 2011), wavelet-based statistical sharpness measure (WSSM) and high order singular value decomposition (HOSVD) (Zeng, 2012), respectively. The parameter settings of these methods are as follows. Four decomposition levels, the "averaging" scheme for the low-pass sub-band, the absolute maximum choosing scheme for the band-pass sub-band and the 3×3 window based consistency check are adopted for the LAP, CVT, SWT, and NSCT method. Four decomposition levels with 4, 8, 8, 16 directions from coarser scale to finer scale are adopted for the NSCT method. Furthermore, the default parameters given by the respective authors are adopted for the GRW, WSSM and HOSVD based methods.

In order to assess the fusion performance of different methods objectively, five fusion quality metrics, i.e., information theory based metric (QMI (Nahavandi,2008)), structure based metrics (QY (Liu, 2008) and QC (Canagarajah, 2005)) and feature based metrics (QG (Petrovic´, 2000) and QP (Liu, 2007)) are adopted. A good survey and comparative study of these quality metrics can be found in Z. Liu et al.'s work (Liu, 2007). The default parameters given in the related publications are adopted for these quality indexes.

1. Normalized mutual information QMI (Nahavandi,2008) is an information theory based metric. One problem with traditional mutual information metric (Wu, 2012) is that it is unstable and may bias the measure towards the source image with the highest entropy. Hossny et al. modified it to the normalized mutual information (Nahavandi,2008). In this paper, Hossny et al.'s definition is adopted.

$$Q_{MI} = 2\left[\frac{MI(A,F)}{H(A)+H(F)}\right] + \left[\frac{MI(B,F)}{H(B)+H(F)}\right] \tag{20}$$

where H(A), H(B) and H(F) are the marginal entropy of A, B and F, andMI(A,F)is the mutual information between the source image A and the fused imageF.

$$MI(A,F)=H(A)+H(F)-H(A,F) \tag{21}$$

where H(A,F) is the joint entropy between A and F, H(A) and H(F) are the marginal entropy of A and F, respectively, and MI(B,F) is similar to MI(A,F). The quality metric QMI measures how well the original information from source images is preserved in the fused image.

2. Yang et al.'s metric QY uses structural similarity (SSIM) (Yan, 2002) for fusion assessment. It is defined as follows:

$$Q_Y = \begin{cases} \lambda_w SSIM(A_w, F_w) + (1-\lambda_w)SSIM(B_w, F_w) = a \\ \max\{SSIM(A_w, F_w), SSIM(B_w, F_w)\} = b \end{cases}$$

a if $SSIM(A_w, B_w|w) \geq 0.75$

b if $SSIM(A_w, B_w|w) < 0.75$ (22)

where w is a window of size 7×7, A, B are the input images and F is the fused image, SSIM is the structural similarity (Yan, 2002) and the local weight λ_w is calculated as follows:

$$\lambda_w = \frac{s(A_w)}{s(A_w)+s(B_w)} \tag{23}$$

where $s(A_w)$ and $s(B_w)$ are the variance of source images A and B within the window w, respectively. Q_Y measures how well the structural information of source images is preserved.

CONCLUSION

We have presented a novel approach is cloud based image fusion approach based on guided filtering technique. The proposed technique utilizes the filter to acquire the two-scale presentations, which is simple and effective. More importantly, the guided filter method is used in a desired way to make full use of the correlations between neighborhood pixels for weight optimization trends. Experiments explained that the proposed technique can well keep the original and complementary information of all input images. Encouragingly, the proposed technique is very robust to image registration. Furthermore, the proposed approach is computationally effective, making it quite qualify for desired applications. At last, how to get improve the effectiveness of the concern proposed method by adaptively choosing the parameters of the guided filter can be further researched.

FUTURE WORK

The future work is as follows

1. We can use SURF, CHOG, Fast SIFT or Dense SIFT method for find the keypoint descriptors of an image.
2. Before implement we can use Optimization method for evaluating optimize descriptors.

3. We can use Artificial Neural Network as a supervised learning for classify and retrieve image.

SUMMARY

The proposed image fusion approaches are highlighted in the following.

1. Traditional multi-scale image fusion methods require more than two scales to obtain satisfactory fusion results. The key contribution of this paper is to present a fast two-scale fusion method which does not rely heavily on a specific image decomposition method. A simple aver- age filter is qualified for the proposed fusion framework.
2. A novel weight construction method is proposed to combine pixel saliency and spatial context for image fusion. Instead of using optimization based methods, guided filtering is adopted as a local filtering method for image fusion.
3. An important observation of this paper is that the roles of two measures, i.e., pixel saliency and spatial consistency are quite different when fusing different layers. In this paper, the roles of pixel saliency and spatial consistency are controlled through adjusting the parameters of the guided filter.

REFERENCES

Crow, F. C. (1984). Summed-area tables for texture mapping. *Proc. SIG- GRAPH 84. 11th Annu. Conf. Comput. Graph. Interact. Tech.*, *18*(3), 207–212.

Cvejic, N., Loza, A., Bull, D., & Canagarajah, N. (2005, April). A similarity metric for assessment of image fusion algorithms. *Int. J. Signal Process.*, *2*(3), 178–182.

Draper, N., & Smith, H. (1981). *Applied Regression Analysis*. New York: Wiley.

Durand, F., & Dorsey, J. (2002, July). Fast bilateral filtering for the display of high- dynamic-range images. *ACM Transactions on Graphics*, *21*(3), 257–266. doi:10.1145/566654.566574

Farbman, Fattal, Lischinski, & Szeliski. (2008, August). Edge-preserving decompositions for multi-scale tone and detail manipulation. *ACM Transactions on Graphics*, *15*(2), 252–267.

Goshtasby, A. A., & Nikolov. (2007). Image fusion: Advances in the state of the art. *Proceeding of IEEE conference on Image Processing*, *8*(2), 113-122.

He, K., Sun, J., & Tang, X. (2010). Guided image filtering. *Proc. Eur. Conf. Comput. Vis.*, 1–14.

Hossny, N., Nahavandi, S., & Creighton, D. (2008, August). Comments on 'information measure for performance of image fusion. *Electronics Letters*, *44*(18), 1266–1268. doi:10.1049/el:20081754

Kumar, M., & Dass, S. (2009, September). A total variation-based algorithm for pixel- level image fusion. *IEEE Transactions on Image Processing*, *18*(9), 2137–2143. doi:10.1109/TIP.2009.2025006 PMID:19520640

Kwok, L., Tsang, I., & Wang. (. (2004, November). Fusing images with different focuses using support vector machines. *IEEE Transactions on Neural Networks*, *15*(6), 1517–1525. doi:10.1109/TNN.2004.837781 PMID:15565778

Li, S., Kang, X., Hu, J., & Yang, B. (2013). Image matting for fusion of multi-focus images in dynamic scenes. *Information Fusion*, *14*(2), 147–162. doi:10.1016/j.inffus.2011.07.001

Liang, J., He, Y., Liu, D., & Zeng, X. (2012, May). Image fusion using higher order singular value decomposition. *IEEE Transactions on Image Processing*, *21*(5), 2898–2909. doi:10.1109/TIP.2012.2183140 PMID:22249708

Liu, Z., Blasch, E., Xue, Z., Zhao, J., Laganiere, R., & Wu, W. (2012, January). Objective assessment of multiresolution image fusion algorithms for context enhancement in night vision: A comparative study. *IEEE Transactions on Pattern Analysis and Machine Intelligence, 34*(1), 94–109. doi:10.1109/TPAMI.2011.109 PMID:21576753

Looney, D., & Mandic, D. P. (2009, April). Multiscale image fusion using complex extensions of EMD. *IEEE Transactions on Signal Processing, 57*(4), 1626–1630. doi:10.1109/TSP.2008.2011836

Pajares & de la Cruz, J.M. (2004). A wavelet-based image fusion tutorial. *Proceeding in IEEE Conference in Pattern Recognition, 37*(9), 1855-1872.

Petrovic´, V. (2007, April). Subjective tests for image fusion evaluation and objective metric validation. *Information Fusion, 8*(2), 208–216. doi:10.1016/j.inffus.2005.05.001

Piella, G. (2009, June). Image fusion for enhanced visualization: A variational approach. *International Journal of Computer Vision, 83*(1), 1–11. doi:10.1007/s11263-009-0206-4

Qu, G., Zhang, D., & Yan, P. (2002, March). Information measure for performance of image fusion. *Electronics Letters, 38*(7), 313–315. doi:10.1049/el:20020212

Rockinger, O. (1997). Image sequence fusion using a shift-invariant wavelet transform. *Proc. Int. Conf. Image Process., 3*, 288–291. doi:10.1109/ICIP.1997.632093

Shen, C. (2011, December). Generalized random walks for fusion of multi-exposure images. *IEEE Transactions on Image Processing, 20*(12), 3634–3646. doi:10.1109/TIP.2011.2150235 PMID:21550887

Socolinsky, & Wolff, A. (2002). Multispectral image visualization through first-order fusion. *IEEE Trans. Image Process., 11*(8), 1109-1119 .

Tessens, L., Ledda, A., Pizurica, A., & Philips, W. (2007). Extending the depth of field in microscopy through curvelet-based frequency-adaptive image fusion. *Proc. IEEE Int. Conf. Acoust. Speech Signal Process., 1*, 861–864.

Tian, J., & Chen, L. (2012, September). Adaptive multi-focus image fusion using a wavelet- based statistical sharpness measure. *Signal Processing, 92*(9), 2137–2146. doi:10.1016/j.sigpro.2012.01.027

Wang, Z., & Bovik, A. (2002, March). A universal image quality index. *IEEE Signal Processing Letters, 9*(3), 81–84. doi:10.1109/97.995823

Wang, Z., Bovik, A., Sheikh, H., & Simoncelli, E. (2004, April). Image quality assessment: From error visibility to structural similarity. *IEEE Transactions on Image Processing, 13*(4), 600–612. doi:10.1109/TIP.2003.819861 PMID:15376593

Xu, M., Chen, H., & Varshney, P. (2011, December). An image fusion approach based on markov random fields. *IEEE Transactions on Geoscience and Remote Sensing, 49*(12), 5116–5127. doi:10.1109/TGRS.2011.2158607

Xydeas, C., & Petrovic´, V. (2000, February). Objective image fusion performance measure. *Electronics Letters, 36*(4), 308–309. doi:10.1049/el:20000267

Yang, C., Zhang, J., Wang, X., & Liu, X. (2008, April). A novel similarity based quality metric for image fusion. *Information Fusion, 9*(2), 156–160. doi:10.1016/j.inffus.2006.09.001

Zhang, Q., & Guo, B. (2009, July). Multifocus image fusion using the non-subsampled contourlet transform. *Signal Processing*, *89*(7), 1334–1346. doi:10.1016/j.sigpro.2009.01.012

Zhao, J., Laganiere, R., & Liu, Z. (2007, December). Performance assessment of combinative pixel-level image fusion based on an absolute feature measurement. *International Journal of Innovative Computing, Information, & Control*, *3*(6), 1433–1447.

KEY TERMS AND DEFINITIONS

Cloud Computing: Is a flourishing technology nowadays because of its scalability, flexibility, availability of resources and other features.

Cloud Resources: Is a model for enabling ubiquitous, convenient, on-demand network access to a shared pool of configurable computing resources(eg, networks, servers, storage, applications, and services).

Filtering: A Confidence-Based Filtering method, named CBF, is investigated for cloud computing environment.

Image Fusion: Is a model for enabling ubiquitous, convenient, on-demand network access to a shared pool of configurable computing resources(eg, networks, servers, storage, applications, and services).

Images: The concept image consists of all the cognitive structure in the individual's mind that is associated with a given concept.

Section 2
Pattern Recognition, Watermarking and Face Recognition

Chapter 9
Determination of Stability of Rock Slope Using Intelligent Pattern Recognition Techniques

Swaptik Chowdhury
VIT University, India

Pratik Goyal
VIT University, India

R. Hariharan
VIT University, India

Pijush Samui
VIT University, India

ABSTRACT

This article adopts Minimax Probability Machine (MPM) and Extreme Learning Machine (ELM) for prediction of stability status of rock slope. The proposed MPM and ELM models use unit weight (γ), cohesions (c_A) and (c_B), angles of internal friction (ϕ_A) and ϕ_B, angle of the line of intersection of the two joint-sets (ψ_p), slope angle (ψ_f), and height (H) as input parameters. For this chapter the determination of stability of rock slope has been adopted as classification problem. The developed MPM and ELM have been compared with each other. The results of this article shows that the developed MPM is robust model for prediction of stability status of rock slope.

INTRODUCTION

Slope instability is a complex phenomenon which can occur at many scales and due to many reasons. Its accurate estimation is difficult due to the complexity of physical system itself and the difficulty involved in determining the necessary input data associated with the geotechnical parameters (Sakellariou & Ferentinou, 2005). Approximately 35 landslides were recorded according to emergency events database (EM-DAT) in 2008, in which 3924 peoples died and 3828660

peoples were affected. The stability of rock slope plays very significant role in underground as well as surface works such as foundation of structures (Power houses, dams and buildings works), transportation options (canals, pipelines, roadways, & railways etc.) particularly in hilly and high terrain areas. For mining engineering works, it is essential to maintain the rock slope in stable condition during the construction time as well as in the operation time during large and small scale size underground and open excavation works. Before the advent of computationally complex methods,

DOI: 10.4018/978-1-4666-8654-0.ch009

slope stability was usually analyzed by methods of limit equilibrium .In this method, factor of safety is derived to analyze the slope stability (Sakellariou & Ilias, 1997; Roussos, 2000).The factor of safety (FS) is the ratio of reaction over action, which is represented through moments or forces and eventually in terms of stresses depending on the geometry of assumed slip surface. But one of the major disadvantage of limit equilibrium method is that it is necessary to determine the location of critical slip surface for the analysis and the corresponding minimum value of FS by testing a considerable number of possible slip surfaces. Researchers developed various methods assuming different slip surfaces such as Taylor (1937) and Bishop (1955) assumed circular shape of slip surface but (Janbu, 1954; Sarma 1975) assumed any random shape of the slip surface. But one of the major assumptions is that the soils are isotropic and homogeneous which may not be true in practical cases (Sakellariou & Ferentinou, 2005).

Several researchers have employed soft computing models such as extreme learning machine (ELM) and Minimax probability machine classification model (MPMC) in the past effectively for various geotechnical problems. Extreme learning Machine (ELM) is a simple learning algorithm for single-hidden layer feed forward neural network (SLFN) whose learning speed is faster than the traditional feed forward network learning algorithms and it also get better generalization performance. It is generally noticed that SLFN with N hidden neuron and arbitrary input weights can learn N distinct observation with insignificant error (Tamura & Tateishi, 1997; Huang, 2003). Parameters of hidden nodes are randomly selected and weights are analytically determined in ELM. The ELN algorithm has better generalization performance, smallest training error, have smallest norm of weights and runs extremely fast and thus the advantage of EXTREME LEARNING MACHINE (Huang, 2003). The Minimax Probability Machine (Lanckriet et al, 2002) is derived from a theorem which assumes positive definite

covariance matrices for each of the two classes but without making any other statistical assumptions, guarantees a lower bound on the probability of misclassification for the classification approach of linear projection to one dimension followed by comparison to a decision boundary. There are many applications in literature of MPMC (Wang et al, 2010; Yang et al, 2010; Zhou et al, 2013). The use of MPMC is advantageous as it makes minimum statistical assumptions about the distribution of underlying true classification function as accurate estimation of these functions is possible only in cases of trivial analysis. The major advantage of MPMC is that it gives a control over future classifiers.

This article examines the capability of two intelligent pattern recognition techniques {Extreme Learning Machine (ELM) and Minimax Probability Machine (MPM)} for prediction of stability of rock slope. The inputs of MPM and ELM models are unit weight (γ), cohesions (c_A) and (c_B), angles of internal friction (ϕ_A) and ϕ_B, angle of the line of intersection of the two jointsets (ψ_p), slope angle (ψ_f), height (H), where A and B refer to the two joint sets. MPM and ELM have been used as classification techniques.

EXTREME LEARNING MACHINE

Researchers use Feedforward neural network extensively due to their ability to approximate complex nonlinear mappings directly from the input values satisfactorily and they can be used to develop model for variety of natural and artificial phenomenon which otherwise are difficult to understand using generally employed parametric technique. However the major drawback of Feedforward neural network is that there is no faster learning algorithm for them as traditional learning algorithms are usually very slow and may need huge computational time to train the neural network depending upon the size of the sample, variance of the sample and learning algorithm. Research focus on the two aspect of Feedforward neural network to study its approximation qualities: universal approximation on compact input sets and approximation in a limited set of training sample. Many researchers have studied the universal approximation capabilities of standard multi-layer feed forward neural network (Hornik,1991; Leshno et al, 1993 ; Ito, 1992; Hornik,1991) showed that the if the activation function is continuous, bounded and non-constant, then continuous mappings can be approximated by neural network for compact input sets. In practical application, finite training data set is used to train neural network. Huang & Babri, (1998) showed that a single hidden layer feed forward neural network (SLFN) with at most N hidden neurons and with any nonlinear activation function can learn N distinct observation with zero error for approximation of function in finite training dataset. However care should be taken that the input weights (linking the input layer to the first hidden layer) need to be adjusted in all the previous theoretical research works as well as in all practical learning algorithms of Feedforward neural networks.

All the different layers of parameters (weights and biases) are dependent as all the parameters of the Feedforward network needs to be adjusted. Recently the use of gradient descent based methods has increased in various learning algorithms of Feedforward neural network. However it is well known that gradient descent-based learning methods are usually very slow due to improper learning steps or it may easily converge to local minima. And such learning algorithm may need many iterative learning steps to obtain better and efficient learning performance

Studies have shown that SLFNs with N hidden neurons and with arbitrarily chosen input weights can learn N different and individual observations with arbitrarily small error (Tamura & Tateishi, 1997; Huang, 2003). Unlike the usual practise

and thought process that all the parameters of the Feedforward network needs to be tuned, it is not necessary to adjust input weights and the first hidden layer biases while implementation. Studies with simulation results of real and artificial large application have shown that this method has very fast learning rate and produces good generalization performance (Huang et al, 2003).It was also shown that SLFN with arbitrary assigned input weights and hidden layer biases and with almost any nonzero activation function can universally approximate any continuous function on any compact input data set. These research results imply that in the applications of Feedforward neural network input weights may not be necessarily adjusted at all.

After the input weights and hidden layer biases are chosen arbitrarily, SLFNs are simply taken as linear systems and the output weights (linking the hidden layer to the output layer) of the SLFNs can be analytically determined through simple generalized inverse operation of the hidden layer output matrices. Based on this concept, ELM is a simple learning algorithm for SLFN. ELM is different from traditional learning algorithm as it tends to reach the smallest training error and also the smallest norm of weights. Barlett theory on the generalization performance of Feedforward neural networks state that for Feedforward neural network reaching smaller training error, the norm of weight should be smaller for the better generalization performance of the network (Bartlett, 1998).So, ELM potrays good generalization performance for Feedforward neural network.

This section is organized as follows. Subsection 1 introduces Moore Penrose generalized inverse and the minimum norm least-squares solution of a general linear system which is important in the development of the ELM learning Theory. Subsection 2 proposes the ELM learning theory as in literature.

MOORE PENROSE GENERALIZED THEORY

The Moore-Penrose generalized inverse and the minimum norm least-squares solution of a general linear system Ax = y in Euclidean space, where $A \in R^{m \times n}$ and y $\in$ Rm is discussed. As depicted by (Tamura & Tateishi, 1997; Huang, 2003), the SLFNs are actually a linear system and the input weights and the hidden layer biases can be chosen arbitrarily.

The resolution of a general linear system Ax = y, where A may be singular and may even not be square, can be made easily by using the Moore-Penrose generalized inverse (Serre, 2002). The matrix G of order n × m can be called the Moore-Penrose generalized inverse of matrix A of order m × n, if (Serre, 2002)

AGA=A, GAG= G, (AG)T = AG, (GA)T = GA (1)

In this chapter, the Moore-Penrose generalized inverse of matrix A is represented by $A^{\dagger}$.

MINIMUM NORM LEAST-SQUARES SOLUTION OF GENERAL LINEAR SYSYTEM

For a general linear system Ax = y, x^ can be called as a least-squares solution (l.s.s) if

$$\left\| A\hat{x} - y \right\| = \min_{x} \left\| Ax - y \right\|$$ (2)

where D.D is a norm in Euclidean Space.

Let x_o XR^n is said to be a minimum norm least squares solution of a linear system Ax=y if for any yXR^m.

Dx0D $\leq$D xD, $\forall$x $\in$ {x: DAx −yΔ $\leq$D Az −yD, $\forall$z $\in$ R^n} (3)

That means, a solution xo is said to be a minimum norm least squares solution of a linear system Ax=y if it has the smallest norm along all the least squares solution .Also, (Wang et al,2010) let there exist a matrix G such that Gy is a minimum norm least-squares solution of a linear system Ax=y. Then it is necessary and sufficient that $G = A^{\dagger}$, the Moore- Penrose generalized inverse of matrix A.

EXTREME LEARNING MACHINE

In this section an extremely fast learning algorithm for the single hidden layer feed-forward networks (SLFNs) with hidden neurons, where N is the number of training samples is discussed using Moore- Pentose inverse and the smallest norm least-squares solution of a general linear system Ax=y.

APPROXIMATION PROBLEM OF SLFNs

For N arbitrary distinct samples (xi, ti) where xi= [xi1, xi2,….., xin]T XRn and ti =[ti1, ti2,….,tim] T $\in$Rm, standard SLFns with hidden neurons and activation functions g(x) are mathematically modeled as:

$$\sum_{i=1}^{\tilde{N}} \beta_i g\left(w_i \cdot x_j + b_i\right) = o_j \, j = 1 \ldots N$$ (4)

where w_i= [w_{i1}, w_{i2},……..,w_{in}]^T is the weight factor connecting the i th hidden neuron and the input neurons β_i =[β_{i1}, β_{i2},……, β_{im}]^T is the weight vector connecting the i th hidden neuron and the output neurons, and b$_i$ representing the threshold of the i th hidden neuron. w_i .x_j denotes the inner product of the w_i and x_j. The output neurons are chosen linear in this paper.

That standard SLFNs with N~ hidden neurons with activation function g(x) can approximate these N samples with zero errors means that $\sum_{j=1}^{\tilde{N}}\left\| o_j - t_j \right\| = 0$ i.e., there exist β_i, w_i and b_i such that

$$\sum_{i=1}^{\tilde{N}} \beta_i g\left(w_i \cdot x_j + b_i\right) = t_j \; j = 1 \ldots N \qquad (5)$$

The N equations presented above can be written summarily as:

$$\mathbf{H}\beta = \mathbf{T} \qquad (6)$$

where

$$H\left(w_i, \ldots, w_{\tilde{N}}, b_1, \ldots, b_{\tilde{N}}, x_1, \ldots, x_N\right)$$

$$= \begin{bmatrix} g\left(w_1 \cdot x_1 + b\right) & \ldots & g\left(w_{\tilde{N}} \cdot x_1 + b_{\tilde{N}}\right) \\ . & \ldots & . \\ . & & . \\ g\left(w_1 \cdot x_N + b\right) & \ldots & g\left(w_{\tilde{N}} \cdot x_N + b_{\tilde{N}}\right) \end{bmatrix}$$

$$(7)$$

$$\beta = \begin{bmatrix} \beta_t^T \\ . \\ . \\ \beta_{\tilde{N}}^T \end{bmatrix} \text{ and } T = \begin{bmatrix} t_t^T \\ . \\ . \\ t_{\tilde{N}}^T \end{bmatrix} \qquad (8)$$

As given in (Huang & Babri,1998) and (Huang, 2003), H representing the hidden layer output matrix of the neural network; the ith column of H represents the ith the hidden neuron's output vector with respect to inputs x_1, x_2, x_3....,x_N.

GRADIENT-BASED LEARNING ALGORITHMS

As reported in several works (Tamura & Tateishi, 1997; Huang, 2003; Huang & Babri, 1998) if the number of hidden neurons equals the number of distinct training samples, $\tilde{N}$ =N, matrix H is the square and invertible, and SLFN's then approximate these training samples with error which tends to zero. But in most of the cases the number of hidden neurons is much less than the number of distinct training samples, $\tilde{N}$ <<N, H is a non-square matrix and there may not exist w_i, b_i, β_i (i=1,.....,N~) such that Hβ = T. Thus, instead one may need to find w_i, b_i, β_i (i=1,....., $\tilde{N}$) such that:

$$\left\| H\left(w_1, \ldots, w_{\tilde{N}}, b1, \ldots b_{\tilde{N}}\right)\hat{\beta} - T \right\|$$

$$= \min_{w_i, b_i, \beta} \left\| H\left(w_1, \ldots, w_{\tilde{N}}, b1, \ldots, b_{\tilde{N}}\right)\beta - T \right\|$$

$$(9)$$

which is similar to minimizing the cost function:

$$E = \sum_{j=1}^{N}\left(\sum_{i=1}^{\tilde{N}} \beta_i g\left(w_i \cdot x_j + b_i\right) - t_j \right)^2 \qquad (10)$$

When H is unknown gradient-based learning algorithms are generally used to search the minimum of D Hβ = TD. For the process of minimization adopted by gradient-based algorithms, vector W comprising of weights (w_i, β_i) and biases (b_i) parameters of W is adjusted itiretively as follows:

$$W_k = W_{k-1} - \eta \frac{\partial E(W)}{\partial W} \qquad (11)$$

Here η is the learning rate. Back propagation learning algorithm is the most commonly used learning algorithm for feed forward learning algorithm in which gradients are calculated efficiently by propagation from output to the input. But it has major drawbacks such as (Huang, 2003):

1. The learning algorithm converges very slowly when the learning rate η is small whereas when η is large, the algorithm becomes unstable and diverges.

2. Another peculiarity of the error surface that impacts the performance of the back-propagation learning algorithm is the presence of local minima. It is undesirable that the learning algorithm stops at a local minimum if it is located far above a global minimum.

3. Back-propagation algorithms sometime over train the neural network and give the worst generalization performance. Thus, validation and appropriate stopping methods are needed in the cost function minimization method

4. Gradient-based learning is cumbersome and needs much time in many applications

ELM is a coherent learning algorithm for Feedforward neural networks which is capable of providing solutions for above stated issues.

MINIMUM NORM LEAST SQUARES SOLUTION OF SLFN

As stated in above sections, adjustment of the input weights wi and the hidden layer biases bi are not necessary in ELM and the hidden layer output matrix H can remain unchanged once the arbitrary values are assigned to the parameters in the initial phase of training. This is different than the other Feedforward network in which all the parameters are needed to be adjusted. Recent work (Guang et al, 2004) showed that SLFNs (with infinite differential activation function) with the input weights chosen arbitrarily can train with distinct data with relatively small error. Also it has been proved by simulation results on the artificial and real world data sets that no change in results is obtained by adjusting the input weights and hidden layer biases. It has been also shown that unlike conventional function approximation theories, which require to tune input weights and hidden layer biases, the Feedforward network with randomly chosen input weights and hidden layer

biases and with all nonzero activation function can universally approximate any continuous function on any controlled input sets.

For a particular fixed input weights w_i and the hidden layer biases b_i, training an SLFN is equivalent to finding a least square solution $\beta^{\wedge}$ of the linear system $H\beta = T$:

$$\left\| H\left(w_1,\ldots,w_{\tilde{N}},b1,\ldots,b_{\tilde{N}}\right)\hat{\beta} - T\right\|$$
$$= \min_{\beta}\left\| H\left(w_1,\ldots,w_{\tilde{N}},b1,\ldots,b_{\tilde{N}}\right)\beta - T\right\|$$

(12)

According to Equation (30) the smallest norm least squares solution to the above linear system is:

$$\hat{\beta} = H^{\dagger}T \tag{13}$$

and it has following properties:

1. Minimum training error. The special solution is one of the least-squares solutions of a general linear system $H\beta = T$, which meant that the smallest training error can be reached using this special solution:

$$\left\| H\hat{\beta} - T\right\| = \left\| HH^{\dagger}T - T\right\| = \min_{\beta}\left\| H\beta - T\right\|$$

(14)

Although all learning algorithms try to reach the minimum training error, most of them cannot obtain it because they have local minimum or infinite training iteration which is usually not allowed in applications.

2. Smallest norm of weights and best generalization performance. Furthermore, the specific solution $\hat{\beta} = H^{\dagger}T$ has the smallest norm among all the least-squares solutions

of Hβ = T has the smallest norm among all the least-squares solution Hβ = T represented as:

$$\left\|\hat{\beta}\right\| = \left\|H^{\dagger}T\right\| \leq \left\|\beta\right\| \qquad (15)$$

$$\forall \beta \in \left\{\beta : \left\|H\beta - T\right\| \leq \left\|Hz - T\right\|, \forall z \in R^{\tilde{N} \times N}\right\} \qquad (16)$$

As shown by (Bartlett, 1998; Barlett, 1997) Vapnik-Chervonenkis (VC) dimension (hence number of parameters) is not important for generalization performance in feedforward networks with small weights and small squared error on training examples. The magnitude of weights is important in the network as smaller the weights are, the better generalization performance network tends to have. And as shown in above sections ELM not only reaches the small squared error on the training datasets but also obtains smallest weights. And thus this method gives better generalization performance. It is difficult for gradient based learning algorithms such as back propagation to obtain better generalization as they try to reduce the training errors without taking into consideration the magnitude of weights.

3. The minimum norm least squares solution of Hβ = T is unique, which is:

$$\hat{\beta} = H^{\dagger}T \qquad (17)$$

LEARNING ALGORITHM FOR SLFNs

The simple learning method for SLFNs called the extreme learning machine ELM can be summarized as follows:

Algorithm ELM: Given a training set $\aleph = \{(xi, ti) | xi \in Rn, ti \in Rm, i = 1, \cdots, N\}$, activation function g(x), and hidden neuron number $\tilde{N}$,

Step 1: Assign random input weight wi and bias bi, i= 1,......, $\tilde{N}$

Step 2: The hidden layer output matrix H is calculated

Step 3: The output weight β is calculated where

$$\hat{\beta} = H^{\dagger}T$$

where H, β and T are defined as in Equation (7) and (8).

However it should be noted that gradient-based learning algorithms like back-propagation can be used for feedforward neural networks with more than one hidden layers while ELM algorithm at its present form is still only valid for single-hidden layer feedforward networks (SLFNs). But, it has been shown that SLFNs can approximate any continuous function (Hornik, 1991; Huang et al, 2003) and can be implement for any classification application (Guang et al, 2004). Thus, reasonably speaking the proposed ELM algorithm can be used for many cases and it employs radial basis function as activation function.

MINIMAX PROBABILITY MACHINE CLASSIFICATION

Consider the problem of selecting a linear discriminant by minimizing the possibilities that data vectors fall on the wrong side of the boundary. One way is to achieve this via generative approach in which distributional assumptions are made about the class conditional densities thereby estimating and controling the relevant probabilities.

Instead of avoiding any reference to class-conditional densities, it might be useful to try to avoid misclassification probabilities encompassed in worst case setting. Such a minimax approach could be viewed as providing an alternative justification for discriminative approaches. In this section, it is shown that such a minimax program can be executed in the setting of binary classification. This approach involves exploiting the following powerful theorem by (Marshall & Olkin, 1960), which has recently been put in the light of recent convex optimization techniques by (Popescu & Berstimas, 2001):

$$\sup_{y \sim (\bar{y} \Sigma y)} = \Pr\{y \in S\} = \frac{1}{1+d^2}, \qquad (18)$$

with

$$d^2 = \inf_{y \in S} (y - \bar{y})^T \Sigma_y^{-1} (y - \bar{y}) \qquad (19)$$

where y is a random vector, S is a given convex set, and where the supremum is spread over all the distributions for y having mean and covariance matrix (Σy) (assumed to be positive definite for simplicity). This theorem provides with the abilities to minimize the probability of misclassifying a point, without making Gaussian or other specific distributional assumptions. This potential is exploited in the design of linear classifiers in which the set S is a half-space. This theorem is useful as it can also be applied in unsupervised learning, One of the important attributes of this theorem is that one reaches an explicit upper bound on the probability of misclassification of future data: 1/ (1+d2).

Another attribute of this formulation is the possibility to study directly the effect of using plug-in estimates for the means and covariance matrices rather than their real, but unknown values. It is assumed that real and covariance values are unknown, but bounded in a convex region and thus the resulting classifiers are affect. It involves the incorporation of a regularization term in the estimator and resulting in the increase in the upper bound of the probability of misclassification of future data.

A third important advantage of this approach is that as in linear discriminant analysis (Mikach et al, 1999) it is possible to generalize the basic methodology to allow nonlinear decision boundaries through the use of Mercer kernels. The classifiers resulting are contesting with existing classifier, including support and the vector machines.

Problem Definition

Let x and y denote random vectors in a binary classification problem, obtaining data from each of two classes, with means and covariance matrices denoted by ($\bar{x}$, Σx) and ($\bar{y}$, Σy), respectively, with x, $\bar{x}$,, y, $\bar{y}$, r $\in$ R^n, and Σx, Σy $\in$ R^{n*n} both symmetric and positive semi definitive. With a slight abuse of notation, x and y denote the classes.

It is needed to determine a hyperplane h(a, b)= {z l a^{T}z = b), where a $\in$R^n\{0} and b $\in$R, which separates the two classes of points with maximum probability with respect to all distributions having these means and covariance matrices. This can be expressed as:

$$\max_{\alpha, a \neq 0, b} \alpha \text{ s.t. } \inf_{x \sim (\bar{x} \Sigma x)} = \Pr\{a^T x \geq b\} \geq \alpha \qquad (20)$$

$$\inf_{y \sim (\bar{y} \Sigma y)} = \Pr\{a^T y \geq b\} \geq \alpha \qquad (21)$$

where the notation ($\bar{x}$,Σx) refers to the class of distributions that have prescribed mean $\bar{y}$ and covariance Σx, but are otherwise are arbitrary; likewise for y.

Future points z for which a^{T}z $\geq$ b are then classified as belonging to the class associated with x, otherwise they are classified as belonging to the class associated with y. In formulation (18 and

19) the term 1-α is the worst case (maximum) misclassification probability, and the classifier minimizes the maximum probability.

Using the above notation with $\bar{y}$, Σy, positive definite, a ≠0, b given, such that a^Ty ≤ and α∈ [0,1], the condition equation

$$\inf_{y\sim(\bar{y}\cdot\Sigma y)} = \Pr\left\{a^T y \geq b\right\} \geq \alpha \qquad (22)$$

Holds true if and only if,

$$b - a^T\bar{y} \geq k(\alpha)\sqrt{a^T \Sigma_y\, a}, \qquad (23)$$

where

$$k(\alpha) = \sqrt{\frac{\alpha}{1+\alpha}} \qquad (24)$$

Now, considering the second constraint in (18 and 19), ≠0., this constraint can be represented as

$$b - a^T\bar{y} \geq k(\alpha)\sqrt{a^T \Sigma_y\, a}, \qquad (25)$$

with

$$k(\alpha) = \sqrt{\frac{\alpha}{1+\alpha}} \qquad (26)$$

This can handle the first constraint (19) in a similar way (write $a^Tx \leq b$ as $-a^Tx \geq b$ and apply the result (25). Considering that (22) and (23) can be applied in both cases: when maximizing α, a hyperplane is preferred for which $a^T\bar{y} \leq b \leq a^T\bar{x}$, since otherwise α=0.

The optimization problem then (18) takes the form of:

$$\max_{\alpha, a\neq 0, b} \alpha.\sigma.\pi.\; b + a^T\bar{x} \geq k(\alpha)\sqrt{a^T \Sigma_x\, a}, \qquad (27)$$

$$b - a^T\bar{y} \geq k(\alpha)\sqrt{a^T \Sigma_y\, a}, \qquad (28)$$

Since k(α) is a monotone increasing function of a, variables can be changed and rewritten as:

$$\max_{k, a\neq 0, b} \kappa \;\text{s.t.}$$
$$a^T\bar{y} + \kappa\sqrt{a^T \Sigma_y\, a} \leq b \leq a^T\bar{x} - \kappa\sqrt{a^T \Sigma_x\, a} \qquad (29)$$

The k (optimal values) and the worst case misclassification probability 1-α are related by eq

$$\alpha = \frac{\kappa*^2}{1+\kappa*^2} \qquad (30)$$

Further, b can be eliminated from (29):

$$\max_{k, a\neq 0, b} \kappa\;\sigma.\pi.$$
$$a^T\bar{y} + \kappa\sqrt{a^T \Sigma_y\, a} \leq b \leq a^T\bar{x} - \kappa\sqrt{a^T \Sigma_x\, a} \qquad (31)$$

Since k has to be maximized, the inequalities in (29) will become equalities at the optimal. An optimal value of b will be given by:

$$b * a^T\bar{x} - \kappa*\sqrt{a*^T \Sigma_x\, a*}$$
$$= a*^T\bar{y} + \kappa*\sqrt{a*^T \Sigma_y\, a*} \qquad (32)$$

where a* and k* are optimal values of α and k respectively. If the constraints in (30) are re-arranged, the optimization problem would be converted to following form:

$$\max_{k, a\neq 0} \sigma.\tau.\; a^T\left(\bar{x} - \bar{y}\right) \geq \kappa\left(\sqrt{a^T \Sigma_x\, a} + \sqrt{a^T \Sigma_y\, a}\right)$$

If $\bar{x} = \bar{y}$, then ≠0 implies k = 0, which yields α = 0. Here, the minimax probability decision problem (20 and 21), does not have a useful solution and the optimal worst-case misclassification probability is $1-\alpha^* = 1$.

If it is proceeded with the assumption $\bar{x} \neq \bar{y}$, the condition (11) will be become homogeneous in a: if a satisfies (11), sa with $s \geq 0$. Also, (11) implies $a^T(\bar{x} - \bar{y}) \geq 0$. Since, $\bar{x} \neq \bar{y}$, $a^T(\bar{x} - \bar{y}) = 1$ can be set without loss of generality. This implies $a \neq 0$, and in turn, $\sqrt{a^T \Sigma_x a} + \sqrt{a^T \Sigma_y a} \neq 0$ .optimization problem can be expressed as:

$$\max_{k,a} \kappa \ \sigma.\tau. \ \kappa \left(\sqrt{a^T \Sigma_x a} + \sqrt{a^T \Sigma_y a} \right)^{-1} \tag{33}$$

which will eliminate k:

$$\min_a \left\| \Sigma_x^{1/2} a \right\|_2 + \left\| \Sigma_x^{1/2} a \right\|_2 \ \text{s.t.} \ a^T (\bar{x} - \bar{y}) = 1 \text{ s.t.} \tag{34}$$

The above problem is convex, feasible (since $\bar{x} \neq \bar{y}$), and its objective is stated below, hence there exists an optimal point, a_*. When either Σ_x or Σ_y is positive definite, the strict convexity of the objective function implies that the optimal function is unique.

So it was concluded that, if $\bar{x} = \bar{y}$, then the minimax probability decision problem (20) does not have a useful solution: the optimal worst case misclassification probability obtained is $1-\alpha_* = 1$. Else, an optimal hyperplane $H(a_*, b_*)$ exists, and which can be obtained by solving the problem:

$$\kappa^{*-1} := \min_a \sqrt{a^T \Sigma_x a}$$
$$+ \sqrt{a^T \Sigma_y a} \ \text{s.t.} \ a^T (\bar{x} - \bar{y}) = 1 \tag{35}$$

and setting b to be the value:

$$b^* = a^{*T} \bar{x} - \kappa^* \sqrt{a^{*T} \Sigma_x a^*} \tag{36}$$

where a_* is an optimal solution of (35). The optimal worst-case misclassification probability is obtained through:

$$1 - \alpha^* = \frac{1}{1 + \kappa^{*2}}$$
$$= \frac{\left(\sqrt{a^{*T} \Sigma_x a^*} + \sqrt{a^{*T} \Sigma_y a^*} \right)^2}{1 + \left(\sqrt{a^{*T} \Sigma_x a^*} + \sqrt{a^{*T} \Sigma_y a^*} \right)^2} \tag{37}$$

If either Σx or Σy is positive definite, the optimal hyperplane is unique.

Once an optimal hyperplane called a minimax probabilistic decision hyperplane is obtained, the new data point z_{new} is classified by evaluating sign $(a_*^T z_{new} - b_*)$: if this is $+1$, z_{new} is classified to class x, otherwise to class y. This algorithm for binary classification is called the Minimax Probability Machine (MPM) for binary classification. MPM employs radial function as activation function.

Solving the Optimization Problem

Problem (35) is a convex optimization problem, a second order cone program (SOCP) (Boyd & Vandenberghe, 2001). General purpose programs such asSeDuMi (Sturm, 1999) or Mosek (Anderson & Anderson, 2000) can tackle this problem efficiently. The codes which employ interior point methods for SOCP (Nesterov & Nemirovsky, 1994; Lobo et al, 1998) yielded a worst case complexity of O (n^3). That reduces the total complexity to O $(n^3 + Nn^2)$ where N is the number of data points. This solution shows similar complexity as the quadratic programs where one has to solve while using linear support vector machines (Scholkopf & Smola, 2002). SVM literature employs same iterative procedures to solve weighted least square problems to achieve an approximate solution as in the Least Squares SVM described by (Suykens & Vandewalle, 1999) or an exact solution by (Perez-Cruz et al, 2001).

It can be written as $a=a_0 + Fu$, where u X R $^{n-1}$, $a_0 = (\bar{x} = \bar{y})/ D \ \bar{x} = \bar{y}, D_2^2$, and FX R$^{n \times (n-1)}$ is an orthogonal matrix whose columns span the subspace the vectors orthogonal to $\bar{x} = \bar{y}$, . Hence, the constraint in (34) can be eliminated and written as an unconstrained SOCP.

$$\min_{u} \left\| \Sigma_x^{1/2} ao + Fu \right\|_2 + \left\| \Sigma_x^{1/2} ao + Fu \right\|_2 \qquad (38)$$

An equivalent form is:

$$\inf_{u, \beta \geq 0, \eta \geq 0} \beta + \frac{1}{\beta} \left\| \Sigma_x^{1/2} ao + Fu \right\|_2^2$$
$$+ \eta + \frac{1}{\mu} \left\| \Sigma_x^{1/2} ao + Fu \right\|_2^2 \qquad (39)$$

This equivalence can be understood by fixing u and minimizing the objective in (39) with respect to β and η. It is to be noticed that a factor $\frac{1}{2}$ has been dropped over each term in (39). This is irrelevant for the optimal values of u, β and η, but has to be considered while computing κ_*, α_*.

The function which is to be minimized is jointly convex in u, β, η. An iterative least-squares approach was used to minimize (39), with regularization of the Hessian for the computational stability. The algorithm, is presented as a pseudo code called, "Block Coordinate Descent", [35]. At iteration, first κ, is minimized with respect to β, η by setting $\beta_k = \left\| \Sigma_x^{1/2} (a0 + Fu_{k-1}) \right\|_2$ and $\eta_k = \left\| \Sigma_x^{1/2} ao + Fu_{k-1} \right\|_2$. Those minimizers are unique. Later it is minimized with respect to u by solving a least squares problem in u, with β, η fixes (u-step). This least square step is regularized with a regularization term δI (with $\delta > 0$ small) added to the Hessian of the least-squares step and it makes the Hessian positive definite. Thus, u-step

also attains the minimum. As shown by [36], these features imply the convergence of the above block coordinate descent method.

Robustness to Estimation Error

In practical experiments, it is possible that the error rate computed on the test set is greater than 1-α* which contradict the previous claim that 1-α_* is an upper bound on misclassification error. This apparent paradox has to do with estimation errors. Mean and covariance is from the data as they are not known where covariance is a priori. The estimate controls the validity of the bound .This is an issue especially in the case of "small sample".

The Robustness Decision Problem

The original problem in (18 and 19) is taken and it is assumed that the mean and the covariance matrix f each class only known with some specified set. In particular, it is assumed that $(x, \Sigma x) \in \in \chi$ where χ is a subset of R^n x S$_n^+$, where S$_n^+$ is the set of n x n symmetric, positive semdefinite matrices. Similarly, a set bY is the set of n x n symmetric, positive semidefinite matrices. Similarly, a set Y is established, taking in consideration the uncertainty in the mean and covariance matrix of the random variable y.The robust counterpart to the original problem is defined as:

$$\max_{\alpha, a \neq 0, b} \alpha \ \text{s.t.} \ \inf_{x \sim (\bar{x}, \Sigma x)} \text{Pr} \left\{ a^T x \geq b \right\} \geq \alpha \forall \left(\bar{x}, \Sigma x \right) \in \chi$$
$$(40)$$

$$\inf_{x \sim (\bar{y}, \Sigma y)} \text{Pr} \left\{ a^T y \geq b \right\} \geq \alpha \forall \left(\bar{y}, \Sigma y \right) \in y \qquad (41)$$

It is assured a worst-case misclassification probability for all distributions, which is unknown, but have bounded mean and covariance matrix and are otherwise arbitrary.

Using the previous approach, it is certain to obtain an equivalent formulation of the robust problem:

$$\max_{\kappa, a \neq 0, b} \kappa \text{ s.t. } \forall (\bar{x}, \Sigma x) \in X, -b + a^T \bar{x} \geq \kappa \sqrt{a^T \Sigma_x a}$$

(42)

$$\forall (\bar{y}, \Sigma y) \in Y, -b + a^T \bar{y} \geq \kappa \sqrt{a^T \Sigma_y a}$$

(43)

The complexity of the above problem relies on the structure of the sets X and Y. Now, a specific choice for these sets is considered, that is both realistic from statistical point of view and solvable numerically. To be specific the equations in consideration are shown in Box 1.

Here $v > 0$ $\rho > 0$ are fixed. The notation $\bar{x} 0$, $\Sigma x0$ represents the "nominal" estimate of the mean and covariance matrix, respectively. The matrix norm employed in the above equation is frobenius norm: $\|A\|_F^2 = \text{Tr}(A^T A)$.

In this model, the mean of the class X belongs to an ellipsoid centered around $\bar{x} 0$, whose shape is determined by the (unknown) Σx. The covariance matrix itself belongs to a matrix norm ball (in the space of symmetric matrices of order n) centered around $\Sigma x0$. It is to be noted that positive semidifiniteness constraint on the covariance matrices are not included in the model. For small value of the uncertainty size ρ and provided both covariance

estimates $\Sigma x0$ and $\Sigma y0$ are positive definite. This assumption are okay as the matrix will lie in the cone of positive semidefinite matrices.

Here, the model for the mean uncertainty is motivated by standard statistical approach to estimate a region of confidence based on Laplace (second order). Approximation to a likelihood function (Kass et al, 1988). The uncertainty model in the covariance matrix is perhaps less important from a statistical viewpoint, but it leads a regularization term of a classical form. The specific value of v and ρ χam be determined based on the Central Limit Theorem or on Re-sampling Methods.

Estimation Errors in the Means

Firstly, the covariance matrix for which each class is known is considered. Later, the results will be extended to the case $\rho > 0$.

For a given a and $\bar{x}^0$,

$$\min_{x(\bar{x} - x^{-0})^T \Sigma_x^{-1} (\bar{x} - x^{-0}) \leq v^2} a^T \bar{x} = a^T x^{-0} - v \sqrt{a^T \Sigma_x a}$$

(46)

Using this result, the following problem is obtained:

$$\max_{\kappa, a \neq 0, b} \kappa \text{ s.t. } -b + a^T \bar{y} \geq \kappa \sqrt{a^T (\Sigma_x + \rho I_n) a}$$

(47)

Box 1.

$$X = \left\{ (\bar{x} \Sigma x) : (\bar{x} - x^{-0})^T \Sigma_x^{-1} (\bar{x} - x^{-0}) \leq v^2, \left\| \Sigma x - \Sigma 0 \right\|_F \leq \rho \right\}, \text{ (44)}$$

$$Y = \left\{ (\bar{y} \Sigma y) : (\bar{y} - y^{-0})^T \Sigma_y^{-1} (\bar{y} - y^{-0}) \leq v^2, \left\| \Sigma y - \Sigma 0 \right\|_F \leq \rho \right\}, \text{ (45)}$$

$$-b+a^T y^{-0} \geq (k+v)\sqrt{a^T \sum_y a} \qquad (48)$$

It is to be noted that the optimization problem (27), (47) and (48) are actually the same; only the optimal values of κ differ. Let $\kappa-1*$ be the optimal value of problem (35). The solution to the robust equation above which is optimum is represented by

$$\kappa^{rob}* = \kappa^* - v. \qquad (49)$$

If the optimal value of the original (non-robust) problem (35) is below v, that is $\kappa^* < v$, it is concluded that the robust version is not feasible. The worst-case probability of misclassification is represented by $1-\alpha^*rob = 1$. If $\kappa^* > v$ where the robust hyperplane is the same as the non-robust one; the only change is in the worst-case misclassification probability, which is now as:

$$1-\alpha^{rob}* = \frac{1}{1+(\kappa*-v)^2} \qquad (50)$$

This gives a new interpretation of the optimal κ, in problem (35). The optimal κ^* is the worst-case uncertainty in the means that can be tolerated. If the level of uncertainty is more then κ^* then the robust problem becomes unfeasible.

It is to be assumed that the means are uncertain; in the model, the center $\bar{x}$ is allowed to vary in the ellipsoid $\varepsilon x(v)$, whose shape and orientation is same as $\varepsilon x(\kappa)$. It means that the robust problem can be reformulated as a variant of the original one, where $\varepsilon x(\kappa)$ is enlarged by changing κ to $\kappa+v$.

Estimation Errors in the Covariance Matrix

In this text the Case where there is uncertainty in the covariance but the mean is accurately estimated from the samples ($v = 0$) is considered and evaluated here:To address the robustness conditions

in (42) and (43), the following problem needs to be solved:

$$\text{Max } a^T\Sigma a: \Delta\Sigma - \Sigma^o \Delta_\Phi \text{ O}\rho \qquad (51)$$

where 'a' is provided for now. The optimal value of the above problem is:

$$\max \Sigma: D\Sigma - \Sigma oDF \text{ O}\rho \text{ aT}\Sigma a: aT(\Sigma O + \rho In)a \qquad (52)$$

where In is the n x n identity matrix.

Problem (42) and (43) reads now:

$$\max_{\kappa, a\neq 0, b} \kappa \text{ s.t. } -b+a^T\bar{y} \geq \kappa\sqrt{a^T\left(\sum_x + \rho I_n\right)a} \qquad (53)$$

$$-b+a^T y^{-0} \geq (k+v)\sqrt{a^T\sum_y a} \qquad (54)$$

Hence, the robust problem is as same as the original one, with a term ρIn been added to the covariance matrices.

The term ρIn can be interpreted as a regularization term. In the original model founded the original problem was not taken convex if e estimates of the covariance matrices was not positive definite. This leads to potentially various solutions, possible discontinuities, and numerical problems. The solution becomes unique as well as a continuous function of the data inputed when such a term is added.

Kernelization

"Kernelization" of the minimax approach is described here. It is basically used to project the problem to a higher-dimensional feature space Rf through a mapping φ: Rn → Rf such that a linear decision boundary $H(a,b) = \{\phi(z)\in R^f| a^T\phi(z) = b\}$ in the feature space Rf corresponds to a non-linear decision boundary $D(a,b) = \{z\in R^n|$

$a^T\phi(z) = b$} in the original space: Let the data be mapped as $R^n (a \in R^f / \{0\}$ and $b \in R)$. A nonlinear decision boundary in R^n is obtained when the minimax probability decision problem (20 and 21) in the higher dimensional feature space R^f is solved as given:

$$x \mapsto \varphi(x) \sim \left(\overline{\varphi(x)}, \Sigma\varphi(x) \right) \tag{55}$$

$$y \mapsto \varphi(y) \sim \left(\overline{\varphi(y)}, \Sigma\varphi(y) \right) \tag{56}$$

To carry out this program, it is needed to reformulate the minimax problem in terms of a given kernel function K $(z1,z2)=\varphi(z1)T\varphi(z2)$ satisfying Mercer's condition.

$$\max_{\alpha, a \neq 0, b} \text{ s.t. } \inf_{\varphi(x) \sim \left(\overline{\varphi(x)}, \Sigma\varphi(x) \right)} \Pr\left\{ a^T\varphi(x) \geq b \right\} \geq \alpha \tag{57}$$

$$\inf_{\varphi(y) \sim \left(\overline{\varphi(y)}, \Sigma\varphi(y) \right)} \Pr\left\{ a^T\varphi(y) \geq b \right\} \geq \alpha \tag{58}$$

The kernel trick will only work if problem (57 and 58) can be entirely expressed in terms of inner products of the mapped data $\varphi(z)$ only. Fortunately, this is indeed the case (even if uncertainty is taken in means and covariance matrices into account), but only when it is used for the means and covariance matrices.

DEVELOPMENT OF MODEL

The main scope of this work is to implement the above methodologies (ELM and MPMC) in the problem of estimating the slope stability. To forecast the Status of Stability (S) of rock or soil slopes, the factor that influence S needs to be determined.

The input layer consists of eight input parameters for wedge failure namely unit weight (γ), cohesions (c_A and c_B), angles of internal friction (φ_A and φ_B), angle of line of intersection of the two joint sets (ψ_P), slope angle(ψ_F) and Height (H), where A and B refer to two joint sets. The data for developing the models is taken from literature (Sakellariou & Ferentinou, 2005; Sah et al, 1994). The data refer to dry slopes without any tension crack. The available data are divided into two sets: training and testing. Seventy percent (i.e. 15) of the data are used for training and thirty percent (i.e. 7) of the data were used for testing. The datasets are normalized between 0 and 1. For developing MPM and ELM, a value of 1 is assigned to the stable condition of rock slope while a value of -1 is assigned to the failure condition of rock slope. The output of ELM and MPM is +1 or -1. The program of ELM and MPM has been developed by using MATLAB.

RESULTS AND DISCUSSIONS

For developing MPM, radial basis function has been adopted as kernel function. The performance of the developed MPM depends on the proper choice of width (σ) of radial basis function. The design value of σ has been determined by trial and error approach. Training and testing performance have been determined by using the following equation.

Training/Testing Performance(%)=

$$\left(\frac{\text{No of data predicted accurately by MPM}}{\text{Total data}} \right) \times 100 \tag{59}$$

The developed MPM gives best performance at $\sigma = 0.54$. The performance of MPM for training and testing datasets is 100%. So, the developed MPM has ability for prediction of stability of rock slope.

The training and testing performance is same. So, the developed MPM does not show overtraining. Therefore, it has good generalization capability. Table 1 and Table 2 show the performance of training and testing datasets respectively.

For developing ELM, radial basis function has been used as an activation function. The success of ELM model depends on the number of hidden nodes. The number of hidden nodes is determined by trial and error approach. The developed ELM gives best performance for six hidden nodes. The developed ELM misclassifies one data for training as well as testing dataset. So, the training performance=93.33% and testing performance=85.71%. Therefore, the developed MPM gives better performance than the ELM

Table 1. Performance of training dataset

γ (kN/m³)	c_A (kPa)	c_B (kPa)	$\phi_A(°)$	$\phi_B(°)$	$\psi_p(°)$	$\psi_f(°)$	H(m)	Actual Class	Predicted Class by MPM	Predicted Class by ELM
25.14	23.94	47.88	20	30	31.2	65	30.5	1	1	1
25	14.36	16.76	28	18	30	45	37	-1	-1	-1
22.8	0	0	35	35	38	47	110	-1	-1	-1
26	0	0	30.6	22.8	30.6	33	270	1	1	1
26	20	20	27	27	60	70	44	1	1	1
26	0	0	39	39	60	70	44	-1	-1	-1
26.66	0	0	45	45	35	50	150	1	1	1
25	0	0	32.4	32.4	30	48	50	1	1	1
18.84	0	0	30	30	37.5	45	61	-1	-1	-1
23.24	19.15	28.73	22.6	19.1	29	40	46	-1	-1	-1
27	0	0	30	30	37.5	26	110	1	1	-1
27	0	0	20	30	37.5	26	110	1	1	1
27	0	0	20	30	43	26	50	1	1	1
27	20	20	20	30	43	26	60	1	1	1
27	0	0	10	10	43	26	60	-1	-1	-1

Table 2. Performance of testing dataset

γ (kN/m³)	c_A (kPa)	c_B (kPa)	$\phi_A(°)$	$\phi_B(°)$	$\psi_p(°)$	$\psi_f(°)$	H(m)	Actual Class	Predicted Class by MPM	Predicted Class by ELM
20	0	0	40	4	45	60	100	-1	-1	-1
19.9	40	19	22	22	37	42	140	-1	-1	-1
26.66	0	0	35	35	30	42	150	1	1	1
18.84	30.07	3.6	30	36.7	37.5	45	61	-1	-1	1
27	0	0	20	30	37.5	26	50	1	1	1
27	0	0	15	15	43	26	60	-1	-1	-1
24	49	49	20	30	65	31	40	1	1	1

models. MPM is a probabilistic model. However, ELM is not a probabilistic model. The developed MPM has control over future prediction whereas the ELM has no control over future prediction.

CONCLUSION

This article uses MPM and ELM for prediction of stability status of rock slope. MPM and ELM have been adopted as classification techniques. The developed MPM and ELM give good performance. The performance MPM is better than the ELM model. The developed models (MPM and ELM) can be used as quick tool for prediction of stability status of rock slope. In summary, it can be concluded that the developed ELM and MPM can be used to solve different problems in engineering.

REFERENCES

Anderson, E. D., & Anderson, A. D. (2000). The MOSEK interior point optimizer for linear programming: An implementation of the homogeneous algorithm. In H. Frenk, C. Roos, T. Terlaky, & S. Zhan (Eds.), High performance optimization, (pp. 197-232). Kluwer Academics Publisher.

Barlett, P. L. (1997). For valid generalization, the size of the weights is more than the size of networks. Advances in Neural Information Processing Systems, 9, 134-140.

Bartlett, P. L. (1998). The sample complexity of pattern classification with neural networks. The size of the weights is more important than the size of network. *IEEE Transactions on Information Theory*, 44(2), 525–536. doi:10.1109/18.661502

Bertsekas, D. P. (1999). *Nonlinear Programming*. Belmont, MA: Athena Scientific.

Bishop, A. W. (1955). The use of slip circle in the stability analysis of eath surface. *Geotechnique*, 5(1), 7–17. doi:10.1680/geot.1955.5.1.7

Boyd, S., & Vandenberghe, L. (2001). *Convex Optimization.* Course notes for EE364, Stanford University. Available at http://www.stanford.edu/class/ee364

Hornik, K. (1991). Approximation capabilities of multilayer feedforward networks. *Neural Networks*, 4(2), 251–257. doi:10.1016/0893-6080(91)90009-T

Huang, G. B. (2003). Learning capability and storage capacity of two hidden layer feed-forward networks. *IEEE Transactions on Neural Networks*, 14(2), 274–281. doi:10.1109/TNN.2003.809401 PMID:18238011

Huang, G. B., & Babri, H. A. (1998). Upper bounds on the number of hidden neurons in Feedforward networks with arbitrary bounded nonlinear activation function. *IEEE Transactions on Neural Networks*, 9(1), 224–229. doi:10.1109/72.655045 PMID:18252445

Huang, G. B., Chen, L., & Siew, C. K. (2003). *Universal approximation using incremental Feedforward networks with arbitrary input weights.* Technical Report ICIS/46, Nayang Technological University.

Huang, G. B., Zhu, Q. Y., & Siew, C. K. (2003). *Real time learning capabilities of neural networks.* Technical report ICIS/45, Nayang Technological University.

Huang, G.-B., Zhu, Q.-Y., & Siew, C.-K. (2004). Extreme Learning machine: A new learning scheme of feedforward Neural Networks. In *Proceedings of International Joint Conference on Neural Networks (IJCNN2004).*

Ito, Y. (1992). Approximation of continuous function on Rd by linear combination of shifted rotation of a sigmoid function with and without scaling. *Neural Networks*, *5*(1), 105–115. doi:10.1016/S0893-6080(05)80009-7

Janbu, N. (1954). Application of composite slip circle for stability analysis. In *Proceedings of Fourth European conference on stability of earth surface.*

Kass, R., Tierney, L., & Kadane, J. (1988). Asymptotics in Bayesian comptation. Bayesian Statistics, 3, 261-278.

Lanckriet, G. R. G., Ghaoui, L. E., Bhattacharyya, C., & Jordan, M. I. (2002a). In T. G. Dietterich, S. Becker, & Z. Ghahramani (Eds.), *Minimax probability machine* (Vol. 14, pp. 801–807). Cambridge, MA: MIT Press.

Leshno, M., Lin, V. Y., Pinkus, A., & Schocken, S. (1993). Multilayer Feedforward networks with a nonpolynomial activation function can approximate any function. *Neural Networks*, *6*(6), 861–867. doi:10.1016/S0893-6080(05)80131-5

Lobo, M., Vanderberghe, L., Boyd, S., & Lebret, H. (1998). Applications of Second order cone programming. *Linear Algebra and Its Application, 284*, 193-228.

Marshall, A. W., & Olkin, I. (1960). Multivarible Chebyshev inequalities. *Annals of Mathematical Statistics*, *31*(4), 1001–1014. doi:10.1214/aoms/1177705673

Mika, S., Ratsch, G., Wetson, J., Scholkof, B., & Muller, K.-R. (1999). Fisher discriminant analysis with kernels. Neural Networks for Signal Processing, 9, 41-48. doi:10.1109/NNSP.1999.788121

Nesterov, Y., & Nemirovsky, A. (1994). *Interior point polynomial methods in convex programming: Theory and Applications.* Philadelphia, PA: SIAM. doi:10.1137/1.9781611970791

Perez-Cruz, F., Alarcon-Diana, P. L., Navia-Vazquez, A., & Artes-Rodriguez, A. (2001). In T. K. Leen, T. G. Dietterich, & V. Tresp (Eds.), *Fast training of support vector classifiers* (Vol. 13, pp. 734–740). MIT Press.

Popescu, I., & Berstimas, D. (2001). *Optimal inequalities in probability theory. A convex optimization approach.* Technical Report TM62, INSEAD.

Roussos, E. (2000). *Neural Networks for landslide hazard estimation.* (Master Thesis). Kings College.

Sah, N. K., Sheorey, P. R., & Upadhyama, L. W. (1994). Maximum Likelihood estimation of slope stability. *Int. J. Rock Mech. Min Sci. Geomech*, *31*(1), 47–53. doi:10.1016/0148-9062(94)92314-0

Sakellariou, M. G., & Ferentinou, M. D. (2005). A study of slope stability prediction using neural networks. *Geotechnical and Geological Engineering*, *23*(4), 419–445. doi:10.1007/s10706-004-8680-5

Sakellariou, M. G., & Ilias, P. (1997). Application of neural networks in the estimation of slope stability. *Proceedings of Third Hellenic Geotechnical Conference, 2*, 269-276.

Sarma, S. K. (1975). Seismic stability of earth dams and embankments. *Geotechnique*, *25*(4), 743–761. doi:10.1680/geot.1975.25.4.743

Scholkopf, B., & Smola, A. (2002). *Learning with Kernels.* Cambridge, MA: MIT Press.

Serre, D. (2002). *Matrices: Theory and applications.* Springer-Verlag.

Sturm, J. (1999). Using SeDuMi 1.02, A MATLAB toolbox for optimization over symmetric cones. *Optimization Methods and Software, 11-12*(1-4), 625–653. doi:10.1080/10556789908805766

Suykens, J. A. K., & Vandewalle, J. (1999). Least squares support vector machine classifiers. *Neural Processing Letters*, *9*(3), 293–300. doi:10.1023/A:1018628609742

Tamura, S., & Tateishi, M. (1997). Capabilities of a four layered feedforward neural network. *Four layer versus three. IEEE Transactions on Neural Networks, 8*(2), 251–255. doi:10.1109/72.557662 PMID:18255629

Taylor, D. W. (1937). Stability of earth slopes. *J.Boston Soc. Civil Eng, 24*, 197.

Wang, J., Wang, S.-T., Deng, Z.-H., & Qi, Y.-S. (2010). Image thresholding based minimax probability criterion. *Pattern Recognition and Artificial Intelligence, 23*(6), 880–884.

Yang, L., Wang, L., Sun, Y., & Zhang, R. (2010). Simultaneous feature selection and classification via Minimax Probability Machine. *International Journal of Computational Intelligence Systems, 3*(6), 754–760. doi:10.1080/18756891.2010.97 27738

Zhou, Z., Wang, Z., & Sun, X. (2013). Face recognition based on optimal kernel minimax probability machine. *Journal of Theoretical and Applied Information Technology, 48*(3), 1645–1651.

KEY TERMS AND DEFINITIONS

Classification: It means to either attribute to a condition of stable or failure. A value of 1 is assigned to the stable condition of rock slope while a value of - 1 is assigned to the failure condition of rock slope.

Extreme Learning Machine: A soft computing model used for classification problems depending on the input.

Minimax Probability Machine: A soft computing model used for classification.

Prediction: Forecasting depending on a previous set of defined input.

Probability: The chance of an event happening or not happening.

Rock Slope: Inclined surface of rock surface.

Slope Instability: Failure of slopes due to external as well as intrinsic factors.

Chapter 10

3D Image Acquisition and Analysis of Range Face Images for Registration and Recognition

Suranjan Ganguly
Jadavpur University, India

Debotosh Bhattacharjee
Jadavpur University, India

Mita Nasipuri
Jadavpur University, India

ABSTRACT

Although, automatic face recognition has been studied for more than four decades; there are still some challenging issues due to different variations in face images. There are mainly two categories of face recognition based on acquisition procedure. One technology that deals with video based face recognition and another approach where different sensors are used for acquisition purpose of different stationary face images, for instance: optical image, infra-red image and 3D image. In this context, researchers have focused only on 3D face images. 3D face images convey a series of advantages over 2D i.e. video frame, optical as well as infra-red face images. In this chapter, a detailed study of acquisition, visualization, detail about 3D images, analyzing it with some fundamental image processing techniques and application in the field of biometric through face registration and recognition are discussed. This chapter also gives a brief idea of the state of the art about the research methodologies of 3D face recognition and its applications.

INTRODUCTION

In our busy schedule of daily life, everyone is very much worried about his or her security. At present, there are different surveillance systems for this reason. It is hooked up from ATM to authentication and also attendance system. The classical approaches like, username and password or even better security system such as, punch card with PIN code are limited to human memorization capabilities and can be stolen, forgot or even it can be duplicated easily, or sometime

DOI: 10.4018/978-1-4666-8654-0.ch010

Figure 1. Human face: a biometric measurement

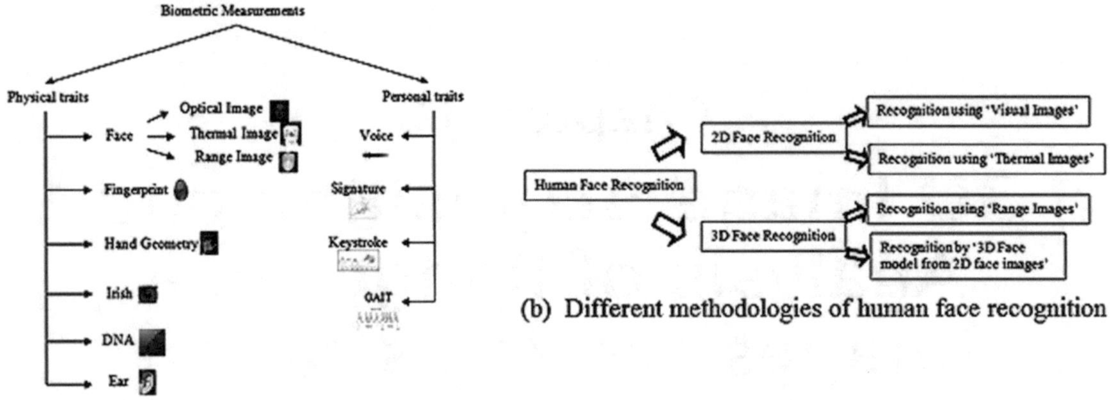

(a) Different Biometric Measurements

(b) Different methodologies of human face recognition

it may also be corrupted. To overthrow these major issues for security purpose, an alternative approach for authentication system is introduced i.e. 'Biometric' based authentication system. It is basically reliant to the intelligence of a computer to compute a series of operation for automatically identification purpose. The context of Biometric is 'life measurement' (Seal et al., 2014). Biometric based system uses two different kinds of characteristics. Depending on the characteristic, biometric measurements are broadly grouped into two sections namely: physical and personal qualities. It is illustrated in Figure 1.

Furthermore, individually, face recognition (FR) domain can further be grouped into two sub-domains such as 2D face recognition and 3D face recognition. It is briefly described in Figure 1(b). Again, 2D FR can be performed using a visual image, as well as infrared image. Other than range face images, 3D face model from 2D images is another approach for 3D face based FR.

The aim of this chapter is to include detail structural information about 3D image technology, its detailing and successful application for biometric measurement especially by 'Range Face Images'. A comparative study on results of recent works on range face image registration and recognition on well-known databases are also reported here.

There are different challenges where computational intelligence fails to correctly recognize the probe range image with gallery face images. But with the advancement of technology, 3D face images can be used to overcome some of these problems. It is captured by 3D scanners. Though there are several biometric measurements, but due to the unique characteristic with non-contacting and non-counterfeit properties, face base authentication system is highly praised over others. In Figure 2, the importance of face image in a different paradigm is highlighted.

In Table 1, a list is also shown for illustrating some of the advantages of 3D face images compared to optical and thermal face images.

Table 1. Face recognition challenges

Different Challenges for Face Recognition	Solvable Using 2D Images		Solvable Using 3D Images
	Optical	Thermal	
Illumination Variation	No	Yes	Yes
Pose variation	No		Yes
Expression Variation	No	Yes	Yes
Disguises	No		Yes
Aging	No		No
Temperature Variation	No	Yes	Yes

Figure 2. Characteristics of human face images measurement

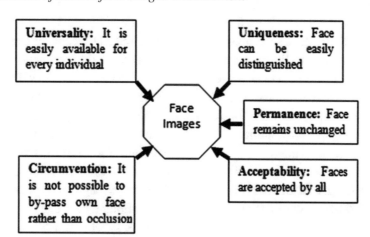

Here, authors have aimed to introduce the detailed description of this new scheme of face recognition in this chapter. Within the chapter, researchers can find a full reference about 3D face technologies related to image acquisition of 3D face image, the image formats, different visualizations of the captured face image, creation of 2.5D range face image from 3D image and its application in the domain of image processing with comparison of conventional 2D face images. In addition, authors have also provided a series of the literature review on available 3D face databases, recent work on face registration as well as recognition.

Thus, the primary concern of this chapter is to provide a complete reference, where the researchers will able to find all the possible quires on 3D face image regarding acquisition to different applications.

At first, the 3D face image acquisition techniques have been described followed by different image formats of the captured 3D image. Now, visualization of these captured 3D face images have been shown. Next, the effect of some fundamental image processing techniques on 2.5D range face images has been illustrated. Alongside,

the literature review on different methodologies (face registration and recognition) with the available databases is depicted.

3D IMAGE ACQUISITION TECHNIQUES

3D image is not same as 2D (whether optical or thermal). For 2D images, illumination (in case of optical image) or heat radiation (for infrared image) are measured and quantified as the intensity value and can be processed as matrix format quickly. But, the 3D images are obtained by different 3D scammers, namely, MINOLTA VIVID-700, DAVID SLS-1, Laser scanner etc and depth value (the Z' values) are preserved in X-Y plane for each point from scanned object. Sometimes, this Z values along carries some significant characteristic to identify the individuals uniquely. Hence, in the 3D image, three point-clouds (X, Y, and Z) for three axes are preserved. The 'Range' images which are the primary focus area of this chapter used to create from these depth values (i.e. Z-values). It is also referred as 'Depth-map Images' or '2.5D' image. The range image is not same as conventional

2D image. It does not have intensity values like 2D, and some metadata are also missing form it compared to original 3D image. Range image is created only from 'Z' data captured by the sensors. There are many ways to capture 3D face images. In this chapter, three different approaches are outlined with detail description. In the following section some object (especially, human face) scanning mechanisms are described.

SLS (Structured Light Scanner) based 3D Face Image Acquisition

In this mechanism the scanner has two components such as, projector and a camera. The projector emits structured light (different patterns of light shown in Figure 4) on the scanning face surface (marked 'C' in Figure 3). There are at most 24 different patterns (horizontal and vertical) that are used by scanner for projection. In Figure 3, the projection of structured light is given as a set of dotted lines. Now, due to the projection, the face is illuminated accordingly, and thus faces are free from any kind of external light source and thus 3D images have illumination free inherent

property. The illumination is provided as solid dark line in Figure 3. Even, in total dark environment, the 3D face scan can be digitized. Here, the 3D digitizing mechanism is illustrated using DAVID SLS-1. The DAVID 3M camera (marked 'B' in Figure 3) is used to capture the 3D image of the face. The very initial step before 3D face scan can be digitized, the camera is required to calibrate. Calibration is the process for adjusting the DAVID 3M camera and projector with a fixed focus length and distance from the face. The calibration process enables both the components to work synchronously for capturing 3D image of the object. By this capturing mechanism, three separated files are generated namely '.mtl', '.obj,' '.png.' The '.png' file is nothing but the 2D image of the scanning face. '.obj' is a 3D image file and '.mtl' is material library. A detailed description of different file format will be discussed in the following section of the chapter. The resolution of the image is 1280×960 with mesh point cloud approximately 350000. The resolution of the scan object is 0.02% of the original scanned object. In Figure 3, a schematic diagram of SLS based 3D face scanning system is shown.

Figure 3. 3D face image capturing mechanism using DAVID SLS 1

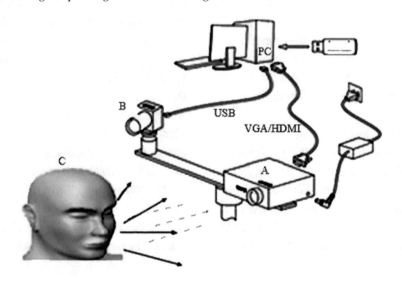

Figure 4. Some of the projected light patterns during 3D face image acquisition process using DAVID SLS 1

Laser Scanner Based 3D the Face Image Acquirement

Like DAVID SLS, laser scanners are also used to calibrate with face. There are two laser colors, namely, red and green. It is needed to keep the laser and brush it on the subject for acquisition. It captures the more detail fine information of the surface less than 0.2 millimeter. The files that will be created are '.obj', '.bmp' and '.mtl' file. The information that is used to hold by these files is same as SLS based procurement. Instead of '.png' it keeps the 2D image of a face in '.bmp.'

image. Instead of projector (a source of emitting structure light) Class 1 laser is used (marked 'A' in Figure 5). In Figure 5, a schematic diagram of laser scanner system is introduced.

Next-Engine 3D Scanner Based Face Image Acquisition

Next-Engine 3D scanner has three functional blocks namely the scanner itself, the 3D scanner software and the scanning object (here, the human face). The 3D scanner and a computer loaded with scanner's software are connected to each other. The

Figure 5. 3D face image capture using DAVID Laser Scanner Starter-Kit

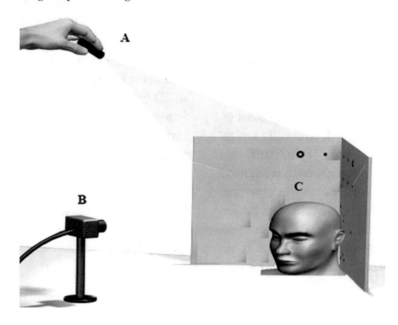

software is used during the scanning of the human face. For Next-Engine scan, studio HD 1.3.2 software is used. Using this software, different types of scan are possible by changing the setting portion of that software. Scanning mode can also be chosen. It can be termed as 'Positioning'. There are three possible modes namely, '360', 'Bracket', and 'Single'. '360' is used for scanning from every angle. 'Bracket' will scan the object (face) in three chunks and 'Single' will scan it from one angle. There are also various parameters those can be used for changing in scanning mechanism. 'Division' is primarily used for a number of divisions in 360 degree rotation. The 'Tilt' control sets the angle of the tilt where the scan will take place. In this process, a single scan or a set of scans take place on the base which actually rotates. 'Points/In2' is used to count the number of pixels which are scanned and 'Target' describes the general colour of the object. Scanning can be possible in a single view as well as in a different view by using MultiDrive part. After the scan is complete, it is possible to omit the unwanted sections. Along with these functionalities, the software also allows viewing the scanned face image in different modes, such as Textured, Solid, Wireframe, and Points.

FILE FORMATS OF 3D IMAGES

With the comparison of 2D image formats, 3D image formats are very much different to each other. 2D image formats are very much standardized, accessible and also well-known to most of the researchers. There are different 2D image formats such as '.png', '.jpeg,' '.bmp,' '.tiff' etc. that are dependent on the number of bits required to store the 2D image's pixel's color information for digitization purpose. For binary image 2-bit, for color image 8-bits for each RGB component and for grey image 8-bits per pixel are required. Thus, based on their digitization procedure, 2D image

formats are grouped into two groups (Reghbati, 1981) (Sayood) namely: lossless image compression and lossy image compression formats.

But 3D image formats do not actually dependent on the number of bits. Actually, 3D images do not belong to any pixel data, like 2D images. Based on different instrumental setup of the 3D scanners, different types of data are preserved in the 3D image files. But the common data that it belongs is the three data points namely: X, Y, and Z. The 'Z' is the depth data that are used to measure in X-Y plane. The depth data is measured from the face surface. Among available different 3D image formats '.wrl', '.bnt,' '.abs' and '.obj' image formats are discussed in this section. All these images are used to read as normal text file and then using the available data points it can be processed accordingly.

'.wrl' Image Format

WRL file format is a member from VRML file (VRML format, 2014). VRML stands for Virtual Reality Modeling Language. It is very much popular file format to represent a 3D image. It is well known for its usage in printing technology. Along with the header portion, it consists of two set of data. One set that belongs to three data clouds i.e. X, Y and Z data and another set which is having 3D polygon data. These two data sets are used for two different purposes. The first data set is helpful to create mesh representation of 3D data, creation of range image and surface image, whereas second data set is useful to generate triangular image (shown in Figure 15). All these images have been demonstrated in the next section of this chapter. Two most famous 3D face database's image namely: Frav3D (Frav3D database, 2014) and GavabDB (GavabDB database, 2014) are of '.wrl.' image format. In Figure 6, description of '.wrl' file is given.

Figure 6. '.wrl' format description

```
#VRML V1.0 ascii
# Polygon Editing Tool
# Object name : F:\FRAV3D_raw\CAM\001\001_01_00
Separator {
    Transform {
        translation 0 0 0
        scaleFactor 0.5 0.5 0.5
    }
    Group {
        Group {
            Separator {
                Transform {
                    translation 0 0 0
                }
                Coordinate3 {
                    point [                    Header Part
1.280 94.328 -1822.467    3D points X, Y an Z data
2.559 94.315 -1822.209,
3.838 94.290 -1821.696,
5.111 94.171 -1819.251,
```

'.bnt' Image Format

It is another well-known 3D image format. '.bnt' image format (BNT format, 2014) is different from '.wrl.' image format. The header portion of this format contains extra meta-data like data length of the image and the minimum depth value i.e. 'Z' value. The length of the data is the number of X, Y and Z data points. Among available databases, it is found that Bosphorus database has 3D face images in the form of '.bnt.' format.

'.obj' Image Format

It is studied that '.obj.' file format contains a set of useful meta-data (other than X, Y and Z) about 3D face images that are absent in above mentioned image formats. The image file size of this format is also large enough compared to others. Along with three data points (X, Y, and Z), this image format consists of color, texture and reflection map of individual face images which have been scanned. Other than these data, 2D coordinate

values for UV mapping of texture information along with 3D triangular data are also kept. The count of each of these meta-data is preserved at the end of each section. The 3D images captured by DAVID SLS 1 are of '.obj.' format. In Figure 7, the '.obj' image format is discussed.

'.abs' Image Format

The '.abs' formatted image (ABS format, 2014) is also another well-known 3D image format. It is investigated that, this image format is also different from 3D image formats mentioned above. At the beginning of the file, number of rows and the number of columns are used to define the set of 'valid points' section. This section is having numbers of 1 and 0 for indicating valid and non-valid points in 3D space (i.e. points along X, Y, and Z axes). Following the header and validation section within the image, there are three the data points regarding X, Y, and Z co-ordinates. The importance of the validation section within the image is that the valid 3D points among three sets

Figure 7. Introduction of '.obj' image format

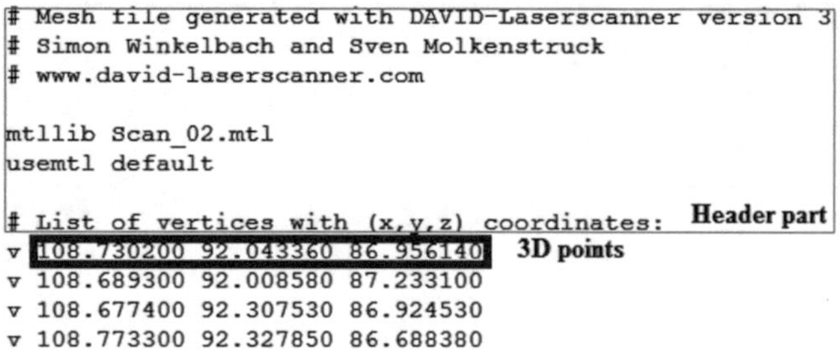

```
# Mesh file generated with DAVID-Laserscanner version 3
# Simon Winkelbach and Sven Molkenstruck
# www.david-laserscanner.com

mtllib Scan_02.mtl
usemtl default

# List of vertices with (x,y,z) coordinates:
v 108.730200 92.043360 86.956140
v 108.689300 92.008580 87.233100
v 108.677400 92.307530 86.924530
v 108.773300 92.327850 86.688380
```


Header part
3D points

of pointcloud representing three co-ordinates are used to make proper dimension of the digitized face. In Figure 8, these three section from '.abs' file is illustrated.

VISUALIZATION 3D FACE IMAGE

After successful acquisition of 3D face images, it is required to be visualized by the researchers. Visualization of 3D face images has a significant role for further processing (face registration and recognition) of images. It cannot be easily visualized like 2D. The 3D images are used to visualize by some dedicated software. Some of the researchers have used their own visualization technique according to their requirements. In this visualization section of the chapter, authors have presented different approaches for visualizing the captured 3D face images. In Figure 9, outcome of various techniques for visualizing the 3D images is summarized.

All these visualization technique has been implemented on Frav3D database and represented in Figure 11 to 16. These images are anticipated from single subject selected randomly from the database. The 2D optical images corresponding to these face images are shown in Figure 10.

3D Face Visualization

It is a technique for visualizing the captured 3D face images in 3D like representation. This view has been made using different viewer software like Cortona3D viewer, etc. Authors have used this method to anticipate the 3D faces for analyzing purpose from Frav3D database. It will help to understand the actual scanned 3D face images by comparing with 2D optical images. Along with this, different face images that have been generated by the authors will also be compared with such representation for analyzing. In Figure 11, the 3D display of face images from Frav3D database is highlighted.

Figure 8. Detailing about '.abs' image format

```
480 rows
640 columns
pixels (flag X Y Z):
0 0 0 0 0 0 0 0 0 0 0 0 0 0 0 0 0 0 0 0 0 0
1 1 1 1 1 1 1 1 1 1 1 1 1 1 1 1 1 1 1 1 1 1
1 1 1 1 1 1 1 1 1 1 1 1 1 1 1 1 1 1 1 1 1 1
0 0 0 0 0 0 0 0 0 0 0 0 0 0 0 0 0 0 0 0 0 0
0 0 0 0 0 0 0 0 0 0 0 0 0 0 0 0 0 0 0 0 0 0
-999999.000000 -999999.000000 -999999.000000
999.000000 -999999.000000 -999999.000000 -99
000000 -999999.000000 -999999.000000 -999999
00 -999999.000000 -999999.000000 -999999.000
999999.000000 -999999.000000 -999999.000000
99.000000 -999999.000000 -999999.000000 -999
00000 -999999.000000 -999999.000000 -999999.
```


Header part
Validating section
3D points

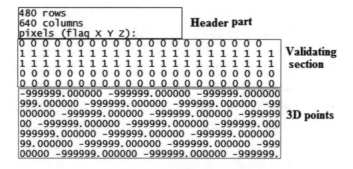

Figure 9. Visualization approaches of 3D face images

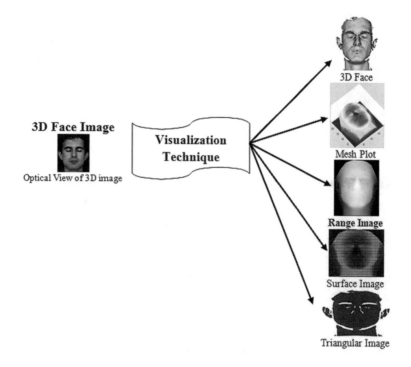

Figure 10. 2D optical face images from Frav3D database

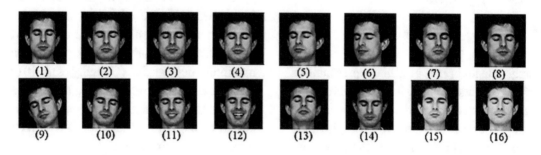

Figure 11. Corresponding 3D face images of 2D face images shown in Figure 10

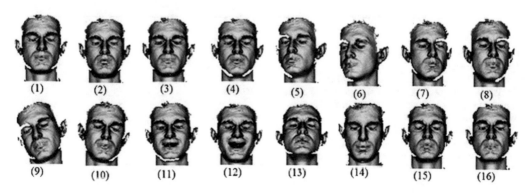

Figure 12. Corresponding 3D Mesh representation of face images shown in Figure 11

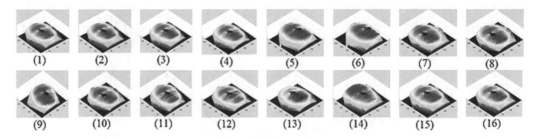

3D MESH VIEWING TECHNIQUE

Mesh images (shown in Figure 12) are the mesh plot of the 3D points (namely: X, Y, and Z) that looks like wire like structure of face images. These structures are made up of wires. This wire look of mesh image is implemented using Z (or depth value) in X-Y plane. The color of the mesh image is proportional to the depth of the face image. Form these kinds of images, the facial key points or landmarks can easily be detected. From the figure, the darkest point might be localized as nose region or 'pronasal'.

2.5D or Range Images

The range images are the gray like representation of the images made from 3D images. This chapter is focused on such kind of range face images. The analysis of 3D face images for registration and recognition will be based on range images.

Range images are also known as 2.5D or depth images (Kang, 1993) (Cantzler). In range image, the pixel data is not preserved rather it consists of the 'Z' values (i.e. depth values) from 3D images. It actually encodes the depth value in 2D representation form and thus, it has a dimension in between 2D and 3D and named as 2.5D. In Table 3, produced range images from different 3D image collected over some available face databases are illustrated. The algorithm for generating these range face images is described in algorithm 1. In Table 2, this algorithm is presented.

The generated range images of 3D face images (described in Figure 11) is shown in Figure 13.

It is further investigated that the nose region (especially 'pronasal' landmark point) is having maximum depth value (Ganguly et al. 2014a) as because it is the closest point to the 3D scanner. The variation of depth values near nose region is also high other than another face surface like: near forehead, cheek, etc.

Table 2. Algorithm 1 to generate range face image from 3D images

Input: 3D Image
Output: Range Image
Step 1: Extract the header information of the file
Step 2: Ignore the header's data
Step 3: Locate the first starting data points of the image
Step 4: Read all the 3 sets of points after discarding header portion from the file
Step 5: Separate the points as points cloud for each three axes
Step 6: Normalize the X, Y, and Z data
Step 7: Create grid by normalized X-Y data
Step 8: Place the Z data at corresponding (X-Y) plane of 2D grid
Step 9: Finally created grid data as the depth or range image

Table 3. Generated range images from different 3D image format

Image Format	Source	Generated Range Image
".wrl"	GavabDB database	
".bnt"	Bosphorus database (Bosphorus database, 2014)	
".abs"	UND face database (UND database, 2014)	
".obj"	Own database *	

* This database is created in our laboratory

Figure 13. Generated range face images of Figure 11

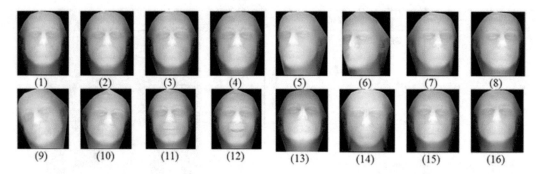

Face Surface Images from 3D Images

As the name suggested 'surface image' is an image of upper most layer of the 3D mesh plot. It is a continuous set of points that has length and breadth which are associated with X; Y co-ordinate and Z (or depth value) as the element of the X-Y plane. The color representation of mesh image and surface face image is same as because of depth values are same for both the cases. In Figure 14, the accomplished surface face images of Figure 14 are described.

Triangular Mesh Representation

Triangular plot of closest points is also possible. This knowledge is used to create triangular mesh representation. Authors have generated these face images (shown in Figure 15) using the meta-data from 3D file. It comprises with a set of triangles sharing common edges or points. It noticed that '.wrl.' file, '.obj' consist of sharing vertices that are used by the authors to generate the triangle mesh. Each triangle from mesh used to share one complete edge with another neighbor triangle and

Figure 14. Description of surface face images of Figure 11

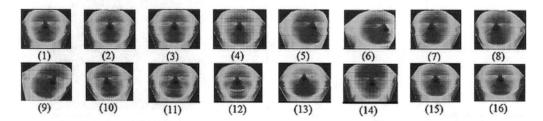

Figure 15. Description of triangular-mesh face images of Figure 11

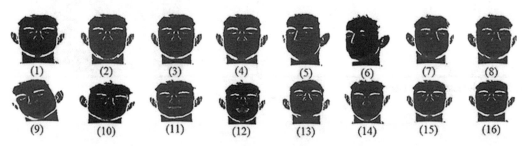

edge with the next triangle. It has the drawback that might not possible to convert each triangle to strips.

Normal Face Range Image

It is another type of range face image that can be generated from 3D image. Along with the depth data, the normal(s) from the 3D surface (X, Y, and Z) are used to accomplish these face data shown in Figure 16. The normal(s) from each vertex in the surface are un-normalized. This kind of face range image can be termed as 'Normal Depth Map' or 'NDM'.

All these different kinds of face images which have been demonstrated earlier from 3D face image are having different expressions and illumination variations as well as they are rotated along yaw, pitch and roll. The description of these face images is given in Table 4.

ANALYSIS OF 3D FACE IMAGES FROM RANGE IMAGE

Range images are neither 3D image nor 2D image and that are used to arrange more valuable depth data as discussed section 4. The conventional image processing techniques that create an array of results for input image might produce different outputs for same subject's 2D face image and 2.5D

face image. The images that will be considered during this analytical phase are selected from Frav3D database.

In this section, the analysis of face images will be carried on based on some fundamental and well known image processing technique. In the following sub-section, a set of investigation on this topic is carried on and explained with examples.

Brightness Measurement

It is an essential attribute for measuring the visual perception. Again visual perception is dependent on light reflected from the subject. Thus, brightness is evoked from the illumination of the subject. The formula used to measure the brightness (Gonzalez et al., 2012) of our research work is given in Equation 1.

Table 4. Description of the face images

Label	Description
1-4	Frontal pose face images
5-8	Rotated face image along Y-axis
9-10	Face rotated along Z-axis
11	Frontal face with an expression (smiling)
12	Frontal face with expression (mouth open)
13-14	Face rotated along X-axis
15-16	Frontal face with illumination variation

Figure 16. Normal Depth Map image of Figure 11

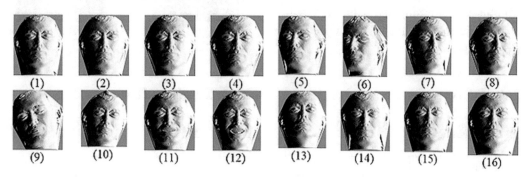

$$B = \frac{1}{(M \times N)} \sum_{x=0}^{M-1} \sum_{y=0}^{N-1} I(x,y) \tag{1}$$

where, M and N is the number of rows and columns of the input image (either 2.5D range images or 2D gray image). During the normalization phase of range image generation, the depths have been mapped in between 0 to 255 (i.e. total 256 depth variations). Besides his, for the comparison purpose, the 2D color space face image is also converted into gray image using Equation 2. Thus, both the 2.5D and 2D face images consist of 256 different depth and pixel data.

$$G = R*C_r + G*C_g + B*C_b \text{ and } C_r=0.2989;$$
$$C_g=0.5870; C_b=0.1140 \tag{2}$$

where R, G, and B are the Red, Green and Blue color channels of a 2D color image respectively. The measured brightness values for both range face image and 2D image are depicted in Table 5. These two face images are shown in Figure 17.

During brightness measurement process for 2.5D image depth values and gray pixel data from 2D images have been considered. Brightness measurement is actually the average of the input image. So, before making any comparative study, both the images have been resized into 100×100 row-column ratio using bi-cubic interpolation method (Gonzalez et al., 2012).

For color 2D image, brightness is quantified as the arithmetic mean of the individual (R, G and B) color space. The 'saturation' is closely related with brightness. Increasing the saturation will actually increase the brightness, and it defines the purity of color.

Contrast Estimation

There are many possible definitions of contrast measurement. In general, contrast is measured by the difference between color and brightness. Some of the he common and well established definitions of contrast (Gonzalez et al., 2012) estimation are Weber contrast (Peli, 1990) Michelson contrast (Peli, 1990) and RMS contrast (Gonzalez et al., 2012) (Peli, 1990). In this chapter, authors have implemented RMS (Root Mean Square) contrast for experimental purpose. The formula for RMS contrast is given in Equation 3.

$$C = \sqrt{\frac{1}{M \times N} \sum_{x=0}^{M-1} \sum_{y=0}^{N-1} \left(I(x,y) - B\right)^2} \tag{3}$$

From the Equation 3, it is observed that increasing the difference will eventually increase the contrast. Like brightness, the range or 2.5D face image and 2D image have been also fixed in to 100×100 resolution. In Table 6, the estimate contrast value of Figure 17 is described.

Figure 17. Considered face images during the analysis phase of this chapter

(i) 2D Face Image   (ii) 2.5D or Range face image

Table 5. Brightness measurement value

Image Dimension	Measured value
2D	34.689900000000002
2.5D (Range image)	1.333139158762471e+02

Table 6. Estimated contrast value

Image Dimension	Estimated value
2D	28.6796
2.5D (Range image)	83.4206

A high contrast value shows a well-distributed depth or intensity values across the min-max range. Whereas the low contrast value indicates concentrated values within the range. The min-max range for both the images is 0 and 255.

Histogram Processing

In the domain image processing, 'histogram' is the process to represent the values either depth or intensity. It can be represented as a discrete function

$$H(v_i) = n_i \qquad (4)$$

where n_i is the number of depth or intensity value v_i in the range 0 to L-1. 'L' is the maximum range value (for both the considered images, it is 255). Thus, the histogram provides a complete summary of the distribution of data from the image. This parameter belongs a major drawback for histogram based classification purpose. The different object with the same distribution of intensity or depth value will be grouped into the same class ignoring its unique shape and texture. In this section, the histogram for range image is termed as 'depth histogram' where as for 2D it is called as 'intensity histogram.' In Figure 18, these two histogram of corresponding face images from Figure 18 is shown.

As it is pointed earlier in 5.2 sections, the significance of contrast values of 2D and range face images are also illustrated in Figure 18.

It is also possible to plot a histogram for color image. In this case, it will count the distribution of the color space, especially R-G-B.

HISTOGRAM EQUALIZATION

Histogram equalization (Gonzalez et al., 2012) (Krutsch et al., 2011) is used as a tool to adjust the contrast of the images. This technique actually spreads the intensity or depth values along the total range for achieving better contrast. There are available many histogram equalization techniques namely: Histogram expansion (disadvantage is that if the gray intensity values are far from each other then it fails), LAHE (though it produce better equalized image but it's computation is very slow), Cumulative distribution (It is good but it is also required to create cumulative histogram) etc. Among these methods, authors have focused on cumulative distribution histogram equalization method (Gonzalez et al., 2012). In Figure 19, the equalized range and 2D face images are shown. In particular this technique is very much used in medical image domain to deal with more accuracy. But, we have experimented it for human face processing, especially for face recognition purpose.

Figure 18. Analysis of histogram

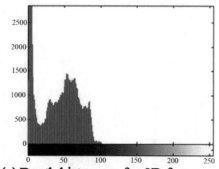 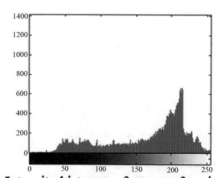

(a) Depth histogram for 2D face mage   (b) Intensity histogram for range face image

In Figure 19 (c) and (d), the contrast (shown in (b) and (a)) of the face images have been enhanced and thus purpose of the histogram equalization is served.

Due to the depth enhancement, the outward sections (such as, nose region, mouth region, and chin etc.) from range face image is brighter than original range face image i.e. it affects locally than globally. But in case of 2D, the enhancement is being made globally.

CONTRAST STRETCHING

Contrast stretching (Gonzalez et al., 2012) (Kerin) is another image enhancing process by which a low-contrast image can be stretched within the full range of intensity or depth value. It has a difference between histogram equalization techniques. Contrast stretching method applies linear scaling of the histograms over the range. In Figure 20, the stretched range image and 2D is shown.

Along with this set of study, another set of investigation is done on summary of the whole image (i.e. on histogram) to locate the differences. As this chapter is concentrated on range face images generated from 3D images, this investigation is done on depth histogram, and it is illustrated in Figure 20. The linear scaling process of contrast stretching operation is anticipated in Figure 21.

With the investigation, it is studied that low contrast 2D image is enhanced with major effect whereas for depth values the contrast stretching is now as useful as histogram equalization.

Image Negative

Negative of a range image is also another range image that spreads its depth values between 0-255. It is performed by the negative transformation or complement operation. The intensity or depth value say **i** is subtracted from maximum range of the image color space. The equation is described in Equation 5.

Figure 19. Summary of histogram equalization

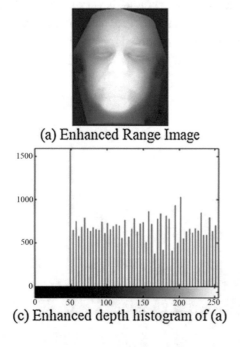

(a) Enhanced Range Image

(c) Enhanced depth histogram of (a)

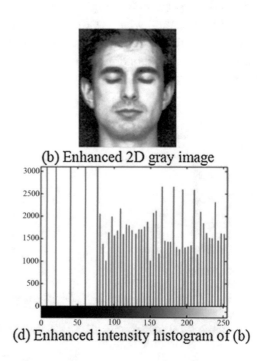

(b) Enhanced 2D gray image

(d) Enhanced intensity histogram of (b)

Figure 20. Study of contrast-stretching process

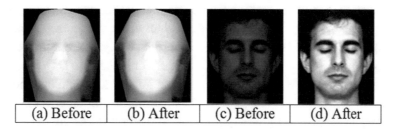

| (a) Before | (b) After | (c) Before | (d) After |

Figure 21. Histogram analysis

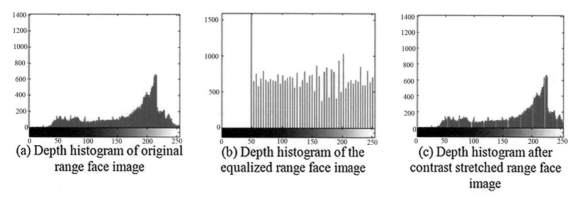

(a) Depth histogram of original range face image

(b) Depth histogram of the equalized range face image

(c) Depth histogram after contrast stretched range face image

$$N(x,y) = MAX_N - I(x,y) \qquad (5)$$

where MAX_N is the maximum depth or intensity value i.e. 255. $N(x,y)$ is the negative image of the input image $I(x,y)$ and (x,y) is the current row and column position during processing. In Figure 22, negative transformation of the image (shown in Figure 22) is demonstrated.

Figure 22. Negative transformation of the face images

(a) Negative of range image   (b) Negative of 2D

It observed that due to the inherent property of range image (consists of the depth values instead of intensity values), the negative transformation of it still exhibits more the facial properties like nose tip, eye-corners etc than negative of 2D image. The contour of the face image can also be extracted by negative range image very quickly. Now, the darkest point will be the nose tip.

Binary Image

In the field of digital image processing, binary image (Gonzalez et al., 2012) holds possible two values for each pixel. It is either '0' or '1'. Some time it is also referred as 'logical image' or 'black and white' image or 'bi-level', etc. The pixel value '0' means the color will be black and for '1' it will be white. A set image processing techniques namely: thinning process, edge detection, curvature etc., can produce a binary image.

In this sub-section, the operation that has been performed for binarization is show in equation 6.

$$\mathbf{B}(\mathbf{x},\mathbf{y}) = \begin{cases} 1 & \text{if } I(x,y) \geq T \text{ where } T = (0.2*I(x.y)) \\ 0 & \text{otherwise} \end{cases}$$

(6)

In this equation B(x,y) is the binary image and I(x,y) is input the the image (either range or 2D image). In Figure 23, binarized range and optical image of Figure 23 is exhibited.

It can be observed that the facial landmarks can no longer be detected from binary range image (Figure 23(a)), rather than one important geometrical property such as contour (Ebrahim-doost et al., 2010) can easily be retrieved from it.

Edge Detection

In general, edge detection method is applied for the image segmentation purpose. This approach deals with the local changes of intensity values from 2D image. For range face image, it is implemented on depth values and the local changes of depth values have been considered. Among different edge detection methodologies (Gonzalez et al., 2012) (Esakkirajan et al., 2009) authors have found two techniques namely: Canny and Sobel edge detection methods to comprise the output (shown in Figure 24) from 2.5D range face image and 2D image of Figure 24.

Basically, Sobel operator has performed convolution method by two windows where one window

Figure 23. Binary face images

(a) Binary range face image   (b) Binary optical face image

is rotated by 90⁰ by other to consider the vertical as, well as horizontal edges from images. Depth values from range face images are not having abrupt changes except the boundary, thus Sobel operator is useful to get the perimeter of the range face images for segmentation purpose based on contour. On the other hand, canny edge detection method is considered as optimal algorithm and does Gaussian soothing at the first step of the algorithm. The small but useful change near nose region, face perimeter can be identified by Canny edge detection process from the range face image. This property might be very much helpful for landmark detection, feature estimation from 3D face images using range images.

Curvature Computation

Curvature (Szeptycki et al., 2008) (Ganguly et al., 2014a) is a measurement of the deviation for objects (here, face image) from being flat or straight. The bend as well as sharpness of the object's image is found during curvature computation. There are four types of curvature maps namely Maximum

Figure 24. Result of edge detection methodologies

(a) Sobel operator   (b) Canny operator

Applied on range face images

(c) Sobel operator   (d) Canny operator

Applied on 2D optical face images

Principal curvature, Minimum Principal curvature, Gaussian, and Mean curvature. All of these have been found during the investigation phase. Principal curvature at a normal plane P is k1 and k2. k1 is used to represent Maximum Principal Curvature (Pmax) value where as k2 is represented as Minimum Principal Curvature value (Pmin). These are perpendicular to each other. The remaining two curvatures, the Gaussian Curvature value (K) and Mean Curvature value (H) is a product and the average of k1 and k2 respectively. This approach has been used on 3D face images, and corresponding four curvature face images has been arrayed in Figure 25.

The same technique has also been used on 2D gray face image. In this case, depth values (the 'Z') in X-Y plane is missing for curvature computation. For the comparative study of the curvature analysis, authors have complemented the depth values by intensity values. The X-Y plane is also accomplished by the size of the original input 2D image. In Figure 26, the outcome of the four curvatures of 2D input image has been described.

It is seen that due to the presence of intensity values instead of depth values as well as lack of X-Y plane's information, the curve value that has also been reported in Figure 26 is not so much informative as 3D curvatures shown in Figure 25.

Bit-Plane Slicing

Both the range and gray face images are having depth and intensity values that spread between 0 to 255 i.e. 256 gray color variations from black to white (as shown in Figure 17). The '0' means pure black and 255 means pure white. These 256 color code can be composed by 8-bits (i.e. 1-byte). Bit-plane slicing (Gonzalez et al., 2012) (Seal et al., 2011) (Bit-plane slicing, 2014) is the approach where the appearance of each bit for each byte will be highlighted into 8 different binary images. In Figure 27, creation of 8-bits from 1-byte is illustrated. Thus, 8-bit image can produce 8-binary images.

The 2.5D range face image can also be represented as a set of 8-bit images. These images

Figure 25. Curvature analysis for 3D face image shown in Figure 11 (1)

(a) Principal minimum curvature   (b) Principal maximum curvature   (c) Mean curvature   (d) Gaussian curvature

Figure 26. Curvature analysis for 2D optical face image shown in Figure 17 (i)

(a) Principal minimum curvature   (b) Principal maximum curvature   (c) Mean curvature   (d) Gaussian curvature

Figure 27. Procedure of bit-plane slicing technique

$$(255)_{10} \rightarrow (11111111)_2 \rightarrow$$

8th bit	....	3rd bit	2nd bit	1st bit
1	1	1	1	1	1	1	1

are of two level i.e. binary images. In Figure 27, the bit-planes from range face images i.e. the 8-binary images from input range image that has been obtained from this processing technique is shown in Figure 28.

The effect of bit-plane slicing technique is quite significant. The geometrical property such as the face contour from face range image is preserved in these images. Based on the depth values, different stripes have also been made in binary images. This can be used as to localize facial characteristic like mouth, nose tip, eyes, etc. Thus, instead of original face range image, the bit plane based on the relative importance of each depth's bit value can be preserved for processing. The space complexity can also be reduced. The bit-planes generated

from 8th bits are equivalent to binary conversion of the original image using equation 6 with the change of the threshold value from 0.2 to 0.5. It is expressed in Equation 7.

$$T = (0.5*I(x,y)) \qquad (7)$$

This technique has also been implemented for 2D gray face image, and the retrieved images have been shown in Figure 29.

Like 2.5D, bit-planes from 2D images are not providing valid information by initial bit-planes. Binary image from bit-pane from 1st bit is a noisy image, whereas bit-plane from 4th bit holding some facial properties. The bit level images from bit-planes 5th to 7th bit are carrying more valu-

Figure 28. Each bit-planes from range face image

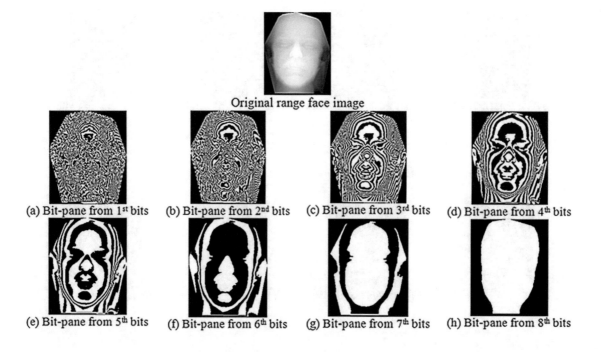

Original range face image

(a) Bit-pane from 1st bits   (b) Bit-pane from 2nd bits   (c) Bit-pane from 3rd bits   (d) Bit-pane from 4th bits

(e) Bit-pane from 5th bits   (f) Bit-pane from 6th bits   (g) Bit-pane from 7th bits   (h) Bit-pane from 8th bits

Figure 29. 8-bit planes from 2D image

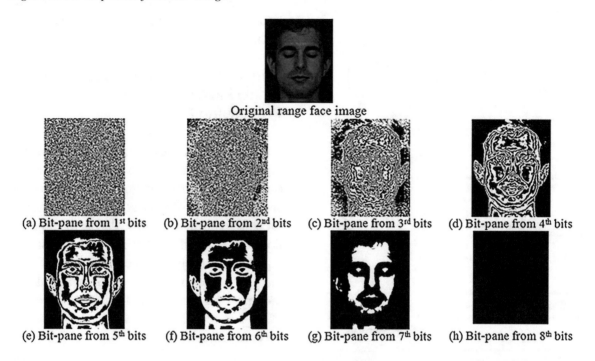

able information than others. Thus, these three images with lesser number of bits may be stored for further processing.

LITERATURE SURVEY AND DIFFERENT METHODOLOGIES

Efficient and robust 3D face recognition algorithm consists of several sub-problems. It is also required to test valid databases to establish its success. As it is discussed in Table 1, the face recognition problem is very much challenging task due to variations of facial expression, illumination, and furthermore due to pose variations along yaw, pitch and roll. Thus, the face registration of rotated face images is also a crucial part during the designing of any recognition algorithm. The localization of landmarks is also a major step during the registration process. However, the

recognition algorithms of face images can also be grouped into to two parts, namely: feature based recognition and holistic approach.

In Figure 30, a general architecture of 3D face recognition process is depicted.

In this section, a broad description of available 3D face databases is reported. Along with this, the research work that has already been carried out on various steps of 3D face recognition (namely: image preprocessing, landmark detection, pose registration and recognition) is also stated.

Available 3D Face Databases

Database plays a significant role for any kind of research work, especially for biometric based authentication purpose. An algorithm which is needed to be established requires a suitable database where it can perform well and up to the mark for evaluation of the researchers' expectation.

Figure 30. Pipeline architecture of 3D face recognition algorithm from range

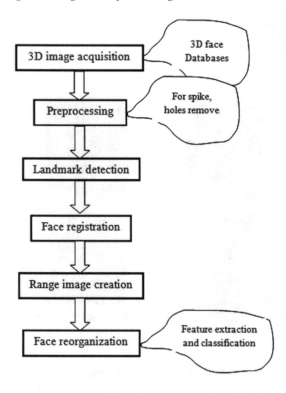

The availability of a standard database containing large sets of 3D face images with varying degree of like poses, facial expressions, illumination etc. are essential for developing new face recognition algorithms and to test it for acceptance by the research community. Like 2D face images database, such as PIE Database (PIE database, 2014), FERET (FERET database, 2014) etc., for 3D face recognition goal, there are few publicly available databases. But the numbers of databases are increasing with time. Some of these databases contain the visual image correspond to the 3D image with or without a degree of variations. Brief descriptions for most of the available databases are given in Table 7.

The file type denoted as 'Set of points' is used to represent the three points along three axes (X, Y and Z) are available, thus range images can easily be created using the algorithm 1, described

earlier. 'Not available' is indicated by 'NA.' The information regarding a particular field is absent in the source.

Different Approaches Followed for 3D Face Image Pre-Processing Purpose

Image pre-processing is the preliminary task during automatic face registration as well as recognition process. It includes face image localization and RoI (Region of Interest) extraction, filtering for noise reduction occurred during the digitization process, method(s) to fill the holes of face region, outlier removal, etc. In Table 8, a summary of different pre-processing techniques is presented that has been applied for the objective of 3D face registration as well as recognition in very recent years.

LANDMARK DETECTION AND REGISTRATION OF 3D FACE IMAGES

Face registration is an intermediate and very crucial step towards accurate and robust face recognition. Pose variation problem which is one of the major challenges for face recognition can be overcome during the face registration step. Face registration (Spreeuwers, 2011) (Ganguly et al., 2014b) is a method by which face images with pose variations can be aligned and fixed to frontal pose. But for the registration purpose it is needed to detect landmarks such as: nose tip, eye corners etc. by which the face images can be rotated and transformed to frontal or near frontal pose. There are mainly three types of registration methods. One approach is one to all registration. It is an iterative method where probe image (the unregistered face image) is translated and rotated according to the frontal posed gallery images. During the registration by face model methodology,

Table 7. Description of available 3D facial images' databases

Database Name	Type of File	Size of File	Number of Person or Subject	Task for Variation of Face Images
3D RMA (3D RMA face database, 2014)	Set of points	4000 points	106-Male 14-Female	Pose
Univ. of York 1 (Univ. of York 1 database, 2014)	Range Image	NA	97	Pose, Expression, Occlusion
Univ. of York 2 (Univ. of York 2 database, 2014)	Range Image	NA	350	Pose, Expression
GavabDB	Set of points	NA	45-Male 16-Female	Smile, frontal accentuated laugh, frontal random gesture
FRAV3D	Set of points	NA	106	Pose, Lighting changes
Bosphorus Database	Set of points	NA	60-Male 45-Female	Pose, Expression, Occlusion
BJUT-3D Chinese Face Database (BJUT-3D, 2014)	NA	NA	250-Male 250-Female	Neutral expression and without accessories
CASIA-3D FaceV1 (CASIA-3D, 2014)	Range Image	NA	123	Poses, Expression, Illumination. Combined variations of expressions under illumination. Pose variation under expressions and smile, laugh, anger, surprise closed eyes
UMB-DB (UMB-DB, 2014)	NA	NA	98-Male 45-Female	Expression, Occlusion
Texas 3D (Texas 3D, 2014)	Range Image	751 × 501	118	Neutral, Expression
ND2006 (ND2006 3D face database, 2014)	NA	NA	888	Expression, Disgust and Other
BU3D FE (BU3D database, 2014)	Range Image	NA	44-Male 56-Female	Expression, Pose (+45° to –45°)
FRGCv.2 (FRGC v.2, 2014)	Range and Texture Image	NA	466	Expression
USF Human ID 3-D Database (USF database, 2014)	NA	NA	NA	NA
3D Dynamic Facial Expression Database (Zhang et al. 2014)	3D dynamic facial sequences, also known as 4D data	1040 × 1329 pixels	101	7-Expression variations and disguise
XM2VTSD (xm2vtsdb 3D face model, 2014)	Set of points	NA	293	speaking head shot and a rotating head shot
PRISM-ASU 3D facial shape (PRISM-ASU 3D facial shape, 2014)	NA	NA	1500	NA
3D Facial Expression Database (3D Facial Expression Database, 2014)	3D face surface geometry and surface texture (mesh and Texture)	1300 × 900 pixels	100	perform seven universal expressions, i.e., neutral, happiness, surprise, fear, sadness, disgust, and angry
3DMD face (3DMD face images, 2014)	NA	NA	NA	NA
UND database	NA	NA	NA	NA
3D TEC (3D Tec database of 3D Twins Expression, 2014)	NA	NA	214 (107 pair of twins)	Neutral and smiling expression
NDOff-2007 (Collection NDOff-2007 3D faces, 2014)	NA	NA	Total 6940 3D images of 387 subjects	Head orientation in a variety of ways
BFM (BFM database, 2014)	Set of points	2000 points	Total 200 (100 Male and 100 Female)	Pose and illumination variations

*'NA' denotes Not Available

Table 8. Different pre-processing approaches for 3D face images

Author(s)	Database(s)	Proposed Methodology
(Liu et al., 2013)	1. SHREC2007 (USF Human ID 3-D database) 2. FRGC v2.0 3. Bosphorus	Spherical map is used to fit on 3D faces for discarding outliers
(Creusot et al., 2013)	1. Bosphorus 2. FRGC v2	RANSAC is used to discard outliers.
(Berretti et al., 2013)	1. UND 2. FRGC v2	RANSAC is fitted to discard outliers and then face image is cropped in an elliptical shape
(Mohammadzade et al., 2013)	FRGC v2	At first, the 3D face is cropped in a spherical shape of radius of 60 mm centred at the nose tips then a 2-D Wiener filter is applied on depth values for de-noising purpose.
(Bagchi et al., 2013)	FRAV3D	The face surface has been cropped to a fixed dimension of size (15×70) by the authors to discard some the outliers. Then the RoI is de-noised by weighted median filter.
(Alyuz et al., 2012)	1. UMB-DB 2. FRGCv2 Neutral database	The RoI is extracted using elliptical shape cropping and then it is de-noised by Gaussian Filter
(Bagchi et al., 2012)	1. Frav3D 2. GavabDB 3. Bosphorus	A comparison of 'pronasal' landmark localization has been investigated by the authors following filters that have been applied to 3D face images. 1. Max Filter 2. Min filter 3. Gaussian filter 4. Mean filter 5. Weighted median filter
(Soltana et al., 2012)	FRGC v2.0	Authors have chosen median filtering to remove sharp spikes and then, interpolation technique has been incorporated to fill the holes on the face surface.
(Zhang et al., 2012)	FRGC v1.0 database	1. Interpolation technique has been applied to remove holes due to the distribution of points from face image. 2. Only the face region is cropped by considering nose tip as a reference point.
(Berretti et al., 2010)	1. FRGC v2.0 2. SHREC08	Geometrical information of the 3D faces is used to encode the required information to form a graph. Then, nodes of the graph represent equal width isogeodesic facial stripes and arcs between pairs of nodes are labelled with descriptors (3D Weighted Walkthroughs or 3DWWs)
(Queirolo et al., 2010)	FRGC v2	Face region has been extracted by isolating some areas like hair, neck, ears and then a median filter is applied for smoothing purpose. Based on depth value face range image is segmented. Thus authors have got four face regions namely circular and elliptical region near nose, upper head (including eyes, nose, and forehead) and

instead of matching the probe image with gallery images, registration is done by a model that has been taken from a training face. Another approach for face registration is based on facial geometric properties. In this technique facial landmarks are detected (like nose tip, eye corners etc.) and then geometric rotation technique is applied for

face registration. The face can be rotated in any direction (along X, Y, and Z axes). In Figure 31, the different possibilities of face rotation are illustrated.

In Table 9, a literature review of various landmark detection techniques and 3D face registration methods have been discussed.

Figure 31. 3D face images of different face rotations

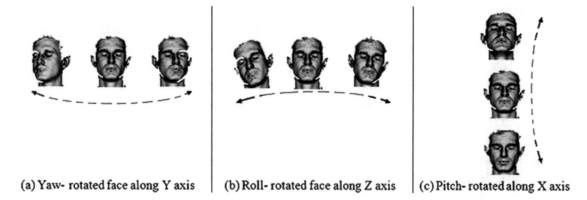

(a) Yaw- rotated face along Y axis | (b) Roll- rotated face along Z axis | (c) Pitch- rotated along X axis

Table 9. Most recent methods used for 3D face registration

Author(s)	Database(s)	Proposed Methodology
(Creusot et al., 2013)	1. Bosphorus 2. FRGC v2.0	At first machine learning based generic key-point detection mechanism is proposed by the authors. Then, it is used to localize the labelled key points (or landmarks) from 3D face images. The proposed system is used to extract macro-features like nose, eyes, mouth rather than micro-features (e.g. wrinkles).
(Berretti et al., 2013)	1. FRGC v2.0 2. GavabDB	Authors have located key points (such as inner and outer eye corners, nose tip, and mouth corners) from depth face images by following the techniques described in (Xu et al., 2006) (Farkas et al., 1987) (Lu et al., 2005) (Lu et al., 2006).
(Koppen et al., 2012)	3DMD	Authors have proposed a new intrinsic coordinate system named as horizontal symmetry for face registration. It resembles with plane of symmetry based on Gaussian curvature. Based on the horizontal axis when the landmarks are determined, two coordinate spaces are aligned for registration.
(Alyuz et al., 2012)	1. UMB-DB 2. FRGC v2.0	Authors have localized the nose region. Then, possible patch centres of mouth and eyes and then with a template matching algorithm eyes, nose and mouth are detected for neutral and frontal face images along with for occluded face. Other than land mark localization, authors have also proposed three different registration approaches namely Face model-based, Nose model-based, Adaptive model-based for neutral as well as occluded face depth image.
(Hernandez et al., 2012)	NA	Authors have registered the input frames with the reference frame using ICP (Iterative Closest Point) algorithm (Zhang, 1994).
(Creusot et al., 2012)	1. BFM 2. FRGC v2.0	Authors have proposed generic 3D face model for landmark localization. For model extraction mechanism, two metrics is used such as saliency metric and ubiquity metric. Then, based on local shape descriptor values and scores, landmark score function is generated and at most 10 landmarks have been detected by the proposed method.
(Spreeuwers, 2011)	FRGC v2.0	Author has registered the face images considering the properties of symmetry. Authors have considered the maximum distance of the nose tip from the curve ends and registered it using the nose-tip.
(Gokberk et al., 2006)	3D_RMA	Authors have proposed non-rigid registration. Registration is performed using AFM (average face model) and different feature descriptor like surface normal, curvature, facial profile curves used to recognize 3D faces from the database.

*'NA' denotes Not Available

Recognition of 3D Face Image Using Range Images

Automatic face recognition by various computing devices is the process for verifying or identifying input or probe faces from gallery images (either 2D or 3D or video frames). With successful implementation of 3D face registration mechanism, it is also easier to recognize the rotated face images. Recognition algorithm is typically carried out by selecting proper feature (known as 'attribute selection') from face images to be classified and recognized by different supervised learning modules (like ANN, KNN, SVM, Edit distance classifiers etc.). At first, supervised classifiers (Nakajima et al., 2000) get trained from the labeled feature set to classify the unknown images by following the learned module.

Since 1989, 3D face recognition problem is acknowledged by the researchers. Cartoux (Cartoux et al., 1989) proposed profile based minimum distance matching between surface approaches. Face recognition problem can be solved in two different methods. One approach is holistic or profiles based recognition, and another process is feature based recognition. In holistic based recognition schemes, all the facial shape's data i.e. the global data is used for discriminating inter class variations whereas feature-based methods achieve the matching procedure through local features which are used to extract typically from the prominent points on facial surfaces. In Table 10, a recent overview on 3D face recognition is presented.

Table 10. Some recent methodologies on 3D face recognition

Author(s)	Database(s)	Proposed Methodology
Holistic Approach		
(Berretti et al., 2010)	1. FRGC v2.0 2. SHREC08	Berretti et al. have proposed a graph based face matching algorithm. Nodes within the graph represent equal width isogeodesic facial stripes and arcs between pairs of nodes are labelled with descriptors which can be referred as 3D Weighted Walkthroughs (3DWWs). The average performance of their algorithm is 99.53%.
(Boehnen et al., 2009)	FRGC v2.0	Authors represented a 3D signature for recognition purpose that has been developed from 3D face shape. According to the authors the proposed method runs more than three orders of magnitude faster than traditional ICP based distance implementation and does not lose accuracy.
(Mahoor et al., 2009)	1. GavabDB 2. FRGC v2.0	Researchers propose a recognition algorithm from frontal range data. It is based on ridge lines on the surface of face images. The matching of the face ridge images is one using Hausdorff distance and the iterative closest points (ICP) on GavabDB face database and FRGC v2.0.
(Samir et al., 2009)		Chafik Samir et al. created a facial surface as representation of indexed facial curves that has been derived from a surface distance function. A Riemannian metric is obtained from differential geometry of the face shapes for computing the distances between faces and finding the optimal deformations between faces and also defining and computing the average of a given set of faces.
(Osaimi et al., 2009)	FRGC v2.0	Authors proposed an expression invariant 3D face recognition approach. Here, only frontal faces are considered. At first, PCA's eigenvectors have been trained, and algorithm executed on FRGC v2.0 database with 0.001 FAR are 98.35% and 97.73% for neutral and non-neutral expressions respectively
(Xu et al., 2009)	1. CASIA 3D 2. FRGC v2.0	Xu et al. have proposed depth and intensity based face recognition algorithm. Gabor wavelet transform been used on these images and then linear discriminate analysis (LDA), and AdaBoost learning is applied for selecting most useful feature. The experiment is implemented on CASIA 3D face database and the FRGC v2.0 database. The highest recognition rate on CASIA 3D is 98.3% on neutral face set, and 79.0% on the face set with large pose variations and smiling and for FRGC v2.0 database the success rate is 97.5%.

continued on following page

Table 10. Continued

Author(s)	Database(s)	Proposed Methodology
(Haar et al., 2008)	SHREC2007	Frank B. ter Haar et al. proposes 3D face matching technique using facial curves. The algorithm is mainly concentrated on profile and contour based face matching. Authors combined three curves of 45 face samples from the database and achieve the highest mean average precision (MAP) of 0.78.
Feature Based Approach		
(Liu et al., 2013)	1. SHREC2007 (USF Human ID 3-D database) 2. FRGC v2.0 3. Bosphorus	Scientists have presented a novel representation of 3D face images known as Spherical Depth Map where they have applied original Spherical Harmonic Features (SHF) for processing shape and fine surface details. After that they have investigated Relief-F, mRmR and Random Forests method for feature selection.
(Berretti et al., 2013)	1. Combined UND and FRGC v2.0 2. GavabDB	For face matching purpose, key points and facial curves are computed. Authors have used SIFT, facial curves and Euclidian distance for this purpose. To remove the outliers RANSAC algorithm is also implemented.
(Mohammadzade et al., 2013)	FRGC v2.0	Authors have proposed Iterative Closest Normal Points and smoothed it and referred as 'CNP'. It used for matching purpose. For dimensionality reduction and discriminate analysis use, LDA is preferred. Two sets of investigation are carried on such as co-ordinate points of CNP and normal vectors at CNP.
(Tang et al., 2013)	1. BJUT-3D 2. FRGC v2.0	Hengliang Tang et al. also proposed 3D face recognition method by LBP. Authors have cropped the face region in an elliptical shape and blocked into 5×3. The local details from each block are gathered as a set of features using LBP operator and then region based histogram is calculated for combining pixel-level, region-level and global-level information. The nearest neighbor classifier is used to classify only the frontal face images collected from databases.
(Soltana et al., 2012)	Subset of FRGC v2.0	Authors have presented four different methods for 3D face recognition use. Among four approaches, the first approach is partly holistic and partly local feature based, the second is feature based technique, and third and fourth approaches are typically holistic approach. Researchers have also reported individual approaches' recognition rate. Along with this, a fusion of individual algorithms' similarity matching score is also presented and implemented for 3D face recognition purpose
(Ramadan et al., 2012)	GavabDB	Authors have introduced wavelet transforms (spherical wavelet and Haar wavelet) for 3D face compression as well as recognition. For recognizing 3D face images, the rotated faces are registered using ICP and then PCA based dimensionality reduction operation is performed. With this proposed algorithm authors claimed to have maximum 86% recognition rate using 4-level decomposition of Haar wavelet.
(Lin et al., 2011)	Own database of 10 individuals. 20 face images from each individual	Cheng-Jain Lin et al. proposed a hybrid intelligent technique that is used to recognize 2D as well as 3D face images. Neural network alienation with hybrid Taguchi-PSO (particle swarm optimization) i.e. HTPSO is used to classify the obtained feature vector. A series of operations have been performed to obtain the feature vector. Features from Gabor wavelet transform is combined with surface feature vector by PCA for final derivation of feature set.
(Bornak et al., 2010)	FRAV3D	Here, authors proposed expression invariant 3D face recognition algorithm. Features have been extracted from the nose region. Authors have located co-ordinates of four points (top-left, down-right, top-right ad down-left points) and implemented two lines from top-left to down-right and top-right to down-left. Thus, depth values from cross-profile are used as feature vector. A weighted method has also been used for better recognition purpose.
(Zhou et al., 2010)	FRGC v2.0	Authors proposed a 3D face recognition method using LBP. For the recognition purpose, the face images are normalized, and different LBP operator is used. For the feature calculation, histogram and LBP number are used. Another experiment is also proposed the authors using varying number of weighted blocks. For classification purpose, the distance measure metric is used as dissimilarity measurement.
(Lee et al., 2008)	Own database with 46 person's photo	Authors implemented a 3D face recognition algorithm that used to classify the feature set by fuzzy neural network. The feature set is derived from the eigenface images from maximum and minimum curvature maps of the 3D face images.

CONCLUSION

Being inspired by the characteristic of 3D images which can be applied for different challenging issues of face recognition, authors have used 2.5Drange images for automatic face recognition purpose. In this chapter, authors have discussed a detailed description on 3D face images in different perspectives. The effect of popular and well known fundamental image processing techniques on range images have also been illustrated here with a comparative study with the corresponding regular 2D face images. To highlight more on 3D face images, different possible acquisition techniques, image formats and its structure have also been demonstrated here. An up-to-date literature survey following a pipelined architecture of 3D face recognition techniques is also reported here.

Thus, a complete reference of 3D imaging technology in the domain of biometric based face recognition is established for all possible references.

ACKNOWLEDGMENT

Authors are thankful for a project supported by DeitY (Letter No.: 12(12)/2012-ESD), MCIT, Govt. of India, at Department of Computer Science and Engineering, Jadavpur University, India for providing the necessary infrastructure for this work.

REFERENCES

Alyuz, N., Gokberk, B., & Akarun, L. (2012). Adaptive Registration for Occlusion Robust 3D Face Recognition. In *Proc of BeFIT'12 Workshop*. doi:10.1007/978-3-642-33885-4_56

BU3D database. (n.d.). Retrieved 22nd July, 2014, from http://www.cs.binghamton.edu/~lijun/Research/3DFE/3DFE_Analysis.html

Bagchi, P., Bhattacharjee, D., Nasipuri, M., & Basu, D. K. (2012). A Novel approach to nose-tip and eye-corners detection using H-K Curvature Analysis in case of 3D images. Proc of International Journal of Computational Intelligence and Informatics, 2(1).

Bagchi, P., Bhattacharjee, D., Nasipuri, M., & Basu, D. K. (2013). *A Method for Nose-tip based 3D face registration using Maximum Intensity algorithm*. In IEEE international Conference of Computation and Communication Advancement.

Berretti, S., Bimbo, A., & Pala, P. (2013). Sparse Matching of Salient Facial Curves for Recognition of 3-D Faces with Missing Parts. IEEE Transactions on Information Forensics and Security, 8(2), 374-389.

Berretti, S., Bimbo, A. D., & Pala, P. (2010). 3D Face Recognition Using Isogeodesic Stripes. *IEEE Transactions on Pattern Analysis and Machine Intelligence*, *32*(12), 2162–2177. doi:10.1109/TPAMI.2010.43 PMID:20975115

BFM database. (n.d.). Retrieved 1st August, 2014, from http://faces.cs.unibas.ch/bfm/main.php?nav=1-0&id=basel_face_model

Bit-plane slicing. (n.d.). Retrieved 5th August, 2014, from http://nptel.iitk.ac.in/courses/Web-course-contents/IIT-KANPUR/Digi_Img_Pro/chapter_8/8_13.html

BJUT-3D Chinese face database. (n.d.). Retrieved 24th July, 2014, from http://www.bjut.edu.cn/sci/multimedia/mul-lab/3dface/facedatabase.htm

BNT format. (n.d.). Retrieved 10th August, 2014, from http://filext.com/file-extension/BNT

Boehnen, C., Peters, T., & Flynn, P. J. (2009). 3D signatures for fast 3D face recognition. In *Proc. 3rd Int. Conf. Adv. Biometrics*. doi:10.1007/978-3-642-01793-3_2

Bornak, B., Rafiei, S., Sarikhani, A., & Babaei, A. (2010). *3D face recognition by used region-based with facial expression variation*. In Second International Conference on Signal Processing Systems. Retrieved 22nd August, 2014 from http://homepages.inf.ed.ac.uk/rbf/CVonline/LOCAL_COPIES/CANTZLER2/range.html

Bosphorus database. (n.d.). Retrieved 16th August, 2014 from http://bosphorus.ee.boun.edu.tr/Home.aspx

Cartoux, J. Y., Lapreste, J. T., & Richetin, M. (1989). Face authentication or recognition by profile extraction from range images. In *Proceedings of the workshop on the interpretation of 3D scenes.*

CASIA-3D FaceV1. (n.d.). Retrieved 24th July, 2014, from http://www.idealtest.org/dbDetailForUser.do?id=8

Chang, K. I., Bowyer, K. W., & P. J. Flynn, (2005). An evaluation of multimodal 2D+3D faces biometrics. *PAMI, 27*(4).

Collection NDOff-2007 3D faces. (n.d.). Retrieved 22nd July, 2014, from http://www3.nd.edu/~cvrl/CVRL/Data_Sets.html

Creusot, C., Pears, N., & Austin, J. (2012). 3D Landmark Model Discovery from a Registered Set of Organic Shapes. In *Proc of Point Cloud Processing (PCP) Workshop at the Computer Vision and Pattern Recognition Conference (CVPR).*

Creusot, C., Pears, N., & Austin, J. (2013). A Machine-Learning Approach to Keypoint Detection and Landmarking on 3D Meshes. *International Journal of Computer Vision, 102*(1-3), 146–179. doi:10.1007/s11263-012-0605-9

3. *DMD face images*. (n.d.). Retrieved 22nd July, 2014, from http://www.3dmd.com/

Ebrahimdoost, Y., Dehmeshki, J., Ellis, T. S., Firoozbakht, M., Youannic, A., & Qanadli, S. D. (2010). Medical Image Segmentation Using Active Contours and a Level Set Model: Application to Pulmonary Embolism (PE) Segmentation. In *Fourth International Conference on Digital Society*. DOI doi:10.1109/ICDS.2010.64

Esakkirajan, S., Veerakumar, T., & Jayaraman, S. (2009). Digital Image Processing (1st ed.). Academic Press.

Farkas, L. G., & Munro, I. R. (1987). *Anthropometric Facial Proportions in Medicine*. Springfield, IL: Thomas Books.

FERET database. (n.d.). Retrieved 20th July, 2014, from http://www.itl.nist.gov/iad/humanid/feret/feret_master.html

Frav3D database. (n.d.). Retrieved 16th August, 2014, from http://archive.today/B1WeX

FRGC v.2 face database. (n.d.). Retrieved 22nd July, 2014, from http://www3.nd.edu/~cvrl/CVRL/Data_Sets.html

Ganguly, S., Bhattacharjee, D., & Nasipuri, M. (2014a). 3D Face Recognition from Range Images Based on Curvature Analysis. ICTACT Journal on Image and Video Processing, 4(3), 748-753.

Ganguly, S., Bhattacharjee, D., & Nasipuri, M., (2014b). Range Face Image Registration using ERFI from 3D Images. *Proceedings of 3rd Frontiers of Intelligent Computing: Theory and applications, Advances in Intelligent Systems and Computing*. DOI: .10.1007/978-3-319-12012-6_36

GavabDB database. (n.d.). Retrieved 16th August, 2014, from http://www.gavab.etsii.urjc.es/recursos_en.html

Gökberk, B., Irfanoğlu, M. O., & Akarun, L. (2006). 3D shape-based face representation and feature extraction for face recognition. *Image and Vision Computing*, 24(8), 857–869. doi:10.1016/j.imavis.2006.02.009

Gonzalez, C., & Woods, R. E. (2012). Digital Image Processing (3rd ed.). Academic Press.

Haar, F. B., & Veltkamp, R. C. (2008). A 3D face matching framework. In *Proc. IEEE Int. Conf. Shape Model. Appl.*

Hernandez, M., Choi, J., & Medioni, G. (2012). Laser scan quality 3-D face modelling using a low-cost depth camera. In *Proc of EUSIPCO*.

Kang, C. Y., Chen, Y. S., & Hsu, W. H. (1993). *Mapping a Lifelike 2.5D Human Face via an Automatic Approach.* IEEE.

Kerin, J. (n.d.). *Contrast Enhancement.* Retrieved 1st August, 2014 from http://web.pdx.edu/~jduh/courses/Archive/geog481w07/Students/Kerin_ContrastEnhancement.pdf

Koppen, W. P., Chan, C. H., Christmas, W. J., & Kittler, J. (2012). An intrinsic coordinate system for 3D face registration. In *Proc of 21st Intl Conf on Pattern Recognition (ICPR)*.

Krutsch, R., & Tenorio, D., (2011). *Histogram Equalization.* Document Number: AN4318.

Lee, Y. H., Han, C. W., & Kim, T. S. (2008). 3D Facial Recognition with Soft Computing. In Digital Human Modeling (LNAI), (vol. 4650, pp. 194–205). Berlin: Springer.

Lin, C. J., Wang, J. G., & Chen, S. M. (2011). 2D/3D Face Recognition using Neural Network based on Hybrid Taguchi-Particle Swarm Optimization. *International Journal of Innovative Computing, Information, & Control, 7*(2).

Liu, P., Wang, Y., Huang, D., Zhang, Z., & Chen, L. (2013). Learning the Spherical Harmonic Features for 3-D Face Recognition. *IEEE Transactions on Image Processing, 22*(3), 914–925. doi:10.1109/TIP.2012.2222897 PMID:23060332

Lu, X., & Jain, A. K. (2005). *Multimodal Facial Feature Extraction for Automatic 3D Face Recognition.* Tech. Rep. MSU-CSE-05-22.

Lu, X., Jain, A. K., & Colbry, D. (2006). Matching 2.5D face scans to 3D models. *IEEE Transactions on Pattern Analysis and Machine Intelligence, 28*(1), 31–43. doi:10.1109/TPAMI.2006.15 PMID:16402617

Mahoor, M. H., & Mottaleb, M. A. (2009). Face recognition based on 3D ridge images obtained from range data. *Pattern Recognition, 42*(3), 445–451. doi:10.1016/j.patcog.2008.08.012

Mohammadzade, H., & Hatzinakos, D. (2013). Iterative Closest Normal Point for 3D Face Recognition. *IEEE Transactions on Pattern Analysis and Machine Intelligence, 35*(2), 381–397. doi:10.1109/TPAMI.2012.107 PMID:22585097

ND2006 3D face database. (n.d.). Retrieved 22nd July, 2014, from http://www3.nd.edu/~cvrl/CVRL/Data_Sets.html

Nakajima, C., Pontil, M., Heisele, B., & Poggio, T. (2000). *People Recognition in Image Sequence by Supervised Learning.* In A.I. Memo No. 1688, C.B.C.L Paper No. 188.

Osaimi, F., Al, F., Bennamoun, M., & Mian, A. (2009). An expression deformation approach to non-rigid 3D faces recognition. *International Journal of Computer Vision, 81*(3), 302–316. doi:10.1007/s11263-008-0174-0

Peli, E. (1990). Contrast in complex images. *Journal of the Optical Society of America. A, Optics and Image Science*, 7(10), 2032. doi:10.1364/JOSAA.7.002032 PMID:2231113

PRISM-ASU 3D facial shape. (n.d.). Retrieved 16th July, 2014, from http://www.public.asu.edu/~mchaudha/prism.html

Queirolo, C. C., Silva, L., Bellon, O. R. P., & Segundo, M. P. (2010). 3D Face Recognition Using Simulated Annealing and the Surface Interpenetration Measure. *IEEE Transactions on Pattern Analysis and Machine Intelligence*, 32(2), 206–219. doi:10.1109/TPAMI.2009.14 PMID:20075453

Ramadan, R. M., & Rehab, F. (2012). 3D Face Compression and Recognition using Spherical Wavelet Parametrization. International Journal of Advanced Computer Science and Applications, 3(9).

Reghbati, H. K. (1981). *An Overview of Data Compression Techniques*. IEEE.

Samir, C., Srivastava, A., Daoudi, M., & Klassen, E. (2009). An intrinsic framework for analysis of facial surfaces. *International Journal of Computer Vision*, 82(1), 80–95. doi:10.1007/s11263-008-0187-8

Sayood, K. (n.d.). Data Compression. *Encyclopedia of Information Systems, 1*, 423-444.

Seal, A., Bhattacharjee, D., Nasipuri, M., & Basu, D. K. (2011). Minutiae from Bit-Plane Sliced Thermal Images for Human Face Recognition. In *Proceedings of the International Conference on Soft Computing for Problem Solving, Advances in Intelligent and Soft Computing*.

Seal, A., Bhattacharjee, D., Nasipuri, M., & Basu, D. K., (2014). Thermal Face Recognition for Biometric Security System. In *Research Developments in Biometrics and Video Processing Techniques*, (pp. 1-24). Academic Press.

Soltana, W. B., Ardabilian, M., Lemaire, P., Huang, D., Szeptycki, P., Chen, L., … Colineau, J. (2012). 3D face recognition: A robust multi-matcher approach to data degradations. In *Proc of ICB 2012*. doi:10.1109/ICB.2012.6199766

Spreeuwers, L. (2011). Fast and Accurate 3D Face Recognition Using registration to an Intrinsic Coordinate System and Fusion of Multiple Region Classifiers. Int. J. Comput Vis, 389–414. DOI doi:10.1007/s11263-011-0426-2

Szeptycki, P., Ardabilian, M., & Chen, L. (2008). *A coarse-to-fine curvature analysis-based rotation invariant 3D faces landmarking*. Retrieved from http://liris.cnrs.fr/Documents/Liris-4503.pdf

Tang, H., Yin, B., Sun, Y., & Hua, Y. (2013). 3D face recognition using local binary patterns. *Signal Processing*, 93(8), 2190–2198. doi:10.1016/j.sigpro.2012.04.002

Texas 3D face database. (n.d.). Retrieved 23rd July, 2014, from http://live.ece.utexas.edu/research/texas3dfr/

UMB-DB face database. (n.d.). Retrieved 22nd July, 2014, from http://www.ivl.disco.unimib.it/umbdb/

Univ. of York 1 database. (n.d.). Retrieved 22nd July, 2014, from http://www-users.cs.york.ac.uk/~tomh/3DfaceDatabase.html

Univ. of York 2 database. (n.d.). Retrieved 22nd July, 2014, from http://www-users.cs.york.ac.uk/~tomh/3DfaceDatabase.html

USF 3-D Database. (n.d.). Retrieved 15th July, 2014, from http://marathon.csee.usf.edu/Gait-Baseline/USF-Human-ID-3D-Database-Release.PDF

VRML format. (n.d.). Retrieved 16th August, 2014, from http://www.nada.kth.se/~stefanc/VRML_lecture.pdf

xm2vtsdb 3D face model. (n.d.). Retrieved 15th July, 2014, from http://www.ee.surrey.ac.uk/CVSSP/xm2vtsdb/

Xu, C., Li, S., Tan, T., & Quan, L. (2009). Automatic 3D face recognition from depth and intensity Gabor features. *Pattern Recognition*, *42*(9), 1895–1905. doi:10.1016/j.patcog.2009.01.001

Xu, C., Tan, T., Wang, Y., & Quan, L. (2006). Combining local features for robust nose location in 3D facial data. *Pattern Recognition Letters*, *27*(13), 1487–1494. doi:10.1016/j.patrec.2006.02.015

Zhang, W., Huang, D., Wang, Y., & Chen, L. (2012). 3D Aided Face Recognition across Pose Variations. In *Proc of CCBR 2012*. doi:10.1007/978-3-642-35136-5_8

Zhang, X., Yin, L., Cohn, J. F., Canavan, S., Reale, M., Horowitz, A., & Liu, P. (2013). A High-Resolution Spontaneous 3D Dynamic Facial Expression Database. In *10th IEEE International Conference and Workshops on Automatic Face and Gesture Recognition (FG)*. doi:10.1109/FG.2013.6553788

Zhang, Z. (1994). Iterative point matching for registration of free-form curves and surfaces. *International Journal of Computer Vision*, *13*(2), 119–152. doi:10.1007/BF01427149

Zhou, X., S'anchez, S. A., & Kuijper, A. (2010). *3D Face Recognition with Local Binary Patterns*. In *2010 Sixth International Conference on Intelligent Information Hiding and Multimedia Signal Processing*. doi:10.1109/IIHMSP.2010.87

KEY TERMS AND DEFINITIONS

3D Face Recognition: Recognition algorithm that can handle 3D images instead of 2D. The drawbacks of the 2D face images can be overcome in 3D. From 3D, 2.5D or Range face image.

3D Face Registration: Registration is the process by which rotated faces can be aligned to frontal pose. With the help of three axes, 3D geometric rotations, translation can be performed.

Bit-Plane Slicing: It is one of the well-known and fundamental techniques of image processing. With this technique, the valid bits from gray scale images can be separated, and it will be useful for processing these data in very less time complexity.

Curvature: It defines the bendness and sharpness of the object. The facial properties like nose tip, eye-corners (inner and outer), chin, lip corner, etc. can be detected from curvature computation.

Depth Image: Images with depth values from 3D face images are used to form depth image. It is also termed as 2.5D or Range image.

Pre-Processing: It is the process by which the input raw images are filtered for noise, spike removal, etc. It is a very crucial step for further processing of input images.

Chapter 11
Face Recognition in Unconstrained Environment

Santosh Kumar
Indian Institute of Technology Varanasi, India

Shrikant Tiwari
Indian Institute of Technology Varanasi, India

Ramesh Chand Pandey
Indian Institute of Technology Varanasi, India

Sanjay Kumar Singh
Indian Institute of Technology Varanasi, India

ABSTRACT

Research emphasizes in face recognition has shifted towards recognition of human from both still images and videos which are captured in unconstrained imaging environments and without user cooperation. Due to confounding factors of pose, illumination, image quality, and expression, as well as occlusion and low resolution, current face recognition systems deployed in forensic and security applications operate in a semi-automatic manner. This book chapter presents a comprehensive review of face recognition approaches in unconstrained environment. The objective of this book chapter is to address issues, challenges and recent advancement in face recognition algorithms which may help novel researchers to do innovative research in unconstrained environment. Finally, this chapter provides the stepping stone for future research to unveil how biometrics approaches can be deployed in unconstrained face recognition systems.

1. INTRODUCTION

Face recognition is a significant and emerging research field in computer vision and pattern recognition system. It needs the ability to recognize an individual despite several variations in the appearance of face. The computer vision systems are operated in two environmental conditions as: (1). Control and constrained based face recognition system and unconstrained face recognition system, no restrictions over environmental conditions such as scale, pose, lighting, focus, resolution, facial expression, accessories, makeup, occlusions, background and photographic quality are required. Present face recognition systems take image of cooperative individuals faces in controlled environment as part of the face recognition process. It is therefore possible to control lighting, pose, background, facial expression, cover and non-covering of faces and quality of images. However, in a real world application, we have to deal with both ideal and imperfect data. Performance of

DOI: 10.4018/978-1-4666-8654-0.ch011

current face recognition systems are affected for such non-ideal and challenging cases.

In general, unconstrained environment challenges in face recognition can be categorized into six parts: illumination, image quality, expression, pose, aging, and disguise. The current research focuses on designing algorithms to mitigate the effect of covariates in face recognition. The results of the recent face recognition test reports, Face Recognition Grand Challenge 2004 (Phillips et al., 2006) and Face Recognition Vendor Test 2006 (Phillips, 2007) has shown that under normal changes in a constrained environment, the performance of existing face recognition systems have been greatly enhanced.

2. CHALLENGES IN FACE RECOGNITION

Over the last few years, face recognition has gained a rapid success with the development of new approaches and techniques. Due to this success, the rate of face recognition has been increased to well above 90% identification accuracy. Despite of all this success, all face recognition techniques usually suffer from common challenges of image visibility. These challenges are lighting conditions variations, skin variations and face angle variations (Phuong &, Quang, 2010). The lighting conditions in which the pictures are taken are not always similar because the variations in time and place. The example of lighting variations could be the pictures taken inside the room and the pictures taken outside. Due to these variations, a same person with similar facial expressions may appear differently in different pictures. As a result, if the person has single image in the database of face recognition, matching could be difficult with the face detection under different lighting conditions (Beymer, 1994). In the face recognition community, several covariates for face recognition have been identified such as pose, expression, illumination and aging and discussed below:

- **Illumination:** In face recognition, images of face with proper illumination are captured under controlled environment. However, face images with illumination variations mitigates the accuracy of recognition algorithms because illumination variations may alter the appearance of face images and these algorithms are not able to extract discriminant features from images, such features may be hidden.

- **Image Quality:** In face recognition, quality of a face image depends on various features such as motion blur, sensor noise, environmental noise, image resolution, and gray scale/color depth. Any degradation in the quality of face images, as shown in Figure 1, can lead to reduced recognition performance.

- **Expression:** Variations in expression can cause deformation in local facial structure which changes the facial appearance and local geometry of the face.

- **Pose:** Frontal images of face are contained more ample information of various features used for face recognition. However, in a profile or semi-profile face image, some features are not visible and matching a frontal face image with a profile face image may produce incorrect results.

- **Aging:** Temporal variations in human face is a regular process with age progression, these variations may cause major structural changes. Aging variations among the three face images of an individual are difficult to handle in an automated face recognition system.

- **Disguise:** The most challenging among all the covariates is the variations due to disguise in which an individual can use make-up accessories to alter the facial features and impersonate another person or hide one's identity. Simple accessories such as beard and mustache can change the appearance of an individual.

Figure 1. Face images annotated (red ellipses) in the FDDB database (Liao, Jain & Li. (2014)

2.1. Skin Color Variations

Another challenge for skin based face recognition system is the difference in the skin color due to the difference in the races of the people. Due to this variation, sometimes the true skin pixels are filtered out along with the noise present in an image. In addition, the false skin background/non-background is not completely filtered out during noise filtering process. So, it is a tough task is to choose a filter which will cover the entire skin tones of different people and kick out false skin noise (Phuong-Trinh et al., 2010).

2.2. Variation in Face Angle or Orientation Variation

The angle of the human face from camera can be different in different situations. A frontal face detection algorithm can't work on non-frontal faces, which is present in the image because the geometry of facial features in frontal view is always different than the geometry of facial features in non-frontal view. This is why orientation variation remains the difficult challenge in face recognition system (Beymer, 1994).

3. WHY FACE RECOGNITION?

The requirement for determining people's identity, the obvious question is what technology is best suited to provide this information? There are many ways that humans can identify each other, and so is for machines. There are many different identification technologies available, many of which have been in commercial use for years. The most common methods for person verification and identification are password/PIN, known as Personal Identification Number systems. The major problems with that or other similar techniques is that they are not unique, and is possible for somebody to forget loose or even have it stolen for somebody else. In order to overcome these problems there has developed considerable interest in "biometrics" based identification systems. It uses pattern recognition techniques to identify people using their characteristics. Some of those methods are fingerprints and retina and iris recognition. Although, these techniques can not easy to used in recognition of individual. For example in bank transactions and entry into secure areas, such technologies have the disadvantage that they are intrusive both physically and socially. The user must position the body relative to the sensor, and then pause for a second to declare himself or herself. That doesn't mean that face recognition doesn't need specific positioning. As we are going to analyze later on the poses and the appearance of the image taken is very important. While the pause and present interaction are useful in high-security, they are exactly the opposite of what is required when building a store that recognize its best customers, or an information kiosk that remembers you, or a house that knows the people who live there.

Face recognition from video and voice recognition have a natural place in these next generation smart environments, they are unobtrusive, are usually passive, do not restrict user movement, and are now both low power and inexpensive. Perhaps most important, however, is that humans identify other people by their face and voice, therefore are likely to be comfortable with systems that use face and voice recognition.

3.1. Face Recognition and Detection

The objective of face detection is to find and locate faces in an image. It is the first step in automatic face recognition applications. Face detection has been well studied for frontal and near frontal faces. The Viola and Jones' face detector (Viola, & Jones, 2001) is the most well-known face detection algorithm, which is based on Haar-like features and cascade AdaBoost (Friedman, Hastie, & Tibshirani, 2000) classifier. However, in unconstrained scenes such as faces in a crowd, state-of-the-art face detectors fail to perform well due to large pose variations, illumination variations, occlusions, expression variations, out-of-focus blur, and low image resolution. For example, the Viola-Jones face detector fails to detect most of face images in the FDDB database (Jain et al., 2010). (Examples shown in Figure 1) due to the difficulties mentioned above.

- **Face recognition includes following sub point as:**
  ◦ Face recognition processing
  ◦ Analysis in face subspaces
  ◦ Technical challenges
  ◦ Technical solutions
- **Face detection**
  ◦ Appearance and learning based approaches
  ◦ Neural networks methods
  ◦ AdaBoost-based methods
  ◦ Dealing with head rotations
  ◦ Performance evaluation

3.2. Face Recognition Processing

Face recognition is a visual pattern recognition problem. It is a three-dimensional object of varying illumination, pose, expression is to be identified based on its two-dimensional image (or three-dimensional images obtained by laser scan).

- A face recognition system generally consists of 4 modules - detection, alignment, feature extraction, and matching are shown in Figure 2.
- Localization and normalization (face detection and alignment) are processing steps before face recognition (facial feature extraction and matching) is performed.
- Face detection segments the face areas from the background. In the case of video, the detected faces may need to be tracked using a face tracking component. Face alignment is aimed at achieving more accurate localization and at normalizing faces, whereas face detection provides coarse estimates of the location and scale of each face. Facial components and facial outline are located; based on the location points.
- The input face image is normalized in respect to geometrical properties, such as size and pose, using geometrical transforms or morphing.

Figure 2. Face Recognition processing flow

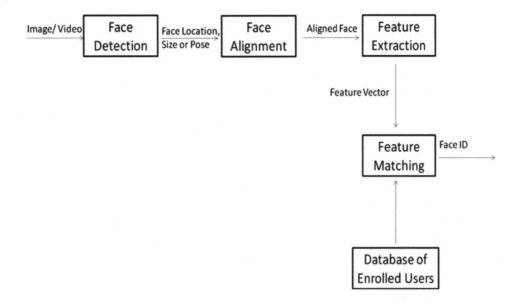

• The face is further normalized with respect to photometrical properties such as illumination and gray scale.

After a face is normalized, feature extraction is performed to provide effective information that is useful for distinguishing between faces of different persons and stable with respect to the geometrical and photometrical variations.

For face matching, the extracted feature vector of the input face is matched against those of enrolled faces in the database; it outputs the identity of the face when a match is found with sufficient confidence or indicates an unknown face otherwise.

3.3. Face Recognition System and Algorithms

There are numerous challenges in designing automated face recognition system and algorithms. Such challenges manifest in the following stages performed by most face recognition algorithms: (i) face detection (ii) face alignment (iii) appearance normalization (iv) feature extraction techniques description (v) feature extraction and (vi) matching. Each stages of face recognition system are discussed below.

3.3.1. Detection, Alignment, and Normalization

The first step in automated face recognition is the detection and alignment of face. Often viewed as a preprocessing step, this stage is critical to both detecting the presence of a face in a digital image, and alignment of the face with the spatial co-ordinate values of given database. After, image database of faces are normalized with min-max normalization techniques. Furthermore, feature descriptors (e.g. LBP, SURF feature descriptors) with window size 8x8 are used to keep the descriminat feature from image of face database. In feature extraction phase, feature is extracted from image for face recognition process. Finally, in matching phase, test image of faces are matching with trained system based on matching criteria such Euclidean distance or template based matching. The overall process of automatic face recognition system is illustrates in Figure 3 and 4 respectively.

Figure 3. The common steps utilized by most face recognition algorithms

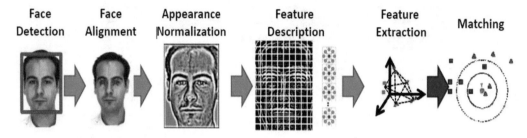

Figure 4. Different methods for face alignment. (a) Face images before (left column) and after (right column) alignment through planar rotation and scaling. (b) Face images aligned using a morphable model (images from (Blanz V. and Vetter. T., (2003)), and (c) a video sequence aligned using a 3D model whose parameters were solved from a structure from motion algorithm images from (Park, & Jain, 2007) co-ordinate system used in the succeeding face description

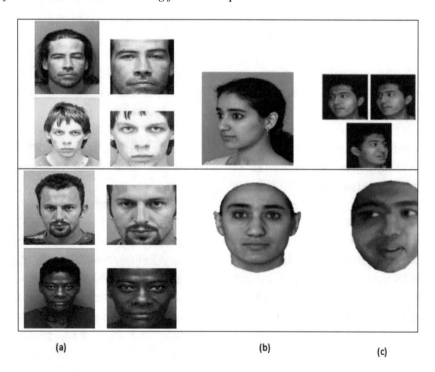

(a) (b) (c)

The face detector proposed by Viola and Jones (Viola, & Jones, 2004) which uses a cascaded classifier in conjunction with images represented using a verbose set of Haar-like features, set the precedent for all modern detectors with its robust accuracy and scalable computational complexity. While many methods have been proposed to improve upon Viola and Jones detector, it still serves as an optimistic baseline of state of the art performance (Parris et al., 2011).

Face alignment is typically performed by first detecting the location of some fixed set of anthropometric landmarks on the face. In its simplest form, these landmarks are the centers of the two eyes. Using the two eye locations, a 2D Plane transformation is performed to the x angle and distance between the two eyes.

More advanced methods use 3D transformations, or procustes alignment, on a more verbose set of landmarks (such as a set of landmarks outlining the locations on the mouth, nose, and face outline). The landmarks in given face images are generally detected by different models such as Active Shape Models (ASM) proposed by (Cootes et al., 1995), (Cootes et al., 2001) and active appearance models (AAM) (Council, 2009). Additional techniques include the use of 3D morphable models (Blanz,, & Vetter, 2003) and structure from motion (Park, & Jain, 2007). Appearance normalization seeks to compensate for variations in illumination. A variety of methods have been proposed to perform such compensation, including the contrast equalization and difference of Gaussian filters proposed by (Tan et al., 2010) cones models by Georghiades et al. (2001) and lighted modeling by Gross et al. (Gross, Matthews, & Baker, 2004).

3.3.2. Feature Representation

The feature representation stage encodes different facial characteristics (often implicitly) in a feature descriptor vector. Such descriptive information can range from a vector of ordered image pixel values to distance measurements between facial components (e.g. the distance from the nose to the mouth), or to even more complex features such as convolutions of a face image with a set of Gabor filters. The range of representations used in face recognition is quite. Klare and Jain developed an organization of such features to facilitate studies of facial individuality and help standardize the face recognition process (Klare, & Jain, 2010). We introduce this taxonomy to provide a better understanding of the different methods by which a face images can be represented.

Klare and Jain's (Klare, & Jain, 2010) taxonomy organized the vast gamut of facial feature repre-

sentations leveraged in automated and manual face recognition into three levels: Level 1, Level 2, and Level 3. In level 1 feature consists of gross facial characteristics that are easily observable in a face, such as skin color, gender, and the general appearance of the face. Features in level 2 consist of localized face information that requires specialized cortex processing, such as the structure of the face, the relationship among facial components, and the precise shape of the face. Level 3 features consist of certain irregularities in the facial skin, which includes micro features such as facial marks, skin discoloration, and moles. Furthermore, features used in automatic fingerprint matchers (AFIS) are compact and have a physical interpretation in terms of the ridge flow patterns in the fingerprint. Indeed state-of-the-art AFIS utilize essentially the same features that are utilized by human fingerprint examiners. This is not necessarily true for face recognition; features extracted by humans are not easy to precisely describe, and thus cannot be utilized in automatic face recognition systems.

3.3.3. Face Feature Levels

Level 1 facial features encompass the global nature of the face, and can be extracted from low resolution face images (< 30 interpupilary pixel distance (IPD)). In automated face recognition, Level 1 features include appearance-based methods such as PCA (Eigenfaces) (Turk, & Pentland, 1991) and LDA (Fisherface) (Belhumeur, Hespanda, & Kriegman, 1997). For example; these features can generally discriminate between: (i) a short round face and an elongated thin face; (ii) face images possessing predominantly male and female characteristics; or (iii) faces from members of different ethnicities. Level 1 feature cannot, however, accurately identify an individual over a large population of candidates, where a query image can easily be differentiated from a subject that has a very different appearance, but cannot be distinguished from a more similar looking subject. The derivable of facial features in level by humans and machines are the gender, race, and general age. The postulated feed-forward nature of human face recognition also uses Level 1 features, where the initial layers can quickly discard a match candidate if they have a largely different facial appearance (Bruce, & Young, 1986). Level 1 facial features are quite analogous to Level 1 fingerprint features. In each of these two traits, Level 1 features are simple to compute even in low resolution images. However, Level 1 features alone are generally useful for indexing or reducing the search space. Level 1 feature should be explicitly leveraged to improve the matching speed by using them in early stages of a cascaded face recognition system. Level 2 features representations are explicit to face recognition, and require more detailed face observations. These features are locally derived and describe structures in the face that are only relevant to face recognition (as opposed to general object recognition) due to their spatial uniqueness. Examples of such face features in automated face recognition include the use of Gabor wavelets in elastic bunch graph matching (EBGM) (Wiskott et al., 1997) Local Binary Patterns (LBP) (Ahonen et al., 2006), SIFT feature descriptors (Klare, & Jain, 2011) Meyers and Wolf (2008) proposed a distribution models (Mayers and Wolf, 2008), texture appearance models (Cootes et al., 2001) biologically inspired features proposed by Riesenhuber and Poggio. Riesenhuber and Poggio (1999) has used explicit face geometry for recognition of faces (Sakai, Nagao, & Kanade, 1972) which includes the Bertillon system (Bertillon, 1896).

Level 2 features are essential for face recognition. Given the strong evidence that suggests face recognition activity in humans takes place in the fusion form face area (Kanwisher et al., 1997) which is a cortical region that appears to be dedicated to face recognition. In an attempt to replicate human visual processing for face recognition, the use of Level 2 biologically inspired features in the form of Gabor wavelets have been successfully

utilized in machine face recognition (Klare, & Jain, 2011). Along with other features such as the local binary patterns and gradient-based methods, these features are face specific, provided they are defined with respect to their spatial coordinates on the face. For example, EBGM extracts Gabor descriptors at specified locations on the face and LBP and SIFT-descriptor methods extract these descriptors at uniformly distributed locations on a face that has been normalized using the eye coordinates (Lowe, 2004). Level 2 facial features are analogous to minutiae location and orientation in fingerprint recognition. In both face and fingerprint, the Level 2 features are defined with respect to a particular spatial coordinate reference, and in each case the local features can generally be computed independently of one another.

This categorization of facial features is intended to provide a better understanding and standardization of both manual and automated face recognition processes. The benefit of this categorization is two folds: (i) facilitating an individuality measure for face images that can be used in legal testimony, and (ii) improving the accuracy of commercial matchers through a more careful selection of facial features. The current fingerprint feature categorization (Maltoni, 2009) accepted by both forensic scientists as well as fingerprint vendors, served as a guiding principle for our categorization of facial features. Compared to face recognition Fingerprint matching has over 100 years of history and success.

3.3.4. Feature Extraction Approaches

A facial recognition based system is a computer application to automatically identifying a person from a digital image or a video frame. One way to achieve this is by comparing selected facial features from the image to a facial database (Akgul, 2007). It is typically used in security systems and can be compared to other biometrics such as fingerprint or human iris (Akgul, 2011).

Currently, developers came up with the design that is capable of extracting and picking up faces from the crowd and have it compared to an image source - database. The software has the ability to know how basic human face looks like in order for it to work accordingly. Thus, developers have been designed these programs (by storing commands) to pinpoint a face and measure its features. There are different methods of facial recognition which involve a series of steps that serve to capturing, analyzing and comparing a face to a database of stored images.

3.3.4.1. Principal Component Analysis (PCA)

Principal component analysis (PCA) method used for global feature extraction which is a powerful technique for extracting global structures from high-dimensional data set. It has been widely used to reduce dimensionality and extract features from faces for face recognition (Akleman, 1997), (Akleman, & Reisch, 2004). Approximate reconstruction of faces in the ensemble was performed using a weighted combination of eigenvectors (Eigen pictures), obtained from that ensemble (Bach, 2008). The weights that characterize the expansion of the given image in terms of Eigen pictures are seen as global facial features. In an extension of that work, Kirby and Sirovich (1990) included the inherent symmetry of faces in the Eigen pictures. All images in face database are representing in matrix as a very long vector. PCA (Principal Component Analysis) is recognized as an optimal method to perform dimension reduction, yet being claimed as lacking discrimination ability. LDA (Linear Discriminant Analysis) is a supervised based classification method which utilizes face class information to represent face vector space efficiently. In LDA face recognition technique, two types of classes are used: (1) Inter-class and (2) Intra-class. The main objective of LDA is to minimize intra class variation of database and maximize interclass variation.

L.H. Chan et al. (Balcan, 2006) have shown the superiority of LDA over PCA, even when the training dataset is small.

3.3.4.2. Linear Discriminant Analysis

Linear Discriminant is a *"classical"* technique in pattern recognition where it is used to find a linear combination of features which characterize or separate two or more classes of objects or events. The resulting combination may be used as a linear classifier or, more commonly, for dimensionality reduction before it can be classified. LDA approach works on only top Eigen values of small datasets. It will not work properly on large datasets because its performance scalability reduces on large datasets. Bertillon (1896) proposed deformable templates techniques, where facial features are determined by interactions with the face images. In Image based approach concepts like class information, class separability, independent components, and face image contents are utilized. As whole face image is used so this method is also termed as holistic method. PCA tries to simplify the input data by extracting the features and LDA tries to distinguish the input data by dimension reduction. By combining both these techniques, subspace LDA based face recognition system is developed (Bhatt, et al., 2010).

3.3.4.3. Local Binary Pattern (LBP)

The LBP operator is one of the better performing texture descriptors and it has been widely used in various applications. It has proven to be highly discriminative and its key advantages, namely, its invariance to monotonic gray-level changes and computational efficiency, make it suitable for demanding image analysis tasks (Ahonen et al., 2006). To be able to deal with textures at different scales, the LBP operator was later extended to use neighborhoods of different sizes (Ahonen et al., 2006). Defining the local neighborhood as a set of sampling points evenly spaced on a circle centered at the pixel to be labeled allows any radius and number of sampling points. Another extension to the original operator is uniform patterns (Ahonen et al., 2006). A local binary pattern is called uniform if the binary pattern contains at most two bitwise transitions from 0 to 1 or vice versa when the bit pattern is considered. The method using local binary patterns (LBPs) is first proposed by (Ahonen et al., 2006) to encode the pixel-wise information in the texture images. The texture analysis community has developed a variety of different descriptors for the appearance of image patches. However, face recognition problem has not been associated to that progress in texture analysis field as it has not been investigated from such point of view. So the question arises that what is the need of texture based face recognition approach. It was investigated that the representation of face images by means of local binary pattern (Duda, Hart, & Stork, 2000) features, yielding in outstanding results. The ground-breaking work of Schmid and Mohr et al showed that invariant local feature matching could be extended to general image recognition problems in which a feature was matched against a large database of images. Further, the Scale Invariant Feature Transform (SIFT) (Lowe, 2004) has emerged as a cut edge methodology in general object recognition as well as for other machine vision applications. One of the interesting features of the SIFT approach is the capability to capture the main gray level features of an object's view by means of local patterns extracted from a scale-space decomposition of the image.

- **Classification of Human faces**

A face recognition system is expected to identify faces present in images and videos automatically. It can operate in either or both of two modes:

1. **Face verification (or authentication):** involves a one-to-one match that compares a query face image against a template face image whose identity is being claimed.

2. **Face identification (or recognition):** involves one-to-many matches that compare a query face image against all the template images in the database to determine the identity of the query face.

- **Analysis in face subspaces**

Subspace analysis techniques for face recognition are based on the fact that a class of patterns of interest, such as the face, resides in a subspace of the input image space: A small image of 64 × 64 having 4096 pixels can express a large number of pattern classes, such as trees, houses and faces. Among the 2564096 > 109864 possible "configurations", only a few correspond to faces. Therefore, the original image representation is highly redundant, and the dimensionality of this representation could be greatly reduced. With the eigenface or PCA approach, a small number (40 or lower) of eigenfaces are derived from a set of training face images by using the Karhunen-Loeve transform or PCA. A face image is efficiently represented as a feature vector (i.e. a vector of weights) of low dimensionality. The features in such subspace provide more salient and richer information for recognition than the raw image. Intra-subject variations in pose, illumination, expression, occlusion, accessories is shown in Figure 5.

- **Highly Complex Nonlinear Manifolds:** The entire face manifold (distribution) is highly non-convex and so face manifold of individual under various changes. Linear methods such as PCA, independent component analysis (ICA) and Linear Discriminant Analysis (LDA) project the data linearly from a high-dimensional space (e.g. the image space) to a low-dimensional subspace. As such, they are unable to preserve the non-convex variations of face manifolds necessary to differentiate among individuals.

Figure 5. Intra-subject variations in pose, illumination, expression, occlusion, accessories (e.g. glasses), color and brightness

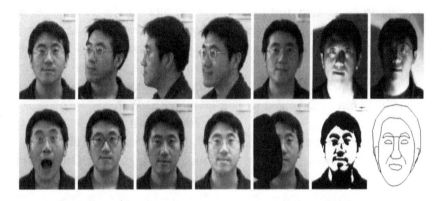

- **In a Linear Subspace:** Euclidean distance and Mahalanobis distance do not perform well for classifying between face and non-face manifolds and between manifolds of individuals. This limits the power of the linear methods to achieve highly accurate face detection and recognition.

- **High Dimensionality and Small Sample Size:** A canonical face image of 112×92 resides in a 10,304-dimensional feature space. Nevertheless, the number of examples per person (typically fewer than 10) available for learning the manifold is usually much smaller than the dimensionality of the image space; a system trained on so few examples may not generalize well to unseen instances of the face.

3.4. Technical Solutions

1. **Feature Extraction:** Construct a "good" feature space in which the face manifolds become simpler i.e. less nonlinear and non-convex than those in the other spaces. This includes two levels of processing:
   - Normalize face images geometrically and photo metrically, such as using morphing and histogram equalization

   - Extract features in the normalized images which are stable with respect to such variations, such as based on Gabor wavelets.

2. **Pattern Classification:** Construct classification engines able to solve difficult nonlinear classification and regression problems in the feature space and to generalize better.

3. **Learning-Based Approach - Statistical Learning:**
   - Learns from training data to extract good features and construct classification engines.
   - During the learning, both prior knowledge about face and variations has seen in the training data which are taken into consideration.
   - The appearance-based approach such as PCA and LDA based methods, has significantly advanced face recognition techniques.
   - They operate directly on an image-based representation (i.e. an array of pixel intensities) and extracts features in a subspace derived from training images.

4. **Appearance-based Approach Utilizing Geometric Features:**

◦ Detects facial features such as eyes, nose, mouth and chin.

◦ Detects properties of and relations (e.g. areas, distances, angles) between the features are used as descriptors for face recognition.

5. **Nonlinear Kernel Techniques:**

◦ Linear methods can be extended using nonlinear

◦ Kernel techniques (kernel PCA and kernel LDA) to deal with nonlinearly in face recognition.

◦ A non-linear projection (dimension reduction) from the image space to a feature space is performed; the manifolds in the resulting feature space become simple, yet with subtleties preserved.

◦ A local appearance-based feature space uses appropriate image filters, so the distributions of faces are less affected by various changes. Examples:

  ▪ Local feature analysis (LFA).
  ▪ Gabor wavelet-based features such as elastic graph bunch matching (EGBM) .
  ▪ Local binary pattern (LBP).

4. FACE RECOGNITION APPROACHES

4.1. PCA (Eigenfaces)

Principal component analysis (PCA) is a statistical procedure that uses orthogonal transformation to convert a set of observations of possibly correlated variables into a set of values of linearly uncorrelated variables called principal components. The number of principal components is less than or equal to the number of original variables. This transformation is defined in such a way that the first principal component has the largest possible variance (that is, accounts for as much of the variability in the data as possible), and each succeeding component in turn has the highest variance possible under the constraint that it be orthogonal to (i.e., uncorrelated with) the preceding components. Principal components are guaranteed to be independent if the data set is jointly normally distributed. PCA is sensitive to the relative scaling of the original variables (Turk, & Pentland, 1991). PCA is the simplest of the true eigenvector-based multivariate analyses. Often, its operation can be thought of as revealing the internal structure of the data in a way that best explains the variance in the data. If a multivariate dataset is visualized as a set of coordinates in a high-dimensional data space (1 axis per variable), PCA can supply the user with a lower-dimensional picture, a projection or "*shadow*" of the object when viewed from its most informative viewpoint. This is done by using only the first few principal components so that the dimensionality of the transformed data is reduced.

PCA is closely related to factor analysis. Factor analysis typically incorporates more domain specific assumptions about the underlying structure and solves eigenvectors of a slightly different matrix. PCA is also related to canonical correlation analysis (CCA). CCA defines coordinate systems that optimally describe the cross-covariance between two datasets while PCA defines a new orthogonal coordinate system that optimally describes variance in a single dataset.

• **PCA Algorithmic Description**

Given M face images arranged as column vectors $\Gamma_1, \Gamma_2, \Gamma_3, \Gamma_4 \ldots \Gamma_M$. The average face $\Psi = \frac{1}{M} \sum_N^M \Gamma_n$ is subtracted from each image $\Phi_i = \Gamma_i - \Psi$. Next we joining the face images into a single matrix $A = [\Phi_1 \ \Phi_2 \ \Phi_3 \ldots \Phi_M]$ PCA find a set of orthonormal vectors that best represents the data. These vectors are the eigenvectors u_k of the covariance matrix $C = AA^T$. In Eigen space terminology, each image is projected by the top M' significant eigenvectors u_k to obtain weights $w_k = u_k^T(\Gamma_i - \Psi)$ that best linearly weight the eigenfaces into a representation of the original image. Knowing the weights of the training images and a new test face image, a nearest neighbor approach determines the identity of the face. Eigenface has the advantage of being simple and fast at the cost of low accuracy when pose, expression, and illumination vary significantly. An Eigen space model Ω may be defined for set $S = \{S_1, S_2, S_3, ..., S_N\}$ of N training images (observations):

$$\Omega = \Omega(\mu, U, \lambda, S) \qquad (1)$$

For a set $S = \{S_1, S_2, S_3, ..., S_N\}$ of N training images, the average vector image μ and the deviation matrix Φ of each image from the average image μ is given by:

$$\Phi = (S-\mu) \quad (2).$$

The covariance matrix C is given by:

$$C = \frac{1}{N}\sum_{i=1}^{N}\Phi_i\Phi_i^T = AA^T \qquad (3)$$

where $A = [\Phi_1, \Phi_2, \Phi_3, ..., \Phi_M]$ and Φ^T is the transpose matrix of Φ. The eigenvectors of the product $L = A^TA$ are obtained as:

$$Lv_i = A^TAv_i = \lambda_i v_i, \, L_{ij} = (\Phi_i)^T\Phi_j \qquad (4)$$

Premultiplying both sides by matrix A

$$AA^TAv_i = \lambda_i Av_i. \qquad (5)$$

where v_i and λ_i are respectively the N eigenvectors and N eigenvalues of matrix L and Av_i and λ_i are respectively the eigenvectors and eigenvalues of the covariance matrix $C=AA^T$

The eigenvectors $u_i = Av_i$ of matrix C are the eigenfaces that are obtained by projection of the deviation matrix Φ on the eigenvectors v_i of L

$$u_i = \sum_{j=1}^{N}v_i\Phi_j, \, i = 1,2,3,...,N. \qquad (6)$$

The resulting eigenvectors are orthogonal; to get orthonormal eigenvectors they need to be normalized to unit length. We can see how the grayscale values are distributed within the specific Eigen faces (Figure 6 and Figure 7).

10 Eigenvectors are obviously not sufficient for a good image reconstruction, 50 Eigenvectors may already be sufficient to encode important facial features. You'll get a good reconstruction with approximately 300 Eigenvectors for the AT&T Face database. There are rule of thumbs how many Eigen faces you should choose for successful face recognition, but it heavily depends on the input data.

4.2. Linear Discriminant Analysis (LDA)

Linear discriminant analysis (LDA) and the related Fisher's linear discriminant are methods used in statistics, pattern recognition and machine learning to find a linear combination of features which characterizes or separates two or more classes of objects or events. The resulting combination may be used as a linear classifier, or, more commonly, for dimensionality reduction before later classification (Zhao et al., 1999) (Roth, & Steinhage, 1999). LDA is closely related to ANOVA (analysis of variance) and regression analysis, which also attempt to express one dependent variable as a linear combination of other features or measurements. In the other two methods however, the dependent variable is a numerical quantity, while for LDA it is a categorical variable (i.e. the class label). Logistic regression and probit regression are more similar to LDA, as they also explain a categorical variable. These methods are prefer-

Figure 6. Eigen faces

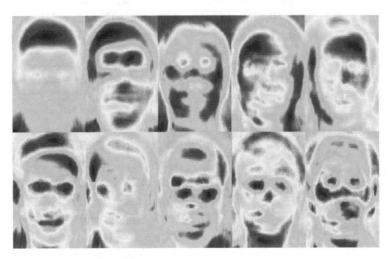

Figure 7. Eigen faces

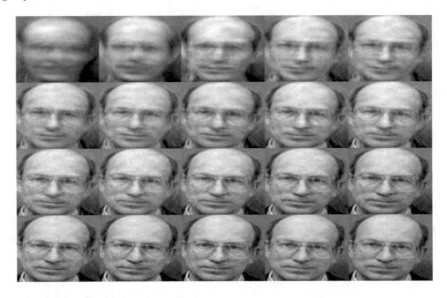

able in applications where it is not reasonable to assume that the independent variables are normally distributed, which is a fundamental assumption of the LDA method. LDA is also closely related to principal component analysis (PCA) and factor analysis in that they both look for linear combinations of variables which best explain the data. LDA explicitly attempts to model the difference between the classes of data. PCA on the other hand does not take into account any difference in class, and factor analysis builds the feature combinations based on differences rather than similarities. Discriminant analysis is also different from factor analysis in that it is not an interdependence technique: a distinction between independent variables and dependent variables (also called criterion variables) must be made. LDA works when the measurements made on independent variables for each observation are continuous quantities. When dealing with categorical independent variables, the equivalent technique is discriminant correspondence analysis.

4.2.1. LDA Algorithmic Description

Let X be a random vector with samples drawn from c classes

$$X = \{X_1, X_2, ..., X_c\}$$

$$X = \{X_1, X_2, ..., X_i\}$$

The scatter matrices S_B and S_w are calculated as:

$$S_B = \sum_{i=1}^{c} (\mu_i - \mu)^T \tag{7}$$

$$S_w = \sum_{i=1}^{c} \sum_{x}^{c} i \in X_j (x_j - \mu_i)^T \tag{8}$$

where μ is the total mean

$$\mu = \frac{1}{N} \sum_{i=1}^{n} X_i \text{, where } i \in (1, 2, 3, ..., n) \tag{9}$$

and μ_i is the mean of class $\mu_i = \frac{1}{\|X_i\|} \sum_{x}^{n} j \in X_i$

$i \in \{1, 2, ..., c\}$ (10)

Fisher's algorithm now looks for a projection W that maximizes the class separability criterion:

$$W_{opt} = \arg\max_w \frac{\left\| W^T S_B W \right\|}{\left\| W^T S_w W \right\|} \tag{11}$$

The optimization problem can then be rewritten as:

$$W_{pca} = \arg\max_w |W^T S_T W| \tag{12}$$

$$W_{fld} = \arg\max_w \frac{\left\| W^T W_{pca}^T S_B W_{pca} W \right\|}{\left\| W^T W_{pca}^T S_w W_{pca} W \right\|} \tag{13}$$

The transformation matrix W that projects a sample into the $(c-1)$-dimensional space is then given by:

$$W = W_{fld}^T W_{pca}^T \tag{14}$$

Each Fisherface has the same length as an original image, thus it can be displayed as an image in Figure 8. The demo shows (or saves) the first, at most 16 Fisherfaces:

Figure 8. Fisherfaces of face image of database

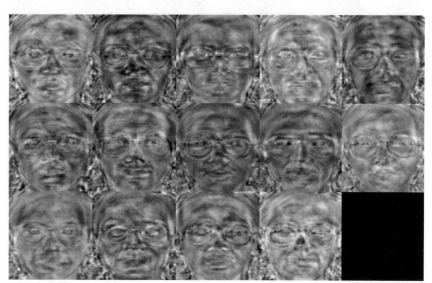

The Fisherfaces method learns a class-specific transformation matrix, so that they do not capture illumination as obviously as the Eigenfaces method. The Discriminant Analysis instead finds the facial features to discriminate between the persons. It's important to mention, that the performance of the Fisherfaces heavily depends on the input data as well. Practically it said: if you learn the Fisherfaces for well-illuminated pictures only and you try to recognize faces in bad-illuminated scenes, then method is likely to find the wrong components (just those features may not be predominant on bad illuminated images). This is somewhat logical, since the method had no chance to learn the illumination.

The Fisherfaces allow a reconstruction of the projected image, just like the Eigenfaces did (see Figure 9). However, since we only identified the features to distinguish between subjects, you can't expect a nice reconstruction of the original image. For the Fisherfaces method we'll project the sample image onto each of the Fisherfaces instead. The differences may be subtle for the human eyes, but we should be able to see some differences:

4.3. Local Binary Patterns (LBP)

Eigen faces and Fisher faces take a somewhat holistic approach to face recognition. You treat your data as a vector somewhere in a high-dimensional image space. We all know high-dimensionality is bad, so a lower-dimensional subspace is identified, where (probably) useful information is preserved. The Eigenface based approach maximizes the total scatter, which can lead to problems if the variance is generated by an external source, because components with a maximum variance over all classes aren't necessarily useful for classification. So to preserve some discriminative information we applied a LDA and optimized as described in the Fisherfaces method. It is one of the better performing texture descriptors and widely used in various applications. It has proven to be highly discriminative because its invariance to monotonic gray level changes and computational efficiency, make it suitable for demanding image analysis tasks. Face can be seen as a composition of micro-patterns which can be well described by LBP operator (Ahonen et al., 2006).

Figure 9. Reconstruction of the projected image

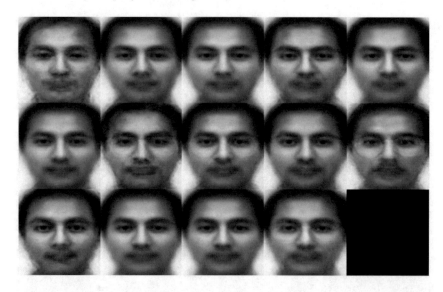

Figure 10. Binary number

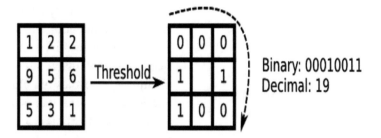

The LBP operator was originally designed for texture description. The operator assigns a label to every pixel of an image by thresholding the 3x3-neighborhood of each pixel with the center pixel value and considering the result as a binary number shown in Figure 10.

1. Extend LBP operator to use neighborhoods of different sizes.
2. Define the local neighborhood as a set of sampling points evenly spaced on a circle centered at the pixel to be labeled allows any radius and number of sampling points. 3. If a sampling point does not fall in the center of a pixel using Bilinear interpolation.

4.3.1. LBP Algorithmic Description

A more formal description of the LBP operator can be given as:

$$LBP(x_c, y_c) = \sum_{p=0}^{p-1} 2^p (i_p - i_c) \qquad (15)$$

where (x_c, y_c) is central pixel with intensity i_p, i_c being the intensity of the neighbor pixel. s is the sign function defined as (Equations 15 and 16):

$$s(x) = \begin{cases} 0 & \text{if } x \geq 0 \\ 1 & \text{else} \end{cases} \qquad (16)$$

This description enables you to capture very fine grained details in images. In fact the authors were able to compete with state of the art results for texture classification. Soon after the operator was published it was noted that a fixed neighborhood fails to encode details differing in scale. So the operator was extended to use a variable neighborhood. The idea is to align an arbitrary number of neighbors on a circle with a variable radius, which enables to capture the following neighborhoods (see Figure 11).

For a given point (x_c, y_c) the position of the neighbor (x_p, y_p), $p \in P$ can be calculated by:

Figure 11. Number of neighbors on a circle with a variable radius

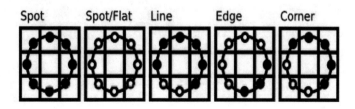

$$x_p = x_c + R\cos(\frac{2\pi p}{P})$$

$$x_p = x_c - R\sin(\frac{2\pi p}{P})$$

The operator is an extension to the original LBP codes, so it's sometimes called Extended LBP (also referred to as Circular LBP). If a point's coordinate on the circle doesn't correspond to image coordinates, the point gets interpolated. Computer science has a bunch of clever interpolation schemes; the OpenCV implementation does a linear interpolation:

$$f(x,y) = [1-x, x]\begin{bmatrix} f(0,0) & f(0,1) \\ f(1,0) & f(1,1) \end{bmatrix}\begin{bmatrix} 1-y \\ y \end{bmatrix}$$

By definition the LBP operator is robust against monotonic grayscale transformations. We can easily verify this by looking at the LBP image of an artificially modified image (see Figure 12).

4.4. Scale Invariant Feature Transform (SIFT)

The image features have many properties that make them suitable for matching different images of an object or scene. The features are invariant to image scaling and rotation, and partially invariant to change in illumination and 3D camera viewpoint. They are well localized in both the spatial and frequency domains, reducing the probability of disruption by occlusion, clutter, or noise. Large numbers of features can be extracted from typical images with efficient algorithms. In addition, the features are highly distinctive, which allows a single feature to be correctly matched with high probability against a large database of features, providing a basis for object and scene recognition (Lowe, 2004). The cost of extracting features is minimized by taking a cascade filtering approach, in which the more expensive operations are applied only at locations that pass an initial test.

4.4.1. SIFT Algorithmic Description

Following are the major stages of computation used to generate the set of image features:

1. **Scale-Space Extrema Detection:** In it, Laplacian of Gaussian is found for the image with various values. LOG acts as a blob detector which detects blobs in various sizes due to change. In short, acts as a scaling parameter. For e.g., in the above image,

Figure 12. Identification of face images using LBP approach

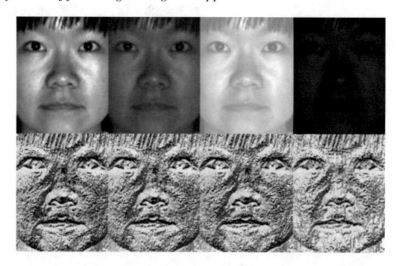

Gaussian kernel, with low and high value for small corner, while Gaussian kernel with high fits well for larger corner. So, we can find the local maxima across the scale and space which gives us a list of values which means there is a potential keypoint at (x,y) at scale. But this LOG is a little costly, so SIFT algorithm uses Difference of Gaussians (DOG) which is an approximation of LOG. Difference of Gaussian is obtained as the difference of Gaussian blurring of an image with two different. This process is done for different octaves of the image in Gaussian Pyramid. It is represented in Figure 13.

Once this DoG is found, images are searched for local extrema over scale and space. For e.g. one pixel in an image is compared with its 8 neighbours as well as 9 pixels in next scale and 9 pixels in previous scales. If it is a local extrema, it is a potential key point. It basically means that keypoint is best represented in that scale and shown in Figure 14.

2. **Keypoint Localization:** Once potential keypoints locations are found, they have to be refined to get more accurate results. They used Taylor series expansion of scale space to get more accurate location of extrema, and if the intensity at this extrema is less than a threshold value (0.03 as per the paper), it is rejected. This threshold is called contrast Threshold in OpenCV DOG has higher response for edges, so edges also need to be removed. For this, a concept similar to Harris corner detector is used. They used a 2x2 Hessian matrix (H) to compute the pricipal curvature. We know from Harris corner detector that for edges, one Eigen value is larger than the other. So here they used a simple function, if this ratio is greater than a threshold, called edgeThreshold in OpenCV, that keypoint is discarded. It is given as 10 in paper. So it eliminates any low-contrast keypoints and edge keypoints and what remain are strong interest points.

3. **Orientation Assignment:** Once potential keypoints locations are found, they have to be refined to get more accurate results. They used Taylor series expansion of scale space to get more accurate location of extrema, and if the intensity at this extrema is less than a threshold value (0.03 as per the paper), it is rejected. This threshold is called contrast Threshold in OpenCV DOG (Difference of Gaussian) has higher response for edges,

Figure 13. Different octaves of the image in Gaussian Pyramid

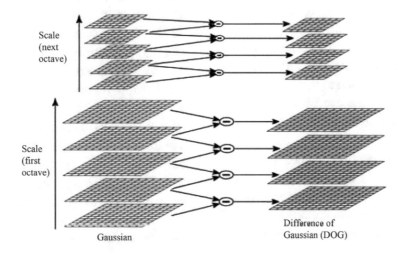

Figure 14. Representation of Keypoint in different scale

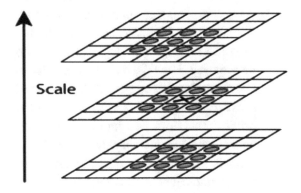

so edges also need to be removed. For this, a concept similar to Harris corner detector is used. They used a 2x2 Hessian matrix (H) to compute the prical curvature. We know from Harris corner detector that for edges, one Eigen value is larger than the other. So here they used a simple function, If this ratio is greater than a threshold, called edgeThreshold in OpenCV, that keypoint is discarded. It is given as 10 in paper. So it eliminates any low-contrast keypoints and edge keypoints and what remain are strong interest points.

4. **Keypoint Descriptor:** Now keypoints descriptor is created. A 16x16 neighborhood around the keypoint is taken. It is divided into 16 sub-blocks of 4x4 sizes. For each sub-block, 8 bin orientation histogram is created. So a total of 128 bin values are available. It is represented as a vector to form keypoint descriptor. In addition to this, several measures are taken to achieve robustness against illumination changes, rotation etc.

This approach has been named the Scale Invariant Feature Transform (SIFT), as it transforms image data into scale-invariant coordinates relative to local features. An important aspect of this approach is that it generates large numbers of features that densely cover the image over the full range of scales and locations. A typical image of size 500x500 pixels will give rise to about 2000 stable features (although this number depends on both image content and choices for various parameters). The quantity of features is particularly important for object recognition, where the ability to detect small objects in cluttered backgrounds requires that at least 3 features be correctly matched from each object for reliable identification. For image matching and recognition, SIFT features are first extracted from a set of reference images and stored in a database. A new image is matched by individually comparing each feature from the new image to this previous database and finding candidate matching features based on Euclidean distance of their feature vectors. This paper will discuss fast nearest-neighbor algorithms that can perform this computation rapidly against large databases.

The keypoints descriptors are highly distinctive, which allows a single feature to find its correct match with good probability in a large database of features. However, in a cluttered 2 image, many features from the background will not have any correct match in the database, giving rise to many false matches in addition to the correct ones. The correct matches can be filtered from the full set of matches by identifying subsets of keypoints that agree on the object and its location, scale, and orientation in the new image (see Figure 15). The probability that several features will agree on these parameters by chance is much lower than the probability that any individual feature match will be in error. The determination of these consistent clusters can be performed rapidly by using an efficient hash table implementation of the generalized Hough transform. Each cluster of 3 or more features that agree on an object and its pose is then subject to further detailed verification. First, a least-squared estimate is made for an affine approximation to the object pose. Any other image features consistent with this pose are identified, and outliers are discarded. Finally, a

Figure 15. Keypoints and matching in AT& T database

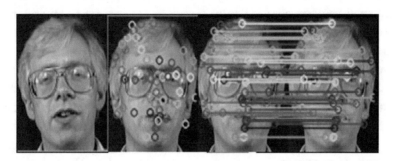

detailed computation is made of the probability that a particular set of features indicates the presence of an object, given the accuracy of fit and number of probable false matches. Object matches that pass all these tests can be identified as correct with high confidence. See the two results in the following images.

5. EXPERIMENTAL RESULT AND DISCUSSION

5.1. Performance Evaluation

The face recognition techniques discussed above have been implemented on the AT&T database

which has been described in the database description earlier. The face recognition algorithms i.e. PCA, LDA, LBP, and SIFT have been implemented on these databases for the evaluation of their recognition and identification accuracy. Each image in every subject of the database has been compares to every other image i.e. total 1,60,000 iterations have been done for the total accuracy check of each database on every algorithm and then their results have been evaluated.

5.2. Comparison of PCA and LDA

- There has been a tendency in the computer vision community to prefer LDA over PCA.

Figure 16. Comparison of PCA and LDA

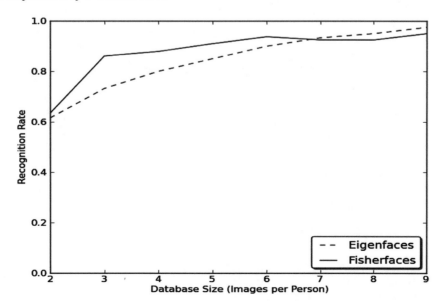

- This is mainly because LDA deals directly with discrimination between classes while PCA does not pay attention to the underlying class structure.
- When the training set is small, PCA can outperform LDA.
- When the number of samples is large and representative for each class, LDA outperforms PCA.
- **LBP has better performance:**
  - Its tolerance to monotonic gray-scale changes.
  - The computational efficiency of the LBP operator is better because no gray-scale normalization is needed prior to applying the LBP operator to the face image.

Table 1 illustrates the identification accuracy of PCA, LDA, ICA based on appearance face recognition and SIFT LBP texture face recognition. Table 1 demonstrates LBP yields better identification accuracy with 90.93% in unconstrained scenario (see Figure 17). They extract prominent type of face image features which are invariant to image scale and rotation to provide robust matching across a substantial range of affine distortion, change in 3D viewpoint, addition of noise, and

Table 1. Experimental Result of AT&T face database

Database	Identification Accuracy (%)				
	PCA	**LDA**	**ICA**	**SIFT**	**LBP**
AT&T	77.97	82.45	84.25	87.76	90.93

Figure 17. CMC to show identification accuracy of cattle face (based on Table1)

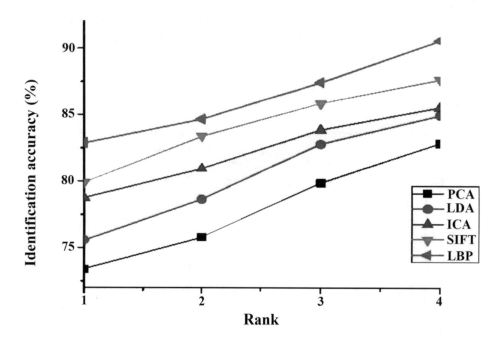

change in illumination. While appearance face recognition algorithms are PCA, LDA and ICA yields identification accuracy with AT&T face database based on holistic feature.

6. CONCLUSION AND FUTURE DIRECTION

The local feature or hybrid feature based approaches to face recognition have been gaining interest lately which is understandable, given the limitations of the holistic representations and these methods are more robust against variations in pose or illumination than holistic methods. Trying to build a holistic description of a face using texture methods is not reasonable. For face, retaining the information about spatial relations is important. But texture descriptors tend to average over the image area. It considers the face is like ordinary textures, texture description should usually be invariant to translation or even rotation of the texture. The small repetitive textures, the small-scale relationships determine the appearance of the texture and thus the large-scale relations do not contain useful information. This book chapter has presented an overview about face recognition. It isn't a trivial task, and today remains unresolved and it can be solved by new or extended feature extraction methods. There is much literature about extending or improving well known algorithms. In above, example, including the weighting procedures to PCA or turning methods like LDA into semi-supervised algorithms. Feature extraction method combination. Many algorithms are being built around this idea. As many strong feature extraction techniques have been developed, the challenge is to combine them. Applications of face Recognition:

- Digital photography: it is used to capture the face images of different people.

- Surveillance: Face of individual is recognized under digital surveillance scenario.
- Album organization: Album of different collections of images are organized in better way.

Face recognition is also resulting in other dares, like expression recognition or body motion recognition. Overall, face recognition techniques and the emerging methods can be used in other areas. Therefore, it isn't just an unresolved problem but also the source of new applications and challenges.

REFERENCES

Ahonen, T., Hadid, A., & Pietikainen, M. (2006). Face description with local binary patterns: Application to face recognition. *Pattern Analysis and Machine Intelligence. IEEE Transactions on*, *28*(12), 2037–2041.

Akgul, T. (2007). Introducing the Cartoonist, Tayfun Akgul. *Antennas and Propagation Magazine, IEEE*, *49*(3), 162–162. doi:10.1109/MAP.2007.4293959

Akgul, T. (2011). Can an Algorithm Recognize Montage Portraits as Human Faces? *IEEE Signal Processing Magazine*, *1*(28), 160–158. doi:10.1109/MSP.2010.938777

Akleman, E. (1997, January). Making caricatures with morphing. In ACM SIGGRAPH 97 Visual Proceedings: The art and interdisciplinary programs of SIGGRAPH'97 (p. 145). ACM. doi:10.1145/259081.259231

Akleman, E., & Reisch, J. (2004, August). Modeling expressive 3D caricatures. In ACM SIGGRAPH 2004 Sketches (p. 61). ACM.

Bach, F. R. (2008). Consistency of the group lasso and multiple kernel learning. *Journal of Machine Learning Research*, *9*, 1179–1225.

Balcan, M. F., Blum, A., & Vempala, S. (2006). Kernels as features: On kernels, margins and low-dimensional mappings. *Machine Learning*, *65*(1), 79–94. doi:10.1007/s10994-006-7550-1

Belhumeur, P., Hespanda, J., & Kriegman, D. (1997). Eigenfaces vs. fisherfaces: Recognition using class specific linear projection. *IEEE Transactions on Pattern Analysis and Machine Intelligence*, *19*(7), 711–720. doi:10.1109/34.598228

Bertillon, A. (1896). *The Bertillon System of Identification*. Chicago, IL: Academic Press.

Beymer, D. (1994). Face Recognition under Varying Pose. In *Proceedings of IEEE Conf. on Comp. Vision and Pattern Recognition*, (pp. 756-761). IEEE.

Bhatt, H. S., Bharadwaj, S., Singh, R., & Vatsa, M. (2010, September). On matching sketches with digital face images. In *Biometrics: Theory Applications and Systems (BTAS), 2010 Fourth IEEE International Conference on*. IEEE. doi:10.1109/BTAS.2010.5634507

Blanz, V., & Vetter, T. (2003). Face recognition based on fitting a 3D morphable model. *Pattern Analysis and Machine Intelligence. IEEE Transactions on*, *25*(9), 1063–1074.

Blanz, V., & Vetter, T. (2003). Face recognition based on fitting a 3d morphable model. *IEEE Transactions on Pattern Analysis and Machine Intelligence*, *25*(9), 1063–1074. doi:10.1109/TPAMI.2003.1227983

Bruce, V., & Young, A. (1986). Understanding faces recognition. *British Journal of Psychology*, *77*(3), 305–327. doi:10.1111/j.2044-8295.1986.tb02199.x PMID:3756376

Cootes, T., Taylor, C., Cooper, D., & Graham, J. (1995). Active shape models-their training and application. *Computer Vision and Image Understanding*, *61*(1), 38–59. doi:10.1006/cviu.1995.1004

Cootes, T. F., Edwards, G. J., & Taylor, C. J. (2001). Active appearance models. *IEEE Transactions on Pattern Analysis and Machine Intelligence*, *23*(6), 681–685. doi:10.1109/34.927467

Council, N. R. (2009). *Strengthening Forensic Science in the United States: A Path Forward*. National Academies Press.

Duda, R., Hart, P., & Stork, D. (2000). *Pattern Classification* (2nd ed.). Wiley-Interscience.

Friedman, J., Hastie, T., & Tibshirani, R. (2000). Additive logistic regression: A statistical view of boosting. *Annals of Statistics*, *28*(2), 337–374. doi:10.1214/aos/1016218223

Georghiades, A., Belhumeur, P., & Kriegman, D. (2001). From few to many: Illumination cone models for face recognition under variable lighting and pose. *IEEE Transactions on Pattern Analysis and Machine Intelligence*, *23*(6), 643–660. doi:10.1109/34.927464

Gross, R., Matthews, I., & Baker, S. (2004). Appearance-based face recognition and light-fields. *IEEE Transactions on Pattern Analysis and Machine Intelligence*, *26*(4), 449–465. doi:10.1109/TPAMI.2004.1265861 PMID:15382650

Jain, V., & Learned-Miller, E. (2010). FDDB: A benchmark for face detection in unconstrained settings. In *Handbook of fingerprint recognition*. Springer.

Kanwisher, N., McDermott, J., & Chun, M. M. (1997). The fusion form face area: A module in human extrastriate cortex specialized for face perception. *The Journal of Neuroscience*, *17*(11), 4302–4311. PMID:9151747

Klare, B., & Jain, A. K. (2010). On a taxonomy of facial features. In *Proc. of IEEE Conference on Biometrics: Theory, Applications and Systems*. IEEE.

Klare, B., Li, Z., & Jain, A. K. (2011). Matching forensic sketches to mugshot photos. *IEEE Transactions on Pattern Analysis and Machine Intelligence*, *33*(3), 639–646. doi:10.1109/TPAMI.2010.180 PMID:20921585

Liao, S., Jain, A. K., & Li, S. Z. (2014). *A Fast and Accurate Unconstrained Face Detector*. arXiv preprint arXiv:1408.1656.

Lorenzo, J., Teli, M. N., Marcel, S., & Atanasoaei, C. (2011) Face and eye detection on hard datasets. In *Proceeding of Int. Joint Conference on Biometrics*. IEEE.

Lowe, D. G. (2004). Distinctive image features from scale-invariant keypoints. *International Journal of Computer Vision*, *60*(2), 91–110. doi:10.1023/B:VISI.0000029664.99615.94

Meyers, E., & Wolf, L. (2008). Using biologically inspired features for face processing. *International Journal of Computer Vision*, *76*(1), 93–104. doi:10.1007/s11263-007-0058-8

Park, U., & Jain, A. K. (2007). 3D model-based face recognition in video. In Advances in Biometrics (pp. 1085-1094). Springer Berlin Heidelberg.

Parris, J., Wilber, M., Helfin, B., Rara, H., Barkouky Aly Farag, A. E., Movellan, J. M., … Kanade, T. (1972). Computer analysis and classification of photographs of human faces. In *Proc. First USA-JAPAN Computer Conference*.

Phillips, P., Flynn, P., Scruggs, P., Bowyer, K., & Worek, W. (2006). Preliminary face recognition grand challenge results. In *Proceedings of International Conference on Automatic Face and Gesture Recognition*. doi:10.1109/FGR.2006.87

Phillips, P., Scruggs, W., OToole, A., Flynn, P., Bowyer, K., Schott, C., & Sharpe, M. (2007). *FRVT 2006 and ICE 2006 large-scale results*. NIST Technical Report NISTIR, 7408.

Phuong-T, P. N., & Quang-L, H. (2010). *Robust Face Detection under Challenges of Rotation*. Pose and Occlusion.

Riesenhuber, M., & Poggio, T. (1999). Hierarchical models of object recognition in cortex. *Nature Neuroscience*, *2*(11), 1019–1025. doi:10.1038/14819 PMID:10526343

Roth, V., & Steinhage, V. (1999). Nonlinear discriminant analysis using kernel functions. In Advances in neural information processing systems.

Tan, X., & Triggs, B. (2010). Enhanced local texture feature sets for face recognition under difficult lighting conditions. Image Processing. *IEEE Transactions on*, *19*(6), 1635–1650.

Turk, M., & Pentland, A. (1991). Eigenfaces for recognition. *Journal of Cognitive Neuroscience*, *3*(1), 71–86. doi:10.1162/jocn.1991.3.1.71 PMID:23964806

Viola, P., & Jones, M. (2001). Rapid object detection using a boosted cascade of simple features. In *Proceedings of IEEE Computer Society Conference on Computer Vision and Pattern Recognition*. IEEE.

Wiskott, L., Fellous, J.-M., Kuiger, N., & von der Malsburg, C. (1997). Face recognition by elastic bunch graph matching. *IEEE Transactions on Pattern Analysis and Machine Intelligence*, *19*(7), 775–779. doi:10.1109/34.598235

Zhao, W., Chellappa, R., & Phillips, P. J. (1999). *Subspace linear discriminant analysis for face recognition*. Computer Vision Laboratory, Center for Automation Research, University of Maryland.

KEY TERMS AND DEFINITIONS

Biometric Profile: Information used to represent an individual or group in an information system.

Biometric Traits: Class of biometric characteristics (e.g., face or stripe pattern) used as source for constructing a biometric profile.

Biometrics: Biometrics means "life measurement" but the term is usually associated with the use of unique physiological characteristics to identify an individual.

Classification: Classification refers to as assigning a physical object or incident into one of a set of predefined categories.

Identification: Process of retrieving identity by one to many (1 to M) matching of an unknown biometric profile against a set of known profiles.

Chapter 12

Intelligence–Based Adaptive Digital Watermarking for Images in Wavelet Transform Domain

V. Santhi
VIT University, India

D. P. Acharjya
VIT University, India

ABSTRACT

Advances in technologies facilitate the end users to carry out unauthorized manipulation and duplication of multimedia data with less effort. Because of these advancements, the two most commonly encountered problems are (1) copyright protection and (2) unauthorized manipulation of multimedia data. Thus a scheme is required to protect multimedia data from those two above said problems. Digital Watermarking is considered as one of the security mechanisms to protect copyrights of multimedia data. The literature review reveals that the calculation of scaling and embedding parameters are not completely automated. In order to automate the procedure of calculating scaling and embedding parameters the computational intelligence need to be incorporated in the watermarking algorithm. Moreover the quality of the watermarked images could also be preserved by combining computational intelligence concepts. Thus watermarking schemes utilizing computational intelligence concepts could be called as intelligence based watermarking schemes and it is presented in this chapter in detail.

INTRODUCTION

Information sharing becomes very easy in Internet that permits the unauthorized manipulations of multimedia data with reduced efforts. In such circumstances protecting copyrights of multimedia data become very essential as cost involved in content development is very high. In Internet, huge volume of data available in the form of images, thus it is required to secure images in particular. Digital watermarking is considered as a most popular security mechanism to protect copyrights

DOI: 10.4018/978-1-4666-8654-0.ch012

of digital images. In general digital watermarking techniques are carried out by inserting a piece of digital data in to a cover data. In order to keep the watermark inside a cover image, its content needs to be altered without affecting its quality. The amount of alteration of cover images decides the quality of cover images. Digital image watermarking techniques are broadly classified into spatial domain and frequency domain techniques. Researcher have carried out watermarking schemes in both working domains, but in order to make watermarking schemes robust it has to be carried out in frequency domain. In this chapter, watermarking schemes carried out in wavelet transform domain combined with computational intelligence are presented. In the subsequent sections, the basics of digital watermarking, watermarking in transform domain, computational intelligence based watermarking schemes and conclusion are discussed in detail.

BASICS OF DIGITAL WATERMARKING

Digital Watermarking is defined as a process of inserting a piece of digital data called watermark into digital images that are to be protected. The watermark to be inserted can be of logo, text data, numbers or any other type of images. The cover data could be of digital images, digital video sequences and digital audio signal. The inserted watermark should be extractable in future for verification of it to the intended purposes. One of the important properties of digital watermarking is its robustness against various attacks. Robustness is defined as the existence of the watermark even after various attacks as discussed in Hartung & Kutter (1999).

Steganography is a technique using which secret information could be hidden within another unrelated cover image for secret communication. Some of the techniques of steganography include spacing patterns in printed documents, coding

messages in music compositions etc as outlined in Anderson & Petitcolas (1998)'s work. The other applications include ownership protection, proof of ownership, fingerprinting, authentication and tampering detection if the robustness property is also considered.

Digital Watermarking can be considered as a special technique of steganography where the secret information could be inserted into any other media data which may be related to each other. The most common examples of watermarking are the presence of specific patterns in currency notes, which are visible only when the note is exposed to light and company logos in the background of printed text documents. In some applications invisible watermarking could also be carried out. The watermarking techniques prevent forgery and unauthorized replication of any digital content.

Working Principle of Digital Watermarking

The general image watermarking system consists of a watermark, embedding algorithm and extraction algorithm. The embedding algorithm takes cover image and watermark as input and produce watermarked image as output. Similarly the watermark extraction algorithm takes watermarked image as input and extract watermark from it. Based on the requirements of original images the watermarking schemes could be classified into non-blind watermarking schemes or blind watermarking schemes. In this chapter the non–blind adaptive watermarking schemes using wavelet transform techniques combined with computational intelligence are presented.

Requirements and Applications

In order to make invisible watermarking to be more effective, the inserted watermark should be visually imperceptible, reliable, unambiguous and resistant to common attacks. The requirements robustness and imperceptibility are conflict to each other, thus some equilibrium need to be achieved by modulating appropriate frequency components.

- **Imperceptible:** The watermark inserted should not introduce any perceptible artifacts into the original image and not degrade the perceived quality of the image.
- **Robustness:** The inserted watermark should still present in the watermarked image after common image processing attacks such as linear or non-linear filtering, image enhancements, noise addition, geometric distortion, resizing, and image compression.
- **Undeletable:** The watermark must be difficult or even impossible to remove by a hacker, at least without obviously degrading the original signal.
- **Unambiguous:** Retrieval of the watermark should unambiguously identify the owner, and the accuracy of identification should degrade gracefully in the face of attack.

Digital watermarking can be used in a wide variety of applications. The performance of a given watermarking system can be evaluated on the basis of application for which it is designed. The some of the most common applications could be found in Langelaar et al (1998)'s work, Cox et al (2007)'s work, Kutter et al (1999)'s & Barnett (1999)'s work which include,

- **Owner's Identification:** The inserted information can prove ownership in court when dispute arise.
- **Transaction Tracking:** To trace the source of illegal copies, the owner can embed different watermarks in the copies of the data that are supplied to different customers. Transaction tracking is more often called fingerprinting.
- **Copy Protection:** The information stored in a watermark can directly control digi-

tal recording devices for copy protection purposes.

- **Broadcast Monitoring:** In order to protect a commercial advertisement, digital watermarking is an obvious method of coding identification information in each video or sound clip prior to broadcast for active monitoring system whether advertisements are broadcasted as contracted. As given in Kalker et al (1999), a broadcast surveillance system can check all broadcast channels and charge the TV stations according to their findings.
- **Data Authentication:** Inserting authentication mark to protect content of digital data. The authentication marks designed to become invalid after even the slightest modification of a cover data are called fragile watermarks. If a cover data containing an authentication mark is modified, then the authentication mark is also modified along with it which reveals how the cover data has been tampered with, as given by Wolfgang & Delp (1999). The digital watermarking scheme could also be used for image indexing, information retrieval and in medical applications.

Classifications of Digital Watermarking Schemes

The digital watermarking schemes can be broadly categorized based on human perception and working domain and is presented below.

- **Working Domain:** Watermark could be inserted by modifying intensity values of pixels or it could be inserted by changing the frequency components. The pixel domain is also called spatial domain and hence called spatial domain watermarking and later is called frequency domain watermarking.

Figure 1. Decomposition of digital image using discrete wavelet transform technique

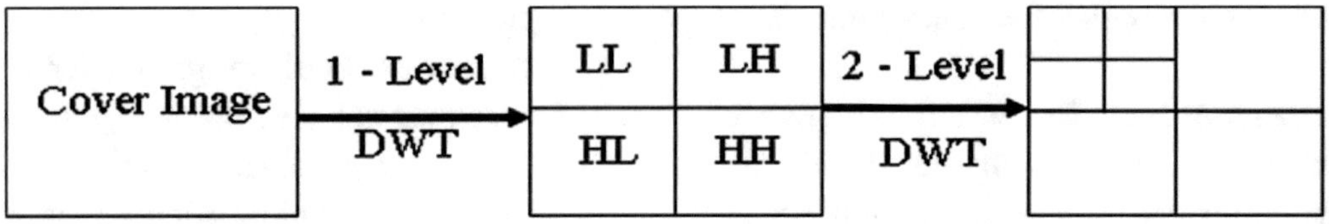

- **Human Perception:** The watermark could be inserted either perceptibly or imperceptibly, therefore watermarking schemes could be classified as visible and invisible watermarking schemes. Both visible and invisible watermarking schemes could be implemented either through adaptive approaches or through non-adaptive approaches.

DIGITAL WATERMARKING SCHEMES IN TRANSFORM DOMAIN

In order to transform images from spatial domain to frequency domain, many transformation techniques are used in general as stated in Ho et al's work. The most predominantly used transformation technique for images is 2D discrete wavelet transform. In each level of decomposition, the wavelet transform represent images in various resolution. Based on the requirements any particular resolution level is chosen for analysis. Figure 1 shows the second level decomposition of wavelet transform. At each level, the high pass filter generates detail information about the image, while the low pass filter produces the coarse approximations of the input image. Significant coefficients are available in higher level sub bands which are exploited for inserting watermark and thus provide robustness. On the other hand lower level sub bands have less energy coefficients leading to intolerability of watermark to various attacks. In general many wavelets are available, based on the requirements it has to be selected to suit the applications.

The decomposed signal is interpreted as low frequency, middle frequency and high frequency bands. The low frequency band is also called as approximation sub band which contains average information about an image and introduces visible distortions. The other bands are called middle and high frequency bands. The secret data could be inserted in any of these bands.

According to human perception the watermarking scheme could be classified into perceptible and imperceptible. In order to protect copyrights of the digital images imperceptible watermarking could be employed to greater extent. The early watermarking scheme which hides undetectable electronic watermark using Least Significant Bit (LSB) manipulation is proposed by van Schyndel et al (1994). Zhao & Koch (1995) proposed a scheme to embed robust label into digital images for copyright protection through bit modification method. Ruanaidh et al (1996) have proposed invisible watermarking scheme in DCT domain. They have embedded bits using bidirectional approach. In more robust region the more number of bits are embedded by modifying significant coefficients. Cox et al (1997) proposed DCT domain based spread spectrum approach. They emphasize that the watermarks should be embedded in perceptually significant components and *N* highest valued coefficients are used for inserting watermarks to make watermark more robust to common attacks. Kankanhalli & Ramakrishnan (1998) proposed content based watermarking scheme based on noise sensitivity of every pixel based on edges, texture and luminance information. Visual model based watermarking techniques are proposed in Podilchuk & Zeng (1998)'s work and Scene based invisible watermarking is proposed for digital images in Swanson et al (1998)'s work. An early attempt to integrate image coding and watermarking using wavelets has been made by Su et al (1999). Zhu et al (1999) exploited the hierarchical nature of the wavelet representation of an image and Gaussian distributed random vector added to all the high pass bands. Kim et al (1999)'s work, number of watermarks embedded is proportional to the energy contained in each band through the selection of different weights for different energy levels.

Podilchuk & Zeng (1998) describe perceptual based digital watermarking techniques for images and video signal that are designed to exploit human visual system in order to provide a transparent invisible but robust watermark. Their approach could be classified as image adaptive watermarks, that is, watermarks which depend not only on the frequency response of the human eye but also the properties of the image itself. The scaling factor is empirically selected to insert watermark. Kim et al (1999) propose a multi resolution watermarking method for digital images, in discrete wavelet transform domain. Pseudo random codes are added to the large coefficients which are selected in each DWT band of an image, with the number of watermarks embedded proportional to the energy in each band. In Hsu & Wu (1999) watermarking scheme visually recognizable pattern is embedded into the image by modifying certain middle frequency part of an image and proved that it is robust to image processing and JPEG Compression attacks. In Tsekeridou & Pitas (2000) exploited the multi resolution property of the wavelet transform and embed a circular self-similar watermark in the first and the second level details sub band coefficients of wavelet decomposition. Lee et al (2006) proposed watermarking schemes which exploits local invariant features of an image. Lin et al (2011) proposed an RST resilient watermarking method in which most appropriate SIFT features are selected for inserting

watermark image and those features are named as SIFT for Watermarking (SIFTW). In Tian et al (2011)'s work, watermarking is carried out in three stages. Region of interest (ROI) is captured from each image automatically. The number of salient regions to be captured and the size of each ROI are adaptive to each image. The watermark is embedded into each adaptively chosen ROI and the watermarked image is formed. In the LL band of K-level wavelet decomposition of the watermarked image, the edge map of one of the ROI is inserted adaptively using quantization step. Image feature based watermarking scheme is proposed in Tsai et al (2011b)'s work, in which non-overlapping features are extracted using Harris Laplacian detector and watermark is inserted in these regions only. Wang et al (2012) have proposed informed watermarking algorithm using Hid-den Markov Model (HMM) and genetic algorithm.

Requirements of Invisible Watermarking Schemes

In order to make invisible watermarking to be more effective, the inserted watermark should be visually imperceptible, reliable, unambiguous and resistant to common attacks. The requirements, robustness and imperceptibility are conflict to each other, thus some equilibrium need to be achieved by modulating appropriate frequency components.

- **Imperceptible:** The watermark inserted should not introduce any perceptible artifacts into the original image and not degrade the perceived quality of the image.
- **Robustness:** The inserted watermark should still present in the watermarked image after common image processing attacks such as linear or non-linear filtering, image enhancements, noise addition, geometric distortion, resizing, and image compression.

- **Undeletable:** The watermark must be difficult or even impossible to remove by a hacker, at least without obviously degrading the original signal.
- **Unambiguous:** Retrieval of the watermark should unambiguously identify the owner, and the accuracy of identification should degrade gracefully in the face of attack.

COMPUTATIONAL INTELLIGENCE AND WATERMARKING SCHEMES

In Engineering, Science and medical fields the success rate of problem solving techniques has been increased by incorporating intelligence in the systems to mimic like a natural biological intelligence and hence the system could be called as computational intelligent systems. Computational intelligence is an alternate method for solving many complex real world problems. In recent days it has established itself as a mathematical tool for solving many complex problems. Most of the real world problems could not be solved using traditional approaches, in those problems computational intelligence comes into picture and help us to solve. The components of computational intelligence include artificial neural networks, evolutionary computation, swarm intelligence, artificial immune systems and fuzzy systems. In the subsequent sections the basics of each component of computational intelligence is presented in details.

Particle Swarm Optimization Technique

Particle swarm optimization (PSO) is a stochastic optimization approach, modeled on the social behaviour of bird flocks. PSO is a population-based search procedure where the individuals, referred to as particles, are grouped into a swarm. Each particle in the swarm represents a candidate solution to the optimization problem. A particle therefore makes use of the best position encountered by itself and the best position of its neighbours to position itself toward an optimum solution. The effect is that particles "fly" toward an optimum, while still searching a wide area around the current best solution. The performance of each particle is measured according to a predefined fitness function which is related to the problem being solved. Applications of PSO include function approximation, clustering, optimization of mechanical structures, and solving systems of equations.

In general in social networks of PSO, each particle is moved by two elastic forces, one force move the particle to the fittest location and it is updated in each iteration. For particle i, its velocity vector v_i is updated with some magnitude and other force make the particle to move to the best location with some magnitude. In PSO the velocity and position are represented as a vector as per formula shown in Equation 1 which is explained in Engelbrecht (2007)'s work.

$$v_i(t+1) = wv_i(t) + c_1r_1(y_i(t) - x_i(t)) + c_2r_2(y_g(t) - x_i(t)) \tag{1}$$

x_i, implies the current position of the particle, y_i denote the personal best position and y_g denote the global best position found by particle i. The parameter w controls the influence of the previous velocity vector, once the velocities of all particles have been updated, the particles move with their new velocity to their new positions according to the formula given in Equation 2.

$$x_i(t+1) = x_i(t) + v_i(t) \tag{2}$$

After all particles have been moved to their new position, the function is evaluated in new positions and the corresponding personal best positions and the global best position are updated. Typical termination criteria for PSO algorithms have been executed until a maximum number of iterations it undergoes or the global best position has not been changed for a certain number of iterations, or a function value has been found which is better than a required threshold value. Janson et al (2008), listed advantages of using Particle Swarm Optimization technique in their work and listed as follows.

Advantages

- PSO uses only the functions values at the positions of the particles to guide the search and therefore is very suitable for dealing with non-differentiable objective functions
- PSO is a population-based and random influenced search method and therefore a PSO algorithm is not so likely to become trapped in a local minimum
- PSO can control the balance between the global and local exploration of the search space and therefore can be used successfully for different types of objective functions
- PSO does not use complex operations and therefore can be implemented easily and efficiently

One of the reasons for popularity of PSO technique is that it is very simple in nature and easy to implement as there are very few parameters need to be adjusted. In recent days, PSO technique is widely applied to optimization function, neural network training, fuzzy system control and other applications of genetic algorithms as presented by Qinqing et al. (2011, June). Thus Particle Swarm Optimization technique can be used across a wide range of applications, as well as for specific applications focused on a specific requirement as stated in Eberhart et al. (2001)'s work.

A Steganographic Method Based upon JPEG and Particle Swarm Optimization Algorithm

In this work, Li Wang (2007) proposed a novel steganographic method using JPEG and Particle Swarm Optimization (PSO) algorithm. Steganography, a branch of information hiding technology, aims to protect important data in transmission. Message capacity and stego-image quality are two important criteria in evaluating a steganographic method. In order to improve the quality of stego-images, an optimal substitution matrix for transforming the secret messages is first derived by means of the PSO algorithm. The standard JPEG quantization table is also modified to contain more secret messages. The transformed messages are then hidden in the DC-to-middle frequency components of the quantized DCT coefficients of the cover-image.

Finally, a JPEG file with secret messages is generated through JPEG entropy coding. The proposed algorithm is compared with Chang et al.'s JPEG-based steganographic algorithm. The experimental results show that, the proposed method has larger message capacity and better image quality than Chang et al.'s work. The experimental results show that our method can achieve both larger message capacity and better image quality than the JQTM method. In addition, the proposed method has a high security level because one cannot recover the secret messages correctly without knowing the substitution matrix.

A Novel Fragile Watermarking Based on Particle Swarm Optimization

Aslantas et al. (2008) presented a novel fragile watermarking scheme based on Discrete Cosine Transform (DCT) and Particle Swarm Optimization (PSO) technique. Embedding watermarks in frequency domain can usually be achieved by modifying the least significant bits (LSBs) of the transformation coefficients. During embedding process rounding off errors appear due to conversion of real numbers into integers for transforming images from frequency domain to spatial domain. A population based stochastic optimization technique (PSO) is proposed to correct these rounding errors. Simulation results show that the feasibility

Figure 2. Original host image and binary watermark

141	70	176	16	211	205	176	247
55	236	83	31	86	110	131	211
170	60	235	7	50	62	253	33
79	33	193	221	130	162	47	215
120	105	102	106	54	94	143	201
129	162	50	202	148	110	124	88
176	46	102	208	250	77	101	188
49	103	39	101	119	110	126	15

		0	1				
	1						
1							

of employing PSO for watermarking and its accuracy. The intensity values of pixels and binary watermark is shown in Figure 2.

DWT-SVD Based Image Watermarking Using Particle Swarm Optimizer

Aslantas et al (2008) have presented, an optimal Discrete Wavelet Transform and Singular Value Decomposition (DWT-SVD) based image watermarking scheme using Particle Swarm Optimizer (PSO). Several watermarking schemes have been proposed with the purpose of copyright protection and access control for multimedia objects. In this work, DWT-SVD based watermarking algorithm initially decomposes the host images into sub-bands then the singular values of each sub-band of the host image are modified by different scaling factors to embed the watermark. Modifications are optimized using PSO to obtain the highest possible robustness without losing the transparency. The wavelet decomposed image is shown in Figure 3.

In this work, PSO is used to select number of coefficients for inserting a watermark. Experimental results show improvement both in transparency and robustness under certain attacks. Because each sub-band includes a watermark, a method which is robust to attacks is achieved. In order to embed small sized watermarks, two or more level DWT decomposition can also be applied.

DCT-Based Robust Watermarking with Swarm Intelligence Concepts

Digital watermarking could be considered as one of the two major categories of information security. Unlike cryptography that the encrypted information represents like noisy patterns, by using watermarking, the watermarked contents look almost identical to its original counterpart, while it still retains the capability to counteract intentional signal processing by others and keeps the existence of the hidden watermark. From this point of view, watermarking is suitable for covert communication since it tends not to cause the suspicion by others. Besides, there must be requirements to keep both the embedded watermark alive and the watermarked contents acceptable. Huang et al (2009) have used a new technique of swarm intelligence, named bacterial foraging, for obtaining an optimized watermarking algorithm with a

Figure 3. Wavelet decomposed image

properly designed fitness function comprising the possible requirements including the watermarked image quality and the capability for the existence of extracted watermark. With our integration, simulation results demonstrate the advantages and effectiveness of the proposed algorithm.

Optimized Watermarking Using Swarm-Based Bacterial Foraging

In this work, Huang et al (2010) have proposed optimized watermarking technique using bacterial foraging concepts. In order to design an effective

fitness function with the pre-determined requirements fuzzy concept is used in conjunction with swarm intelligence. In this work, digital images are used as multimedia content. By the use of bacterial foraging (BF) and fuzzy concepts, the optimized outcome for image-based watermarking is obtained. In this work, the quality of the watermarked image, the capability to resist against attacks, and the number of embedded bit (or capacity) are considered as optimization process.

In practical case, the watermark capacity is considered as constant value, and the trade-off between watermark imperceptibility and water-

Figure 4. Procedure flow for robust watermarking with bacterial foraging

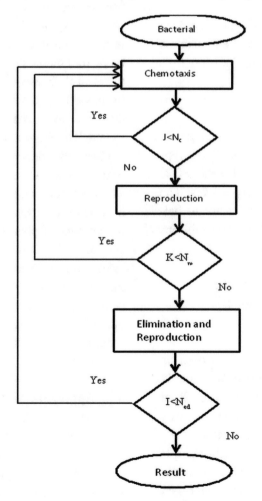

mark robustness are considered as optimization process. These two requirements are conflicts to each other and briefly summarized as follows.

- **Imperceptibility:** To make the water-marked image imperceptible, the watermark should be hidden into less significant parts, such as the least significant bits in the spatial domain or the high frequency components in the transform domain.
- **Robustness:** In order to make the algorithm robust, the watermark needs to be hidden into more important parts of the media. Hence, better robustness can be expected if the data is hidden into lower frequency bands

The proposed algorithm is designed to reduce bit error rate (BCR) and increase the robustness using fitness function as given in Equation 3.

$$f_i = PSNR_i + BCR_i \qquad (3)$$

where fi represents the fitness value and i denote the iteration number. Similarly the PSNRi represents the peak signal to noise ratio and BCRi represents the bit correct rate respectively. The lambda represents the weighting factor to balance the effects from the conflicting conditions of imperceptibility and robustness.

Efficient Digital Watermarking Based on SVD and PSO with Multiple Scaling Factor

Roychowdhury et al (2015) have proposed an invisible robust non-blind Digital Watermarking algorithm to maintain acceptable levels of imperceptibility and robustness simultaneously using Singular Value Decomposition (SVD) and Particle Swarm Optimization (PSO) with multiple scaling factor. This scheme provides an avenue for optimization of the strength-of-the-watermark through scaling factor for attaining high robustness

against attacks while maintaining the visual quality of the cover object. The proposed algorithm shows significant performance improvement over the usage of constant scaling factors in Singular Value Decomposition based Digital Watermarking algorithm. Intelligent based watermarking techniques can also be used for watermarking medical images as discussed in Naheed et al (2014)' work, but the quality of medical images need to be preserved while inserting a watermark.

Ant Colony Optimization

Ant colony optimization (ACO) takes inspiration from the foraging behaviour of some ant species. As ants live in colonies in searching for food they use a cooperative method and while moving, they initially explore the area surrounding their nest in a random manner leaving a chemical pheromone trail on the ground. Ants smell pheromone to select their way and it implies that, ants tend to select the paths marked by strong pheromone concentrations. The same way during return trip the smell of pheromone is used by ants. The smell of pheromone depends on the quantity and quality of the food as outlined by Al-Qaheri et al (2010). These pheromone trails progressively decrease by evaporation with time elapsing resulting in the amount of pheromone becomes larger on a shorter path. Then the probability that an ant selects this shorter path becomes higher. One model of learning which exhibits these features is the pheromone mechanism used by insects to guide their collective decision processes and it is described using a mechanism comprises of four components:

- **Aggregation:** An entity (insect or simulation agent) marks an event by adding to an existing base of pheromone. This component effectively fuses multiple observations into a single variable.
- **Evaporation:** Over time, pheromones gradually fade (unless new deposits rein-

force them). This component is a novel mechanism for truth maintenance. In traditional AI, an agent remembers everything that it has learned unless there is reason to forget it. This approach is computationally intractable for logics beyond a certain level of expressiveness. In contrast, an ant colony immediately begins to forget everything it learns as soon as it learns it, unless it is reinforced, a constant-time process.

- **Propagation:** Pheromones disperse spatially, with the maximum concentration of a deposit remaining at the original point of deposit.

- **Sensing:** Other entities make decisions or act based on the pheromone levels they sense in their environment.

Digital Watermarking Using Ant Colony Optimization in Fractional Fourier Domain

The properties of ant colony optimization technique are used for embedding a watermark as discussed in Al-Qaheri et al (2010)'s work. The watermark insertion process is carried out in modified Fractional Fourier domain. In addition, the sharp and noiseless pheromone maps during retrieval reinforce the security against deliberate tampering if any. Finally, the results of the proposed algorithms are presented in terms of improved RMSE index of the watermarked retrieved image after comparing with other contemporary works. The elaborated discussion is given below. The proposed algorithm has three distinct phases, it is defined as follows:

- **Embedding Phase:** In this phase, the domain parameters $\alpha 1$ and $\alpha 2$ are identified and initialized, the best value for normalized embedding domain factor based on heuristic approach is obtained and it is guided by core algorithm Ant Colony Optimization (ACO) technique.

- **Extraction Phase:** In this phase, the pheromone trace mechanism is initiated to yield the better result in terms of original embedded image irrespective of tampering efforts against the post retrieval of the watermarked image

- **Ant Colony Optimization Process:** A certain quantity of Ants are placed randomly on a bi-dimensional lattice represented by an $N \times N$ array and this array store values between 0 and 255, 8-bit representation of the level of the pixels. During optimization process ant moves to an adjacent cell and reinforces the pheromone level on that spot. One cell may be occupied by one and only one ant (in this case, an ant will not move if it finds itself totally surrounded by others ants), or ants are allowed to share the same cell. Ant chooses a particular cell of the subjected embedded image to trace according to its current direction and the pheromone intensity on the eight surrounding cells. It is implied that, if an ant comes from south, and the eight cells have no pheromone, the chance of going north is higher, followed by the chance of going northeast or northwest, and so on, until the likelihood of returning south, which would be very low.

Fuzzy Logic

Uncertainty in the problem is effectively solved by fuzzy set concepts. Fuzzy means vagueness. Fuzzy theory is considered as a mathematical tool to handle the uncertainty arising due to vagueness. Understanding human voice could be considered as one of the example where fuzziness manifests. A fuzzy concept was propounded by Lotfi A Zadeh in 1965. Fuzzy sets support a flexible sense of membership of elements to a set while in crisp set theory, an element either belongs or does not belongs to a set, in fuzzy set theory many degrees of membership between 0 and 1 are allowed. The membership function values need not always be described by discrete values it could be even continuous quite often. Logic is the science of reasoning. Like mathematical sets could be classified as crisp sets or fuzzy sets logic could also be viewed as crisp logic or fuzzy logic. The concept of fuzzy logic could be used in digital watermarking. In the following section the fuzzy logic based watermarking techniques are presented.

Multistage Spread Spectrum Watermark Detection Technique Using Fuzzy Logic

In this work, Maity & Maity (2009) proposed a new model of spread spectrum (SS) watermarking in which each watermark bit is spread using a distinct code pattern over N-mutually orthogonal signal points. Decision variable for each bit of watermark decoding is formed from the weighted average of N-decision statistics. Multiple detection stages are applied where the detected bit patterns of one stage are used in the immediate subsequent stage to cancel the multiple bit interference (MBI) effect experienced by the individual bit. Fuzzy logic is used to beat the effect of such MBI through Multiple Group Combined Interference Cancelation (MGCIC) technique in the intermediate stage(s). The group is formed from the decision magnitudes corresponding to a group of code patterns and the ensemble of code patterns are classified in different groups like very strong, strong, weak and very weak based on fuzzy membership function derived from the magnitude of the decision variables. Attack channel is modeled as Rayleigh distribution followed by AWGN (additive white Gaussian noise). Simulation results show that BER (bit error rate) value is reduced more, of course, at the cost of slight increase in computational complexity if the code patterns are classified in a greater number of groups. Fuzzy logic becomes potential to beat uncertainties associated with multiple bit interference effect.

A Fuzzy Logic Approach to Encrypted Watermarking For Still Images in Wavelet Domain on FPGA

A new fuzzy logic approach is introduced to embed the encrypted watermark in the wavelet domain. The multi-resolution representation based on discrete wavelet transform (DWT) incorporates a model of Human Visual System (HVS). In order to provide a complete security both encryption and watermarking technique could be combined. To provide security to digital right management, encryption and digital watermarking techniques need to be incorporated. Encryption transforms the original contain into unreadable format and watermarking leaves the digital object intact and recognizable. The objective is to develop simple, real time and robust secure watermarking system, which can be achieved through the hardware implementation. In order to meet a real time constrains parallel computing architecture for wavelet transform has been proposed. The experimental results demonstrate the high robustness of the proposed algorithm to various image / signal processing attacks as discussed in Lande et al (2010).

A Novel HVS Based Gray Scale Image Watermarking Scheme Using Fast Fuzzy-ELM Hybrid Architecture

In this work, Mishra and Goel (2015) have proposed a novel image watermarking scheme using HVS characteristics in transform domain. The Human Visual System (HVS) is modeled based on the Fuzzy Inference System (FIS) by considering luminance sensitivity, edge sensitivity and contrast sensitivity. The output of the FIS is a single output known as weighing factor (WF). A dataset is prepared using the image coefficients and the WF. A fast neural network called extreme learning machine (ELM) is trained using input dataset. The ELM produces a column vector of size 1024 x 1 used as normalized watermark embedded in low frequency coefficients of gray scale images. The signed images are subject to quality assessment before and after executing image processing attacks to examine the issue of robustness and imperceptibility. The obtained results proved that the Fuzzy-ELM architecture for image watermarking produce good results.

Genetic Algorithm

Genetic Algorithm (GA) is a search technique for finding the global maximum/minimum solutions for problems. Although the GA operation performs randomly, choosing candidates to avoid stranding on a local optimum solution, there is no guarantee that the global maximum/minimum will be found. In general, the possibility of obtaining the global maximum/minimum by using GA is related to the complexity of a problem. That is the more complex a problem is, the higher the difficulty of obtaining the optimum solution. The GA is one of the most widely used artificial intelligent techniques for optimization. They have been successfully applied to obtain good solutions in optimal localization and intensity of audio watermark. Usually, the GA starts with some randomly selected genes as the first generation, called population. Each individual in the population corresponding to a solution in the problem domain is called chromosome. An objective, called fitness function, is used to evaluate the quality of each chromosome. The chromosomes of high quality will survive and form a new population of the next generation. By using the tree operators: selection crossover, and mutation, we recombine a new generation to find the best solution. In order to apply the GA for embedding audio watermarking into the DWT the chromosomes is used to adjust position values of audio watermarking on DWT.

Intelligent Audio Watermarking Using Genetic Algorithm in DWT Domain

In this work, Ketcham and Vongpradhip (2007) proposed an innovative watermarking scheme for audio signal based on genetic algorithms (GA) in discrete wavelet transforms. It is robust against watermarking attacks, which are commonly employed in literature. In this algorithm, GA is employed for the optimal localization and intensity of watermark. The watermark detection process can be performed without using the original audio signal, and could be classified as blind watermarking algorithm. The experimental results demonstrate that watermark is inaudible and robust to many digital signal processing, such as cropping, low pass filter, additive noise. The diagrammatic representation of watermarking process is shown in Figure 5.

A Singular-Value Decomposition-Based Image Watermarking Using Genetic Algorithm

Aslantas (2008) proposed a novel optimal watermarking scheme based on singular-value decomposition (SVD) using genetic algorithm (GA). The singular values (SVs) of the host image are modified by multiple scaling factors to embed the watermark image. Modifications are optimised using GA to obtain the highest possible robustness without losing the transparency. Experimental results show both the significant improvement in transparency and the robustness under attacks. In this work, the property of GAs is utilized to optimise watermark embedding process with respect to the two conflicting requirement: transparency and robustness. An $N \times N$ host image can have N number SVs that may reveal different tolerance to modification. Since quality degradation of the image to various values of the scaling factor is not known in advance thus an algorithm is needed to achieve the optimum SFs that produce maximum transparency and robustness. For this purpose, GA which is a well-known modern heuristic optimisation algorithm is employed in this work.

The basic of genetic algorithm is shown in Figure 6. It consists of five components that are a random number generator, fitness evaluation unit and genetic operators for reproduction, crossover

Figure 5. Watermark embedding model

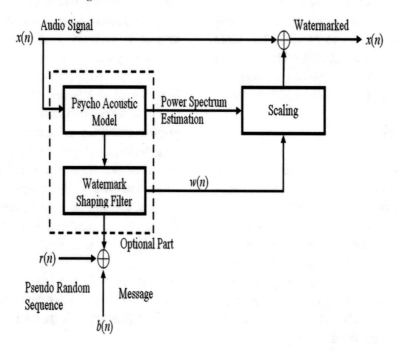

Figure 6. Basics of genetic algorithm

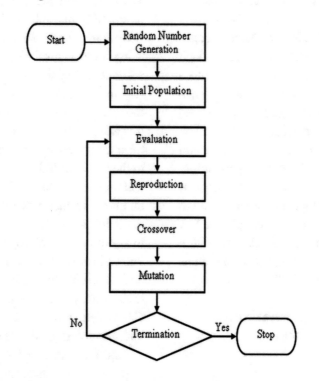

and mutation operations. The initial population required at the start of the algorithm is a set of number strings generated by the random number generator. Each string is a representation of a solution to the optimisation problem being addressed. Associated with each string is a fitness value *(f*val*)* computed by the evaluation unit. A fitness value is a measure of the goodness of the solution that it represents. The aim of the genetic operators is to transform the set of strings into sets with higher fitness values.

The reproduction operator performs a natural selection function known as "seeded selection". Individual strings are copied from one set (representing a generation of solutions) to the next according to their fitness values, the higher the fitness value, the greater the probability of a string being selected for the next generation. The crossover operator chooses pairs of strings at random and produces new pairs. The simplest crossover operation is to cut the original "parent" strings at a randomly selected point and exchange their tails. The number of crossover operations is governed by a crossover rate (CR). The mutation operator randomly mutates or reverses the values of bits in a string. The number of mutation operations is determined by a mutation rate (MR). A phase of the algorithm consists of applying the evaluation, reproduction, crossover and mutation operations. A new generation of solutions is produced with each phase of the algorithm. The watermark embedding model is shown in Figure 7.

Experimental results show the feasibility of multiple SFs estimated by GA and its superiority over the use of a single SF. The watermarked imag and original images are shown in Figure 8. Further research can be carried out with the *U* and *V* components of the SVD. The developed system can also be applied to watermarking in DWT, DFT, DCT and the spatial domains, by changing the SVD embedding algorithm into the other domain embedding algorithms. Due to the flexibility of the developed system, the attacking modules used in this work can easily be replaced with the other attacking schemes.

Figure 7. Watermark embedding process

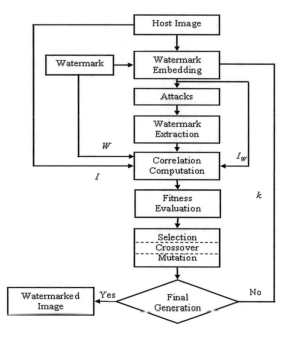

Figure 8. (a) Original image (b) watermark (c) watermarked image

a   b   c

A Watermarking Algorithm for Fingerprinting Intelligence Images

Another important application of digital watermarking is fingerprinting. The owner or the distributor of the multimedia data can insert unique watermarks into different copies which will be helpful to identify the source of illegal copies. Fingerprinting could be used by an intelligence agency to trace illegal copies. In this paper, digital watermarking algorithm for requirements for fingerprinting application is proposed by Wang et al (2001).

Most fingerprinting algorithms in the literature review have given access to both distributor and users the fingerprinted data. The intelligence media data are highly valuable thus to prevent it from espionage asymmetric system need to be used in order to protect it. In this work, the distributor collects a key also called finger printing information from each user and embeds it in the corresponding copy of media data. This fingerprinting information could be called as watermark. This random data could be used to generate orthonormal filter banks randomly for each user. The embedding process is carried out in transform domain using filter banks. These filter banks are stored for future use. In order to provide more security the received user identification data could be further scrambled before insertion. If a particular media data is scrambled, then the corresponding filter bank is used to extract the watermark and compared with the original for similarity measure. If the calculated similarity

value is above the threshold it could be claimed as finger print is found. The algorithm is tested against various attacks.

An Authentication Watermarking Scheme with Transaction Tracking Enabled

In this work, a novel watermarking scheme that supports authentication and transaction tracking functionalities is proposed by Emmanuel et al (2007). The principle of finite state machine is used for inserting watermark in his scheme. The proposed watermarking scheme could be classified as blind and asymmetric. In the blind watermarking scheme the original image is not required for watermark extraction. Similarly, two different key could be used for watermark embedding and watermark extraction. The algorithm is implemented and tested for its visual quality, compression overhead, execution time overhead and payload capacity. It is found that the algorithm has high visual quality, high payload capacity, low compression overhead and low execution time overhead.

The proposed watermarking scheme uses several arithmetic and swapping operations which, increases the difficulty of the attackers in estimating the operations imposed on the coefficients for embedding the watermark bit. The three operations, addition, subtraction and swapping provide the necessary confusion without adjusting the coefficients to the extent that perceptual distortion occurs.

The proposed a watermarking scheme could be used for both authentication and transaction tracking using the concept of state tables and state transition. As a single-pass algorithm, it is fast and is also able to achieve high visual quality in terms of PSNR. Furthermore, the addition of watermark has only small effect on the compression ratio. In terms of security, the algorithm allows the extraction of the messages with a different extraction key than the embedding key and it employs multiple modification actions to carry out the watermarking.

Evolutionary Computation

Evolutionary algorithms use a population of individuals, where an individual is referred to as a chromosome. A chromosome defines the characteristics of individuals in the population. Each characteristic is referred to as a gene. The value of a gene is referred to as an allele. For each generation, individuals compete to reproduce offspring. Those individuals with the best survival capabilities have the best chance to reproduce. Offspring are generated by combining parts of the parents, a process referred to as crossover. Each individual in the population can also undergo mutation which alters some of the allele of the chromosome. The survival strength of an individual is measured using a fitness function which reflects the objectives and constraints of the problem to be solved. After each generation, individuals may undergo *culling*, or individuals may survive to the next generation (referred to as *elitism*). Additionally, behavioural characteristics (as encapsulated in phenotypes) can be used to influence the evolutionary process in two ways: phenotypes may influence genetic changes, and/ or behavioural characteristics evolve separately.

Different classes of evolutionary algorithms (EA) have been developed:

- **Genetic Algorithms:** which model genetic evolution.
- **Genetic Programming:** which is based on genetic algorithms, but individuals are programs (represented as trees).
- **Evolutionary Programming:** which is derived from the simulation of adaptive behavior in evolution (*phenotypic* evolution).
- **Evolution Strategies:** which are geared toward modeling the strategy parameters that control variation in evolution, i.e. the evolution of evolution.
- **Differential Evolution:** which is similar to genetic algorithms, differing in the reproduction mechanism used.
- **Cultural Evolution:** which models the evolution of culture of a population and how the culture influences the genetic and phenotypic evolution of individuals.
- **Coevolution:** where initially "dumb" individuals evolve through cooperation, or in competition with one another, acquiring the necessary characteristics to survive.

Ketcham & Ganokratanaa (2014) have proposed Evolutionary Computation based Video Watermarking Using Quick Response Code in Discrete Multiwavelet Transformation domain.

Artificial Immune Systems

The natural immune system (NIS) has an amazing pattern matching ability, used to distinguish between foreign cells entering the body (referred to as *non-self*, or *antigen*) and the cells belonging to the body (referred to as *self*). As the NIS encounters antige the adaptive nature of the NIS is exhibited, with the NIS memorizing the structure of this antigen for faster future response the antigen. This artificial immune system could also be used in digital watermarking schemes.

CONCLUSION

Digital Watermarking is considered as most important method to protect copyrights of digital images. As per the survey many existing watermarking schemes uses constant scaling factor which may destroy the quality of underlying cover image data. Moreover, in adaptive watermarking schemes cited in literature demonstrates that the automatism in inserting watermark is not complete and it implies that the dependency of user is required. Thus it is required to calculate scaling and embedding parameter using the content of cover image to make watermarking useful to the intended purpose. In order to calculate scaling and embedding factors adaptively it is required to incorporate computational intelligence such as neural networks, fuzzy logic, and optimization techniques and so on. It is observed from the literature review that the adaptive digital watermarking using computational intelligence is still in infant stage. Some of the works using intelligence concepts are presented elaborately in this chapter. In future the calculation of parameters from the content of the cover image could be carried out by incorporating intelligence more efficiently using hybrid approaches. In addition intelligence based watermarking could be carried for protecting video sequences also.

REFERENCES

Al-Qaheri, H., Mustafi, A., & Banerjee, S. (2010). Digital watermarking using ant colony optimization in fractional Fourier domain. *Journal of Information Hiding and Multimedia Signal Processing*, *1*(3), 179–189.

Anderson, R. J., & Petitcolas, F. A. (1998). On the limits of steganography. *IEEE Journal on Selected Areas in Communications*, *16*(4), 474–481. doi:10.1109/49.668971

Aslantas, V. (2008). A singular-value decomposition-based image watermarking using genetic algorithm. *AEÜ. International Journal of Electronics and Communications*, *62*(5), 386–394. doi:10.1016/j.aeue.2007.02.010

Aslantas, V., Dogan, A. L., & Ozturk, S. (2008). DWT-SVD based image watermarking using particle swarm optimizer. In *Multimedia and Expo, 2008 IEEE International Conference on*. IEEE. doi:10.1109/ICME.2008.4607416

Aslantas, V., Ozer, S., & Ozturk, S. (2008). A novel fragile watermarking based on particle swarm optimization. In *Multimedia and Expo, 2008 IEEE International Conference on*. IEEE. doi:10.1109/ICME.2008.4607423

Barnett, R. (1999). Digital watermarking: applications, techniques and challenges. *J. Electron. Commun. engin.*, *11*(4), 173–183.

Barni, M., Bartolini, F., & Piva, A. (2001). Improved wavelet-based watermarking through pixel-wise masking. *IEEE Transactions on Image Processing*, *10*(5), 783–791. doi:10.1109/83.918570 PMID:18249667

Cox, I., Miller, M., Bloom, J., Fridrich, J., & Kalker, T. (2007). *Digital watermarking and steganography* (pp. 15–46). Burlinton: Morgan Kaufmann.

Cox, I. J., Kilian, J., Leighton, F. T., & Shamoon, T. (1997). Secure spread spectrum watermarking for multimedia. *IEEE Transactions on Image Processing*, *6*(12), 1673–1687. doi:10.1109/83.650120 PMID:18285237

Eberhart, R. C., & Shi, Y. (2001). Particle swarm optimization: developments, applications and resources. In *Evolutionary Computation, 2001. Proceedings of the 2001 Congress on* (pp. 81-86). IEEE. doi:10.1109/CEC.2001.934374

Emmanuel, S., Vinod, A. P., Rajan, D., & Heng, C. K. (2007). An Authentication Watermarking Scheme with Transaction Tracking Enabled. In Digital EcoSystems and Technologies Conference, 2007. DEST'07. Inaugural IEEE-IES (481-486). IEEE.

Engelbrecht, A. P. (2007). *Computational intelligence: an introduction*. John Wiley & Sons. doi:10.1002/9780470512517

Hartung, F., & Kutter, M. (1999). Multimedia watermarking techniques. *Proceedings of the IEEE*, *87*(7), 1079–1107. doi:10.1109/5.771066

Ho, A. T., Shen, J., Tan, S. H., & Kot, A. C. (2002). Digital image-in-image watermarking for copyright protection of satellite images using the fast Hadamard transform. *Proc. IEEE International Symposium on Geoscience and Remote Sensing*. doi:10.1109/IGARSS.2002.1027166

Hsu, C. T., & Wu, J. L. (1999). Hidden digital watermarks in images. *IEEE Transactions on Image Processing*, *8*(1), 58–68. doi:10.1109/83.736686 PMID:18262865

Huang, H. C., Chen, Y. H., & Abraham, A. (2010). Optimized watermarking using swarm-based bacterial foraging. *Journal of Information Hiding and Multimedia Signal Processing*, *1*(1), 51–58.

Huang, H. C., Chen, Y. H., & Lin, G. Y. (2009). DCT-Based Robust Watermarking with Swarm Intelligence Concepts. In *Information Assurance and Security, 2009. IAS'09. Fifth International Conference on*. IEEE. doi:10.1109/IAS.2009.85

Janson, S., Merkle, D., & Middendorf, M. (2008). Molecular docking with multi-objective Particle Swarm Optimization. *Applied Soft Computing*, *8*(1), 666–675. doi:10.1016/j.asoc.2007.05.005

Kalker, T., Depovere, G., Haitsma, J., & Maes, M. (1999). A video watermarking system for broadcast monitoring. Proc. Security and Watermarking of Multimedia Contents. *SPIE, San Jose*, *3657*, 103–112.

Kankanhalli, M. S., & Ramakrishnan, K. R. (1998). Content based watermarking of images. *Proc. Sixth ACM international conference on Multimedia*. doi:10.1145/290747.290756

Ketcham, M., & Ganokratanaa, T. (2014). The Evolutionary Computation Video Watermarking Using Quick Response Code Based on Discrete Multiwavelet Transformation. In *Recent Advances in Information and Communication Technology* (pp. 113-123). Springer International Publishing. doi:10.1007/978-3-319-06538-0_12

Ketcham, M., & Vongpradhip, S. (2007). Intelligent audio watermarking using genetic algorithm in DWT domain. *International Journal Of Intelligent Technology*, *2*(2), 135–140.

Kim, Y. S., Kwon, O. H., & Park, R. H. (1999). Wavelet based watermarking method for digital images using the human visual system. *Electronics Letters*, *35*(6), 466–468. doi:10.1049/el:19990327

Kutter, M., Bhattacharjee, S. K., & Ebrahimi, T. (1999). Towards second generation watermarking schemes. *Proc. International Conference on Image Processing*.

Lande, P. U., Talbar, S. N., & Shinde, G. N. (2010). A Fuzzy logic approach to encrypted Watermarking for still Images in Wavelet domain on FPGA. *International Journal of Signal Processing. Image Processing and Pattern Recognition*, *3*(2), 1–9.

Langelaar, G. C., Lagendijk, R. L., & Biemond, J. (1998). Real-time labeling of MPEG-2 compressed video. *Journal of Visual Communication and Image Representation*, *9*(4), 256–270. doi:10.1006/jvci.1998.0397

Lee, H. Y., H. Kim and H.K. Lee (2006). Robust image watermarking using local invariant features. *Optical Engineering*, *45*(3), 037002:1–037002:11.

Li, X., & Wang, J. (2007). A steganographic method based upon JPEG and particle swarm optimization algorithm. *Information Sciences*, *177*(15), 3099–3109. doi:10.1016/j.ins.2007.02.008

Lin, Y. T., Huang, C. Y., & Lee, G. C. (2011). Rotation, scaling, and translation resilient watermarking for images. *IET Image Proc., 5*(4), 328–340. doi:10.1049/iet-ipr.2009.0264

Maity, S. P., & Maity, S. (2009). Multistage spread spectrum watermark detection technique using fuzzy logic. *Signal Processing Letters, IEEE, 16*(4), 245–248. doi:10.1109/LSP.2009.2014097

Mishra, A., & Goel, A. (2015). A Novel HVS Based Gray Scale Image Watermarking Scheme Using Fast Fuzzy-ELM Hybrid Architecture. In *Proceedings of ELM-2014*. Springer International Publishing. doi:10.1007/978-3-319-14066-7_15

Naheed, T., Usman, I., Khan, T. M., Dar, A. H., & Shafique, M. F. (2014). Intelligent reversible watermarking technique in medical images using GA and PSO. *Optik-International Journal for Light and Electron Optics, 125*(11), 2515–2525. doi:10.1016/j.ijleo.2013.10.124

Podilchuk, C. I., & Zeng, W. (1998). Image-adaptive watermarking using visual models. *IEEE Journal on Selected Areas in Communications, 16*(4), 525–539. doi:10.1109/49.668975

Qinqing, G., Guangping, Z., Dexin, C., & Ketai, H. (2011, June). Image enhancement technique based on improved PSO algorithm. In *Industrial Electronics and Applications (ICIEA), 2011 6th IEEE Conference on* (234-238). IEEE. doi:10.1109/ICIEA.2011.5975586

Roychowdhury, M., Sarkar, S., Laha, S., & Sarkar, S. (2015, January). Efficient Digital Watermarking Based on SVD and PSO with Multiple Scaling Factor. In *Proceedings of the 3rd International Conference on Frontiers of Intelligent Computing: Theory and Applications (FICTA) 2014*. Springer International Publishing. doi:10.1007/978-3-319-11933-5_89

Ruanaidh, J. O., Dowling, W. J., & Boland, F. M. (1996). Watermarking of digital images for copyright protection. *Proc. IEEE Vision, Image and Signal Processing, 143*(4), 250–256. doi:10.1049/ip-vis:19960711

Tian, L., Zheng, N., Xue, J., Li, C., & Wang, X. (2011). An integrated visual saliency based watermarking approach for synchronous image authentication and copyright protection. *Signal Processing Image Communication, 26*(8), 427–437. doi:10.1016/j.image.2011.06.001

Tsai, J. S., Huang, W. B., & Kuo, Y. H. (2011b). On the selection of optimal feature region set for robust digital image watermarking. *IEEE Transactions on Image Processing, 20*(3), 735–743. doi:10.1109/TIP.2010.2073475 PMID:20833602

Tsekeridou, S., & Pitas, I. (2000). Embedding self-similar watermarks in the wavelet domain. *IEEE International Conference on Acoustics, Speech, and Signal Processing*. doi:10.1109/ICASSP.2000.859216

van Schyndel, R. G., Tirkel, A. Z., & Osborne, C. F. (1994). A digital watermark. *Proc. IEEE International Conference on Image Processing*. doi:10.1109/ICIP.1994.413536

Wang, Y., Doherty, J. F., & Van Dyck, R. E. (2001). A watermarking algorithm for fingerprinting intelligence images. In *Conference on Information Sciences and Systems*.

Wolfgang, R. B., & Delp, E. J. (1999). Fragile watermarking using the VW2D watermark. *Proc. SPIE, Security and Watermarking of Multimedia Contents*. doi:10.1117/12.344670

Wu, L. Y., Cheng, L. Z., & Zhi-Hong, Y. X. (2004). Translucent Digital Watermark Base on Wavelets and Error-Correct Code. *Chin. J. Comput., 11*(12), 533–1539.

Xia, X. G., Boncelet, C. G., & Arce, G. R. (1997). A multiresolution watermark for digital images. *Proc. International Conference on Image Processing.*

Zadeh, L. A. (1994). Fuzzy logic, neural networks, and soft computing. *Communications of the ACM*, *37*(3), 77–84. doi:10.1145/175247.175255

Zhao, J., & Koch, E. (1995). Embedding robust labels into images for copyright protection. *Proc. International Congress on Intellectual Property Rights for Specialised Information, Knowledge and New Technologies.*

Zhu, W., Xiong, Z., & Zhang, Y. Q. (1999). Multiresolution watermarking for images and video. *IEEE Transactions on Circuits and Systems for Video Technology*, *9*(4), 545–550. doi:10.1109/76.767121

KEY TERMS AND DEFINITIONS

Computational Intelligence: Process of incorporating intelligence through the application of optimization technique, fuzzy logic and neural networks.

Digital Watermarking: Process of inserting a piece of digital information in a cover data is called digital watermarking.

Evolutionary Computation: Evolutionary algorithms use a population of individuals, where an individual is referred to as a chromosome. A chromosome defines the characteristics of individuals in the population. Each characteristic is referred to as a gene.

Fuzzy Logic: Fuzzy means vagueness. Fuzzy theory is considered as a mathematical tool to handle the uncertainty arising due to vagueness.

Particle Swarm Optimization: Particle swarm optimization (PSO) is a stochastic optimization approach, modeled on the social behaviour of bird flocks. PSO is a population-based search procedure where the individuals, referred to as particles, are grouped into a swarm. Applications of PSO include function approximation, clustering, optimization of mechanical structures, and solving systems of equations.

Robustness: Even if the watermarked image undergoes any image processing operations it should be very difficult for users to remove the inserted watermark from the watermarked images.

Transform Domain: In order to decorrelate the signal transformation technique is used. Domain in which signal gets decorrelated.

Chapter 13
Feature Extraction Techniques:
Fundamental Concepts and Survey

Heba Ahmed Elnemr
Electronics Research Institute, Egypt

Nourhan Mohamed Zayed
Electronics Research Institute, Egypt

Mahmoud Abdelmoneim Fakhreldein
Electronics Research Institute, Egypt

ABSTRACT

The feature extraction is the process to represent raw image in a reduced form to facilitate decision making such as pattern detection, classification or recognition. Finding and extracting reliable and discriminative features is always a crucial step to complete the task of image recognition and computer vision. Furthermore, as the number of application demands increase, an extended study and investigation in the feature extraction field becomes very important. The goal of this chapter is to present an intensive survey of existing literatures on feature extraction techniques over the last years. All these techniques and algorithms have their advantages and limitations. Thus, in this chapter analysis of various techniques and transformations, submitted earlier in literature, for extracting various features from images will be discussed. Additionally, future research directions in the feature extraction area are provided.

INTRODUCTION

Feature is defined as a function of the basic measurement variables or attributes that specifies some quantifiable property of an object and is useful for classification and/or pattern recognition. Obtaining a good data representation is a very domain specific task and it is related to the available measurements. Various features cur-

rently employed can be classified into low-level features and high-level features. However, there is no clear guideline along which features should be classified as low- or high-level ones. Generally, quantitatively and qualitatively more complex processing is needed to derive high-level features from an image than low-level features. Low-level features are the fundamental features that can be extracted directly from an image without any object

DOI: 10.4018/978-1-4666-8654-0.ch013

description, while high-level features extraction concerns finding shapes and objects in computer images and it is based on low level features(Nixon & Aguado, 2013).The Low-level features can be categorized as follows: General features, Global features and Domain-specific features. General features are application independent features such as color, texture, and shape. These features, according to the abstraction level, can be further divided into: pixel-level features, which are the features calculated at each pixel(e.g. color, location, etc.) and local features, which are features computed over a subdivision of the image bands that are resulted from image segmentation or edge detection. The Global features are features that are calculated over the entire image or just regular sub-area of an image. The domain-specific features are application dependent features such as human faces, fingerprints, character recognition and conceptual features (Chora´s, 2007). Obviously, this classification is not that sharp, there exist overlaps between them. Also, it must be considered that for some applications such as computer vision applications, the feature used should be both expressive and meaningful (associated with significant scene elements) and detectable (the location algorithm must exist). It's worth be noted that, the lower the abstraction level of the features employed, the easier to locate them in the image, yet the more difficult to use them for understanding the meaning of that image, and vice versa (Lei, Hendriks & Reinders, 2009).Figure 1 shows the categorization of feature extraction methods.

Human expertise, which is often required to convert "raw" data into a set of useful features, can be escorted by automatic feature extraction methods. Feature extraction is the process of transforming raw data into more informative signatures or characteristics of a system, which will most efficiently or meaningfully represent the information that is important for analysis and classification. In pattern recognition and in image processing, feature extraction is a special form of dimensionality reduction. When the input data to an algorithm is too large to be processed and it is suspected to be redundant (much data, but not much information) then the input data will be transformed into a reduced representation set of features (features vector). If the extracted features are carefully chosen it is expected that the features vector will extract the relevant information from the input data in order to perform the desired task using this reduced representation instead of the full size input.

A good feature representation is essential to attain high performance in any pattern recognition or image processing tasks. However, manually defining a good feature set is often not feasible. The problem of feature extraction can be decomposed into two steps: feature construction and feature selection (Guyon, Gunn, Nikravesh & Zadeh, 2006). Researchers have been tackled both steps for many years, however there is still a great interest in feature extraction. A number of new applications (e.g. bioinformatics, combinatorial chemistry, text processing, decision making, pattern recognition, speech processing, image retrieval and vision) with very large input spaces critically need space dimensionality reduction for efficiency and efficacy analysis (Gale & Salankar, 2014; Shenbagavalli & Ramar, 2014; Arun, Emmanuel & Durairaj, 2013; Zhu, Xu, Lu, Wen, Fan & Li, 2014). Feature construction involves transforming a given set of input features to generate a new set of more powerful features, which can then be utilized for processing.

Furthermore, reducing the number of features as well as removing the irrelevant, redundant, or noisy data increases the efficiency and effectiveness of the implemented algorithms. Feature selection is the process of selecting a subset of the constructed features according to a certain criteria. This is an important and frequently used dimensionality reduction technique for various applications, e.g. data mining, face recognition

Figure 1. Feature extraction methods categorization

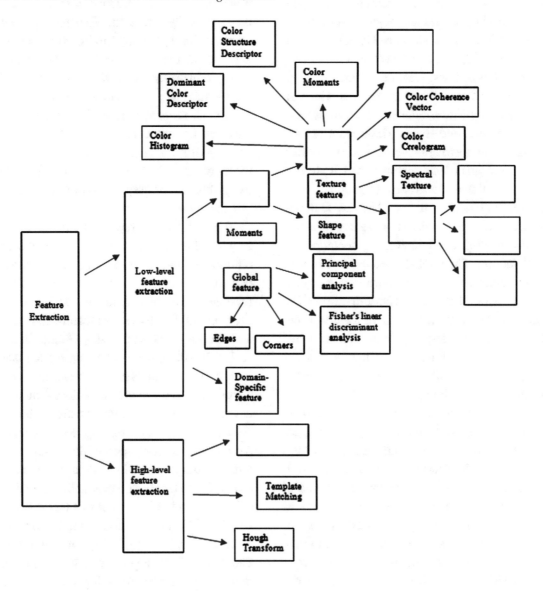

and character recognition (Chitra & Balakrishnan, 2012; Hawashin, Mansour & Aljawarneh, 2013).

In this article we present a survey of the research conducted for feature extraction methods over the past years. This chapter is divided into 4 sections. Section 2 depicts a thorough description of different low-level feature extraction methods, categorized based on the techniques used. While section 3 presents the high-level feature concepts and debates its extraction methods described in the literatures. Finally, conclusions and future work are discussed in section 4.

LOW-LEVEL FEATURE EXTRACTION

Low-level features are the basic features that can be extracted automatically from an image without any shape information. In the literature the techniques/approaches go from the very basic to the more advanced ones, in this section we shall discuss some of the most popular approaches.

General Features

Features that are independent on the application nature are denoted as general features. These features, according to the extraction level, can be categorized into: pixel-level features that are computed at each pixel and local features that are calculated over a subdivision of an image. In the next sections different kinds of general features will be discussed in details.

Color Features Extraction

The color feature is one of the most widely used visual features in image processing applications. It is relatively robust to background complication and independent of image size and orientation. Color features are defined based on a particular color space or model. A number of color spaces have been used in literature, such as RGB, LUV, HSV, LAB and YCrCb (Yasmin, Sharif & Mohsin, 2013). Once the color space is specified, color feature can be extracted from images or regions. The most straightforward and frequently used way to represent color features is color histograms. For each point of the considered color space, the number of pixels of a specified color is calculated. Such representation of information on color is simple, natural and robust to translation and rotation changes. However, a color histogram does not tell pixels' spatial information. Therefore, visually different images can have similar color histograms. In addition, the dimension of a histogram is usually very high. Besides, such histograms are very sparse and, thus, sensitive to noise (Jain& Singh, 2011; Mistry & Ingole, 2013; Zhang, Islam & Lu, 2012).

To overcome the quantization effects as in the color histogram, a number of important color features have been suggested in the literatures, as color moments (CM), color coherence vector (CCV) and color correlogram. Stricker and Orengo proposed color moments approach (Stricker & Orengo, 1995). The basis of CM lays in the assumption that the distribution of color in an image can be interpreted as a probability distribution, which are characterized by a number of unique moments. The common moments are mean, standard deviation and skewness. Usually they are calculated for each color channels (components) separately. Therefore, nine features form the feature vector. These features are useful when they are calculated for region or object. Such a representation of color is less sensitive to noise, however, they are not enough to represent all the color information of an image. Besides, Pass and Zabith offered histogram refinement method, the CCV, which incorporates spatial information into the basic color histogram. It divides each histogram bin into two components: coherent and non-coherent parts. The coherent component contains pixels that are spatially connected, while the non-coherent component includes pixels that are isolated. Since CCV captures spatial information, it usually outperforms a color histogram. However, the dimension of a CCV is twice of a conventional histogram (Pass & Zabith, 1996). Furthermore, Huang et al. introduced color correlogram, which is the color version of grey level co-occurrence matrix (GLCM). It describes the color histogram as a function of distance between pixels, it can be treated as a3D histogram where the first two dimensions denote the colors of any pixel pair and the third dimension is their spatial distance (Huang, Kuamr, Mitra et al., 1997).

The color correlogram outperforms not only the traditional color histogram method but also the histogram refinement methods, because it captures both intensity levels and spatial patterns in an image. However, it is much more complex due to high dimensionality and multiple matrix processing (Zhang et al., 2012).

On the basis of MPEG-7 international standards, a number of color features including scalable color descriptor (SCD), color structure descriptor (CSD) and dominant color descriptor (DCD) are proposed (Manjunath, Ohm, Vasudevan & Yamada, 2001).

The SCD is a histogram-based descriptor. The goal of this color histogram descriptor is to acquire a representation of the color composition of an image that is scalable in the number of coefficients it contains. The SCD extracts a quantized histogram in HSV color space from a given picture (usually in the RGB format). The probability values of each bin are calculated and indexed. The resulting histogram is then transformed via a discrete Haar transformation to achieve the scalability. Although experimental results show that such down scaling significantly affects the retrieval performance, the descriptor does not include any spatial information, which is the same problem of the conventional histogram (Manjunath, Salembier & Sikora, 2002). The CSD is also a histogram-based descriptor. This descriptor creates a color histogram modified to take into account the distribution of each quantized color inside the images, and so it captures both color content and information about the structure of this content (Park, Jeong, Lee & Olybia, 2007). The CSD histogram is obtained by moving a structuring element (e.g. square) throughout the image, it counts the number of times a particular color is contained within the structuring element. The performance of CSD depends on the size and structure of the window. Moreover, it is computationally more expensive than SCD (Zhang et al., 2012).

The DCD is also another alternative color histogram feature. The goal of the DCD is to represent an image by its most dominant colors. The number of colors (bins) selected as DCD depends on the threshold of the bins height (Islam, Zhang & Lu, 2008). MPEG-7 recommends that 1–8 colors are sufficient to represent a region. In contrast to other color histograms, the DCD has a very compact representation, making it more suitable for applications that need high-speed (e.g. retrieval and browsing).

Considering the various color features, color moments are insufficient to represent the image regions information. Furthermore, Color features such as CCV and color correlogram are useful for whole image representation, but they all involve complex computation. On the other hand, histogram based descriptors are either too high dimensional or too expensive to compute. DCD proved to be a good balance between the two extremes, the feature dimension of DCD is low and the computation is relatively inexpensive. Besides it has been demonstrated that DCD is sufficient to represent the color information of a region. Table 1 provides a summary of different color methods quoted from the literature (Islam et al., 2008), including their strengths and weaknesses.

Texture Features Extraction

Texture is a very valuable representation for a wide range of images. Texture extraction techniques have been utilized in wide range of applications in various fields; industrial, biomedical, remote

Table 1. Contrast of different color descriptors

Color Method	Pros.	Cons.
Histogram	Simple to compute, intuitive	High dimension, no spatial info, sensitive to noise
CM	Compact, robust	Not enough to describe all colors, no spatial info
CCV	Spatial info	High dimension, high computation cost
Correlogram	Spatial info	Very high computation cost, sensitive to noise, rotation and scale
DCD	Compact, robust, perceptual meaning	Need post-processing for spatial info
CSD	Spatial info	Sensitive to noise, rotation and scale
SCD	Compact on need, scalability	No spatial info, less accurate if compact

sensing areas, etc. Generally, it can be said that human visual systems use texture for recognition and interpretation. Whereas color is usually a pixel property, texture can only be measured from a group of pixels. Many techniques have been suggested to extract texture features. Texture feature extraction methods, based on the domain from which they are extracted, can be broadly classified into spatial texture feature extraction methods and spectral texture feature extraction methods. For the premier approach, texture features are extracted by computing the pixel statistics or finding the local pixel structures in original image domain, whereas the latter transforms an image into frequency domain and then calculates features from the transformed image. Both spatial and spectral features have advantage and disadvantages. Table 2 summarizes their pros. and cons. (Tian, 2013). These techniques will be discussed in the following sections.

Spatial Texture Feature Extraction Approaches

Spatial texture methods are easy to realize and many of them even have semantics. They do not need regular region shape and can be applied to irregular regions directly. However, they are usually sensitive to noise and distortions. Furthermore, many of these methods comprise complex search and optimization procedures, which have no general solutions.

Table 2. Contrast of texture features

Texture Method	Pros.	Cons.
Spatial texture	Meaningful, easy to understand, can be extracted from any shape without losing information	Sensitive to noise and distortions
Spectral texture	Robust, need lower computation	No semantic meaning, need square image regions with sufficient size

In spatial approach, texture features are obtained by computing the pixel statistics or getting the local pixel structures in original image domain. The spatial texture feature extraction techniques can be further classified into three categories as statistical texture, structural texture and model-based texture (Bharati, Liu & MacGregor, 2004). In texture analysis field, statistical texture is the most widely used method for quality grading or classification (Srinivasan & Shobha, 2008; Bharathi & Subashini, 2013; Elnemr, 2013).

On the other hand, structural texture and model based texture might also be used, but not as often as statistical texture. Table 3 summarizes different spatial texture methods (Zhang et al., 2012).

Statistical Texture Features

Statistical approaches analyze the spatial distribution of grey values, by computing local features at each point in the image, and deriving a set of statistical values from the distributions of the local features (Srinivasan & Shobha, 2008). Based on the number of pixels defining the local features, statistical methods can be further classified in two categories. Firstly, the first order statistical methods that are based on calculating the statistics

Table 3. Contrast of spatial texture methods

Texture Method	Pros.	Cons.
Structural method	Intuitive	Sensitive to noise, rotation and scale, difficult to define texture primitives
GLCM based method	Intuitive, compact, robust	High computation cost, not enough to describe all textures.
Tamura	Perceptually meaningful	Too few features
SAR	Compact, robust, rotation invariant	High computation cost, difficult to define pattern size
FD	Compact, perceptually meaningful	High computation cost, sensitive to scale

from the individual pixel values, ignoring any information about the relative positions of the various gray levels within the image. Common first-order statistical features include moments such as mean, variance, dispersion, mean square value or average energy, entropy, skewness and kurtosis (Gonzalez& Woods, 2007). Secondly, the second and higher order statistical methods which are based on estimating the properties of two or more pixel values occurring at specific locations relative to each other. Popular second order statistical methods utilized are spatial gray level dependency matrices (SGLDM) or gray level co-occurrence matrices (GLCM), gray level run length matrices (GLRLM) and gray level difference matrices (GLDM) (Srinivasan & Shobha, 2008; Bharathi & Subashini, 2013; Elnemr&Hefnawy, 2013). Additionally, Tamura et al. (Tamura, Mori & Yamawaki, 1978) proposed a texture representation based on 6 statistical features, coarseness, contrast, directionality, line-likeness, regularity, and roughness. These features were considered to be the most visually expressive features (He, Zhang, Lok & Lyu, 2005).

Statistical features are compact and robust, yet they are not sufficient to describe the large variety of textures. Furthermore, the performance of the feature extraction methods using the first and second order statistics yields low accuracy. Thus, the first and second order methods are combined in order to improve the accuracy level (Bharathi & Subashini, 2013).

Structural Texture Features

Structural textures are characterized by a set of texture primitives (texels, texon or texture elements) and their placement rules (Gonzalez & Woods, 2007; Lee, 2004). The texels may be defined by their gray level, shape or homogeneity of some local property, see figure 2. On the other hand, the placement rules define the spatial relationships

Figure 2. Examples of structural textures

between the texels and these spatial relationships may be expressed in terms of adjacency, closet distance or periodicities. Many real-world textures contain the structural characteristic. A large number of woven fabrics and commercial furniture are good examples of simply structural or semi-deterministic textures (Lee, 2004).

Structural methods involve many image preprocessing procedures to extract texels. Accordingly they are time-consuming. Furthermore, it is difficult to find an appropriate texel in an input texture since the image textures to be analyzed generally have texels of different sizes and various configuration, accordingly these methods can only describe very regular textures. In view of that, not many researchers have developed texture analysis techniques using structural methods. Besides, the statistical approaches seem to be the more efficient approaches for texture matching.

Model Based Texture Features

Model based texture techniques aimed to interpret an image texture using generative and stochastic models. The estimated model parameters are utilized to characterize the texture property of the image. The crucial problem of these methods is how to estimate the parameters of these models and how to select the correct model suitable for the nominated texture (Materka & Strzelecki; 1998, Zhang & Tan, 2002).

Common texture models are Markov random field (MRF) (Chen & Kundu, 1995; Islam, Venkataraman & Islam, 2010; Blanchet, Forbes & Schmid, 2005), simultaneous auto-regressive (SAR) (Mao & Jain, 1992) and fractal dimension (FD) (Chaudhuri & Sarkar, 1995).

A common drawback of such statistical model based methods is their high computational complexity, as these models involve optimization.

Spectral Texture Feature Extraction Approaches

In spectral texture feature extraction techniques, an image is transformed into frequency domain and then features are calculated from the transformed image. The common spectral methods include Fourier transform (FT) (Lee & Chen, 2005; Zhou, Feng & Shi, 2001; Ursani, Kpalma, Ronsin, Memon & Chowdhry, 2009), discrete cosine transform (DCT) (Yun & Runsheng, 2002; Huang, 2005; Sorwar, Abraham & Dooley, 2001), wavelet (Chen, Lu & Zhang, 2004; Bhagavathy & Chhabra, 2007; Hong & Xuanbing, 2010; Arai, Abdullah & Okumura, 2014; Yu, Lin & Kamarthi, 2010), Gabor filters (Zhang, Wong, Indrawan & Lu, 2000; Wang, Ding & Liu, 2005; Kambale & Inamdar, 2011) and curvelet transform (Donoho & Duncan, 2000; Sumana, Islam, Zhang & Lu, 2008).

Methods based on FT and DCT are very fast to compute, and so they arise as good candidates in applications where the speed (i.e. on-line implementation) is a critical issue. However, they are not scale and rotation invariant, as well as they perform poorly in practice due to their lack of spatial localization. Figure 3 and 4 represent applying FT and DCT to a retina and lung images, respectively. On the other hand wavelet gives both the spatial and frequency information of the images. Hence, it is both efficient and robust, but it only captures horizontal and vertical features. Among them, Gabor features are most robust because it captures image features in multi-orientations and multi-scales. Nevertheless, their benefit is limited in practice because there is usually no single filter resolution at which one can localize a spatial structure in natural textures. Recently, researches on multi-resolution analysis have demonstrated that curvelet features have considerable advantages over Gabor features and wavelet features, because curvelet features are more effective in capturing anisotropic elements such as the edges lines of an image effectively (Donoho & Duncan, 2000; Sumana et al., 2008; Bhadu, Tokas & Kumar, 2012). Also, curvelet spectra cover the frequency plane of an image completely. Implementation of wavelet transform, Gabor filter and curvelet transform are illustrated in figures 5, 6, 7, 8 and 9. Table 4 abstracts different spectral texture methods (Zhang et al., 2012).

Generally, spatial features have semantic meaning comprehensible by humans as well as can be extracted from any shape without losing information. Nevertheless, spatial features are usually sensitive to noise. On the other hand, spectral texture features are robust, and also take less computation because convolution in spatial domain is done as multiplication process in frequency domain. But they do not have semantic meaning as spatial features. For small images or regions, especially when the regions are irregular, spatial features are suitable to be employed. While, images or regions with sufficient size, spectral texture features are appropriate choices. Additionally, some researchers integrate spatial and spectral texture features (Prabhu & Kumar, 2014), others combine methods of spectral texture feature extraction (Gupta, Agrwal, Meena & Nain, 2011) to improve the systems performance.

Shape Features Extraction

Shape is an important human visual feature that is considered to be one of the basic features used to identify and recognize real world objects. Shape

Figure 3. Applying Fourier and Discrete cosine transform transforms to retina image

(a) Original image   (b) Fourier transform   c) Discrete cosine transform

Figure 4. Applying Fourier and Discrete cosine transform transforms to lungs image

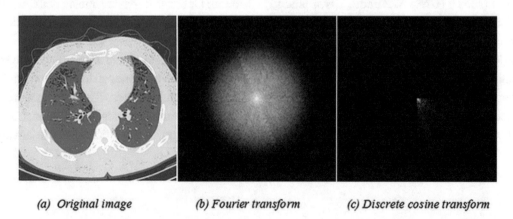

(a) Original image   (b) Fourier transform   (c) Discrete cosine transform

Figure 5. Applying wavelet transform to the retina image presented in figure 3 (a)

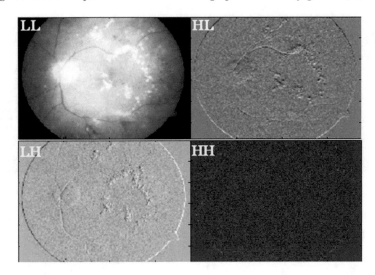

Figure 6. Applying wavelet transform to lungs image presented in figure 4 (a)

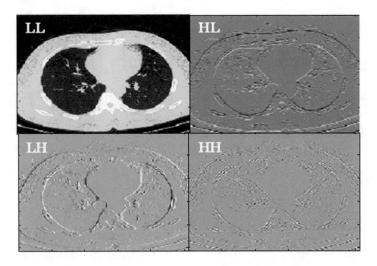

Figure 7. Applying Gabor filters of different orientations to retina image presented in figure 3 (a)

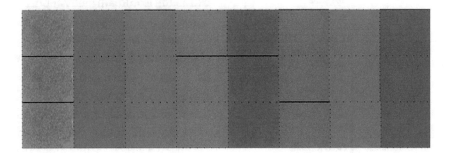

Figure 8. Applying Gabor filters of different orientations to lungs image presented in figure 4 (a)

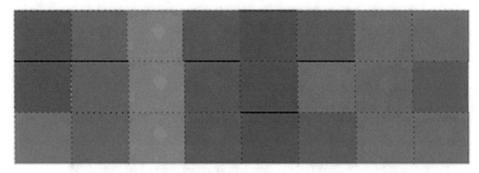

Figure 9. (a) BigMac Image, and stages of Curvelet Analysis (b) Curvelet Coefficients, and stages of Curvelet Synthesis (Donoho & Duncan, 2000)

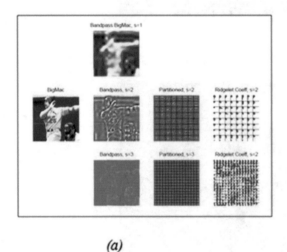

(a)

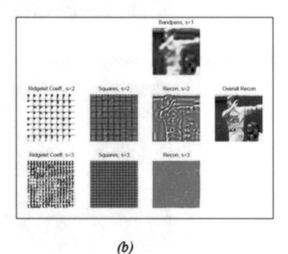

(b)

Table 4. Contrast of spectral texture methods

Texture Method	Pros.	Cons.
FT/DCT	Fast computation	Sensitive to rotation and scale
Wavelet	Fast computation, multi-resolution	Sensitive to rotation, limited orientation
Gabor	Multi-scale, multi-orientation, robust	Need rotation normalization, loosing of spectral information due to incomplete cover of spectrum plane (Sumana et al.,2008)
Curvelet	Multi-scale, multi-orientation, robust	Need rotation normalization

characterization compared to other features, like texture and color, are much more efficient in semantically distinguishing the content of an image. Shape feature techniques are employed for extracting features in many applications. However, shape representation and description is a difficult task due to the projection of a 3-D real world object onto a 2-D image plane as well as the fact that a shape is often corrupted with noise, defects, arbitrary distortion and occlusion. The challenging task of shape description is the precise extraction and representation of shape information.

Shape extraction techniques can be broadly categorized into two major groups: contour-based and region-based methods (Zhang & Lu, 2004). Contour-based approaches compute the shape features from the boundary of the shape only, whereas the region-based approaches excerpt features from the whole shape region. Figure 10 shows the hierarchy of the classification of shape feature extraction methods according to their processing approaches (Yang, Kpalm& Ronsin, 2008).

Contour-based methodologies are more popular than region-based methodologies in literature. This is due to the fact that human beings are believed to distinguish shapes mainly by their contour features. Another reason is that in different shape applications, the interest concentrates on the shape contour while the shape interior content is not important. However, there are some limitations with contour based methods. First, contour based techniques are more sensitive to noise than region based techniques, because they are based on using only a small part of shape information that is contour information, which is affected significantly with any small changes in the shape. Second, shape content may be more important than the contour features in some applications. On the other hand, region-based methods considered

Figure 10. An overview of shape description techniques

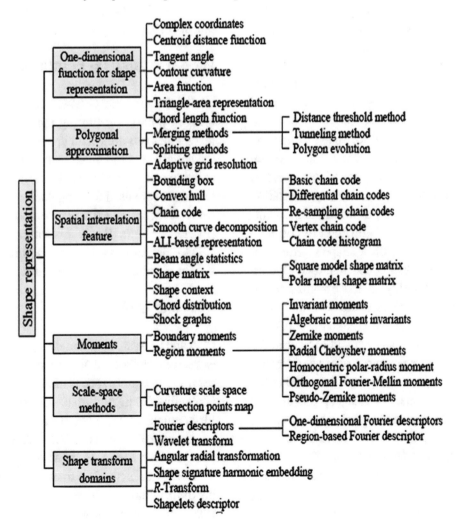

being more robust since they use all the available shape information and they can be applied to general applications. Moreover, region based techniques can cope well with shape defection, which is a general problem for contour-based shape representation techniques. Besides, region based methods are not necessarily more complex than contour based methods.

The most successful representatives for these two categories are Fourier descriptor (FD) and moment invariants. The shape description techniques using FD are simple to compute, robust to noise and compact. It has been implemented in many applications in different areas. Liu et al. (Liu, Zhang, Tjondronegoro & Geve, 2007) utilized FD of shape contour for bird classification. (Lee et al., 2012) employed FD shape feature extraction technique to provide enhanced classification accuracy for breast tumor ultrasound diagnosis system.

(Zhang et al., 2008; Khurana& Komal, 2012) proposed content-based medical image retrieval systems using FD. Likewise, the moment-based shape descriptors are used for shape feature extraction. The moment-based shape descriptors are usually succinct, robust and easy to compute. It is also invariant to scaling, rotation and translation of the object. However, the drawback of moment-based methods is that it is difficult to correlate high order moments with a shape's prominent features, because of their global nature. In (Jyothi, Latha, Mohan &Reddy, 2013) pseudo-Zernike moments has been used to achieve an image retrieval system. Celebi and Aslandogan (Celebi & Aslandogan, 2005) studied and compared the performance of three moment-based descriptors, invariant moments, Zernike moments, and radial Chebyshev moments, for image retrieval. The results indicate that radial Chebyshev moments achieve the highest retrieval performance.

Rao et al. proposed employing Zernike moments as shape descriptors to extract features of Telugu characters (Rao, Prasad & Kumar, 2013). Another investigation and comparative study on three shape descriptors, moments, FD and angular radial transform, for shape retrieval has been accomplished in (Amanatiadis, Kaburlasos, Gasteratos & Papadakis, 2011, 2009). Results illustrate that image moment descriptors outperform the other two methods regarding scaling, translation, and rotation invariance and compactness. Furthermore, FDs are more robust to general boundary variations than angular radial transform. However, the angular radial transform strongly captures the perceptual shape features.

More complex shape features are usually used in domain specific applications such as trademark retrieval (Wang &Hong, 2012) and object classification, where shape is the most important feature. For example, (Raj, Naveen, Arun & Vinod, 2009) described classification of vehicular shape-based objects using FD.

Global Statistical Features

Global features are obtained from the arrangement of points constituting the whole image or just regular sub-area of an image. Global features are not affected too much by noise or distortions as compared to topological features. A number of techniques are used for global feature extraction; some of these are: Principal component analysis (PCA), Fisher's linear discriminant analysis (LDA), also known as Fisher Discriminant Analysis), moments, edges, corners, etc.

PCA and LDA

PCA and LDA are both widely used global feature extraction methods that have been applied successfully in pattern recognition and data analysis (Zainudin, Radi, Abdullah, Abd Rahim, Ismail, Idris, Sulaiman & Jaafar, 2012; Murukesh, Thanushkodi, 2013; Ayushi, 2013; Aswathy, 2013; Hidayat, Nur, Muda, Huoy & Ahmad, 2011).

Both these methods extract features by projecting the original sample vectors onto a new feature space through a linear transformation matrix.

However, the goal of optimizing the transformation matrix in the two methods is different. In PCA, the transformation matrix is optimized by finding the largest variance associated with it. On the other hand, LDA searches for those vectors in the underlying space that best discriminate among classes (rather than those that best describe the data). Its aim is to maximize the ratio of the between-class and within-class variations by projecting the original features to a subspace (Yang, Zhang, Frangi, & Yang, 2004).

The PCA and LDA approaches extract features directly based on vector patterns, i.e., before applying them, any non-vector pattern such as an image is first converted into a vector pattern by some techniques like concatenation. However, such a conversion has been proved not to be beneficial for some image processing tasks. Therefore, a Two-dimensional principal component analysis (2DPCA) and a two-dimensional linear discriminant analysis (2DLDA) are developed based on 2-D image matrices rather than 1-D vectors (Li & Yuan, 2005; Mutelo, Khor, Woo & Dlay, 2006; Chen, Zhu, Zhang & Yang; 2005).

Moments

Moment based features are a traditional and widely used tool for feature extraction and have been extensively used in image processing applications through the years (Zulkifli, Zalikha, Iskandar, Saad & Mohtar, 2011; Fei & Kehong, 2011; Fu & Lv, 2009; Seddik, Hassan,& Fakhreldein, 2013). Moment features are invariant under scaling, translation, rotation and reflection. Furthermore, they have been proven to be useful in pattern recognition applications due to their sensitivity to the pattern features (Sridevi & Subashini, 2012). Geometrical, central and normalized moments are the only family of moments that were applied for many decades (Hu, 1962).The main problems of these descriptors are their disability to fully describe an object such that its reconstruction

could be possible, using the moments set, as well as calculation of higher order of these moments is a difficult task. To overcome these problems Teague (Teague, 1980) introduced Zernike moments, which could recover the image using the concept of orthogonal moments. Zernike moments are superior to other moments because they are shift, rotation, and scale invariants and are insensitivity towards information content and image noise (Teh & Chin, 1988; Kale, Deshmukh, Chavan, Kazi & Rode, 2014; Nabatchian, Abdel-Raheem & Ahmadi, 2008).

Edges

Edges are points where there is a boundary (or an edge) between two image regions. The edge is the basic characteristics of the image. There is a lot of information of the image in the edge. Edge detection is an essential tool used in various image processing and computer vision applications in the areas of feature detection and feature extraction (Nixon & Aguado, 2013; Ohashi & Shimodaira, 2003). The focal goal of edge detection is to detect points in a digital image at which the image brightness changes abruptly or, more strictly. Thus, edge detection aims to extract edges in an image by identifying pixels where the intensity variation is high. This process detects outlines of an object and boundaries between objects and the background in the image.

There are many methods for edge detection, but most of them can be classified into two groups; first derivative-based edge detection and second derivative-based edge detection. The first derivative-based edge detection operator relies on detecting image edges by computing the image gradient values. On the other hand, the second derivative-based edge detection operator searches for zero crossings in a second order derivative expression computed from the image in order to find edges (Nixon & Aguado, 2013; Bin & yeganeh, 2012).

First-Order Derivative Edge Detection

There are two fundamental methods for generating first-order derivative edge gradients. One method involves generation of gradients along two orthogonal directions; the second utilizes a set of directional derivatives.

Some popular First-order edge detection methods are Sobel, Perwitt, Roberts and Canny operators (Nixon & Aguado, 2013; Kaur & Malhotra, 2013). The main advantages of Sobel, Perwitt and Roberts operators are their simplicity of implementation and capability of detecting edges and their directions. However, they are sensitive to noise and not accurate in locating edges. On the other hand, Canny's edge detection algorithm has greater computational complexity and time consumption in comparing to Sobel, Prewitt and Robert's operators. Even though, the Canny's edge detection algorithm has a better performance (better localization and improved signal to noise ratio). Sobel, Perwitt and Roberts are useful for applications such as heavy data transfer in the form of images and videos. In these applications timely arrival of data is important which can be satisfied as these operators give faster performance in terms of computation. Alternatively, Canny is used for object recognition, and pattern matching purposes where it is necessary to keep the features even in case of noisy images (Kaur & Malhotra, 2013; Shrivakshan & Chandrasekar, 2012; Chandwadkar, Dhole, Gadewar, Raut & Tiwaskar, 2013). Figure 11 and 12 demonstrates the different first-Order derivative edge detection operators.

Second-Order Derivative Edge Detection

Instead of searching the maxima of the gradient, we may search zero crossings of the second order derivative. In Second-order derivative based methods, edges are found by searching for zero crossings in a second-order derivative

Figure 11. Comparison of First-Order Derivative edge detection operators of retina image

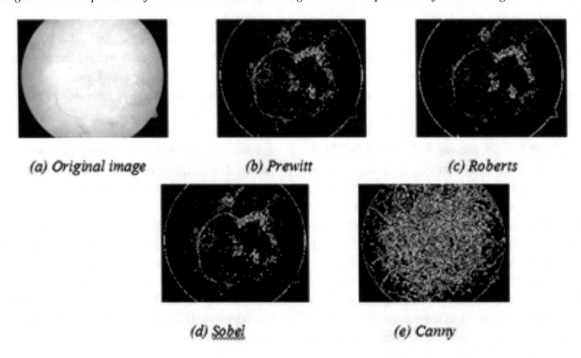

(a) Original image   (b) Prewitt   (c) Roberts

(d) Sobel   (e) Canny

Figure 12. Comparison of First-Order Derivative edge detection operators of lungs image

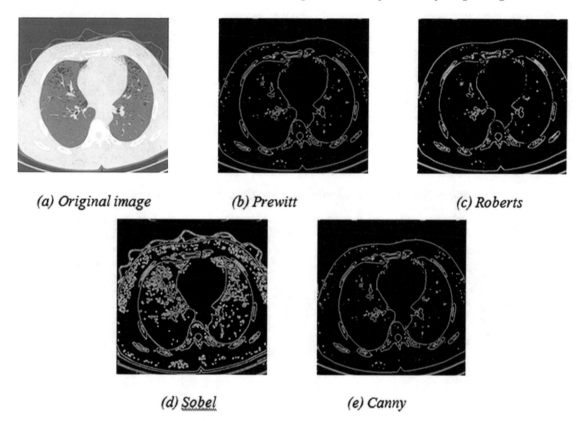

(a) Original image   *(b) Prewitt*   *(c) Roberts*

(d) Sobel   *(e) Canny*

expression computed from the image. Common Second-order derivative edge detection operators include Laplacian of Gaussian (LOG) operator, difference of Gaussian operator (DOG) (Nixon & Aguado, 2013). LOG first performs the Gaussian smoothing, which is followed by the Laplacian operation. A smoothing stage is applied as a pre-processing step to edge detection. The Laplacian, the 2nd spatial derivative, of an image highlights regions of rapid intensity change and is therefore often used for edge detection. Thus, the Gaussian filtering is combined with Laplacian to break down the image where the intensity varies to detect the edges effectively. The main problem of LOG operator is its computation complexity. In order to avoid the large computation of LOG operator, the DOG operator can be used as an approximation to the LOG by taking the difference of two Gaussians having different standard deviation. The

zero crossing operators outperform the gradient operators such that they are closer to mechanisms of visual perception and they produce closed contours. However, they are more sensitive to noise and there is no information on the orientation of the contour (Shrivakshan & Chandrasekar, 2012). Figure 13 and 14 presents the different second-order derivative edge detection operators.

In general, global features have some drawbacks: a) feature extraction is a time consuming and a high complexity computation task on the high-dimensional image matrix; b) extracting global features on the entire image may miss some other effective contents that represent different semantic meanings. To overcome these disadvantages, Jing et al. (He, Jiang, Guo & Liu, 2011) proposed utilizing global feature extraction methods to extract the features from image local regions (block) with the anticipation of: a) com-

Figure 13. Comparison of Second-Order Derivative edge detection operators of retina image

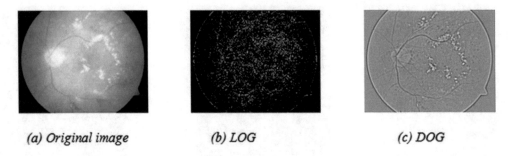

(a) Original image   *(b) LOG*   *(c) DOG*

Figure 14. Comparison of Second-Order Derivative edge detection operators of lungs image

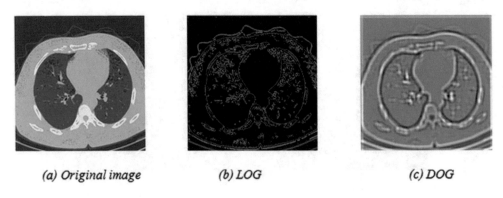

(a) Original image   *(b) LOG*   *(c) DOG*

bining the advantages of local and global features; b) discovering multiple semantic meanings in one image. Also, Chowdhury et al. (Chowdhury, Sing, Basu & Nasipuri, 2010) introduced a scheme for feature extraction based on fusing local and global discriminant features. The images are divided into a number of non-overlapping sub-images and then global feature methods are applied to each of these sub-images as well as to the whole image to extract local and global discriminant features, respectively. All these extracted local and global discriminant features are then fused to get a large feature vector.

Domain-Specific Features

The various feature extraction methods offered in the literature are usually universal in the sense that they can be applied to many different applications with different degrees of success according to the nature of the application at hand. However, for some specific image recognition and computer vision tasks, human expert plays an important role to recognize the information of the image that is invariant to image variations within the class and discriminate between classes. The major problem with universal features is that they do not match the way by which humans intuitively discriminate among classes, identify various objects, etc. That is, the universal features are usually unrelated to the distinguishing features that humans utilize in particular application. Domain-specific features are application dependent features such as human faces, fingerprints, and conceptual features. These features are often a fusion of low-level features for a specific domain.

Abdelazeem (Abdelazeem, 2009) investigates the recognition of Arabic handwritten digits problem. The extracted features are based on the essential properties of Arabic numerals. The results demonstrate that the proposed domain-specific intuitive feature vector outperform the universal features with respect to the recognition rate and speed. Furthermore, in character recognition applications various domain-specific features are suggested in literatures (Vamvakas, Gatos & Perantonis, 2009; Verma& Ali, 2012; Khobragade, Koli & Makesar, 2013).Some common features implemented for character recognition are as follows:

Zoning: In this method the character matrix is divided into small portions or zones. The densities of pixels in each zone are computed and used as features (Suen, Berthod & Mori, 1980; Oliveira, Bortolozzi & Suen, 2002; Rajashekararadhya &Ranjan, 2008; Ashoka, Manjaiah &Bera, 2012).

Projection histograms: This technique relies on computing the number of black pixels in the vertical, horizontal, left diagonal or right diagonal directions of the specified area of the character (Hussain, Toussaint & Donaldson, 1972; Koerich, 2003).

Crossings and distances: Crossings count the number of transitions from background to foreground pixels along vertical and horizontal directions through the character image, and Distances calculate the distances of the first pixel detected from the upper and lower boundaries, of the image, along vertical directions and from the left and right boundaries along horizontal directions (Kim, Kim & Suen, 2000).

Additionally, to be able to recognize faces automatically this requires extraction of some major facial features. Some researchers implied domain-specific feature extraction techniques based on extracting geometrical and structural facial features (generic knowledge about Faces) like facial organs' position, symmetry, and edge shape. These features are such as: a face contains four main organs, i.e., eyebrows, eyes, nose and mouth; a face image is symmetric in the left and right directions; eyes are below two eyebrows; nose lies between and below two eyes; lips lie below nose; the contour of a human head can be

approximated by an ellipse, the distance between facial components, the relative positions and sizes of these elements and so on. By using the facial components along with positional relationship between them the faces can be located easily (Dhawan & Dogra, 2012; Bhatt & Shah, 2011; Lu, Zhou & Yu, 2003).

A geometrical face model and an efficient facial feature detection approach, based on the fact that human faces are constructed in the same geometrical configuration as well as the geometrical facial symmetry, is presented in (Jeng, Liao, Han, Chern & Liu, 1998). The proposed approach can accurately detect facial features, especially the eyes, even when the images have complex backgrounds such as bad lighting condition, skew face orientation, and facial expression. Wong et al. (Wong, Lam & Siu, 2001) devised an algorithm for human face detection based on the location of an eye pair. In (Liposcak & Loncaric, 1999) a face recognition from profiles technique is presented. This technique concentrates on obtaining points of interest, called fiducial points, from the outline curve of the front portion of the silhouette that bounds the face image. Gu et al. (Gu, Su & Du, 2003) proposed a method to extract the feature points from faces automatically. This method affords a feasible way to locate the positions of two eyeballs, near and far corners of eyes, midpoint of nostrils and mouth corners from face image. Face detection and recognition can often be achieved by detecting geometrical relationships among facial organs as mentioned, because they are simple, straightforward, efficient and not affected by irrelevant information in the image. Yet, they are sensitive to unpredictability of face appearance and environmental conditions.

Among many other applications, fingerprint recognition is another good example of feature extraction based on the human domain specific expertise. Two major tasks in fingerprint recognition are classification and authentication. (Jiang, 2009) surveyed and investigated some advanced feature extraction approaches that are based on the human expert knowledge to solve problems of image-based biometrics, including fingerprint verification/identification and face detection/recognition.

The speed of feature extraction of some domain-specific features makes them good candidates to be used in the early stages of classification or recognition processes.

HIGH-LEVEL FEATURE EXTRACTION

High-level feature extraction concerns with realizing shapes or objects in digital images. High-level features get closer to the semantic understanding of images than the low-level features, although most of the high-level features are still very much below these mantic level. Often high-level features can be calculated making use of some low-level features. In order to extract a shape from an image, it is necessary to identify it from the background elements. This can be done by considering the intensity information or by comparing the pixels against a given template. In the first approach, if the brightness of the shape is known, then the pixels that construct the shape can be obtained by classifying the pixels according to a fixed intensity threshold. Besides, if the background image is known, this can be subtracted to get the pixels that define the shape of an object superimposed on the background. The second methodology is template matching, which is a model-based approach. This approach points toward extract a shape from an image by searching for the best correlation between a known model and the pixels in an image. Correlation can be implemented by considering the image or frequency domains. Another approach that will be considered in this article is the Hough transform. This technique is capable of extracting simple shapes such as lines and quadratic forms, as well as arbitrary shapes (Nixon & Aguado, 2013).

Thresholding and Subtraction

Thresholding is a simple shape extraction technique. This implies that the object's brightness must be known in advance and that it has a different range of intensities to the background. It is accomplished by selecting a value for the threshold that separates an object from its background. Otsu's method (Otsu, 1979) is one of the most popular techniques of thresholding. Zhang et al. (Zhang, Xu & Wu, 2011) described a method based on Otsu to extract the position information of structure light stripe centerline. Sthitpattanapongsa and Srinark proposed a fast and robust thresholding method that can overcome the shortcoming of the 1-D and 2-D Otsu's methods (Sthitpattanapongsa & Srinark, 2011).

Alternatively, if the background image is known precisely, this can be subtracted from the image to obtain the pixels that define the shape of an object superimposed on the background. In (Sharma & Bansal, 2013) background subtraction is used as the first step of gait recognition system. In addition, background subtraction is utilized to identify moving objects from the portion of a video frame that differs significantly from a background model (Spagnolo, Orazio, Leo & Distante, 2006; Ukinkar & Makrand, 2012).

Despite the fact that thresholding and subtraction are attractive, because of their simplicity and hence their speed, the performance of both techniques is sensitive to partial shape data, noise, variation in illumination and occlusion of the target shape by other objects shapes (Nixon & Aguado, 2013). Figure 15 presents using subtraction and thresholding for shape extraction.

Template Matching

Template Matching is a high-level machine vision technique that allows extracting an object by comparing portions of images with another image. It is conceptually a simple process. The

Figure 15. Shape extraction by subtraction and thresholding (Nixon & Aguado, 2013)

 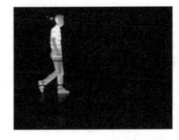 

(a) Image of walking subject   *(b) After background subtraction*❘   *(c) After thresholding*

template is a subimage that contains the shape we are trying to find. These templates may be certain objects in a scene or strings of patterns, such as letters forming words in a written text or words or phrases in a spoken text (Theodoridis & Koutroumbas, 2009) or eyes in face images (Bhoi, Mohanty, 2010). The template is centered on an image part and the template is matched against this part. The procedure is repeated for the entire image, and the part that led to the best match is deemed to be the portion where the shape (given by the template) lies within the image. The template matching process needs to solve two problems. Firstly, a template should be designed. The typical template matching methods directly use images as templates (Al-Mamun, Jahangir, Islam & Islam, 2009). Secondly, the template matching operation needs a similarity measure.

Number of techniques has been established and still evolving to measure similarities between the input image and the template, as geometric distance, mutual information, correlation (Mahalakshmi, Muthaiah & Swaminathan, 2012), asymmetric correlation (ASC) (Elboher & Werman, 2013), etc.

Template matching is widely used in several image-processing applications. In (Mahbub, Imtiaz, Roy, Rahman & Ahad, 2013) an approach for gesture recognition from motion depth images based on template matching is presented. Liu et al.

proposed an improved template matching method for detecting infrared point targets (Liu, Lu, Gong & Liu, 2012). Jin et al. demonstrated a face-detection algorithm based on combining template-matching technique with skin-color information in segmenting eye-pair candidates using a linear transformation (Jin, Lou, Yang & Sun, 2007). (Mahalakshmi et al., 2012) submitted a review article surveys extensively various approaches based on template matching. Furthermore, a new FPGA based spectral architecture is proposed to achieve a fast similarity measure between template and input image. (Lu & Little, 2006) proposed a template-based algorithm to track and recognize athlete's actions by exploitation of the PCA-HOG descriptor (the histogram of oriented gradient (HOG) is projected to a linear subspace by the principal component analysis (PCA)).

The main advantages of template based feature extraction method are its insensitivity to noise and occlusion, simplicity, efficiency as well as it is easy to implement. Yet, a very common problem of templates is being rigid and uniform, which affects the detection rate. Besides, the computational cost of template-matching method is large, a direct implementation is slow. To speed up this, some researchers suggested utilizing hardware implementations. In (Mahalakshmi et al., 2012) the authors implemented FBGA based architecture to reduce the computational time.

Hough Transform

The Hough transform (HT) is a convenient tool for feature extraction from images used in image analysis, computer vision, and digital image processing. The HT was submitted in 1962 for straight-line detection in pictures, see figure 16 (Hough, 1962). Later, HT was generalized to detect features with arbitrary shapes, see figure 17 (Ballard, 1981).In (Elnemr, 2012) HT was exploited to detect lines in Arabic bank checks. These lines indicate the different bank check fields. Bendale et al. (Bendale, Nigam, Prakash and Gupta, 2012) proposed an iris segmentation algorithm that uses an improved circular HT to detect the inner boundary of iris from a given eye image. Moreover, Hough-based methods were successfully adapted to imply the location of an object by estimating the locations of its parts (Okada, 2009; Maji and Malik, 2009; Barinova, Lempitsky and Kohli, 2010).

A main drawback of the HT is its time and space complexity, the computational complexity grows rapidly with more complex shapes. However, it has a number of interesting possessions: HT can be applied for recognizing several simultaneously existing lines. HT is very robust to the noise produced by isolated noisy measurements and missed measurements.

FUTURE RESEARCH DIRECTIONS

The suggested future work is directed for two scopes; enhancing the feature extraction techniques regarding accuracy and speed, as well as increasing their capabilities and applications. The following points of research are suggested for future work:

1. Various features computed using different extraction methods are complementary,

Figure 16. Applying the Hough transform for lines (Nixon & Aguado, 2013)

Figure 17. Using the Hough transform for circles (Nixon & Aguado, 2013)

(a) Image of eye   *(b) Sobel edges*   *(c) Edges with HT detected circle*

and combining several features within the maximum relevance and minimum redundancy framework is a good way of fusing information provided by different methods and increasing recognition accuracy.

2. A new approach of feature extraction by using Matrix Pencil Method in Frequency Domain (MPMFD). The proposed method takes into account not only the magnitude of the signal in frequency domain, but also its phase.

3. Investigating Genetic Programming for automatic feature extraction using different amounts of existing knowledge from only using raw pixel intensities and ground truth to more advanced domain knowledge such as filters, transformations, etc.

4. Utilizing the feature extraction techniques in mobile applications such as:

    a. Feature Extraction Method for Mobile visual Product Search

    b. Feature Extraction Method for mobile video Search

    c. Augmented reality: Enable a user to take a picture, use some feature extraction algorithms (e.g., an object recognition algorithm and/or an edge detection algorithm) and send the extracted meta-data in form of a MPEG-7 document to a server which returns semantic information about the content of the image (e.g., a specific building has been detected, etc.).

CONCLUSION

For several visual applications, extracting robust and discriminative features from image is the most difficult yet the most critical step. Feature extraction techniques are widely employed in many areas such as pattern recognition, machine learning and data mining. Features should be easily computed, robust, insensitive to various distortions and variations in the images, rotationally invariant, also they should support the discrimination aspect. The objective of feature extraction is to capture the essential characteristics of a desired object. This chapter provides a comprehensive survey on various feature extraction techniques. Several typical and advanced approaches of feature extraction from image are explored, discussed and evaluated. It is worth be noted that reliable and effective feature extraction is the most crucial and substantial issue in the field of image recognition and computer vision.

REFERENCES

Abdelazeem, S. (2009). A Novel Domain-Specific Feature Extraction Scheme for Arabic Handwritten Digits Recognition. *International Conference on Machine Learning and Applications*, Miami Beach, FL. doi:10.1109/ICMLA.2009.136

Al-Mamun, H. A., Jahangir, N., Islam, M. S., & Islam, M. A. (2009). Eye Detection in Facial Image by Genetic Algorithm Driven Deformable Template Matching. *International Journal of Computer Science and Network Security*, *9*(8), 771–779.

Amanatiadis, A., Kaburlasos, V. G., Gasteratos, A., & Papadakis, S. E. (2009). *A Comparative Study of Invariant Descriptors for Shape Retrieval. International Workshop on Imaging Systems and Techniques*, Shenzhen, China. doi:10.1109/IST.2009.5071672

Amanatiadis, A., Kaburlasos, V. G., Gasteratos, A., & Papadakis, S. E. (2011). Evaluation of Shape Descriptors for Shape-Based Image Retrieval. *IET Image Processing*, *5*(5), 493–499. doi:10.1049/iet-ipr.2009.0246

Arai, K., Abdullah, I. N., & Okumura, H. (2014). Comparative Study of Feature Extraction Components from Several Wavelet Transformations for Ornamental Plants. *International Journal of Advanced Research in Artificial Intelligence, 3*(2), 5–11. doi:10.14569/IJARAI.2014.030202

Arun, C. H., Sam, W. R., & Christopher, D. D. (2013). Texture Feature Extraction for Identification of Medicinal Plants and Comparison of Different Classifiers. *International Journal of Computers and Applications, 62*(12), 1–9. doi:10.5120/10129-4920

Ashoka, H. N., Manjaiah, D. H., & Bera, R. (2012). Zone Based Feature Extraction and Statistical Classification Technique for Kannada Handwritten Numeral Recognition. [IJCSET]. *International Journal of Computer Science & Engineering Technology, 3*(10), 476–482.

Aswathy, R. (2013). A Literature review on Facial Expression Recognition Techniques. *IOSR Journal of Computer Engineering, 11*(1), 61-64.

Ayushi. (2013). A Survey on Feature Extraction Techniques. *International Journal of Computer Applications, 66*(11), 43-46.

Ballard, D. H. (1981). Generalizing the Hough Transform to Detect Arbitrary Shapes. *Pattern Recognition, 13*(2), 111–122. doi:10.1016/0031-3203(81)90009-1

Barinova, O., Lempitsky, V., & Kohli, P. (2010). On the Detection of Multiple Object Instances Using Hough Transforms. *Proceedings of IEEE Conference on Computer Vision and Pattern Recognition.* doi:10.1109/CVPR.2010.5539905

Bendale, A., Nigam, A., Prakash, S., & Gupta, P. (2012). Iris Segmentation Using an Improved Hough Transform. *Proceedings of International Conference on Intelligent Computing.* doi:10.1007/978-3-642-31837-5_59

Bhadu, A., Tokas, R., & Kumar, V. (2012). Facial Expression Recognition Using DCT, Gabor and Wavelet Feature Extraction Techniques. *International Journal of Engineering and Innovative Technology, 2*(1), 92–95.

Bhagavathy, S., & Chhabra, K. (2007). *A Wavelet-based Image Retrieval System. Technical Report—ECE278A.* Santa Barbara, CA: Vision Research Laboratory, University of California.

Bharathi, P. T., & Subashini, P. (2013). Texture Feature Extraction of Infrared River Ice Images using Second-Order Spatial Statistics. World Academy of Science. *Engineering and Technology, 74*, 747–757.

Bharati, M. H., Liu, J. J., & MacGregor, J. F. (2004). Image texture analysis: Methods and comparisons. *Chemometrics and Intelligent Laboratory Systems, 72*(1), 57–71. doi:10.1016/j.chemolab.2004.02.005

Bhatt, B. G., & Shah, Z. H. (2011). *Face Feature Extraction Techniques: A Survey. National Conference on Recent Trends in Engineering & Technology.*

Bhoi, N., & Mohanty, M. N. (2010). Template Matching Based Eye Detection in Facial Image. *International Journal of Computers and Applications, 12*(5), 15–18. doi:10.5120/1676-2262

Bin, L., & Yeganeh, M. S. (2012). Comparison for Image Edge Detection Algorithms. *IOSR Journal of Computer Engineering, 2*(6), 1–4. doi:10.9790/0661-0260104

Blanchet, J., Forbes, F., & Schmid, C. (2005). Markov Random Fields for Recognizing Textures Modeled by Feature Vectors. *International Conference on Applied Stochastic Models and Data Analysis*, France.

Celebi, M. E., & Aslandogan, Y. A. (2005). *A Comparative Study of Three Moment-Based Shape Descriptors. International Conference on Information Technology: Coding and Computing.* doi:10.1109/ITCC.2005.3

Chandwadkar, R., Dhole, S., Gadewar, V., Raut, D., & Tiwaskar, S. A. (2013). Comparison of Edge Detection Techniques. *Proceedings of Sixth IRAJ International Conference.*

Chaudhuri, B. B., & Sarkar, N. (1995). Texture segmentation using fractal dimension. *IEEE Transactions on Pattern Analysis and Machine Intelligence, 17*(1), 72–77. doi:10.1109/34.368149

Chen, J. L., & Kundu, A. (1995). Unsupervised Texture Segmentation Using Multichannel Decomposition and Hidden Markov Models. IEEE Trans. *Image Processing, 4*(5), 603–619. doi:10.1109/83.382495 PMID:18290010

Chen, L., Lu, G., & Zhang, D. S. (2004). *Effects of Different Gabor Filter Parameters on Image Retrieval by Texture.* The 10th IEEE International Conference on Multi-Media Modelling, Australia.

Chen, S. C., Zhu, Y. L., Zhang, D. Q., & Yang, J. Y. (2005). Feature extraction approaches based on matrix pattern: MatPCA and MatFLDA. *Pattern Recognition Letters, 26*(8), 1157–1167. doi:10.1016/j.patrec.2004.10.009

Chitra, S., & Balakrishnan, G. (2012). A Survey of Face Recognition on Feature Extraction Process of Dimensionality Reduction Techniques. *Journal of Theoretical and Applied Information Technology, 36*(1), 92–100.

Chora's, R. S. (2007). Image Feature Extraction Techniques and their Applications for CBIR and Biometrics Systems. *International Journal of Biology and Biomedical Engineering, 1*(1), 6–16.

Chowdhury, S., Sing, J. K., Basu, D. K., & Nasipuri, M. (2010). *Feature Extraction by Fusing Local and Global Discriminant Features: An Application to Face Recognition. IEEE International Conference on Computational Intelligence and Computing Research (ICCIC)*, Coimbatore. doi:10.1109/ICCIC.2010.5705827

Dhawan, S., & Dogra, H. (2012). Feature Extraction Techniques for Face Recognition. International Journal of Engineering. *Business and Enterprise Applications, 2*(1), 1–4.

Donoho, D. L., & Duncan, M. R. (2000). Digital Curvelet Transform: Strategy, Implementation and Experiments. *Proceedings of the Society for Photo-Instrumentation Engineers, 4056*, 12–29. doi:10.1117/12.381679

Elboher, E., & Werman, M. (2013). Asymmetric correlation: A noise robust similarity measure for template matching. *IEEE Transactions on Image Processing, 99*, 1–12. PMID:23591492

Elnemr, H. A. (2012). Using Hybrid Decision Tree -Houph Transform Approach for Automatic Bank Check Processing. *International Journal of Computer Science and Information Security, 10*(5), 31–37.

Elnemr, H. A. (2013). Statistical Analysis of Law's Mask Texture Features for Cancer and Water Lung Detection. *International Journal of Computer Science Issues, 10*(6), 196–202.

Elnemr, H. A., & Hefnawy, A. A. (2013). A Significance Test-Based Feature Selection Method for Diabetic Retinopathy Grading. *CiiT International Journal of Digital Image Processing, 5*(5), 243 – 249.

Fei, G., & Kehong, W. (2011). The Research of Classification Method of Arc Welding Pool Image Based on Invariant Moments. *Power Engineering and Automation Conference (PEAM)*, Wuhan.

Fu, Y., & Lv, J. (2009). *Recognition of SAR Image Based on SVM and New Invariant Moment Feature Extraction. Second International Symposium on Knowledge Acquisition and Modeling*, Wuhan.

Gale, A. G., & Salankar, S. S. (2014). A Review on Advance Methods of Feature Extraction in Iris Recognition System. *IOSR Journal of Electrical and Electronics Engineering, 3*(14), 65-70.

Gonzalez, R. C., & Woods, R. E. (2007). *Digital Image Processing* (3rd ed.). Prentice-Hall.

Gu, H., Su, G., & Du, C. (2003). Feature points extraction from face. *Proceedings of Conference on Image and Vision Computing.*

Gupta, S. K., Agrwal, S., Meena, Y. K., & Nain, N. (2011). *A Hybrid Method of Feature Extraction for Facial Expression Recognition. Seventh International Conference on Signal-Image Technology and Internet-Based Systems (SITIS)*, Dijon. doi:10.1109/SITIS.2011.64

Guyon, I., Gunn, S., Nikravesh, M., & Zadeh, L. A. (2006). *Feature Extraction Foundations and Applications*. Berlin: Springer -Verlag. doi:10.1007/978-3-540-35488-8

Hawashin, B., Mansour, A., & Aljawarneh, S. (2013). An Efficient Feature Selection Method for Arabic Text Classification. *International Journal of Computers and Applications, 83*(17), 1–6. doi:10.5120/14666-2588

He, J., Jiang, Z., Guo, P., & Liu, L. (2011). *A Study of Block-Global Feature based Supervised Image Annotation Systems. IEEE International Conference on Man, and Cybernetics*, Anchorage, AK.

He, X.-J., Zhang, Y., Lok, T.-M., & Lyu, M. R. (2005). A New Feature of Uniformity of Image Texture Directions Coinciding with the Human Eyes Perception. Lecture Notes in Artificial Intelligence, 3614, 727–730. doi:10.1007/11540007_90

Hidayat, E., Nur, F. A., Muda, A. K., Huoy, C. Y., & Ahmad, S. (2011). A Comparative Study of Feature Extraction Using PCA and LDA for Face Recognition. *7th International Conference on Information Assurance and Security (IAS).* doi:10.1109/ISIAS.2011.6122779

Hong, Z., & Xuanbing, Z. (2010). *Texture feature extraction based on wavelet transform. International Conference on Computer Application and System Modeling (ICCASM).*

Hough, P. V. C. (1962). *Method and Means for Recognizing Complex Patterns*. U.S. Patent 3,069,654.

Hu, M. K. (1962). Visual pattern Recognition by Moment Invariants. *I.R.E. Transactions on Information Theory, 8*(2), 179–187. doi:10.1109/TIT.1962.1057692

Huang, J., Kuamr, S., & Mitra, M. (1997). *Image indexing using colour correlogram. IEEE Computer Society Conference on Computer Vision and Pattern Recognition.* doi:10.1109/CVPR.1997.609412

Huang, Y. L. (2005). A Fast Method for Textural Analysis of DCT-Based Image. *Journal of Information Science and Engineering, 21*(1), 181–194.

Hussain, A. B. S., Toussaint, G. T., & Donaldson, R. W. (1972). Results Obtained Using a Simple Character Recognition Procedure on Munson's Handprinted Data. *IEEE Transactions on Computers, C-21*(2), 201–205. doi:10.1109/TC.1972.5008927

Islam, M., Venkataraman, S., & Alazab, M. (2010). *Stochastic Model Based Approach for Biometric Identification*. Technological Developments in Networking, Education and Automation.

Islam, M. M., Zhang, D., & Lu, G. (2008). Automatic Categorization of Image Regions Using Dominant Colour Based Vector Quantization. *Proceedings of the Digital Image Computing: Techniques and Applications.*

Jain, M., & Singh, S. K. (2011). A Survey On: Content Based Image Retrieval Systems Using Clustering Techniques for Large Data sets. *International Journal of Managing Information Technology, 3*(4), 23–39. doi:10.5121/ijmit.2011.3403

Jeng, S.-H., Liao, H. Y. M., Han, C. C., Chern, M. Y., & Liu, Y. T. (1998). Facial Feature Detection Using Geometrical Face Model: An Efficient Approach. *Pattern Recognition, 31*(3), 273–282. doi:10.1016/S0031-3203(97)00048-4

Jiang, X. (2009). *Feature Extraction for Image Recognition and Computer Vision.* 2nd IEEE International Conference on Computer Science and Information Technology, Beijing.

Jin, Z., Lou, Z., Yang, J., & Sun, Q. (2007). Face Detection Using Template Matching and Skin-Color Information. ScienceDirect. *Neurocomputing, 70*(4-6), 794–800. doi:10.1016/j.neucom.2006.10.043

Jyothi, B., Latha, Y. M., Mohan, P. G. K., & Reddy, V. S. K. (2013). Medical Image Retrieval Using Moments. *International Journal of Application or Innovation in Engineering & Management, 2*(1), 195–200.

Kale, K. V., Deshmukh, P. D., Chavan, S. V., Kazi, M. M., & Rode, Y. S. (2014). Zernike Moment Feature Extraction for Handwritten Devanagari (Marathi) Compound Character Recognition. *International Journal of Advanced Research in Artificial Intelligence, 3*(1), 68–76.

Kambale, S. A., & Inamdar, V. S. (2011). Gabor Filter for Feature Extraction: A Review. *Proc. of the International Conference on Advanced Computing and Communication Technologies (ACCT 2011).*

Kaur, K., & Malhotra, S. (2013). A Survey on Edge Detection Using Different Techniques. *International Journal of Application or Innovation in Engineering & Management, 2*(4), 496–500.

Khobragade, R. N., Koli, N. A., & Makesar, M. S. (2013). A Survey on Recognition of Devnagari Script. *International Journal of Computer Applications & Information Technology, 2*(1), 22–26.

Khurana, S., & Komal. (2012). Content Based Medical Image Retrieval Using Shape Descriptors. *International Journal of Latest Research in Science and Technology, 1*(2), 115–119.

Kim, J. H., Kim, K. K., & Suen, C. Y. (2000). Hybrid Schemes of Homogeneous and Heterogeneous Classifiers for Cursive Word Recognition. *Proceedings of the 7th International Workshop on Frontiers in Handwritten Recognition.*

Koerich, A. L. (2003). *Unconstrained Handwritten Character Recognition Using Different Classification Strategies. International Workshop on Artificial Neural Networks in Pattern Recognition.*

Lee, B. (2004). A New Method for Classification of Structural Textures. *International Journal of Control, Automation, and Systems, 2*(1), 125–133.

Lee, J.-H. (2012). *Fourier-Based Shape Feature Extraction Technique for Computer-Aided B-Mode Ultrasound Diagnosis of Breast Tumor.* Engineering in Medicine and Biology Society (EMBC), Annual International Conference of the IEEE, San Diego, CA.

Lee, K. L., & Chen, L. H. (2005). An Efficient Computation Method for the Texture Browsing Descriptor of MPEG-7. *Image and Vision Computing, 23*(5), 479–489. doi:10.1016/j.imavis.2004.12.002

Lei, B. J., Hendriks, E. A., & Reinders, M. J. T. (1999). *On Feature Extraction from Images.* Technical report on "inventory properties" for MCCWS.

Li, M., & Yuan, B. (2005). 2D-LDA: A Statistical linear discriminant analysis for image matrix. *Pattern Recognition Letters*, *26*(5), 527–532. doi:10.1016/j.patrec.2004.09.007

Liposcak, Z., & Loncaric, S. (1999). A Scale-Space Approach to Face Recognition from Profiles. In *Proceedings of the 8th International Conference on Computer Analysis of Images and Patterns, Lecture Notes In Computer Science* (1689, pp. 243-250). London, UK: Springer-Verlag.

Liu, R., Lu, Y., Gong, C., & Liu, Y. (2012). Infrared Point Target Detection with Improved Template Matching. *Infrared Physics & Technology*, *55*(4), 380–387. doi:10.1016/j.infrared.2012.01.006

Liu, Y., Zhang, J., Tjondronegoro, D., & Geve, S. (2007). A Shape Ontology Framework for Bird Classification. In *Proceedings of the Ninth Conference on Digital Image Computing Techniques and Applications*. doi:10.1109/DICTA.2007.4426835

Lu, W. L., & Little, J. J. (2006). Simultaneous Tracking and Action Recognition Using the PCA-HOG Descriptor. *Proceedings of the 3rd Canadian Conference on Computer and Robot Vision.*

Lu, Y. Z., Zhou, J. L., & Yu, S. S. (2003). A survey of face detection, extraction and recognition. *Computing and Informatics*, *22*(2), 163–195.

Mahalakshmi, T., Muthaiah, R., & Swaminathan, P. (2012). Review Article: An Overview of Template Matching Technique in Image Processing. Research Journal of Applied Sciences. *Engineering and Technology*, *4*(24), 5469–5473.

Mahbub, U., Imtiaz, H., Roy, T., Rahman, S., & Ahad, A. R. (2013). Template Matching Approach of One-Shot-Learning Gesture Recognition. *Pattern Recognition Letters*, *34*(15), 1780–1788. doi:10.1016/j.patrec.2012.09.014

Maji, S., & Malik, J. (2009). Object Detection Using a Max-Margin Hough Transform. *Proceedings of IEEE Conference on Computer Vision and Pattern Recognition*. doi:10.1109/CVPR.2009.5206693

Manjunath, B. S., Ohm, J., Vasudevan, V. V., & Yamada, A. (2001). Color and Texture Descriptors. *IEEE Transactions on Circuits and Systems for Video Technology*, *11*(6), 703–715. doi:10.1109/76.927424

Manjunath, B. S., Salembier, P., & Sikora, T. (2002). *Introduction to MPEG-7: Multi- media Content Description Language*. John Wiley & Sons Ltd.

Mao, J., & Jain, A. K. (1992). Texture Classification and Segmentation using Multiresolution Simultaneous Autoregressive Models. *Pattern Recognition*, *25*(2), 173–188. doi:10.1016/0031-3203(92)90099-5

Materka, A., & Strzelecki, M. (1998). Texture Analysis Methods—A Review. Institute of Electronics, Technical University of Lodz.

Mistry, Y., & Ingole, D. T. (2013). Survey on Content Based Image Retrieval Systems. *International Journal of Innovative Research in Computer and Communication Engineering*, *1*(8), 1827–1836.

Murukesh, C., & Thanushkodi, K. (2013). An Efficient Gait Recognition System Based on PCA and Multi-Layer Perceptron. *Life Science Journal*, *10*(7), 1024–1029.

Mutelo, R. M., Khor, L. C., Woo, W. L., & Dlay, S. S. (2006). *A novel fisher discriminant for biometrics recognition: 2DPCA plus 2DFLD. IEEE International Symposium on Circuits and System*. doi:10.1109/ISCAS.2006.1693586

Nabatchian, A., Abdel-Raheem, E., & Ahmadi, M. (2008). Human Face Recognition Using Different Moment Invariants: A Comparative Study. Congress on Image and Signal Processing, Sanya.

Nixon, M. S., & Aguado, A. S. (2013). *Feature Extraction & Image Processing for Computer Vision* (3rd ed.). Elsevier Ltd.

Ohashi, G., & Shimodaira, Y. (2003). *Edge-based feature extraction method and its application to image retrieval. In Proceedings of 7th World Multi-conference on Systemics.* Cybernetics and Informatics.

Okada, R. (2009). *Discriminative Generalized Hough Transform for Object Detection. 12th International Conference on Computer Vision.*

Oliveira, L. S., Bortolozzi, F., & Suen, C. Y. (2002). Automatic Recognition of Handwritten Numerical Strings: A Recognition and Verification Strategy. *IEEE Transactions on Pattern Recognition and Machine Intelligence, 24*(11), 1438–1454. doi:10.1109/TPAMI.2002.1046154

Otsu, N. (1979). A Threshold Selection Method from Gray-Level Histograms. *IEEE Trans. SMC, 9*(1), 62–66.

Park, K.-W., Jeong, J.-W., & Lee, D.-H. (2007). Olybia: Ontology-based automatic image annotation system using semantic inference rules. *Proceedings of the 12th International Conference on Database Systems for Advanced Applications.* Bangkok, Thailand: Springer.

Pass, G., & Zabith, R. (1996). Histogram Refinement for Content Based Image Retrieval. *Proceedings 3rd IEEE Workshop on Applications of Computer Vision.* doi:10.1109/ACV.1996.572008

Prabhu, J., & Kumar, J. S. (2014). Wavelet Based Content Based Image Retrieval Using Color and Texture Feature Extraction by Gray Level Coocurence Matrix and Color Coocurence Matrix. *Journal of Computer Science, 10*(1), 15–22. doi:10.3844/jcssp.2014.15.22

Raj, Y. B., Naveen, N. K., Arun, G. K., & Vinod, R. K. (2009). Vehicular Shape-Based Objects Classification Using Fourier Descriptor Technique. *Journal of Scientific and Industrial Research, 68*(6), 484–495.

Rajashekararadhya, S. V., & Ranjan, P. V. (2008). Efficient Zone Based Feature Extraction Algorithm for Handwritten Numeral Recognition of Four Popular South Indian Scripts. *Journal of Theoretical and Applied Information Technology, 4*(12), 1171–1181.

Rao, P. B., Prasad, D. V., & Kumar, Ch. P. (2013). Feature Extraction Using Zernike Moments. [IJLTET]. *International Journal of Latest Trends in Engineering and Technology, 2*(2), 228–234.

Seddik, A. F., Hassan, R. A., & Fakhreldein, M. A. (2013). Spectral Domain Features for Ovarian Cancer Data Analysis. *Journal of Computer Science, 9*(8), 1061–1068. doi:10.3844/jcssp.2013.1061.1068

Sharma, O., & Bansal, S. K. (2013). Gait Recognition System for Human Identification Using BPNN Classifier. *International Journal of Innovative Technology and Exploring Engineering, 3*(1), 217–220.

Shenbagavalli, R., & Ramar, K. (2014). Feature Extraction of Soil Images for Retrieval based on Statistics. *International Journal of Computers and Applications, 88*(14), 8–12. doi:10.5120/15418-3822

Shrivakshan, G. T., & Chandrasekar, C. (2012). A Comparison of various Edge Detection Techniques used in Image Processing. *International Journal of Computer Science Issues, 9*(5), 269–276.

Sorwar, G., Abraham, A., & Dooley, L. S. (2001). *Texture classification based on DCT and soft computing.* The 10th IEEE International Conference on Fuzzy Systems. doi:10.1109/FUZZ.2001.1009012

Spagnolo, P., Orazio, T. D., Leo, M., & Distante, A. (2006). Moving Object Segmentation by Background Subtraction and Temporal Analysis. *Image and Vision Computing, 24*, 411-423.

Sridevi, N., & Subashini, P. (2012). Moment Based Feature Extraction for Classification of Handwritten Ancient Tamil Scripts. *International Journal of Emerging trends in Engineering and Development, 7*(2), 106-115.

Srinivasan, G. N., & Shobha, G. (2008). Statistical Texture Analysis. Proceedings of World Academy of Science. *Engineering and Technology, 36*, 1264–1269.

Sthitpattanapongsa, P., & Srinark, T. (2011). A Two-Stage Otsu's Thresholding Based Method on a 2D Histogram. In *Proceedings of the 7th IEEE International Conference on Intelligent Computer Communication and Processing* (pp. 345-348). doi:10.1109/ICCP.2011.6047894

Stricker, M., & Orengo, M. (1995). Similarity of Color Images. *Proc. of the SPIE Conf., 2420*, 381–392. doi:10.1117/12.205308

Suen, C. Y., Berthod, M., & Mori, S. (1980). Automatic Recognition of Hand Printed Characters- the State of the Art. *Proceedings of the IEEE, 68*(4), 469–487. doi:10.1109/PROC.1980.11675

Sumana, I. J., Islam, M. M., Zhang, D. S., & Lu, G. (2008). Content Based Image Retrieval Using Curvelet Transform. In *Proceedings of IEEE International Workshop on Multimedia Signal Processing (MMSP08).* doi:10.1109/MMSP.2008.4665041

Tamura, H., Mori, S., & Yamawaki, T. (1978). Texture Features Corresponding to Visual Perception. *IEEE Transactions on Systems, Man, and Cybernetics, 8*(6), 460–473. doi:10.1109/TSMC.1978.4309999

Teague, M. R. (1980). Image analysis via the general theory of moments. *Journal of the Optical Society of America, 70*(8), 920–930. doi:10.1364/JOSA.70.000920

The, C. -H., & Chin, R. T. (1988). On Image Analysis by the Methods of Moments. *IEEE Transactions on Pattern Analysis Machine Intelligent, 10*(4), 496-513.

Theodoridis, S., & Koutroumbas, K. (2009). *Pattern Recognition* (4th ed.). Singapore: Elsevier.

Tian, D. P. (2013). A Review on Image Feature Extraction and Representation Techniques. *International Journal of Multimedia and Ubiquitous Engineering, 8*(4), 385–395.

Ukinkar, V. G., & Makrand. (2012). Object Detection in Dynamic Background Using Image Segmentation: A review. *International Journal of Engineering Research and Applications, 2*(3), 232–236.

Ursani, A. A., Kpalma, K., Ronsin, J., Memon, A. A., & Chowdhry, B. S. (2009). Improved Texture Description with Features Based on Fourier Transform. Wireless Networks. *Information Processing and Systems Communications in Computer and Information Science, 20*, 19–28. doi:10.1007/978-3-540-89853-5_5

Vamvakas, G., Gatos, B., & Perantonis, S. J. (2009). *A Novel Feature Extraction and Classification Methodology for the Recognition of Historical Documents. 10th International Conference on Document Analysis and Recognition.* doi:10.1109/ICDAR.2009.223

Verma, R., & Ali, J. (2012). A-Survey of Feature Extraction and Classification Techniques in OCR Systems. *International Journal of Computer Applications & Information Technology, 1*(3), 1–3.

Wang, X., Ding, X., & Liu, C. (2005). Gabor Filters-Based Feature Extraction for Character Recognition. *Pattern Recognition Letters*, *38*(3), 369–379. doi:10.1016/j.patcog.2004.08.004

Wang, Z., & Hong, K. (2012). A Novel Approach for Trademark Image Retrieval by Combining Global Features and Local Features. *Journal of Computer Information Systems*, *8*(4), 1633–1640.

Wong, K.-W., Lam, K.-M., & Siu, W.-C. (2001). An Efficient Algorithm for Human Face Detection and Facial Feature Extraction under Different Conditions. *Pattern Recognition*, *34*(10), 1993–2004. doi:10.1016/S0031-3203(00)00134-5

Yang, J., Zhang, D., Frangi, A. F., & Yang, J.-Y. (2004). Two-dimensional PCA: A new approach to appearance-based face representation and recognition. IEEE Tanns. *PAMI*, *26*(1), 131–137. doi:10.1109/TPAMI.2004.1261097

Yang, M., Kpalm, K., & Ronsin, J. (2008). A Survey of Shape Feature Extraction Techniques. *Pattern Recognition*, 43–90.

Yasmin, M., Sharif, M., & Mohsin, S. (2013). Use of Low Level Features for Content Based Image Retrieval: Survey. *Research Journal of Recent Sciences*, *2*(11), 65–75.

Yu, G., Lin, Y. Z., & Kamarthi, S. (2010). Wavelets-Based Feature Extraction for Texture Classification. *Advanced Materials Research*, *97*(101), 1273–1276. doi:10.4028/www.scientific.net/AMR.97-101.1273

Yun, F., & Runsheng, W. (2002). An Image Retrieval Method Using DCT Features. *Journal of Computer Science and Technology*, *17*(6), 865–873. doi:10.1007/BF02960778

Zainudin, M. N. S., Radi, H. R., Abdullah, S. M., Abd Rahim, R., Ismail, M. M., Idris, M. I., Sulaiman, H. A., & Jaafar, A. (2012). Face Recognition using Principle Component Analysis (PCA) and Linear Discriminant Analysis (LDA). *International Journal of Electrical & Computer Sciences, 12*(5), 50-55.

Zhang, D., & Lu, G. (2004). Review of Shape Representation and Description Techniques. *Pattern Recognition*, *37*(1), 1–19. doi:10.1016/j.patcog.2003.07.008

Zhang, D., Wong, A., Indrawan, M., & Lu, G. (2000). Content-Based Image Retrieval Using Gabor Texture Features. *Proceedings of the First IEEE Pacific- Rim Conference on Multimedia.*

Zhang, D. S., Islam, M., & Lu, G. J. (2012). A review on automatic image annotation techniques. *Pattern Recognition*, *45*(1), 346–362. doi:10.1016/j.patcog.2011.05.013

Zhang, G. (2008). *Shape Feature Extraction Using Fourier Descriptors with Brightness in Content-Based Medical Image Retrieval. International Conference on Intelligent Information Hiding and Multimedia Signal Processing.* doi:10.1109/IIH-MSP.2008.16

Zhang, J., & Tan, T. (2002). Brief Review of Invariant Texture Analysis Methods. *Pattern Recognition*, *35*(3), 735–747. doi:10.1016/S0031-3203(01)00074-7

Zhang, L., Xu, Y., & Wu, C. (2011). Features Extraction for Structured Light Stripe Image Based On OTSU Threshold. *Fourth International Symposium on Knowledge Acquisition and Modeling.* doi:10.1109/KAM.2011.32

Zhou, F., Feng, J.-F., & Shi, Q.-Y. (2001). Texture Feature Based on Local Fourier Transform. *IEEE Transactions on Image Processing*, *2*, 610–613.

Zhu, Q., Xu, Y., Lu, Y., Wen, J., Fan, Z., & Li, Z. (2014). Novel Matrix Based Feature Extraction Method for Face Recognition Using Gabor face Features. *Genetic and Evolutionary Computing Advances in Intelligent Systems and Computing*, *238*, 349–357. doi:10.1007/978-3-319-01796-9_38

Zulkifli, Z., Iskandar, S., Saad, P., Skudai, & Mohtar, I. A. (2011). *Plant Leaf Identification using Moment Invariants & General Regression Neural Network*. 11th International Conference on Hybrid Intelligent Systems (HIS), Melacca. doi:10.1109/HIS.2011.6122144

KEY TERMS AND DEFINITIONS

Domain-Specific Features: Application dependent features such as human faces, fingerprints, character recognition and conceptual features.

Feature: A function of the basic measurement variables or attributes that specifies some quantifiable property of an object and is useful for classification and/or pattern recognition.

Feature Extraction: The process to represent raw image in a reduced form to facilitate decision making such as pattern detection, classification or recognition.

General Features: Application independent features such as color, texture, and shape.

Global Features: Features that are calculated over the entire image or just regular sub-area of an image.

High-Level Features: Features that concern with finding shapes and objects in computer images and it is based on low level features.

LDA: Fisher's linear discriminant analysis, also known as Fisher Discriminant Analysis.

Local Features: Features computed over a subdivision of the image bands that are resulted from image segmentation or edge detection.

Low-Level Features: The fundamental features that can be extracted directly from an image without any object description.

PCA: Principal component analysis.

Pixel-Level Features: Features calculated at each pixel (e.g. color, location, etc.).

Section 3
Bio Imaging and Applications

Chapter 14
Metal Artifact Reduction:
A Problem of Tremendous Importance in Medical Imaging

Shrinivas D. Desai
B. V. B. College of Engineering and Technology, India

Linganagouda Kulkarni
Vivekanand Institute of Technology, India

ABSTRACT

Metallic implants are known to generate bright and dark streaking artifacts in x-ray computed tomography (CT) images. These artifacts cause loss of information, reduces the resolution, forms noise which hinders diagnostic capability. The reduction of metal artifact is of immense importance in the present scenario. We propose seeded watershed segmentation-interpolation based sinogram correction method to reduce the metal artifacts caused by metallic implants. We tend to find projection bins affected by the metallic objects in the raw projection data and to replace the corrupted values by appropriate estimates. The novelty of proposed method lies in segmentation of metal part from the CT image by seeded watershed segmentation method, using IlastiK tool. Proposed method is experimented using dataset pertaining to different clinical cases. Solution is studied for correctness by quantitatively as well as qualitatively. The result presents significant improvement in artifact reduction aiding to better diagnostic ability.

1. INTRODUCTION

The science of medical imaging owes much of its existence to the discovery of X-rays by W C Roentgen over 120 years ago in 1895. It was the development of practical computed tomography (CT) scanners in the early 1970s by G Hounsfield in 1973 and others that brought computers into medical imaging and clinical practice. G Hounsfield shared the Nobel Prize in 1972, along with Allan Cormack who independently discovered some of the reconstruction algorithms. His invention showed that it is possible to compute high-quality cross-sectional images with greater accuracy when the projection data is acquired and complete in all aspect. However the solution to the problem of how to reconstruct a function from its projection data is based on the proposal by Radon in 1917. The

DOI: 10.4018/978-1-4666-8654-0.ch014

problem of image reconstruction from projection data is an inverse problem with many solutions.

The problem of image reconstruction from projections has repeatedly arisen over last 5 decades in various applications of scientific, technical and medical fields. Scientific applications are Cryo Electron Crystallography (Reconstruction of molecular structure by using data from electron microscopes), Radio astronomy (Maps of radio emission of celestial objects), Astronomy (X-ray structure of supernova remnants and reconstructing electron-density distribution in the solar corona), Seismic Tomography (Slice of the earth using seismic data) and Volcanology (Three-dimensional (3D) volumes from tomographic images of active, explosive volcanoes) etc. Technical applications includes Non-Destructive Testing such as industrial radiography or industrial CT scanning, to indicate presence of cracks in the radiograph, passage of sound through the weld and back, or indicate a clear surface without penetrant captured in cracks. Diamond packaging and construction, Micro CT for non-invasive imaging of wood anatomy, scanning of baggage for potential threat items in aviation security settings

Medical applications of image reconstruction is tremendous, CT is one application which has revolutionized medical imaging. Image reconstruction from projections is also used in nuclear medicine to map the distribution of concentration of gamma ray emitting radionuclide in a given cross section of human body. Another prominent application of image reconstruction from projections is Magnetic resonance imaging (MRI); a technique used to investigate the anatomy and physiology of the body without exposure to ionizing radiation. Positron emission tomography (PET) and single-photon emission computed tomography (SPECT, a nuclear medicine imaging technique to produces a three-dimensional image of functional processes in the body. Data set collected in PET is much poorer than CT, so reconstruction techniques are more difficult. Image reconstruction is applicable even for Small animal imaging. Of all the applications,

probably the greatest effect in the world at large has been in the area of diagnostic medicine; CT has revolutionized radiology.

Basically the CT works on the principle of X-Ray imaging. The output intensity that is measured after an X-ray beam passed through an object depends on the material distribution of the object along the ray. Consequently, the complete illumination of an object by an X-ray beam yields a 2D intensity image in which the contrast is induced by the varying structures and attenuation properties in the object. Such an intensity image, which basically represents a projection of a 3D object onto a 2D plane, is an X-ray photo as presented in Figure 1.

One limitation of X-ray photos is that they do not provide depth information, since the measured intensity of the beam that traversed the object is independent of the material order along the ray. However, when X-ray projections of the object are acquired at many different orientations, a complete 3D attenuation map of the object can be reconstructed. This technique, called Tomographic imaging, is widely used as a medical diagnostic tool, but has also various industrial applications.

X-ray transmission CT is a non-destructive imaging technique providing 3D structural information of an object under examination. The desired 3D image is computed from a set of X-ray projections of the object, which are recorded by the X-ray CT scanner at different orientations as shown in Figure 2.

CT has many important applications such as medical diagnostics and small animal imaging, which supports pre-clinical drug testing. Other applications are found in the industry (diamond, packaging, construction), where CT scanners are employed for nondestructive testing. Figure 3 presents a typical setup of a clinical CT scanner: a source-detector pair rotates around a patient that is lying on a bed.

Several scanning geometries can be considered such as parallel beam, fan beam and cone beam geometry as presented in Figure. 4 (a) and (b).

Figure 1. Conventional X–ray (a) Acquisition set up (b) an example of chest study

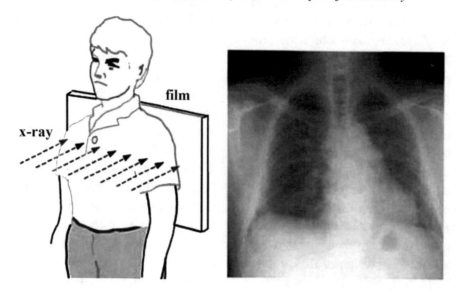

Figure 2. CT Acquisition set up

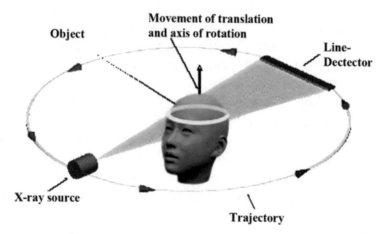

Figure 3. Conventional CT set up

Figure 4. CT scanning geometry (a) parallel beam (b) fan beam

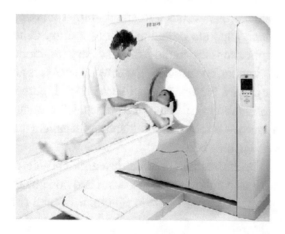

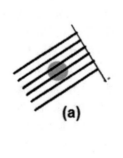 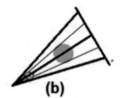

Parallel and fan-beam geometry were typically used in early generations of commercial X-ray CT systems. Both geometries record the attenuation data slice-by slice. In a parallel beam geometry, the X-rays travel along parallel paths. In fan beam geometry, characterized by opening angle 2, the X-rays are emitted from a single focal point for each projection. Opposed to parallel and fan beam, cone beam CT or multislice CT as presented in Figure 5, is essentially three dimensional.

X-ray point source, emitting a cone beam, illuminates the entire object or a stack of slices at each orientation, which results in 2D projections on the detector. Note that the signal on the detector line for z = 0 corresponds to a fan beam geometry. The corresponding illuminated object slice is referred to as the central slice. Although the majority of current X-ray tomography systems uses a cone beam geometry, research for fan and parallel beam remains highly relevant since the standard 3D reconstruction algorithms basically perform a set of weighted 2D reconstructions along tilted planes.

Figure 5. 3D cone beam tomography

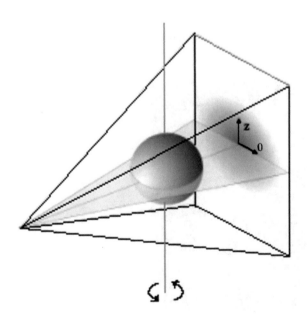

As aforementioned, reconstruction of image from projection is an analytical reconstruction method and is basic working principle of computed tomography. The foundation of analytical reconstruction methods is the *Radon transform*, which relates a 2D function f(x, y) to the collection of *line integrals* of that function. The Radon transform shall be presented as

$$p\left(r,\theta\right) = \int\limits_{-\infty}^{\infty}\int f\left(x,y\right)\delta\left(x\cos\theta + y\sin\theta - r\right)dx\,dy \tag{1}$$

where θ is the angle of the line, and r is the perpendicular offset of the line. The radon transform computes the line integrals from multiple sources along parallel paths, or beams, in a certain direction and computes *projections* of an image matrix and presents as sinogram.

The *2D image reconstruction problem* is to recover f(x, y) from its projections $p(r,\theta)$. This is achieved by inverse Radon transform. Basically it works by subsequently "smearing" the acquired $p(r, \theta)$ across a film plate. This is simple back projection

$$b\left(x,y\right) = B\left\{p\left(r,\theta\right)\right\} = \int\limits_{0}^{\pi}p\left(x\cos\theta + y\sin\theta,\theta\right)d\theta \tag{2}$$

1.1. Problem with CT Images

Although images produced by CT are generally faithful representations of the scanned volume, the technique is susceptible to a number of artifacts. In CT, the term *artifact* is applied to any systematic discrepancy between the CT numbers in the reconstructed image and the true attenuation coefficients of the object. CT images are inherently more prone to artifacts than conventional radiographs because the image is reconstructed from something on the order of a million independent detector measurements. The reconstruction technique assumes that all these measurements are consistent, so any error of measurement will usually reflect itself as an error in the reconstructed image. Artifacts can seriously degrade the quality of CT images, sometimes to the point of making them diagnostically unusable.

CT artifacts originate from a range of sources. Physics-based artifacts result from the physical processes involved in the acquisition of CT data. Patient-based artifacts are caused by such factors as patient movement or the presence of metallic materials in or on the patient. Scanner-based artifacts result from imperfections in scanner function. Helical and multisection technique artifacts are produced by the image reconstruction process. Design features incorporated into modern CT scanners minimize some types of artifacts, and some can be partially corrected by the scanner software. However, in many instances, careful patient positioning and optimum selection of scanning parameters are the most important factors in avoiding CT artifacts. Different types of artifact that can occur, are as follows: *(a)* streaking, which is generally due to an inconsistency in a single measurement; *(b)* shading, which is due to a group of channels or views deviating gradually from the true measurement; *(c)* rings, which are due to errors in an individual detector calibration; and *(d)* distortion, which is due to helical reconstruction.

In patient based artifact one common problem is streak artifacts caused by the presence of high-attenuation objects in the field of view of scanner device. Streak artifacts arising from metal implants such as dental fillings, surgical clips, coils, wires, and orthopedic hardware may obscure important diagnostic information in CT. Metal streak artifacts occur because filtered back projection (FBP) assumes that each detector measurement is equally accurate (Kak AC *et al.,* 1988).

In reality, rays that pass through or near metal implants are highly attenuated and have a much larger error due to a combination of scatter, beam-hardening effects, noise from low photon counts (i.e., photon starvation), edge effects, and Patient motion (De Man B *et al.,* 1999). Scattered photons and tube current (Background signal from the detector when no photons are detected) increase the detector signal (Joseph PM *et al.,* 1982), resulting in dark streaks between metal implants as shown in Figure 6.

Figure 6. Bilateral hip replacements (with streaks obscuring perirectal lymphadenopathy from rectal cancer)

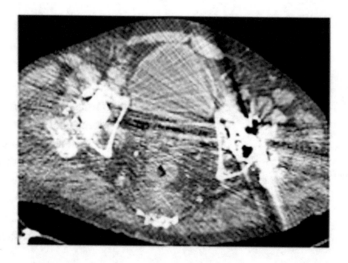

Beam hardening effects are seen in CT images acquired with polychromatic x-ray sources. As the x-ray passes through metal, low-energy x-ray photons are absorbed first, and the remaining high energy photons are not attenuated as easily. These "extra" photons also result in dark streaks between metal structures

Now the problem of reconstruction from projection differs from earlier. The beam hardening, photon starvation are primary reason for occurrence of these streaking artifacts. This not only degrades the image quality but also hinders the diagnostic capability. Now we shall consider the original object to be reconstructed as

$$f(x,y) = \mu_b(t,s) + \mu_m(t,s) \qquad (3)$$

Figure 7 present Projection of an object f(x, y) containing a circular metal insert by a single ray at a projection angle θ. Several strategies to reduce the severity of artifacts in CT images have been proposed. Photon counting noise can be reduced by increasing the tube current, but this increases the patient's exposure to radiation. A beam-hardening correction can be applied iteratively

Figure 7. Projection of an object f(x, y) containing a circular metal insert by a single ray at a projection angle θ

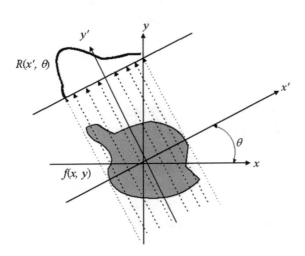

on the basis of the current reconstructed image (Hsieh J *et al.,* 2000).

2. EXISTING MAR METHODS

During the past three decades, various approaches have been proposed for elimination or at least reduction of the undesirable effects caused by metallic implants on CT images (Abdoli *et al.,* 2012). These approaches are generally referred to as metal artifact reduction (MAR) techniques. There have been a few attempts to suppress these artifacts without the use of algorithmic mathematical MAR approaches. These approaches are referred to as implicit methods. The majority of the proposed approaches however are based on various mathematical algorithms. They are referred as explicit MAR methods.

2.1. Implicit Method

It is difficult for any proposal to be appreciated in research community, without mathematical background. Yet implicit methods are proposed by some researchers to address issues of metal artifact reduction. Research experiments were carried out to investigate the influence of using an extended CT scale on radiotherapy treatment planning of patients with metallic hip implants (Coolens *et al.,* 2003). Scaling down the CT numbers, which expands the CT scale, enables the user to distinguish between the metallic object and surrounding tissues and also between high-density and low-density prostheses, thus allowing the accurate derivation of metallic object's electron density. However, this method does not deal with streaking artifacts caused by the implants owing to the simplicity of the approach which assumes that the implants are surrounded by soft tissues whose effective atomic numbers are close to water.

It was reported that applying a higher tube voltage (100–120 kVp) is more effective for reducing the streak artifacts in the reconstructed CT images than increasing the tube current defined in terms of effective mAs (S. G. Moon *et al.*, 2008). The use of dual-energy CT for MAR has also been considered. This approach allows the extrapolation of beam hardening to obtain an image similar to the assumed image which would be acquired by a monoenergetic beam with high energy quanta (F. Bamberg *et al.*, 2011).

Implicit methods might have contributed with significant result in some specific cases, however design of more generic approaches are necessary to address different types of metal artifacts commonly produced by standard procedure used in clinical CT scanners

2.2. Explicit Methods

Explicit MAR methods are most widely experimented and have been the main focus of research groups during the past few decades. Various techniques have been proposed in this category which can be classified in different ways. The majority of techniques operate on the projection data i.e. in the sinogram domain. Some techniques incorporated the correction within an iterative reconstruction algorithm. Some of the methods are reported to handle the artifacts in the image domain. To have better clarity of these methods, they are classified into five categories based on their working principle. Five categories are; interpolation based sinogram correction, non-interpolation based sinogram correction, hybrid sinogram correction, iterative image reconstruction, and image-based approaches.

2.2.1. Interpolation Based Sinogram Correction

From the literatures it is observed that majority of research work belong to this category. Several research groups followed almost the same procedure and experimented with various interpolation techniques to improve the efficiency of the algorithm. The main agenda is to find affected

projection bins corrupted by the metallic objects in the projection data and to replace the corrupted values by appropriate estimates (W. J. H. Veldkamp *et al.*, 2010; Koehler *et al.*, 2011). Some research works are reported to work by manipulating raw projection data stored in proprietary format. Whereas majority of researchers have worked on projection data generated analytically.

Two approaches have been explored for the detection of affected bins. The first approach identifies the affected bins directly in the sinogram domain. In this approach, the affected bins are distinguished because their intensities are higher than the other bins owing to the higher attenuation of metallic objects. These are referred to as sinogram based projection completion methods.

One challenge in this approach could be a situation when CT number of unaffected bony area in artifact affected image is same as that of metal implant CT number. This eventually leads to same pixel value in sinogram too, making this approach less effective. The second approach segments the metallic objects from the image using various thresholding methods and forward project the binary image to obtain the position of the affected projection bins. This method is referred as Image domain projection completion method.

In this approach many researchers have experimented by applying various segmentation and interpolation technique. Figure 8 represent the block diagram for this approach. Both approaches (sinogram based and image based) projection completion methods are fast and straight forward, however both of these techniques are reported to cause extra artifacts.

2.2.2. Normalized Metal Artifact Reduction (NMAR)

Some researchers designed better methods to address the issue of extra artifacts generated through projection completion methods. They are called as normalized metal artifact reduction methods and is shown in Figure 9. Here metal is segmented in

Figure 8. System model of Interpolation based sinogram correction

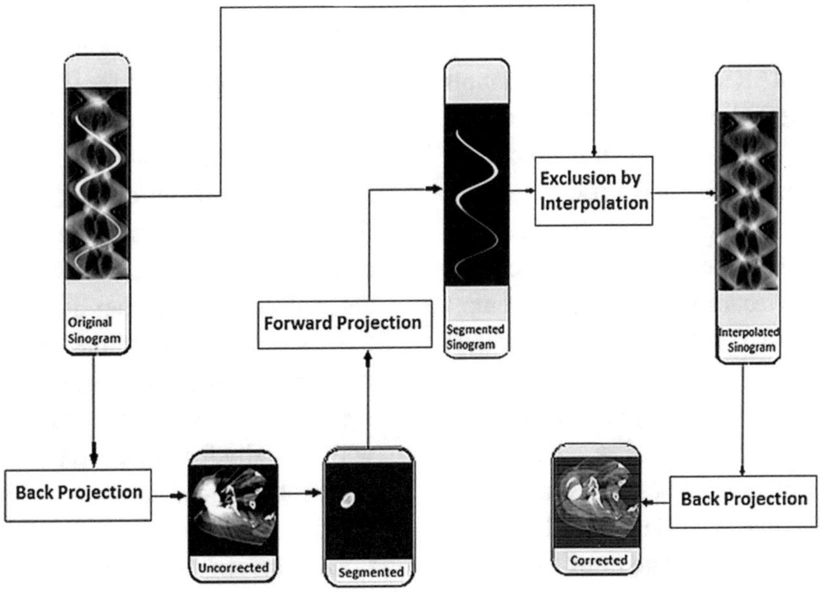

the image domain by various thresholding methods like multilevel, mean shift etc. A three dimensional forward projection localizes the metal trace in the original projections. Before applying interpolation, the projections are normalized based on a three dimensional forward projection of a prior image. The original raw projection data are divided by the projection data of the prior image and, after interpolation subjected to de-normalization pro-cess (E. Meyer *et al.*, 2010; Lell *et al.*, 2012; M. M. Lell *et al.*, 2013; Meyer *et al.*, 2011). NMAR clearly outperforms the other methods for both moderate and severe artifacts. Computationally efficient and inexpensive compared to iterative methods, NMAR can be used as an additional step in any conventional sinogram interpolation-based MAR method.

Figure 9. System model of normalized metal artifact reduction

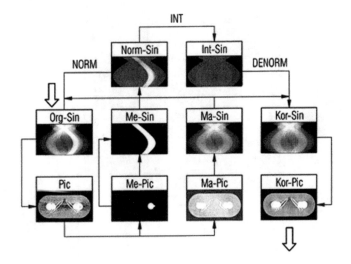

2.2.3. Non-Interpolation Based Sinogram Correction

Aforementioned MAR techniques which attempts to correct the affected projection bins in the sinogram or image domain using an interpolation method, other approaches make use of supplementary correction strategies in the sinogram domain. These are called as non-interpolation based sinogram correction method, which attempts to correct the affected projection bins rather than interpreting them.

Raeside *et al.,* 1981 developed a MAR technique whose performance was assessed using Monte Carlo simulation studies. In this approach, the projection bins intersecting the metallic objects are determined on the simulated raw data and a nearest-neighbour pattern recognition approach is utilized to modify the values of the affected projections. Liu *et al.,* 2003 detected the affected projections in the sinogram space in two steps. Usually correction is complex, and depends on detection of affected projection bins. The success of non-interpolation based sinogram approach depends mainly on detection of affected artifacts, which is usually a prediction.

2.2.4. Iterative Image Reconstruction

Currently CT developers use filtered backprojection (FBP) algorithms for CT image reconstruction. However, some developers have attempted to alleviate the incomplete projection data problem using either the exterior Radon transform or iterative reconstruction approaches. The reconstruction of image from projections can be considered a particular case where the objective is to determine the "best" estimate of the image based on the measured projections. Study shows that iterative reconstruction algorithm performs better even with partially incomplete data.

Iterative reconstruction techniques shall be classified as two main groups: algebraic and statistical techniques. Instances of the first group are the algebraic reconstruction technique (ART) and the simultaneous iterative reconstruction technique (SIRT). The best known example of the second group is the maximum likelihood-expectation maximization (ML-EM) algorithm. Figure 10 represents the block diagram for this approach. In iterative MAR methods raw data are not manipulated, and no extra artifact is introduced. However one major drawback is high computational time requirement and the subsequent high costs.

Figure 10. System model of Iterative reconstruction

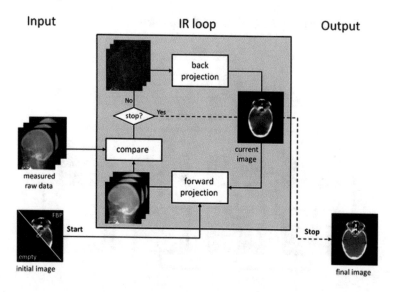

De Man *et al.*, 2000 applied a statistical iterative reconstruction algorithm, referred to as the transmission maximum likelihood (ML-TR) technique. The algorithm uses the Markov random field smoothness prior and reconstructs the images at double resolution to provide sharp edges and better handling of other sources of errors, such as beam hardening and partial volume effect (E. U. Mumcuoglu *et al.*, 1996). After the last iteration the image is down-sampled to its normal resolution. The ML-TR algorithm optimizes the likelihood under the assumption that the detector readouts have a Poisson distribution. Therefore, less weight is assigned to low-count readouts (J. Nuyts *et al.*, 1998).

2.3. Hybrid Sinogram Correction

Integrating different approaches to yield a better performance by choosing suitable tools of each algorithm is quite common and effective method in various fields. In the context of MAR methods, several approaches have been proposed, in which a integration of interpolation based sinogram correction, non-interpolation based sinogram correction, and iterative image reconstruction techniques are used. In this section, we present hybrid MAR methods according to the following integration: (1) integration of interpolation based and non-interpolation based sinogram correction approaches, (2) integration of interpolation based sinogram correction and iterative reconstruction, and (3) integration of non-interpolation based sinogram correction and iterative reconstruction.

2.4. Image-Based Approaches

As mentioned earlier, the majority of proposed MAR approaches estimates the corrupted raw data to ease streaking artifacts visible on CT images. However, some techniques deal with the problem in the image domain. In this category of MAR

methods the projection data are not manipulated. The affected pixels are replaced, usually by a constant value in the image domain.

To summarise the main characteristics and limitations of different MAR methods, belonging to these categories and associated subcategories, are presented in Table 1.

Explicit MAR methods are at the forefront and have been the main focus of research groups during the past three decades. Various approaches have been proposed which can be classified in different ways. The majority of techniques operate on the raw CT projection data or in the sinogram domain. Other techniques incorporated the correction within an iterative reconstruction algorithm.

3. PROPOSED METHODOLOGY

The main idea is to find projection bins affected by the metallic objects in the raw projection data and to replace the corrupted values by appropriate estimates. The proposed approach segments the metallic objects from the image and forward project the binary image to obtain the position of the affected projection bins. The main contribution from our proposal is incorporation of a seeded watershed algorithm for the segmentation of metallic object. The following Figure 11 shows the proposed methodology.

3.1. Seeded Watershed Based Segmentation

The seeded watershed algorithm is an image segmentation algorithm for interactive object carving from image data (Ruparelia *et al.*, 2012), where instead of working on an image itself, the technique is often applied on its gradient image. Here we look for three types of points; Points belonging to a regional minimum, Catchment basin / watershed of a regional minimum (Points at which a drop of

Table 1. Review of reported metal artifact reduction methods

Category	Characteristics	Limitations
Implicit Methods		
Implicit methods	Manipulation of the parameters prior to scanning procedure	Limited applicability
Explicit Methods		
Interpolation-based sinogram correction	Fast and straightforward	Might cause extra artifacts
Non-interpolation-based sinogram correction	Various approaches to replace the effected projection bins	The influence on the attenuation corrected PET data has not been investigated
Iterative image reconstruction	The raw data are not manipulated. No extra artifact is introduced	High computational time and the subsequent high costs
Hybrid Sinogram Correction		
Interpolation & non-interpolation-based sinogram correction	Compensate for one single method's shortcomings	The limitations are case dependent
Interpolation-based sinogram correction & iterative reconstruction	Improve the quality of the corrected CT image compared to the methods which use FBP reconstruction	The inherent limitations of iterative approaches are still present; the quantitative impact has not been assessed
Non-interpolation-based sinogram Correction & iterative reconstruction	Improve the quality of the corrected CT image compared to FBP reconstruction method	The inherent limitations of iterative approaches are still present; the quantitative impact has not been assessed
Image-Based Approaches		
Image-based approaches	The raw data are not manipulated. The affected pixels are replaced, usually by a constant value	Challenging task of differentiation between the metallic objects, artifactual regions and the surrounding tissues; do not account for underestimations

Figure 11. Proposed Seeded watershed segmentation based MAR

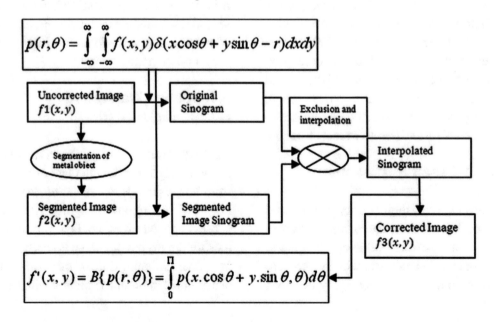

water will certainly fall to a single minimum) and Divide lines / Watershed lines (Points at which a drop of water will be equally likely to fall to more than one minimum and crest lines on the topographic surface). This technique is to identify all the third type of points for segmentation. The basic steps involved in segmentation process shall be summarized as piercing holes in each regional minimum of I, later the 3D topography is flooded from below gradually, and followed by building the dam to prevent the merging, when the rising water in distinct catchment basins is about to merge. The dam boundaries correspond to the watershed lines to be extracted by a watershed segmentation algorithm. Eventually only constructed dams can be seen from above. The algorithmic representation of watershed segmentation shall be presented a shown as follows.

3.2. Ilastik Software Tool

The Ilastik -0.5.12 do provide user to spot object markers for the various side of an object. From these markers an initial segmentation is calculated that can be refined interactively (Sommer C *et al.,* 2011). The seeded watershed relies on discernible object boundaries in the image data and not on inner appearance of an object like for example the classification workflow as shown in Figure 12. While the Classification module is useful for segmenting objects with discernible brightness, color or textural differences in comparison to their surroundings, the carving module's purpose is to aid in the extraction of objects from images that are only separable by their boundary - i.e. objects that do not differ from the rest of the image by their internal appearance. The algorithm is applicable for a wide range of segmentation problems that fulfill these properties. In the case of data where the boundaries are not clearly visible or in the case of very noisy data, a boundary detection filter can be applied to improve results.

After the necessary preprocessing, two different types of seeds exist, Foreground seeds and Background seeds - per default the background seed receives a higher priority such that the background seed is preferred in the case of ambiguous boundaries. After marking the objects of interest with a foreground seed and the outside with a background seed the button SEGMENT can be clicked to obtain a seeded watershed segmentation starting from the seeds. The intermediate steps observed during seed watershed segmentation method in Ilastik tool is presented in Figure 13.

3.3 Experimental Set Up

Experiment is carried out by writing matlab programs in MATLAB R2009a (The MathWorks Inc., Natick, Massachusetts, USA), version 7.8.0 and executed on Intel© coreTM i5-2410M processor 2.30 GHz, RAM. The MATLAB functions 'tic' and 'toc' are used to get the precise time required to complete the algorithm.

Figure 12. Segmentation process in Ilastik Software

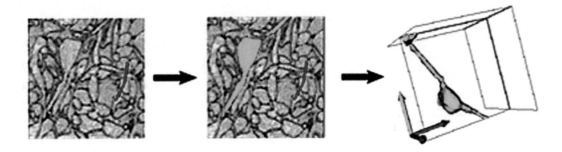

Figure 13. Seeded watershed segmentation by Ilastik software with a) two levels b) three levels c) four levels and d) five levels

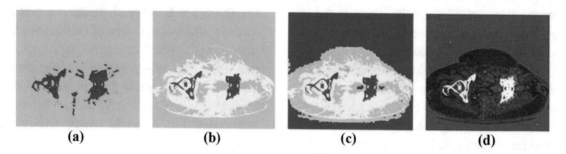

(a)　　　　　(b)　　　　　(c)　　　　　(d)

3.3.1. Dataset

The CT images affected by metal artifact are collected from local diagnostic centre. Scanning is done on a 64-slice CT scanner (GE, Lightspeed VCT 64 slice). The helical pitch and rotation time varied dependent on patient size and examination type. Scan parameters were: tube voltage: 120 kVp, tube current–time: 72mAs, collimation: 2010 mm; pitch: 0.78; gantry rotation time: 0.5 s. All data collected for experimentation is by informed consent from patient. Clinical cases having hip prosthesis, dental filling, embolization coils and cholecystectomy clips were collected. The Table 2 presents the most affected slice in the dataset for different clinical cases. The Figure 14 presents the artifact affected slices (highlighted by

yellow color), and one considered for experiment (highlighted by red color) from partial dataset of patient having hip prosthesis. Figure 15 presents the dataset of Patient ID 1, Slice No 169 to 200 are artifact affected slices. Slice No 169 is considered as most affected slice.

3.3.2. Performance Evaluation

Quantitative performance analysis is performed by computing the Normalised Root Mean Squared Error (NRMSE) of the difference between the FBP reconstructed image without metal inserts and the MAR-corrected images.

$$NRMSE = \sqrt{\frac{\sum_{j=1}^{\tilde{N}}\left(f_j - f_j^{ref}\right)^2}{\sum_{j=1}^{\tilde{N}}\left(f_j^{ref} - \mu\right)^2}} \qquad (4)$$

where f_j is the corrected image; f_j^{ref} is the reference image; μ is the mean of all the reference image intensities and $\tilde{N}$ is the (reduced) number of pixels in the image (as the regions corresponding to the metal inserts are not considered). A large difference (between f_j and f_j^{ref}) in a few pixels results in a high NRMSE. An NRMSE value of 1 would correspond to a uniformly-dense corrected image with an intensity value equal to μ.

Table 2. Performance evaluation by NRMSE and Computation time

Clinical Case	NRMSE	Computation Time (in seconds)
F-36, Left hip prosthesis	36.33	80.24
M-75, Embolization coil	24.19	76.18
M-28, Dental filling	20.86	86.158
F-50, Cholecystectomy clip	17.01	82.45
M-32, Dental filling	21.08	83.94
F-68, Embolization coils	24.84	85.66
Average	**24.05**	**82.438**

Figure 14. Input dataset under study to experiment with proposed MAR method

Patient ID	Most affected slice (Axial view)	Domain
Female 36 years Left hip prosthesis	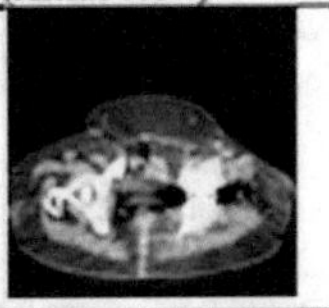	Hip Prosthesis
Male 75 years Pipeline Embolization Device for intracranial aneurysms	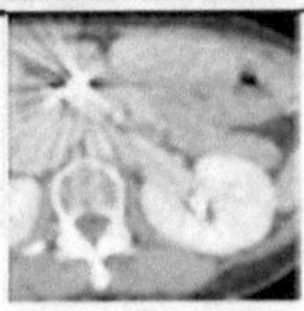	Embolization coils
Male 28 years Dental filling material = amulgum		Dental filling
Female 50 years 1 clip CT abdomen	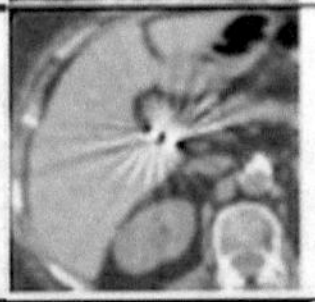	Cholecystectomy clips
Male 32 years Dental filling material = Nickel - chrome	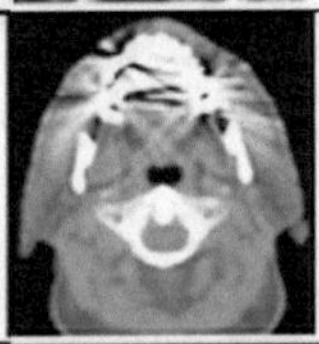	Dental filling
Female 68 years Embolization coils For intracranial aneurysms	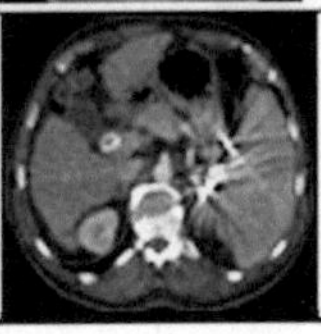	Embolization coils

Qualitative analysis is carried out by consulting two radiologists and one orthopedician evaluating all the cases. For each case, the original affected image and corrected image were displayed side by side. The radiologists were allowed to browse through each image series and zoom in and out. They ranked the overall image quality using a 5-point score: 0 = totally obscured, no structures identifiable; 1 = marked artifacts, questionable recognition; 2 = faint anatomic recognition; 3 = anatomic recognition with low confidence; 4 = anatomic recognition with medium confidence; and 5 = anatomic recognition with high confidence in a potential diagnosis. The images were evaluated and the final ranking was obtained by consensus.

4. RESULTS AND DISCUSSION

The slice with most affected by artifact is considered as primary input, it is subjected to forward projection and its sinogram is kept apart. Later we use Ilastik tool and mark different regions over most affected slice, followed by running seeded watershed segmentation. This yields metal part segmented from the original image. This part is applied to forward projection and its sinogram is mutually excluded from prior original sinogram. The result is sinogram representing the affected projection bins. These locations are treated as missing or incomplete data and then we proceed for interpolation. Different interpolation techniques

Figure 15. Dataset of Patient ID 1, Slice No 169 to 200 are artifact affected slices. Slice No 169 is considered as most affected slice

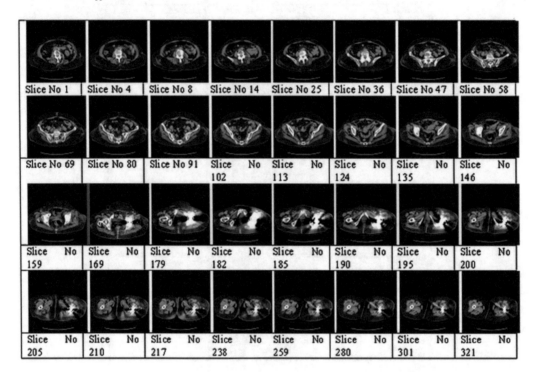

like linear interpolation, cubic, nearest neighbour, shape preserving are applied to recover incomplete data by estimation. Figure 16 presents artifact affect slice, various intermediate results and final corrected slice.

Experiment 1: To evaluate the quality of corrected image normalized root mean square error between original affected slice and reconstructed slice. The computation time for reconstruction from interpolated projections is also recorded. The computation time consumed to segment metal part through Ilastik software and time consumed for interpolating each projection is excluded from calculation. Table 2 presents the statistics.

Experiment 2: We compared the projection (sinogram) profiles of original affected slice with profile of corrected slice as shown in Figure 17. However this graph is more

suitable when we have ground truth as reference image. Hence we could not draw much conclusion out of it.

Experiment 3: An experiment to compare mean and standard deviation of CT numbers in the region of interest could reveal better understanding. The mean CT value in the most pronounced hypodense streak artifacts around the metal implant (ROI1) was (-391.67, ±149.74 HU) in the 169th slice with the FBP algorithm as shown in Figure 18 which is significantly improved by TB-MAR (HU) and SWS-MAR reconstruction by (HU). Similarly the ROI2 had mean CT value (-31.89, ±53.92) for FBP, which was significantly improved by TB-MAR (HU) and SWS-MAR reconstruction by (HU). The mean CT values of ROI3 had no statistically significant difference. A small SD of the CT values indicates a homogeneous intensity

Figure 16. Intermediate results of proposed methodology. a) metal artifact affected slice b) original projection c) segmented image in Ilastik software d) binary representation of segmented part e) affected projection bin f) mutually excluded projection g) first projection to be interpolated h) interpolated sinogram by cubic spline method.

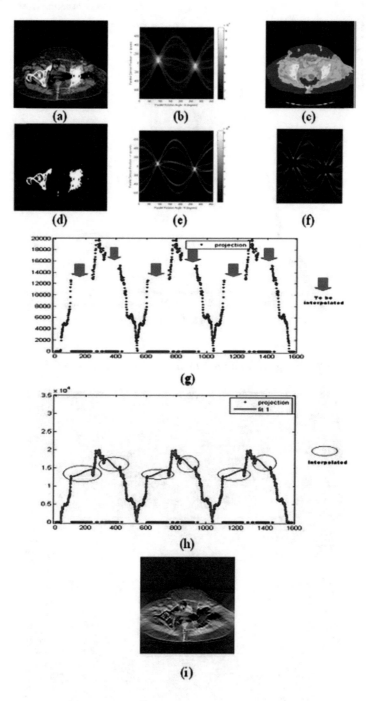

Figure 17. Profile of metal artifact affected slice and corrected image

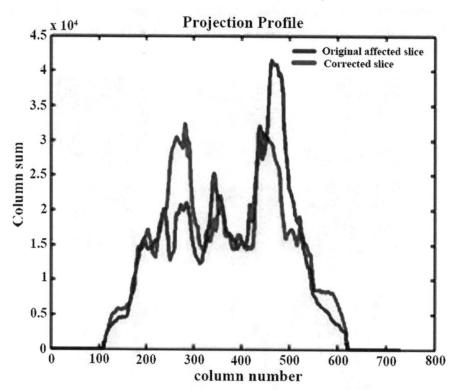

Figure 18. Region of interest along with mean and standard deviation of CT number

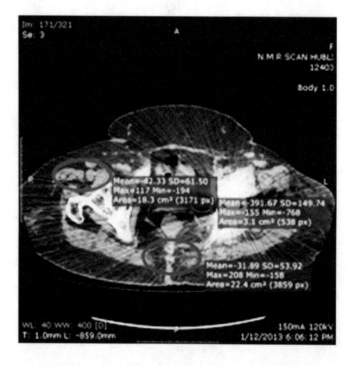

distribution in the respective ROI, SWS-MAR has the lowest mean SD value in all three ROIs, which is significantly different from FBP and LI-MAR.

A comparison of the mean along with standard deviation of CT values in different regions of interest (ROIs) is recorded in the Table.3. The readings are recorded for Filtered back-projection (FBP), Threshold based segmentation metal artifact reduction (TB-MAR) and Seeded watershed segmentation metal artifact reduction (SWS-MAR). Data are given as mean ± standard deviation unless otherwise indicated. The readings

clearly indicate significant reduction in standard deviation for SWS-MAR proving it to be better than TB-MAR and FBP.

Experiment 4: As the measure of metal artifact reduction method is a qualitative one, performance evaluation is incomplete without qualitative valuation by domain expert for diagnostic acceptability of corrected images. Hence this experiment is carried out, where the two bind reviews from radiologists, with final single opinion is recorded in a likart scale. The understanding of lickart scale is as presented below. The Table 4 presents the

Table 3. Mean with standard deviation of CT number in the Region of Interest

Clinical Case	ROI	FBP	TB-MAR	SWS-MAR
F-36 Left hip prosthesis	1	391.67 ±149.74	335.67 ±112.57	**305.62 ± 42.65**
	2	-31.89 ±53.92	-29.65 ±33.92	**-20.89 ±23.14**
	3	-42.33 ± 61.50	-38.53 ± 41.50	**-30.72 ± 21.27**
M-75 Embolization coil	1	197.84 ± 126.41	161.81 ± 80.21	124.41 ± 42.67
	2	68.15 ± 97.45	51.19 ± 62.47	32.17 ± 38.30
	3	-78.43 ± 84.62	-56.63 ± 64.57	-45.13 ± 43.97
M-28 Dental filling	1	-189 ± 67.49	-142 ± 47.34	-131 ± 22.31
	2	67.42 ± 68.66	52.22 ± 50.06	42.82 ± 29.36
	3	344 ± 87.41	298 ± 53.11	224 ± 31.14
F-50 Cholecystectomy clip	1	267 ± 99.74	211 ± 62.14	203 ± 33.64
	2	-316 ± 167.42	-286 ± 122.52	-223 ± 56.53
	3	68.66 ± 85.18	51.31 ± 55.36	46.51 ± 27.16
M-32 Dental filling	1	846.14 ± 102.41	756.94 ± 81.22	724.90 ± 39.29
	2	67.44 ± 84.16	53.27 ± 75.15	49.97 ± 38.45
	3	-126.47 ± 102.63	-112.67 ± 77.23	-108.61 ± 37.27
F-68 Embolization coils	1	544.19 ± 122.2	518.12 ± 86.47	503.62 ± 41.57
	2	642.88 ± 160.47	624.85 ± 134.32	611.81 ± 50.36
	3	-127.83 ± 206.48	-116.81 ± 127.38	-101.51 ± 51.28

Table 4. Qualitative evaluation of proposed MAR method

	Patient ID -1	Patient ID -2	Patient ID -3	Patient ID -4	Patient ID -5	Patient ID -6
Reviewer -1	5	3	3	3	4	4
Reviewer -2	5	4	3	4	4	4

rating by two radiologists. The rating matches with quantitative evaluation aforementioned.

0 = totally obscured, no structures identifiable;
1 = marked artifacts, questionable recognition;
2 = faint anatomic recognition;
3 = anatomic recognition with low confidence;
4 = anatomic recognition with medium confidence; and
5 = anatomic recognition with high confidence in a potential diagnosis

CONCLUSION AND FUTURE SCOPE

Strategy proposed in this paper to segment metal implant from artifact affected slice using seeded watershed segmentation has yielded significant improvement in artifact correction. The ability of seeded watershed segmentation in ilastik© software is at the core of the success. The software utilizes three spatial plus one spectral dimension of image for feature calculation. The experimental results for first clinical case is exceptionally better compared to other cases. The quantitative results attained are in line with qualitative evaluation by domain experts.

Presently the method is investigated for few clinical cases. In future experiment shall be carried out for few other clinical cases such as elbow implant, and knee implant. Experimenting with hybrid approach; where integrating the proposed method with iterative methods shall be carried out in future to further improve the artifact correction.

REFERENCES

Abdoli, M., Dierckx, R. A., & Zaidi, H. (2012). Metal artifact reduction strategies for improved attenuation correction in hybrid PET/CT imaging. *Medical Physics*, *39*(6), 3343–3360. doi:10.1118/1.4709599 PMID:22755716

Avinash, C., Kak, & Slaney, M. (2001). Principles of computerized tomographic imaging. Society for Industrial and Applied Mathematics.

Bamberg, F., Dierks, A., Nikolaou, K., Reiser, M. F., Becker, C. R., & Johnson, T. R. (2011). Metal artifact reduction by dual energy computed tomography using monoenergetic extrapolation. *European Radiology*, *21*(7), 1424–1429. doi:10.1007/s00330-011-2062-1 PMID:21249370

Coolens, C., & Childs, P. J. (2003). Calibration of CT Hounsfield units for radiotherapy treatment planning of patients with metallic hip prostheses: The use of the extended CT-scale. *Physics in Medicine and Biology*, *48*(11), 1591–1603. doi:10.1088/0031-9155/48/11/308 PMID:12817940

De Man, B., Nuyts, J., Dupont, P., Marchal, G., & Suetens, P. (1998). Metal streak artifacts in X-ray computed tomography: a simulation study. In *Nuclear Science Symposium, 1998. Conference Record. 1998 IEEE 3*, 1860-1865. IEEE. doi:10.1109/NSSMIC.1998.773898

De Man, B., Nuyts, J., Dupont, P., Marchal, G., & Suetens, P. (2000). Reduction of metal streak artifacts in x-ray computed tomography using a transmission maximum a posteriori algorithm. *IEEE Transactions on Nuclear Science*, *47*(3), 977–981. doi:10.1109/23.856534

Hounsfield, G. N. (1973). Computerized transverse axial scanning (tomography): Part 1. Description of system. *The British Journal of Radiology*, *46*(552), 1016–1022. doi:10.1259/0007-1285-46-552-1016 PMID:4757352

Hsieh, J., Molthen, R. C., Dawson, C. A., & Johnson, R. H. (2000). An iterative approach to the beam hardening correction in cone beam CT. *Medical Physics*, *27*(1), 23–29. doi:10.1118/1.598853 PMID:10659734

Joseph, P. M., & Spital, R. D. (1982). The effects of scatter in x-ray computed tomography. *Medical Physics*, *9*(4), 464–472. doi:10.1118/1.595111 PMID:7110075

Kalender, W. A., Hebel, R., & Ebersberger, J. (1987). Reduction of CT artifacts caused by metallic implants. *Radiology*, *164*(2), 576–577. doi:10.1148/radiology.164.2.3602406 PMID:3602406

Lell, M. M., Meyer, E., Kuefner, M. A., May, M. S., Raupach, R., Uder, M., & Kachelriess, M. (2012). Normalized metal artifact reduction in head and neck computed tomography. *Investigative Radiology*, *47*(7), 415–421. doi:10.1097/RLI.0b013e3182532f17 PMID:22659592

Lell, M. M., Meyer, E., Schmid, M., Raupach, R., May, M. S., Uder, M., & Kachelriess, M. (2013). Frequency split metal artefact reduction in pelvic computed tomography. *European Radiology*, *23*(8), 2137–2145. doi:10.1007/s00330-013-2809-y PMID:23519437

Liu, J. J., Watt-Smith, S. R., & Smith, S. M. (2003). *CT Reconstruction Using FBP with Sinusoidal Amendment for Metal Artefact Reduction* (pp. 439–448). DICTA.

Meyer, E., Raupach, R., Lell, M., Schmidt, B., & Kachelrieß, M. (2010). Normalized metal artifact reduction (NMAR) in computed tomography. *Medical Physics*, *37*(10), 5482–5493. doi:10.1118/1.3484090 PMID:21089784

Meyer, E., Raupach, R., Schmidt, B., Mahnken, A. H., & Kachelrieß, M. (2011, October). Adaptive normalized metal artifact reduction (ANMAR) in computed tomography. In *Nuclear Science Symposium and Medical Imaging Conference (NSS/MIC)*. IEEE. doi:10.1109/NSSMIC.2011.6152691

Moon, S. G., Hong, S. H., Choi, J. Y., Jun, W. S., Kang, H. G., Kim, H. S., & Kang, H. S. (2008). Metal artifact reduction by the alteration of technical factors in multidetector computed tomography: A 3-dimensional quantitative assessment. *Journal of Computer Assisted Tomography*, *32*(4), 630–633. doi:10.1097/RCT.0b013e3181568b27 PMID:18664853

Morin, R. L., & Raeside, D. E. (1981). A pattern recognition method for the removal of streaking artifact in computed tomography. *Radiology*, *141*(1), 229–233. doi:10.1148/radiology.141.1.7291530 PMID:7291530

Mumcuoglu, E. Ü., Leahy, R. M., & Cherry, S. R. (1996). Bayesian reconstruction of PET images: Methodology and performance analysis. *Physics in Medicine and Biology*, *41*(9), 1777–1807. doi:10.1088/0031-9155/41/9/015 PMID:8884912

Nuyts, J., De Man, B., Dupont, P., Defrise, M., Suetens, P., & Mortelmans, L. (1998). Iterative reconstruction for helical CT: A simulation study. *Physics in Medicine and Biology*, *43*(4), 729–737. doi:10.1088/0031-9155/43/4/003 PMID:9572499

Radon, J. (1917). On determination of functions by their integral values along certain multiplicities. *Ber. der Sachsische Akademie der Wissenschaften Leipzig*, (Germany), 69, 262-277.

Ruparelia, S. (2012). *Implementation of watershed based image segmentation algorithm in FPGA*. Academic Press.

Sommer, C., Straehle, C., Koethe, U., & Hamprecht, F. (2011, March). ilastik: Interactive learning and segmentation toolkit. In *Biomedical Imaging: From Nano to Macro, 2011 IEEE International Symposium on*. IEEE.

Veldkamp, W. J., Joemai, R. M., van der Molen, A. J., & Geleijns, J. (2010). Development and validation of segmentation and interpolation techniques in sinograms for metal artifact suppression in CT. *Medical Physics*, *37*(2), 620–628. doi:10.1118/1.3276777 PMID:20229871

Yazdi, M., & Beaulieu, L. (2008). Artifacts in spiral x-ray CT scanners: Problems and solutions. *International Journal of Biological and Medical Sciences*, *4*(3), 135–139.

Chapter 15
Improved Lymphocyte Image Segmentation Using Near Sets for ALL Detection

Shiwangi Chhawchharia
Vellore Institute of Technology, India

Subrajeet Mohapatra
Birla Institute of Technology Mesra, India

Gadadhar Sahoo
Birla Institute of Technology Mesra, India

ABSTRACT

Light microscopic examination of peripheral blood smear is considered vital for diagnosis of various hematological disorders. The objective of this paper is to develop a fast, robust and simple framework for blood microscopic image segmentation which can assist in automated detection of hematological diseases i.e. acute lymphoblastic leukemia (ALL). A near set based clustering approach is followed for color based segmentation of lymphocyte blood image. Here, a novel distance measure using near sets has been introduced. This improved nearness distance measure has been used in a clustering framework for achieving accurate lymphocyte image segmentation. The nearness measure determines the degree to which two pixels resemble each other based on a defined probe function. It is essential as image segmentation is considered here as a colour based pixel clustering problem. Lymphocyte image segmentation algorithm developed here labels each pixel into nucleus, cytoplasm or background region based on the nearness measure.

1. INTRODUCTION

Cellular components of the blood (erythrocyte, leukocytes, and platelets) are important for medical diagnosis of various hematological disorders. These blood cells which are easily reachable are indicators of disturbances or degradation in their organs of origin which are more difficult to analyze (being less accessible). Thus, changes in the features of blood cells can easily be studied and

DOI: 10.4018/978-1-4666-8654-0.ch015

important inferences can be drawn about various hematological abnormalities. Any disorder detected in erythrocytes, leukocytes or platelets is considered as a sign of critical condition which needs immediate attention. This paper would help in the recognition of such deformities of leukocytes or white blood cells (WBC).

Deformities in WBC are usually neoplastic or non-neoplastic. One of the potentially fatal WBC disorder is leukemia. It is a neoplastic disorder and considered as our subject of study.

Leukemia is neoplastic proliferations of hemopoietic cells in human body. It is a type of hematological disease. This malignant transformation of cells can be attributed to specific genetic changes. This results in formation of clone of leukemia cells or cancerous tumor of white blood cells. Leukemia is a condition where number of myeloid or lymphoid blasts increases causing a hematological malignancy. It can be acute or chronic depending on the severity of the disease. Leukemia can be categorized on the basis of morphologic findings, genetic abnormalities, putative etiology, and cell of origin, immunophenotypic qualities, and clinical characteristics. Thus its classification is quite complicated. However, French, American, British (FAB) classification and World Health Organization (WHO) classification are two protocols for leukemia categorization which are widely applied (Trachuk, 2007). Both fundamentally divide leukemia's into myeloid and lymphoid types, depending on the origin of the blast cell. In the present work we consider acute lymphoblastic leukemia (ALL) as our research focus.

Advanced techniques like flow cytometer, immunophenotyping, molecular probing etc, are present but they are not economic choice for initial screening of leukemia patients as microscopic examination of blood slides. The disadvantage of manual examination of blood slides is that it is subject to human error and the count is based on a much smaller sample size. Thus automated framework would help diagnosing patients with more accuracy. They will support medical clini-

cians in providing prediction of acute lymphoblastic leukemia in a simple and robust way. The benefit of the automated system is that it reduces the risk of wrong diagnoses, provides much quicker diagnoses for patients' conditions, and removes wavering opinions of doctors.

Image segmentation of peripheral blood smear for differential blood count is vital in today's medical industry as it helps in correctly analyzing the conditions of healthy and unhealthy patients. The normality and abnormality conditions of WBC provide hematologists with a great amount of useful data and knowledge about a patient's condition. However, high performance measure is a requirement in automated blood image segmentation for accurate hematological disease detection. There are various segmentation algorithms which provide high efficiency with different kinds of images and as there is no standard segmentation process, specialized process especially for segmentation of blood image can be developed.

Clustering is a classification technique. Given a vector of N measurements describing each pixel or group of pixels (i.e., region) in an image, a similarity of the measurement vectors and therefore their clustering in the N-dimensional measurement space implies similarity of the corresponding pixels or pixel groups. Therefore, clustering in measurement space may be an indicator of similarity of image regions, and may be used for segmentation purposes.

The vector of measurements describes some useful image feature and thus is also known as a feature vector. Similarity between image regions or pixels implies clustering (small separation distances) in the feature space. Clustering methods were some of the earliest data segmentation techniques to be developed (see Figure 1. Clusters)

1.1. Similar Data Points Grouped Together into Clusters

Most popular clustering algorithms suffer from two major drawbacks

Figure 1. Clusters

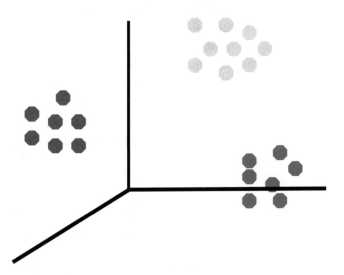

- First, the number of clusters is predefined, which makes them inadequate for batch processing of huge image databases
- Secondly, the clusters are represented by their centroid and built using an Euclidean distance therefore inducing generally an hyperspheric cluster shape, which makes them unable to capture the real structure of the data.

This is especially true in the case of color clustering where clusters are arbitrarily shaped.

There are two standard methods explained in this thesis K-means and Fuzzy C-Means (FCM). K-means is a hard clustering algorithm whereas FCM is soft clustering algorithm as mentioned in section III.

In this thesis, near set based clustering approach is followed for color based segmentation of lymphocyte blood image. Lymphocyte stands out as blue colored component in the whole blood smear. A novel distance measure using near sets for blood image segmentation has been introduced. This improved Nearness distance measure has been used in a clustering framework for achieving lymphocyte image segmentation. It determines the

degree to which two pixels resemble each other based on probe function which is essential as image segmentation is considered as a pixel classification problem. The pixels are evaluated on the basis of their attributes which are measured by probe functions. Near C-means (NCM) employs standard K-means algorithm with nearness measure as metric to evaluate the nearness between two pixels. K-means is a clustering algorithm which is used in various problem domains including image segmentation. An important drawback of this clustering technique is it gets trapped in local minima. A new combination of K-means with a new distance measure (Nearness measure) is employed for WBC image segmentation.

In recent years, few studies focusing on automated blood image segmentation have been reported in the literature. One of the major issues in such segmentation is touching and overlapping cells due to accumulation of high amount of leukocytes or red blood cells. Variable staining and uneven lightening condition makes the segmentation even worse. Blood image segmentation methods available in the literature are mostly colour, shape, threshold, region growing or edge based schemes. Some of which are reported in this paper. Kan Angulo et al. (2003) used a leukocyte segmentation method which was two staged algorithm. It had automatic calculation of threshold and binary filtering. Even though algorithm is two staged, difficulty due to variable staining and lighting condition still remains increasing the difficulty in calculating optimum threshold initially. Since method applies two stage processing, the average segmentation time is more. Jiang (2003) introduces a two-step segmentation process using HSV color model. As it is two-stepped process its computational time increases. Color segmentation procedure applied by Sinha (2003) uses mean-shift to segment the blood images. Comaniciu (2001) proposed the usage of shape analysis to segment leukocytes. Another scheme using active contour models is presented by Ongun (2001). Mohaptra (2012) proposed an image segmentation algorithm using a novel Functional Link Neural Architecture. Umpon (2005) applied patch based blood cell segmentation using fuzzy logic clustering. This algorithm provides precise nucleus segmentation but cytoplasm extraction is not possible. It makes this algorithm specification bound and cannot be used for larger detection of deformities. Hence limited by its ability to segment lymphocytes. Chinwaraphat et al. (2008) introduced an advanced fuzzy c− means clustering technique. The determination of the belongingness of the pixels at the conjunction of cytoplasm and nucleus is difficult. This scheme reduces the probability of false clustering at the junction. The segmentation performance is comparable to traditional Fuzzy c−Means. However the manual cropping is essential for effective test images. Ghosh et al. (2010) presented a marker controlled watershed segmentation technique which extracts the entire WBC effectively from the entire background which includes RBC and platelets. However, the said technique fails in obtaining the cytoplasm and nucleus from the background as no specific methods has been presented for accurate threshold estimation. Due to various methods of slide preparation techniques and complex nature of the

blood smear images, much work can be done to meet real time clinical demands.

Present paper presents a near set based clustering approach for color based segmentation of lymphocyte images. Lymphocyte stands out as a blue colored component in the whole blood smear. A novel distance measure using near sets for blood image segmentation has been introduced. This improved Nearness measure (NM) as a distance measure has been used in a clustering framework for achieving lymphocyte image segmentation. It determines the degree to which two pixels resemble each other based on a probe function which is essential as image segmentation is considered as a pixel clustering problem. The pixels are evaluated on the basis f there attributes which are measured by probe functions. Near C means (NCM) employs simple K-means algorithm with nearness measure as metric to evaluate the nearness between two pixels. K-means is a clustering algorithm which is used in various problem domains including image segmentation. An important drawback of this clustering technique is it gets trapped in local minima (Henry, 2010). Use of NM in K-means framework has been employed for achieving improved segmentation accuracy in lymphocyte image segmentation. Rest of the paper is organized as follows: Section II and Section III describe the schema of the proposed method. Experimental results and analysis are presented in Section V. Finally, Section VII provides the concluding remarks.

1.2. Problem Definition

The knowledgeable and proficient people, specialized in health science have established the medical community to take care of human health. With the technological advances in medical field, faster and efficient analysis tools are easily attainable (e.g. MRI machines, complete blood count machine etc).These automated medical tools helps diagnosing patients with more accuracy. They are essential for supporting medical doctors in providing prediction of the conditions and how to cure them. The benefit of utilizing the advanced technologies is that it reduces the risk of wrong diagnoses, provides much quicker diagnoses for patients' conditions, and thus removes wavering opinions of doctors.

With the increase in number of people suffering from lymphocyte disorders, faster and efficient computer aided tools are need of the hour. There are many patients who need these tools for their effective diagnosis. As this increases the workload of the hematologists, fast, robust and automated system is required for clinicians to carry out the necessary treatments.

The hematologists use their pathological experience for characterization of lymphocytes viz. mature lymphocyte or lymphoblast. As a result, the hematologist will have a lot of valuable information about the patient's condition. However, the disadvantage of the manual evaluation is that it is subject to inconsistent and subjective reports.

Thus there is always a need for a cost effective and robust automated system for leukemia screening which can improve the diagnostic accuracy. This is achieved by using blood image segmentation techniques. Blood image segmentation module is an integral part of the entire automated system.

Peripheral blood image segmentation is a persistent problem in medical image processing. It is a challenge to extract cytoplasm alone from the blood smear image. The colour variation between nucleus and cytoplasm boundary and between cytoplasm and background is negligible. An effective way to do it is by cluster based segmentation such as K means using Euclidean distance.

The challenges in data clustering are the local optimum problem and tendency of cluster to have vague and imprecise boundaries. Such overlapping conditions can be handled by nearness measure replacing Euclidean distance as Euclidean distance measure is based on the spatial closeness of pixels, and not their attributes. Near

sets are computationally efficient in comparison to standard methods. Want for a better algorithm with different measure was the motivation for the employment of near set theory based clustering for lymphocyte segmentation. Thus Near C-Means was employed for lymphocyte segmentation.

2. MATERIAL AND METHODS

2.1. Blood Smear Preparation

Blood samples were randomly collected at Ispat General Hospital, Rourkela, India. Later the blood film generated from blood drop smear slide was stained using Leishman for visualization of cell components. A digital microscope (Carl Zeiss India) was used for capturing 100 blood images. It was done with an effective magnification of 1000 under 100X oil immersed setting. Some blood data sets were discarded because of peripheral problems and rest were used and segmented for the study. A panel of hematologists performed the manual segmentation. They segmented each blood image into nucleus, cytoplasm and background. For leukemia detection, only lymphocytes are considered as they provide necessary information. Hence, it is assumed that the data set contains a particular type of leukocyte i.e. lymphocyte (see Figure 2).

2.2. Sub Imaging

As the blood smear images are relatively large, there is more than one leukocyte per image for processing. However, the region of interest (ROI) must contain a lone lymphocyte as each lymphocyte image has to be evaluated to discriminate between a lymphoblast and a mature lymphocyte. Therefore, the entire blood smear image data set is clustered using K−means with RGB color features and all the blue WBC nucleus of the entire image is obtained (This algorithm is explained is section III). The cluster represents the nucleus of

Figure 2. Sample blood images

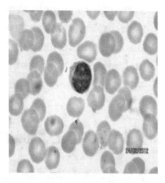 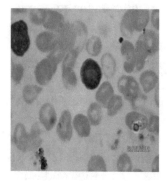

(a)Sample 1   (b) Sample 2

entire leukocytes image and the centroid of each nucleus is obtained. A square sub image around each nucleus is cropped from the original image such that entire cell will be within the cropped sub image. Again remapping with the original image, the color components and color sub images are restored. The process is done with an assumption that there are cells touching each other (see Figure 3).

2.3. Color Conversion

The images generated by digital microscopes are usually represented in RGB (Red, Green and Blue) color model. In this paper, L*a*b* color space has been used for reducing color features in clustering algorithm. The L*a*b* color model consists of a luminosity layer L*, chromaticity layer a* and chromaticity layer b*. The color components i.e. a* and b* are used as features in the clustering process. This model has only two color components as opposed to RGB which has three components. Computation time is an important issue in all feature based clustering problems with large data sets. Use of two color features (a* and b*) instead of three (red, green and blue) reduces the computational time drastically.

2.4. Lymphocyte Image Segmentation

Alterations in the blood cells lead to the recognition of hematological disorders. Analysis of segmented nuclei and cytoplasm leads to the discovery of such alterations. After the sub imaging, blood image segmentation is classified as the unsupervised pixel clustering algorithm. Each pixel of sub image containing single nucleus is considered as belonging to one of the groups i.e. cytoplasm, nucleus or background which includes RBC. Theses segmented regions can be used for feature extraction for accurate details of variation in lymphocyte. In the following section, cluster based image segmentation which includes K-means and Near C-means clustering is presented.

3. CLUSTERING BASED IMAGE SEGMENTATION

Clustering is an unsupervised segmentation algorithm where data patterns are clustered into homogeneous groups. In various domains such as data mining, marketing, pattern recognition, image processing, psychology, biology etc clustering

Figure 3. Stained sub images

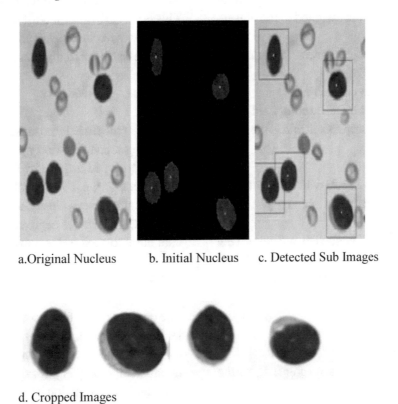

a.Original Nucleus   b. Initial Nucleus   c. Detected Sub Images

d. Cropped Images

based segmentation technique has been proved very useful. Popular clustering algorithms used for image segmentation include K means (Kanungo, 2002), Fuzzy C Means (XiaoLi,2010).

3.1. K-Means Clustering

K-Means algorithm is an unsupervised clustering algorithm that classifies the input data points into multiple classes based on their inherent distance from each other. It is centroid-based clustering algorithm which effectively clusters large databases as well as high dimensional database. By repeated iterations, it dynamically changes its centroid which leads to different cluster formation. As the initial centers are randomly chosen the output set is different each time for the same data set.

Algorithm Process:

Step 1: Initial Value of Centroids.

Initial centroid values are selected at random from the set of instances.

Step 2: Objects - Centroid Distance.

Then the distance between each class centroid to each object. A simple distance measure that is commonly used is Euclidean distance. This step leads to the generation of a distance matrix which represents the distance between each object and each cluster centroid.

Step 3: Object Allocation.

Objects are allocated to a specific cluster based on the distance measure. For any given object, the distance which is least for the pair of the object and the centroids the object is assigned to the cluster.

Step 4: Iteration 1: Determination of Centroids.

Once the members of each group are determined, the new centroids can be computed based on these new memberships. Centroid is the mean of each cluster.

Step 5: Repeat the step 2 and 3 with new centroids.
Step 6: Iteration 2: Determine centroids.

The whole process is carried out iteratively until the centroid values converges, i.e. do no change iteratively or completes the given number of iterations.

Algorithm Summary:

1. Assign initial means v_i (centroid).
2. Assign each data pattern (point) X_k to the cluster U_i for the closest mean.
3. New updated centroid.

$$V_i = \sum X_k \tag{1}$$

$$|C_i|$$

where C_i is the number of objects in cluster U_i.

4. Repeat step 2 and 3 until the updated centroid become stable.

The Euclidean distance used in K-means is the straight-line distance between two pixels

$$\text{Euclidean distance} = \sqrt{((x1 - x2)^2 + (y1 - y2)^2)} \tag{2}$$

where (x1,y1) & (x2,y2) are two pixel points or two data points.

Therefore Euclidean distance generally stimulate an hyperspheric cluster shape, which is not useful if real structure of data has to be captured. This is the case in color clustering of blood smear images where clusters are arbitrarily shaped and not necessarily spatially close to each other.

3.2. Fuzzy C-Means

The one of the first algorithms in the soft partition clustering arena was fuzzy c-means (FCM) and it was developed in 1973 by Dunn and improved hence. In FCM, each data point in data set is associated with every cluster using a membership function, which gives degree of belongingness of data point to each of the clusters.

3.2.1. Fuzzy Sets

The concept of the fuzzy set was first introduced in 1965 by Zadeh. A fuzzy set is defined to be a class of objects with a continuum of grades of membership. In every fuzzy set a membership (characteristic) function is present that characterizes it. This member function assigns each object a grade of membership ranging from 0 to 1.

For example, Let $U = \{x\}$ be a space of points, where x is a generic element of U. A fuzzy set Q in U is characterized by a membership characteristic function $f_Q(x)$ that provides a real number in the interval [0,1] to each point in U. Thus, when Q is an crisp set, $f_Q(x)$ can take on only two values, 0 and 1, with $f_Q(x)=1$ or 0 according as x belongs or not to the set Q. But in a fuzzy theory, set Q has data points where a larger value of $f_Q(x)$ indicates higher grade of membership of x in Q.[r1]

3.2.2. Fuzzy C-Means

Fuzzy cluster analysis allows gradual memberships of data points to clusters measured as degrees in [0, 1]. This gives the flexibility to express that data points can belong to more than one cluster. Furthermore, these membership degrees offer a much finer degree of detail of the data model. Aside from assigning a data point to clusters in shares, membership degrees can also express how ambiguously or definitely a data point should belong to a cluster. The concept of these membership degrees is substantiated by the definition and interpretation of fuzzy sets as mentioned. Thus, fuzzy clustering allows fine grained solution spaces in the form of fuzzy partitions of the set of given examples $X = \{x_1, \ldots, x_n\}$. Whereas the clusters U_i of data partitions have been classical subsets so far, they are represented by the fuzzy sets U_i of the data-set X in the following. Complying with fuzzy set theory, the cluster assignment u_{ij} is now the membership degree of a datum x_j to cluster Ui, such that: $u_{ij} \in [0, 1]$. Since memberships to clusters are fuzzy, there is not a single label that is indicating to which cluster a data point belongs. Instead, fuzzy clustering methods associate a fuzzy label vector to each data point x_j that states its memberships to the C clusters. This is possible only when certain conditions are satisfied as explained in below.

Let $X = \{x_1, \ldots, x_n\}$ be the set of given data points and let c be the number of clusters where $(1 < c < n)$ represented by the fuzzy sets U_i, (i = 1, . . ., c). Then following conditions

$$0 < \sum_{k=1}^{c} \mu_{ik} < N, \forall i \epsilon \{1 \ldots c\} \qquad (3)$$

and $\forall i$ with $dik_{=\|} Xk - vi_\|2$, s$_{ub}$ject to

$$\sum_{i=1}^{c} \mu_{ik} = 1, \forall k \epsilon \{1 \ldots n\}, \qquad (4)$$

The $u_{ij} \in [0_{,1]}$ are interpreted as the membership degree of datum xj to cluster _i relative to all other clusters. Constraint (3) guarantees that no cluster is empty. This corresponds to the requirement in classical cluster analysis that no cluster, represented as (classical) subset of X, is empty Condition (4) ensures that the sum of the membership degrees for each datum equals 1. This means that each

datum receives the same weight in comparison to all other data and, therefore, that all data are (equally) included into the cluster partition. This is related to the requirement in classical clustering that partitions are formed exhaustively). As a consequence of both constraints no cluster can contain the full membership of all data points. Furthermore, condition (4) corresponds to a normalization of the memberships per datum. Thus the membership degrees for a given datum formally resemble the probabilities of its being a member of the corresponding cluster.

After defining probabilistic partitions we can turn to developing an objective function for the fuzzy clustering task. Certainly, the closer a data point lies to the center of a cluster, the higher its degree of membership should be to this cluster. Following this rationale, one can say that the distances between the cluster centers and the data points (strongly) assigned to it should be minimal. Hence the problem to divide a given data-set into c clusters can (again) be stated as the task to minimize the squared distances of the data points to their cluster centers, since, of course, we want to maximize the degrees of membership. The probabilistic fuzzy objective function Jf is thus based on the least sum of squared distances .The partition matrix is obtained by minimizing an objective function more formally, a fuzzy cluster model of a given data-set X into c clusters is defined to be optimal when it minimizes the objective function:

$$J = \sum_{k=1}^{N} \sum_{i=1}^{c} (\mu_{ik})^m \left\| X_k - v_i \right\|^2, \qquad (5)$$

where $1 < m < \infty$ is the degree of fuzziness, vi is the ith cluster center, $\mu \in [0,1]$ is the membership of the kth data pattern to it, vi and ui is computed as below and ‖.‖ is the euclidean distance normalized. Under the constraints (3) and (4) that have to be satisfied the condition (3) avoids the trivial solution of minimization problem, i.e., uij = 0, ∀$_{i,}$ j. The normalization constraint (4) leads to a 'distribution' of the weight of each data point over the different clusters. Since all data points have the same fixed amount of membership to share between clusters, the normalization condition implements the known partitioning property of any probabilistic fuzzy clustering algorithm. The parameter m (where m > 1), is called the fuzzifier or weighting exponent. The exponentiation of the memberships with m in Jf can be seen as a function g of the membership degrees, g(uik) = u_{ik}^m which removes functional error.

The actual value of m then determines the 'fuzziness' of the classification. It has been shown for the case m = 1 (when Jh and J_f become identical), that cluster assignments remain hard or crisp when minimizing the target function, even though they are allowed to be fuzzy, i.e., they are not constrained in {0, 1}. For achieving the desired fuzzification of the resulting probabilistic data partition the function $g\left(u_{ik} = u_{ik}^2\right)$ has been proposed first. The generalization for exponent m > 1 that lead to fuzzy memberships has been proposed later. With higher values for m the boundaries between clusters become softer, with lower values they get harder. Usually m = 2 is chosen.

The update formulae for the cluster parameters depend, of course, on the parameters used to describe a cluster (location, shape, size) and on the chosen distance measure. Therefore a general update formula cannot be given. In the case of the basic fuzzy C-means model the cluster center vectors serve as prototypes, while an inner product norm induced metric is applied as distance measure. Consequently the derivations of Jf w.rt. the centers vi yield:

$$v_i = \frac{\sum_{k=1}^{N}\left(\mu_{ik}\right)^m X_k}{\sum_{k=1}^{N}\left(\mu_{ik}\right)^m}, \tag{6}$$

The choice of the optimal cluster center points for fixed memberships of the data to the clusters has the form of a generalized mean value computation for which the fuzzy C-means algorithm has its name. The membership degrees have to be chosen according to the following update formula that is independent of the chosen distance measure:

$$\mu_{ik} = \frac{1}{\sum_{j=1}^{c}(d_{ik} / d_{jk})^{2/(m-1)}}, \tag{7}$$

where $\forall i$ with $d_{ik} = |Xk - v_i||2$, subject to $\sum_{i=1}^{c}\mu_{ik} = 1$, $\forall k$, and $0 < \sum_{i=1}^{c}\mu_{ik} < N, \forall i$.

These are two conditions has to be satisfied as mentioned above.. The above equation clearly shows the relative character of the probabilistic membership degree. It depends not only on the distance of the datum Xj to cluster i, but also on the distances between this data point and other clusters.

3.2.3. Algorithm

The FCM algorithm consists of the following steps.

1. Assign initial centroids $vi, i=1,2,…,c$.
2. Choose value of degree of fuzziness (fuzzifier) m and threshold tmax.
3. Set iteration counter count=1.
4. Compute μik by Equation 3 for c number of clusters and N data patterns.
5. Update means, vi, using Equation 4.
6. Increment t
7. Repeat steps 2-4 until $|\mu ik(count)-\mu ik(count-1)|>tmax$.

The (probabilistic) fuzzy C-means algorithm is known as a stable and robust classification method. Compared with the hard C-means it is quite insensitive to its initialization and it is not likely to get stuck in an undesired local minimum of its objective function in practice. Due to its simplicity and low computational demands, the probabilistic fuzzy C-means is a widely used initializer for other more sophisticated clustering methods. On the theoretical side it has been proven that either the iteration sequence itself or any convergent subsequence of the probabilistic FCM converges in a saddle point or a minimum – but not in a maximum – of the objective function.

K-means and fuzzy c means algorithms are unable to differentiate between the overlapping boundaries. Since it uses Euclidean distance which is spatial distance measure, it sometimes provides bad segmentation results. Euclidean distance generally stimulates an hyperspheric cluster shape, which is not useful if real structure of data has to be captured. This is the case in color clustering of blood smear images where clusters are arbitrarily shaped and not necessarily spatially close to each other.

Nearness measure is based on measurable qualitative attributes of the images i.e. color which is measured by probe functions.

This gives qualitative distance between the pixels and they can be as abstract as needed. Thus Near C-Means using near measure was employed for lymphocyte segmentation. Near sets and Near C-Means algorithm are presented in the following sections.

3.3. Near Sets

The nearness of objects is defined by their measurable qualitative attributes and not their spatial distance to one another. It is not a crisp concept,

but a near or rough concept. Near set is specialized case of rough sets, where the number of granules (neighborhoods) has been increased (Pawlak, 2007). These granules are responsible for classifying a concept as either near or crisp. This results in formation of near set. The objects present in near set are have features which are measured by probe functions. These features provide the basis for measuring the similarity between objects in near set theory (Henry, 2010). Let X, Y be sets of objects in a topological space with pseudo-metric d such that

$D(X, Y) = \inf\{d(a, b)|x \ 2 \ X, y \ 2 \ Y \}$.
Then near(X, Y) is defined as follows.
Near (X, Y) iff $D(X, Y) = 0$

Sets X, Y in Figure 4 (a) are Near to each other with respect to objects common to both sets. The presence of tolerance class determine the degree to which sets X, Y are near to each other. In Figure 4 (b), sets X, Y are not near to each other whatever the quota of tolerance class maybe.

3.4. Near C-Means Clustering

Near set Y is characterized by the similarity between the objects. The each object is given nearness for each cluster. An object is made member of a cluster depending upon the nearness measure. The centroid of cluster to which an object is closest is made the parent cluster. The centroid m_i of cluster U_i is computed as

Figure 4. Sample sets

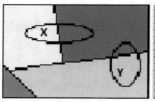 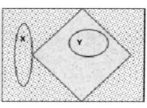

(a)Near Sets   (b) Non Near Sets

$$m_i = \frac{\sum_{x_{k \in U_i}} X_k}{C_i} \qquad (8)$$

where Xk i$_s$ data pattern and Ci i_s the number of objects in cluster Ui .

*N*earness Measure (NM) for a pair of data member Xk $_a$nd centroid mi $_i$s computed as:

$$NM(X_k, m_i) = (|P|)^{-1} \sum \frac{(\min(p_n, q_n))}{(\max(p_n, q_n))} \qquad (9)$$

where p$_n$ and q$_n$ are probe function of data patterns (pixel) X$_k$ and m$_i$. P is the number of probe functions being used.

Here we have chromaticity layer a* and chromaticity layer b* of L a*b* colour model as probe functions.

3.5. Algorithm

1. Assign the initial centroids m_i for the *C* clusters.
2. Each data object X_k is assigned to one of the clusters *Ui*, by computing the Nearness Measure between the data member X_k and centroids m_i NM (X$_k$,m$_i$).
3. Allocate $X_k \in U_i$ such that distance NM (X$_k$,m$_i$) is maximum over the remaining clusters.
4. Compute new updated centroid for each cluster U_i using given equation.
5. Iterate until there are no more changes in centroids of the clusters U$_i$ or until specified number of iteration have been done.

4. PROPOSED LEUKOCYTE SEGMENTATION

The peripheral blood smear images are relatively larger and contain more than one leukocyte, thus process of sub imaging is a requirement. Sub images contains single leukocyte per image and are obtained as proposed earlier. Microscopic blood images generated from digital microscope are represented using RGB color model which has three feature inputs i.e. red, blue, and green. This colour model is then represented as L*a*b colour model. The a* and b* component of L*a*b colour model are considered as two feature inputs for image segmentation using Near C-means clustering. The proposed algorithm is applied on each sub image to segment the nucleus and cytoplasm from the background. The detailed segmentation approach in form of an algorithm is as follows (see Figure 5):

1. Apply *L*a*b** color space conversion on I_{rgb} to obtain L*a*b* image i.e. I_{lab}.
2. Construct the input feature vector using *a** and *b** components of I_{lab}.
3. Each data pattern X$_k$ of the feature vector is assigned to appropriate class C using Near C-means algorithm.
4. Obtain the labeled image from the classified feature vector.
5. Reconstruct the segmented RGB color image for each class.

After segmentation process, each pixel of the digital blood image is labeled as belonging to one of the three clusters i.e. nucleus, cytoplasm, and background stain. These three clusters were suggested by the hematologist. Hence, the number of clusters or classes C was considered three in the experiments.

Output of lymphocyte image segmentation.

5. RESULTS AND ANALYSIS

Near C-means clustering is employed for lymphocyte image segmentation. The proposed technique is applied on peripheral blood smear images obtained as mentioned earlier. The success of

Figure 5. Flow chart of NCM

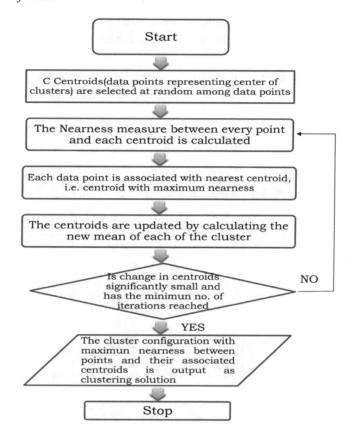

the scheme is demonstrated by conducting three experiments. As the use of proper segmentation scheme is very critical for any medical image evaluation and same is true for ALL Detection. Near measure based clustering was employed for more efficient nucleus and cytoplasm region extraction of peripheral blood smear. The performance of the proposed segmentation technique was validated for 20 images and found to be better than standard color based clustering schemes as mentioned.

The proposed scheme was implemented using Matlab 7.14.0.739 and experimental simulation was performed using an Intel Core i3 2.40 GHz PC, along with 2 GB RAM running on Windows 7 Home basic 32-bit operating system. A total of 20 lymphocyte sub images belonging to the test image data set are used for the experimental evalu-

ation of the proposed scheme. Three experiments are conducted on the test images to demonstrate the efficacy of the proposed scheme.

In the first experiment the proposed scheme is compared with standard image segmentation schemes such as K means, Fuzzy C Means and is presented in Figures 2, 3, 4 and 5. These four images helps in evaluation of subjective performance. The misclassification error percentage (ε) is evaluated in the second experiment by comparing the segmentation results with the available 4 manual segmented test images using the following relation:

$$\varepsilon = \frac{\text{Total number of misclassified pixels}}{\text{Total number of pixels in a region}} \times 100$$

(10)

where the number of pixels in a region in the labeled reference image is provided by a panel of hematologists (ground truth) and number of misclassified pixels is the pixels in labeled image obtained using the proposed segmentation approach and is presented in Table 1. In the last experiment, the proposed algorithm is compared with the said standard methods in terms of computation time (in seconds) and shown in Figure 6.

The Figures 6, 7, 8 and 9 show the original image and its segmentation by K means, FCM, NCM (See Table 1).

Table 1. Variations in misclassification error percentage results of different methods

Image Sample	Error	Methods		
		K Means	FCM	NCM
Old_DSC01538aBL1	CSE	27.1155	17.824	6.8352
	NSE	5.2765	8.2474	1.0193
Old_DSC01538cBL1	CSE	11.574	13.3681	8.5069
	NSE	3.394	10.2119	2.0820
Old_DSC01550eBL1	CSE	13.4241	4.5136	7.8599
	NSE	4.3978	3.3121	0.6422
Old_DSC01556aBL1	CSE	10.3030	6.5152	5.2121
	NSE	3.5463	5.8194	1.3111

Figure 6. Comparative lymphocyte segmentation results

Figure 7. Comparative lymphocyte segmentation results

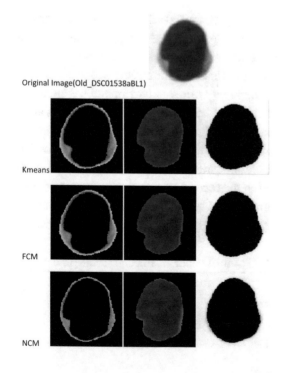

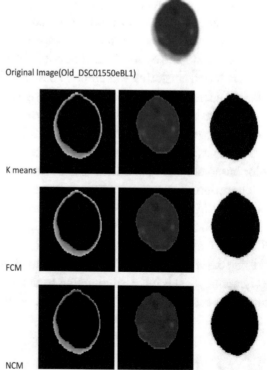

Figure 8. Comparative lymphocyte segmentation results

Original Image(Old_DSC01538cBL1)

K means

FCM

NCM

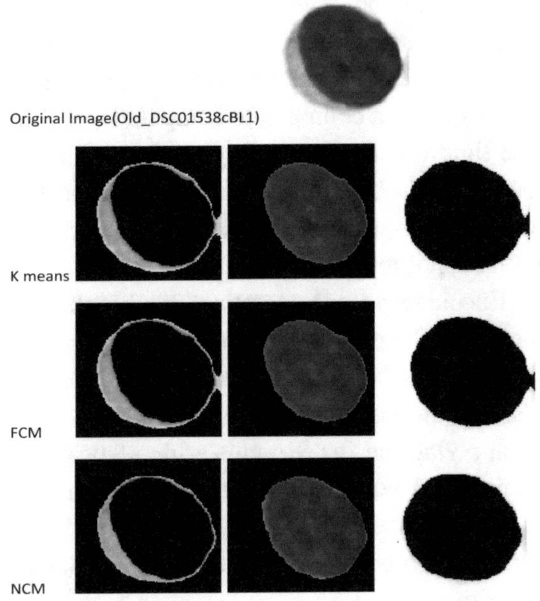

Figure 9. Comparative lymphocyte segmentation results

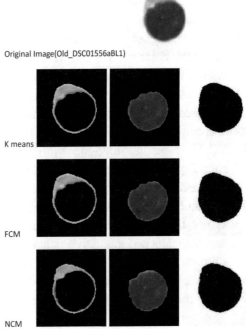

Original Image(Old_DSC01556aBL1)

K means

FCM

NCM

6. CONCLUSION AND FUTURE WORK

Study and implementation of existing and development new algorithms for efficient lymphocyte image segmentation for Leukemia detection is the main objective of the project. Leukocytes are one of the main issues to determine various diseases. Leukemia is one such disease, where pathologists observe the abnormalities present in the leukocytes in the form of color, textures or population and categorize a diseased lymphocyte based on their clinic pathological knowledge of the abnormalities present in the blood parameters. Therefore proper segmentation of leukocyte nuclei is very much needed to justify the disease detection. The development of near measure in Near C-Means is presented in this thesis. Our proposed algorithm provides a better computer assisted scheme to help pathologists for better decision making.

The use of an automated system to examine microscopic blood samples is vital since that it can lead to a faster detection of ALL. Also, using automated image processing to segment lymphocyte could give various advantages including more examination accuracy, less human error and faster analysis time. Segmentation of single lymphocyte image could lead to appropriate analysis of human health where the difference between lymphocyte from lymphoblast could distinguish between healthy person and a person suffering from ALL. Segmentation of WBC from other elements in blood such as RBC, stains and platelets has proven to be a challenging exercise. In our work, sub imaging of the Leishman smeared microscopic blood samples was adopted to segment single nucleus of lymphocyte from the whole blood sample. Then, the region extraction of nucleus and cytoplasm was done using computational segmentation algorithms using color feature.

In this work, to classify lymphocyte, region extraction of nucleus and cytoplasm has to be done. This process mimics the hematologist experts who depend on area, shape, color as feature for classifying lymphocyte cell in their labs. On this basis, color based features of microscopic blood were extracted and will be analyzed for ALL detection.

NCM gave higher segmentation results compared to the K-means or FCM. Accuracy of segmentation for NCM for cytoplasm is 92.9% and for Nucleus is 98.74% was achieved when NCM was used with color based morphological features in conjunction with L*a*b color model. This model reduces the three input problem to two feature input based problem. Furthermore, the NCM based clustering was not sensitive to initial randomly chosen cluster center, whereas this was not the case with either of previous algorithm. K-means was found to be stuck in the local optimum problem and tendency of cluster to have vague and imprecise boundaries. Such overlapping conditions was handled by nearness

measure replacing Euclidean distance as Euclidean distance measure is based on the spatial closeness of pixels, and not their attributes. This is clearly seen in the segmentation of the blood sample in Figure 10. The NCM gave repeatable and consistent results in a comparable computational time. The time was marginally higher than FCM. On the other hand, performance of K-means as well as FCM was dependant on randomly selected initial conditions.

Encouraging segmentation results obtained motivates the usage of near sets in future works. Future work can be done to improve the misclassification error percentage of the algorithm by applying the fuzzy c-clustering algorithm in conjunction with nearness measure. Furthermore, there is an intension to apply the proposed algorithm on a larger WBC database and refining the algorithm.

Figure 10. Computation time of different methods

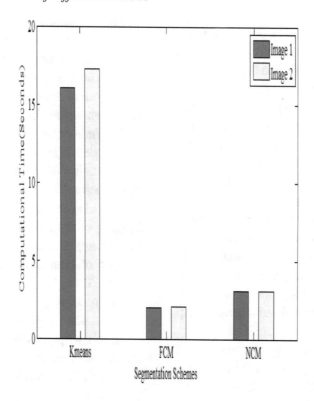

Use of near measure in Near C Means for efficient lymphocyte image segmentation for Leukemia detection is the main objective of the paper. The computational time of NCM is marginally higher than FCM but the encouraging segmentation results obtained motivates the usage of near sets in future works. The future works may also include fuzzy c means using near sets.

ACKNOWLEDGMENT

We are grateful to Dr. S. Satpathi, Ispat General Hospital Rourkela for providing microscopic images. The authors would like to thank Prof. D. Patra, National Institute of Technology Rourkela whose guidance which helped significantly in the improvement of the paper.

REFERENCES

Angulo, J., & Flandrin, G. (2003). *Microscopic image analysis using mathematical morphology: application to haematological cytology.* IEEE International Conference On Acoustics, Speech and Signal Processing.

Chinwaraphat, S., Sanpanich, A., Pintavirooj, C., & Sangworasil, M. (2012). A modified fuzzy clustering for white blood cell segmentation. *Proc Third Int Symp Biomed Eng.*

Comaniciu, D., & Meer, P. (2001). Cell image segmentation for diagnostic pathology. In *Advanced Algorithm Approaches to Medical Image Segmentation: State-Of-The-Art Application in Cardiology, Neurology, Mammography and Pathology.*

Ghosh, M., Das, D., Chakraborty, C., Pala, M., Maity, A. K., Pal, S. K., & Ray, A. K. (2010). Statistical pattern analysis of white blood cell nuclei morphometry. *Proc IEEE Students Technol Symp.*

Henry, C.J., & Peters, J.F. (2010). *Near Sets: Theory and Applications.* Academic Press.

Jiang, K., Liao, Q., & Dai, S. (2003). *A novel white blood cell segmentation scheme using scale-space filtering and watershed clustering.* In Machine Learning and Cybernetics, 2003 International Conference on. doi:10.1109/ICMLC.2003.1260033

Kanungo, T., Mount, D. M., Netanyahu, N. S., Piatko, C. D., Silverman, R., & Wu, A. Y. (2002). An efficient k-means clustering algorithm: Analysis and implementation. Pattern Analysis and Machine Intelligence. *IEEE Transactions on, 24*(7), 881–892.

Mohapatra, S. (2012). *Lymphocyte Image Segmentation Using Functional Link Neural Architecture for Acute Leukemia Detection.* The Korean Society of Medical & Biological Engineering and Springer.

Ongun, G., Halici, U., Leblebiicioglu, K., Atalay, V., Beksac, M., & Beksak, S. (2001). *An automated differential blood count system.* In *International Conference of the IEEE Engineering in Medicine and Biology Society.*

Pawlak, Z., & Skowron, A. (2007). Rudiments of rough sets. *Information Sciences, 177*(1), 3–2. doi:10.1016/j.ins.2006.06.003

Sinha, N., & Ramakrishnan, A. G. (2003). Automation of differential blood count. In *Proceedings Conference on Convergent Technologies for Asia Pacific Region.* doi:10.1109/TENCON.2003.1273221

Tkachuk, C. D., & Hirschmann, J. V. (2007). Wintrobe's Atlas of Clinical Hematology. Lippincott Williams and Wilkins.

Umpon, N. T. (2005). Patch based white blood cell nucleus segmentation using fuzzy clustering. *ECTI T Electr Electron Commun., 3*(1), 5–10.

XiaoLi, C., Ying, Z., JunTao, S., & Jiqing, S. (2010). *Method of image segmentation based on fuzzy c-means clustering algorithm and artificial fish swarm algorithm.* In Intelligent Computing and Integrated Systems (ICISS), 2010 International Conference on.

KEY TERMS AND DEFINITIONS

Clustering: Clustering is a classification technique where similar kinds of objects are grouped together. The similarity between the objects maybe determined in different ways depending upon the use case. Therefore, clustering in measurement space may be an indicator of similarity of image regions, and may be used for segmentation purposes.

Image Segmentation: Image segmentation is a technique of dividing a digital image into multiple segments so as to simplify an image.

This simplification helps in a study of images for further analysis.

Lymphocyte: It is a type of white blood cell (leucocyte) which is found in lymphatic system. It is characterized by single round nucleus. Lymphocytes are mainly responsible for body's immune responses.

Near Sets: Sets for which the nearness of their objects are defined by their measurable qualitative attributes and not their spatial distance to one another are said to be near sets . It is not a crisp concept, but a near or rough concept.

Nearness Measure: This is the novel distance measure presented in the chapter. It is used as a metric to evaluate the qualitative distance between the pixels, at the same time allowing them to be as abstract as required. Nearness measure is based on measurable qualitative attributes of the images i.e. color which is measured by probe functions. It is used in a clustering framework for achieving lymphocyte image segmentation.

Chapter 16
Biometric Identification System Using Neuro and Fuzzy Computational Approaches

Tripti Rani Borah
Gauhati University, India

Kandarpa Kumar Sarma
Gauhati University, India

Pranhari Talukdar
Gauhati University, India

ABSTRACT

In all authentication systems, biometric samples are regarded to be the most reliable one. Biometric samples like fingerprint, retina etc. is unique. Most commonly available biometric system prefers these samples as reliable inputs. In a biometric authentication system, the design of decision support system is critical and it determines success or failure. Here, we propose such a system based on neuro and fuzzy system. Neuro systems formulated using Artificial Neural Network learn from numeric data while fuzzy based approaches can track finite variations in the environment. Thus NFS systems formed using ANN and fuzzy system demonstrate adaptive, numeric and qualitative processing based learning. These attributes have motivated the formulation of an adaptive neuro fuzzy inference system which is used as a DSS of a biometric authenticable system. The experimental results show that the system is reliable and can be considered to be a part of an actual design.

INTRODUCTION

Of late biometric attributes have become important components of authentication systems. This is because biometric attributes are based on a physiological or behavioral characteristic which are unique to a person. Biometric aids are accepted as important components of highly secured identification and verification systems as solutions to security breaches, transaction frauds etc. in a diverse range of applications that have direct impact on the lives of the common man.

DOI: 10.4018/978-1-4666-8654-0.ch016

This is more so with cases which are confidential in nature like that seen in financial transactions, restricted access zones, working with personal data and privacy. Biometric authentication systems are also available in real time mode especially with applications including distributed computing resources where application logins, data protection, remote access, transaction security etc are linked to individual personal attributes. The primary benefit derived is security which re-enforces reliability and trust. In most case, biometric identification is found to be the most reliable method of trustworthy transaction of any type.

Biometric authentication refers to the identification of humans by their characteristics or traits. Biometrics is used in human computer interaction (HCI) systems as a form of identification and access control. Biometric characteristics of a person are unique and remain unchanged over a lifetime. Biometric identifiers are the distinctive, measurable characteristics used to label and describe individuals (Jain, Hong, & Pankanti, 2000). They are often categorized as physiological versus behavioral characteristics. A physiological biometric would identify a person by an iris scan, DNA or fingerprint etc. Behavioral biometrics is related to the behavior of a person, including but not limited to typing rhythm, gait and voice. Though behavioral biometrics is less expensive and less dangerous for the user, physiological characteristics offer highly exact identification of a person.

Fingerprint identification is a matured biometric technique used for criminal investigations. Major representations of the finger are based on the entire image, finger ridges or salient features derived from the ridges (minutiae). These characteristics are used to generate an orientation field of the fingerprint, which subsequently provides the discriminating details for authentication of persons. Fingerprint identification is a popular technique because of their easy access, low price of fingerprint sensors, non-intrusive scanning and relatively good performance. In recent years, significant performance improvements have been achieved in commercial automatic fingerprint recognition systems (FRS). The fingerprint of an individual is unique and remains unchanged over a lifetime (Jain, Hong, Pankanti, & Bolle, 1997).

Retina is another unique biometric pattern that can be used as a part of a verification system. Retina identification is an automatic method that provides true identification of the person by acquiring an internal body image which is difficult to counterfeit (Hill, 1978). Retina identification has found application in high security environments of all types.

In the most basic form, a biometric identification system has an acquisition stage, a pre-processing stage, feature extraction, a classifier and a decision making stage. Conventionally, the design solutions use a combination of a number of technologies some of which are also learning based. The primary benefit of a learning based system is that it can capture finer variations of the input, retain the knowledge and use it subsequently. Among the learning systems, Artificial Neural Networks (ANNs) have been the most preferred ones. These are non-parametric prediction tolls that generate non-linear computing and can make proper discrimination between closely varying patterns. One of the limitations of the ANN is that it cannot provide qualitative computing. It means it fails to make discrimination between minute variations within classes like, in case of illumination variation, it shall assume all changes of bright light to be same meaning that it shall provide a binary decision between bright and dark. To enable it make discrimination between subtle variations of light, structural modifications of the ANN type should be made. To deal with situations of subtle variations between two extreme cases like dark and bright, fuzzy systems are found be excellent choice. Fuzzy systems work best when it is combined with ANNs. These aspects are discussed in subsequent sections. One of the combinations of ANN and fuzzy system is the neuro-fuzzy system (NFS). The ANN is also configured with fuzzy attributes as a NFS for applications involving finer variation of inputs and also enabling it to deal with uncertainty. Such aspects are explored here in case of a framework for biometric authentication involving fingerprint and retina.

Here, we propose a Fingerprint Recognition System (FRS) and a Retina Recognition System (RRS) based on adaptive neuro fuzzy inference system (ANFIS). ANFIS, an integrated system, comprising of fuzzy attributes and ANN, can be used as a decision support system (DSS) of a biometric verification framework. The ANFIS based method properly addresses and solves certain problems related to non-linearity, randomness and uncertainty of data observed in the inputs. An ANFIS is configured and trained to handle a range of variations in the texture of the fingerprint and retina inputs. Here, in the fingerprint recognition system, Crossing Number Algorithm (CNA) is used for the minutiae feature extraction. In case of retina recognition system, Principal Component Analysis (PCA) is used for the feature extraction of the blood vessels. The specialty of the work is associated with the fact that if the ANFIS is configured properly in terms of number and types of membership functions (MF) it can tackle the variations in the fingerprint and retinal images. This way the approach provides the insights for developing certain learning aided system which is autonomous and requires these samples for verification and authorization during the training stage only. The knowledge thus acquired is used subsequently for decision making. Experimental results show that the proposed approach is fast, reliable and robust for a range of conditions. Here, we used samples from databases of ISI Kolkata, MESSIDOR, Indraprastha Institute of Information Technology, Delhi, India, and CASIA. Some of the issues involved are acquisition of proper quality fingerprint and retina images, so that these can be used as inputs in the recognition system, preprocessing of the input images for making them suitable for manipulation and interpretation, use of different kinds of techniques for the

enhancement of input images, morphological operations for extracting image components useful in describing image shape, application of efficient feature extraction techniques to develop a prototype model for fingerprint and retina based biometric identification system and application of neuro-fuzzy classifier for improvement of the overall performance of the recognition system.

BACKGROUND AND LITERATURE REVIEW

The reliability factor related to biometric based systems has contributed towards research and the growth of application of such systems. The trust factor associated with biometric systems is found to be greater than traditional systems. Various works on biometric identification based on fingerprint and retina recognition using fuzzy have been going on all over the world. The work reports a method which uses ridge bifurcation as fingerprints minutiae and a fuzzy encoder with BPNN as recognizer for fingerprint recognition (Hsieh & Hu, 2005). A technique of fingerprint image enhancement and minutiae extraction was designed by Thai (2003). Fingerprint recognition using modular neural networks and fuzzy integrals for response integration is a work proposed in (Bravo & Castillo, 2005). In this work the author described an approach for pattern recognition using modular neural networks with a fuzzy logic method. Fingerprints Recognition Using Minutiae Extraction: a Fuzzy Approach is another work where the authors described the fingerprint verification based on local ridge discontinuities features (minutiae) only using gray scale images (Baldassarri, Vallesi, & Tascini, 2007). Fingerprint recognition using fuzzy art map neural network architecture is another work proposed in (Dagher, Helwe, & Yassine, 2002). In this work, ANN architecture, Fuzzy Artmap (FAM), was used to classify fingerprints. Another work identification of individuals using fingerprints by linguistic descriptions fuzzy comparison was proposed by Martinez (1999). In this work, a new method of personal identification through fingerprints by comparing two fingerprints (one known and the other unknown) by means of linguistic elements fuzzy comparison was used. A new approach that has been used the feed forward back propagation neural network which was implemented through Matlab was reported by (Rajharia & Gupta, 2012). Fingerprint Pattern Recognition Using Back Propagation Algorithms is another work proposed (Khetri, Padme, Jain, & Pawar, 2012). In this work, authors described the better performance of CASIA fingerprint database than FVC 2002 database using feedforward backpropagation neural network. Fingerprint recognition using neural network is another work where the author described a neural network based approach for automated fingerprint recognition (Leung, Lau, & Luk, 1991). They extracted the minutiae from the fingerprint image via a multilayer perceptron (MLP) classifier and backpropagation learning technique is used for its training. A neural network based approach for fingerprint recognition system is a work where the author used candidate score, ideal weight model score and recognition quotient for recognition of the pattern (Jha, Narasimham, Krishna, & Pillai, 2010). A new fingerprint image recognition approach using artificial neural network is another work where the author described the fingerprint image recognition based on artificial neural network and wavelet transform (Lihua, 2010). The authors developed a fingerprint identification and recognition system (Jin, Chekima, Dargham, & Liau, 2002). The author described the image enhancement process by performing gray level enhancement, spatial filtering, image sharpening, edge detection, segmentation, and thinning processes. After the image has been processed, back propagation neural network is used for training.

On modeling the retina using neural networks is a work proposed in (Joshi & Lee, 1991). In this work the authors described about the architecture of the retina and build a system that would model and simulate the information processing in the retina. Retinal vessel segmentation using Gabor filter and artificial neural network is another work proposed in (Nandy & Banerjee, 2012). The work demonstrates an automated segmentation scheme of retinal vasculature using Gabor filter bank, which is optimized on the basis of entropy. Supervised segmentation of vasculature in retinal images using neural networks is a work proposed where the authors reported about a neural network based supervised segmentation algorithm for retinal vessel delineation (Ding, Xia, & Li, 2014). Self-Organizing neural network based pathology classification in retinal images is another work where the authors designed an automated system based on Self-Organizing neural network (Kohonen network) for eye disease classification (Anitha, Hemanth, Vijila, & Ahsina, 2009). Retinal vessel segmentation using the 2-D Morlet wavelet and neural network is a work where the authors reported a new method for automatic segmentation of the vasculature in retinal images (Ghaderi, Hassanpour, & Shahiri, 2007). Emulation of salamander retina with multilayer neural network is another work where the authors used multilayer cellular neural network platform to emulate the functions of salamander retina (Sung-Nien, Chien-Nan, & Chun-Chieh, 2009). Retina vessel detection using Fuzzy Ant Colony Algorithm is another work where the authors described a fuzzy clustering method based on Ant Colony Algorithm (Hooshyar & Khayati, 2010). Vascular landmark classification in retinal images using fuzzy RBF (Radial Basis Function) is a work proposed in (Candemir, Cetinkaya, Kilincceker, & Cinsdikici, 2013). In this work, the author suggested the use of radial based neural networks for classification of the landmark points from retina vessels in the retinal vascular images to diagnose the disease in the diabetic retinopathy patients and to track the periodic differences in retinal vessel images. Locating the Optic Nerve in a Retinal image using the Fuzzy convergence of the blood vessels is a work where the author used an automated method to locate the optic nerve in images of the ocular fundus (Hoover & Goldbaum, 2003). They used a novel algorithm called fuzzy convergence to determine the origination of the blood vessel network. A method to obtain vector curve of blood vessel's skeleton using the green channel gray-scale retina images was proposed (Xu, Guo, Hu, & Cheng, 2005). Another approach is reported in (Ortega, Marina, Penedo, Blanco, & Gonzalez, 2006). They used a fuzzy circular Hough transform to localize the optical disk in the retina image. This algorithm is computationally more efficient with respect to the algorithm presented in (Xu, Guo, Hu, & Cheng, 2005).

Here, we noticed that the major literature have been restricted to the preprocessing techniques with no focus on the variations of the ridge pattern. These are restricted to the popular NFS and FNS learning and decision making arena with no focus on performance variations that may be derived from the application of fuzzy based hybrid systems with varying fuzzification norms and inference rules.

MOTIVATION

There are several issues involved in a biometric authentication system which have already been outlined. Preprocessing of fingerprint and retina samples is a crucial component in fingerprint as well as retina recognition. Further, the success of such a recognition system depends on the better feature extraction and classification techniques. Hence, the focus is to explore a range of pre-processing techniques along with feature extraction and classification techniques which shall improve performance of fingerprint as well as retina recognition blocks of a biometric authentication system. This work initially considered ANN based identification, but the success rate obtained by could not be increased beyond 95%. This aspect has driven the design of an ANFIS

based identification system. Fingerprint and retina features are non-linear with varying patterns with subtle alterations. The ANFIS has the capability to address and solve such problems where there are distinct presence of non-linearity, randomness and uncertainty in the data. The ANFIS based identification system used in this work provides better success rate (around 98%). Further, some experimental work has been carried out to develop an authentication / identification system which uses fingerprint and retina as inputs.

The rest of the description is grouped under sections related to theoretical consideration, system details, experimental works and results, conclusion and future direction.

BASIC THEORETICAL CONSIDERATIONS

The previous section provided a brief description of the background, identified issues, related works and the primary motivation of the work. In this section, we provide the basic theoretical aspects related to the work.

Fingerprint Recognition

Fingerprints are graphical flow-like ridges and valleys present on the surface of human fingers. Typically, there are two prominent types of minutiae (ridge endings and ridge bifurcations) that constitute a fingerprint pattern. A ridge ending is defined as the ridge point where it ends abruptly. A ridge bifurcation is defined as the ridge point where a ridge diverges into branch ridges. A fingerprint can be represented by the minutiae locations, types and attributes like orientation. A proper quality fingerprint image typically has about 40 to 100 minutiae, but a dozen of minutiae are considered sufficient to identify a fingerprint pattern. A sample fingerprint image is shown in Figure 1.

Figure 1. A sample fingerprint image

Fingerprint recognition is one of the popular biometric techniques and is an automated method of verifying a match between two fingerprint images. It is the process used to determine whether two sets of fingerprint ridge detail come from the same finger or not. The most remarkable strengths of fingerprint recognition are its maturity in providing a high level of recognition accuracy, use with low-cost small-size acquisition devices, allowing its use in a broad range of applications not requiring complex user-system interaction.

Retina Recognition

Retina is the vascular pattern of the eye which is not easy to change and replicate. The patterns are different for right and left eye. The retina of an individual is unique and remains unchanged over a lifetime. Figure 2 shows the structure of a retina.

Retina recognition is a system that captures and analyzes the patterns of blood vessels on the thin nerve on the back of the eyeball. These vessels processes light entering through the pupil. Retinal patterns are highly distinctive traits. Every eye has its own totally unique pattern of blood vessels. Even the eyes of identical twins are distinct. The strengths of retina recognition are suitability for high level security environment and difficulty in destroying its features.

Artificial Neural Network (ANN)

ANNs are non-parametric prediction or soft computing tools based on the analogy of biological nervous systems consisting of interconnected group

Figure 2. Structure of a retina

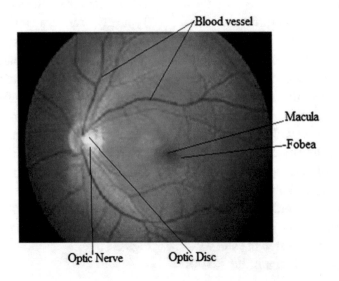

of artificial neurons and information-processing units using connectionist approach that can be used for a host of pattern classification and recognition purposes (Haykin, 2003). ANNs can be trained to perform complex functions in various fields, including pattern recognition, identification, classification, speech, vision, and control systems and to solve problems that are difficult for conventional computers or human beings (Fausett, 1993). ANNs are characterized by non-linear processing performing pattern matching using a method which determines values of connectionist using a process called training or learning. There is a close analogy between the structure of a biological neuron (i.e. a brain or nerve cell) and the processing element of the neural network. A biological neuron has three types of components: its dendrites, soma and axons. Many dendrites receive signals from other neurons. The signals are electric impulses that are transmitted across a synaptic gap by means of a chemical process. The action of the chemical transmitter modifies the incoming signal in a manner similar to the action of the weights in an ANN. The soma or cell body sums the incoming signals. When sufficient input is received, the cell transmits a signal over its axon to other cells. At any instant of time a cell may transmit or not, so that transmitted signals can be treated as binary. However, the frequency of firing varies and can be viewed as a signal of either greater or lesser magnitude. This corresponds to looking at discrete time steps and summing all activity i.e., signals

received or signals sent, at a particular point of time (Fausett, 1993). The transmission of the signals from a particular neuron is accomplished by an action potential resulting from differential concentrations of ions on either side of the neuron's axon sheath. The ions most directly involved are potassium, sodium and chloride (Fausett, 1993). A generic biological neuron, together with axons from other neurons is as in Figure 3.

The fundamental information-processing unit of the operation of the ANN is the McCulloch-Pitts Neuron (1943). Figure 4 shows the model of a McCulloch-Pitts neuron, which forms the basis for designing ANNs which are of different types like supervised and unsupervised. The main reasons behind their success are non-linear processing, ability to learn, adaptive in nature, contextual information, fault tolerance, diversity of types and topologies, uniformity of analysis and design, input-output mapping and evidential response.

The three basic elements of the neuron model are explained as:

1. A set of synapses or connecting links, each of which is characterized by weight or strength of its own. Specially, a signal x_j at the input of synapse j connected to v neuron, k is multiplied by the synaptic weight w_{kj}, refers to the neuron in question and the second subscript refers to the input end of the synapse to which the weight refers. Unlike

Figure 3. A generic biological neuron

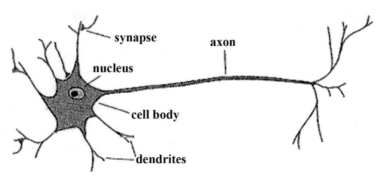

Figure 4. A model of a neuron

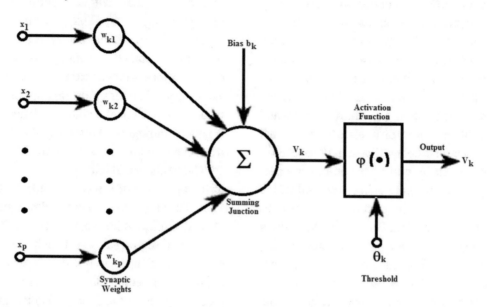

a synapse in the brain, the synaptic weight of an artificial neuron may lie in a range that includes negative as well as positive values (Haykin, 2003).

2. An adder for summing the input signal, weighted by the respective synapses of the neuron; the operations described here constitutes a linear combiner (Haykin, 2003).

3. An activation function for limiting the amplitude of the output of a neuron. The activation function is also referred to as a squashing function in that it squashes (limits) the permissible amplitude range of the output signal to some finite value (Haykin, 2003).

From this model the interval activity of a neuron k can be shown to be,

$$u_k = \sum_{j=1}^{m} w_{kj} x_j \qquad (1)$$

and

$$y_k = \varphi(u_k + b_k) \qquad (2)$$

where $x_1, x_2, ..., x_k$ are the input signals, $w_{k1}, w_{k2}, ..., w_{km}$ are the synaptic weights of neuron k, b_k is the bias, $\varphi(.)$ is the activation function and y_k is the output signal of the neuron. The use of bias b_k has the effect of applying and affine transformation to the output u_k of the linear combiner in the model of Figure 4 as shown by

$$v_k = u_k + b_k \qquad (3)$$

From the above equations we have,

$$v_k = \sum_{j=0}^{m} w_{kj} x_j \qquad (4)$$

here a new synapse has been added. Its input is $x_0 = +1$ and its weight is

$$w_{k0} = b_k \text{ and } y_k = \varphi(v_k) \qquad (5)$$

The activation function acts as a squashing function, such that the output of a neuron in a neural network is between certain values (usually 0 and 1, or -1 and 1). Among several types of activation function, three basic types are explained here (Haykin, 2003).

Threshold Function: This type of activation function takes on a value of 0 if the summed input is less than a certain threshold value v, and the value 1 if the summed input is greater than or equal to the threshold value and is defined as

$$\varphi(v) = \begin{cases} 1, & \text{if } v \geq 0; \\ 0, & \text{if } v < 0. \end{cases} \qquad (6)$$

This type of threshold function is referred as a Heaviside function. The output of neuron k employing such a threshold function is expressed as

$$y_k = \begin{cases} 1, & \text{if } v_k \geq 0; \\ 0, & \text{if } v_k < 0. \end{cases} \qquad (7)$$

where v_k is the induced field of the neuron.

If the threshold function of Equations (6) are rewritten have the range -1 to +1, it is referred as Signum function and is defined as

$$\varphi(v) = \begin{cases} 1 & v_k > 0; \\ 0 & v_k = 0; \\ -1 & v_k < 0. \end{cases} \qquad (8)$$

1.   Piecewise-Linear Function: This function can take on the values of 0 or 1, but can also take on values between that depending on the amplification factor in a certain region of linear operation. This function is defined as

$$\varphi(v) = \begin{cases} 1, & v \geq +\dfrac{1}{2}; \\ v, & +\dfrac{1}{2} > v > -\dfrac{1}{2}; \\ 0, & v \leq -\dfrac{1}{2}. \end{cases} \qquad (9)$$

where the amplification factor inside the linear region of operation is assumed to be unity.

2.   Sigmoid Function: The sigmoid is defined as a strictly increasing function that exhibits a graceful balance between linear and nonlinear behavior. This function can range between 0 and 1, but it is also sometimes useful to use the -1 to 1 range. An example of the sigmoid function is the logistic function defined as

$$\varphi(v) = \frac{1}{1 + \exp(-a * v)} \qquad (10)$$

where a is the slope parameter of the sigmoid function.

With respect to the active or decoding phase, ANNs can be classified into two systems. They are feed forward and feedback systems. Feed forward ANNs are static whereas feedback systems are dynamic or recurrent in nature. Figures 5 and 6 show the structure of a feed forward neural network and feedback neural network respectively. There are two broad methods of learning which classifies ANNs further into supervised and unsupervised category. Learning is the act of presenting the network with some sample data and modifying the weights to better approximate data to a desired form using an appropriate function. In supervised learning the ANN is provided with a pattern which it learns constantly till it can fully handle the pattern fed to it. In case of unsupervised learning, there are no reference patterns for the ANNs to learn. They do it by following a competitive learning among themselves. Feed forward ANNs are used for prediction, classification and function approximation. Examples are back propagation networks, radial basis networks and linear recursive least mean square (LMS) networks.

Figure 5. Structure of a feed forward neural network

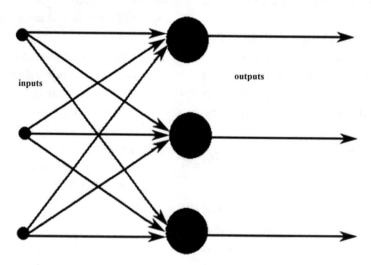

Figure 6. Structure of a feedback neural network

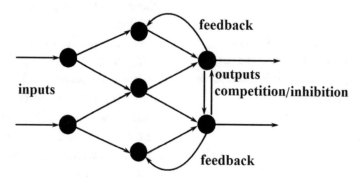

Feedback networks are used in feature matching, constraint satisfaction and optimization. Examples are recurrent back propagation networks, adaptive resonance networks and associative memories. In Feed forward neural networks, solutions are known, weights are learned and it evolves in the weight space. Whereas in feedback neural networks, solutions are unknown, weights are prescribed and it evolves in the state space. An ANN can be a single or multilayered approach. ANNs can be used as classifier because of its adaptive in nature. It can generate multiple classes and decision boundaries, so robust in multiple classifications.

In this work, the author used back propagation feed forward neural network with Levenberg-Marquardt optimization training method. The basic back propagation algorithm is based on minimizing the error of the network using the derivatives of the error function. The Levenberg-Marquardt algorithm has been found being faster and having better performance than the other neural network algorithms in training. The Multilayer Perceptron neural network is used here with two hidden layers. Figure 7 shows the structure of a Multilayer Perceptron (MLP).

Figure 7. MLP with two hidden layers

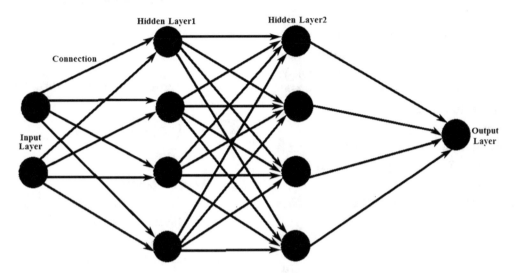

Multi Layer Perceptron (MLP)

A MLP consists of one or more hidden layers in between the input and output layers, whose computation nodes are correspondingly called hidden neurons or hidden units. By adding one or more hidden layers, the network is enabled to extract higher order statistics (Haykin, 2003). The architectural graph in Figure 7 shows a representation of a simple MLP with two hidden layers. The equation for output in a MLP with one hidden layer is given as:

$$O_x = \sum_{i=1}^{N} \beta_i g[w]_i.[x] + b_i \qquad (11)$$

where β_i is the weight value between the ith hidden neuron.

The process of adjusting the weights and biases of a MLP is known as training. The most common training algorithm for MLP is error backpropagation. This algorithm entails a back propagation of the error correction through each neuron in the network. Classification by an ANN involves training it so as to provide an optimum decision rule for classifying all the outputs of the network. The training should minimize the risk function (Haykin, 2003):

$$R = \frac{1}{2N} \sum \left(d_j - F(x_j) \right)^2 \qquad (12)$$

where d_j is the desired output pattern for the prototype vector x_j, $((.))$ is the Euclidean norm of the enclosed vector and N is the total number of samples presented to the network in training. The decision rule therefore can be given by the output of the network:

$$y_{kj} = F_k(x_j) \qquad (13)$$

For the jth input vector x_j. Training the ANN is done in two broad passes-one a forward pass and the other a backward calculation with error determination and connecting weight updating in between. Batch training method is adopted as it accelerates the speed of training and the rate of convergence of the MSE to the desired value (Haykin, 2003). The steps are:

1. **Initialization:** Initialize the weight matrix W with random values between [-1, 1] if a tan-sigmoid function is used as an activation function and between [0, 1] if log-sigmoid function is used as activation function. W is a matrix of $C \times P$ where P is the length of the feature vector used for each of the C classes.

2. **Presentation of Training Samples:** Input is $P_m = [P_{m1}, P_{m2}, ..., P_{mL}]$. The desired output is $d_m = [d_{m1}, d_{m2}, ..., d_{mL}]$.

   a. Compute the values of the hidden nodes as

$$net_{mj}^h = \sum_{i=1}^{L} w_{ji}^h p^{mi} + \phi_j^h \qquad (14)$$

   b. Calculate the output from the hidden layer as

$$o_{mj}^h = f_j^h \left(net_{mj}^h \right) \qquad (15)$$

where $f(x) = \dfrac{1}{e^x}$ or $f(x) = \dfrac{e^x - e^{-x}}{e^x + e^{-x}}$ depending upon the choice of the activation function.

   c. Calculate the values of the output node as

$$o_{mk}^o = f_k^o \left(net_{mj}^o \right) \qquad (16)$$

3. Forward Computation: Compute the errors

$$e_{jn} = d_{jn} - o_{jn} \qquad (17)$$

   a. Calculate the Mean Square Error (MSE) as

$$MSE = \frac{\sum_{j=1}^{M} \sum_{n=1}^{L} e_{jn}^2}{2M} \qquad (18)$$

   b. Error terms for the output layer is

$$\delta_{mk}^o = o_{mk}^o \left(1 - o_{mk}^o \right) e_{mn} \qquad (19)$$

   c. Error terms for the hidden layer

$$\delta_{mk}^h = o_{mk}^h \left(1 - o_{mk}^h \right) \sum_j \delta_{mj}^o w_{jk}^o \qquad (20)$$

4. Weight Update:

   a. Between the output and the hidden layers

$$w_{kj}^o (t+1) = w_{kj}^o (t) + \eta \delta_{mk}^o o_{mj} \qquad (21)$$

where η is the learning rate ($0 < \eta < 1$). For faster convergence a momentum term (α) may be added as

$$w_{kj}^o (t+1) = w_{kj}^o (t) + \eta \delta_{mk}^o o_{mj} + \alpha \left(w_{kj}^o (t+1) - w_{kj} \right) \qquad (22)$$

   b. Between the hidden layer and input layer

$$w_{ji}^h (t+1) = w_{ji}^h (t) + \eta \delta_{mj}^h P_i \qquad (23)$$

A momentum term may be added as

$$w_{ji}^h (t+1) = w_{ji}^h (t) + \eta \delta_{mj}^h p_i + \alpha \left(w_{ji}^o (t+1) - w_{ji} \right) \qquad (24)$$

One cycle through the complete training set forms one epoch. The above is repeated till MSE meets the performance criteria.

Here, while MSE approaches the convergence goal, training of the MLPs suffer if

$$Corr(p_{m,i}(j), p_{m,i}(j+1)) = high$$

and

$Corr(p_{m,i}(j), p_{m,i+1}(j))$=high.

This is due to the requirements of the (error) back propagation algorithm as suggested by Equations 19 and 20. Therefore, the motivation of formulation of any feature set should always keep this fact within sight.

Fuzzy System (FS)

Fuzzy systems were derived from the work in the field of Fuzzy Logic carried out by Zadeh (1965). Fuzzy Logic is built on the Fuzzy set theory, which was introduced to the world, for the first time by Zadeh in 1965. The invention or proposition of Fuzzy set was motivated by the need to capture and represent the real world with its fuzzy data due to uncertainty. Uncertainty can be caused by imprecision in measurement due to several factors. Zadeh showed the limitations of Crisp set theory in representing such descriptions and classifications. Unlike crisp sets, fuzzy sets define intermediate steps or stages defined using membership functions. Zadeh proposed the concept of a Membership Function (MF) to represent this uncertainty instead of saying when a quantity belongs to a class or not. An element can be in the set with a degree of membership and out of the set with a degree of membership. Hence, crisp

sets are a special case, or a subset of fuzzy sets, where elements are allowed a membership degree of 100% or 0% but nothing in between. Figure 8 illustrates the use of Fuzzy sets to represent the notion of a tall person. Some of the advantages of Fuzzy logic can be summarized as (Zadeh, 1965):

1. The rationale behind the rules associated with Fuzzy logic is conceptually easy to understand.
2. Flexibility is a property of Fuzzy logic.
3. It can tolerate imprecise data.
4. It can be used to model non-linear functions of unknown complexity.
5. Fuzzy logic can be related to previous experience and knowledge.
6. Fuzzy logic can work in concert with conventional techniques and improve performance.
7. Fuzzy logic is defined using the basic principles of natural language.

There are four ways of representing fuzzy membership functions as: (i) Graphical representation, (ii) Tabular and list representation, (iii) Geometric representation and (iv) Analytic representation.

Graphical representation is the most common in the literature. Tabular and list representations are used for finite sets. In this type of representation, each element of the set is paired with its degree of membership. Two different notations have been used in the literature for tabular and list repre-

Figure 8. Fuzzy set representation

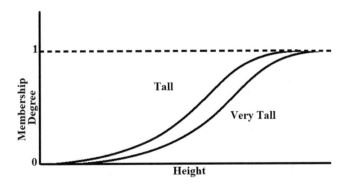

sentation. The following example illustrates the two notations for the same membership function.

$$A = \{<x_1, 0.9>, <x_2, 0.6>, <x_3, 0.7>, <x_4, 0.8>\} \tag{25}$$

$$A = \frac{0.8}{x_1} + \frac{0.7}{x_2} + \frac{0.6}{x_3} \tag{26}$$

The third method of representation is the geometric representation and is also used for representing finite sets. For a set that contains n elements, n-dimensional Euclidean space is formed and each element may be represented as a coordinate in that space. Finally analytical representation is another alternative to graphical representation in representing infinite sets, e.g., a set of real numbers. Fuzzy Arithmetic uses arithmetic on closed intervals. In a sense, Fuzzy logic can be considered to be a generalization of a logic system that includes the class of all logic systems with truth-values in the interval [0, 1].

Fuzzy systems can be broadly categorized into two categories. The first includes linguistic models based on collections of IF - THEN rules, whose antecedents and consequents utilize fuzzy values. It uses fuzzy reasoning and the system behavior can be described in natural terms. The Mamdani Model (Mamdani & Assilian, 1975) falls in this group. The knowledge is represented as

$$R^i : \text{If } x_1 \text{ is } A_1^i \text{ and } x_2 \text{ is } A_2^i \text{ ....and } x_n \text{ is } A_m^i \tag{27}$$

$$: \text{then } y_i \text{ is } B_i \tag{28}$$

where R^i ($i = 1, 2,....l$) denotes the ith fuzzy rule, x_j ($j = 1, 2,....l$) is the input, y_j ($j = 1, 2,....l$) is the output of the fuzzy rule R^i and $A_1^i, A_2^i,..., A_m^i$, B^i ($i = 1, 2,....l$) are fuzzy membership functions usually associated with linguistic terms.

The second category, based on Sugeno–type systems (Takagi & Sugeno, 1985), uses the rule structure that has fuzzy antecedent and functional consequent parts. This can be viewed as the expansion of piecewise linear partition represented as

$$R^i : \text{If } x_1 \text{ is } A_1^i \text{ and } x_2 \text{ is } A_2^i \text{ ....and } x_n \text{ is } A_m^i \tag{29}$$

$$: \text{then } y_i = a_0^i + a_1^i x_1 + ...a_n^i x_n . \tag{30}$$

The approach approximates a nonlinear system with a combination of several linear systems, by decomposing the whole input space into several partial fuzzy spaces and representing each output space with a linear equation. Such models are capable of representing both qualitative and quantitative information and allow relatively easier application of powerful learning techniques for their identification from data (Takagi & Sugeno, 1985). They are capable of approximating any continuous real – valued function on a compact set to any degree of accuracy (Takagi & Sugeno, 1985). This type of knowledge representation does not allow the output variables to be described in linguistic terms and the parameter optimization is carried out iteratively using a nonlinear optimization method (Mitra & Hayashi, 2000).

Fuzzy control has proved to be the most successful application of Fuzzy Logic shown in Figure 9 which consists of four modules: the rule base, the inference engine, the fuzzification, and the defuzzification (Kartalopoulos, 1996). But there are problems associated with fuzzy systems as well. Some of them can be as below:

1. **Stability:** No theoretical guarantee can be assumed regarding the fact that a general fuzzy system does not go chaotic and remains stable, despite extensive experience.
2. **Learning Capability:** Fuzzy systems lack capabilities of learning and have no memory

Figure 9. Fuzzy controller

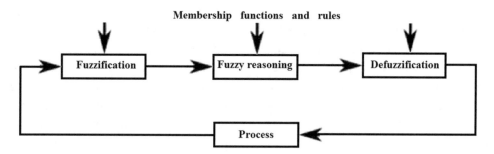

as started previously. This is why hybrid systems, particularly neuro-fuzzy system, are becoming more and more popular.

3. **Membership Functions and Fuzzy Rules:** Defining appropriate membership functions and fuzzy rules are not always easy. It is complicated task to determine membership functions and related rules.

Neuro –Fuzzy Systems

The need for developing hybrid systems that combine fuzzy techonology and a ANN was motivated by the short comings and the complementary nature of each of the two methodologies. The performance of ANN becomes degraded and less robust when the inputs are not well defined, i.e., fuzzy inputs. On the other hand, fuzzy systems are not capable of learning. Moreover, the fuzzy rules that define the input/output relationship mustbe known in advance. Therefore, combining the two techonologies to create hybrid systems that feel the gaps of one paradigm by means of the other was very highly motivated (Kartalopoulos, 1996). Both fuzzy systems and ANNs are soft computing approaches to modelling expert behavior. The goal is to mimic the actions of an expert who solves complex problems (Mitra & Hayashi, 2000). Both ANNs and fuzzy systems are dynamic, parallel processing systems that estimate input output functions. The estimate a function without any mathematical model and learn from experience with sample data. A fuzzy system adaptively infers

and modifies its fuzzy associations from representative numarical samples. ANNs, on the other hand, can blindly generate and refine fuzzy rules from training data (Kosko, 1991). Fuzzy sets are considered to be advantageous in the logical field and in handling higher order processing easily. The higher flexibility is a characteristic feature of neural networks produced by learning and hence, this suits data-driven processing better (Mitra & Hayashi, 2000; Nauck, Klawonn, & Kruse, 1997).

Fuzzy logic and ANNs are suited for contrasting application requirements. For example, fuzzy system are appropriate if sufficient expert knowledge about the process is available, while neural systems are useful if sufficient process data are available or measurable. Neural systems are treated in a numaric quantitative manner, whereas fuzzy systems are treated in a symbolic qualitative manner. Fuzzy system, however exhibits both symbolic and numeric features. Therefore, ANN and fuzzy systems together creates a framework which leads to a symbiotic relationship in which fuzzy systems provide a powerful framework for expert knowledge representation, while neural networks provide learning capabilities and exceptional suitability for computationally efficient hardware implemantation. The significance of this integration becomes even more apparent by considering there disparities. Neural networks do not provide a strong scheme for knowledge representation, while fuzzy logic controllers do not possess capabilities for automated learning (Mitra & Hayashi, 2000).

Fuzzification

One of the primary blocks of this proposed approach is a fuzzfier. In this ANFIS based FRS and RRS, Gaussian and generalized bell MFs are used. It has the advantage of being smooth and nonzero at all points. A generalized bell MF is specified by three parameters $\{a, b, c\}$ and is expressed as:

$$\text{Bell}(x \, ; a, b, c) = \frac{1}{1 + \left| \frac{x-c}{a} \right|^{2b}} \qquad (31)$$

where 'c' determines the center of the curve, 'a' is the half width and 'b' (together with 'a') controls the slopes at the crossover points (where MF value is 0.5) and the parameter 'b' is usually positive. A desired bell MF can be obtained by a proper selection of the parameter set $\{a, b, c\}$. Specifically, we can adjust 'c' and 'a' to vary the center and width of the MF and then use to control the slopes at the crossover points. Figure 10 shows a generalized bell MFs.

We have also considered the Gaussian MF. Gaussian MF is specified by two parameters $\{c, s\}$ and is expressed as:

$$\text{Gaussian}(x; c, s, m) = \exp\left[-\frac{1}{2} \left| \frac{x-c}{s} \right|^{m} \right] \qquad (32)$$

'c' represents the center of the MF's, width of the MF's and m is the fuzzification factor (e.g.; $m=2$). Because of their smoothness and concise notation, gauss MF's and bell MF's are becoming increasingly popular methods for specifying fuzzy sets. Gaussian functions are well known in the fields of probability and statistics and they possess useful properties such as invariance under multiplication and Fourier transform. The bell MF has one more parameter than the Gaussian MF, so it can approach a non-fuzzy set if $b \rightarrow \infty$ (Jang & Sun, 1995). A detailed set of experiments are carried out in this work. Respective performances are noted which are derived by considering these two MFs and their impact in ascertaining the system efficiency.

Adaptive Neuro-Fuzzy Inference System (ANFIS)

Fuzzy systems provide an expert level decision making system by following the variations in the texture of the input data. ANN and Fuzzy System (FS) are the important components of soft computing. They have received large acceptance in the diverse fields of uncertainty. ANNs are comfortable with the situations that have sufficient model free measurement data (Mitra & Hayashi, 2000) and FSs work where sufficient process data are available and expert knowledge

Figure 10. Physical meaning of parameters in a gbell MF

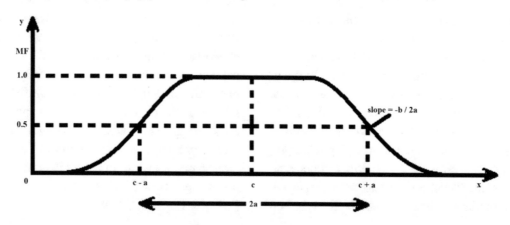

is necessary (Jang & Sun, 1995). Thus ANN and FS having the numeric quantitative capability and symbolic-qualitative capacity respectively can be applied to solve problems where higher precision of estimation is difficult. Hybrid systems formed by combinations of fuzzy and ANN methods have adaptability, parallelism, non-linear processing, robustness and learning in data rich environment for modeling uncertainty (Ross, 2008). Fuzzy and ANN can be combined to form either Neuro-Fuzzy System (NFS) or Fuzzy-Neural System (FNS) based units. Here, NFS based approach is used. The ANFIS combines the advantages of ANN with those of fuzzy systems. It has found numerous applications in a variety of fields. The fuzzy model can either be Mamdani fuzzy model or TSK fuzzy model. However, TSK model is smoother and computationally efficient representation than Mamdani's model.

Let, the considered FIS is given two inputs 'x' and 'y' and one output 'f'. For a first-order Sugeno fuzzy model, a common rule set with two fuzzy if-then rules is as follows:

Rule 1: If (x is A_1) and (y is B_1) then ($f_1 = p_1 x + q_1 y + r_1$) (33)

Rule 2: If (x is A_2) and (y is B_2) then ($f_2 = p_2 x + q_2 y + r_2$) (34)

where A_i and B_i are the fuzzy sets, f_i are the outputs within the fuzzy region specified by the fuzzy rule, p_i, q_i and r_i are the design parameters that are determined during the training process. Figure 11 shows the Type-3 fuzzy reasoning mechanism for a first order Sugeno fuzzy model.

The corresponding equivalent ANFIS architecture to implement these two rules is shown in Figure 12 in which a circle indicates a fixed node, whereas a square indicates an adaptive node (Jang, 1993). The general architecture of ANFIS, which is primarily a fuzzy system having five layers as described below:

Layer 1: Every node i in this layer is an adaptive node with a node output defined by

$$O_i^1 = \mu A_i(x), \text{ for } i = 1, 2 \text{ or} \tag{35}$$

$$O_i^1 = \mu B_{i-2}(y), \text{ for } i = 3, 4 \tag{36}$$

where x or y is the input to the node and A_i or B_{i-2} is a fuzzy set associated with this node. The outputs of this layer are the membership values of the premise part. Here, the MFs for A_i and B_i can be any appropriate parameterized MFs. For example, if the bell shaped MF is employed, $\mu A_i(x)$ is given by

Figure 11. TSK type -3 Fuzzy reasoning

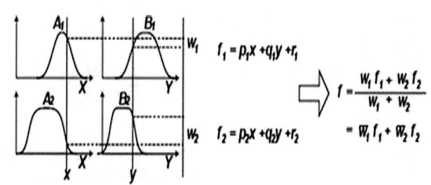

Figure 12. Equivalent ANFIS

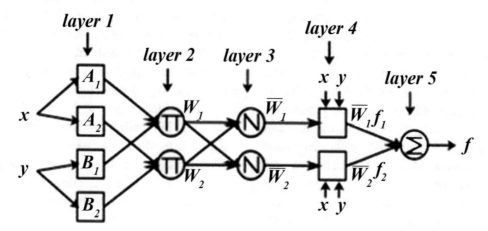

$$\mu A_i\left(x\right)=\frac{1}{1+\left(\frac{x-c_i}{a_i}\right)^{2bi}} \quad (37)$$

where a_i, b_i and c_i are the parameters of the MFs, governing the bell shaped functions accordingly and are referred to as premise parameters.

Layer 2: Every node in this layer is a fixed node labeled Π, which multiplies the incoming signals and gives the product as output. For instance,

$$O_i^2 = w_i = \mu A_i(x) \times \mu B_i(y), \, i=1, 2 \quad (38)$$

Each node output represents the firing strength of a rule.

Layer 3: Every node in this layer is a fixed node labeled N, indicating that they play a normalization role to the firing strengths from the previous layer. The output of this layer can be represented as

$$O_i^3 = \overline{w}_i = \frac{w_i}{w_1 + w_2}, \, i=1,2 \quad (39)$$

which are the so called normalized firing strengths. Here w_1, w_2 are the firing strengths to the rules 1 and 2.

Layer 4: Every node in this layer is an adaptive node. The output of each node in this layer is simply the product of the normalized firing strength and a first order polynomial (for a first order Sugeno Model). Thus the output of this layer is given by:

$$O_i^4 = \overline{w}_i f_i = \overline{w}_i\left(p_i x + q_i y + r_i\right), \, i=1,2 \quad (40)$$

parameters in this layer will be referred to as consequent parameters.

Layer 5: In this layer, there is only one single fixed node labeled with Σ that performs the summation of all incoming signals. Hence, the overall output of the model is given by

$$O_i^5 = \sum_{i=1} \overline{w}_i f_i = \frac{\sum_i w_i f_i}{\sum_i w_i} = \text{overall output} \quad (41)$$

Thus, ANFIS uses a hybrid learning procedure for estimation of the premise and consequent parameters (Stergiou & Siganos, 1996).

Crossing Number Algorithm (CNA)

The most commonly employed method of minutiae extraction is the Crossing Number Algorithm (CNA) (Amengual et al., 1997). This method involves the use of the skeleton image where the ridge flow pattern is eight connected. The minutiae are extracted by scanning the local neighbourhood of each ridge pixel in the image using a 3×3 window. The CN value is defined as half the sum of the differences between pairs of adjacent pixels in the eight - neighbourhood. Then, depending on the CN value, the ridge pixel can be classefied.

Principal Component Analysis (PCA)

PCA is a fast, linear, eigen vector based method. It uses an orthogonal transformation to convert a set of observation of possibly correlated variables into a set of linearly uncorrelated variables called principal components. The number of principal components is less than or equal to the number of original variables. This transformation is defined in such a way that the first principal component has the largest possible variance and each succeeding component in turn has the highest variance possible under the constraint that it is orthogonal to (uncorrelated with) the preceding components. PCA is sensitive to the relative scaling of the original variables. Often, its operation can be thought of as revealing the internal structure of the data in a way that best explains the variance in the data. If a multivariate dataset is visualized as a set of coordinates in a high–dimensional data space, PCA can supply the user with a lower- dimensional picture, a projection or shadow of this object when viewed from its most informative view point. This is done by using only the first few principal components so that the dimensionality of the transformed data is reduced.

PREPROCESSING AND FEATURE EXTRACTION OF FINGERPRINT AND RETINA

Here, we discuss some of the relevant pre-processing and feature extraction steps.

This section includes a detail explanation of all the experimental work done for the fingerprint and retina based recognition system. This section also provides a description of theoretical background of the method. The results and related discussions are described in the next. The proposed biometric identification system includes the following stages. They are image acquisition, image preprocessing, enhancement operations, morphological operations, feature extraction and classification.

Image Acquisition

In this stage, an image is captured for storage into a computer by a digital scanner, digital camera etc. It is very important as the quality of the input image must be good and free from any noise for better performance. Based on the mode of acquisition, a fingerprint image can be classified as off-line and on-line. An off-line image is typically obtained by smearing ink on the fingertip and creating an inked impression of the fingertip on paper and later scans it for future use. On the other hand, an on-line or live-scan image is acquired by sensing the tip of the finger directly, using a sensor that is capable of digitizing the fingerprint on contact. Basically, there are three types of sensors used for image acquisition. They are optical ultrasonic and capacitance sensors. Among, these three sensors, optical sensor is the most widely use because of its high efficiency and acceptable accuracy. Optical sensor captures a digital image by reflecting the light from the finger passes through a phosphor layer to an array of pixels which captures a visual image of the fingerprint. Retina scan is based on the blood vessel pattern in the retina at the back of the eye. Retina is not directly visible and so a coherent infrared light source is necessary to illuminate the retina. The infrared energy is absorbed faster by blood vessels in the retina than by the surrounding tissue. The image of the retina blood vessel pattern is then analyzed. Retina scans require that the person place their naked eye close to the scanner, stare at a specific point and remain still and focus on a specified location for approximately 10 to 15 seconds while the scan is completed. A retinal scan involves the use of a low-intensity coherent light source, which is projected onto the retina to illuminate the blood vessels which are then photographed and analyzed. A coupler is used to read the blood vessel patterns. A retina scan cannot be faked as it is currently impossible to forge a human retina. In this work, Fundus camera is used to capture the retina image.

Image Preprocessing

During image preprocessing, various samples from the selected databases are taken for making them suitable for manipulation and interpretation by subsequent stages. The steps include removal of noise and variation of intensity recorded, sharpening, improving the contrast and strengthening the texture of the image. Another important aspect is image restoration which extracts image information from a degraded form to make it suitable for subsequent processing and interpretation. The images which are corrupted by impulse or undesirable random variations in intensity values called noise. The images are corrupted by where the images are stored at default memory location in system of hardware and the images are damage by a noisy transmission channel. During acquisition, transmission, storage and retrieval processes, an image signal gets contaminated with noise. An image which is being sent electronically from one place to another place is contaminated by a variety

of noise sources. Noise can be caused in images by random fluctuations in the image signal. The main objective of the image pre-processing is to extract clear information from the images corrupted by noise. Such technique for noise removal is called filtering or denoising. An image gets corrupted with different types of noise. Noise can be classified as substitutive or impulsive noise (e.g. salt and pepper noise), additive noise (e.g. Gaussian noise) and multiplicative noise (e.g. speckle noise). Salt and pepper noise is a special case of impulsive noise, where a certain percentage of individual pixels are randomly digitized into widely varying maximum and minimum intensities (Toh & Isa, 2010). The need to remove salt and pepper noise is very important before subsequent image processing because the contamination of image by salt and pepper noise is caused in great amount and the occurrence of noise can severely damage the information or data contained in the original image. The simplest way to remove salt and pepper noise is by windowing the noise image with a median filter, is extensively applied to eliminate salt and pepper noise due to its outstanding computational efficiency. In this work, the author used median filter to remove the salt and pepper noise from the input images without significantly reducing the sharpness of the image.

Noise Removal Technique (Median Filter)

The best-known order-statistical filter in digital image processing is the median filter. It is a useful tool for reducing salt and pepper noise in an image. The median filter plays a key role in image processing and vision (Tukey, 1974). In median filter, the pixel value of a point p is replaced by the median of pixel value of 8-neighborhood of a point 'p'. The operation of this filter can be expressed as:

$$g(p) = \text{median}\{f(p), \text{ where } p \in N_8(p)\} \qquad (42)$$

The median filter reduces random impulsive noise. This noise removal is performed without blurring edges as much as a comparable linear low pass filter.

ENHANCEMENT OPERATIONS

Image enhancement aims to process an image so that the output is more suitable than the original image for a specific application. It includes sharpening, smoothing, highlighting features or normalizing illumination for display or analysis. It is used to improve the quality of image. A method which is quite useful for enhancing an image may not necessarily be the best approach for enhancing another image. Image enhancement techniques are based on performing image transformations using image operators that either manipulates the spatial domain (i.e. pixel values) or the frequency domain (i.e. the light wave components). Enhancing an image in the spatial domain could be achieved by image operators that transform an image by changing pixel values or move them around. Frequency domain enhancement techniques are based on modifying the Fourier transform of an image. A certain amount of trial and error usually is required before a particular image enhancement technique is selected. In this work, the author used intensity domain enhancement technique (i.e. Histogram Equalization).

The Histogram of a digital image with intensity levels in the range [0, *L*-1] is a discrete function. Histograms are frequently normalized by the total number of pixels in the image. Assuming an $M \times N$ image, a normalized. Histogram is related to probability of occurrence of in the image,

$$h(r_k) = n_k, \tag{43}$$

$$p(r_k) = \frac{n_k}{MN}, k = 0,1,2,\dots L\text{-}1 \tag{44}$$

where,

r_k is the kth intensity value

n_k is the number of pixels in the image having intensity value r_k,

$h(r_k)$ is the histogram of a digital image with intensity value r_k,

$p(r_k)$ gives an estimate of the probability of occurrence of intensity value r_k. The sum of all components of a normalized histogram is equal to 1.

Histogram equalization is a common technique for enhancing the appearance of an image. Suppose we have an image which is predominantly dark. Then its histogram would be skewed towards the lower end of the gray scale and all the image detail is compressed into the dark end of the histogram. If it stretches out the gray levels at the dark end to produce a more uniformly distributed histogram then the image would become much clearer. Histogram techniques are global enhancement techniques, in the sense that pixels are modified by a transformation function based on the gray-level content of an entire image. Since, in this work retina and fingerprint are used as inputs so it is important to enhance details over small areas in them, which is called the local enhancement. Adaptive histogram equalization technique operates on small areas in the image so it is used here for such purpose.

MORPHOLOGICAL OPERATIONS

Morphological operation is used as a tool for extracting image components useful in describing image shape such as boundaries, skeletons, thinning etc. The value of each pixel in the output image is based on a comparison of the corresponding pixel in the input image with its neighbors. By choosing the size and shape of the neighborhood, one can construct a morphological operation that is sensitive to specific shapes in the input image.

Mathematical morphology is a set theoretical approach to multidimensional digital signal or image analysis, based on shape. Erosion and Dilation operations are fundamental to morphological processing. Using these two basic operations, Opening and Closing and more other advanced morphological operations can be implemented. Dilation operation adds pixels to the boundaries of objects of an image, while erosion operation removes pixels on object boundaries. The number of pixels added or removed from the objects in an image depends on the size and shape of the structuring element used to process the image. The structuring element is a two dimensional patterns of hits, all relative to an origin that is often referred to as the center of the structuring element. It is a set as well. In the morphological dilation and erosion operation, the state of any given pixel in the output image is determined by applying a rule to the corresponding pixel and its neighbors in the input image. The rule used to process the pixels defines the operation as a dilation or erosion. In erosion operation, the value of the output pixel is the minimum value of all the pixels in the input pixel's neighborhood. In a binary image, if any of the pixels is set to 0, the output pixel is set to 0. The erosion of set A by the structuring element B, such that all z in A when B is in A and origin of $B=z$. It is denoted by $A \ominus B$ and defined as

$$A \ominus B = \{z|(B)_z \subseteq A\} \tag{45}$$

In dilation operation, the value of the output pixel is the maximum value of all the pixels in the input pixel's neighborhood. In a binary image, if any of the pixels is set to the value 1, the output pixel is set to 1. The dilation of set A by the structuring element B, such that all z in A when B hits A and origin of $B=z$. It is denoted by $A \oplus B$ and defined as

$$A \oplus B = \left\{z \left| \left(\hat{B}\right)_z \cap A \neq \varnothing \right.\right\} \tag{46}$$

Opening operation smoothes the contour object, breaks necks and eliminates thin protrusions. Opening decreases sizes of the small bright detail, with no appreciable effect on the darker gray levels, while the closing operation decreases sizes of the small dark details, with relatively little effect on bright features. Closing also tends to smooth sections of contours but, as opposed to opening, it generally fuses narrow breaks and long thin gulfs, eliminates small holes and fills gaps in the contour. The opening of set A by structuring element B, is denoted by $A \circ B$ and is defined as

$$A \circ B = (A \ominus B) \oplus B \tag{47}$$

Similarly, the closing of set A by structuring element B, is denoted by $A \bullet B$ and is defined as

$$A \bullet B = (A \oplus B) \ominus B \tag{48}$$

Another important morphological operation is the thinning operation. Thinning is an image processing operation in which binary valued image regions are reduced to lines. The purpose of thinning is to reduce the image components to their essential information for further analysis and recognition. The thinning of a set A by a structuring element B, denoted $A \otimes B$, can be defined in terms of the hit or miss transform

$$A \otimes B = A - (A \circledast B)$$

$$= A \cap (A \circledast B)^c \tag{49}$$

A more useful expression for thinning A symmetrically is based on a sequence of structuring elements:

$$\{B\} = \{B^1, B^2, B^3, \ldots, B^n\} \tag{50}$$

where B^i is a rotated version of B^{i-1}. Using this concept, thinning is defined by a sequence of structuring elements as

$$A \otimes \{B\} = ((\dots ((A \otimes B^{1}) \otimes B^{2}) \dots \otimes) B^{n}) \tag{51}$$

The process is to thin A by one pass with B^{1}, and then thin the result with one pass of B^{2} and so on, until A is thinned with one pass of B^{n}. The entire process is repeated until no further changes occur. Each individual thinning pass is performed using the above equation.

FEATURE EXTRACTION

It is a process through which certain vital information and details of an image section is captured for subsequent interpretation. Feature extraction aims to create discriminative features good for classification. The main goal of the feature extractor is to characterize an object to be recognized by measurements whose values are similar for objects in the same category and different for objects in different categories. Here, in the fingerprint recognition system, Crossing Number Algorithm (CNA) is used for the minutiae feature extraction. In case of retina recognition system, Principal Component Analysis (PCA) is used for the feature extraction of the blood vessels.

Feature Extraction of Fingerprint using CN Algorithm

The ridge pixel can be divided into bifurcation, ridge ending and non-minutiae point based on the value of CN. The CN algorithm is working on pixel representation '1' or '0', but the decision of minutiae point can be selected for each pixel value. CN method extracts the ridge endings and

bifurcations from the skeleton image by examining the local neighborhood of each ridge pixel using a 3×3 window.

The CN for a ridge pixel P is given by

$$0.5 \sum_{i=1}^{8} |P_{i} - P_{i+1}| \, CN = 0.5 \sum_{i=1}^{8} |P_{i} - P_{i+1}|, \quad P_{9} = P_{1} \tag{52}$$

where P_{i} is the pixel value in the neighborhood of P. For a pixel P, its eight neighboring pixels are scanned in an anti-clockwise direction as shown in Table 1.

After the CN for a ridge pixel has been computed, the pixel can then be classified according to the property of its CN value. With this formula, if CN=1 it corresponds to the end point and if CN=3, it corresponds to bifurcation point of minutiae. Other properties of CN are described in Table 2. In applying this algorithm, border area may be ignored, since there is no need to extract minutiae point on border area of the image that will gives more false minutiae points.

Feature Extraction of Retina sing PCA Algorithm

Principal Component Analysis (PCA) is a traditional procedure that uses linear transformations to map data from high dimensional space to low dimensional space (Suganthy & Ramamoorthy, 2012). The low dimensional space can be determined by Eigen vectors of the covariance matrix. The following steps involved in PCA include:

Table 1. Position of pixels

P4	P3	P2
P5	P	P1
P6	P7	P8

Table 2. CN with properties

CN	Properties
0	Isolated point
1	Ending point
2	Connective point
3	Bifurcation point
4	Crossing point

Step 1: Get the mean value $\bar{S}$ of the given dataset S.

Step 2: Subtract the mean value say from S. From these values a new matrix is obtained. Let say A.

Step 3: Covariance is obtained from the matrix i.e., $C=AA^T$ Eigen values are obtained from the covariance matrices that are $V_1 V_2 V_3 V_4$ ....V_N

Step 4: Finally, Eigen vectors and Eigen values are calculated for covariance matrix C.

Step 5: Only the largest Eigen values are kept to form lower dimensional dataset.

RETINA AND FINGERPRINT RECOGNITION USING ANFIS FOR BIOMETRIC IDENTIFICATION

Both retina and fingerprint samples are used in an ANFIS based biometric identification system. During the learning phase, the ANFIS tracks the minute variations in the samples, retains the learning and uses it subsequently. The main focus of the work is to study the performance of the fingerprint and retina recognition system that provides reliability, accuracy and reduced overall match speed. In this proposed model, a multi stage approach is used. The decision obtained from the system is used to generate the response. During image acquisition the operations are performed separately. Fingerprint image can be captured by a digital scanner, digital camera and sensor etc. for subsequent manipulation. Fingerprint image preprocessing includes resizing the original images to required size, image normalization, enhancement and thinning etc. Normalization is done so that the gray level values lies within a given set of values. It is required as the image usually has distorted levels of gray values. It allows standardizing the distorted levels of variation in the gray scale values. It involves pixel-wise operations and does not change the structures. Retina images captured by the Fundus camera are pre-

processed for subsequent manipulation. The next stage is feature extraction. In case of fingerprint, the thinned images are next considered for the minutiae feature extraction. The minutiae feature extraction algorithm extracts the main minutiae features required for matching two fingerprints. Here, CNA is used for minutiae extraction of fingerprints (Maltoni, Maio, Jain, & Prabhakar, 2009). Retina features include patterns of blood vessels (Hill, 2003). In this proposed model, PCA is used to extract the retina features. The proposed system model using ANFIS in block diagram form is shown in Figure 13. Here, ANFIS is used as classifier for recognition. It applies a combination of the least-squares (LS) method and the back propagation gradient descent (BPGD) method for training FIS membership function parameters to emulate a given training dataset. The ANFIS considered have five layers and its key specifications are provided in Table 3.

EXPERIMENTAL DETAILS AND RESULTS

The performance of FRS and RRS are analyzed in terms of computational speed and reliability. The overall computational time taken by the system is reduced to a greater level. ANFIS parameters

Table 3. ANFIS specifications

Input Data size	For fingerprint - CN features of length 101; For retina - PCA features of length 101.
SNR of input samples	0-3dB
Classifier type	ANFIS with five layers
ANFIS training method	Least-squares with the back propagation gradient descent method
Average training epochs	10-60
Total no. of membership functions	2,4,6,8 and 10
Type of membership functions	Gbell MF, Gaussian MF

Figure 13. Proposed system model

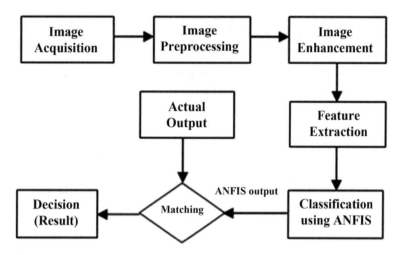

are adjusted so as to reduce the error measure defined by the sum of the square of the difference between the actual and desired output. The Root Mean Square Error (RMSE) is calculated using the expression:

$$\text{RMSE} = \sqrt{\frac{1}{N}\sum_{t=1}^{N}\left(A_t - F_t\right)^2} \qquad (53)$$

where A_t and F_t are actual and fitted values respectively and N is the number of training or testing sample. The RMSE is used as the primary criterion to ascertain the extent of learning acquired by the ANFIS.

The obtained results are compared with (Borah, Sarma, & Talukdar, 2013) and found that the ANFIS generate comparable RMSE values but the computational speed is significantly better. The ANFIS shows at least 50% increase in computational speed which establishes its usefulness. Further, the RMSE convergence is completed in less number of epochs. Thus the proposed approach is suitable for verification and authorization for the design of FRS and RRS. A total of 60 identical fingerprint as well as 100 retina images have been provided to the system for training, validation and testing. After extensive training,

the system is subjected to certain variations with signal to noise ratio (SNR) range between 0 to 3 dB to achieve robustness and proper recognition. The convergence RMSE due to change in MFs for 50 epochs are shown in Table 4. Also, the time required for 50 epochs for different inputs due to change in MFs are shown in Table 5. The average success rates achieved among few numbers of training epochs with ANN and ANFIS for both fingerprint and retina inputs are shown in Table 6. Again, the performance for both the Gaussian MF and Bell shaped MF are also considered. Here, the best average RMSE is obtained for Gauss MF with 6 and 10 numbers of MFs with an average RMSE of 4×10^{-3} and 1.6×10^{-3} obtained within 10.1 and 1.6 seconds respectively. The RMSE curves for both the FRS and RRS with 6 and 10 numbers of MFs are shown in Figure 14. and Figure 15. Also with Gaussian MFs, the computational time required is a bit lower compared to Bell MF. The advantage of using the ANFIS for FRS and RRS thus is obvious. With proper selection of MF type and numbers higher efficiency and lower computational time can be obtained for a range of patterns.0

Here, we have considered the performance for the Gaussian MF and Bell shaped MF for both the two input patterns. From the nature of

Table 4. Calculation of average RMSE for 50 epochs for different inputs

Input Name	Number of Membership Functions (MFs)	Minimum RMSE attained by after 50 epochs	
		Gaussmf	Gbellmf
Fingerprint	2	4×10^{-2}	9×10^{-2}
	4	2.3×10^{-2}	2.8×10^{-2}
	6	4×10^{-3}	5.6×10^{-2}
	8	8×10^{-3}	6.5×10^{-2}
	10	6×10^{-3}	1×10^{-2}
Retina	2	3.7×10^{-3}	3.7×10^{-3}
	4	3.6×10^{-3}	3.6×10^{-3}
	6	3.5×10^{-3}	3.6×10^{-3}
	8	3.4×10^{-3}	3.4×10^{-3}
	10	1.6×10^{-3}	1.6×10^{-3}

Table 5. Time required for 50 epochs for different inputs

Input Name	Number of Membership Functions (MFs)	Time required to reach 50 epochs by (in sec.)	
		Gaussmf	Gbellmf
Fingerprint	2	10.2	10.9
	4	10.1	10.8
	6	10.1	10.6
	8	10.1	10.5
	10	10	10.1
Retina	2	1.5	1.5
	4	1.5	1.6
	6	1.6	1.6
	8	1.6	1.6
	10	1.6	1.6

Table 6. Average success rates achieved among few numbers of training epochs with ANN and ANFIS for fingerprint and retina

Observation No	Epochs by ANN	Epochs by ANFIS	% Success Rate with ANN (Fingerprint)	% Success Rate with ANFIS (Fingerprint)	% Success Rate with ANN (Retina)	% Success Rate with ANFIS (Retina)
1	15	10	86	87.5	86	88
2	32	20	88	90	90	92
3	47	30	90	91	92	93
4	61	40	92	93	93	94
5	76	50	92.5	94	94	96
6	91	60	93.2	96	95	98

Figure 14. RMSE plot for fingerprint image

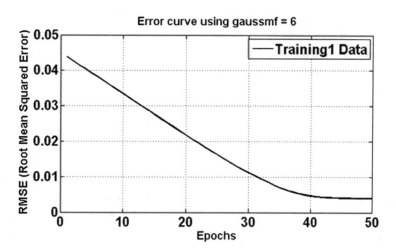

Figure 15. RMSE plot for retina image

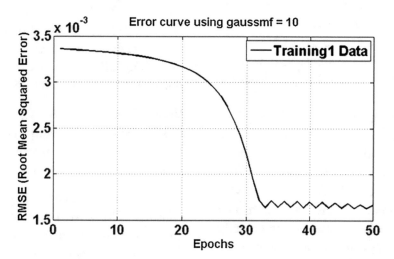

the RMSE plots, we noticed that with the Gaussian MF, the performance of the FRS and RRS is better than the Bell MF. Further, we see that the best average RMSE is obtained for Gaussian MF with 6 numbers of MFs for fingerprint. It is with an average RMSE of 4 X 10^{-3} is obtained within 10.1 seconds. Again the best average RMSE is obtained for the retina with 10 numbers Gaussian MF. It is found to be on an average, MSE of 1.6 X 10^{-3} is obtained within 1.6 seconds. Also with Gaussian MF, the computational time required is a

bit lower compared to Bell MF. With proper selection of MF type and numbers, higher efficiency and lower computational time can be obtained for a range of patterns.

From the nature of the RMSE plot of FRS, we see that starting with two numbers of epochs the convergence is gradually decreased up to 40 epochs and around 40 to 50, it is fixed. Beyond 50 epochs it becomes nearly constant at 4 X 10^{-3}. For the retina, starting with two numbers of epochs the convergence reaches stable value around 25 epochs is found and after that it suddenly drops down. Beyond 32 epochs it fluctuates to reach the convergence. Thus the number of MFs determines the computational time and accuracy related to the system. The feature set and the properly formulated ANFIS system generates a framework which is suitable for application in biometric authentication using retina and fingerprint samples.

CONCLUSION AND FUTURE DIRECTION

Here, we have discussed a retina and fingerprint based authentication system using an ANFIS. Initially, we perform a few pre-processing and feature extraction operations. We capture relevant features for both fingerprint and retina separately. For fingerprint detection we used CNA which provides a reliable set of features. Next, we used PCA features for retina based system. Both the two feature sets for the individual cases of retina and fingerprint are applied to the ANFIS system which acts as a DSS. The ANFIS is tested with several numbers of MFs. We derived the number of MFs required for deriving a proper ANFIS model to perform the work. The number of MFs also determines the computational time related to the system. The feature set and the properly formulated ANFIS system generates a framework which is suitable for application in biometric authentication. The experimental results show that the proposed model in an extended form shall be suitable for actual applications. The strength of the proposed system is its speed, computational efficiency, robustness and high precision which shall make it suitable for certain application. The overall performance of the system can be enhanced further by considering more number of samples and variations and by using better preprocessing techniques with ANFIS based blocks. The future scope of this work is to improve the ANFIS architecture to achieve high classification accuracy. The

present work has been verified using simulation based models. Next, the work can be extended to be part of an actual system with its primary blocks implemented for applications both in soft and hardware forms.

REFERENCES

Amengual, J. C., Juan, A., Prez, J. C., Prat, F., Sez, S., & Vilar, J. H. (1997). Real time minutiae extraction in fingerprint images. In *Proceedings of the 6th International Conference on Image Processing and its Applications*. doi:10.1049/cp:19971021

Anitha, J., Hemanth, D. J., Vijila, C. K. S., & Ahsina, A. (2009). Self Organizing neural network based pathology classification in retinal images. In *Proceedings of World Congress on Nature & Biologically Inspired Computing* (NaBIC). doi:10.1109/NABIC.2009.5393697

Borah, T. R., Sarma, K. K., & Talukdar, P. H., (2013). Retina and Fingerprint based Biometric Identification System. *International Journal of Computer Applications*, 74– 77.

Candemir, C., Cetinkaya, C., Kilincceker, O., & Cinsdikici, M. (2013). Vascular landmark classification in retinal images using fuzzy RBF. In *Proceeding of Signal Processing and Communications Applications Conference* (SIU). doi:10.1109/SIU.2013.6531382

Dagher, I., Helwe, W., & Yassine, F. (2002). Fingerprint recognition using fuzzy artmap neural network architecture. In *Proceeding of 14th International Conference on Microelectronics* (ICM). doi:10.1109/ICM-02.2002.1161519

Ding, C., Xia, Y., & Li, Y. (2014). Supervised segmentation of vasculature in retinal images using neural networks. In *Proceeding of IEEE International Conference on Orange Technologies* (ICOT). doi:10.1109/ICOT.2014.6954694

Fausett, L. (1993). *Fundamentals of Networks Architectures, Algorithms and Applications.* Pearson Education.

Ghaderi, R., Hassanpour, H., & Shahiri, M. (2007). Retinal vessel segmentation using the 2-D Morlet wavelet and neural network. In *Proceeding of International Conference on Intelligent and Advanced Systems* (ICIAS). doi:10.1109/ICIAS.2007.4658584

Haykin, S. (2003). *Neural Networks – A Comprehensive Foundation.* New Delhi: Pearson Education.

Hill, R. B. (1978). *Apparatus and method for identifying individuals through their retinal vasculature patterns.* US Patent No. 4109237.

Hill, R. B. (2003). *Retina Identification.* Biometrics Springer.

Hooshyar, S., & Khayati, R. (2010). Retina Vessel Detection Using Fuzzy Ant Colony Algorithm. In *Proceeding of Canadian Conference on Computer and Robot Vision* (CRV). doi:10.1109/CRV.2010.38

Hoover, A., & Goldbaum, M. (2003, August). Locating the Optic Nerve in a Retinal Image Using the Fuzzy Convergence of the Blood Vessels. *IEEE Transactions on Medical Imaging, 22*(8), 951–958. doi:10.1109/TMI.2003.815900 PMID:12906249

Hsieh, C. T., & Hu, C. S. (2005). An Application of Fuzzy Logic and Neural network to Fingerprint Recognition. In *Proceeding of the 4th WSEAS International Conference on Electric, Signal Processing and Control* (ESPOCO'05). WSEAS.

Jain, A., Hong, L., & Pankanti, S. (2000). Biometric Identification. *Communications of the ACM, 43*(2), 91–98. doi:10.1145/328236.328110

Jain, A., Hong, L., Pankanti, S., & Bolle, R. (1997). An identity authentication system using fingerprints. In *Proceeding of the Institute of Electrical and Electronics Engineers.* IEEE.

Jang, J. S. R., & Sun, C. T. (1995, March). Neuro FuzzyModeling and Control. *Proceedings of the IEEE, 85*(3), 378–406. doi:10.1109/5.364486

Jang, R. J. (1993). ANFIS: Adaptive – Network Based Fuzzy Inference System. *IEEE Transactions on Systems, Man, and Cybernetics, 23*(3), 665–685. doi:10.1109/21.256541

Jha, A. K., Narasimham, S., Krishna, S. S., & Mahadevan Pillai, V. P. (2010). *A neural network based approach for fingerprint recognition system. International Congress on Ultra Modern Telecommunications and Control Systems and Workshops (ICUMT)*, Moscow, Russia.

Jin, A. L. H., Chekima, A., Dargham, J. A., & Liau, F. C. (2002). Fingerprint identification and recognition using back propagation neural network. In *Student Conference on Research and Development* (SCOReD). doi:10.1109/SCORED.2002.1033066

Joshi, A., & Lee, C. H. (1991). On modeling the retina using neural networks. In *Proceeding of IEEE International Joint Conference on Neural Networks* (pp. 2343 – 2348). IEEE.

Kartalopoulos, S. (1996). *Understanding Neural Networks and Fuzzy Logic: Basic Concepts and Applications.* IEEE Press.

Khetri, G. P., Padme, S. L., Jain, D. C., & Pawar, V. P. (2012). Fingerprint Pattern Recognition Using Back Propagation Algorithms. *International Journal of Electronics and Computer Science Engineering, 2*(1), 225–232.

Kosko, B. (1991). *Neural Networks and Fuzzy Systems.* Englewood Cliffs, NJ: Prentice Hall.

Leung, W. F., Leung, S. H., Lau, W. H., & Luk, A. (1991). Fingerprint recognition using neutal network. In *Proceedings of IEEE Workshop on Neural Networks for Signal Processing.* IEEE.

Lihua, Z. (2010). A new fingerprint image recognition approach using artificial neural network. In *Proceeding of International Conference on E-Health Networking, Digital Ecosystems and Technologies* (EDT).

Maltoni, D., Maio, D., Jain, A. K., & Prabhakar, S. (2009). *Handbook of Fingerprint Recognition* (2nd ed.). Berlin: Springer Professional Computing. doi:10.1007/978-1-84882-254-2

Mamdani, E. H., & Assilian, S. (1975). An experiment in linguistic synthesis with a fuzzy logic controller. *International Journal of Man - Machine Study, 7*(1), 1 -13.

Martinez, A. L. P. (1999). Identification of individuals using fingerprints by linguistic descriptions fuzzy comparison. In *Proceedings of IEEE 33rd Annual International Carnahan Conference on Security Technology.* doi:10.1109/CCST.1999.797917

Mehtre, B. M. (1993). Fingerprint image analysis for automatic identification. *Machine Vision and Applications, 6*(2), 124–139. doi:10.1007/BF01211936

Melin, P., Bravo, D., & Castillo, O. (2005). Fingerprint recognition using modular neural networks and fuzzy integrals for response integration. In *Proceeding of IEEE International Joint Conference Neural Networks* (IJCNN'05) (pp. 2589-2594). doi:10.1109/IJCNN.2005.1556311

Mitra, S., & Hayashi, Y. (2000). Neuro – Fuzzy Rule Generation: Survey in Soft Computing Framework. *IEEE Transactions on Neural Networks, 2*(3), 748–768. doi:10.1109/72.846746 PMID:18249802

Montesanto, A., Baldassarri, P., Vallesi, G., & Tascini, G. (2007). Fingerprints Recognition Using Minutiae Extraction: a Fuzzy Approach. In *Proceeding of 14th International Conference on Image Analysis and Processing* (ICIAP). doi:10.1109/ICIAP.2007.4362784

Nandy, M., & Banerjee, M. (2012). Retinal vessel segmentation using Gabor filter and artificial neural network. In *Proceedings of Third International Conference on Emerging Application of Information Technology* (EAIT). doi:10.1109/EAIT.2012.6407885

Nauck, D., Klawonn, F., & Kruse, R. (1997). *Foundations of Neuro Fuzzy Systems.* Chichester, UK: Wiley.

Ortega, M., Marina, C., Penedo, M. G., Blanco, M., & Gonzalez, F. (April, 2006). Biometric Authentication using Digital Retinal Images. In *Proceedings of the 5th WSEAS International Conference on Applied Computer Science* (ACOS 06).

Rajharia, J., & Gupta, P. C. (2012, August). A New and Effective Approach for Fingerprint Recognition by using Feed Forward Back Propagation Neural Network. *International Journal of Computers and Applications, 52*(10), 20–28. doi:10.5120/8239-1492

Ross, T. J. (2008). *Fuzzy logic with Engineering Applications* (2nd ed.). New Delhi: Wiley India.

Stergiou, C., & Siganos, D. (n.d.). *Neural Networks.* Retrieved from: http://www.doc.ic.ac.uk/nd/surprise96/journal/vol4/cs11/report.html

Suganthy, M., & Ramamoorthy, P. (2012). Principal Component Analysis Based Feature Extraction, Morphological Edge Detection and Localization for Fast Iris Recognition. *Journal of Computer Science, 8*(9), 1428 – 1433.

Sung-Nien, Y., Chien-Nan, L., & Chun-Chieh, C. (2009). Emulation of salamander retina with multilayer neural network. In *Proceeding of IEEE International Symposium on Circuits and System* (ISCAP). IEEE.

Takagi, T., & Sugeno, M. (1985). Fuzzy identification of systems and its applications to modeling and control. *IEEE Transactions on Neural Networks, 15*, 116–132.

Thai, R. (2003). *Fingerprint image Enhancement and Minutiae Extraction*. (Thesis). University of Western Australia.

Toh, K., & Isa, N. (2010, March). Noise Adaptive Fuzzy Switching Median Filter for Salt and Pepper Noice Reduction. *IEEE Signal Processing Letters*, *17*(3), 281–284. doi:10.1109/LSP.2009.2038769

Tukey, J. W. (1974) Nonlinear (nonsuperposable) methods for smoothing data. In *Proceeding of Congressional Record EASCOM*.

Xu, Z. W., Guo, X. X., Hu, X. Y., & Cheng, X. (2005). The Blood Vessel Recognition of Ocular Fundus. In *Proceedings of the 4th International Conference on Machine Learning and Cybernetics* (ICMLC05).

Zadeh, L. A. (1965). Fuzzy Sets. *Information and Control*, *8*(3), 338–353. doi:10.1016/S0019-9958(65)90241-X

KEY TERMS AND DEFINITIONS

Adaptive Neuro Fuzzy Inference System (ANFIS): ANFIS belongs to the class of systems commonly known as neuro fuzzy systems. NFS combines the powers od ANN with those of Fuzzy systems. This procedure leads to long cycles of system modification and evaluation. This process goes on and on until decent levels of accuracy are met.

Artificial Neural Network (ANN): ANN is a soft-computing tool that can learn patterns and predicts.

Blood Vessel: They are present on the thin nerve on the back of the eyeball that processes light entering through the pupil in a retina.

Eigen Vector: A nonzero vector x is an eigen vector of a square matrix A if there exists a scalar λ such that $Ax = \lambda x$. Then λ is an eigen value of A.

Filter: It is an enhancement technique in digital image processing that can be used for noise removal, sharpening, smoothing etc.

Fingerprint Recognition System (FRS): It is the process used to determine whether two sets of fingerprint from the same finger or not. Fingerprint consists of ridges and valleys.

Fuzzy Inference System (FIS): A FIS is a way of mapping an input space to an output space using fuzzy logic. FIS uses a collection of fuzzy membership functions and rules, instead of Boolean logic, to reason about data.

Fuzzy System (FS): Fuzzy System can solve problems very effectively by adding impreciseness to the systems. It provides an expert leve decision making system by following the variations in the texture of the input data.

Gaussian Noise: It is statistical noise that has a probality density function of the normal distribution. It means, the values that the noise can take on are gaussian distribution.

Mean Square Error (MSE): It is used as the primary criterion to ascertain the extent of learning acquired by a learning system like ANN. It is defined as the average squared error between the network's output and the target value over all the samples.

Membership Function (MF): The membership function is a graphical representation of the magnitude of participation of each input. It associates weighting with each of the inputs that are processed.

Neuro Fuzzy System (NFS): A neuro fuzzy system is essentially a multilayer neural network and thus it can apply standard learning algorithms developed for neural networks, including the back-propagation algorithm.

Noise: It is the disturbance in a digital image. Noise can be caused in imges by random fluctuations in the image signal.

Retina Recognition System (RRS): It is a high security identification system based on retina. Retina is the vascular pattern (blood vessels) of the eye which is not easy to replicate.

Ridge: Ridges are like graphical flow patterns present on the surface of the human finger.

Root Mean Square Error (RMSE): It is used as the primary criterion to ascertain the extent of learning acquired by the ANFIS. It is defined by the sum of the square of the difference between the actual and desired output.

Salt and Pepper Noise: It is a form of noise typically seen on images which represents itself as randomly occurring white and black pixels.

Speckle Noise: This type of noise can be seen on medical images because of the signals from elementary scatterers.

Thinning: It is the image enhancement technique in which binary valued image regions are reduced to lines.

Chapter 17
A Novel Fuzzy Logic Classifier for Classification and Quality Measurement of Apple Fruit

Narendra Kumar Kamila
C. V. Raman College of Engineering, India

Pradeep Kumar Mallick
St. Peter's University, India

ABSTRACT

Fruit and vegetables market is getting highly selective and requiring their suppliers to distribute the fruits of high standards of quality and good appearance. So the growing need to supply quality fruits within a short period of time has given rise to development of Automated Grading of fresh market fruits. The objective of this chapter is to classify apples into three grades based on its attributes such as color, size and weight. Initially apple image database is created. Next each image is analyzed using image processing software where images are first preprocessed and useful features like color and size are extracted from the images. Fuzzy logic is used for classification. Color, size features are represented as a fuzzy variables which are used for classification. The apples of different classes are graded into three grades viz. Grade1, Grade2 and Grade3 on the basis of combination of parameters mentioned above.

1. INTRODUCTION

In agricultural industry the efficiency and the proper grading process are very important to increase the productivity. Currently, the agriculture industry has a better improvement, particularly in terms of sorting and grading of fruits, but the process is needed to be upgraded. Grading of the fruit is important to improve the quality of fruits. However, fruits grading by humans in agricultural area are inefficient, labor intensive and prone to errors. Automated grading system not only speeds up the time of the process but also minimize error. Therefore, there is a need of developing an efficient method for grading fruits and vegetables. In recent years, computer vision and image processing techniques have been found increasingly useful in the fruit industry, especially for applications in quality inspection and shape sorting. Computer vision is a novel technology for acquiring and analyzing

DOI: 10.4018/978-1-4666-8654-0.ch017

an image of a real scene by computers to control machines or to process it. It includes capturing, processing and analyzing images to facilitate the objective and non-destructive assessment of visual quality characteristics in agricultural and food products. The techniques used in image analysis include image acquisition, image pre-processing and image interpretation, leading to quantification and classification of images and objects of interest within images. The overall appearance of fruit object is a combination of its chromatic attributes (color) and its geometric attributes (shape, size, texture), together with the presence of defects that can diminish the external quality (Khoje et. al. 2013). Thus automated fruit gradation plays an important role to increase the value of products. However, automatic fruit classification offers an additional benefit of reducing subjectiveness arising from human experts.

Grading systems give us many kinds of information such as size, color, shape, defect, and internal quality. Among these color, size, weight and texture are the most important features for accurate classification and/or sorting of fresh fruits such as oranges, apples, mangoes etc. Automatic grading system not only speeds up the process but also gives accurate results. Therefore, it needs to develop an efficient fruits grading or classification methods.

Traditionally, classification and grading is performed based on observations through experience. Many new agricultural automation technologies are being developed by university researchers that pose questions about the efficiency and effectiveness with which we carry out grading system practically (Naganur et al. 2012). This has given rise to new avenues to study how to classify and grade fruits and vegetables accurately without loss of generality. Classification is also vital for the evaluation of agricultural product. However, fruit size is the most important physical property while color resembles visual property. Thus classification of fruits is necessary in evaluating agricultural

product meeting quality standards and increasing market value. The laborers classify fruits and vegetables based on color, size, etc. manually which is error prone. If these quality measures are mapped into automated systems, then process of classification and grading would be faster and error free. Moreover, manual grading is an expensive and time consuming process and even the operation is affected due to non-availability of labors during peak seasons. The development of graders dated back to five decades ago and the first grader designed was simply a crude slat with a hag attached to the end (Lodhe et al, 2013). Products were inspected on the slat and moved by hand into the bag. These were called slat graders, which led to development of mechanical graders. Grading has been changed very little in the last fifty years. However, the grading process has been fully mechanized. A mechanical grader consisted of a chain conveyor belt, with a bag at the end. Smaller produce fell through the chain, making the grading process easier. Indian grading is still being done by hand. Labor shortages and a lack of overall consistency in the process resulted in a search for automated solutions. In vegetable grading, the need to be responsive to market demand places a greater emphasis on quality assessment resulting in the greater need for improved and more accurate grading and sorting practices. Size variation in vegetables like potatoes, onions provided a base for grading them in different categories. Every vegetable producing country had made their own standards of different grades keeping in view the market requirements.

This automated system is designed to overcome the problems of manual techniques. The image could be captured using a regular digital camera or high resolution mobile phone camera. This image is given as an input to the system for obtaining the fruit's features. The system consists of several steps like feature extraction, texture analysis, sorting and grading.

2. LITERATURE SURVEY

This section presents some past works relating how to evaluate quality of different fruits. Leemans et al. (2002) have initiated working on online fruit grading according to the external quality of fruits (specifically apple) using machine vision. They have taken two varieties of apples (Golden delicious and Jonagold) for their experiment. Moreover, they have created image database belonging to three acceptable categories (Extra., I & II, reject). The proposed method shows correct classification rates of 78 and 72% for delicious golden and jonagold appels based on external quality. It is observed from their experiments that healthy fruits are graded better than weak fruits. But Gamea et al. (2011) proposed design and manufacturing of prototype for orange grading using phototransistors. The prototype uses different successively operating components, such as phototransistors and actuators, each performing a specific task. The operating principle depends on the phototransistor, signal gathering and output circuit for distributing unit. When it works, the system receives digital signals produced by fruits that shadow the light from a phototransistor sensor during fruit measuring. After digital signals processed by the electronic circuit, every fruit's sizing level gets deduced. Then, the system outputs switch signals to open the sorting switches according to fruit size. In this way they have set up the prototype for grading of oranges. Prior to the above findings, Gay et al. (2002) have proposed a system that able to grade fruits on the basis of surface color. Dang et al.(2010) have proposed fruit size detecting and grading system based on image processing which uses ARM9 as main processor and developed the fruit size detecting program. Li et al. (2011) have proposed a multi feature information fusion method based on BP-neural network and D-sevidential theory to improve the accuracy of apple grading. Their experimental results tell that decision information fusion method based on shape, size or color features has good

performance on accuracy compared to single feature based method in apple grading. Naganur et al.(2012) have proposed a system which finds size of different fruits and accordingly different fruits can be sorted using fuzzy logic. Similarly Njoroge et al. (2002) have developed an automated grading system using image processing technique in which they have focused fruit's internal and external defects. X-ray imaging is used for inspecting the biological defects. Ismail Kavdir et. al.(2003) have applied Fuzzy logic (FL) as a decision making support to grade apples. FL showed 89% of accuracy. Razak et al.(2012) proposed and implemented methodologies and algorithms that utilize digital fuzzy image processing to determine the grade of local mango production in Perlis(2012). Brendon J. Woodford et al.(1999) have detailed the image processing and neural network classification methods using wavelets applied to the task of identifying the pest that caused the damage to apple fruits and leaves in orchards. Paulraj et al.(2009) have implemented a simple color recognition algorithm using a Neural Network model and applied to determine the ripeness of a banana. However Devrim Unay et. al.(2006) have proposed a method for apple defect detection and quality classification with MLP-neural networks. Zhang et al.(2010) proposed a novel classification method based on a multi-class kernel support vector machine (kSVM) for accurate and fast classification of fruits. Khojastehnazhand et al. (2010) have presented an efficient algorithm for sorting and grading lemon fruits based on color and size using RGB color space method. Chandra Nandi et al.(2012) implemented a computer vision based system for automatic grading and sorting of mangoes based on maturity level. Dah-Jye-Lee (2011) has implemented a Color mapping technique to evaluate the quality and maturity stage of agricultural products like tomatoes and date fruits. In the same way Abdullah et al. (2002) had used the color vision system *HSI* (Hue, Saturation and Intensity) color space method to classify oil palms. Effendi et al. (2009) have developed a Grading

System of Jatropha (GSJ) by using color histogram method to distinguish the level of ripeness of the fruits based on the color intensity. Gupta (2013) presented a novel methodology to detect infected fruit part based on color features with K-mean clustering segmentation algorithm. Vyas et. al. (2014) have considered quality inspection and classification of mangoes using color and size features. Mohana et al. (2014) have proposed a novel technique for grading of dates using shape and texture features. Their method begins with reducing the specular reflection and small noise using a bilateral filter. Finally their output shows proposed technique achieves highest accuracy. However, Nandi et al. (2014) have used computer vision technique with support vector machine based classifier for mango fruit grading. To solve this problem they have also used multi attribute decision making theory. The experimental result is showing 90% to 95% performance. But variation of size, color and texture is another issue in their problem. In 2015 few researchers have started working on gradation of different fruits using different technologies. Singh et al. (2015) have classified apples using neural network and compared their output by using other classifiers. And they are suggesting support vector machine based approach performs well, i.e. the accuracy is 90%. Another research finding came out with title "A survey on detection of disease and fruit grading" (Solanki et al. 2015) in the year 2015. As it is survey paper, they have taken different colors, textures and classifiers into account and have the comparison among all classifiers. They have also discussed the merits and demerits of their methodologies. The works discussed above using different image processing techniques emphasizes on different aspects of different fruits, but nobody tells about quality measurements and accurate classification.

The rest of the chapter is as follows: section III explains overview of the proposed system. Section IV presents the algorithms used in each phase of system. Section V explains Fuzzy logic technique in detail. However section VI describes the result obtained which is followed by the conclusion in section VII.

3. SYSTEM ARCHITECTURE

A.   Proposed system is divided in following steps:
- Create fruit image database
- Image preprocessing
- Color, size feature extraction
- Image classification using fuzzy logic technique

B.   Figure 1 shows block diagram of the system:

Figure 1. System block diagram

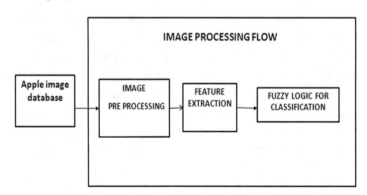

C. Flow of proposed system is as follows:
- This work implements fruit quality measurement using MATLAB-10 software for processing of image.
- Images from two sides of fruits are captured using digital camera and a database of fruit images is created for image analysis. Proposed system uses apple image database for testing. Database of images are used as input to the MATLAB software.
- MATLAB software is used for image preprocessing, feature extraction and classification using different image processing techniques. Feature extraction technique extracts color and size feature from images for classification.
- Fuzzy logic is used as a classifier. Features are treated as a fuzzy set. This fuzzy set is applied to fuzzy inference engine and classification is completed as per fuzzy rules which are created as per requirement. After classification, different classes of apples are classified into three grades grade1, grade2 and grade3.
- Graphical user interface (GUI) is created to show the calculated parameters and result of grading.

D. Components used in the system:
- Different classes of apple image database.
- Matlab-10 software with image processing tool box
- Personal computer

4. PROPOSED ALGORITHM OF SYSTEM

Algorithm of each phase of the system is given below.

A. Image acquisition algorithm:
1. Capture images using digital camera to create a database of apple images of different classes.
2. Transfer images to PC through RS232 and acquire it in a MATLAB software environment.

B. Image pre-processing: Usually the images that are obtained from the first phase are not suitable for classification purpose because of various factors, so some preprocessing steps are necessary. Steps are as follows.
1. Convert image from RGB to Gray
2. Edge detection & Red plane extraction
3. Convert image to binary to get ROI

C. Feature extraction algorithm
1. Mean intensity value of Red pixels is considered as a color feature. Mean Value is calculated as follows:

$$Mean\,R = \frac{R}{Total\,no.of\,pixels} \qquad (1)$$

where,

Mean R= Mean value of Red plane,
R = Sum of red color intensities of all pixels contained in the ROI

2. Mean size of an object is considered as a measure of a size. Mean size is calculated by taking average of horizontal and vertical diameters of the object. However, mean size of an image is calculated using following formula:

$$Mean\,size = \frac{\left[\begin{array}{l} \left(Max\left(row\right) - Min\left(row\right)\right) \\ + \left(\max\left(col\right) - Min\left(col\right)\right) \end{array} \right]}{2} \qquad (2)$$

where,

Max (row) = Maximum value of row in the object

Min (row) = minimum value of row in the object

Max (col) = Maximum value of column in the object

Min (col) = Minimum value of column in the object

D.   Classification algorithm

1.   Image feature values are converted to a fuzzy set by defining a membership function.

2.   Reference values are assigned to membership functions of each input feature. Degree of memberships is calculated for each membership function in an inference engine.

3.   Fuzzy rules are created according to the requirement of the system. Those rules are applied on membership function in an inference engine.

4.   Output of each feature is calculated.

5.   Final output is the aggregation of outputs of three features.

6.   Fuzzy output is converted to defuzzified output i.e grades by defuzzification by comparing final output values with the threshold values decided. In this manner each apple image is classified into grade1, grade2 or grade3.

5. FUZZY AS A CLASSIFIER

This section describes the most popular and accurate Fuzzy logic method for classification.

Fuzzy logic (FL) has been used in a wide range of problem domains. Applications area of fuzzy logic is very wide: process control, management and decision making, operations research, economies and, for this paper the most important task is pattern recognition and classification. FL is used to handle uncertainty, ambiguity and vagueness. Once the features are fixed, they led in input to a classifier which outputs a value associated to the classification of the quality (integer value) or a quality index (real value).

The classification can be divided into two approaches: conventional classification and computational intelligence-based classification. The computational intelligence-based approach includes statistical approach, neural networks and fuzzy systems. It is based on the concept of "partial truth", i.e. truth values between "absolutely true" and "absolutely false". Fuzzy Logic provides a structure to model uncertainty, the way human thinks and the perception process. Fuzzy Logic is based on natural language and through a set of rules of an inference system is built which is the basis of the fuzzy computation. Fuzzy set theory and fuzzy logic provide powerful tools to represent and process human knowledge in the form of fuzzy IF-THEN rules. A *degree of membership* became a new way of solving the problems.

A fuzzy set is a set whose elements have degrees of membership. An element of a fuzzy set can be full member (100% membership) or a partial member (between 0% and 100% membership). That is, the membership value assigned to an element is no longer restricted to just two values, but can be 0, 1 or any value in-between.

A fuzzy set is a pair (U, μ), where U is a set and μ: U → [0,1].

For each x ∈ U, the value of μ(x) is called the grade of membership of x in (U, μ).

For a finite set U= $\{x1, x2, ..., xn\}$ (3)

the fuzzy set (U, μ) is always denoted by

$$\left\{ \frac{\mu(x1)}{x1} .... \frac{\mu(xn)}{xn} \right\} \tag{4}$$

Let x ∈ U, then x is called not included in fuzzy set if,

$$\mu(x) = 0 \tag{5}$$

x is called fully included if

$$\mu(x) = 1 \tag{6}$$

Mathematical function which defines the degree of an element's membership in a fuzzy set is called *membership function* (Meunkaewjinda et al. 2008). x is called fuzzy member if

$$0 < \mu(x) < 1 \qquad (7)$$

The function μ is called membership function of the fuzzy set (U, μ).

Fuzzy logic has many advantages, firstly it is essential and applicable to many systems, moreover it is easy to understand and flexible; finally it is able to model non linear functions of arbitrary complexity.

The Fuzzy Inference System (FIS) is one of the main concepts of fuzzy logic and the general scheme is shown in Figure 2. A FIS is a way of mapping input data to output data by exploiting the fuzzy logic concepts. Fuzzification is used to convert the system inputs, which is represented by crisp numbers into fuzzy set through a fuzzification function. The fuzzy rule base is characterized in the form of *if-then* rules and the set of these fuzzy rules provide the rule base for the fuzzy logic system. Moreover the inference engine simulates the human reasoning process: through a suitable composition procedure, all the fuzzy subsets corresponding to each output variable are combined together in order to obtain a single fuzzy set for each output variable.

Finally the Defuzzification operation is used to convert the fuzzy set coming from the inference engine into a crisp value.

Fuzzy classification is an application of fuzzy theory. In fuzzy classification an instance can belong to different classes with different membership degrees; conventionally the sum of the membership values of each single instance must be unitary. The main advantage of fuzzy classification based method includes its applicability for complex processes.

The flow of classification using fuzzy logic is described below.

- Input (image channels) and output variables are introduced in Matlab's environment,
- Membership functions are defined using results from supervised classification,
- Matlab Fuzzy Logic Toolbox is used based on fuzzy logic inference rules,
- These rules are tested and verified through the simulation of classification procedure at random sample areas and at the end,
- Image classification is conducted.

6. RESULT AND DISCUSSION

For convenience a GUI is created for the system. System execution steps are as follows:

Figure 2. Fuzzy logic concept

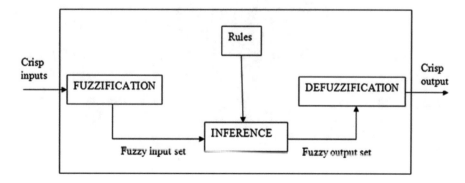

System uses apple fruit for testing. Image database of apple fruit is created by capturing images of apple from two sides using digital camera. 50-60 apples of different classes, color and sizes are used for the analysis. Weight of all the apples used for creating database is noted down. Fruit weight is considered as one of the feature for the classification. Database of images are used as input to the MATLAB software.

Stage1: Image preprocessing

After acquiring apple images, images are preprocessed where color images are converted to grayscale images to make processing easier and faster as shown in Figure 3 and Figure 4. To make images more meaningful for the analysis, we have to remove the background of the object that is nothing but the noise. Canny edge detector is used to detect the edges of the object shown in Figure 5.

For color feature we are interested only in Red (R) plane, so R plane is separated from the color image depicted in Figure 6. To get R plane without background we make use of edge detected image. In order to make computation easy, extracted Red plane image is converted to binary image. That is nothing but the region of interest (ROI) as shown in Figure 7 and all necessary operations are performed on this binary image only.

Stage2: Feature extraction

For color feature, mean value of red plane is calculated. Similarly for size feature mean size of the object is calculated. Mean value of red plane and mean size is calculated for all images in the database. Mean color and mean size for all images are calculated using equations no.1 and no.2 respectively.

Calculated Mean intensity, mean size and weights value of five images of the database is

Figure 3. Original Apple image

Figure 4. Grayscale image of Apple

Figure 5. Edge detected image

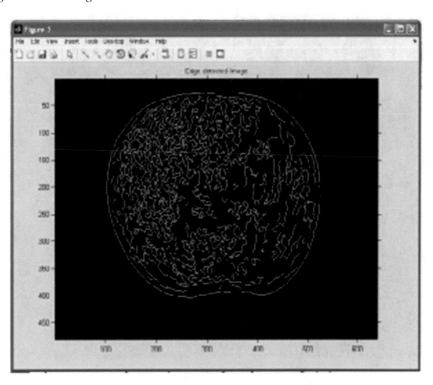

Figure 6. Extracted Red Plane

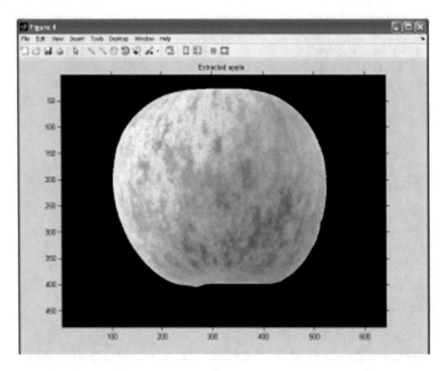

Figure 7. Region of Interest (ROI)

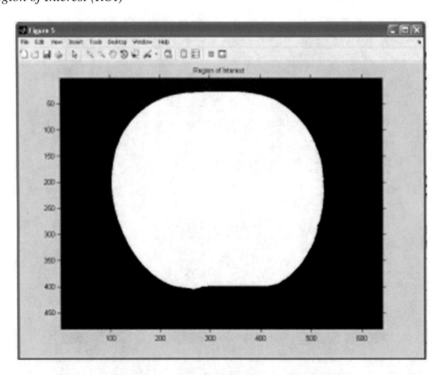

shown in Table 1. Different types of apples have different weights, colors with intensity and sizes. Taking the images of various apples together mean intensity, mean size and weights have been calculated for our experiment.

Stage3: Fuzzy Classification

For classification all steps mentioned in classification algorithm is follwed. Input and output membership functions for Mamdani fuzzy inference is shown in Figure 8.

Output for each input feature is calculated seperately. Cout, sout and wout are the outputs calculated for color, size and weight feature respectively. Final output is the aggregation of outputs of three input features.

$$Output = cout + sout + wout \qquad (8)$$

Membership function plot for output is shown in Figure 9. From the figure it is seen that grades are prominently visible for different threshold values based on mean color, size and weight. Membership function separates different types of apples into three grades in which range varies from -300 to 300. All grades are falling under range value 200 for each grade.

For decision of grading two threshold values are used as there are three grades.

$$th1 = -100 \qquad (9)$$

Table 1. Calculates Mean color, size and weights values of images

Image No.	Mean Intensity	Mean Size	Weight(gms)
1	172.4278	279.5000	150
2	166.5435	366.5000	250
3	152.5317	295.0000	310
4	166.2407	291,5000	290
5	157.7708	350.5000	160

$$th2 = 100 \qquad (10)$$

Experimental results carried out on the apple images are shown in Figure 10 and Figure 11. Different images of apples are tested using above algorithm and apples are graded into three grades. Table 2 represents the criteria of grading using threshold values being described in Equations (9) and (10). In other words all apples need to be classified into three grades by using above threshold values. This threshold value is a prototype for our experiment. However it is user dependent. User may take different types of threshold values based on different types and qualities of apples across the globe irrespective of geographical location. The main objective of this discussion is to make the system automated. Figure 10 also shows how the edge of original image (of an apple) is extracted with gray scale image and region of interest after grading.

Figure 11 depicts the edge detection, gray scale and region of interest of grade 1 apple from original image. However the images falling under grade 3 are not discussed much which is beyond the scope of this chapter. But care must be taken for analysis of grade 3 apple.

7. CONCLUSION

This chapter presents a new technique for sorting and grading of fruit apples. The grading and sorting of the apples are done based on external parameters namely size, color and weight. Apple images have been captured first using regular

Table 2. Criteria for grading

Output	Grade
Output > th2	Grade1
th1 < = output < = th2	Grade2
Output < th1	Grade3

Figure 8. Fuzzy logic implementation for proposed system

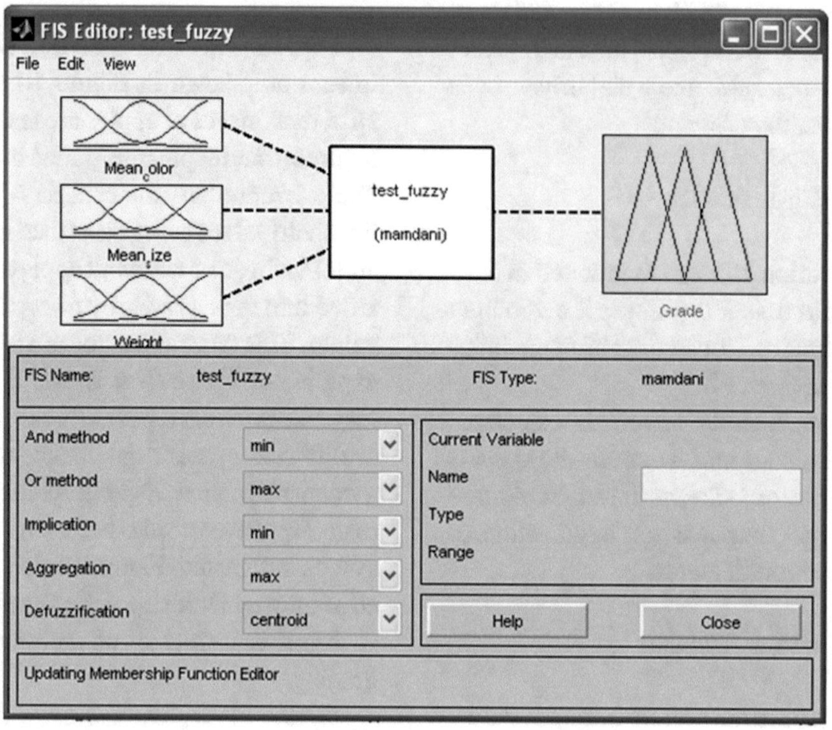

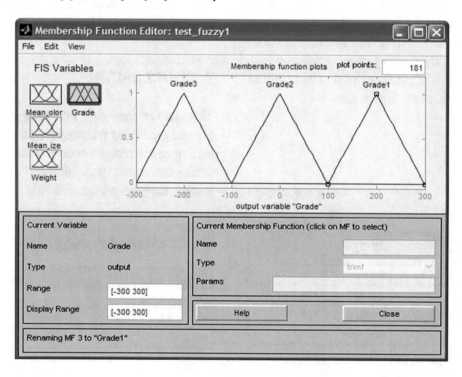

Figure 9. Membership function plot for final output

Figure 10. Classified to Grade2 Apple

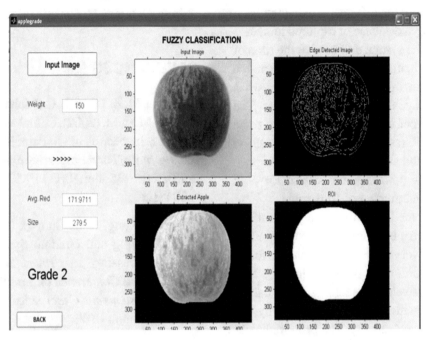

Figure 11. Classified to Grade1 Apple

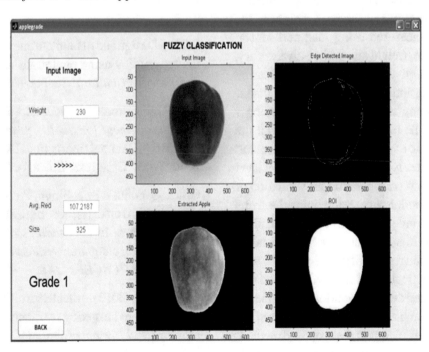

digital camera, preprocessed it. Useful features like size and color are efficiently extracted from the image; weight database of captured images is kept stored in the system and used at the time of classification. Then necessary fuzzy operations are performed on the images. Matlab-10 software is used for the image analysis and processing. The apples of different classes are graded into three grades namely Grade1, Grade2 and Grade3 on the basis of combination of parameters mentioned above. Fuzzy logic technique is used for both classification and grading of fruit apple.

Fuzzy logic method is found very useful and accurate for the fruit grading. Fuzzy logic method is conceptually very simple. This method is found to be very flexible and gives results very fast. The main objective of this technique is to handle imprecise data which cannot be handled by any other techniques accurately. The proposed technique accurately classifies and grades the fruit. The results are good for different type apples with same and dissimilar color and sizes.

Current system works on the image database and weight database. Future work will include image acquisition in real time and weight of the fruits will be measured using load cell sensor. Since color, size, weight and texture always vary, fuzzy multi objective optimization method can be used for grading and classification of all fruits for better result along with quality and accordingly a software can be implemented to carry out the above job in spite of manual labor for quick result and better service. Noise images of different level may be taken into consideration for validation of developed methodologies. Sometimes the fruits look like of having good health, but internally it may be rotten. In such case care must be taken into consideration for identification of quality and gradation/classification. If more number of features are included during gradation, performance would be better and accuracy will be increased. So to enhance the efficiency of the proposed method, above discussed points need to be taken care of for which real time data set are always required.

Hence to make the system more robust background illumination may be considered for better result.

REFERENCES

Abdullah, M. Z., Guan, L. C., Mohamed, A. M. D., & Noor, M. A. M. (2002). Color Vision System for Ripeness Inspection of Oil Palm Elaeis Guineenszs. *Journal of Food Processing and Preservation*, *26*(3), 213–235. doi:10.1111/j.1745-4549.2002. tb00481.x

Dang, H., Song, J., & Guo, Q. (2010). A Fruit Size Detecting and Grading System Based on Image Processing. In *Proceedings of Second International Conference on Intelligent Human-Machine Systems and Cybernetics (IHMSC 2010)*. Nanjing, China: IEEE.

Effendi, Z., Ramli, R., Ghani, J. A., & Yaakob, Z. (2009). Development of Jatropha Curcas Color Grading System for Ripeness Evaluation. *European Journal of Scientific Research*, *30*(4), 662–669.

Gamea, G. R., Aboamera, M. A., & Ahmed, M. E. (2011). Design and manufacturing of prototype for orange grading using phototransistor. *Australian Journal of Agricultural Engineering*, *2*(3), 74–81.

Gay, P., Berruto, R., & Piccarolo, P. (2002). *Fruit color assessment for quality grading purposes*. 2002 ASAE Annual International Meeting/CIGR XVth World Congress, Chicago, IL.

Gill, J., Sandhu, P. S., & Singh, T. (2014). A review of automatic fruit classification using soft computing techniques. In *Proceedings of international conference on computer, systems and electronics engineering (ICSCEE2014)*.

Gupta, J. P. (2013). Infected fruit part detection using K-means clustering segmentation technique. *International Journal of Artificial Intelligence and Interactive Multimedia*, *2*(3), 65-72.

Kavdir, I., & Guyer, D. E. (2003). Apple Grading Using Fuzzy Logic. *Turky Journal of Agriculture, 27*, 375–382.

Khojastehnazhand, M., Omid, M., & Tabatabaeefar, A. (2010). Development of a lemon sorting system based on color and size. *African Journal of Plant Science, 4*(4), 122–127.

Khoje, S., & Bodhe, S. (2013). Comparative Performance Evaluation of Size Metrics and Classifiers in Computer Vision based Automatic Mango Grading. *International Journal of Computers and Applications, 61*(9), 1–7. doi:10.5120/9953-4320

Lee, D.-J., Archibald, J. K., & Xiong, G. (2011). Rapid Color Grading for Fruit Quality Evaluation Using Direct Color Mapping. *IEEE Transactions on Automation Science and Engineering, 8*(2), 292–302. doi:10.1109/TASE.2010.2087325

Leemans, V., Magein, H., & Destain, M. F. (2002). Online fruit grading according to their external quality using machine vision. *Biosystems Engineering, 83*(4), 397–404. doi:10.1006/bioe.2002.0131

Li, X., & Zhu, W. (2011). Apple grading method based on features fusion of size, shape and color. *Procedia Engineering, 15*, 2885–2891. doi:10.1016/j.proeng.2011.08.543

Lodhe, D., Nalawade, S., Pawar, G., Atkari, V., & Wandka, S. (2013). Grader: A review o different methods of grading for fruits and vegetables. *Agric Eng Int: CIGR Journal, 15*(3), 217–230.

Meunkaewjinda, A., Kumsawat, P., Attakitmongcol, K., & Srikaew, A. (2008). Image Classification Based On Fuzzy Logic. *The International Archives of the Photogrammetry. Remote Sensing and Spatial Information Sciences, 34*(30), 1–5.

Mohana, S. H., & Prabhakar, C. J. (2014). A novel technique for grading of dates using shape and texture features. *Machine Learning and Applications: An International Journal, 1*(2), 15–29. doi:10.5121/mlaij.2014.1202

Naganur, H. G., Sannakki, S. S., Rajpurohit, V. S., & Arunkumar, R. (2012). Fruits Sorting and Grading using Fuzzy Logic. *International Journal of Advanced Research in Computer Engineering & Technology, 1*(6), 117–122.

Nandi, C. S., Tudu, B., & Koley, C. (2012). An Automated Machine vision based system for fruit sorting and grading. In *Proceedings of Sixth International conference on sensing technology (ICST)*. Kolkata: IEEE.

Nandi, C. S., Tudu, B., & Koley, C. (2014). Computer vision based mango fruit grading system. In *Proceedings of International Conference on Innovative Engineering Technologies (ICIET)*.

Njoroge, J. B., Ninomiya, K., Kondo, N., & Toita, H. (2002). *Automated Fruit Grading System using Image Processing. In The Society of Instrument and Control Engineers (SICE2002)*. Osaka, Japan: IEEE.

Paulraj, M. P., Hema, C. R., Krishnan, R. P., & Sofiah, S. (2009). Color Recognition Algorithm using a Neural Network Model in Determining the Ripeness of a Banana. In *Proceedings of the International Conference on Man-Machine Systems* (ICoMMS).

Razak, R. B., Othman, M. B., Bakar, M. N. B. A., Ahmad, K. A. B., & Mansor, A. R. (2012). Mango Grading By Using Fuzzy Image Analysis. In *Proceedings of International Conference on Agricultural, Environment and Biological Sciences (ICAEBS'2012)*.

Singh, S. P., Bansal, S., Ahuja, M., Parnami, S., & Singh, H. (2015). Classification of apples using neural networks. In *Proceedings of International Conference on Recent Trends in Engineering Science and Management*.

Solanki, U., Jaliya, U. K., & Thakore, D. G. (2015). A survey on detection of disease and fruit grading. *International Journal of Innovative and Emerging Research in Engineering*, 2(2), 109–114.

Unay, D., & Gosselin, B. (2006). Automatic defect segmentation of Jonagold apples on multi-spectral images: A comparative study. *Postharvest Biology and Technology*, 42(3), 271–279. doi:10.1016/j.postharvbio.2006.06.010

Vyas, A. M., Talati, B., & Naik, S. (2014). Quality Inspection and classification of mangoes using color and size features. *International Journal of Computers and Applications*, 98(1), 1–5. doi:10.5120/17144-7161

Woodford, B. J., Kasabov, K. K., & Wearing, C. H. (1999). *Fruit Image Analysis using Wavelets*. Research Gate Digital Library.

Zhang, Y., & Wu, L. (2012). Classification of Fruits Using Computer Vision and a Multiclass Support Vector Machine. *Sensors (Basel, Switzerland)*, 12(12), 12489–12505. doi:10.3390/s120912489 PMID:23112727

KEY TERMS AND DEFINITIONS

Classification: Classification refers to as assigning a physical object or incident into one of a set of predefined categories.

Feature: A function of the basic measurement variables or attributes that specifies some quantifiable property of an object and is useful for classification and/or pattern recognition.

Feature Extraction: When the data is too large to be processed, the data will be transformed into a reduced representation set of features. The process of transforming the input data into the set of features is called feature extraction.

Fuzzy Logic: Fuzzy logic is a problem solving tool of artificial intelligence which deals with approximate reasoning rather than fixed and exact reasoning.

Inference Engine: An Inference Engine is a tool from artificial intelligence. The first inference engines were components of expert systems. The typical expert system consisted of a knowledge base and an inference engine. The inference engine applied logical rules to the knowledge base and deduced new knowledge. Inference engines work primarily in one of two modes: forward chaining and backward chaining. Forward chaining starts with the known facts and asserts new facts. Backward chaining starts with goals, and works backward to determine what facts must be asserted so that the goals can be achieved.

Membership Function: The membership function is a graphical representation of the magnitude of participation of each input. It associates weighting with each of the inputs that are processed.

Neural Network: Is a computational model built in accordance with the central nervous system of human being.

Pre-Processing: It is the process by which the input images are filtered to remove noise, spike removal, etc. It is a very crucial step for further processing of input images.

Support Vector Machine (SVM): A supervised machine learning method that constructs classification models with associated learning algorithms that analyze data and recognize patterns.

Chapter 18
Application of Charge System Search Algorithm for Data Clustering

Yugal Kumar
Birla Institute of Technology, India

Gadadhar Sahoo
Birla Institute of Technology Mesra, India

ABSTRACT

This chapter presents a charged system search (CSS) optimization method for finding the optimal cluster centers for a given dataset. In CSS algorithm, while the Coulomb and Gauss laws from electrostatics are applied to initiate the local search, global search is performed using Newton second law of motion from mechanics. The efficiency and capability of the proposed algorithm is tested on seven datasets and compared with existing algorithms like K-Means, GA, PSO and ACO. From the experimental results, it is found that the proposed algorithm provides more accurate and effective results in comparison to other existing algorithms.

INTRODUCTION

Clustering is a powerful technique which is applied in finding hidden patterns and knowledge from a given set of patterns and data. It has proven its significance in many research fields such as pattern recognition (Webb, 2002; Zhou & Liu, 2008), image processing (Sonka, Hlavac, & Boyle, 2014), process monitoring (Teppola, Mujunen, & Minkkinen, 1999), machine learning (Alpaydin, 2004), quantitative structure activity relationship (Dunn III, Greenberg, & Callejas, 1976), document retrieval (Hu, Zhou, Guan, & Hu, 2008),

bioinformatics (He, Pan, & Lin, 2006), image segmentation (Pappas, 1992) and many more. The aim of clustering is to group the similar items which have similar characteristics. Different similarity measures are applied to group the items into clusters but the sum of the squared distances is widely accepted similarity measure. Generally, the clustering algorithms can be classified into two groups: hierarchical clustering algorithms and partition-based clustering algorithms (Kogan, Nicholas, Teboulle, & Berkhin, 2006; Rokach, 2010). In hierarchical algorithms, a tree structure of data is formed by merging or splitting data

DOI: 10.4018/978-1-4666-8654-0.ch018

based on similarity criterion. In partition-based algorithms, clustering is achieved by relocating data between clusters to the clustering criterion, i.e. Euclidian distance.

From the literature, it is observed that partition-based algorithms are more efficient and popular than hierarchical algorithms (Jain, Murty, & Flynn, 1999). The most popular and widely used partition-based algorithm is K-means. It is easy, fast, simple to implement and also having linear time complexity (Forgy, 1965; Jain, 2010). In K-means algorithm, a dataset is divided into K number of predefined clusters and iteratively minimized the intra-cluster distance (Jain, Murty, & Flynn, 1999). But, this algorithm has some limitations such as the results of K-means algorithm is highly dependent on the choice of initial cluster centers and also stuck in local minima (Y. Kao, Zahara, & I. Kao, 2008; Niknam & Amiri, 2010). Thus, to overcome the pitfalls of the K-means algorithm, several heuristic algorithms have developed. K-harmonic mean algorithm has been proposed for clustering instead of K-means (Zhang, Hsu, & Dayal, 1999). A simulated annealing (SA)-based approach has been developed for clustering (Selim, & Alsultan, 1991). A tabu search (TS)-based method has been introduced for effective clustering (Sung, & Jin, 2000). A genetic algorithm (GA)-based algorithms were presented in (Cowgill, Harvey, & Watson, 1999; Krishna, & Murty, 1999). Fathian et al., have developed a clustering algorithm based on honey-bee mating optimization (HBMO) (Fathian, Amiri, & Maroosi, 2007). Cat swarm optimization based algorithm has been reported for clustering (Santosa & Ningrum, 2009; Kumar & Sahoo, 2014c, Kumar & Sahoo, 2015). In 2004, Shelokar et al., have proposed ant colony optimization (ACO) based approach for clustering (Shelokar, Jayaraman, & Kulkarni, 2004). Particle swarm optimization (PSO) is also applied for clustering (Van der Merwe & Engelbrecht, 2003). Hatamlou et al., have developed big bang-big crunch algorithm for data clustering (A., Hatamlou, Abdullah, &

M., Hatamlou, 2011). A novel clustering approach based on artificial bee colony (ABC) is presented in (Karaboga & Ozturk, 2011). A data clustering approach based on gravitational search algorithm has been reported (Hatamlou, Abdullah, & Nezamabadi-Pour, 2011; Hatamlou, Abdullah, & Nezamabadi-Pour, 2012). Charged system search and teacher learning based optimization methods are also reported in literature to achieve optimal cluster centers (Kumar & Sahoo, 2014a; Kumar & Sahoo, 2014b; Satapathy & Naik, 2011; Sahoo & Kumar, 2014). But, every algorithm has some drawbacks, for example, K-means algorithm trap in local optima, in genetic algorithm, convergence is highly dependent on initial positions of cluster centers. In case of ACO, the solution vectors are affected as the number of iterations increased. In spite these algorithms, it is also noticed that fuzzy and rough set based algorithms have been proposed for clustering problem and these algorithms obtain good results over traditional methods (Bezdek, 1981; Ruspini, 1969; Sotirios, 2010; Pal & Bezdek, 1995; Bezdek, 1974; Graves & Witold, 2010; Lee, & Pedrycz, 2009).

This chapter investigates the applicability and adaptability of charged system search (CSS) algorithm (Kaveh & Talatahari, 2010) for data clustering. CSS is the latest meta-heuristic optimization technique developed in 2010. This technique is based on three principles: Coulomb law, Gauss law and Newton second law of motion. Every meta-heuristic algorithm contains two unique features, i.e. exploration and exploitation. Exploration is referred to generate the promising searching space, while the exploitation is defined as determination of the most promising solution set from promising searching space. In CSS, exploration is carried out using Coulomb and Gauss laws, while Newton second law of motion is applied to perform exploitation process. The performance of the proposed algorithm is tested on two artificial and several real datasets and compared with some existing algorithms in which quality of solution is improved using CSS algorithm.

Charge System Search (MCSS) Algorithm

Charged system search (CSS) algorithm is a recent meta-heuristic algorithm developed by (Kaveh & Talatahari, 2010) based on three principles: Coulomb law, Gauss law and Newton second law of motion. In CSS, charged particles (CPs) act as search agents and explore the D-dimensional search space to obtain optimal solutions. The movement of charged particles in D-dimensional search space enforce the electric force on the other charged particles and the resultant force is proportional to the charge (mass) and speed of the charged particles. The magnitude and direction of the resultant force depend on the two factors- first, velocity of the charged particles and secondly, magnitude and direction of the electric field. Therefore, the position of the ith charged particle in search space is described as $X_i = (X_{i,1}, X_{i,2}, X_{i,3}, ..., X_{i,D})$ and the velocity is represented as $V_i = (V_{i,1}, V_{i,2}, V_{i,3}, ..., V_{i,D})$. It is suggested that the position and velocities of the charged particle should be in the range of $[X_{min}, X_{max}]^D$ and $[V_{min}, V_{max}]^D$ respectively. Initially, it is assumed that the velocities of all charged particles are set to 0. The main steps of the CSS algorithm is as follows.

Step 1: Initialization

Algorithm starts by identifying the initial positions of charged particles (CPs) in d-dimensional space in random order and setting the initial velocities of CPs to zero. Equation 1 is used to determine the initial positions of CPs. A variable charge memory (CM) is used to store the best results.

$$C_k = X_{j,min} + r_j*(X_{j,max} - X_{j,min}), \text{ where } j = 1, 2, ..., D \text{ and } k = 1, 2, ..., K \quad (1)$$

where, C_k denotes the kth CPs for a given dataset, r_j is a random number in the range of 0 and 1, $X_{j,min}$ and $X_{j,max}$ denote the minimum and maximum value of the jth attribute of the dataset and K represents the total number of CPs (clusters) in a dataset.

Step 2: Compute the Actual Electric Force (F_k) acts on CPs.

When CPs move in D-dimensional space, an electric field is produced surrounding it and exerted an electric force on the other CPs. This electric force is directly proportional to the magnitude of its charge and the distance between CPs. The magnitude of the electric force generated on other charge particle is measured using Equation 2.

In Equation 2, q_i and q_k represents the fitness values of ith and k^{th} CP, r_{ik} denotes the separation distance between i^{th} and k^{th} CPs, w_1 and w_2 are the two variables whose values are either 0 or 1, R represents the radius of CPs which is set to unity and it is assumed that each CPs has uniform volume charge density but changes in every iteration and P_{ik} denotes the moving probability of each CPs.

Variables $q_i, q_k, r_{ik}, R, X_i, C_k, w_1, w_2$ and P_{ik} are used to determine the electric force (E_{ik}) and these variables can be defined as follows:

- q_i denotes the fitness of ith particle which can be calculated using the following equation.

Box 1. Equation 2

$$F_{ik} = q_k \sum_{i,i \neq k} \left(\frac{q_i}{R^3}*i_1 + \frac{q_i}{r_{ik}^2}*i_2 \right)*p_{ik}*(X_i - C_k), \begin{cases} k = 1,2,3,.....K \\ w_1 = 1, w_2 = 0 \leftrightarrow r_{ik} < R \\ w_1 = 0, w_2 = 1 \leftrightarrow r_{ik} \geq R \end{cases}$$

$$q_i = \frac{\text{fit}(i) - \text{fit}(\text{worst})}{\text{fit}(\text{best}) - \text{fit}(\text{worst})}, \quad i = 1, 2, 3, \ldots, N \quad (3)$$

where fit(i) presents the fitness of the ith particle while fit(best) and fit(worst) denote the best and worst fitness values of the given dataset.

- Separation distance (r_{ik}) can be defined as the change in the magnitude of two charge particles and it is calculated using Equation 4 which is described as follows.

$$r_{ik} = \frac{X_i - C_k}{(X_i + C_k)/2 - X_{best} + \in} \quad (4)$$

In Equation 4, X_i and X_k represent the position of ith and k^{th} particle and X_{best} describes the best position and $\in$ is a small positive constant to avoid singularities.

- Moving probability (P_{ik}) describes the direction of electric force (E_{ik}) whether an electric force (E_{ik}) produced at a point is either inside of charge particles or outside the charge particles. Equation 5 is used to compute the moving probability (P_{ik}) for CPs and it can be either "0" or "1". Table 6 denotes the moving probability (P_{ik}) values for example dataset.

$$p_{ik} = \begin{cases} 1 & \text{if} \\ \frac{\text{fit}(i) - \text{fit}(\text{best})}{\text{fit}(k) - \text{fit}(i)} > randV \ \text{fit}(k) > \text{fit}(i) \\ 0 & \text{otherwise} \end{cases}$$

where fit(i), fit(k), and fit(worst) present the fitness of the ith data instance, k^{th} CP and the worst fitness value in a given dataset respectively and rand is the random function.

- The value of (X_i - C_k) represents the difference between the positions of ith particle to k^{th} CPs.

Step 3: Determine the new positions and velocities of CPs.

Newton law of motion is applied to determine the movement of CPs. The magnitude of the total force with Newton laws is used to produce the next positions and velocities of CPs. The new positions and velocities of CPs are computed using Equations 6 and 7.

$$C_{k,new} = rand_1 * Z_a * \frac{F_k}{m_k} * \Delta t^2 + rand_2 * Z_v * V_{k\,old} * \Delta t + C_{k\,old} \quad (6)$$

where, $rand_1$ and $rand_2$ are the two random variable in the range of 0 and 1, Z_a and Z_v act as control parameters to control the influence of actual electric force (F_k) and $V_{k\,old}$ denotes the velocity of kth CPs, m_k is the mass of kth CPs which is equal to the q_k, Δt represents the time step which is set to 1 and $C_{k\,old}$ denotes the position of kth current CP.

$$V_{k\,new} = \frac{C_{k\,new} - C_{k\,old}}{\Delta t} \quad (7)$$

where, $V_{k\,old}$ denotes the new velocity of kth CP, $C_{k\,old}$ and $C_{k\,new}$ represent the old and new position of kth CP and Δt represents the time step.

Step 4: Update charge memory (CM)

CPs with better objective function values replace the worst CPs from the CM and store the positions of new CPs in CM.

Step 5: Termination condition

If the maximum iterations reached and the condition is satisfied then the algorithm is stopped and the optimal cluster centers are obtained. Otherwise repeat the step 2-4.

CSS ALGORITHM FOR CLUSTERING

In this section, CSS algorithm is explained to solve the clustering problem. The aim of this algorithm is to find the optimal cluster centers in a given dataset. Euclidean distances is considered as the similarity measure and the items are arranged into clusters using minimum Euclidean distance. The algorithm starts with identifying the initial positions of K number of charged particles (clusters). The initial positions of charged particles (CPs) are defined in random manner. It is also mentioned that

CPs can be assumed the charged sphere of radius 'a' and its initial velocity is set to zero. Pseudo code of CSS algorithm of clustering problem is summarized in Box 2.

Illustrative Example

To illustrate the working principles of the proposed algorithm, consider a two dimensional dataset consisting of 10 data objects and two attributes. Here, it is also mentioned that the number of clusters (K) is set to 3. Objects in the example dataset are given as (5.1, 3.5), (4.9, 3), (4.7, 3.2), (4.6, 3.1), (5, 3.6), (5.4, 3.9), (4.6, 3.4), (5, 3.4), (4.4, 2.9) and (4.9, 3.1). These data objects are assumed to be divided into three clusters, here, N=10, K = 3 and D = 2, where N is the total number of data objects, K is the total number of clusters and D

Box 2. Pseudo Code of CSS Algorithm for Clustering

```
Step 1: Load the dataset and specify the user defined parameters like number
of clusters (K), number of CPs, c, rand and ∈.
Step 2: \* initialize the initial positions and velocities of Charged
        Particles CPs * /
                For each charged particles k=1 to K   /* K represents the
                total number of cluster centers */
                        For each j=1 to m /* m represents the total number of
                        features in dataset */
                                Determine the value of initial position of
                                charged particles (C_k) using equation 1;
                                Calculate the value of mass for each C_k using
                                equation 8;
                        end
                end
            V_k=0;
            Iteration =0;
Step 3: Evaluate the value of objective function using sum of squared distanc-
es using equation 9 and assign the items to the clusters with minimum objec-
tive function value.
Step 4: Store the positions of initial charged particles (C_k) into a variable,
called CM.
```

continued on following page

Box 2. Continued

Step 5: while (the termination conditions are not met), do
\ * Calculate the value of moving probability $P_{i,k}$ for each charged particle C_k * /
For each charged particles k=1 to K
For each i=1 to n
Determine the value of fitness of each instance (q_{ik})
with each charged articles C_k using equation 3;
end for
if (fit (q_{ik}) > fit (k))
$P_{ik} \to 1;$
else
$P_{ik} \to 0;$
end if
end for
Step 6: \ * Determine the value of actual electric force F_k */
Determine the value of mass for each instance q_i using equation 3.
Calculate the value of radius 'a' using equation 8.
For each charged particles k=1 to K
Calculate the value of separation distance ($r_{i,k}$) using equation 4.
If ($r_{i,k}$ < a)
$i_1 \to 1$
else
$i_2 \to 0$
end if
If ($r_{i,k} \geq a$)
$i_2 \to 1$
else
$i_1 \to 0$
end if
end for
For each charged particles k=1 to K
Determine the value of actual electric force using equation 2.
end for
Step 7: Calculate the new positions and velocities of charged particles using equation 6 and 7.
Step 8: Recalculate the value of objective function using new positions of charge particles.
Step 9: Compare the value of objective function of newly generated charge particles to charge particles reside in CM.
Step 10: Memorize the best solution achieved so far
Iteration= Iteration +1;
End while
Step 11: Output the best solution obtained.

is the dimension of data set. Here, the aim of clustering is to reduce the intra-cluster distance of the data set. The major steps of the proposed algorithm are described below.

Step 1: Initialize the example dataset and set the user defined parameters such as number of clusters (K), number of CPs, c, rand and ∈

Step 2: As described earlier, the algorithm starts with the identification of the initial positions and velocities of CPs in random fashion. Thus, to identify the initial positions of randomly defined CPs (cluster centers), Equation 1 is used to initialize the initial positions of CPs and the initial position of CPs are (4.6467, 3.5664), (4.4835, 3.526) and (5.0609, 3.6298). While, the initial velocities of CPs are set to 0 and it can be given as $V_k = 0$, k = 1, 2, 3, ..., K. In CSS algorithm, it is noted that the CPs are described as charged spheres. So, every CP contains some mass and mass of each CP is calculated using the following equation. The mass of CPs for example dataset are 0.91315, 0.70944 and 1.3907.

$$m_k = \frac{\text{fit}(k) - \text{fit}(\text{worst})}{\text{fit}(\text{best}) - \text{fit}(\text{worst})} \quad (8)$$

Step 3: In this step, Euclidean distance is used as similarity measure in CSS algorithm to find the closeness of particles to CPs and assigned the objects to CPs with minimum objective value. Table 1 provides the value of objective function of initial positioned CPs for our example dataset. Euclidean distance is computed using Equation 9 which is defined as.

$$d_{i,k} = \sum_{k=1}^{K}\sum_{i=1}^{N}\sum_{j=1}^{D}\sqrt{X_{ij} - C_{kj}}^2 \quad (9)$$

Now, each data object is arranged into different clusters using the minimized similarity measure values. Using the information of Table 1, data objects are arranged into different clusters which are summarized into given string.

3 1 1 2 3 3 2 3 2 1

Step 4: To store the positions of CPs, a variable called charge memory (CM) is declared to memorize the positions of CPs. Later on, these CPs positions will be used for comparisons with newly generated CPs positions and the best positions are included in the CM and excluded the worst positions from CM. The main work of CM is to keep track the good positions of CPs which are obtained during the execution of CSS algorithm. After the completion of algorithm, the optimal positions of CPs are determined from CM.

Step 5: In this step, moving probability (P_{ik}) is computed for each charged particles (C_k). Moving probability $(P_{i,k})$ is either 0 or 1 and it gives the information about the movement of CPs. Equation 5 is used to compute the moving probability for example dataset which is mentioned in Table 2.

Table 1. Normalized value of similarity measure

N	K		
	1	2	3
1	0.45811	0.61706	0.1355
2	0.62046	0.67091	0.64999
3	0.37027	0.39132	0.56122
4	0.46875	0.44161	0.70222
5	0.35486	0.5218	0.067819
6	0.82382	0.9899	0.43358
7	0.17285	0.17159	0.51503
8	0.3905	0.53165	0.2377
9	0.71063	0.6315	0.98457
10	0.53074	0.59576	0.55366

Table 2. Moving probability P_{ik} of each CPs with each items of the dataset

N	K		
	1	2	3
1	0	0	1
2	1	1	0
3	1	1	0
4	1	1	0
5	0	0	1
6	0	0	0
7	1	1	0
8	0	0	1
9	1	1	0
10	1	1	0

Step 6: The actual electric force is the combined effect of the following variables such as q_i, q_k, $r_{i,k}$, R, X_i, C_k, w_1, w_2 and P_{ik}. Table 3 shows the values obtained for charge (q_i) and separation distance $(r_{i,k})$. Table 4-5 represent the values obtained for the variables i_1, i_2 and $(X_i$-$C_k)$ for each CP. The amount of actual electric force F_k generated on each CP is measured

Table 3. Values of magnitude of charge (q_i) of each CPs and separation distance $(r_{i,k})$

N	q_i	Separation Distance $(r_{i,k})$		
		K		
		1	2	3
1	1.3	0.85265	1.5314	0.13776
2	0.6	0.79976	0.021312	1.7952
3	0.6	0.56345	0.42517	1.5859
4	0.4	1.2859	0.20939	2.2103
5	1.3	0.88357	1.6231	0.13828
6	2	1.6087	2.1519	0.72074
7	0.7	0.49457	0.5983	1.4444
8	1.1	0.54907	1.2877	0.47032
9	0.5	4.0248	4.0406	4.0154
10	0.7	0.39833	0.39626	1.4168

using above discussion and the values of F_k for initial CPs (cluster centers) are 0.85871, 0.29861 and 0.33496.

In this step, new positions and velocities are computed for CPs. Newton second law of motion is employed to get the new positions and velocities of CPs. New positions of CPs and velocities are obtained from Equation 6 and 7. Here, Z_a and Z_v act as the control parameters which are used to control the exploration and exploitation process of CSS algorithm and it can be computed using Equation 10.

$$Z_a = (1 - \text{iteration/iteration max}), Z_v = (1 + \text{iteration/iteration max}) \quad (10)$$

Hence, the updated positions of CPs are (4.8604, 3.78), (4.5288, 3.5305) and (5.174, 3.6763). Finally, the updated velocities of CPs are 0.4273, 0.0498, and 0.1596.

Step 8-10: In step 8-10, first, the objective function value is computed using the new position of CPs. After computing the objective function value, compare the objective function value with the old ones and finally, memorize the

Table 4. Values of i_1 and i_2

N	K (i_1)			K (i_2)		
	1	2	3	1	2	3
1	0	1	0	1	0	1
2	0	0	1	1	1	0
3	0	0	1	1	1	0
4	0	0	1	1	1	0
5	0	1	0	1	0	1
6	1	1	0	0	0	1
7	0	0	1	1	1	0
8	0	0	0	1	1	1
9	1	1	1	0	0	0
10	0	0	0	1	1	1

Table 5. Values of X_i-C_k for each cluster center K

N	K		
	1	2	3
1	0.38685	0.59056	0.90696
2	0.31315	0.10944	0.7907
3	0.31315	0.10944	0.7907
4	0.51315	0.30944	0.9907
5	0.38685	0.59056	0.9269
6	1.0868	1.2906	0.6093
7	0.21315	0.9372	0.6907
8	0.18685	0.39056	0.2907
9	0.91315	0.70944	1.3907
10	0.21315	0.94426	0.6907

best charge particles for clustering process. This process will be continued until termination condition is not met.

Step 11: After completion of algorithm, final cluster center is obtained from CM.

CLUSTERING ALGORITHMS

The objective of clustering algorithm is to group the similar data objects together. In literature, there are many techniques which have been applied for clusters analysis such as partition-based clustering, hierarchical clustering, density-based clustering, and artificial intelligence-based clustering. This section describes the clustering algorithms which are used to compare the results of the proposed algorithm. These clustering algorithms are K-Means, Genetic Algorithm (GA), Particle Swarm Optimization (PSO) and Ant Colony Optimization (ACO).

K-Means

K-means algorithm is one of the most popular and oldest methods developed by Macqueen (MacQueen, 1967). It is one of the simple, fast and robust method. In K-Means algorithm, sum of Euclidean distance is used as similarity criteria to find the predefined number of cluster centers in a given dataset. K-means algorithm is started with randomly initialized cluster centers then arranges the data vectors into predefined number of clusters according to minimum Euclidean distances. The cluster centers are updated taking mean of data vectors within the clusters and this process is repeated if there is no improvement in cluster centers.

Genetic Algorithm (GA)

John Holland has proposed genetic algorithm based on the Darwin theory of evolution (Holland, 1975) and widely applied to solve the function optimization problems. In GA, the string of chromosome describes the parameters of random search space. An objective function is associated with each string which defines the importance of the string. Three operators are applied in GA to find the optimal solutions. These are the selection, crossover and mutation operators. Genetic algorithm is applied to solve the clustering problem and evaluated the performance of the genetic algorithm using three experiments on synthetic and real life data sets (Murthy & Chowdhury, 1996). From the results, it is concluded that the outcome of K-means algorithm is improved using GA. Al-Sultan et al., have studied several algorithms such as K-means algorithm, simulated annealing algorithm, tabu search algorithm, and genetic algorithm and compared the performance of these algorithms for the clustering problems (AL-Sultan & Khan, 1996). A genetic K-means (GKA) algorithm has been proposed for clustering and proved that the hybrid algorithm is converged on the optimal solution (Krishna & Murty, 1999). Maulik & Bandyopadhyay (2000) have applied the GA algorithm for clustering problem and tested the performance of algorithm using four artificial and three real life datasets. The results show that genetic algorithm is more superior to K-means algorithm.

Particle Swarm Optimization (PSO)

PSO is a population-based stochastic search algorithm and widely used to solve a broad range of optimization problems (Kennedy & Eberhart, 1997). This algorithm is based on social behavior of birds, insects etc. and presented the individual swarm knowledge among all the members of the group. For example, if one member finds a desirable path to go then rest of swarm will follow this path. In PSO, this behavior of birds are described in the form of particles and each particle is associated with certain positions and velocities in a random search space. The algorithm is started using randomly initialized population. Each particle in PSO moves through the searching space and remembers the best position it is achieved. Each particle shares the good positions to other particles and updates their own position and velocity based on these good positions. The updation of velocity is based on the historical behaviors of the particles as well as their neighbors such that the particles move towards better searching areas. To investigate the performance of PSO algorithm, Van der Merwe et al. have applied the PSO algorithm for clustering in two ways- First, the PSO algorithm is used to obtain optimal cluster centers for predefined number of clusters and second, PSO is used to refine the initial cluster centers for K-Means algorithm (Van der Merwe & Engelbrecht, 2003). The results show that the PSO has obtained better convergence rate. A hybrid algorithm based on PSO-SA has been developed to obtain good clusters partition (Niknam, Amiri, Olamaei, & Arefi, 2009). In this algorithm, SA is applied to obtain global solution for PSO algorithm. In 2010, Niknam et al., have proposed a hybrid approach based on PSO, SA and K-Means for cluster analysis and the experimental results show that the proposed approach has obtained better result to PSO, SA, PSO-SA and K-Means (Niknam & Amiri, 2010).

Ant Colony Optimization (ACO)

Ant colony optimization is a meta-heuristic algorithm proposed for combinatorial optimization problems (Dorigo & Gambardella, 1996). This algorithm simulates the behavior of real ants i.e. how ants find the shortest path between food sources to the nest. In ACO, artificial ants are used to construct the solutions by traversing the fully connected graph G (V, E) where V is a set of vertices and E is a set of edges. Each artificial ant moves from vertex to vertex along the edges of the graph and constructs a partial solution. Each ant is also deposited a certain amount of pheromone on each vertex that they have traversed. The amount of pheromone deposited is depend on the quality of the solution obtained. Ants are used the pheromone information to find the promising regions in the search space. To examine the efficiency of ACO algorithm in clustering domain, an ant based clustering approach has been proposed by Shelokar et al., (2004). The simulation results indicate that the proposed algorithm has obtained good results in terms of quality of solutions. Tsai et al., have applied the ant system with different favorable strategy for data clustering and named as ant colony optimization with different favor (ACODF) (C. F., Tsai, C. W., Tsai, Wu, & Yang, 2004). Firstly, ACODF algorithm is used different favorable ants to solve the clustering problem. Then, the proposed ant colony system has been applied with the simulated annealing concept.

EXPERIMENTAL RESULTS

This section describes the results of the CSS algorithm for clustering problem. To assess the performance of CSS algorithm, it is applied on five datasets. These datasets are iris, wine, CMC, glass and breast cancer Wisconsin which are taken from UCI repository. The characteristics of these datasets are given in Table 6. The proposed algorithm is implemented in Matlab 2010a environment on a core i5 processor with 4 GB using window operating system. For every dataset, the algorithm is run 20 times individually to check the effectiveness of proposed algorithm using different initial cluster centers. Parameter settings for the CSS algorithm is mentioned in Table 7. Sum of intra cluster distances and f-measure are used to evaluate the quality of solutions. The sum of intra cluster distances is defined as the distance between the data instances within the clusters to the corresponding cluster centers. The results are measured in terms of best case, average cases, worst case solutions and standard deviation. The quality of clustering is directly related to the minimum of the sum of distances. Whereas, accuracy of clustering is measured using f-measure. To ensure the effectiveness and adaptability of CSS algorithm in clustering domain, the investigational results of CSS algorithm are compared with K-Means, GA, PSO and ACO algorithms which are given in Table 8.

Datasets

Iris Dataset

Iris dataset contains three variety of the iris flower which is setosa, versicolour and virginica. The dataset contains 150 instances with three classes and four attributes in which each class consists of 50 instances. The attributes of iris dataset are sepal length, sepal width, petal length, and petal width.

Wine Dataset

It contains the chemical analysis of wine in the same region of Italy using three different cultivators. This dataset contains 178 instances with thirteen attributes and three classes. The attributes of dataset are alcohol, malic acid, ash, alcalinity of ash, magnesium, total phenols, flavanoids, nonflavanoid phenols, proanthocyanins, color intensity, hue, OD280/OD315 of diluted wines and proline.

Glass

This dataset consists of six different types of glass information. The dataset contains 214 instances and 7 classes. It contains nine attributes which are refractive index, sodium, magnesium, aluminium, silicon, potassium, calcium, barium, and iron.

Breast Cancer Wisconsim

This dataset characterize the behavior of cell nuclei present in the image of breast mass. It contains 683 instances with 2 classes i.e. malignant and benign and 9 attributes. The attributes are clump thickness, cell size uniformity, cell shape uniformity, marginal adhesion, single epithelial cell size, bare nuclei, bland chromatin, normal nucleoli, and mitoses. Maligant class consists of 444 instances while benign consists of 239 instances.

Table 6. Characteristics of datasets

Dataset	Classes	Features	Total Instances	Instance in Each Class
Iris	3	4	150	(50, 50, 50)
Glass	6	9	214	(70,17, 76, 13, 9, 29)
Cancer	2	9	683	(444, 239)
CMC	3	9	1473	(629,334, 510)
Wine	3	13	178	(59, 71, 48)

Table 7. Parameters setting for CSS algorithm

Parameters	Value
No. of CPs	No. of Clusters
rand	random value between [0,1]
c	0.1
∈	0.001

Table 8. Performance comparisons of different clustering algorithm with CSS algorithm

Dataset	Parameters	K-means	GA	PSO	ACO	CSS
Iris	Best	97.33	113.98	96.89	97.1	96.47
	Average	106.05	125.19	97.23	97.17	96.63
	Worst	120.45	139.77	97.89	97.8	96.78
	Std	14.631	14.563	0.347	0.367	0.14
	F-Measure	0.782	0.778	0.782	0.779	0.787
Wine	Best	16555.68	16530.53	16345.96	16530.53	16282.12
	Average	18061	16530.53	16417.47	16530.53	16289.42
	Worst	18563.12	16530.53	16562.31	16530.53	16317.67
	Std	793.213	0	85.497	0	10.31
	F-Measure	0.521	0.515	0.518	0.519	0.529
Cancer	Best	2999.19	2999.32	2973.5	2970.49	2946.48
	Average	3251.21	3249.46	3050.04	3046.06	2961.16
	Worst	3521.59	3427.43	3318.88	3242.01	3006.14
	Std	251.14	229.734	110.801	90.5	12.23
	F-Measure	0.829	0.819	0.819	0.821	0.847
CMC	Best	5842.2	5705.63	5700.98	5701.92	5672.46
	Average	5893.6	5756.59	5820.96	5819.13	5687.82
	Worst	5934.43	5812.64	5923.24	5912.43	5723.63
	Std	47.16	50.369	46.959	45.634	21.43
	F-Measure	0.334	0.324	0.331	0.328	0.359
Glass	Best	215.74	278.37	270.57	269.72	203.58
	Average	235.5	282.32	275.71	273.46	223.44
	Worst	255.38	286.77	283.52	280.08	241.27
	Std	12.47	4.138	4.55	3.584	13.29
	F-Measure	0.431	0.333	0.359	0.364	0.446

Contraceptive Method Choice (CMC)

It is a subset of National Indonesia Contraceptive Prevalence Survey data that has been performed in 1987. This dataset contains the information about married women who were either pregnant (but did not know about pregnancy) or not pregnant. It contains 1473 instances and three classes i.e., no use, long term method and short term method. Each class contains 629, 334 and 510 instances respectively. It has nine attributes which are Age, Wife's education, Husband's education, Number of children ever born, Wife's religion, Wife's now working, Husband's occupation, Standard-of-living index and Media exposure.

Performance Measures

Sum of Intra Cluster Distances

It is sum of distances between the data instances present in the clusters to its corresponding cluster centers. Minimum the sum of intra cluster distance indicates the better the quality of the solution. The results are measured in terms of best, average and worst solutions.

Standard Deviation

Standard deviation provides the information about the dispersion of data instances present in a cluster from its cluster center. The minimum value of standard deviation indicates that the data instances are close to its center while large value indicates the data is far from its center centers.

F-Measure

F-measure is calculated using recall and precision of an information retrieval system (Dali, 2003; Handl, Knowles, & Dorigo, 2003). It is weighted harmonic mean of recall and precision. The recall and precision, for each cluster j and class i is defined as

$$\text{Recall}\left(r(i,j)\right) = \frac{n_{i,j}}{n_i}$$
and (11)
$$\text{Precision}\left(p(i,j)\right) = \frac{n_{i,j}}{n_j}$$

The value of F-measure ($F(i,j)$) is computed as

$$F(i,j) = \frac{2*\left(\text{Recall}*\text{Precision}\right)}{\left(\text{Recall}+\text{Precision}\right)} \quad (12)$$

Finally, the value of F-measure for a given clustering algorithm which consist of n number of data instances is given as

$$F(i,j) = \sum_{i=1}^{n} \frac{n_i}{n}.\max_i\left(F(i,j)\right) \quad (13)$$

From Table 8, it can be seen that the results obtained using the CSS algorithm is better as compared to the other algorithms. The best values achieved by the algorithm for iris, wine, cancer, CMC and glass datasets are 96.47, 16282.12, 2946.48, 5672.46 and 203.58. The standard deviation parameter shows dispersion of data from the cluster centers. The value of standard deviation parameter for CSS algorithm is also smaller than other methods. Moreover, the CSS algorithm provides better f-measure values which shows higher accuracy than the other algorithms being compared.

CONCLUSION

Charged system search algorithm (CSS) is applied to solve the clustering problem. In the proposed algorithm, Newton second law of motion is used to get the optimal cluster centers but it is the actual electric force (F_k) which plays a vital role to obtain the optimal cluster centers. The working of proposed algorithm is divided into two steps, first step involves the calculation of the value of actual electric force using Coulomb and Gauss laws. While, in second step, the optimal cluster centers are obtained using Newton second law of motion. The CSS algorithm is applied for data clustering when number of clusters (K) is already known. The performance of the CSS algorithm is tested on the several datasets and compared with K-Means, GA, PSO and ACO. The proposed algorithm provides better results as well as the quality of solutions obtained by the proposed algorithm is superior in comparison to the other algorithms.

REFERENCES

Al-Sultana, K. S., & Khan, M. M. (1996). Computational experience on four algorithms for the hard clustering problem. *Pattern Recognition Letters*, *17*(3), 295–308. doi:10.1016/0167-8655(95)00122-0

Alpaydin, E. (2004). *Introduction to Machine Learning*. Cambridge, MA: MIT Press.

Bezdek, J. C. (1974). Numerical taxonomy with fuzzy sets. *Journal of Mathematical Biology*, *1*(1), 57–71. doi:10.1007/BF02339490

Bezdek, J. C. (1981). *Pattern recognition with fuzzy objective function algorithms*. Kluwer Academic Publishers. doi:10.1007/978-1-4757-0450-1

Cowgill, M. C., Harvey, R. J., & Watson, L. T. (1999). A genetic algorithm approach to cluster analysis. *Computers & Mathematics with Applications (Oxford, England)*, *37*(7), 99–108. doi:10.1016/S0898-1221(99)00090-5

Dalli, A. (2003). Adaptation of the F-measure to cluster based lexicon quality evaluation. In *Proceedings of the EACL*. doi:10.3115/1641396.1641404

Dorigo, M., & Gambardella, L. M. (1997). Ant colonies for the travelling salesman problem. *Bio Systems*, *43*(2), 73–81. doi:10.1016/S0303-2647(97)01708-5 PMID:9231906

Dunn, W. J. III, Greenberg, M. J., & Callejas, S. S. (1976). Use of cluster analysis in the development of structure-activity relations for antitumor triazenes. *Journal of Medicinal Chemistry*, *19*(11), 1299–1301. doi:10.1021/jm00233a009 PMID:1003406

Fathian, M., Amiri, B., & Maroosi, A. (2007). Application of honey-bee mating optimization algorithm on clustering. *Applied Mathematics and Computation*, *190*(2), 1502–1513. doi:10.1016/j.amc.2007.02.029

Forgy, E. W. (1965). Cluster analysis of multivariate data: Efficiency versus interpretability of classifications. *Biometrics*, *21*, 768–769.

Graves, D., & Witold, P. (2010). Kernel-based fuzzy clustering and fuzzy clustering: A comparative experimental study. *Fuzzy Sets and Systems*, *161*(4), 522–543. doi:10.1016/j.fss.2009.10.021

Handl, J., Knowles, J., & Dorigo, M. (2003). On the performance of ant-based clustering. Design and Application of Hybrid Intelligent System. *Frontiers in Artificial Intelligence and Applications*, *104*, 204–213.

Hatamlou, A., Abdullah, S., & Hatamlou, M. (2011). Data clustering using big bang–big crunch algorithm. In *Innovative Computing Technology* (pp. 383–388). Springer Berlin Heidelberg. doi:10.1007/978-3-642-27337-7_36

Hatamlou, A., Abdullah, S., & Nezamabadi-Pour, H. (2011). Application of gravitational search algorithm on data clustering. In *Rough Sets and Knowledge Technology* (pp. 337–346). Springer Berlin Heidelberg. doi:10.1007/978-3-642-24425-4_44

Hatamlou, A., Abdullah, S., & Nezamabadi-pour, H. (2012). A combined approach for clustering based on K-means and gravitational search algorithms. *Swarm and Evolutionary Computation*, *6*, 47–52. doi:10.1016/j.swevo.2012.02.003

He, Y., Pan, W., & Lin, J. (2006). Cluster analysis using multivariate normal mixture models to detect differential gene expression with microarray data. *Computational Statistics & Data Analysis*, *51*(2), 641–658. doi:10.1016/j.csda.2006.02.012

Holland, J. H. (1975). *Adaptation in natural and artificial systems: An introductory analysis with applications to biology, control, and artificial intelligence*. University of Michigan Press.

Hu, G., Zhou, S., Guan, J., & Hu, X. (2008). Towards effective document clustering: A constrained K-means based approach. *Information Processing & Management*, *44*(4), 1397–1409. doi:10.1016/j.ipm.2008.03.001

Jain, A. K. (2010). Data clustering: 50 years beyond K-means. *Pattern Recognition Letters*, *31*(8), 651–666. doi:10.1016/j.patrec.2009.09.011

Jain, A. K., Murty, M. N., & Flynn, P. J. (1999). Data clustering: a review. *ACM Computing Surveys, 31*(3), 264-323.

Kao, Y. T., Zahara, E., & Kao, I. W. (2008). A hybridized approach to data clustering. *Expert Systems with Applications*, *34*(3), 1754–1762. doi:10.1016/j.eswa.2007.01.028

Karaboga, D., & Ozturk, C. (2011). A novel clustering approach: Artificial Bee Colony (ABC) algorithm. *Applied Soft Computing*, *11*(1), 652–657. doi:10.1016/j.asoc.2009.12.025

Kaveh, A., & Talatahari, S. (2010). A novel heuristic optimization method: Charged system search. *Acta Mechanica, 213*(3-4), 267–289. doi:10.1007/s00707-009-0270-4

Kennedy, J., & Eberhart, R. C. (1997, October). A discrete binary version of the particle swarm algorithm. In *IEEE International Conference on Computational Cybernetics and Simulation*, *5*, 4104-4108. doi:10.1109/ICSMC.1997.637339

Kogan, J., Nicholas, C., Teboulle, M., & Berkhin, P. (2006). A Survey of Clustering Data Mining Techniques. In Grouping Multidimensional Data, 25-71.

Krishna, K., & Murty, M. N. (1999). Genetic K-means algorithm. *IEEE Transactions on Systems, Man, and Cybernetics. Part B, Cybernetics*, *29*(3), 433–439. doi:10.1109/3477.764879 PMID:18252317

Kumar, Y., & Sahoo, G. (2014b). A chaotic charged system search approach for data clustering. *Informatica*, *38*(3), 249–261.

Kumar, Y., & Sahoo, G. (2014a). A charged system search approach for data clustering. *Progress in Artificial Intelligence*, *2*(2-3), 153–166. doi:10.1007/s13748-014-0049-2

Kumar, Y., & Sahoo, G. (2015). An Improved Cat Swarm Optimization Algorithm for Clustering. Computational Intelligence in Data Mining, 1, 187-197. doi:10.1007/978-81-322-2205-7_18

Kumar, Y., & Sahoo, G. (2014c). A Hybridize Approach for Data Clustering Based on Cat Swarm Optimization. *International Journal of Information and Communication Technology*.

Lee, M., & Pedrycz, W. (2009). The fuzzy C-means algorithm with fuzzy P-mode prototypes for clustering objects having mixed features. *Fuzzy Sets and Systems*, *160*(24), 3590–3600. doi:10.1016/j.fss.2009.06.015

MacQueen, J. (1967, June). Some methods for classification and analysis of multivariate observations. In *Proceedings of the fifth Berkeley symposium on mathematical statistics and probability*.

Maulik, U., & Bandyopadhyay, S. (2000). Genetic algorithm-based clustering technique. *Pattern Recognition*, *33*(9), 1455–1465. doi:10.1016/S0031-3203(99)00137-5

Murthy, C. A., & Chowdhury, N. (1996). In search of optimal clusters using genetic algorithms. *Pattern Recognition Letters*, *17*(8), 825–832. doi:10.1016/0167-8655(96)00043-8

Niknam, T., & Amiri, B. (2010). An efficient hybrid approach based on PSO, ACO and k-means for cluster analysis. *Applied Soft Computing*, *10*(1), 183–197. doi:10.1016/j.asoc.2009.07.001

Niknam, T., Amiri, B., Olamaei, J., & Arefi, A. (2009). An efficient hybrid evolutionary optimization algorithm based on PSO and SA for clustering. *Journal of Zhejiang University Science A*, *10*(4), 512–519. doi:10.1631/jzus.A0820196

Pal, N. R., & Bezdek, J. C. (1995). On cluster validity for the fuzzy c-means model. *IEEE Transactions on Fuzzy Systems*, *3*(3), 370–379. doi:10.1109/91.413225

Pappas, T. N. (1992). An adaptive clustering algorithm for image segmentation. *IEEE Transactions on Signal Processing*, *40*(4), 901–914. doi:10.1109/78.127962

Rokach, L. (2010). A survey of clustering algorithms. In Data mining and knowledge discovery handbook, (pp. 269-298). Springer.

Ruspini, E. H. (1969). A new approach to clustering. *Information and Control*, *15*(1), 22–32. doi:10.1016/S0019-9958(69)90591-9

Sahoo, A. J., & Kumar, Y. (2014, March). Modified Teacher Learning Based Optimization Method for Data Clustering. In Advances in Signal Processing and Intelligent Recognition Systems, 429-437. doi:10.1007/978-3-319-04960-1_38

Santosa, B., & Ningrum, M. K. (2009, December). Cat swarm optimization for clustering. In *IEEE International Conference of Soft Computing and Pattern Recognition*.

Satapathy, S. C., & Naik, A. (2011). Data clustering based on teaching-learning-based optimization. In *Swarm* (pp. 148–156). Evolutionary, and Memetic Computing, Springer Berlin Heidelberg.

Selim, S. Z., & Alsultan, K. (1991). A simulated annealing algorithm for the clustering problem. *Pattern Recognition*, *24*(10), 1003–1008. doi:10.1016/0031-3203(91)90097-O

Shelokar, P. S., Jayaraman, V. K., & Kulkarni, B. D. (2004). An ant colony approach for clustering. *Analytica Chimica Acta*, *509*(2), 187–195. doi:10.1016/j.aca.2003.12.032

Sonka, M., Hlavac, V., & Boyle, R. (2014). *Image processing, analysis, and machine vision*. Springer.

Sung, C. S., & Jin, H. W. (2000). A tabu-search-based heuristic for clustering. *Pattern Recognition*, *33*(5), 849–858. doi:10.1016/S0031-3203(99)00090-4

Teppola, P., Mujunen, S. P., & Minkkinen, P. (1999). Adaptive Fuzzy C-Means clustering in process monitoring. *Chemometrics and Intelligent Laboratory Systems*, *45*(1), 23–38. doi:10.1016/S0169-7439(98)00087-2

Tsai, C. F., Tsai, C. W., Wu, H. C., & Yang, T. (2004). ACODF: A novel data clustering approach for data mining in large databases. *Journal of Systems and Software*, *73*(1), 133–145. doi:10.1016/S0164-1212(03)00216-4

Van der Merwe, D. W., & Engelbrecht, A. P. (2003, December). Data clustering using particle swarm optimization. In *IEEE Congress on Evolutionary Computation CEC-03*.

Zhang, B., Hsu, M., & Dayal, U. (1999). *K-harmonic means-a data clustering algorithm*. Hewlett-Packard Labs Technical Report HPL-1999-124.

Zhou, H., & Liu, Y. (2008). Accurate integration of multi-view range images using k-means clustering. *Pattern Recognition*, *41*(1), 152–175. doi:10.1016/j.patcog.2007.06.006

KEY TERMS AND DEFINITIONS

Charge Particles: Charged particles are the particles with an electric charge.

Clustering: It is a technique to find out hidden patterns and knowledge from a given set of patterns and data.

Coulomb Law: Coulomb law stated that electric force between two small charged spheres (charge particles) is proportional to the inverse square of their separation distance.

Gauss Law: Gauss's law is defined as the electric fields at points on the closed surface and the net charge enclosed by that surface.

Newton Law: The force acting on an object is equal to the mass of that object and its acceleration.

Chapter 19

Learning Aided Digital Image Compression Technique for Medical Application

Kandarpa Kumar Sarma
Gauhati University, India

ABSTRACT

The explosive growths in data exchanges have necessitated the development of new methods of image compression including use of learning based techniques. The learning based systems aids proper compression and retrieval of the image segments. Learning systems like. Artificial Neural Networks (ANN) have established their efficiency and reliability in achieving image compression. In this work, two approaches to use ANNs in Feed Forward (FF) form and another based on Self Organizing Feature Map (SOFM) is proposed for digital image compression. The image to be compressed is first decomposed into smaller blocks and passed to FFANN and SOFM networks for generation of codebooks. The compressed images are reconstructed using a composite block formed by a FFANN and a Discrete Cosine Transform (DCT) based compression-decompression system. Mean Square Error (MSE), Compression ratio (CR) and Peak Signal-to-Noise Ratio (PSNR) are used to evaluate the performance of the system.

INTRODUCTION

The last few decades have seen unprecedented growth in communication and multi-media technologies. Both of these have been symbiotically driven. The use of multimedia contents in every segment of day to day life has necessitated the urgent requirement of providing more and more storage space. This requirement, to a large extent, can be optimized by use of compression technologies. This has motivated the research in digital image compression domain. Of late, the importance of application of innovative technologies has reached a new level. Though traditional approaches have already established their importance and effectiveness, still there are ample of opportunities to explore new methods of achieving compression. Modern day vision devices have placed great leverages on resolution which have constantly increased the data volume. Concurrently, though compression methods have supported the requirements of more and more

DOI: 10.4018/978-1-4666-8654-0.ch019

storage space and communication capacity, improvement in decompression and presentation approaches have become stringent factors. Therefore, design of improved compression and decompression methods have become a need of the hour. A practical compression algorithm for image data should preserve most of the characteristics of the data while working in a lossy manner and maximize the gain and be of lesser algorithmic complexity (Ettaouil, Ghanou, Moutaouakil, & Lazaar, 2011; Durai & Saro, 2006). The process of image compression is based on reduction of redundancy contained in an image. Some of the benefits derived from image compression are cost savings associated with sending less data over switched telephone or wireless networks, reduction of storage requirements and overall processing/execution time, reduction in transmission errors and improvement in security against illicit monitoring. So while image compression provides several benefits, complex methods are required to restore the forms before presentation. It is more so if medical images are involved.

Medical images are needed to be stored in diagnostic centers for a patient's future reference and also for the purpose of transmission through a communication channel for telemedicine and referral for advanced treatment. Hence, it has to be compressed before using it for storage or transmission. Learning systems like Artificial Neural Networks (ANN) can be used to pre-process input patterns to yield simpler patterns with smaller components. This motivates the users to prefer it for image compression. ANN based image systems provide high compression rates and preserve quality. They have the ability to preprocess input patterns to produce reduced data sizes with fewer components. Self Organizing Feature Map (SOFM) is a kind of ANN which consists of components called nodes (neurons) and is based upon unsupervised learning. It gives a low dimensional and discretized representation of the input space of the training samples which is known as map (Sharma & Kumari, 2013). The

SOFM model proposed by Kohonen can be used for image compression. The primary principle behind the use of SOFM is the fact that it is inherently a data reduction method. Considerable compression techniques have been designed, regarding the use of conventional and ANN based methods for compression of images. Here, we include learning and decomposition based image compression technique using ANN in feedforward (FF) configuration and applied as SOFM. The work describes a lossy compression system for compression of medical images. An image is first decomposed into smaller blocks before passing it through FF ANN and SOFM network for generation of a codebook. The output of FF ANN and SOFM are further compressed by applying Discrete Cosine Transform (DCT), Discrete Wavelet Transform (DWT) like techniques to it. The compressed image is then reconstructed using a multi-layer FF ANN. The performance of the proposed system is judged by finding parameters like Mean Square Error (MSE), Compression Ratio (CR) and Peak Signal-to-Noise Ratio (PSNR). The original image is degraded to some extent by applying salt and pepper noise to it and applied to the proposed system. The PSNR value of the reconstructed image containing noise is determined. It is found that the system is robust to degradations like noise that may be present in an image due to false switching of the device and transmission through a noisy channel.

BACKGROUND

In the field of image processing, computer vision, bio-informatics, compression of data is an area which has received continued attention due to demands of multimedia applications. The redundancies observed in data specially image is removed through which compression is generated. Compression techniques maybe either lossy or loss less. Lossy techniques generally achieve high compression ration but are not suitable for critical applications like medical. Further, lossless techniques have less compression ratios and hence are less efficient. There is a continuous demand for design and implementation of techniques which can provide the quality of lossless compression yet achieve memory reduction requirement showing performance similar to that of lossy techniques. In this respect, learning based tools have become parts of appropriate and reliable methods.

LITERATURE REVIEW

Learning based systems like ANN and its subtypes have found applications in range of domains ranging from engineering to social sciences. Their versatility and their ability to mimic human processing is one of the driving factors. In Saikia and Sarma (2014), authors report the use of a feedforward ANN and multi-level discrete wavelet transform (DWT) for image de-noising applications which is also suitable for medical purposes. Application of a dynamic DWT and ANN combination is tested for image restoration in Baruah and Sarma (2013). In Ahmed, Dey, and Sarma (2011), authors report the use of ANN for texture analysis. In (Gogoi & Sarma, 2012), authors report the use of an adaptive neuro-fuzzy inference system (ANFIS) for extraction of background and foreground information from satellite images. In Bodoloi and Sarma (2012), ANN has been used for protein structure analysis. Innovative handwriting segmentation using ANN has been reported in Bhattacharyya and Sarma (2009). In wireless communication, application of ANN has been demonstrated in Sarma and Mitra (2009, 2011, 2012).

In Talukder and Harada (2007), authors proposed a paper on Haar wavelet based approach for image compression and quality assessment of compressed image. A low complex 2D image compression method using wavelets (Talukder & Harada, 2007) as the basis functions and the approach to measure the quality of the compressed image has been presented. A fuzzy based approach to image compression is presented in Tamilarasi

and Palanisamy (2009). Another such work is reported in Ettaouil, Ghanou, Moutaouakil and Lazaar (2011), Durai and Saro (2006). In Tamilarasi and Palanisamy (2009), authors have proposed a fuzzy based approach of image compression. The combination system adopts a new fuzzy neuron network (FNN) which can appropriately adjust input and output values, and increase robustness, stability and working speed of the network by achieving high compression ratio. It is observed that embedded zero tree wavelet coding with fuzzy back propagation networks is able to achieve good performance with relatively less computational effort. Another work (Jilani & Sattar, 2010) uses fuzzy neural approach for image compression. Different image compression techniques were combined with neural network classifier for various applications (Sicuranzi, Ramponi, & Marsi, 1990). The work Senthilkumaran and Suguna (2011), describes a lossless image compression technique using ANN for X-ray images. The work outperformed the existing Huffman encoding technique in terms of compression ratio, transmission time and compression performance. The authors of Arel, Rose, and Karnowski (2011), presented a technique of deep machine learning which is a new frontier in artificial intelligence research. The article provided an overview of the mainstream deep learning approaches and research directions proposed over the past decade. In Amin, Qureshi, Junaid, Habib, and Anjum (2011), the authors proposed a system on modified run length encoding (RLE) scheme with introduction of bit stuffing for efficient data compression. A high compression ratio is obtained by the work. The work (Polomo & Dominguez, 2011), describes a image compression scheme based on growing hierarchial SOMs. The experimental results of the work provided good performance. The authors of Boopathi and Arockiasamy (2011), presented an image compression approach using wavelet transform and modified SOM. The experimental results of the work provided better peak signal to nosie ration (PSNR) value and reduced mean square error (MSE). In the work Ansari and Anand (2008), the authors proposed a work on the recent trends in image compression and its application in telemedicine and teleconsultation. In this work, a comparative analysis of different compression techniques and their applications in the fields of medical science have been reported. In Thota and Devireddy (2008), Image compression using DCT is reported. Here, storage area to load an image is minimized by reducing redundancy. In the work Khasman and Dimililer (2008), the authors have proposed a work on image compression using ANNs and Haar Wavelet. Here, ANN has been trained to recognize an optimum compression ratio for Haar wavelet compression of an image. The authors of Soliman and Omari (2006), presented an ANN approach to image data compression. The work outperformed the JPEG2000 and DjVu wavelet technology. The work Haykin (2005), describes a image compression system using SOMs. The scheme provided better performance compared to JPEG.

CONTRIBUTION

The primary contribution of the work is design of a few learning aided methods of image compression for medical applications. The first works is related to the Implementation of learning aided, lossless medical image compression algorithm using ANN which intends to analyze an approach for improving the quality of decompression in medical applications. Image compression involves reducing the size of images, while retaining necessary information. Hence, to analyze and suggest a suitable technique for lossless image compression is an important motivating factor for any such design. Another approach is to avoid the supervised learning used in case of the feedforward ANN trained with back propagation algorithm. The unsupervised SOM and DWT are used together to generate an image compression approach. Learning based compression-decompression is

a form of pattern recognition application. In any pattern classification and recognition application, the main difficulty is that the learning complexity grows exponentially with linear increase in the dimensionality of the data. Therefore, a system which is capable of learning the features from the data given to it is needed. The proposed system meets the above requirement. The work describes a lossy compression system for compression of medical images. An image is first decomposed into smaller blocks before passing it through SOM network for generation of a codebook. The output of SOM is further compressed by applying DWT to it. The compressed image is then reconstructed using a multi-layer feed forward ANN.

ORGANIZATION OF THE CHAPTER

In the next section we cover the theoretical aspects related to the work. These include certain essential details of the ANN, compression and decompression and DWT. Next, we describe the proposed approaches based on FF ANN and SOM in separate subsections. We also include a detailed description of the experiments performed and the results derived. Finally, we conclude the chapter.

THEORETICAL CONSIDERATIONS

Here we briefly cover certain theoretical aspects of the work.

Artificial Neural Networks (ANNs)

ANNs are non-parametric prediction or soft computing tools based on the analogy of biological nervous systems consisting of interconnected group of artificial neurons and information-processing units using connectionist approach that can be used for a host of pattern classification and recognition purposes (Haykin, 2005). The key element of this paradigm is the novel structure of the information processing system. It is composed of a large number of highly interconnected processing elements (neurons) working in unison to solve specific problems. ANNs can be trained to perform complex functions in various fields, including pattern recognition, identification, classification, speech, vision and control systems and to solve problems that are difficult for conventional computers or human beings. ANNs are adaptive, resilient and connectionist in processing. The fundamental information-processing unit of the operation of the neural networks is the McCulloch-Pitts Neuron (1943). Figure 1 shows the model of an artificial neuron, which forms the basis for designing ANNs.

The three basic elements of the neuron model are explained as:

1. A set of synapses or connecting links, each of which is characterized by weight or strength of its own. Specially, a signal x_j at the input of synapse j connected to v neuron, k is multiplied by the synaptic weight w_{kj}.
2. An adder for summing the input signal, weighted by the respective synapses of the neuron; the operations described here constitutes a linear combiner.
3. An activation function for limiting the amplitude of the output of a neuron.

Figure 1. A model of a neuron

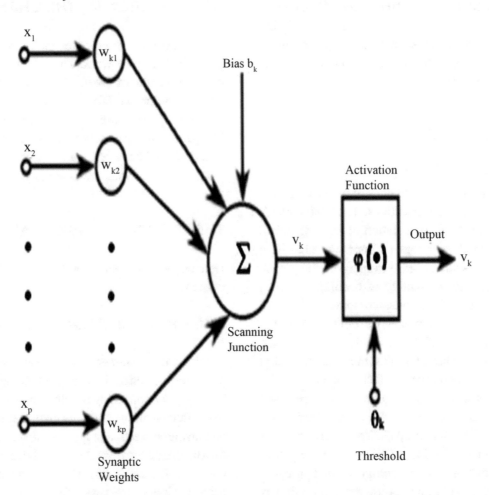

From this model the interval activity of a neuron k can be shown to be

$$u_k = \sum_{j=1}^{m} w_{kj} x_j \qquad (1)$$

and

$$y_k = \varphi(u_k + b_k) \qquad (2)$$

where $x_1, x_2, \ldots, x_k$ are the input signals, $w_{k1}, w_{k2}, \ldots, w_{km}$ are the synaptic weights of neuron k, b_k is the bias, $\varphi(.)$ is the activation function and y_k is the output signal of the neuron. The use of bias b_k has the effect of applying and affine transformation to the output u_k of the linear combiner in the model of Figure 1 as shown by

$$v_k = u_k + b_k \qquad (3)$$

From the above equations we have,

$$v_k = \sum_{j=0}^{m} w_{kj} x_j \qquad (4)$$

where a new synapse has been added. Its input is $x_0 = +1$ and its weight is $w_{k0} = b_k$ and

$$y_k = \varphi(v_k) \qquad (5)$$

The activation function acts as a squashing function, such that the output of a neuron in a neural network is between certain values (usually 0 and 1, or -1 and 1). Among several types of activation function, three basic types are explained here (Haykin, 2005).

1. **Threshold Function:** This type of activation function takes on a value of 0 if the summed input is less than a certain threshold value v, and the value 1 if the summed input is greater than or equal to the threshold value and is defined as

$$\varphi(v) = \begin{cases} 1, & \text{if } v \geq 0; \\ 0, & \text{if } v < 0. \end{cases} \qquad (6)$$

This type of threshold function is referred as a Heaviside function. The output of neuron k employing such a threshold function is expressed as

$$y_k = \begin{cases} 1, & \text{if } v_k \geq 0; \\ 0, & \text{if } v_k < 0. \end{cases} \qquad (7)$$

where v_k is the induced field of the neuron.

If the threshold function of Equations (6) are rewritten have the range -1 to +1, it is referred as Signum function and is defined as

$$\varphi(v) = \begin{cases} 1, & v_k > 0; \\ 0, & v_k = 0; \\ -1, & v_k < 0. \end{cases} \qquad (8)$$

2. **Piecewise-Linear Function:** This function can take on the values of 0 or 1, but can also take on values between that depending on the amplification factor in a certain region of linear operation. This function is defined as

$$\varphi(v) = \begin{cases} 1, & v \geq +\dfrac{1}{2}; \\ v, & +\dfrac{1}{2} > v > -\dfrac{1}{2}; \\ 0, & v \leq -\dfrac{1}{2}. \end{cases} \qquad (9)$$

where the amplification factor inside the linear region of operation is assumed to be unity.

3. **Sigmoid Function:** The sigmoid is defined as a strictly increasing function that exhibits a graceful balance between linear and

nonlinear behavior. This function can range between 0 and 1, but it is also sometimes useful to use the -1 to 1 range. An example of the sigmoid function is the logistic function defined as

$$\varphi(v) = \frac{1}{1 + \exp(-a*v)} \qquad (10)$$

where a is the slope parameter of the sigmoid function.

ANNs can be classified into two systems, viz. feed forward and feedback systems. Feed forward (FF) ANN are static and feedback systems are dynamic or recurrent in nature. Figures 2 and 3 show the structure of a FF ANN and feedback neural network respectively. There are two broad methods of learning which classifies ANNs further into supervised and unsupervised category. Learning is the act of presenting the network with some sample data and modifying the weights to better approximate data the desired function. Supervised learning is like guided by a teacher. The ANN is provided with a pattern which it learns constantly till it can fully handle the pattern fed to it. While

unsupervised learning means learning without teacher's guidance but in case of supervised case there is always a reference to follow. FF ANNs are used for prediction, classification and function approximation. Examples are back propagation based Multi Layer Perceptron (MLP), Radial Basis Function (RBF) ANNs etc. Feedback networks are used in feature matching, constraint satisfaction and optimization. Examples are recurrent back propagation networks etc.

A MLP neural network consists of one or more hidden layers in between the input and output layers, whose computation nodes are correspondingly called hidden neurons or hidden units. Figure 4 shows a simple MLP with two hidden layers. A MLP consists of several layers of neurons. The expression for output in a MLP with one hidden layer is given as:

$$O_x = \sum_{i=1}^{N} \beta_i g[w]_i .[x] + b_i \qquad (11)$$

where β_i is the weight value between the ith hidden neuron. The process of adjusting the weights and biases of a perceptron or MLP is known as training. The perceptron algorithm for training simple perceptrons consists of comparing the output of the perceptron with an associated target value.

Figure 2. Structure of a feed forward neural network

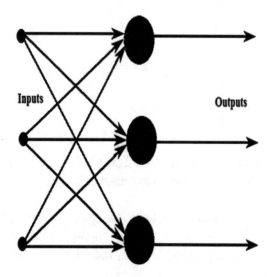

Figure 3. Structure of a feedback neural network

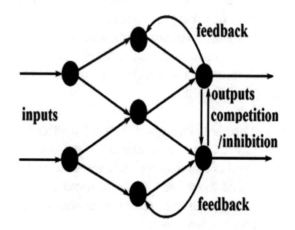

Figure 4. Multilayer Perceptron neural network

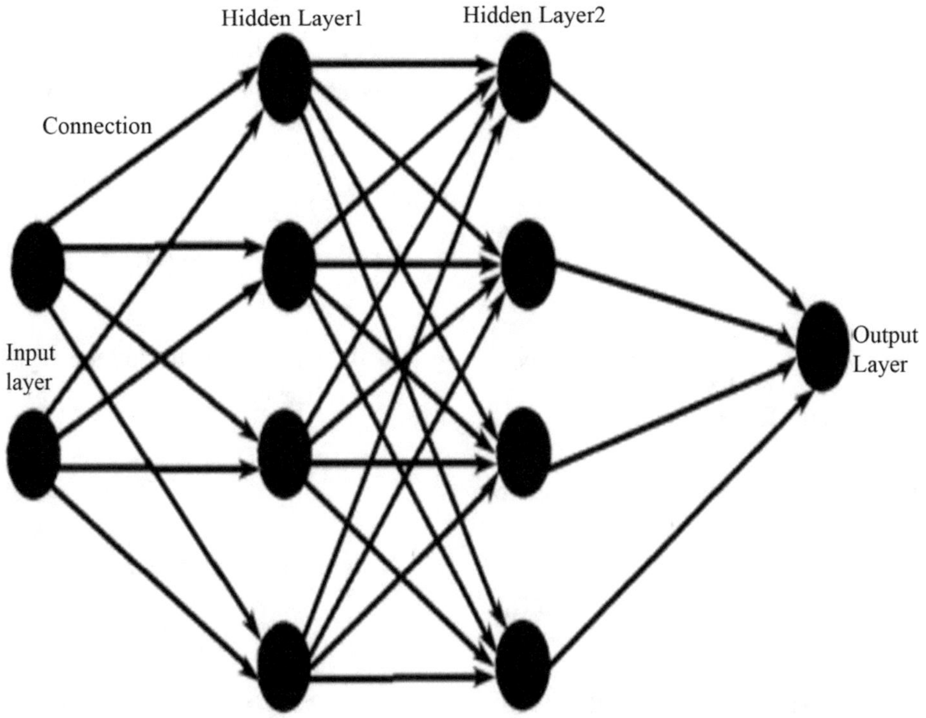

The most common training algorithm for MLP is error back propagation. The training should minimize the risk function:

$$R = \frac{1}{2N} \sum \left(d_j - F\left(x_j \right) \right)^2 \qquad (12)$$

where d_j is the desired output pattern for the prototype vector x_j, $((.))$ is the Euclidean norm of the enclosed vector and N is the total number of samples presented to the network in training. The decision rule therefore can be given by the output of the network:

$$y_{kj} = F_k(x_j) \qquad (13)$$

For the jth input vector. Training the ANN is done in two broad passes-one a forward pass and the other a backward calculation with error

determination and connecting weight updating in between. Batch training method is adopted as it accelerates the speed of training and the rate of convergence of the MSE to the desired value. The steps are:

1. Initialization: Initialize the weight matrix W with random values between [-1, 1] if a tan-sigmoid function is used as an activation function and between [0, 1] if log-sigmoid function is used as activation function. W is a matrix of $C{\times}P$ where P is the length of the feature vector used for each of the C classes.

2. Presentation of training samples: Input is P_m = $[P_{m1}, P_{m2}, ..., P_{mL}]$. The desired output is $d_m = [d_{m1}, d_{m2}, ..., d_{mL}]$.
    a. Compute the values of the hidden nodes as

$$net^h_{mj} = \sum_{i=1}^{L} w^h_{ji} p^{mi} + \phi^h_j \qquad (14)$$

b. Calculate the output from the hidden layer as

$$o^h_{mj} = f^h_j \left(net^h_{mj} \right) \qquad (15)$$

where $f(x) = \dfrac{1}{e^x}$ or $f(x) = \dfrac{e^x - e^{-x}}{e^x + e^{-x}}$ depending upon the choice of the activation function.

c. Calculate the values of the output node as

$$o^o_{mk} = f^o_k \left(net^o_{mj} \right) \qquad (16)$$

3. Forward Computation: Compute the errors

$$e_{jn} = d_{jn} - o_{jn} \qquad (17)$$

Calculate the Mean Square Error (MSE) as

$$MSE = \frac{\sum_{j=1}^{M} \sum_{n=1}^{L} e^2_{jn}}{2M} \qquad (18)$$

Error terms for the output layer is

$$\delta^o_{mk} = o^o_{mk} \left(1 - o^o_{mk} \right) e_{mn} \qquad (19)$$

Error terms for the hidden layer

$$\delta^h_{mk} = o^h_{mk} \left(1 - o^h_{mk} \right) \sum_j \delta^o_{mj} w^o_{jk} \qquad (20)$$

4. Weight Update:

a. Between the output and the hidden layers

$$w^o_{kj} (t+1) = w^o_{kj} (t) + \eta \delta^o_{mk} o_{mj} \qquad (21)$$

where η is the learning rate ($0 < \eta < 1$). For faster convergence a momentum term (α) may be added as

$$w^o_{kj} (t+1) = w^o_{kj} (t) + \eta \delta^o_{mk} o_{mj} + \alpha \left(w^o_{kj} (t+1) - w_{kj} \right) \qquad (22)$$

b. Between the hidden layer and input layer

$$w^h_{ji} (t+1) = w^h_{ji} (t) + \eta \delta^h_{mj} P_i \qquad (23)$$

A momentum term may be added as

$$w^h_{ji} (t+1) = w^h_{ji} (t) + \eta \delta^h_{mj} p_i + \alpha \left(w^o_{ji} (t+1) - w_{ji} \right) \qquad (24)$$

One cycle through the complete training set forms one epoch. The above is repeated till MSE meets the performance criteria. While repeating the above the number of epoch elapsed is counted. A few methods used for MLP training includes

1. Gradient Descent (GDBP),
2. Gradient Descent with Momentum BP (GDMBP),
3. Gradient Descent with Adaptive Learning Rate BP (GDALRBP) and
4. Gradient Descent with Adaptive Learning Rate and Momentum BP (GDALRMBP)

Here, while MSE approaches the convergence goal, training of the MLPs suffer if

$$Corr(p_{m,i}(j), p_{m,i}(j+1)) = high$$

and

$Corr(p_{m,i}(j), p_{m,i+1}(j))$=high.

This is due to the requirements of the (error) back propagation algorithm as suggested by Equations 19 and 20. Therefore, the motivation of formulation of any feature set should always keep this fact within sight.

Self Organizing Map (SOM)

Self organizing map (SOM) is a type of ANN developed by Kohonen, (Figure 5) preferable for reducing dimensions. It is done by producing a map of usually one or two dimensions that plots the similarities of the data by grouping the closely matching data items together. The SOM uses an unsupervised learning method to map high di-

mensional data into a $1 - D, 2 - D$ or $3 - D$ data space, subject to a topological ordering constraint. A major advantage is that the clustering produced by the SOM retains the underlying structure of the input space, while the dimensionality of the space is reduced. The following are among some of methods used for training and weight updating of SOMs as part of competitive learning: (a) Inner Product and (b) Euclidean Distance Based Competition. A SOM follows competitive learning which is based upon a philosophy called 'winners take all'. Competitive learning requires that the weight vector of the winning neuron be made to correlate more with the input vector. This is done by perturbation of only the winning weight vector towards the input vector. At the time of self organization, the weight vector of the cluster (output)

Figure 5. Self organizing map (SOM) layout

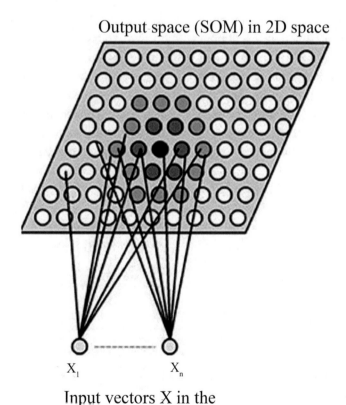

Output space (SOM) in 2D space

X_1 X_n

Input vectors X in the
multidimensional space

unit which matches the input pattern very closely is chosen as the winner. The closeness of weight vector of cluster unit to the input pattern is based on the minimum Euclidean distance.

Discrete Wavelet Transform (DWT)

The DWT is a fast linear operation used to generate wavelet transform of discrete waveforms. It operates on a data vector whose length is an integer power of two. It transforms the data vector into a form numerically dissimilar with identical length. Wavelet transform is invertible and orthogonal like the fast Fourier Transform (FFT). The inverse transform matrix is simply the transpose of the transform (Gonzales, 2009). DWT based image compression schemes has its own transformation and compression functions.

Discrete Cosine Transform (DCT)

DCT expresses a sequence having finite data points in terms of a sum of cosine functions oscillating at different frequencies. It is a Fourier related transform similar to the discrete Fourier transform (DFT), which uses only real numbers. In signal and image processing applications, DCT can be used for lossy data compression because of its strong energy compaction property (Gonzales, 2009).

PROPOSED APPROACH

The work is related to the design of a few learning aided methods of image compression for medical applications. The first works is related to the implementation of learning aided, lossless medical image compression algorithm using ANN. It intends to ascertain the performance of a learning based approach for improving the quality of compression and decompression of images for medical applications. The first approach is based on a supervised technique based on FF ANN. Another approach is to avoid the supervised learning used

in case of the feedforward ANN trained with back propagation algorithm. The unsupervised SOM and DWT are used together to generate an image compression approach. The performance of the systems is evaluated by determining the MSE, compression ration and PSNR. The two approaches are described in two subsections.

FF ANN Based Image Compression and Decompression

The ANN used for compression in the proposed method is a multi-layer FF ANN based on back-propagation algorithm, containing two hidden layers. The ANN parameters for the compression scheme for input image of sizes, 32x32 and 128x128 for decomposition level 4 and 108x108 and 240x240 for decomposition level 9 are shown in Table 1. The layer sizes will vary with four or nine decomposition levels.

At first, an X-ray image of size 32x32 is taken for compression purpose. The whole image is sent to two ANNs for compression and decompression, assigning suitable reference vectors. For compression, average value of input pixels is used as reference and the hidden layer output gives the compressed image. In the reconstruction process, the original image is used as a reference. The quality of the recovered image is found to be low when we give the whole image as input to ANN.

Table 1. Parameters of FF ANN used for compression decompression

ANN Type	Feed-Forward MLP
Training Algorithm	Backpropagation Levenberg-Marquardt Optimization
Training Function	Trainlm
Epochs	Maximum 100 for each sample
MSE goal	10^{-4}
Input Layer Size	12x12; 64x64; 36x36; 80x80
Output Layer Size	1x12 ; 1x64 ; 1x36 ; 1x80
Hidden Layer Size	1.5 times input layer size

To overcome this limitation, multi-level decomposition of the image is done. Decomposition of an image into sub-blocks also reduces computational complexity of the system. We describe a 4-level decomposition done to perform image compression using ANN. The ANN is presented with patterns which it learns during training. The learning is retained and used subsequently.

The image to be compressed is sub-divided into 4-blocks of equal sizes. Each sub-block is given as input to an ANN for compression with the help of a reference. The output of the FF ANN will be of same size as the target vector. In order to achieve maximum CR, we have chosen the target to be the mean value of the pixels of the input image. The compressed outputs of sub-images are combined together, which generates the compressed image. The compressed image is given as input to another ANN along with a reference for reconstruction of the original image. The reference is chosen as the original image. The recovered image is compared with the original image and MSE is calculated. The quality of the image after decompression is not found to be very close to that of the original image. Hence, the decomposition level is increased and it is seen that 9-level decomposition gives satisfactory results. The block diagram for the proposed

image compression scheme is shown in Figure 6. Figures 7 and 8 give the image results for the just described compression system. The MSE and PSNR of the decompressed image are calculated and compared with existing run length encoding (RLE) technique shown in Table 3. Similarly, the PSNR obtained from the multi-level ANN based approach is compared with RLE approach. This is shown in Table 4.

The above results clearly show the advantage of the proposed approach.

The algorithm for training FF ANN in form of MLP, involving back-propagation training is implemented, trained and tested using medical images successfully. The proposed learning based medical image compression techniques, provide efficient compression rate while maintaining image quality. The system works well over medical images as shown by the results and could be applied to real-time applications. The first approach provides satisfactory image quality but computational time requirement is high. Therefore, a new approach, multi-level decomposition based ANN aided compression-decompression is designed which reduces computational latency while retaining the image quality. Although, this method reduces computational time requirement, yet for

Figure 6. Block diagram of proposed image compression system using FF ANN

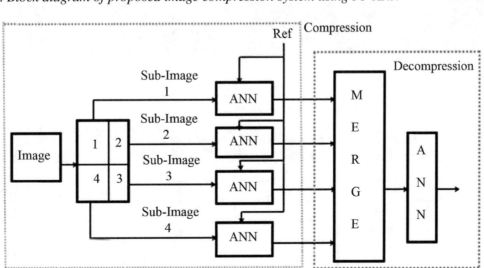

Figure 7. Image results of the FF ANN based system

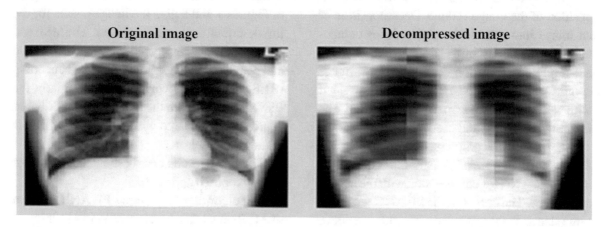

Figure 8. Performance of multi-level decomposition based FF ANN aided compression and decompression used in case of MRI image of the brain

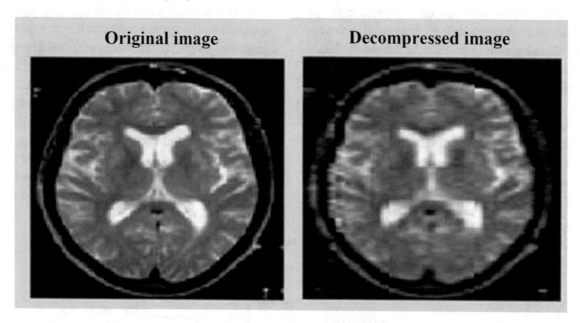

Table 2. Performance evaluation of the above system

Image	Original Image Size	Decomposition Level	Compressed Image Size	MSE	Computational Time in Secs.
X-ray	32x32	4	1x32	0.15	221.70
X-ray	108x108	8	1x108	0.018	3465.15
Retina	32x32	4	1x32	0.135	218.14
Retina	108x108	8	1x108	0.044	2877.47
Brain	32x32	4	1x32	0.108	159.00
Brain	108x108	8	1x108	0.015	5251.44

Table 3. MSE comparison between proposed multi-level decomposition based FF ANN aided and existing RLE

Image	MSE, RLE	MSE, Proposed
MRI	0.36	0.16
CT Scan	0.34	0.14
Ultrasound	0.33	0.13

Table 4. PSNR comparison between proposed multi-level decomposition based FF ANN aided and existing RLE

Image	PSNR, Original Image, (dB)	PSNR, RLE (dB)	PSNR, Proposed (dB)
MRI	65.54	52.58	56.53
CT Scan	66.07	52.81	57.24
Ultrasound	66.30	52.88	55.86

large sized images, it is still a limiting factor. Hence, another technique based on SOM, DWT and FF ANN is designed and presented in next section. This new approach provides satisfactory performance while reducing computational time. The training time for the system to converge to the expected output can be reduced by linking deep learning technique along with ANN.

Image Compression Using SOFM and DWT

Learning based compression-decompression is a form of pattern recognition application. In any pattern classification and recognition application, the main difficulty is that the learning complexity grows exponentially with linear increase in the dimensionality of the data. Therefore, a system which is capable of learning the features from the data given to it is needed. The proposed system meets the above requirement. The work describes a lossy compression system for compression of medical images. An image is first decomposed into smaller blocks before passing it through SOM network for generation of a codebook. The output of SOM is further compressed by applying DWT to it. The compressed image is then reconstructed using a multi-layer feed forward ANN. It is found that the system is robust to degradations like noise that may be present in an image due to false switching of the device and transmission through a noisy channel. The work also describes a comparison between two

lossy image compression schemes. The image to be compressed is decomposed into smaller sized blocks and then applied to either an MLP or a SOM network followed by DWT for compression. The compressed image is reconstructed using an MLP in the first approach. In this method, the image after compression is recovered by a composite block formed using a FF ANN and a DCT based compression-decompression system. The original image is degraded to some extent by adding salt and pepper noise to it in order to check whether the image compression systems are robust to degradations like noise. The performance of the systems is evaluated by determining the MSE, compression ration and PSNR.

The decomposed parts of the original image of size mxn are sent to a SOM network individually for generating the weight matrices, also known as the codebook. The size of the codebook generated by SOM is kept fixed at 64 x n/2. There will be four weight matrices or codebooks with respect to each sub-image. The weight matrix is decomposed into four sub-bands by applying single-level DWT to it. The four components formed after single-level decomposition are the approximation coefficient (LL), the horizontal coefficient (LH), the vertical coefficient (HL) and the diagonal coefficient (HH) (Gonzales, 2009). Among the four components, only the LL part contains useful information required for preserving the image quality. The other coefficients (LH, HL and HH) contain very less information details and if they are discarded, the quality of the reconstructed image is not hampered. The LL part is retained to get the compressed sub-image. For each sub-image, the procedure is repeated for each sub-block which gives a compressed image of size 64 x n/2 with a CR of 8:1. The block diagram of the proposed compression system is shown in Figure 9.

Reconstruction of Original Image Using FF ANN

The ANN used for the decompression process is in multi-layer feed-forward form containing one hidden layer. The input to the ANN is the compressed sub-image along with one reference. The reference is chosen to be the reconstructed matrix generated after applying DCT based compression and decompression (JPEG) to the original image sub-blocks. Figure 4 shows the decompression scheme for the regression process. The ANN is trained with input patterns until reconstruction of the original image is attained. The size of layers will vary with respect to four and nine level decompositions. The image result of the system is shown in Figure 10. The SOM parameters are summarized in Table 5. The performance of the SOM based approach is shown in Table 6.

The reconstructed images after compression are found out to be close to the original images. The system is tested for various medical images and the results are found out to be within the range of an acceptable limit. Hence, the proposed technique for medical image compression can be used for storage and transmission purposes in medical centers. Moreover, the system is robust to degradations such as noise. This feature of the system enables the users to transmit it through communication channels even if it is noisy.

For comparing the experimental results of the compression systems decomposition less FF ANN aided compression-decompression (S1) and multi-level decomposition based FF ANN aided compression-decompression (S2), discussed in the previous section and the just described DWT and SOM based technique (S3), an input image of size 240×240 is considered. For the systems, S1 and S2, the original image is decomposed into nine equal sized blocks, whereas the same image is sub-divided into four blocks in the later case. The decomposed sub-images are applied as input to ANN, in both cases. The FF ANN based techniques require a reference for performing image compression. The reference is taken as

Figure 9. Block diagram of image compression process using SOFM and DWT

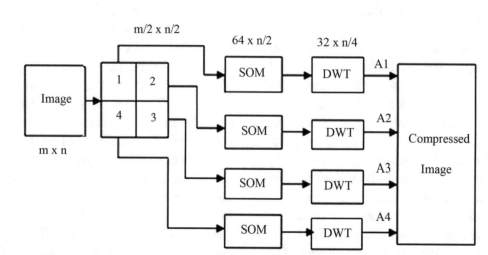

Figure 10. Block diagram of the reconstruction scheme using FF ANN

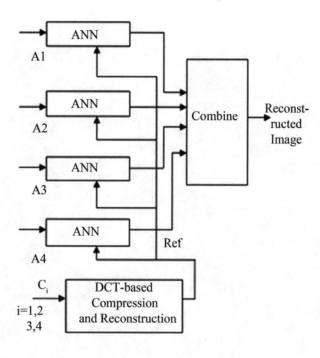

Table 5. SOM parameters

Input Size	SOM Grid Size	SOM Training	Epochs	Topology Function	Distance Function
128 ×128 160 ×160 256 ×256	64 ×128 64 ×160 64 ×256	Competitive, Unsupervised	50 to 500	hextop	linkdist

Table 6. Performance evaluation of the image compresion system using SOM-DWT

Image	Original Size	Compressed Size	CR	MSE	Computational Time (sec)
MRI	256 ×256	64 ×128	8: 1	0.017	199.49
	320 ×320	64 ×160	10: 1	0.017	153.00
	512 ×512	64 ×256	16: 1	0.015	146.20
CT Scan	256 ×256	64 ×128	8: 1	0.010	139.12
	320 ×320	64 ×160	10: 1	0.011	135.30
	512 ×512	64 ×256	16: 1	0.010	141.10
Ultrasound	256 ×256	64 ×128	8: 1	0.007	133.37
	320 ×320	64 ×160	10: 1	0.006	136.20
	512 ×512	64 ×256	16: 1	0.007	135.21

Figure 11. Image results of proposed image compression system using SOM- DWT

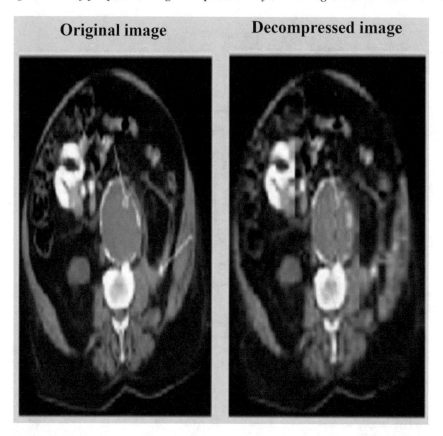

the average intensity value of the pixels for each sub-image. For a sub-image of size 80×80, the reference will be of size 1×80. Thus, we will be able to generate nine outputs each of sizes 1×80. On combining these outputs, a compressed image of size 3×240 is attained. The compressed image is applied to another FF ANN for decompression. In the second method, there is no requirement of a target vector for performing image compression. The sub-bocks of sizes 120×120 are passed to a SOM network one by one for generation of a weight matrix of size 64×120. A single level Haar DWT is applied to the weight matrix, to obtain a compressed sub-image of size 32×60. The procedure is repeated for each sub-images. The compressed sub-images are combined together, which gives the compressed image. The performance of the image compression systems

are evaluated by finding parameters like MSE, CR and PSNR. The computational time required for performing the compression-decompression task, by the systems are also calculated. Table 7 shows the experimental results for three different sample images of MRI, CT scan and X-ray.

The systems are analyzed based on these results. From Table 7, it is seen that the proposed image compression schemes differ from each other in terms of CR, PSNR and computational time. The percentage change in MSE and computational time requirement between systems, S1 and S3 is shown in Table 8.

In S3, the output undergoes image compression without requirement of a reference unlike S1 and S2. The image quality after reconstruction is maintained in both the cases which is judged by finding out the MSE. The system is experimented

Table 7. Performance evaluation for three different sample images of MRI, CT scan and X-ray using Si, S2 and S3 system

Image	Original Image Size	CR, S1	CR, S3	MSE, S1	MSE, S3	PSNR, S1, dB	PSNR, S3, dB	Computational Time, S1 (sec)	Computational Time, S3 (sec)
MRI	240 ×240	80: 1	15: 2	0.16	0.017	56.67	67.41	3465.15	153.00
CT Scan	240 ×240	80: 1	15: 2	0.14	0.010	56.55	67.30	2877.50	138.20
X-ray	240 ×240	80: 1	15: 2	0.01	0.007	57.92	68.60	3251.44	133.37

Table 8. Percentage change in MSE and computational time requirement between systems, S1 and S3

Image	Size	Change in MSE (%),	Change in Computational Time (%)
MRI	240 ×240	89	96
CT Scan	240 ×240	29	95
X-ray	240 ×240	30	96

samples each of clean, Gaussian, salt and pepper and speckle noise corrupted images with noise SNR varying between -3dB and +3dB.

A comparative depiction of the proposed approach is shown in Figure 12 to establish the suitability of the methods for medical application. It is related to a decompressed image of a liver obtained using ultra-sound technique and applied to the system during testing.

The SOM-DWT based compression scheme derived using unsupervised and supervised ANN provides better image quality with fast convergence. Proposed compression system is designed with the objective of making it suitable for medical applications. The computational time required for the entire process using system, S3 is found out to be minimum as compared to S2 and S1. Future aspect of the proposed work includes designing a

for various medical images and the performance is found out to be satisfactory. The experiments are repeated for images mixed with salt and pepper noise and the outcomes are compared. The three proposed systems are compared based on MSE, PSNR and computational time requirement which is shown in Tables 9, 10 and 11. The values shown are derived from three different sets with ten

Table 9. Comparison of MSE of the three systems

Image	Size	MSE, S1	MSE, S2	MSE, S3
MRI	240×240	0.014	0.20	0.017
CT Scan	240×240	0.032	0.16	0.010
X-ray	240×240	0.010	0.17	0.007

Table 10. Comparison of PSNR of the three systems

Image	Size	PSNR, S1 (dB)	PSNR, S2 (dB)	PSNR, S3 (dB)
MRI	240×240	56.63	56.63	67.41
CT Scan	240×240	57.28	57.28	67.30
X-ray	240×240	57.56	57.56	68.60

Table 11. Comparison of computational time of the three systems

Image	Size	Comp. Time, S1, (sec)	Comp. Time, S2, (sec)	Comp. Time, S3, (sec)
MRI	240×240	3125.12	885.34	153.00
CT Scan	240×240	2940.20	1178.97	138.20
X-ray	240×240	3251.44	758.92	133.37

Figure 12. Original and reconstructed images using S1 and S3

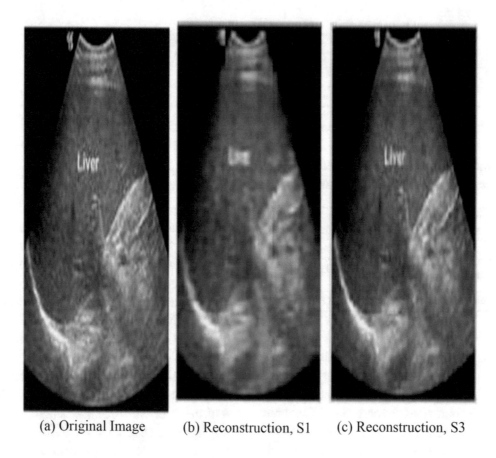

(a) Original Image   (b) Reconstruction, S1   (c) Reconstruction, S3

system by linking fuzzy logic along with SOFM. As the suggested technique is applicable for grayscale images, so to implement it for color images will include another future activity.

SUMMARY

Every image contains some redundant information, which needs to be identified by user to obtain compression. In this work, an image compression technique using learning and ANN in FF and unsupervised form is proposed. Experiments are performed for different varieties of medical images. It is found that by eliminating the highly correlated training vectors, better CR and satisfactory PSNR values can be achieved. It has also been observed that as the image size

increases, higher CR is obtained and errors are also reduced. However, training time increases significantly. Simulation results for standard test images with different sizes are presented. These results are compared with existing RLE technique. Several performance measures are used to test the reconstructed image quality. According to the experimental results, the proposed technique outperformed the existing RLE method. It can be inferred from experimental results as shown in above tables that the proposed methods perform well for medical imagery purposes and results in higher CR. Besides providing higher CR, it also preserves the quality of the image. It can be concluded that the suggested neuro-computing based image compression systems facilitate a new approach for compressing digital images.

CONCLUSION

Digital medical imaging technologies have become increasingly important in medical practice and health care for providing assistant tools for diagnosis, treatment and surgery. Due to the huge volume of medical images which is growing rapidly, especially on MRI and CT Scan, image compression must be applied. The back-propagation algorithm for training MLP is studied and implemented successfully on image compression. We have also presented a new compression model based on SOFM and DWT which provides considerable reduction of the file size. The proposed learning based medical image compression techniques provides efficient compression rate while maintaining image quality. The system works well over medical images as shown by the results and could be applied to real-time applications. The training time for the network to converge to the expected output can be reduced by implementing the adaptive learning algorithm. In the first approach, we have described two image compression systems, S1 and S2, using FF ANN. The image quality after decompression is retained in both the systems, but system S1 is computationally less efficient as its computational latency is high. System S2 reduces the time requirement to compute the compression-decompression process to some extent, providing same CR. In order to reduce the computational time requirement further, a new approach using SOM, DWT and FF ANN is designed and presented in this work.

LIMITATION

The primary limitation of the work is its dependence on training. It must first work on an off-line mode and compute the learning. Then only it becomes capable of doing the compression and decompression. Due to the training, there is always a computational latency. Further, the images considered are gray-scale only.

FUTURE DIRECTION

The presented method considers the compression techniques on 2-D images. Our concept can be extended to 3-D images. The research issues such as efficiency of the compression rate in 3-D watermarking will be studied in the future. The next phase of the proposed work may also include designing a compression system by linking Fuzzy logic along with SOM. For reconstruction of the original image, to suggest a learning system without requiring any target will be another work. The proposed work can be exposed to designing an ANN aided medical image compression based on deep learning techniques. Deep learning architecture is capable of learning the features from the data given to it. Hence, it can reduce learning complexity.

REFERENCES

Ahmed, S. A., Dey, S., & Sarma, K. K. (March, 2011). Image Texture Classification using Artificial Neural Network (ANN). In *Proceedings of 2nd IEEE National Conference on Emerging Trends and Applications in Computer Science.* doi:10.1109/NCETACS.2011.5751383

Amerijckx, C., Legat, J. D., & Verleysen, M. (2003). Image Compression using Self-Organizing Maps. *Systems Analysis Modeling Simulation, 43*(11), 1529–1543. doi:10.1080/0232929032000115182

Amin, A., Qureshi, H. A., Junaid, M., Habib, M. Y., & Anjum, W. (Dec. 2011). Modified Run Length Encoding Scheme with Introduction of Bit Stuffing for Efficient Data Compression. In *Proceedings of International Conference on Internet Technology and Secured Transactions.*

Ansari, M. A., & Anand, R. S. (2008). *Recent Trends in Image Compression and its Application in Telemedicine and Teleconsultation. XXXII National Systems Conference,* Roorkee, India.

Arel, I., Rose, D. C., & Karnowski, T. P. (2010, November). Deep Machine Learning- A New Frontier in Artificial Intelligence Research. *IEEE Computational Intelligence Magazine*, *5*(4), 13–18. doi:10.1109/MCI.2010.938364

Baruah, P., & Sarma, K. K. (2013, December). Image Restoration Using Dynamic Wavelet Thresholding and Artificial Neural Network. *Journal of Computational Intelligence and Electronic Systems*, *2*(2), 132–140. doi:10.1166/jcies.2013.1051

Bhattacharyya, K., & Sarma, K. K. (2009, October). ANN-based Innovative Segmentation Method for Handwritten text in Assamese. *International Journal of Computer Science Issues*, *5*, 9–16.

Bodoloi, H., & Sarma, K. K. (2012). Protein Structure Prediction Using Multiple Artificial Neural Network Classifier. Soft Computing Techniques in Vision Science. *Studies in Computational Intelligence*, *395*, 137–146. doi:10.1007/978-3-642-25507-6_12

Boopathi, G., & Arockiasamy, S. (2011, September). An Image Compression Approach using Wavelet Transform and Modified Self-Organized Kohonen Map. *International Journal of Computer Science Issues*, *8*(2), 323–330.

Durai, S. A., & Saro, E. A. (Dec. 2006). An Improved Image Compression approach with SOFM Network using Cumulative Distribution Function. In *Proceedings of International conference on Advanced Computing and Communications*. doi:10.1109/ADCOM.2006.4289904

Ettaouil, M., Ghanou, Y., Moutaouakil, K., & Lazaar, M. (2011, April). Image Medical Compression by a new Architecture Optimization Model for the Kohonen Networks. *International Journal of Computer Theory and Engineering*, *3*(2), 1793–1801.

Gogoi, R., & Sarma, K. K. (2012). ANFIS based Information Extraction using K-means Clustering for Application in Satellite Images. *International Journal of Computers and Applications*, *50*(7), 13–18. doi:10.5120/7782-0872

Gonzales, R. C. (2009). *Digital Image Processing* (3rd ed.). New Delhi, India: Pearson Education.

Haykin, S. (2005). *Neural Networks: A Comprehensive Foundation*. New Delhi: Pearson Education.

Jilani, S. A. K., & Sattar, S. A. (2010, June). A Fuzzy Neural Networks based EZW Image Compression System. *International Journal of Computers and Applications*, *2*(9).

Khashman, A., & Dimililer, K. (2008). Image Compression using Neural Networks and Haar Wavelet. *WSEAS Transactions on Signal Processing*, *4*(5).

Polomo, E. J., & Dominguez, E. (Aug. 2011). Image Compression based on growing Hierarchial Self-Organizing Maps. In *Proceedings of International Joint Conference on Neural Networks*.

Saikia, T., & Sarma, K. K. (2014), Multilevel-DWT based Image De-noising using Feed Forward Artificial Neural Network, in *Proceedings of 1st IEEE International Conference on Signal Processing and Integrated Networks (SPIN 2014)*. doi:10.1109/SPIN.2014.6777062

Sarma, K. K., & Mitra, A. (November, 2009). ANN based Rayleigh Multipath fading channel estimation of a MIMO-OFDM system. In *Proceedings of 1st IEEE Asian Himalayas International Conference on Internet (AH-ICI) - The Next Generation of Mobile, Wireless and Optical Communications Networks*. doi:10.1109/AHICI.2009.5340306

Sarma, K. K., & Mitra, A. (2011). *Estimation of MIMO Wireless Channels using Artificial Neural Networks. In Cross-Disciplinary Applications of Artificial Intelligence and Pattern Recognition: Advancing Technologies* (pp. 509–545). IGI Global.

Sarma, K. K., & Mitra, A. (2012, April). Modeling MIMO Channels using a Class of Complex Recurrent Neural Network Architectures. *International Journal of Electronics and Communications.*, 66(4), 322–331. doi:10.1016/j.aeue.2011.08.008

Senthilkumaran, N., & Suguna, J. (2011, February). Neural Network technique for Lossless Image Compression using X-Ray Images. *International Journal of Computer and Electrical Engineering*, 3(1), 1793–8163.

Sharma, M., & Kuamri, R. (2013, June). A Technique of Image Compression based on Discrete Wavelet Image Decomposition and Self Organizing Map. *International Journal of Computational Engineering Science*, 3(8).

Sicuranzi, G. L., Ramponi, G., & Marsi, S. (1990, March). Artificial Neural Network for Image Compression. *Electronics Letters*, 26(7), 477–479. doi:10.1049/el:19900310

Soliman, H. S., & Omari, M. (2006). A Neural Networks Approach to Image Data Compression. [Elsevier.]. *Applied Soft Computing*, 6(3), 258–271. doi:10.1016/j.asoc.2004.12.006

Talukder, K. H., & Harada, K. (2006). A Scheme of Wavelet Based Compression of 2D Image. In *Proceedings of IMECS-2006*.

Talukder, K. H., & Harada, K. (2007, February). Haar Wavelet Based Approach for Image Compression and Quality Assessment of Compressed Image, IAENG International. *Journal of Applied Mathematics*, 36(1), 1–8.

Tamilarasi, M., & Palanisamy, V. (2009, November). Fuzzy Based Image Compression on ROI using Optimized Directional Contourlet Transform. *International Journal of Recent Trends in Engineering*, 2(5), 217–212.

Thota, N. R., & Devireddy, S. K. (2008). Image Compression using Discrete Cosine Transform. *Georgian Electronic Scientific Journal: Computer Science and Telecommunications*, 3(17), 35–43.

KEY TERMS AND DEFINITIONS

Artificial Neural Network (ANN): Is non-parametric tool that learns from the surroundings, retains the learning and uses it subsequently.

Discrete Cosine Transform (DCT): Is a forward transform used in image compression. It separates DCT coefficients into most relevant and least relevant types.

Discrete Wavelet Transform (DWT): Is a wavelet transform performed in discrete domain. It has mother and daughter wavelets with which multi level decomposition is achieved and spectral representation of samples obtained. DWT is often used in image compression and restoration applications.

K-Means Clustering (KMC): Is a grouping technique where objects with common characteristics are placed in K-numbers of identical groups considering the sample to sample difference of mean to be a cost functional.

Lossless Compression: It is technique of image compression which has a lower compression ration but provide high decompression quality. It is suitable for medical applications.

Lossy Compression: It is method of image compression where the compression ratio is high but the quality is poor. It is useful for less critical applications like text, voice etc compression and storage.

Mean Square Error (MSE): Is a cost functional used to ascertain the level of training that a prediction system achieves. MSE is to measure the closeness between present output to actual output.

Multi Layer Perceptron (MLP): Is an ANN type that requires a reference to learn patterns. It is trained using (error) back propagation algorithm.

Self Organizing Map (SOM): Is a special form of ANN that uses a competitive learning approach to perform classification and clustering. It requires no referencing.

Supervised Learning: It is a type of learning where the systems follow a pre-determined pattern. It is like learning with the support of a teacher. It is generally observed in MLP type ANN.

Unsupervised Learning: It is used with SOM where there is no reference to follow. It adopts a competitive learning approach to form clusters of samples that have commonality.

Compilation of References

3DMD face images. (n.d.). Retrieved 22nd July, 2014, from http://www.3dmd.com/

Abdelazeem, S. (2009). A Novel Domain-Specific Feature Extraction Scheme for Arabic Handwritten Digits Recognition. *International Conference on Machine Learning and Applications*, Miami Beach, FL. doi:10.1109/ICMLA.2009.136

Abdoli, M., Dierckx, R. A., & Zaidi, H. (2012). Metal artifact reduction strategies for improved attenuation correction in hybrid PET/CT imaging. *Medical Physics*, 39(6), 3343–3360. doi:10.1118/1.4709599 PMID:22755716

Abdullah, M. Z., Guan, L. C., Mohamed, A. M. D., & Noor, M. A. M. (2002). Color Vision System for Ripeness Inspection of Oil Palm Elaeis Guineenszs. *Journal of Food Processing and Preservation*, 26(3), 213–235. doi:10.1111/j.1745-4549.2002.tb00481.x

Acar, R., & Vogel, C. R. (1994). Analysis of bounded variation penalty methods for ill-posed problems. *Inverse Problems*, 10(6), 1217–1229. doi:10.1088/0266-5611/10/6/003

Adelson, E. (1990). *Digital signal encoding and decoding apparatus.* U.S. Patent, (4), 939, 515.

Afonso, M. V., Bioucas-Dias, J. M., & Figueiredo, M. A. (2010). An augmented Lagrangian approach to linear inverse problems with compound regularization. *ICIP 2010 17th IEEE International Conference on Image Processing* (pp. 4169–4172). IEEE.

Afonso, M. V., Bioucas-Dias, J. M., & Figueiredo, M. A. (2011). An augmented Lagrangian approach to the constrained optimization formulation of imaging inverse problems. *IEEE Transactions on Image Processing*, 20(3), 681–695. doi:10.1109/TIP.2010.2076294 PMID:20840899

Agarwal, V., Gribok, A., & Abidi, M. (2007). Image restoration using l1 norm penalty function. *Inverse Problems in Science and Engineering*, 15(8), 785–809. doi:10.1080/17415970600971987

Ahmed, S. A., Dey, S., & Sarma, K. K. (March, 2011). Image Texture Classification using Artificial Neural Network (ANN). In *Proceedings of 2nd IEEE National Conference on Emerging Trends and Applications in Computer Science*. doi:10.1109/NCETACS.2011.5751383

Ahonen, T., Hadid, A., & Pietikainen, M. (2006). Face description with local binary patterns: Application to face recognition. *Pattern Analysis and Machine Intelligence. IEEE Transactions on*, 28(12), 2037–2041.

Aiswarya, K., Jayaraj, V., & Ebenezer, D. (2010). A new and efficient algorithm for the removal of high density salt and pepper noise in images and videos. In *Proceedings of Second International Conference on Computer Modeling and Simulation*. IEEE. doi:10.1109/ICCMS.2010.310

Akgul, T. (2007). Introducing the Cartoonist, Tayfun Akgul. *Antennas and Propagation Magazine, IEEE*, 49(3), 162–162. doi:10.1109/MAP.2007.4293959

Akgul, T. (2011). Can an Algorithm Recognize Montage Portraits as Human Faces? *IEEE Signal Processing Magazine*, 1(28), 160–158. doi:10.1109/MSP.2010.938777

Akleman, E. (1997, January). Making caricatures with morphing. In ACM SIGGRAPH 97 Visual Proceedings: The art and interdisciplinary programs of SIGGRAPH'97 (p. 145). ACM. doi:10.1145/259081.259231

Akleman, E., & Reisch, J. (2004, August). Modeling expressive 3D caricatures. In ACM SIGGRAPH 2004 Sketches (p. 61). ACM.

Al-Mamun, H. A., Jahangir, N., Islam, M. S., & Islam, M. A. (2009). Eye Detection in Facial Image by Genetic Algorithm Driven Deformable Template Matching. *International Journal of Computer Science and Network Security, 9*(8), 771–779.

Alpaydin, E. (2004). *Introduction to Machine Learning.* Cambridge, MA: MIT Press.

Al-Qaheri, H., Mustafi, A., & Banerjee, S. (2010). Digital watermarking using ant colony optimization in fractional Fourier domain. *Journal of Information Hiding and Multimedia Signal Processing, 1*(3), 179–189.

Al-Sultana, K. S., & Khan, M. M. (1996). Computational experience on four algorithms for the hard clustering problem. *Pattern Recognition Letters, 17*(3), 295–308. doi:10.1016/0167-8655(95)00122-0

Alter, F., Durand, S., & Froment, J. (2005). Adapted total variation for artifact free decompression of JPEG images. *J. Math. Imaging and Vision, 23*(2), 199–211.

Alyuz, N., Gokberk, B., & Akarun, L. (2012). Adaptive Registration for Occlusion Robust 3D Face Recognition. In *Proc of BeFIT'12 Workshop.* doi:10.1007/978-3-642-33885-4_56

Amanatiadis, A., Kaburlasos, V. G., Gasteratos, A., & Papadakis, S. E. (2009). *A Comparative Study of Invariant Descriptors for Shape Retrieval. International Workshop on Imaging Systems and Techniques*, Shenzhen, China. doi:10.1109/IST.2009.5071672

Amanatiadis, A., Kaburlasos, V. G., Gasteratos, A., & Papadakis, S. E. (2011). Evaluation of Shape Descriptors for Shape-Based Image Retrieval. *IET Image Processing, 5*(5), 493–499. doi:10.1049/iet-ipr.2009.0246

Amengual, J. C., Juan, A., Prez, J. C., Prat, F., Sez, S., & Vilar, J. H. (1997). Real time minutiae extraction in fingerprint images. In *Proceedings of the 6th International Conference on Image Processing and its Applications.* doi:10.1049/cp:19971021

Amerijckx, C., Legat, J. D., & Verleysen, M. (2003). Image Compression using Self-Organizing Maps. *Systems Analysis Modeling Simulation, 43*(11), 1529–1543. doi:10.1080/0232929032000115182

Amin, A., Qureshi, H. A., Junaid, M., Habib, M. Y., & Anjum, W. (Dec. 2011). Modified Run Length Encoding Scheme with Introduction of Bit Stuffing for Efficient Data Compression. In *Proceedings of International Conference on Internet Technology and Secured Transactions.*

Ancuti, C. O., & Ancuti, C. (2013). Single image dehazing by multi-scale fusion. *Image Processing. IEEE Transactions on, 22*(8), 3271–3282.

Anderson, E. D., & Anderson, A. D. (2000). The MOSEK interior point optimizer for linear programming: An implementation of the homogeneous algorithm. In H. Frenk, C. Roos, T. Terlaky, & S. Zhan (Eds.), High performance optimization, (pp. 197-232). Kluwer Academics Publisher.

Anderson, R. J., & Petitcolas, F. A. (1998). On the limits of steganography. *IEEE Journal on Selected Areas in Communications, 16*(4), 474–481. doi:10.1109/49.668971

Angulo, J., & Flandrin, G. (2003). *Microscopic image analysis using mathematical morphology: application to haematological cytology.* IEEE International Conference On Acoustics, Speech and Signal Processing.

Anitha, J., Hemanth, D. J., Vijila, C. K. S., & Ahsina, A. (2009). Self Organizing neural network based pathology classification in retinal images. In *Proceedings of World Congress on Nature & Biologically Inspired Computing (NaBIC).* doi:10.1109/NABIC.2009.5393697

Ansari, M. A., & Anand, R. S. (2008). *Recent Trends in Image Compression and its Application in Telemedicine and Teleconsultation. XXXII National Systems Conference*, Roorkee, India.

Antani, S., Kasturi, R., & Jain, R. (2002). A survey on the use of pattern recognition methods for abstraction, indexing and retrieval of images and video, Pergamon. *Pattern Recognition, 35*(4), 945–965. doi:10.1016/S0031-3203(01)00086-3

Antonie, M.-L., Zaïane, O. R., & Coman, A. (2001). Application of Data Mining Techniques for Medical Image Classification. In *Proceeding of the 2nd International Workshop on Multimedia Data Mining in Conjunction with ACM SIGKDD Conference*, (pp. 94-101). ACM.

Anwar, M. I., & Khosla, A. (2013). Segmentation Methods for Images: A Systematic Review, Journal of Remote Sensing & GIS. *STM Journals*, *4*(3), 61–67.

Anwar, M. I., & Khosla, A. (2014). Classification of Homogeneous and Heterogeneous Fog for Vision Enhancement. *Current Trends in Signal Processing*, *4*(2), 7–10.

Arai, K., Abdullah, I. N., & Okumura, H. (2014). Comparative Study of Feature Extraction Components from Several Wavelet Transformations for Ornamental Plants. *International Journal of Advanced Research in Artificial Intelligence*, *3*(2), 5–11. doi:10.14569/IJARAI.2014.030202

Arel, I., Rose, D. C., & Karnowski, T. P. (2010, November). Deep Machine Learning- A New Frontier in Artificial Intelligence Research. *IEEE Computational Intelligence Magazine*, *5*(4), 13–18. doi:10.1109/MCI.2010.938364

Arun, C. H., Sam, W. R., & Christopher, D. D. (2013). Texture Feature Extraction for Identification of Medicinal Plants and Comparison of Different Classifiers. *International Journal of Computers and Applications*, *62*(12), 1–9. doi:10.5120/10129-4920

Ashoka, H. N., Manjaiah, D. H., & Bera, R. (2012). Zone Based Feature Extraction and Statistical Classification Technique for Kannada Handwritten Numeral Recognition.[IJCSET]. *International Journal of Computer Science & Engineering Technology*, *3*(10), 476–482.

Aslantas, V., Dogan, A. L., & Ozturk, S. (2008). DWT-SVD based image watermarking using particle swarm optimizer. In *Multimedia and Expo, 2008 IEEE International Conference on*. IEEE. doi:10.1109/ICME.2008.4607416

Aslantas, V., Ozer, S., & Ozturk, S. (2008). A novel fragile watermarking based on particle swarm optimization. In *Multimedia and Expo, 2008 IEEE International Conference on*. IEEE. doi:10.1109/ICME.2008.4607423

Aslantas, V. (2008). A singular-value decomposition-based image watermarking using genetic algorithm. *AEÜ. International Journal of Electronics and Communications*, *62*(5), 386–394. doi:10.1016/j.aeue.2007.02.010

Aswathy, R. (2013). A Literature review on Facial Expression Recognition Techniques. *IOSR Journal of Computer Engineering*, *11*(1), 61-64.

Avinash, C., Kak, & Slaney, M. (2001). Principles of computerized tomographic imaging. Society for Industrial and Applied Mathematics.

Ayushi. (2013). A Survey on Feature Extraction Techniques. *International Journal of Computer Applications*, *66*(11), 43-46.

Bach, F. R. (2008). Consistency of the group lasso and multiple kernel learning. *Journal of Machine Learning Research*, *9*, 1179–1225.

Bagchi, P., Bhattacharjee, D., Nasipuri, M., & Basu, D. K. (2012). A Novel approach to nose-tip and eye-corners detection using H-K Curvature Analysis in case of 3D images. Proc of International Journal of Computational Intelligence and Informatics, *2*(1).

Bagchi, P., Bhattacharjee, D., Nasipuri, M., & Basu, D. K. (2013). *A Method for Nose-tip based 3D face registration using Maximum Intensity algorithm*. In IEEE international Conference of Computation and Communication Advancement.

Bahi, J. M., Couchot, J.-F., & Guyeux, C. (2011). Steganography: A Class of Algorithms having Secure Properties. In *Intelligent Information Hiding and Multimedia Signal Processing (IIH-MSP), 2011 Seventh International Conference on*. doi:10.1109/IIHMSP.2011.87

Balcan, M. F., Blum, A., & Vempala, S. (2006). Kernels as features: On kernels, margins and low-dimensional mappings. *Machine Learning*, *65*(1), 79–94. doi:10.1007/s10994-006-7550-1

Ballard, D. H. (1981). Generalizing the Hough Transform to Detect Arbitrary Shapes. *Pattern Recognition*, *13*(2), 111–122. doi:10.1016/0031-3203(81)90009-1

Bamberg, F., Dierks, A., Nikolaou, K., Reiser, M. F., Becker, C. R., & Johnson, T. R. (2011). Metal artifact reduction by dual energy computed tomography using monoenergetic extrapolation. *European Radiology*, *21*(7), 1424–1429. doi:10.1007/s00330-011-2062-1 PMID:21249370

Bamis, A., Lymberopoulos, D., Teixeira, T., & Savvides, A. (2010). The BehaviorScope framework for enabling ambient assisted living. *Personal and Ubiquitous Computing*, *14*(6), 473–487. doi:10.1007/s00779-010-0282-z

Bandyopadhyay, S. K., Maitra, I. K., Bhattacharyya, D., & Tai-Hoon, K. (2010). Reserved Fields of Palette for Data Hiding in Steganography. In *Computational Intelligence and Communication Networks (CICN), 2010 International Conference on*. doi:10.1109/CICN.2010.82

Bandyopadhyay, S. K., Bhattacharyya, D., Das, P., Mukherjee, S., & Ganguly, D. (2008). A secure scheme for image transformation. In *Proceedings of 9th ACIS International Conference on Software Engineering, Artificial Intelligence, Networking, and Parallel/Distributed Computing*.

Banerjee, A., Burlina, P., & Diehl, C. (2006). A support vector method for anomaly detection in hyperspectral imagery. *IEEE Transactions on Geoscience and Remote Sensing, 44*(8), 2282–2291. doi:10.1109/TGRS.2006.873019

Barinova, O., Lempitsky, V., & Kohli, P. (2010). On the Detection of Multiple Object Instances Using Hough Transforms. *Proceedings of IEEE Conference on Computer Vision and Pattern Recognition*. doi:10.1109/CVPR.2010.5539905

Barlett, P. L. (1997). For valid generalization, the size of the weights is more than the size of networks. Advances in Neural Information Processing Systems, 9, 134-140.

Barnett, R. (1999). Digital watermarking: applications, techniques and challenges. *J. Electron. Commun. engin., 11*(4), 173–183.

Barni, M., Bartolini, F., & Piva, A. (2001). Improved wavelet-based watermarking through pixel-wise masking. *IEEE Transactions on Image Processing, 10*(5), 783–791. doi:10.1109/83.918570 PMID:18249667

Barnum, P. C., Narasimhan, S., & Kanade, T. (2010). Analysis of rain and snow in frequency space. *International Journal of Computer Vision, 86*(2-3), 256–274. doi:10.1007/s11263-008-0200-2

Bartlett, P. L. (1998). The sample complexity of pattern classification with neural networks. The size of the weights is more important than the size of network. *IEEE Transactions on Information Theory, 44*(2), 525–536. doi:10.1109/18.661502

Baruah, P., & Sarma, K. K. (2013, December). Image Restoration Using Dynamic Wavelet Thresholding and Artificial Neural Network. *Journal of Computational Intelligence and Electronic Systems, 2*(2), 132–140. doi:10.1166/jcies.2013.1051

Belaid, L. J., & Mourou, A. (2009). Image Segmentation: A Watershed Transformation Algorithm. *Image Analysis & Stereology, 28*(2), 93–102. doi:10.5566/ias.v28.p93-102

Belhumeur, P., Hespanda, J., & Kriegman, D. (1997). Eigenfaces vs. fisherfaces: Recognitionusing class specific linear projection. *IEEE Transactions on Pattern Analysis and Machine Intelligence, 19*(7), 711–720. doi:10.1109/34.598228

Bendale, A., Nigam, A., Prakash, S., & Gupta, P. (2012). Iris Segmentation Using an Improved Hough Transform. *Proceedings of International Conference on Intelligent Computing*. doi:10.1007/978-3-642-31837-5_59

Bender, W., Gruhl, D., Morimoto, M., & Lu, A. (1996). Techniques for Data Hiding. *IBM Systems Journal, 35*(3&4), 313–336. doi:10.1147/sj.353.0313

Berretti, S., Bimbo, A., & Pala, P. (2013). Sparse Matching of Salient Facial Curves for Recognition of 3-D Faces with Missing Parts. IEEE Transactions on Information Forensics and Security, 8(2), 374-389.

Berretti, S., Bimbo, A. D., & Pala, P. (2010). 3D Face Recognition Using Isogeodesic Stripes. *IEEE Transactions on Pattern Analysis and Machine Intelligence, 32*(12), 2162–2177. doi:10.1109/TPAMI.2010.43 PMID:20975115

Bertillon, A. (1896). *The Bertillon System of Identification*. Chicago, IL: Academic Press.

Bertsekas, D. P. (1999). *Nonlinear Programming*. Belmont, MA: Athena Scientific.

Beymer, D. (1994). Face Recognition under Varying Pose. In *Proceedings of IEEE Conf. on Comp. Vision and Pattern Recognition*, (pp. 756-761). IEEE.

Bezdek, J. C. (1974). Numerical taxonomy with fuzzy sets. *Journal of Mathematical Biology, 1*(1), 57–71. doi:10.1007/BF02339490

Bezdek, J. C. (1981). *Pattern recognition with fuzzy objective function algorithms.* Kluwer Academic Publishers. doi:10.1007/978-1-4757-0450-1

Bezdek, J. C., Hall, L. O., & Klarke, L. P. (1993). Review of MR Segmentation Techniques using Pattern Recognition. *Medical Physics*, 20(4), 1033–1048. doi:10.1118/1.597000 PMID:8413011

BFM database. (n.d.). Retrieved 1st August, 2014, from http://faces.cs.unibas.ch/bfm/main.php?nav=1-0&id=basel_face_model

Bhadouria, V. S., Ghoshal, D., & Siddiqi, A. H. (2014). A new approach for high density saturated impulse noise removal using decision-based coupled window median filter. *Signal. Image and Video Processing*, 8(1), 71–84. doi:10.1007/s11760-013-0487-5

Bhadu, A., Tokas, R., & Kumar, V. (2012). Facial Expression Recognition Using DCT, Gabor and Wavelet Feature Extraction Techniques. *International Journal of Engineering and Innovative Technology*, 2(1), 92–95.

Bhagavathy, S., & Chhabra, K. (2007). *A Wavelet-based Image Retrieval System. Technical Report—ECE278A.* Santa Barbara, CA: Vision Research Laboratory, University of California.

Bharathi, P. T., & Subashini, P. (2013). Texture Feature Extraction of Infrared River Ice Images using Second-Order Spatial Statistics. World Academy of Science. *Engineering and Technology*, 74, 747–757.

Bharati, M. H., Liu, J. J., & MacGregor, J. F. (2004). Image texture analysis: Methods and comparisons. *Chemometrics and Intelligent Laboratory Systems*, 72(1), 57–71. doi:10.1016/j.chemolab.2004.02.005

Bhatt, H. S., Bharadwaj, S., Singh, R., & Vatsa, M. (2010, September). On matching sketches with digital face images. In *Biometrics: Theory Applications and Systems (BTAS), 2010 Fourth IEEE International Conference on.* IEEE. doi:10.1109/BTAS.2010.5634507

Bhattacharyya, D., Das, P., Bandyopadhyay, S. K., & Kim, T. (2009). Text steganography: A novel approach. *International Journal of Advanced Science and Technology*, 3, 79–86.

Bhattacharyya, K., & Sarma, K. K. (2009, October). ANN-based Innovative Segmentation Method for Handwritten text in Assamese. *International Journal of Computer Science Issues*, 5, 9–16.

Bhatt, B. G., & Shah, Z. H. (2011). *Face Feature Extraction Techniques: A Survey. National Conference on Recent Trends in Engineering & Technology.*

Bhoi, N., & Mohanty, M. N. (2010). Template Matching Based Eye Detection in Facial Image. *International Journal of Computers and Applications*, 12(5), 15–18. doi:10.5120/1676-2262

Bin, L., & Yeganeh, M. S. (2012). Comparison for Image Edge Detection Algorithms. *IOSR Journal of Computer Engineering*, 2(6), 1–4. doi:10.9790/0661-0260104

Bishop, A. W. (1955). The use of slip circle in the stability analysis of eath surface. *Geotechnique*, 5(1), 7–17. doi:10.1680/geot.1955.5.1.7

Bit-plane slicing. (n.d.). Retrieved 5th August, 2014, from http://nptel.iitk.ac.in/courses/Webcourse-contents/IIT-KANPUR/Digi_Img_Pro/chapter_8/8_13.html

BJUT-3D Chinese face database. (n.d.). Retrieved 24th July, 2014, from http://www.bjut.edu.cn/sci/multimedia/mul-lab/3dface/facedatabase.htm

Blanchet, J., Forbes, F., & Schmid, C. (2005). Markov Random Fields for Recognizing Textures Modeled by Feature Vectors. *International Conference on Applied Stochastic Models and Data Analysis*, France.

Blanz, V., & Vetter, T. (2003). Face recognition based on fitting a 3D morphable model. *Pattern Analysis and Machine Intelligence. IEEE Transactions on*, 25(9), 1063–1074.

Blanz, V., & Vetter, T. (2003). Face recognition based on fitting a 3d morphable model. *IEEE Transactions on Pattern Analysis and Machine Intelligence*, 25(9), 1063–1074. doi:10.1109/TPAMI.2003.1227983

Blomgren, P., & Chan, T. F. (1998). Color TV: total variation methods for restoration of vector-valued images. *IEEE Transactions on Image Processing*, 7(3), 304–309. Retrieved from http://www.ncbi.nlm.nih.gov/pubmed/18276250

BNT format. (n.d.). Retrieved 10th August, 2014, from http://filext.com/file-extension/BNT

Bodoloi, H., & Sarma, K. K. (2012). Protein Structure Prediction Using Multiple Artificial Neural Network Classifier. Soft Computing Techniques in Vision Science. *Studies in Computational Intelligence, 395*, 137–146. doi:10.1007/978-3-642-25507-6_12

Boehnen, C., Peters, T., & Flynn, P. J. (2009). 3D signatures for fast 3D face recognition. In *Proc. 3rd Int. Conf. Adv. Biometrics*. doi:10.1007/978-3-642-01793-3_2

Boopathi, G., & Arockiasamy, S. (2011, September). An Image Compression Approach using Wavelet Transform and Modified Self-Organized Kohonen Map. *International Journal of Computer Science Issues, 8*(2), 323–330.

Borah, T. R., Sarma, K. K., & Talukdar, P. H., (2013). Retina and Fingerprint based Biometric Identification System. *International Journal of Computer Applications*, 74–77.

Borghys, D., Truyen, E., Shimoni, M., & Perneel, C. (2009). Anomaly detection in hyperspectral images of complex scenes. In *Proceedings of 29th Earsel Symposium*.

Boris, Yendiyarov, & Petrushenko. (2011). Design of a Wavelet Based Data Mining Techniques. *Automatic*, 1-21,

Bornak, B., Rafiei, S., Sarikhani, A., & Babaei, A. (2010). *3D face recognition by used region-based with facial expression variation*. In Second International Conference on Signal Processing Systems. Retrieved 22nd August, 2014 from http://homepages.inf.ed.ac.uk/rbf/CVonline/LOCAL_COPIES/CANTZLER2/range.html

Bosphorus database. (n.d.). Retrieved 16th August, 2014 from http://bosphorus.ee.boun.edu.tr/Home.aspx

Bossu, J., Hautière, N., & Tarel, J. P. (2011). Rain or snow detection in image sequences through use of a histogram of orientation of streaks. *International Journal of Computer Vision, 93*(3), 348–367. doi:10.1007/s11263-011-0421-7

Bovik, A. C. (2010). *Handbook of image and video processing*. Academic Press.

Boyd, S., & Vandenberghe, L. (2001). *Convex Optimization*. Course notes for EE364, Stanford University. Available at http://www.stanford.edu/class/ee364

Brdiczka, O., Langet, M., Maisonnasse, J., & Crowley, J. L. (2009). Detecting human behavior models from multimodal observation in a smart home. *IEEE Transactions on Automation Science and Engineering, 6*(4), 588–597. doi:10.1109/TASE.2008.2004965

Bredies, K., Kunisch, K., & Pock, T. (2010). Total generalized variation. *SIAM Journal on Imaging Sciences, 3*(3), 492–526. doi:10.1137/090769521

Brox, T., Bruhn, A., & Weickert, J. (2006). Variational motion segmentation with level sets. *European Conference on Computer Vision (ECCV), 1*, 471-483.

Bruce, V., & Young, A. (1986). Understanding faces recognition. *British Journal of Psychology, 77*(3), 305–327. doi:10.1111/j.2044-8295.1986.tb02199.x PMID:3756376

Bruhn, A., Weickert, J., Kohlberger, T., & Schnörr, C. (2005). Discontinuity-preserving computation of variational optic flow in real-time. *Scale Space and PDE Methods in Computer Vision, 3459*, 279-290. Retrieved on August 29, 2014 from http://www.springerlink.com/index/jbevcvnfegkdrw0k.pdf

BU3D database. (n.d.). Retrieved 22nd July, 2014, from http://www.cs.binghamton.edu/~lijun/Research/3DFE/3DFE_Analysis.html

Burl, M. C., Fowlkes, C., Roden, J., Stechert, A., & Mukhtar, S. (1999). *Diamond Eye: A Distributed Architecture for Image Data Mining*. Orlando, FL: SPIE DMKD.

Cachin, C. (1998). An information-theoretic model for steganography. In *Proceedings of 2nd Workshop on Information Hiding*. Springer.

Candemir, C., Cetinkaya, C., Kilincceker, O., & Cinsdikici, M. (2013). Vascular landmark classification in retinal images using fuzzy RBF. In *Proceeding of Signal Processing and Communications Applications Conference (SIU)*. doi:10.1109/SIU.2013.6531382

Candes, E. J., Romberg, J., & Tao, T. (n.d.). Retrieved from http://users.ece.gatech.edu/~justin/l1magic/

Candes, E.J. & Wakin, M. (2008). An introduction to compressive sampling. *IEEE Signal Processing Magazine, 25*(2), 21-30.

Candes, E., Romberg, J., & Tao, T. (2006). Robust uncertainty principles: Exact signal reconstruction from highly incomplete frequency information. *IEEE Transactions on Information Theory*, *52*(2), 489–509. doi:10.1109/TIT.2005.862083

Carlotto, M. J. (2005). A Cluster-Based Approach for Detecting Man-Made Objects and Changes in Imagery. *IEEE Transactions on Geoscience and Remote Sensing*, *43*(2), 374–387. doi:10.1109/TGRS.2004.841481

Cartoux, J. Y., Lapreste, J. T., & Richetin, M. (1989). Face authentication or recognition by profile extraction from range images. In *Proceedings of the workshop on the interpretation of 3D scenes*.

Caselles, V., Chambolle, A., & Novaga, M. (2011). Total variation in imaging. Media, *1*(1), 1015-1057.

CASIA-3D FaceV1. (n.d.). Retrieved 24th July, 2014, from http://www.idealtest.org/dbDetailForUser.do?id=8

Celebi, M. E., & Aslandogan, Y. A. (2005). *A Comparative Study of Three Moment-Based Shape Descriptors. International Conference on Information Technology: Coding and Computing*. doi:10.1109/ITCC.2005.3

Chaaraoui, A. A., Climent-Pérez, P., & Flórez-Revuelta, F. (2012). A review on vision techniques applied to human behaviour analysis for ambient-assisted living. *Expert Systems with Applications*, *39*(12), 10873–10888. doi:10.1016/j.eswa.2012.03.005

Chambolle, A. (2004). An algorithm for total variation minimization and applications. *Journal of Mathematical Imaging and Vision, 20*(1/2), 89-97. doi:10.1023/B:JMIV.0000011321.19549.88

Chambolle, A., & Lions, P. L. (1997). Image recovery via total variation minimization and related problems. *Numerische Mathematik, 76*(2), 167-188. doi:10.1007/s002110050258

Chandola, V., Banerjee, A., & Kumar, V. (2009). Anomaly Detection: A Survey. *ACM Computing Surveys*, *41*(3), 1–72. doi:10.1145/1541880.1541882

Chandwadkar, R., Dhole, S., Gadewar, V., Raut, D., & Tiwaskar, S. A. (2013). Comparison of Edge Detection Techniques.*Proceedings of Sixth IRAJ International Conference*.

Chang, K. I., Bowyer, K. W., & P. J. Flynn, (2005). An evaluation of multimodal 2D+3D faces biometrics. *PAMI, 27*(4).

Chang, C. I., Zhao, X. L., Mark, L. G., & Pan, J. J. (1998). Least Squares Subspace Projection Approach to Mixed Pixel Classification for Hyperspectral Images. *IEEE Transactions on Geoscience and Remote Sensing*, *36*(3), 898–912. doi:10.1109/36.673681

Chang, C.-C., & Lin, C. J. (2011). LIBSVM: A library for support vector machines. *ACM Transactions on Intelligent Systems and Technology*, *2*(3), 1–27. doi:10.1145/1961189.1961199

Chang, Ch.-I. (2005). Orthogonal subspace projection (OSP) revisited: A comprehensive study and analysis. *IEEE Transactions on Geoscience and Remote Sensing*, *43*(3), 502–518. doi:10.1109/TGRS.2004.839543

Chang, Ch.-I., & Chiang, Sh.-Sh. (2002). Anomaly detection and classification for hyperspectral imagery. *IEEE Transactions on Geoscience and Remote Sensing*, *40*(6), 1314–1325. doi:10.1109/TGRS.2002.800280

Chang, Ch.-I., Ren, H., & Chiang, Sh. (2001). Real-Time Processing Algorithms for Target Detection and Classification in Hyperspectral Imagery. *IEEE Transactions on Geoscience and Remote Sensing*, *39*(4), 760–768. doi:10.1109/36.917889

Chang, Ch.-I., Xiong, W., & Wen, C.-H. (2014). A Theory of High-Order Statistics-Based Virtual Dimensionality for Hyperspectral Imagery. *IEEE Transactions on Geoscience and Remote Sensing*, *52*(1), 188–208. doi:10.1109/TGRS.2012.2237554

Chan, R. H., Ho, C. W., & Nikolova, M. (2005). Salt-and-pepper noise removal by median-type noise detectors and detail-preserving regularization. *IEEE Transactions on Image Processing*, *14*(10), 1479–1485. doi:10.1109/TIP.2005.852196 PMID:16238054

Chan, T. F., Marquina, A., & Mulet, P. (2000). High-order total variation-based image restoration. *SIAM Journal on Scientific Computing*, *22*(2), 503–516. doi:10.1137/S1064827598344169

Chan, T. F., & Shen, J. (2005). *Image Processing and Analysis - Variational, PDE, Wavelet, and Stochastic Methods*. SIAM. doi:10.1137/1.9780898717877

Chan, T. F., & Wong, C. K. (1998). Total variation blind deconvolution. *IEEE Transactions on Image Processing*, *7*(3), 370–375. doi:10.1109/83.661187 PMID:18276257

Chan, T., Esedoglu, S., Park, F., & Yip, A. (2005). *Recent developments in total variation image restoration. In Handbook of Mathematical Models in Computer Vision* (pp. 17–30). New York: Springer.

Chaovalit, P., Gangopadhyay, A., Karabatis, G., & Chen, Z. (2011). Discrete Wavelet Transform-Based Time Series Analysis and Mining. *ACM Computing Surveys*, *43*(2), 1–37.

Chaudhary, A., Vasavada, J., Raheja, J. L., Kumar, S., & Sharma, M. A. (2012). Hash based Approach for Secure Keyless Steganography in Lossless RGB Images. In Proceedings of 22nd Graphicon. doi:10.1109/ICUMT.2012.6459795

Chaudhary, A., Raheja, J. L., & Verma, B. K. (2010). An Algorithmic Approach to Intrusion Detection. In *Proceedings of 4th IEEE International Conference on Advanced Computing and Communication Technologies.*

Chaudhuri, B. B., & Sarkar, N. (1995). Texture segmentation using fractal dimension. *IEEE Transactions on Pattern Analysis and Machine Intelligence*, *17*(1), 72–77. doi:10.1109/34.368149

Chen, L., Lu, G., & Zhang, D. S. (2004). *Effects of Different Gabor Filter Parameters on Image Retrieval by Texture.* The 10th IEEE International Conference on Multi-Media Modelling, Australia.

Cheng-wu, L. (2009). A fast algorithm for variational image inpainting.*2009 AICI International Conference on Artificial Intelligence and Computational Intelligence*, *3*, 439-443.

Chen, J. L., & Kundu, A. (1995). Unsupervised Texture Segmentation Using Multichannel Decomposition and Hidden Markov Models. IEEE Trans. *Image Processing*, *4*(5), 603–619. doi:10.1109/83.382495 PMID:18290010

Chen, J. Y., & Reed, I. S. (1987). A Detection Algorithm for Optical Targets in Clutter. *IEEE Transactions on Aerospace and Electronic Systems*, *AES-23*(1), 46–59. doi:10.1109/TAES.1987.313335

Chen, P. Y., & Lien, C. Y. (2008). An efficient edge-preserving algorithm for removal of salt-and-pepper noise. *IEEE Signal Processing Letters*, *15*, 833–836. doi:10.1109/LSP.2008.2005047

Chen, S. C., Zhu, Y. L., Zhang, D. Q., & Yang, J. Y. (2005). Feature extraction approaches based on matrix pattern: MatPCA and MatFLDA. *Pattern Recognition Letters*, *26*(8), 1157–1167. doi:10.1016/j.patrec.2004.10.009

Chen, T., Ma, K. K., & Chen, L. H. (1999). Tri-state median filter for image denoising. *IEEE Transactions on Image Processing*, *8*(12), 1834–1838. doi:10.1109/83.806630 PMID:18267461

Chen, T., & Wu, H. R. (2000). Impulse noise removal by multi-state median filtering. In *Proceedings of IEEE International Conference on Acoustics, Speech, and Signal Processing*. IEEE.

Chiang, S. S., Chang, Ch. I., & Ginsberg, I. W. (2001). Unsupervised Target Detection in Hyperspectral Images Using Projection Pursuit. *IEEE Transactions on Geoscience and Remote Sensing*, *39*(7), 1380–1391. doi:10.1109/36.934071

Chinwaraphat, S., Sanpanich, A., Pintavirooj, C., & Sangworasil, M. (2012). A modified fuzzy clustering for white blood cell segmentation.*Proc Third Int Symp Biomed Eng.*

Chitra, S., & Balakrishnan, G. (2012). A Survey of Face Recognition on Feature Extraction Process of Dimensionality Reduction Techniques. *Journal of Theoretical and Applied Information Technology*, *36*(1), 92–100.

Chiu, W.-Y., & Tsai, D.-W. (2010). A macro-observation scheme for abnormal event detection in daily-life video sequences. *EURASIP Journal on Advances in Signal Processing*, *2010*(1), 525026. doi:10.1155/2010/525026

Chora's, R. S. (2007). Image Feature Extraction Techniques and their Applications for CBIR and Biometrics Systems. *International Journal of Biology and Biomedical Engineering*, *1*(1), 6–16.

Chowdhury, S., Sing, J. K., Basu, D. K., & Nasipuri, M. (2010). *Feature Extraction by Fusing Local and Global Discriminant Features: An Application to Face Recognition.IEEE International Conference on Computational Intelligence and Computing Research (ICCIC)*, Coimbatore. doi:10.1109/ICCIC.2010.5705827

Coelho, A. M., & Estrela, V. V. (2012c). A study on the effect of regularization matrices in motion estimation. *IJCA*, 2012.

Coelho, A. M., & Estrela, V. V. (2012a). Data-driven motion estimation with spatial adaptation.[IJIP]. *International Journal of Image Processing*, 6(1). Retrieved from http://www.cscjournals.org/csc/manuscript/Journals/IJIP/volume6/Issue1/IJIP-513.pdf

Coelho, A. M., & Estrela, V. V. (2012b). EM-based mixture models applied to video event detection. In P. Sanguansat (Ed.), *Intech*. doi:10.5772/2693

Cohen, I. (1993). Nonlinear variational method for optical flow computation.*Proc. Eighth Scandinavian Conference on Image Analysis*, 1, 523-530.

Collection NDOff-2007 3D faces. (n.d.). Retrieved 22nd July, 2014, from http://www3.nd.edu/~cvrl/CVRL/Data_Sets.html

Colonnese, S., Rinauro, S., & Scarano, G. (2014). Current research results on depth map interpolation techniques. In P. D. Giamberardino, D. Iacoviello, R. N. Jorge & J. M. R. S. Tavares (Eds.), Computational Modeling of Objects Presented in Images (LNCVB) (vol. 15, pp. 187-200). Berlin, Germany: Springer. doi:10.1007/978-3-319-04039-4_11

Comaniciu, D., & Meer, P. (2001). Cell image segmentation for diagnostic pathology. In *Advanced Algorithm Approaches to Medical Image Segmentation: State-Of-The-Art Application in Cardiology, Neurology, Mammography and Pathology.*

Coolens, C., & Childs, P. J. (2003). Calibration of CT Hounsfield units for radiotherapy treatment planning of patients with metallic hip prostheses: The use of the extended CT-scale. *Physics in Medicine and Biology*, 48(11), 1591–1603. doi:10.1088/0031-9155/48/11/308 PMID:12817940

Cootes, T. F., Edwards, G. J., & Taylor, C. J. (2001). Active appearance models. *IEEE Transactions on Pattern Analysis and Machine Intelligence*, 23(6), 681–685. doi:10.1109/34.927467

Cootes, T., Taylor, C., Cooper, D., & Graham, J. (1995). Active shape models-their training and application. *Computer Vision and Image Understanding*, 61(1), 38–59. doi:10.1006/cviu.1995.1004

Council, N. R. (2009). *Strengthening Forensic Science in the United States: A Path Forward*. National Academies Press.

Cowgill, M. C., Harvey, R. J., & Watson, L. T. (1999). A genetic algorithm approach to cluster analysis. *Computers & Mathematics with Applications (Oxford, England)*, 37(7), 99–108. doi:10.1016/S0898-1221(99)00090-5

Cox, I. J., Kilian, J., Leighton, F. T., & Shamoon, T. (1997). Secure spread spectrum watermarking for multimedia. *IEEE Transactions on Image Processing*, 6(12), 1673–1687. doi:10.1109/83.650120 PMID:18285237

Cox, I., Miller, M., Bloom, J., Fridrich, J., & Kalker, T. (2007). *Digital watermarking and steganography* (pp. 15–46). Burlinton: Morgan Kaufmann.

Creusot, C., Pears, N., & Austin, J. (2012). 3D Landmark Model Discovery from a Registered Set of Organic Shapes. In *Proc of Point Cloud Processing (PCP)Workshop at the Computer Vision and Pattern Recognition Conference (CVPR)*.

Creusot, C., Pears, N., & Austin, J. (2013). A Machine-Learning Approach to Keypoint Detection and Landmarking on 3D Meshes. *International Journal of Computer Vision*, 102(1-3), 146–179. doi:10.1007/s11263-012-0605-9

Crisologo, Monterola, & Soriano. (2011). Statistical Feature Based Craquelure Classification. *International Journal of Modern Physics*, 22(11), 1191-1209.

Crow, F. C. (1984). Summed-area tables for texture mapping. *Proc. SIG- GRAPH 84.11th Annu. Conf. Comput. Graph. Interact. Tech.*, 18(3), 207–212.

Cvejic, N., Loza, A., Bull, D., & Canagarajah, N. (2005, April). A similarity metric for assessment of image fusion algorithms. *Int. J. Signal Process.*, 2(3), 178–182.

Dagher, I., Helwe, W., & Yassine, F. (2002). Fingerprint recognition using fuzzy artmap neural network architecture. In *Proceeding of 14th International Conference on Microelectronics* (ICM). doi:10.1109/ICM-02.2002.1161519

Dalal, N., & Triggs, B. (2005). Histograms of oriented gradients for human detection. In *Proceedings of IEEE International Conference on Computer Vision and Pattern Recognition* (pp 886-893). IEEE Press. doi:10.1109/CVPR.2005.177

Dalli, A. (2003). Adaptation of the F-measure to cluster based lexicon quality evaluation. In *Proceedings of the EACL*. doi:10.3115/1641396.1641404

Dang, H., Song, J., & Guo, Q. (2010). A Fruit Size Detecting and Grading System Based on Image Processing. In *Proceedings of Second International Conference on Intelligent Human-Machine Systems and Cybernetics (IHMSC 2010)*. Nanjing, China: IEEE.

Datta, Joshi, Li, & Wang. (2008). Image Retrieval: Ideas, Influences, and Trends of the New Age. *ACM Computing Surveys, 40*(2), 1-60.

De Man, B., Nuyts, J., Dupont, P., Marchal, G., & Suetens, P. (1998). Metal streak artifacts in X-ray computed tomography: a simulation study. In *Nuclear Science Symposium, 1998. Conference Record. 1998 IEEE 3*, 1860-1865. IEEE. doi:10.1109/NSSMIC.1998.773898

De Man, B., Nuyts, J., Dupont, P., Marchal, G., & Suetens, P. (2000). Reduction of metal streak artifacts in x-ray computed tomography using a transmission maximum a posteriori algorithm. *IEEE Transactions on Nuclear Science, 47*(3), 977–981. doi:10.1109/23.856534

Devasena, L. C., Sumathi, T., & Hemalatha, M. (2011). An Experiential Survey on Image Mining Tools. *Techniques and Applications, 3*(3), 1155-1167.

Dhawan, Ś., & Dogra, H. (2012). Feature Extraction Techniques for Face Recognition. International Journal of Engineering. *Business and Enterprise Applications, 2*(1), 1–4.

Ding, C., Xia, Y., & Li, Y. (2014). Supervised segmentation of vasculature in retinal images using neural networks. In *Proceeding of IEEE International Conference on Orange Technologies* (ICOT). doi:10.1109/ICOT.2014.6954694

Donoho, D. L., & Duncan, M. R. (2000). Digital Curvelet Transform: Strategy, Implementation and Experiments. *Proceedings of the Society for Photo-Instrumentation Engineers, 4056*, 12–29. doi:10.1117/12.381679

Donoho, D., & Tsaig, Y. (2008). Fast solution of l1-norm minimization problems when the solution may be sparse. *IEEE Transactions on Information Theory, 54*(11), 4789–4812. doi:10.1109/TIT.2008.929958

Dorigo, M., & Gambardella, L. M. (1997). Ant colonies for the travelling salesman problem. *Bio Systems, 43*(2), 73–81. doi:10.1016/S0303-2647(97)01708-5 PMID:9231906

Doster, T. J., Ross, D. S., Messinger, D. W., & Basener, W. F. (2009). Anomaly Clustering in Hyperspectral Images. In *Proceedings of SPIE 7334, Algorithms and Technologies for Multispectral, Hyperspectral, and Ultraspectral Imagery XV*. Orlando, FL: SPIE. doi:10.1117/12.818407

Draper, N., & Smith, H. (1981). *Applied Regression Analysis*. New York: Wiley.

Drulea, M., & Nedevschi, S. (2011). Total variation regularization of local-global optical flow. *Proc. 14th International IEEE Conference on Intelligent Transportation Systems (ITSC)*, (pp. 318 - 323). doi:10.1109/ITSC.2011.6082986

Du, B., & Zhang, L. (2011). Random-Selection-Based Anomaly Detector for Hyperspectral Imagery. *IEEE Transactions on Geoscience and Remote Sensing, 49*(5), 1578–1589. doi:10.1109/TGRS.2010.2081677

Duda, R., Hart, P., & Stork, D. (2000). *Pattern Classification* (2nd ed.). Wiley-Interscience.

Dunn, W. J. III, Greenberg, M. J., & Callejas, S. S. (1976). Use of cluster analysis in the development of structure-activity relations for antitumor triazenes. *Journal of Medicinal Chemistry, 19*(11), 1299–1301. doi:10.1021/jm00233a009 PMID:1003406

Durai, S. A., & Saro, E. A. (Dec.2006). An Improved Image Compression approach with SOFM Network using Cumulative Distribution Function. In *Proceedings of International conference on Advanced Computing and Communications*. doi:10.1109/ADCOM.2006.4289904

Durand, F., & Dorsey, J. (2002, July). Fast bilateral filtering for the display of high- dynamic-range images. *ACM Transactions on Graphics, 21*(3), 257–266. doi:10.1145/566654.566574

Duran, O., & Petrou, M. (2007). A Time-Efficient Method for Anomaly Detection in Hyperspectral Images. *IEEE Transactions on Geoscience and Remote Sensing, 45*(12), 3894–3904. doi:10.1109/TGRS.2007.909205

Eberhart, R. C., & Shi, Y. (2001). Particle swarm optimization: developments, applications and resources. In *Evolutionary Computation, 2001.Proceedings of the 2001 Congress on* (pp. 81-86). IEEE. doi:10.1109/CEC.2001.934374

Eberle, W., & Holder, L. (2013). Incremental Anomaly Detection in Graphs. In *Proceedings of the IEEE 13th International Conference on Data Mining Workshops (ICDMW)*. Dallas, TX: IEEE.

Ebrahimdoost, Y., Dehmeshki, J., Ellis, T. S., Firoozbakht, M., Youannic, A., & Qanadli, S. D. (2010). Medical Image Segmentation Using Active Contours and a Level Set Model: Application to Pulmonary Embolism (PE) Segmentation. In *Fourth International Conference on Digital Society*. DOI doi:10.1109/ICDS.2010.64

Effendi, Z., Ramii, R., Ghani, J. A., & Yaakob, Z. (2009). Development of Jatropha Curcas Color Grading System for Ripeness Evaluation. *European Journal of Scientific Research, 30*(4), 662–669.

Efron, B., Hastie, T., Johnstone, I., & Tibshirani, R. (2004). Least angle regression. *Annals of Statistics, 32*(2), 407–499. doi:10.1214/009053604000000067

Eggers, J.J., Bauml, R. Girod, B. (2002). A communication approach to image steganography. *Security and Watermarking of Multimedia Contents V of SPIE Proceedings, 4675*, 26-37.

Elboher, E., & Werman, M. (2013). Asymmetric correlation: A noise robust similarity measure for template matching. *IEEE Transactions on Image Processing, 99*, 1–12. PMID:23591492

Elnemr, H. A., & Hefnawy, A. A. (2013). A Significance Test-Based Feature Selection Method for Diabetic Retinopathy Grading. *CiiT International Journal of Digital Image Processing, 5*(5), 243 – 249.

Elnemr, H. A. (2012). Using Hybrid Decision Tree-Houph Transform Approach for Automatic Bank Check Processing. *International Journal of Computer Science and Information Security, 10*(5), 31–37.

Elnemr, H. A. (2013). Statistical Analysis of Law's Mask Texture Features for Cancer and Water Lung Detection. *International Journal of Computer Science Issues, 10*(6), 196–202.

Emmanuel, S., Vinod, A. P., Rajan, D., & Heng, C. K. (2007). An Authentication Watermarking Scheme with Transaction Tracking Enabled. In Digital EcoSystems and Technologies Conference, 2007. DEST'07. Inaugural IEEE-IES (481-486). IEEE.

Engelbrecht, A. P. (2007). *Computational intelligence: an introduction*. John Wiley & Sons. doi:10.1002/9780470512517

Eng, H. L., & Ma, K. K. (2001). Noise adaptive soft-switching median filter. *IEEE Transactions on Image Processing, 10*(2), 242–251. doi:10.1109/83.902289 PMID:18249615

Enjun, W., Qing, W., Xiumin, C., & Lei, X. (2008, September). Research on road image fusion enhancement technique based on wavelet transform. In *Vehicle Power and Propulsion Conference, 2008. VPPC'08. IEEE* (pp. 1-5). IEEE. doi:10.1109/VPPC.2008.4677691

Esakkirajan, S., Veerakumar, T., & Jayaraman, S. (2009). Digital Image Processing (1st ed.). Academic Press.

Esakkirajan, S., Veerakumar, T., Subramanyam, A. N., & PremChand, C. H. (2011). Removal of high density salt and pepper noise through modified decision based unsymmetric trimmed median filter. *IEEE Signal Processing Letters, 18*(5), 287–290. doi:10.1109/LSP.2011.2122333

Ettaouil, M., Ghanou, Y., Moutaouakil, K., & Lazaar, M. (2011, April). Image Medical Compression by a new Architecture Optimization Model for the Kohonen Networks. *International Journal of Computer Theory and Engineering, 3*(2), 1793–1801.

Farbman, Fattal, Lischinski, & Szeliski. (2008, August). Edge-preserving decompositions for multi-scale tone and detail manipulation. *ACM Transactions on Graphics, 15*(2), 252–267.

Farkas, L. G., & Munro, I. R. (1987). *Anthropometric Facial Proportions in Medicine*. Springfield, IL: Thomas Books.

Fathian, M., Amiri, B., & Maroosi, A. (2007). Application of honey-bee mating optimization algorithm on clustering. *Applied Mathematics and Computation, 190*(2), 1502–1513. doi:10.1016/j.amc.2007.02.029

Fattal, R. (2008, August). Single image dehazing. *ACM Transactions on Graphics*, *27*(3), 72. doi:10.1145/1360612.1360671

Fausett, L. (1993). *Fundamentals of Networks Architectures, Algorithms and Applications*. Pearson Education.

Fei, G., & Kehong, W. (2011). The Research of Classification Method of Arc Welding Pool Image Based on Invariant Moments. *Power Engineering and Automation Conference (PEAM)*, Wuhan.

FERET database. (n.d.). Retrieved 20th July, 2014, from http://www.itl.nist.gov/iad/humanid/feret/feret_master.html

Fleck, S., Busch, F., & Straßer, W. (2007). Adaptive probabilistic tracking embedded in smart cameras for distributed surveillance in a 3D model. *EURASIP Journal on Embedded Systems*, *2007*(1), 29858. doi:10.1186/1687-3963-2007-029858

Fleck, S., & Strasser, W. (2008). Smart camera based monitoring system and its application to assisted living. *Proceedings of the IEEE*, *96*(10), 1698–1714. doi:10.1109/JPROC.2008.928765

Fontana, R. (2004). Recent system applications of short-pulse ultra-wideband (uwb) technology. *IEEE Transactions on Microwave Theory and Techniques*, *52*(9), 2087–2104. doi:10.1109/TMTT.2004.834186

Forgy, E. W. (1965). Cluster analysis of multivariate data: Efficiency versus interpretability of classifications. *Biometrics*, *21*, 768–769.

Franz, M., & Schölkopf, B. (2006). A unifying view of Wiener and Volterra theory and polynomial kernel regression. *Neural Computation*, *18*(12), 3097–3118. doi:10.1162/neco.2006.18.12.3097 PMID:17052160

Frav3D database. (n.d.). Retrieved 16th August, 2014, from http://archive.today/B1WeX

FRGC v.2 face database. (n.d.). Retrieved 22nd July, 2014, from http://www3.nd.edu/~cvrl/CVRL/Data_Sets.html

Friedman, J., Hastie, T., & Tibshirani, R. (2000). Additive logistic regression: A statistical view of boosting. *Annals of Statistics*, *28*(2), 337–374. doi:10.1214/aos/1016218223

Friedman, J., Hastie, T., & Tibshirani, R. (2010). Regularization paths for generalized linear models via coordinate descent. *Journal of Statistical Software*, *33*(1), 1. doi:10.18637/jss.v033.i01 PMID:20808728

Fromont, M. (2007). Model selection by bootstrap penalization for classification. *Machine Learning*, *66*(2-3), 165–207. doi:10.1007/s10994-006-7679-y

Fu, Y., & Lv, J. (2009). *Recognition of SAR Image Based on SVM and New Invariant Moment Feature Extraction. Second International Symposium on Knowledge Acquisition and Modeling*, Wuhan.

Gajjar, T. Y., & Chauhan, N. C. (2012). A Review of Image Mining Frameworks and Techniques. *International Journal of Computer Science and Information Technologies*, *3*(3), 4064-4066.

Galatsanos, N. P., & Katsaggelos, A. K. (1992). Methods for choosing the regularization parameter and estimating the noise variance in image restoration and their relation. *IEEE Transactions on Image Processing*, *1*(3), 322–336. doi:10.1109/83.148606 PMID:18296166

Gale, A. G., & Salankar, S. S. (2014). A Review on Advance Methods of Feature Extraction in Iris Recognition System. *IOSR Journal of Electrical and Electronics Engineering*, *3*(14), 65-70.

Gamea, G. R., Aboamera, M. A., & Ahmed, M. E. (2011). Design and manufacturing of prototype for orange grading using phototransistor. *Australian Journal of Agricultural Engineering*, *2*(3), 74–81.

Gancarczyk, J., & Sobczyk, J. (2013). Data Mining Approach to Image Feature Extraction in Old Painting Restoration. *Foundation of Computing and Decision Sciences*, *38*(3), 159–174. doi:10.2478/fcds

Ganguly, S., Bhattacharjee, D., & Nasipuri, M. (2014a). 3D Face Recognition from Range Images Based on Curvature Analysis. ICTACT Journal on Image and Video Processing, *4*(3), 748-753.

Ganguly, S., Bhattacharjee, D., & Nasipuri, M., (2014b). Range Face Image Registration using ERFI from 3D Images. *Proceedings of 3rd Frontiers of Intelligent Computing: Theory and applications, Advances in Intelligent Systems and Computing*. DOI: .10.1007/978-3-319-12012-6_36

Garg, K., & Nayar, S. K. (2005, October). When does a camera see rain? In *Computer Vision, 2005. ICCV 2005. Tenth IEEE International Conference on*. IEEE. doi:10.1109/ICCV.2005.253

Garg, K., & Nayar, S. K. (2007). Vision and rain. *International Journal of Computer Vision*, *75*(1), 3–27. doi:10.1007/s11263-006-0028-6

GavabDB database. (n.d.). Retrieved 16th August, 2014, from http://www.gavab.etsii.urjc.es/recursos_en.html

Gay, P., Berruto, R., & Piccarolo, P. (2002). *Fruit color assessment for quality grading purposes*. 2002 ASAE Annual International Meeting/ CIGR XVth World Congress, Chicago, IL.

Gebeyehu, B. G., Zhongshi, & Huazheng. (2013b). Data Mining Prospects in Mobile Social Networks. In *Data Mining in Dynamic Social Networks and Fuzzy Systems*. IGI Global.

Gebeyehu, B. G., Zhongshi, H., & Zhu, Z. H. (2013a). The Development of Invisible Data Mining, Functionality for Discovering Interesting Knowledge: In the case of Bioinformatics. *Journal of Convergence Information Technology*, *7*(4), 251–259.

Geetha, P., & Chitradevi, B. (2014). A Review of Image Processing Techniques for Synthetic Aperture Radar (SAR) Images. *International Journal of Innovative Research in Computer and Communication Engineering*, *2*(4), 3823–3829.

Geng, X., Sun, K., Ji, L., & Zhao, Y. (2014). A High-Order Statistical Tensor Based Algorithm for Anomaly Detection in Hyperspectral Imagery. *Scientific Reports*, *4*(6869), 1–7. PMID:25366706

Georghiades, A., Belhumeur, P., & Kriegman, D. (2001). From few to many: Illumination cone models for face recognition under variable lighting and pose. *IEEE Transactions on Pattern Analysis and Machine Intelligence*, *23*(6), 643–660. doi:10.1109/34.927464

Geronimo, D., Lopez, A. M., Sappa, A. D., & Graf, T. (2010). Survey of pedestrian detection for advanced driver assistance systems. *IEEE Transactions on Pattern Analysis and Machine Intelligence*, *32*(7), 1239–1258. doi:10.1109/TPAMI.2009.122 PMID:20489227

Ghaderi, R., Hassanpour, H., & Shahiri, M. (2007). Retinal vessel segmentation using the 2-D Morlet wavelet and neural network. In *Proceeding of International Conference on Intelligent and Advanced Systems* (ICIAS). doi:10.1109/ICIAS.2007.4658584

Ghosh, M., Das, D., Chakraborty, C., Pala, M., Maity, A. K., Pal, S. K., & Ray, A. K. (2010). Statistical pattern analysis of white blood cell nuclei morphometry. *Proc IEEE Students Technol Symp*.

Gilboa, G., Sochen, N., & Zeevi, Y. Y. (2003). Texture preserving variational denoising using an adaptive fidelity term. *Proc. VLSM 2003*. Nice, France.

Gill, J., Sandhu, P. S., & Singh, T. (2014). A review of automatic fruit classification using soft computing techniques. In *Proceedings of international conference on computer, systems and electronics engineering (IC-SCEE2014)*.

Gökberk, B., İrfanoğlu, M. O., & Akarun, L. (2006). 3D shape-based face representation and feature extraction for face recognition. *Image and Vision Computing*, *24*(8), 857–869. doi:10.1016/j.imavis.2006.02.009

Gogoi, R., & Sarma, K. K. (2012). ANFIS based Information Extraction using K-means Clustering for Application in Satellite Images. *International Journal of Computers and Applications*, *50*(7), 13–18. doi:10.5120/7782-0872

Gonzales, R. C., & Woods, R. E. (1993). *Digital image processing*. Academic Press.

Gonzalez, C., & Woods, R. E. (2012). Digital Image Processing (3rd ed.). Academic Press.

Gonzalez, R. C., & Woods, R. E. (2002). *Digital Image Processing*. Pearson Education.

Goovaerts, P., Jacquez, G. M., & Marcus, A. (2005). Geostatistical and local cluster analysis of high resolution hyperspectral imagery for detection of anomalies. *Remote Sensing of Environment*, *95*(3), 351–367. doi:10.1016/j.rse.2004.12.021

Goshtasby, A. A., & Nikolov. (2007). Image fusion: Advances in the state of the art. *Proceeding of IEEE conference on Image Processing*, *8*(2), 113-122.

Goswami, S., & Bhaiya, L. K. P. (2013). A hybrid neuro-fuzzy approach for brain abnormality detection using GLCM based feature extraction. In *Proceedings of the International Conference on Emerging Trends in Communication, Control, Signal Processing & Computing Applications (C2SPCA)*. Bangalore: IEEE. doi:10.1109/C2SPCA.2013.6749454

Graves, D., & Witold, P. (2010). Kernel-based fuzzy clustering and fuzzy clustering: A comparative experimental study. *Fuzzy Sets and Systems*, *161*(4), 522–543. doi:10.1016/j.fss.2009.10.021

Gregory, K. (2005). Investigator's Guide to Steganography (2nd ed.). Academic Press.

Gross, R., Matthews, I., & Baker, S. (2004). Appearance-based face recognition and light-fields. *IEEE Transactions on Pattern Analysis and Machine Intelligence*, *26*(4), 449–465. doi:10.1109/TPAMI.2004.1265861 PMID:15382650

Gu, H., Su, G., & Du, C. (2003). Feature points extraction from face. *Proceedings of Conference on Image and Vision Computing*.

Guichard, F., & Malgouyres, F. (1998). Total variation based interpolation. *Proc. European Signal Processing Conf.*, *3*, 1741-1744.

Guo, Q., Zhang, B., Ran, Q., Gao, L., Li, J., & Plaza, A. (2014). Weighted-RXD and Linear Filter-Based RXD: Improving Background Statistics Estimation for Anomaly Detection in Hyperspectral Imagery. *IEEE Journal of Selected Topics in Applied Earth Observations and Remote Sensing*, *7*(6), 2351–2366. doi:10.1109/JSTARS.2014.2302446

Gupta, A., & Chaudhary, A. (2014). Hiding Sound in Image by k-LSB Mutation using Cuckoo Search. In Proceedings of 2nd IEEE-INNS ISCBI. doi:10.1109/ISCBI.2014.12

Gupta, J. P. (2013). Infected fruit part detection using K-means clustering segmentation technique. *International Journal of Artificial Intelligence and Interactive Multimedia*, *2*(3), 65-72.

Gupta, S. K., Agrwal, S., Meena, Y. K., & Nain, N. (2011). *A Hybrid Method of Feature Extraction for Facial Expression Recognition. Seventh International Conference on Signal-Image Technology and Internet-Based Systems (SITIS)*, Dijon. doi:10.1109/SITIS.2011.64

Gurram, P., & Kwon, H. (2011). Hyperspectral anomaly detection using an optimized support vector data description method. In *Proceedings of 2011 3rd Workshop on Hyperspectral Image and Signal Processing: Evolution in Remote Sensing (WHISPERS)*. Lisbon: IEEE. doi:10.1109/WHISPERS.2011.6080965

Gurram, P., & Kwon, H. (2011). Support-Vector-Based Hyperspectral Anomaly Detection Using Optimized Kernel Parameters. *IEEE Geoscience and Remote Sensing Letters*, *8*(6), 1060–1064. doi:10.1109/LGRS.2011.2155030

Gurram, P., Kwon, H., & Han, T. (2012). Sparse Kernel-Based Hyperspectral Anomaly Detection. *IEEE Geoscience and Remote Sensing Letters*, *9*(5), 943–947. doi:10.1109/LGRS.2012.2187040

Gutub, A. A. (2010). Pixel indicator technique for RGB image steganography. *Journal of Emerging Technologies in Web Intelligence*, *2*(1), 56–64. doi:10.4304/jetwi.2.1.56-64

Gu, Y., Liu, Y., & Zhang, Y. (2006). A Selective Kernel PCA Algorithm for Anomaly Detection in Hyperspectral Imagery. In *Proceedings of the IEEE International Conference on Acoustics, Speech and Signal Processing*. Toulouse: IEEE.

Gu, Y., Liu, Y., & Zhang, Y. (2008). A Selective KPCA Algorithm Based on High-Order Statistics for Anomaly Detection in Hyperspectral Imager. *IEEE Geoscience and Remote Sensing Letters*, *5*(1), 43–47. doi:10.1109/LGRS.2007.907304

Guyon, I., Gunn, S., Nikravesh, M., & Zadeh, L. A. (2006). *Feature Extraction Foundations and Applications*. Berlin: Springer -Verlag. doi:10.1007/978-3-540-35488-8

Gw'enol'e, Q., Lamard, M., Cazuguel, G., Cochener, B., & Roux, C. (2012). Fast wavelet-based image characterization for highly adaptive image retrieval. *IEEE Transactions on Image Processing*, *21*(4), 1613–1623. doi:10.1109/TIP.2011.2180915 PMID:22194244

Haar, F. B., & Veltkamp, R. C. (2008). A 3D face matching framework. In *Proc. IEEE Int. Conf. Shape Model. Appl.*

Hall, M., Frank, E., Holmes, G., Pfahringer, B., Reutemann, P., & Witten, I. H. (2009). The WEKA data mining software: An update. *SIGKDD Explorations*, *11*(1), 10–19. doi:10.1145/1656274.1656278

Handl, J., Knowles, J., & Dorigo, M. (2003). On the performance of ant-based clustering. Design and Application of Hybrid Intelligent System. *Frontiers in Artificial Intelligence and Applications*, *104*, 204–213.

Han, J. (2012). *Data Mining Concepts and Techniques* (3rd ed.). London, UK: Elsevier Inc.

Harsanyi, J. C. (1993). *Detection and Classification of Subpixel Spectral Signatures in Hyperspectral Image Sequences*. (Doctoral dissertation). Université de Maryland Baltimore County.

Hartung, F., & Kutter, M. (1999). Multimedia watermarking techniques. *Proceedings of the IEEE*, *87*(7), 1079–1107. doi:10.1109/5.771066

Hatamlou, A., Abdullah, S., & Hatamlou, M. (2011). Data clustering using big bang–big crunch algorithm. In *Innovative Computing Technology* (pp. 383–388). Springer Berlin Heidelberg. doi:10.1007/978-3-642-27337-7_36

Hatamlou, A., Abdullah, S., & Nezamabadi-Pour, H. (2011). Application of gravitational search algorithm on data clustering. In *Rough Sets and Knowledge Technology* (pp. 337–346). Springer Berlin Heidelberg. doi:10.1007/978-3-642-24425-4_44

Hatamlou, A., Abdullah, S., & Nezamabadi-pour, H. (2012). A combined approach for clustering based on K-means and gravitational search algorithms. *Swarm and Evolutionary Computation*, *6*, 47–52. doi:10.1016/j.swevo.2012.02.003

Hautière, N., Tarel, J. P., & Aubert, D. (2010). Mitigation of visibility loss for advanced camera-based driver assistance. *Intelligent Transportation Systems. IEEE Transactions on*, *11*(2), 474–484.

Hautiere, N., Tarel, J. P., Lavenant, J., & Aubert, D. (2006). Automatic fog detection and estimation of visibility distance through use of an onboard camera. *Machine Vision and Applications*, *17*(1), 8–20. doi:10.1007/s00138-005-0011-1

Hawashin, B., Mansour, A., & Aljawarneh, S. (2013). An Efficient Feature Selection Method for Arabic Text Classification. *International Journal of Computers and Applications*, *83*(17), 1–6. doi:10.5120/14666-2588

Haykin, S. (2003). *Neural Networks – A Comprehensive Foundation*. New Delhi: Pearson Education.

Haykin, S. (2005). *Neural Networks: A Comprehensive Foundation*. New Delhi: Pearson Education.

Hazel, G. G. (2000). Multivariate Gaussian MRF for multispectral scene segmentation and anomaly detection. *IEEE Transactions on Geoscience and Remote Sensing*, *38*(3), 1199–1211. doi:10.1109/36.843012

He, X.-J., Zhang, Y., Lok, T.-M., & Lyu, M. R. (2005). A New Feature of Uniformity of Image Texture Directions Coinciding with the Human Eyes Perception. *Lecture Notes in Artificial Intelligence*, 3614, 727–730. doi:10.1007/11540007_90

Heesung, K., & Nasrabadi, N. M. (2005). Kernel RX-algorithm: A nonlinear anomaly detector for hyperspectral imagery. *IEEE Transactions on Geoscience and Remote Sensing*, *43*(2), 388–397. doi:10.1109/TGRS.2004.841487

He, J., Jiang, Z., Guo, P., & Liu, L. (2011). *A Study of Block-Global Feature based Supervised Image Annotation Systems. IEEE International Conference on Man, and Cybernetics*, Anchorage, AK.

He, K., Sun, J., & Tang, X. (2010). Guided image filtering. *Proc. Eur. Conf. Comput. Vis.*, 1–14.

He, K., Sun, J., & Tang, X. (2011). Single image haze removal using dark channel prior. *Pattern Analysis and Machine Intelligence. IEEE Transactions on, 33*(12), 2341–2353.

Henry, C.J., & Peters, J.F. (2010). *Near Sets: Theory and Applications*. Academic Press.

Henry, R. C., Mahadev, S., Urquijo, S., & Chitwood, D. (2000). Color perception through atmospheric haze. *JOSA A, 17*(5), 831–835. doi:10.1364/JOSAA.17.000831 PMID:10795630

Hernandez, M., Choi, J., & Medioni, G. (2012). Laser scan quality 3-D face modelling using a low-cost depth camera. In *Proc of EUSIPCO*.

He, Y., Pan, W., & Lin, J. (2006). Cluster analysis using multivariate normal mixture models to detect differential gene expression with microarray data. *Computational Statistics & Data Analysis, 51*(2), 641–658. doi:10.1016/j.csda.2006.02.012

Hidayat, E., Nur, F. A., Muda, A. K., Huoy, C. Y., & Ahmad, S. (2011). A Comparative Study of Feature Extraction Using PCA and LDA for Face Recognition. *7th International Conference on Information Assurance and Security (IAS)*. doi:10.1109/ISIAS.2011.6122779

Hidy, G. M. (1972). *Aerosols and Atmospheric Chemistry*. New York: Academic Press.

Hill, R. B. (1978). *Apparatus and method for identifying individuals through their retinal vasculature patterns*. US Patent No. 4109237.

Hill, R. B. (2003). *Retina Identification*. Biometrics Springer.

Hines, G. D., Rahman, Z. U., Jobson, D. J., & Woodell, G. A. (2004, September). Single-scale retinex using digital signal processors. In *Global Signal Processing Conference*.

Ho, A. T., Shen, J., Tan, S. H., & Kot, A. C. (2002). Digital image-in-image watermarking for copyright protection of satellite images using the fast Hadamard transform. *Proc. IEEE International Symposium on Geoscience and Remote Sensing*. doi:10.1109/IGARSS.2002.1027166

Holland, J. H. (1975). *Adaptation in natural and artificial systems: An introductory analysis with applications to biology, control, and artificial intelligence*. University of Michigan Press.

Holte, M. B., Tran, C., Trivedi, M. M., & Moeslund, T. B. (2012). Human pose estimation and activity recognition from multi-view videos: Comparative explorations of recent developments. *IEEE Journal of Selected Topics in Signal Processing, 6*(5), 538–552. doi:10.1109/JSTSP.2012.2196975

Hom, B., & Schunck, B. (1981). Determining optical flow. *Artificial Intelligence, 17*(1-3), 185–203. doi:10.1016/0004-3702(81)90024-2

Hong, Z., & Xuanbing, Z. (2010). *Texture feature extraction based on wavelet transform.International Conference on Computer Application and System Modeling (ICCASM)*.

Hooshyar, S., & Khayati, R. (2010). Retina Vessel Detection Using Fuzzy Ant Colony Algorithm. In *Proceeding of Canadian Conference on Computer and Robot Vision (CRV)*. doi:10.1109/CRV.2010.38

Hoover, A., & Goldbaum, M. (2003, August). Locating the Optic Nerve in a Retinal Image Using the Fuzzy Convergence of the Blood Vessels. *IEEE Transactions on Medical Imaging, 22*(8), 951–958. doi:10.1109/TMI.2003.815900 PMID:12906249

Hornik, K. (1991). Approximation capabilities of multilayer feedforward networks. *Neural Networks, 4*(2), 251–257. doi:10.1016/0893-6080(91)90009-T

Hosseini, H., & Marvasti, F. (2013). Fast restoration of natural images corrupted by high-density impulse noise. *EURASIP Journal on Image and Video Processing, 15*, 1–7.

Hossny, N., Nahavandi, S., & Creighton, D. (2008, August). Comments on 'information measure for performance of image fusion. *Electronics Letters, 44*(18), 1266–1268. doi:10.1049/el:20081754

Hough, P. V. C. (1962). *Method and Means for Recognizing Complex Patterns*. U.S. Patent 3,069,654.

Hounsfield, G. N. (1973). Computerized transverse axial scanning (tomography): Part 1. Description of system. *The British Journal of Radiology*, *46*(552), 1016–1022. doi:10.1259/0007-1285-46-552-1016 PMID:4757352

Hsieh, C. T., & Hu, C. S. (2005). An Application of Fuzzy Logic and Neural network to Fingerprint Recognition. In *Proceeding of the 4th WSEAS International Conference on Electric, Signal Processing and Control* (ESPOCO'05). WSEAS.

Hsieh, J., Molthen, R. C., Dawson, C. A., & Johnson, R. H. (2000). An iterative approach to the beam hardening correction in cone beam CT. *Medical Physics*, *27*(1), 23–29. doi:10.1118/1.598853 PMID:10659734

Hsien-Wei, Y., & Kuo, F. H. (2011). Reversible Data Hiding for Color BMP Image Based on Block Difference Histogram. In *Ubi-Media Computing (U-Media), 2011 4th International Conference on.*

Hsu, C. T., & Wu, J. L. (1999). Hidden digital watermarks in images. *IEEE Transactions on Image Processing*, *8*(1), 58–68. doi:10.1109/83.736686 PMID:18262865

Huang, G. B., Chen, L., & Siew, C. K. (2003). *Universal approximation using incremental Feedforward networks with arbitrary input weights*. Technical Report ICIS/46, Nayang Technological University.

Huang, G. B., Zhu, Q. Y., & Siew, C. K. (2003). *Real time learning capabilities of neural networks*. Technical report ICIS/45, Nayang Technological University.

Huang, H. C., Chen, Y. H., & Lin, G. Y. (2009). DCT-Based Robust Watermarking with Swarm Intelligence Concepts. In *Information Assurance and Security, 2009. IAS'09. Fifth International Conference on*. IEEE. doi:10.1109/IAS.2009.85

Huang, G. B. (2003). Learning capability and storage capacity of two hidden layer feed-forward networks. *IEEE Transactions on Neural Networks*, *14*(2), 274–281. doi:10.1109/TNN.2003.809401 PMID:18238011

Huang, G. B., & Babri, H. A. (1998). Upper bounds on the number of hidden neurons in Feedforward networks with arbitrary bounded nonlinear activation function. *IEEE Transactions on Neural Networks*, *9*(1), 224–229. doi:10.1109/72.655045 PMID:18252445

Huang, G.-B., Zhu, Q.-Y., & Siew, C.-K. (2004). Extreme Learning machine: A new learning scheme of feedforward Neural Networks. In *Proceedings of International Joint Conference on Neural Networks (IJCNN2004)*.

Huang, H. C., Chen, Y. H., & Abraham, A. (2010). Optimized watermarking using swarm-based bacterial foraging. *Journal of Information Hiding and Multimedia Signal Processing*, *1*(1), 51–58.

Huang, J., Kuamr, S., & Mitra, M. (1997). *Image indexing using colour correlogram.IEEE Computer Society Conference on Computer Vision and Pattern Recognition*. doi:10.1109/CVPR.1997.609412

Huang, T., Yang, G., & Tang, G. (1979). A fast two-dimensional median filtering algorithm. *IEEE Transactions on Acoustics, Speech, and Signal Processing*, *27*(1), 13–18. doi:10.1109/TASSP.1979.1163188

Huang, Y. L. (2005). A Fast Method for Textural Analysis of DCT-Based Image. *Journal of Information Science and Engineering*, *21*(1), 181–194.

Huck, A., & Guillaume, M. (2010). Asymptotically CFAR-Unsupervised Target Detection and Discrimination in Hyperspectral Images With Anomalous-Component Pursuit. *IEEE Transactions on Geoscience and Remote Sensing*, *48*(11), 3980–3991.

Hu, G., Zhou, S., Guan, J., & Hu, X. (2008). Towards effective document clustering: A constrained K-means based approach. *Information Processing & Management*, *44*(4), 1397–1409. doi:10.1016/j.ipm.2008.03.001

Hu, M. K. (1962). Visual pattern Recognition by Moment Invariants. *I.R.E. Transactions on Information Theory*, *8*(2), 179–187. doi:10.1109/TIT.1962.1057692

Hussain, A. B. S., Toussaint, G. T., & Donaldson, R. W. (1972). Results Obtained Using a Simple Character Recognition Procedure on Munson's Handprinted Data. *IEEE Transactions on Computers*, *C-21*(2), 201–205. doi:10.1109/TC.1972.5008927

Hu, X., Subbu, R., Bonissone, P., Qiu, H., & Iyer, N. (2008). Multivariate anomaly detection in real-world industrial systems. In *Proceedings of IEEE International Joint Conference on Neural Networks*. Hong Kong: IEEE.

Hwang, H., & Haddad, R. (1995). Adaptive median filters: New algorithms and results. *IEEE Transactions on Image Processing*, 4(4), 499–502. doi:10.1109/83.370679 PMID:18289998

Hytla, P., Hardie, R. C., Eismann, M. T., & Meola, J. (2007). Anomaly detection in hyperspectral imagery: a comparison of methods using seasonal data. In *Proceedings of SPIE 6565, Algorithms and Technologies for Multispectral, Hyperspectral, and Ultraspectral Imagery XIII*. Orlando, FL: SPIE. doi:10.1117/12.718381

Hyvärinen, A., & Oja, E. (2000). Independent component analysis: Algorithms and applications. *Neural Networks, Elsevier Science Ltd, 13*(4-5), 411–430. doi:10.1016/S0893-6080(00)00026-5 PMID:10946390

Islam, M. M., Zhang, D., & Lu, G. (2008). Automatic Categorization of Image Regions Using Dominant Colour Based Vector Quantization. *Proceedings of the Digital Image Computing: Techniques and Applications*.

Islam, M., Venkataraman, S., & Alazab, M. (2010). *Stochastic Model Based Approach for Biometric Identification*. Technological Developments in Networking, Education and Automation.

Ito, Y. (1992). Approximation of continuous function on Rd by linear combination of shifted rotation of a sigmoid function with and without scaling. *Neural Networks, 5*(1), 105–115. doi:10.1016/S0893-6080(05)80009-7

Jain, A. K., Murty, M. N., & Flynn, P. J. (1999). Data clustering: a review. *ACM Computing Surveys, 31*(3), 264-323.

Jain, V., & Learned-Miller, E. (2010). FDDB: A benchmark for face detection in unconstrained settings. In *Handbook of fingerprint recognition*. Springer.

Jain, A. K. (2010). Data clustering: 50 years beyond K-means. *Pattern Recognition Letters, 31*(8), 651–666. doi:10.1016/j.patrec.2009.09.011

Jain, A., Hong, L., & Pankanti, S. (2000). Biometric Identification. *Communications of the ACM, 43*(2), 91–98. doi:10.1145/328236.328110

Jain, A., Hong, L., Pankanti, S., & Bolle, R. (1997). An identity authentication system using fingerprints. In *Proceeding of the Institute of Electrical and Electronics Engineers*. IEEE.

Jain, M., & Singh, S. K. (2011). A Survey On: Content Based Image Retrieval Systems Using Clustering Techniques for Large Data sets. *International Journal of Managing Information Technology, 3*(4), 23–39. doi:10.5121/ijmit.2011.3403

Janbu, N. (1954). Application of composite slip circle for stability analysis. In *Proceedings of Fourth European conference on stability of earth surface*.

Jang, J. S. R., & Sun, C. T. (1995, March). Neuro Fuzzy-Modeling and Control. *Proceedings of the IEEE, 85*(3), 378–406. doi:10.1109/5.364486

Jang, R. J. (1993). ANFIS: Adaptive – Network Based Fuzzy Inference System. *IEEE Transactions on Systems, Man, and Cybernetics, 23*(3), 665–685. doi:10.1109/21.256541

Janson, S., Merkle, D., & Middendorf, M. (2008). Molecular docking with multi-objective Particle Swarm Optimization. *Applied Soft Computing, 8*(1), 666–675. doi:10.1016/j.asoc.2007.05.005

Japkowicz, N., & Stephen, S. (2002). The class imbalance problem: A systematic study. *Intelligent Data Analysis, 6*(5), 429–450.

Jeng, S.-H., Liao, H. Y. M., Han, C. C., Chern, M. Y., & Liu, Y. T. (1998). Facial Feature Detection Using Geometrical Face Model: An Efficient Approach. *Pattern Recognition, 31*(3), 273–282. doi:10.1016/S0031-3203(97)00048-4

Jha, A. K., Narasimham, S., Krishna, S. S., & Mahadevan Pillai, V. P. (2010). *A neural network based approach for fingerprint recognition system. International Congress on Ultra Modern Telecommunications and Control Systems and Workshops (ICUMT)*, Moscow, Russia.

Jiang, K., Liao, Q., & Dai, S. (2003). *A novel white blood cell segmentation scheme using scale-space filtering and watershed clustering*. In Machine Learning and Cybernetics, 2003 International Conference on. doi:10.1109/ICMLC.2003.1260033

Jiang, L., & Zheng-quan, X. (2010). Color Image Information Hiding Based on Perceptual Color Clustering. In *Wireless Communications Networking and Mobile Computing (WiCOM), 2010 6th International Conference on*. doi:10.1109/WICOM.2010.5601277

Jiang, Perng, & Li. (2011). Natural Event Summarization. In *Proceedings of CIKM'11*. ACM.

Jiang, X. (2009). *Feature Extraction for Image Recognition and Computer Vision*. 2nd IEEE International Conference on Computer Science and Information Technology, Beijing.

Jiang, H., Li, C., Haimi-Cohen, R., Wilford, P., & Zhang, Y. (2012). Scalable video coding using compressive sensing. *Bell Labs Technical Journal, 16*(4), 149–169. doi:10.1002/bltj.20539

Jiayi, L., Hongyan, Z., & Liangpei, Z. (2014). Background joint sparse representation for hyperspectral image sub-pixel anomaly detection. In *Proceeding of 2014 IEEE International Geoscience and Remote Sensing Symposium (IGARSS)*. Quebec City, Canada: IEEE. doi:10.1109/IGARSS.2014.6946729

Jilani, S. A. K., & Sattar, S. A. (2010, June). A Fuzzy Neural Networks based EZW Image Compression System. *International Journal of Computers and Applications, 2*(9).

Jin, A. L. H., Chekima, A., Dargham, J. A., & Liau, F. C. (2002). Fingerprint identification and recognition using back propagation neural network. In *Student Conference on Research and Development* (SCOReD). doi:10.1109/SCORED.2002.1033066

Jin-ping, Y., Xi-mei, H., & Xiao-yun, X. (2012). Image Data Mining Technology of Multimedia. Springer-Verlag Berlin Heidelberg.

Jin, Z., Lou, Z., Yang, J., & Sun, Q. (2007). Face Detection Using Template Matching and Skin-Color Information. ScienceDirect. *Neurocomputing, 70*(4-6), 794–800. doi:10.1016/j.neucom.2006.10.043

Jobson, D. J., Rahman, Z. U., & Woodell, G. A. (1997). A multiscale retinex for bridging the gap between color images and the human observation of scenes. *Image Processing. IEEE Transactions on, 6*(7), 965–976.

John, J., & Wilscy, M. (2008, September). Enhancement of weather degraded video sequences using wavelet fusion. In *Cybernetic Intelligent Systems, 2008. CIS 2008. 7th IEEE International Conference on* (pp. 1-6). IEEE. doi:10.1109/UKRICIS.2008.4798926

Johnson, N. F., & Jajodia, S. (1998). Exploring steganography: Seeing the unseen. *IEEE Computer Magazine, 31*(2), 26–34. doi:10.1109/MC.1998.4655281

Johnson, R. J., Williams, J. P., & Bauer, K. W. (2013). AutoGAD: An Improved ICA-Based Hyperspectral Anomaly Detection Algorithm. *IEEE Transactions on Geoscience and Remote Sensing, 51*(6), 3492–3503. doi:10.1109/TGRS.2012.2222418

Joseph, P. M., & Spital, R. D. (1982). The effects of scatter in x-ray computed tomography. *Medical Physics, 9*(4), 464–472. doi:10.1118/1.595111 PMID:7110075

Joshi, A., & Lee, C. H. (1991). On modeling the retina using neural networks. In *Proceeding of IEEE International Joint Conference on Neural Networks* (pp. 2343 – 2348). IEEE.

Jourabloo, A., Feghahati, A. H., & Jamzad, M. (2012). New algorithms for recovering highly corrupted images with impulse noise. *Scientia Iranica, 19*(6), 1738–1745. doi:10.1016/j.scient.2012.07.016

Jyothi, B., Latha, Y. M., Mohan, P. G. K., & Reddy, V. S. K. (2013). Medical Image Retrieval Using Moments. *International Journal of Application or Innovation in Engineering & Management, 2*(1), 195–200.

Kale, K. V., Deshmukh, P. D., Chavan, S. V., Kazi, M. M., & Rode, Y. S. (2014). Zernike Moment Feature Extraction for Handwritten Devanagari (Marathi) Compound Character Recognition. *International Journal of Advanced Research in Artificial Intelligence, 3*(1), 68–76.

Kalender, W. A., Hebel, R., & Ebersberger, J. (1987). Reduction of CT artifacts caused by metallic implants. *Radiology, 164*(2), 576–577. doi:10.1148/radiology.164.2.3602406 PMID:3602406

Kalker, T., Depovere, G., Haitsma, J., & Maes, M. (1999). A video watermarking system for broadcast monitoring. Proc. Security and Watermarking of Multimedia Contents. *SPIE, San Jose, 3657*, 103–112.

Kamal, A. T., Ding, C., Morye, A. A., Farrell, J. A., & Roy-Chowdhury, A. K. (2014). An overview of distributed tracking and control in camera networks. In V. K. Asari (Ed.), *Wide Area Surveillance: Augmented Vision and Reality* (pp. 207–234). Berlin, Germany: Springer. doi:10.1007/8612_2012_10

Kambale, S. A., & Inamdar, V. S. (2011). Gabor Filter for Feature Extraction: A Review.*Proc. of the International Conference on Advanced Computing and Communication Technologies (ACCT 2011).*

Kang, C. Y., Chen, Y. S., & Hsu, W. H. (1993). *Mapping a Lifelike 2.5D Human Face via an Automatic Approach.* IEEE.

Kang, M. G., & Katsaggelos, A. K. (1995). General choice of the regularization functional in regularized image restoration. *IEEE Transactions on Image Processing,* 4(5), 594–602. doi:10.1109/83.382494 PMID:18290009

Kankanhalli, M. S., & Ramakrishnan, K. R. (1998). Content based watermarking of images.*Proc. Sixth ACM international conference on Multimedia.* doi:10.1145/290747.290756

Kanungo, T., Mount, D. M., Netanyahu, N. S., Piatko, C. D., Silverman, R., & Wu, A. Y. (2002). An efficient k-means clustering algorithm: Analysis and implementation. Pattern Analysis and Machine Intelligence. *IEEE Transactions on,* 24(7), 881–892.

Kanwisher, N., McDermott, J., & Chun, M. M. (1997). The fusion form face area: A module in human extrastriate cortex specialized for face perception. *The Journal of Neuroscience,* 17(11), 4302–4311. PMID:9151747

Kao, Y. T., Zahara, E., & Kao, I. W. (2008). A hybridized approach to data clustering. *Expert Systems with Applications,* 34(3), 1754–1762. doi:10.1016/j.eswa.2007.01.028

Karaboga, D., & Ozturk, C. (2011). A novel clustering approach: Artificial Bee Colony (ABC) algorithm. *Applied Soft Computing,* 11(1), 652–657. doi:10.1016/j.asoc.2009.12.025

Kartalopoulos, S. (1996). *Understanding Neural Networks and Fuzzy Logic: Basic Concepts and Applications.* IEEE Press.

Kass, R., Tierney, L., & Kadane, J. (1988). Asymptotics in Bayesian comptation. Bayesian Statistics, 3, 261-278.

Kaur, K., & Malhotra, S. (2013). A Survey on Edge Detection Using Different Techniques. *International Journal of Application or Innovation in Engineering & Management,* 2(4), 496–500.

Kavdir, I., & Guyer, D. E. (2003). Apple Grading Using Fuzzy Logic. *Turky Journal of Agriculture, 27,* 375–382.

Kaveh, A., & Talatahari, S. (2010). A novel heuristic optimization method: Charged system search.*Acta Mechanica, 213*(3-4), 267–289. doi:10.1007/s00707-009-0270-4

Kennedy, J., & Eberhart, R. C. (1997, October). A discrete binary version of the particle swarm algorithm. In *IEEE International Conference on Computational Cybernetics and Simulation, 5,* 4104-4108. doi:10.1109/ICSMC.1997.637339

Kerin, J. (n.d.). *Contrast Enhancement.* Retrieved 1st August, 2014 from http://web.pdx.edu/~jduh/courses/Archive/geog481w07/Students/Kerin_ContrastEnhancement.pdf

Ketcham, M., & Ganokratanaa, T. (2014). The Evolutionary Computation Video Watermarking Using Quick Response Code Based on Discrete Multiwavelet Transformation. In Recent Advances in Information and Communication Technology (pp. 113-123). Springer International Publishing. doi:10.1007/978-3-319-06538-0_12

Ketcham, M., & Vongpradhip, S. (2007). Intelligent audio watermarking using genetic algorithm in DWT domain. *International Journal Of Intelligent Technology, 2*(2), 135–140.

Khalidov, I., & Unser, M. (2006). From differential equations to the construction of new wavelet-like bases. *IEEE Transactions on Signal Processing, 54*(4), 1256–1267. doi:10.1109/TSP.2006.870544

Khare, A., Kunari, M, Khare P. (2010). Efficient Algorithm For Digital Image Steganography. *Journal of Information Science, Knowledge and Research in Computer Science and Application,* 1-5.

Khashman, A., & Dimililer, K. (2008). Image Compression using Neural Networks and Haar Wavelet. *WSEAS Transactions on Signal Processing, 4*(5).

Khazai, S., Homayouni, S., Safari, A., & Mojaradi, B. (2011). Anomaly Detection in Hyperspectral Images Based on an Adaptive Support Vector Method. *IEEE Geoscience and Remote Sensing Letters, 8*(4), 646–650. doi:10.1109/LGRS.2010.2098842

Khazai, S., Safari, A., Mojaradi, B., & Homayouni, S. (2013). An Approach for Subpixel Anomaly Detection in Hyperspectral Images. *IEEE Journal of Selected Topics in Applied Earth Observations and Remote Sensing*, *6*(2), 769–778. doi:10.1109/JSTARS.2012.2210277

Khetri, G. P., Padme, S. L., Jain, D. C., & Pawar, V. P. (2012). Fingerprint Pattern Recognition Using Back Propagation Algorithms. *International Journal of Electronics and Computer Science Engineering*, *2*(1), 225–232.

Khobragade, R. N., Koli, N. A., & Makesar, M. S. (2013). A Survey on Recognition of Devnagari Script. *International Journal of Computer Applications & Information Technology*, *2*(1), 22–26.

Khojastehnazhand, M., Omid, M., & Tabatabaeefar, A. (2010). Development of a lemon sorting system based on color and size. *African Journal of Plant Science*, *4*(4), 122–127.

Khoje, S., & Bodhe, S. (2013). Comparative Performance Evaluation of Size Metrics and Classifiers in Computer Vision based Automatic Mango Grading. *International Journal of Computers and Applications*, *61*(9), 1–7. doi:10.5120/9953-4320

Khurana, S., & Komal. (2012). Content Based Medical Image Retrieval Using Shape Descriptors. *International Journal of Latest Research in Science and Technology*, *1*(2), 115–119.

Kienzle, W., Bakir, G., Franz, M., & Schölkopf, B. (2005). Face detection - efficient and rank deficient. Academic Press.

Kim, D., Jeon, C., Kang, B., & Ko, H. (2008, August). Enhancement of image degraded by fog using cost function based on human visual model. In *Multisensor Fusion and Integration for Intelligent Systems, 2008. MFI 2008. IEEE International Conference on* (pp. 64-67). IEEE. doi:10.1007/978-3-540-89859-7_12

Kim, D. H., & Finkel, L. H. (2003). Hyperspectral Image Processing Using Locally Linear Embedding. In *Proceedings of the 1st International IEEE EMBS Conference on Neural Engineering*. IEEE. doi:10.1109/CNE.2003.1196824

Kim, J. H., Kim, K. K., & Suen, C. Y. (2000). Hybrid Schemes of Homogeneous and Heterogeneous Classifiers for Cursive Word Recognition. *Proceedings of the 7th International Workshop on Frontiers in Handwritten Recognition*.

Kim, M. S. (2013). Robust, Scalable Anomaly Detection for Large Collections of Images. In *proceeding of International Conference on Social Computing (SocialCom)*. Alexandria, VA: IEEE. doi:10.1109/SocialCom.2013.170

Kim, Y. S., Kwon, O. H., & Park, R. H. (1999). Wavelet based watermarking method for digital images using the human visual system. *Electronics Letters*, *35*(6), 466–468. doi:10.1049/el:19990327

Klare, B., & Jain, A. K. (2010). On a taxonomy of facial features. In *Proc. of IEEE Conference on Biometrics: Theory, Applications and Systems*. IEEE.

Klare, B., Li, Z., & Jain, A. K. (2011). Matching forensic sketches to mugshot photos. *IEEE Transactions on Pattern Analysis and Machine Intelligence*, *33*(3), 639–646. doi:10.1109/TPAMI.2010.180 PMID:20921585

Koenderink, J. J., & Richards, W. A. (1992). Why is snow so bright? *JOSA A*, *9*(5), 643–648. doi:10.1364/JOSAA.9.000643

Koerich, A. L. (2003). *Unconstrained Handwritten Character Recognition Using Different Classification Strategies. International Workshop on Artificial Neural Networks in Pattern Recognition*.

Kogan, J., Nicholas, C., Teboulle, M., & Berkhin, P. (2006). A Survey of Clustering Data Mining Techniques. In Grouping Multidimensional Data, 25-71.

Koli, M., & Balaji, S. (2013). Literature survey on impulse noise reduction. *Signal & Image Processing: An International Journal*, *4*(5), 75–95.

Kopf, J., Neubert, B., Chen, B., Cohen, M., Cohen-Or, D., Deussen, O., & Lischinski, D. et al. (2008, December). Deep photo: Model-based photograph enhancement and viewing. *ACM Transactions on Graphics*, *27*(5), 116. doi:10.1145/1409060.1409069

Koppen, W. P., Chan, C. H., Christmas, W. J., & Kittler, J. (2012). An intrinsic coordinate system for 3D face registration. In *Proc of 21st Intl Conf on Pattern Recognition (ICPR)*.

Ko, S. J., & Lee, Y. H. (1991). Center weighted median filters and their applications to image enhancement. *IEEE Transactions on Circuits and Systems, 38*(9), 984–993. doi:10.1109/31.83870

Kosko, B. (1991). *Neural Networks and Fuzzy Systems*. Englewood Cliffs, NJ: Prentice Hall.

Kraut, S., & Scharf, L. L. (1999). The CFAR adaptive subspace detector is a scale-invariant GLRT. *IEEE Transactions on Signal Processing, 47*(9), 2538–2541. doi:10.1109/78.782198

Krishna, K., & Murty, M. N. (1999). Genetic K-means algorithm. *IEEE Transactions on Systems, Man, and Cybernetics. Part B, Cybernetics, 29*(3), 433–439. doi:10.1109/3477.764879 PMID:18252317

Krishnan, N. C., & Cook, D. J. (2014). Activity recognition on streaming sensor data. *Pervasive and Mobile Computing, 10*, 138–154. doi:10.1016/j.pmcj.2012.07.003 PMID:24729780

Król, D., & Lopes, H. S. (2012). Nature-inspired collective intelligence in theory and practice. *Information Sciences, 182*(1), 1–2. doi:10.1016/j.ins.2011.10.001

Krutsch, R., & Tenorio, D., (2011). *Histogram Equalization*. Document Number: AN4318.

Kumar, Y., & Sahoo, G. (2015). An Improved Cat Swarm Optimization Algorithm for Clustering. Computational Intelligence in Data Mining, 1, 187-197. doi:10.1007/978-81-322-2205-7_18

Kumar, M., & Dass, S. (2009, September). A total variation-based algorithm for pixel- level image fusion. *IEEE Transactions on Image Processing, 18*(9), 2137–2143. doi:10.1109/TIP.2009.2025006 PMID:19520640

Kumar, Y., & Sahoo, G. (2014). A chaotic charged system search approach for data clustering. *Informatica, 38*(3), 249–261.

Kumar, Y., & Sahoo, G. (2014). A charged system search approach for data clustering. *Progress in Artificial Intelligence, 2*(2-3), 153–166. doi:10.1007/s13748-014-0049-2

Kumar, Y., & Sahoo, G. (2014). A Hybridize Approach for Data Clustering Based on Cat Swarm Optimization. *International Journal of Information and Communication Technology*.

Kuo, C.-H., Huang, C., & Nevatia, R. (2010). Inter-camera association of multi-target tracks by on-line learned appearance affinity models. In K. Daniilidis, P. Maragos & N. Paragios (Eds.), *Computer Vision: Proceedings of European Conference on Computer Vision (LNCS) 6331*, 381-396). Berlin, Germany: Springer. doi:10.1007/978-3-642-15549-9_28

Kutter, M., Bhattacharjee, S. K., & Ebrahimi, T. (1999). Towards second generation watermarking schemes. *Proc. International Conference on Image Processing*.

Kuybeda, O., Malah, D., & Barzohar, M. (2007). Rank Estimation and Redundancy Reduction of High-Dimensional Noisy Signals With Preservation of Rare Vectors. *IEEE Transactions on Signal Processing, 55*(12), 5579–5592. doi:10.1109/TSP.2007.901645

Kwok, L., Tsang, I., & Wang. (. (2004, November). Fusing images with different focuses using support vector machines. *IEEE Transactions on Neural Networks, 15*(6), 1517–1525. doi:10.1109/TNN.2004.837781 PMID:15565778

Kwon, H., Der, S. Z., & Nasrabadi, N. M. (2003). Adaptive anomaly detection using subspace separation for hyperspectral imagery. *Optical Engineering (Redondo Beach, Calif.), 42*(11), 3342–3351. doi:10.1117/1.1614265

Kwon, H., & Gurram, P. (2010). Optimal kernel bandwidth estimation for hyperspectral kernel-based anomaly detection. In *Proceedings of 2010 IEEE International Geoscience and Remote Sensing Symposium (IGARSS)*. Honolulu, HI: IEEE. doi:10.1109/IGARSS.2010.5649775

Kwon, H., & Nasrabadi, N. M. (2005). Kernel adaptive subspace detector for hyperspectral target detection. In *Proceedings of the IEEE International Conference on Acoustics, Speech, and Signal Processing, (ICASSP '05)*. IEEE.

Lai, Y. H., Chen, Y. L., Chiou, C. J., & Hsu, C. T. (2014). *Single Image Dehazing Via Optimal Transmission Map Under Scene Priors*. Academic Press.

Lanckriet, G. R. G., Ghaoui, L. E., Bhattacharyya, C., & Jordan, M. I. (2002a). In T. G. Dietterich, S. Becker, & Z. Ghahramani (Eds.), *Minimax probability machine* (Vol. 14, pp. 801–807). Cambridge, MA: MIT Press.

Lande, P. U., Talbar, S. N., & Shinde, G. N. (2010). A Fuzzy logic approach to encrypted Watermarking for still Images in Wavelet domain on FPGA. *International Journal of Signal Processing. Image Processing and Pattern Recognition*, *3*(2), 1–9.

Langelaar, G. C., Lagendijk, R. L., & Biemond, J. (1998). Real-time labeling of MPEG-2 compressed video. *Journal of Visual Communication and Image Representation*, *9*(4), 256–270. doi:10.1006/jvci.1998.0397

Lavee, G., Rivlin, E., & Rudzsky, M. (2009). Understanding video events: A survey of methods for automatic interpretation of semantic occurrences in video. *IEEE Trans. on Systems, Man, and Cybernetics, Part C: Applications and Reviews*, *39*(5), 489–504. doi:10.1109/TSMCC.2009.2023380

Lee, H. Y., H. Kim and H.K. Lee (2006). Robust image watermarking using local invariant features. *Optical Engineering*, *45*(3), 037002:1–037002:11.

Lee, J.-H. (2012). *Fourier-Based Shape Feature Extraction Technique for Computer-Aided B-Mode Ultrasound Diagnosis of Breast Tumor*. Engineering in Medicine and Biology Society (EMBC), Annual International Conference of the IEEE, San Diego, CA.

Lee, Y. H., Han, C. W., & Kim, T. S. (2008). 3D Facial Recognition with Soft Computing. In Digital Human Modeling (LNAI), (vol. 4650, pp. 194–205). Berlin: Springer.

Lee, B. (2004). A New Method for Classification of Structural Textures. *International Journal of Control, Automation, and Systems*, *2*(1), 125–133.

Lee, D.-J., Archibald, J. K., & Xiong, G. (2011). Rapid Color Grading for Fruit Quality Evaluation Using Direct Color Mapping. *IEEE Transactions on Automation Science and Engineering*, *8*(2), 292–302. doi:10.1109/TASE.2010.2087325

Lee, K. L., & Chen, L. H. (2005). An Efficient Computation Method for the Texture Browsing Descriptor of MPEG-7. *Image and Vision Computing*, *23*(5), 479–489. doi:10.1016/j.imavis.2004.12.002

Lee, M., & Pedrycz, W. (2009). The fuzzy C-means algorithm with fuzzy P-mode prototypes for clustering objects having mixed features. *Fuzzy Sets and Systems*, *160*(24), 3590–3600. doi:10.1016/j.fss.2009.06.015

Leemans, V., Magein, H., & Destain, M. F. (2002). Online fruit grading according to their external quality using machine vision. *Biosystems Engineering*, *83*(4), 397–404. doi:10.1006/bioe.2002.0131

Lee, Y., Yeh, Y.-R., & Wang, Y.-C. (2013). Anomaly Detection via Online Oversampling Principal Component Analysis. *IEEE Transactions on Knowledge and Data Engineering*, *25*(7), 1460–1470. doi:10.1109/TKDE.2012.99

Lefkimmiatis, S., Bourquard, A., & Unser, M. (2012). Hessian-based norm regularization for image restoration with biomedical applications. *IEEE Transactions on Image Processing*, *21*(3), 983–995. doi:10.1109/TIP.2011.2168232 PMID:21937351

Lehmann, E. L. (1993). The Fisher, Neyman-Pearson theories of testing hypotheses: One theory or two? *Journal of the American Statistical Association*, *88*(424), 1242–1249. doi:10.1080/01621459.1993.10476404

Lei, B. J., Hendriks, E. A., & Reinders, M. J. T. (1999). *On Feature Extraction from Images*. Technical report on "inventory properties" for MCCWS.

Lell, M. M., Meyer, E., Kuefner, M. A., May, M. S., Raupach, R., Uder, M., & Kachelriess, M. (2012). Normalized metal artifact reduction in head and neck computed tomography. *Investigative Radiology*, *47*(7), 415–421. doi:10.1097/RLI.0b013e3182532f17 PMID:22659592

Lell, M. M., Meyer, E., Schmid, M., Raupach, R., May, M. S., Uder, M., & Kachelriess, M. (2013). Frequency split metal artefact reduction in pelvic computed tomography. *European Radiology*, *23*(8), 2137–2145. doi:10.1007/s00330-013-2809-y PMID:23519437

Leshno, M., Lin, V. Y., Pinkus, A., & Schocken, S. (1993). Multilayer Feedforward networks with a non-polynomial activation function can approximate any function. *Neural Networks*, *6*(6), 861–867. doi:10.1016/S0893-6080(05)80131-5

Leung, K., Cunha, A., Toga, A. W., & Parker, D. S. (2014). Developing Image Processing Meta-Algorithms with Data Mining of Multiple Metrics, Hindawi Publishing Corporation. *Computational and Mathematical Methods in Medicine*, *2*, 1–8. doi:10.1155/2014/383465

Leung, W. F., Leung, S. H., Lau, W. H., & Luk, A. (1991). Fingerprint recognition using neutal network. In *Proceedings of IEEE Workshop on Neural Networks for Signal Processing*. IEEE.

Levicky, D., Bugar, G., Banoci, V. (2012). A novel JPEG steganography method secure against histogram steganalysis. In *ELMAR, 2012 Proceedings*.

Li, T., Ma, S., & Ogihara, M. (2010). Wavelet Methods for Data Mining. In O. Maimon & L. Rokach (Eds.), Data Mining and Knowledge Discovery Handbook (2nd Ed.). Springer Science+Business Media, LLC. DOI doi:10.1007/978-0-387

Liang, J., He, Y., Liu, D., & Zeng, X. (2012, May). Image fusion using higher order singular value decomposition. *IEEE Transactions on Image Processing*, *21*(5), 2898–2909. doi:10.1109/TIP.2012.2183140 PMID:22249708

Liao, S., Jain, A. K., & Li, S. Z. (2014). *A Fast and Accurate Unconstrained Face Detector*. arXiv preprint arXiv:1408.1656.

Lihua, Z. (2010). A new fingerprint image recognition approach using artificial neural network. In *Proceeding of International Conference on E-Health Networking, Digital Ecosystems and Technologies* (EDT).

Likas, A., & Galatsanos, N. (2004). A variational approach for bayesian blind image deconvolution. *IEEE Transactions on Signal Processing*, *52*(8), 2222–2233. doi:10.1109/TSP.2004.831119

Li, M., & Yuan, B. (2005). 2D-LDA: A Statistical linear discriminant analysis for image matrix. *Pattern Recognition Letters*, *26*(5), 527–532. doi:10.1016/j.patrec.2004.09.007

Lin, C. J., Wang, J. G., & Chen, S. M. (2011). 2D/3D Face Recognition using Neural Network based on Hybrid Taguchi-Particle Swarm Optimization. *International Journal of Innovative Computing, Information, & Control*, *7*(2).

Lin, Y. T., Huang, C. Y., & Lee, G. C. (2011). Rotation, scaling, and translation resilient watermarking for images. *IET Image Proc.*, *5*(4), 328–340. doi:10.1049/iet-ipr.2009.0264

Liposcak, Z., & Loncaric, S. (1999). A Scale-Space Approach to Face Recognition from Profiles. In *Proceedings of the 8th International Conference on Computer Analysis of Images and Patterns, Lecture Notes In Computer Science* (1689, pp. 243-250). London, UK: Springer-Verlag.

Li, S., Kang, X., Hu, J., & Yang, B. (2013). Image matting for fusion of multi-focus images in dynamic scenes. *Information Fusion*, *14*(2), 147–162. doi:10.1016/j.inffus.2011.07.001

Li, T., Li, Q., Zhu, S., & Ogihara, M. (2002). A Survey on Wavelet Applications in Data Mining. *SIGKDD Explorations*, *4*(2), 9–68. doi:10.1145/772862.772870

Liu, P., Xu, J., Liu, J., & Tang, X. (2009). Pixel based temporal analysis using chromatic property for removing rain from videos. *Computer and Information Science*, *2*(1), P53.

Liu, D., Guojing, H., & Zhang, J. (2008). Texture segmentation based anomaly detection in remote sensing images. *33rd International Conference on Infrared, Millimeter and Terahertz Waves, IRMMW-THz 2008*. Pasadena, CA: IEEE.

Liu, J. J., Watt-Smith, S. R., & Smith, S. M. (2003). *CT Reconstruction Using FBP with Sinusoidal Amendment for Metal Artefact Reduction* (pp. 439–448). DICTA.

Liu, N., Amin, P., & Subbalakshmi, K. P. (2007). Security and Robustness Enhancement for Image Data Hiding. *Multimedia, IEEE Transactions on*, *9*(3), 466–474. doi:10.1109/TMM.2006.888005

Liu, P., Wang, Y., Huang, D., Zhang, Z., & Chen, L. (2013). Learning the Spherical Harmonic Features for 3-D Face Recognition. *IEEE Transactions on Image Processing*, *22*(3), 914–925. doi:10.1109/TIP.2012.2222897 PMID:23060332

Liu, R., Lu, Y., Gong, C., & Liu, Y. (2012). Infrared Point Target Detection with Improved Template Matching. *Infrared Physics & Technology*, *55*(4), 380–387. doi:10.1016/j.infrared.2012.01.006

Liu, W., & Chang, Ch.-I. (2004). A nested spatial window-based approach to target detection for hyperspectral imagery. In *Proceedings of IEEE International Geoscience and Remote Sensing Symposium, IGARSS '04*. IEEE.

Liu, W.-M., & Chang, Ch.-I. (2013). Multiple-Window Anomaly Detection for Hyperspectral Imagery. *Selected Topics in IEEE Journal of Applied Earth Observations and Remote Sensing*, *6*(2), 644–658. doi:10.1109/JSTARS.2013.2239959

Liu, Y., Zhang, J., Tjondronegoro, D., & Geve, S. (2007). A Shape Ontology Framework for Bird Classification. In *Proceedings of the Ninth Conference on Digital Image Computing Techniques and Applications*. doi:10.1109/DICTA.2007.4426835

Liu, Z., Blasch, E., Xue, Z., Zhao, J., Laganiere, R., & Wu, W. (2012, January). Objective assessment of multiresolution image fusion algorithms for context enhancement in night vision: A comparative study. *IEEE Transactions on Pattern Analysis and Machine Intelligence*, *34*(1), 94–109. doi:10.1109/TPAMI.2011.109 PMID:21576753

Liu, Z., Gu, Y., & Zhang, Y. (2010). Comparative Analysis of Feature Extraction Algorithms with Different Rules for Hyperspectral Anomaly Detection. In *Proceedings of 2010 First International Conference on Pervasive Computing Signal Processing and Applications (PCSPA)*. Harbin: IEEE. doi:10.1109/PCSPA.2010.78

Li, W., Prasad, S., & Fowler, J. E. (2013). Integration of Spectral–Spatial Information for Hyperspectral Image Reconstruction From Compressive Random Projections. *IEEE Geoscience and Remote Sensing Letters*, *10*(6), 1379–1383. doi:10.1109/LGRS.2013.2242043

Li, X., & Wang, J. (2007). A steganographic method based upon JPEG and particle swarm optimization algorithm. *Information Sciences*, *177*(15), 3099–3109. doi:10.1016/j.ins.2007.02.008

Li, X., & Zhu, W. (2011). Apple grading method based on features fusion of size, shape and color. *Procedia Engineering*, *15*, 2885–2891. doi:10.1016/j.proeng.2011.08.543

Lobo, M., Vanderberghe, L., Boyd, S., & Lebret, H. (1998). Applications of Second order cone programming. *Linear Algebra and Its Application*, *284*, 193-228.

Lodhe, D., Nalawade, S., Pawar, G., Atkari, V., & Wandka, S. (2013). Grader: A review o different methods of grading for fruits and vegetables. *Agric Eng Int: CIGR Journal*, *15*(3), 217–230.

Looney, D., & Mandic, D. P. (2009, April). Multiscale image fusion using complex extensions of EMD. *IEEE Transactions on Signal Processing*, *57*(4), 1626–1630. doi:10.1109/TSP.2008.2011836

Lorenzo, J., Teli, M. N., Marcel, S., & Atanasoaei, C. (2011) Face and eye detection on hard datasets. In *Proceeding of Int. Joint Conference on Biometrics*. IEEE.

Lowe, D. G. (2004). Distinctive image features from scale-invariant keypoints. *International Journal of Computer Vision*, *60*(2), 91–110. doi:10.1023/B:VISI.0000029664.99615.94

Lu, W. L., & Little, J. J. (2006). Simultaneous Tracking and Action Recognition Using the PCA-HOG Descriptor. *Proceedings of the 3rd Canadian Conference on Computer and Robot Vision*.

Lu, X., & Jain, A. K. (2005). *Multimodal Facial Feature Extraction for Automatic 3D Face Recognition*. Tech. Rep. MSU-CSE-05-22.

Lu, X., Jain, A. K., & Colbry, D. (2006). Matching 2.5D face scans to 3D models. *IEEE Transactions on Pattern Analysis and Machine Intelligence*, *28*(1), 31–43. doi:10.1109/TPAMI.2006.15 PMID:16402617

Lu, Y. Z., Zhou, J. L., & Yu, S. S. (2003). A survey of face detection, extraction and recognition. *Computing and Informatics*, *22*(2), 163–195.

Lymberopoulos, D., Teixeira, T., & Savvides, A. (2008). Macroscopic human behavior interpretation using distributed imager and other sensors. *Proceedings of the IEEE*, *96*(10), 1657–1677. doi:10.1109/JPROC.2008.928761

Lysaker, M., & Tai, X.-C. (2006). Iterative image restoration combining total variation minimization and a second-order functional. *International Journal of Computer Vision*, *66*(1), 5–18. doi:10.1007/s11263-005-3219-7

MacQueen, J. (1967, June). Some methods for classification and analysis of multivariate observations. In *Proceedings of the fifth Berkeley symposium on mathematical statistics and probability.*

Mahalakshmi, T., Muthaiah, R., & Swaminathan, P. (2012). Review Article: An Overview of Template Matching Technique in Image Processing. Research Journal of Applied Sciences. *Engineering and Technology, 4*(24), 5469–5473.

Mahbub, U., Imtiaz, H., Roy, T., Rahman, S., & Ahad, A. R. (2013). Template Matching Approach of One-Shot-Learning Gesture Recognition. *Pattern Recognition Letters, 34*(15), 1780–1788. doi:10.1016/j.patrec.2012.09.014

Mahoor, M. H., & Mottaleb, M. A. (2009). Face recognition based on 3D ridge images obtained from range data. *Pattern Recognition, 42*(3), 445–451. doi:10.1016/j.patcog.2008.08.012

Maity, S. P., & Maity, S. (2009). Multistage spread spectrum watermark detection technique using fuzzy logic. *Signal Processing Letters, IEEE, 16*(4), 245–248. doi:10.1109/LSP.2009.2014097

Maji, S., & Malik, J. (2009). Object Detection Using a Max-Margin Hough Transform. *Proceedings of IEEE Conference on Computer Vision and Pattern Recognition.* doi:10.1109/CVPR.2009.5206693

Ma, L., Crawford, M. M., & Tian, J. (2010). Anomaly detection for hyperspectral images using local tangent space alignment. In *Proceedings of 2010 IEEE International Geoscience and Remote Sensing Symposium (IGARSS).* Honolulu, HI: IEEE. doi:10.1109/IGARSS.2010.5652183

Malik, M., & Goel, V. (2012). *Vision in Bad Weather using IR Cameras- Challenges & Opportunities, Advance Signal processing and Integrated circuits.* IJERA.

Maltoni, D., Maio, D., Jain, A. K., & Prabhakar, S. (2009). *Handbook of Fingerprint Recognition* (2nd ed.). Berlin: Springer Professional Computing. doi:10.1007/978-1-84882-254-2

Mamdani, E. H., & Assilian, S. (1975). An experiment in linguistic synthesis with a fuzzy logic controller. *International Journal of Man - Machine Study, 7*(1), 1 -13.

Manjunath, B. S., Ohm, J., Vasudevan, V. V., & Yamada, A. (2001). Color and Texture Descriptors. *IEEE Transactions on Circuits and Systems for Video Technology, 11*(6), 703–715. doi:10.1109/76.927424

Manjunath, B. S., Salembier, P., & Sikora, T. (2002). *Introduction to MPEG-7: Multi- media Content Description Language.* John Wiley & Sons Ltd.

Mao, J., & Jain, A. K. (1992). Texture Classification and Segmentation using Multiresolution Simultaneous Autoregressive Models. *Pattern Recognition, 25*(2), 173–188. doi:10.1016/0031-3203(92)90099-5

Markovsky, I., Sima, D., & Van Huffel, S. (2010). Total least squares methods. *WIREs Computational Statistics, 2*(2), 212–217. doi:10.1002/wics.65

Marshall, A. W., & Olkin, I. (1960). Multivarible Chebyshev inequalities. *Annals of Mathematical Statistics, 31*(4), 1001–1014. doi:10.1214/aoms/1177705673

Martinez, A. L. P. (1999). Identification of individuals using fingerprints by linguistic descriptions fuzzy comparison. In *Proceedings of IEEE 33rd Annual International Carnahan Conference on Security Technology.* doi:10.1109/CCST.1999.797917

Mason, B. J. (1975). *Clouds, rain, and rainmaking.* Cambridge University Press.

Mateos, J., Molina, R., & Katsaggelos, A. (2005). Approximations of posterior distributions in blind deconvolution using variational methods. *Proceedings of the IEEE International Conference on Image Processing (ICIP 2005), 2,* 770-773. doi:10.1109/ICIP.2005.1530169

Materka, A., & Strzelecki, M. (1998). Texture Analysis Methods—A Review. Institute of Electronics, Technical University of Lodz.

Matteoli, S., Diani, M., & Corsini, G. (2014). Impact of Signal Contamination on the Adaptive Detection Performance of Local Hyperspectral Anomalies. *IEEE Transactions on Geoscience and Remote Sensing, 52*(4), 1948–1968. doi:10.1109/TGRS.2013.2256915

Matteoli, S., Veracini, T., Diani, M., & Corsini, G. (2013). A Locally Adaptive Background Density Estimator: An Evolution for RX-Based Anomaly Detectors. *IEEE Geoscience and Remote Sensing Letters, 11*(1), 323–327. doi:10.1109/LGRS.2013.2257670

Maulik, U., & Bandyopadhyay, S. (2000). Genetic algorithm-based clustering technique. *Pattern Recognition, 33*(9), 1455–1465. doi:10.1016/S0031-3203(99)00137-5

Mehtre, B. M. (1993). Fingerprint image analysis for automatic identification. *Machine Vision and Applications, 6*(2), 124–139. doi:10.1007/BF01211936

Melin, P., Bravo, D., & Castillo, O. (2005). Fingerprint recognition using modular neural networks and fuzzy integrals for response integration. In *Proceeding of IEEE International Joint Conference Neural Networks* (IJCNN'05) (pp. 2589-2594). doi:10.1109/IJCNN.2005.1556311

Messinger, D. W., & Albano, J. (2011). A graph theoretic approach to anomaly detection in hyperspectral imagery. In *Proceedings of 3rd Workshop on Hyperspectral Image and Signal Processing: Evolution in Remote Sensing (WHISPERS)*. Lisbon: IEEE. doi:10.1109/WHISPERS.2011.6080899

Meunkaewjinda, A., Kumsawat, P., Attakitmongcol, K., & Srikaew, A. (2008). Image Classification Based On Fuzzy Logic. *The International Archives of the Photogrammetry. Remote Sensing and Spatial Information Sciences, 34*(30), 1–5.

Meyer, E., Raupach, R., Lell, M., Schmidt, B., & Kachelrieß, M. (2010). Normalized metal artifact reduction (NMAR) in computed tomography. *Medical Physics, 37*(10), 5482–5493. doi:10.1118/1.3484090 PMID:21089784

Meyer, E., Raupach, R., Schmidt, B., Mahnken, A. H., & Kachelrieß, M. (2011, October). Adaptive normalized metal artifact reduction (ANMAR) in computed tomography. In *Nuclear Science Symposium and Medical Imaging Conference (NSS/MIC)*. IEEE. doi:10.1109/NSSMIC.2011.6152691

Meyers, E., & Wolf, L. (2008). Using biologically inspired features for face processing. *International Journal of Computer Vision, 76*(1), 93–104. doi:10.1007/s11263-007-0058-8

Middletoneton, W. E. (1952). *Vision through the Atmosphere*. Toronto, Canada: Univ. Toronto Press.

Mika, S., Ratsch, G., Wetson, J., Scholkof, B., & Muller, K.-R. (1999). Fisher discriminant analysis with kernels. Neural Networks for Signal Processing, 9, 41-48. doi:10.1109/NNSP.1999.788121

Mishra & Silakari. (2012). Image Mining in the Context of Content-Based Image Retrieval: A Perspective. *International Journal of Computer Science Issues, 9*(3), 69-76,

Mishra, A., & Goel, A. (2015). A Novel HVS Based Gray Scale Image Watermarking Scheme Using Fast Fuzzy-ELM Hybrid Architecture. In *Proceedings of ELM-2014*. Springer International Publishing. doi:10.1007/978-3-319-14066-7_15

Mistry, Y., & Ingole, D. T. (2013). Survey on Content Based Image Retrieval Systems. *International Journal of Innovative Research in Computer and Communication Engineering, 1*(8), 1827–1836.

Mitra, S., & Hayashi, Y. (2000). Neuro – Fuzzy Rule Generation: Survey in Soft Computing Framework. *IEEE Transactions on Neural Networks, 2*(3), 748–768. doi:10.1109/72.846746 PMID:18249802

Mohammadzade, H., & Hatzinakos, D. (2013). Iterative Closest Normal Point for 3D Face Recognition. *IEEE Transactions on Pattern Analysis and Machine Intelligence, 35*(2), 381–397. doi:10.1109/TPAMI.2012.107 PMID:22585097

Mohana, S. H., & Prabhakar, C. J. (2014). A novel technique for grading of dates using shape and texture features. *Machine Learning and Applications: An International Journal, 1*(2), 15–29. doi:10.5121/mlaij.2014.1202

Mohapatra, S. (2012). *Lymphocyte Image Segmentation Using Functional Link Neural Architecture for Acute Leukemia Detection*. The Korean Society of Medical & Biological Engineering and Springer.

Moisan, L. (2007) How to discretize the total variation of an image? *PAMM · Proc. Appl. Math. Mech. 7*. DOI 10.1002/pamm.200700424

Molero, J. M., Garzon, E. M., Garcia, I., & Plaza, A. (2013). Analysis and Optimizations of Global and Local Versions of the RX Algorithm for Anomaly Detection in Hyperspectral Data. *Selected Topics in IEEE Journal of Applied Earth Observations and Remote Sensing, 6*(2), 801–814. doi:10.1109/JSTARS.2013.2238609

Molina, R., Vega, M., & Katsaggelos, A. K. (2007). From global to local Bayesian parameter estimation in image restoration using variational distribution approximations. *2007 IEEE International Conference on Image Processing* (Vol. 1). doi:10.1109/ICIP.2007.4378906

Money, J. H. (2006). *Variational methods for image deblurring and discretized Picard's method*. University of Kentucky Doctoral Dissertations. Paper 381. Retrieved from http://uknowledge.uky.edu/gradschool_diss/381

Montesanto, A., Baldassarri, P., Vallesi, G., & Tascini, G. (2007). Fingerprints Recognition Using Minutiae Extraction: a Fuzzy Approach. In *Proceeding of 14th International Conference on Image Analysis and Processing* (ICIAP). doi:10.1109/ICIAP.2007.4362784

Moon, S. G., Hong, S. H., Choi, J. Y., Jun, W. S., Kang, H. G., Kim, H. S., & Kang, H. S. (2008). Metal artifact reduction by the alteration of technical factors in multidetector computed tomography: A 3-dimensional quantitative assessment. *Journal of Computer Assisted Tomography*, *32*(4), 630–633. doi:10.1097/RCT.0b013e3181568b27 PMID:18664853

Morin, R. L., & Raeside, D. E. (1981). A pattern recognition method for the removal of streaking artifact in computed tomography. *Radiology*, *141*(1), 229–233. doi:10.1148/radiology.141.1.7291530 PMID:7291530

Mosabbeb, E. A., Raahemifar, K., & Fathy, M. (2013). Multi-view human activity recognition in distributed camera sensor networks. *Sensors (Basel, Switzerland)*, *13*(7), 8750–8770. doi:10.3390/s130708750 PMID:23881136

Moudani, W., & Sayed, A. R. (2011). Efficient Image Classification using Data Mining. *International Journal of Combinatorial Optimization Problems and Informatics, 2*(1), 27-44.

Mumcuoglu, E. Ü., Leahy, R. M., & Cherry, S. R. (1996). Bayesian reconstruction of PET images: Methodology and performance analysis. *Physics in Medicine and Biology*, *41*(9), 1777–1807. doi:10.1088/0031-9155/41/9/015 PMID:8884912

Mumtaz, , & Syed, , Hameed, & Jameel. (2008). Enhancing Performance of Image Retrieval Systems Using Dual Tree Complex Wavelet Transform and Support Vector Machines. *Journal of Computing and Information Technology*, *16*(1), 57–68.

Munishwar, V. P., & Abu-Ghazaleh, N. B. (2010). Scalable target coverage in smart camera networks. In *Proceedings of the Fourth ACM/IEEE International Conference on Distributed Smart Cameras* (pp. 206-213). ACM Press. doi:10.1145/1865987.1866020

Murthy, C. A., & Chowdhury, N. (1996). In search of optimal clusters using genetic algorithms. *Pattern Recognition Letters*, *17*(8), 825–832. doi:10.1016/0167-8655(96)00043-8

Murukesh, C., & Thanushkodi, K. (2013). An Efficient Gait Recognition System Based on PCA and Multi-Layer Perceptron. *Life Science Journal*, *10*(7), 1024–1029.

Mutelo, R. M., Khor, L. C., Woo, W. L., & Dlay, S. S. (2006). *A novel fisher discriminant for biometrics recognition: 2DPCA plus 2DFLD.IEEE International Symposium on Circuits and System*. doi:10.1109/IS-CAS.2006.1693586

Nabatchian, A., Abdel-Raheem, E., & Ahmadi, M. (2008). Human Face Recognition Using Different Moment Invariants: A Comparative Study. Congress on Image and Signal Processing, Sanya.

Naganur, H. G., Sannakki, S. S., Rajpurohit, V. S., & Arunkumar, R. (2012). Fruits Sorting and Grading using Fuzzy Logic. *International Journal of Advanced Research in Computer Engineering & Technology*, *1*(6), 117–122.

Nagel, H. H., & Enkelmann, W. (1986). An investigation of smoothness constraints for the estimation of displacement vector fields from image sequences. *IEEE Transactions on Pattern Analysis and Machine Intelligence*, *8*(5), 565–593. doi:10.1109/TPAMI.1986.4767833 PMID:21869357

Naheed, T., Usman, I., Khan, T. M., Dar, A. H., & Shafique, M. F. (2014). Intelligent reversible watermarking technique in medical images using GA and PSO. *Optik-International Journal for Light and Electron Optics*, *125*(11), 2515–2525. doi:10.1016/j.ijleo.2013.10.124

Nair, M. S., & Shankar, V. (2013). Predictive-based adaptive switching median filter for impulse noise removal using neural network-based noise detector. *Signal. Image and Video Processing*, *7*(6), 1041–1070. doi:10.1007/s11760-012-0310-8

Nakajima, C., Pontil, M., Heisele, B., & Poggio, T. (2000). *People Recognition in Image Sequence by Supervised Learning*. In A.I. Memo No. 1688, C.B.C.L Paper No. 188.

Nandi, C. S., Tudu, B., & Koley, C. (2012). An Automated Machine vision based system for fruit sorting and grading. In *Proceedings of Sixth International conference on sensing technology (ICST)*. Kolkata: IEEE.

Nandi, C. S., Tudu, B., & Koley, C. (2014). Computer vision based mango fruit grading system. In *Proceedings of International Conference on Innovative Engineering Technologies (ICIET)*.

Nandy, M., & Banerjee, M. (2012). Retinal vessel segmentation using Gabor filter and artificial neural network. In *Proceedings of Third International Conference on Emerging Application of Information Technology* (EAIT). doi:10.1109/EAIT.2012.6407885

Narasimhan, S. G., & Nayar, S. K. (2002). Vision and the atmosphere. *International Journal of Computer Vision*, *48*(3), 233–254. doi:10.1023/A:1016328200723

Narasimhan, S. G., & Nayar, S. K. (2003). Contrast restoration of weather degraded images. *Pattern Analysis and Machine Intelligence. IEEE Transactions on*, *25*(6), 713–724.

Narasimhan, S. G., & Nayar, S. K. (2003, October). Interactive (de) weathering of an image using physical models. In *IEEE Workshop on Color and Photometric Methods in Computer Vision 6*. IEEE.

Nauck, D., Klawonn, F., & Kruse, R. (1997). *Foundations of Neuro Fuzzy Systems*. Chichester, UK: Wiley.

Nayak, M., & Panigrahi, B. S. (2011). Advanced Signal Processing Techniques for Feature Extraction in Data Mining. *International Journal of Computers and Applications*, *19*(9), 30–37. doi:10.5120/2387-3160

Nayar, S. K., & Narasimhan, S. G. (1999). Vision in bad weather. In *Computer Vision, 1999. The Proceedings of the Seventh IEEE International Conference on*. IEEE. doi:10.1109/ICCV.1999.790306

ND2006 3D face database. (n.d.). Retrieved 22nd July, 2014, from http://www3.nd.edu/~cvrl/CVRL/Data_Sets.html

Neeta, D., Snehal, K., & Jacobs, D. (2006). Implementation of LSB steganography and its evaluation for various bits. In *Proceedings of 1st International Conference on Digital Information Management*.

Nesterov, Y., & Nemirovsky, A. (1994). *Interior point polynomial methods in convex programming: Theory and Applications*. Philadelphia, PA: SIAM. doi:10.1137/1.9781611970791

Ng, P. E., & Ma, K. K. (2006). A switching median filter with boundary discriminative noise detection for extremely corrupted images. *IEEE Transactions on Image Processing*, *15*(6), 1506–1516. doi:10.1109/TIP.2005.871129 PMID:16764275

Niknam, T., & Amiri, B. (2010). An efficient hybrid approach based on PSO, ACO and k-means for cluster analysis. *Applied Soft Computing*, *10*(1), 183–197. doi:10.1016/j.asoc.2009.07.001

Niknam, T., Amiri, B., Olamaei, J., & Arefi, A. (2009). An efficient hybrid evolutionary optimization algorithm based on PSO and SA for clustering. *Journal of Zhejiang University Science A*, *10*(4), 512–519. doi:10.1631/jzus.A0820196

Nixon, M. S., & Aguado, A. S. (2013). *Feature Extraction & Image Processing for Computer Vision* (3rd ed.). Elsevier Ltd.

Njoroge, J. B., Ninomiya, K., Kondo, N., & Toita, H. (2002). *Automated Fruit Grading System using Image Processing. In The Society of Instrument and Control Engineers (SICE2002)*. Osaka, Japan: IEEE.

Nuyts, J., De Man, B., Dupont, P., Defrise, M., Suetens, P., & Mortelmans, L. (1998). Iterative reconstruction for helical CT: A simulation study. *Physics in Medicine and Biology*, *43*(4), 729–737. doi:10.1088/0031-9155/43/4/003 PMID:9572499

Oakley, J. P., & Bu, H. (2007). Correction of simple contrast loss in color images. *Image Processing. IEEE Transactions on*, *16*(2), 511–522.

Oakley, J. P., & Satherley, B. L. (1998). Improving image quality in poor visibility conditions using a physical model for contrast degradation. *Image Processing. IEEE Transactions on*, *7*(2), 167–179.

Ohashi, G., & Shimodaira, Y. (2003). *Edge-based feature extraction method and its application to image retrieval. In Proceedings of 7th World Multi-conference on Systemics*. Cybernetics and Informatics.

Ohtake, T. (1970). Factors affecting the size distribution of raindrops and snowflakes. *Journal of the Atmospheric Sciences*, *27*(5), 804–813. doi:10.1175/1520-0469(1970)027<0804:FATSDO>2.0.CO;2

Okada, R. (2009). *Discriminative Generalized Hough Transform for Object Detection.12th International Conference on Computer Vision.*

Oliveira, L. S., Bortolozzi, F., & Suen, C. Y. (2002). Automatic Recognition of Handwritten Numerical Strings: A Recognition and Verification Strategy. *IEEE Transactions on Pattern Recognition and Machine Intelligence*, *24*(11), 1438–1454. doi:10.1109/TPAMI.2002.1046154

Ongun, G., Halici, U., Leblebiicioglu, K., Atalay, V., Beksac, M., & Beksak, S. (2001). *An automated differential blood count system.* In *International Conference of the IEEE Engineering in Medicine and Biology Society.*

OReilly, C., Gluhak, A., Imran, M. A., & Rajasegarar, S.OReilly. (2014). Anomaly Detection in Wireless Sensor Networks in a Non-Stationary Environment. *IEEE Communications Surveys and Tutorials*, *16*(3), 1413–1432. doi:10.1109/SURV.2013.112813.00168

Ortega, M., Marina, C., Penedo, M. G., Blanco, M., & Gonzalez, F. (April, 2006). Biometric Authentication using Digital Retinal Images. In *Proceedings of the 5th WSEAS International Conference on Applied Computer Science* (ACOS 06).

Osaimi, F., Al, F., Bennamoun, M., & Mian, A. (2009). An expression deformation approach to non-rigid 3D faces recognition. *International Journal of Computer Vision*, *81*(3), 302–316. doi:10.1007/s11263-008-0174-0

Otsu, N. (1979). A Threshold Selection Method from Gray-Level Histograms. *IEEE Trans. SMC*, *9*(1), 62–66.

Pajares & de la Cruz, J.M. (2004). A wavelet-based image fusion tutorial.*Proceeding in IEEE Conference in Pattern Recognition*, *37*(9), 1855-1872.

Pal, N. R., & Bezdek, J. C. (1995). On cluster validity for the fuzzy c-means model. *IEEE Transactions on Fuzzy Systems*, *3*(3), 370–379. doi:10.1109/91.413225

Pappas, T. N. (1992). An adaptive clustering algorithm for image segmentation. *IEEE Transactions on Signal Processing*, *40*(4), 901–914. doi:10.1109/78.127962

Park, K.-W., Jeong, J.-W., & Lee, D.-H. (2007). Olybia: Ontology-based automatic image annotation system using semantic inference rules. *Proceedings of the 12th International Conference on Database Systems for Advanced Applications*. Bangkok, Thailand: Springer.

Park, U., & Jain, A. K. (2007). 3D model-based face recognition in video. In Advances in Biometrics (pp. 1085-1094). Springer Berlin Heidelberg.

Park, W. J., & Lee, K. H. (2008, April). Rain removal using Kalman filter in video. In *Smart Manufacturing Application, 2008. ICSMA 2008. International Conference on* (pp. 494-497). IEEE. doi:10.1109/ICSMA.2008.4505573

Parris, J., Wilber, M., Helfin, B., Rara, H., Barkouky Aly Farag, A. E., Movellan, J. M., … Kanade, T. (1972). Computer analysis and classification of photographs of human faces. In *Proc. First USA-JAPAN Computer Conference.*

Pass, G., & Zabith, R. (1996). Histogram Refinement for Content Based Image Retrieval.*Proceedings 3rd IEEE Workshop on Applications of Computer Vision.* doi:10.1109/ACV.1996.572008

Patwardhan, K. A., & Sapiro, G. (2003, September). Projection based image and video inpainting using wavelets. In *Image Processing, 2003. ICIP 2003. Proceedings. 2003 International Conference on.* IEEE. doi:10.1109/ICIP.2003.1247098

Paulraj, M. P., Hema, C. R., Krishnan, R. P., & Sofiah, S. (2009). Color Recognition Algorithm using a Neural Network Model in Determining the Ripeness of a Banana. In *Proceedings of the International Conference on Man-Machine Systems* (ICoMMS).

Pawlak, Z., & Skowron, A. (2007). Rudiments of rough sets. *Information Sciences*, *177*(1), 3–2. doi:10.1016/j.ins.2006.06.003

Paz, A., & Plaza, A. (2010). Cluster versus GPU implementation of an Orthogonal Target Detection Algorithm for Remotely Sensed Hyperspectral Images. In *Proceedings of the IEEE International Conference on Cluster Computing (CLUSTER).* Heraklion, Crete: IEEE. doi:10.1109/CLUSTER.2010.28

Peli, E. (1990). Contrast in complex images. *Journal of the Optical Society of America. A, Optics and Image Science*, *7*(10), 2032. doi:10.1364/JOSAA.7.002032 PMID:2231113

Perez-Cruz, F., Alarcon-Diana, P. L., Navia-Vazquez, A., & Artes-Rodriguez, A. (2001). In T. K. Leen, T. G. Dietterich, & V. Tresp (Eds.), *Fast training of support vector classifiers* (Vol. 13, pp. 734–740). MIT Press.

Perlin, K. (1985). An image synthesizer. *Computer Graphics*, *19*(3), 287–296. doi:10.1145/325165.325247

Petrovic´, V. (2007, April). Subjective tests for image fusion evaluation and objective metric validation. *Information Fusion*, *8*(2), 208–216. doi:10.1016/j.inffus.2005.05.001

Petrovic, N. I., & Crnojevic, V. (2008). Universal impulse noise filter based on genetic programming. *IEEE Transactions on Image Processing*, *17*(7), 1109–1120. doi:10.1109/TIP.2008.924388 PMID:18586619

Phillips, P., Scruggs, W., OToole, A., Flynn, P., Bowyer, K., Schott, C., & Sharpe, M. (2007). *FRVT 2006 and ICE 2006 large-scale results*. NIST Technical Report NISTIR, 7408.

Phillips, P., Flynn, P., Scruggs, P., Bowyer, K., & Worek, W. (2006). Preliminary face recognition grand challenge results. In *Proceedings of International Conference on Automatic Face and Gesture Recognition*. doi:10.1109/FGR.2006.87

Phuong-T, P. N., & Quang-L, H. (2010). *Robust Face Detection under Challenges of Rotation*. Pose and Occlusion.

Piella, G. (2009, June). Image fusion for enhanced visualization: A variational approach. *International Journal of Computer Vision*, *83*(1), 1–11. doi:10.1007/s11263-009-0206-4

Pillai, K. A. S., Riji, R., Nair, M. S., & Wilscy, M. (2012). Fuzzy based directional weighted median filter for impulse noise detection and reduction. *Fuzzy Information and Engineering*, *4*(4), 351–369. doi:10.1007/s12543-012-0120-2

Pizer, S. M., Amburn, E. P., Austin, J. D., Cromartie, R., Geselowitz, A., Greer, T., & Zuiderveld, K. et al. (1987). Adaptive histogram equalization and its variations. *Computer Vision Graphics and Image Processing*, *39*(3), 355–368. doi:10.1016/S0734-189X(87)80186-X

Podilchuk, C. I., & Zeng, W. (1998). Image-adaptive watermarking using visual models. *IEEE Journal on Selected Areas in Communications*, *16*(4), 525–539. doi:10.1109/49.668975

Pok, G., & Liu, J. C. (1999). Decision-based median filter improved by predictions. In *Proceedings of 1999 International Conference on Image Processing*. IEEE.

Polomo, E. J., & Dominguez, E. (Aug.2011). Image Compression based on growing Hierarchial Self-Organizing Maps. In *Proceedings of International Joint Conference on Neural Networks*.

Popescu, I., & Berstimas, D. (2001). *Optimal inequalities in probability theory. A convex optimization approach*. Technical Report TM62, INSEAD.

Popoola, K., & Wang, O. P. (2012). Video-based abnormal human behavior recognition-a review. *IEEE Trans. Systems, Man, and Cybernetics. Part C*, *42*(6), 865–878.

Prabhu, J., & Kumar, J. S. (2014). Wavelet Based Content Based Image Retrieval Using Color and Texture Feature Extraction by Gray Level Coocurence Matrix and Color Coocurence Matrix. *Journal of Computer Science*, *10*(1), 15–22. doi:10.3844/jcssp.2014.15.22

PRISM-ASU 3D facial shape. (n.d.). Retrieved 16th July, 2014, from http://www.public.asu.edu/~mchaudha/prism.html

Qinqing, G., Guangping, Z., Dexin, C., & Ketai, H. (2011, June). Image enhancement technique based on improved PSO algorithm. In *Industrial Electronics and Applications (ICIEA), 2011 6th IEEE Conference on* (234-238). IEEE. doi:10.1109/ICIEA.2011.5975586

Queirolo, C. C., Silva, L., Bellon, O. R. P., & Segundo, M. P. (2010). 3D Face Recognition Using Simulated Annealing and the Surface Interpenetration Measure. *IEEE Transactions on Pattern Analysis and Machine Intelligence*, *32*(2), 206–219. doi:10.1109/TPAMI.2009.14 PMID:20075453

Qu, G., Zhang, D., & Yan, P. (2002, March). Information measure for performance of image fusion. *Electronics Letters*, *38*(7), 313–315. doi:10.1049/el:20020212

Rabah, K. (2004). Steganography- the Art of Hiding Data. *Information Technology of Journal*, *3*(3), 245–269. doi:10.3923/itj.2004.245.269

Radon, J. (1917). On determination of functions by their integral values along certain multiplicities. Ber. der Sachische Akademie der Wissenschaften Leipzig,(Germany), 69, 262-277.

Raheja, J. L., Manasa, M. B. L., Chaudhary, A., & Raheja, S. (2011). ABHIVYAKTI: Hand Gesture Recognition using Orientation Histogram in different light conditions. In *Proceedings of the 5th Indian International Conference on Artificial Intelligence.*

Rajashekararadhya, S. V., & Ranjan, P. V. (2008). Efficient Zone Based Feature Extraction Algorithm for Handwritten Numeral Recognition of Four Popular South Indian Scripts. *Journal of Theoretical and Applied Information Technology*, 4(12), 1171–1181.

Rajharia, J., & Gupta, P. C. (2012, August). A New and Effective Approach for Fingerprint Recognition by using Feed Forward Back Propagation Neural Network. *International Journal of Computers and Applications*, 52(10), 20–28. doi:10.5120/8239-1492

Raj, Y. B., Naveen, N. K., Arun, G. K., & Vinod, R. K. (2009). Vehicular Shape-Based Objects Classification Using Fourier Descriptor Technique. *Journal of Scientific and Industrial Research*, 68(6), 484–495.

Ramadan, R. M., & Rehab, F. (2012). 3D Face Compression and Recognition using Spherical Wavelet Parametrization. International Journal of Advanced Computer Science and Applications, 3(9).

Rao, P. B., Prasad, D. V., & Kumar, Ch. P. (2013). Feature Extraction Using Zernike Moments.[IJLTET]. *International Journal of Latest Trends in Engineering and Technology*, 2(2), 228–234.

Razak, R. B., Othman, M. B., Bakar, M. N. B. A., Ahmad, K. A. B., & Mansor, A. R. (2012). Mango Grading By Using Fuzzy Image Analysis. In *Proceedings of International Conference on Agricultural, Environment and Biological Sciences (ICAEBS'2012).*

Reddy, D., Agrawal, A., & Chellappa, R. (2009). Enforcing integrability by error correction using L1-minimization. *Proceedings of the IEEE Conference on Computer Vision and Pattern Recognition CVPR09*, (pp. 2350-2357). doi:10.1109/CVPR.2009.5206603

Reed, I. S., & Yu, X. (1990). Adaptive multiple-band CFAR detection of an optical pattern with unknown spectral distribution. *IEEE Transactions on Acoustics, Speech, and Signal Processing*, 38(10), 1760–1770. doi:10.1109/29.60107

Reghbati, H. K. (1981). *An Overview of Data Compression Techniques.* IEEE.

Ren, H., Du, Q., Wang, J., Chang, Ch.-I., Jensen, J. O., & Jensen, J. L. (2006). Automatic target recognition for hyperspectral imagery using high-order statistics. *IEEE Transactions on Aerospace and Electronic Systems, 42*(4), 1372–1385. doi:10.1109/TAES.2006.314578

Riesenhuber, M., & Poggio, T. (1999). Hierarchical models of object recognition in cortex. *Nature Neuroscience*, 2(11), 1019–1025. doi:10.1038/14819 PMID:10526343

Rinner, B., & Wolf, W. (2008). An introduction to distributed smart cameras. *Proceedings of the IEEE, 96*(10), 1565–1575. doi:10.1109/JPROC.2008.928742

Robila, S. A., & Varshney, P. K. (2002). Target detection in hyperspectral images based on independent component analysis. In *Proceedings of the 12th SPIE 4726, Automatic Target Recognition.* Orlando, FL: SPIE. doi:10.1117/12.477024

Rockinger, O. (1997). Image sequence fusion using a shift-invariant wavelet transform. *Proc.Int. Conf. Image Process., 3*, 288–291. doi:10.1109/ICIP.1997.632093

Rodriguez, P., & Wohlberg, B. (n.d.). *Numerical methods for inverse problems and adaptive decomposition (NUMIPAD).* Retrieved from http://sourceforge.net/projects/numipad/

Rokach, L. (2010). A survey of clustering algorithms. In Data mining and knowledge discovery handbook, (pp. 269-298). Springer.

Roodaki,, A., Taki, A., Setarehdan, S. K., & Navab, N. (2008). Modified Wavelet Transform Features for Characterizing Different Plaque Types in IVUS Images: A Feasibility Study. IEEE*Signal Processing*, 789–792.

Roshtkhari, M. J., & Levine, M. D. (2013). Online dominant and anomalous behavior detection in videos. In *Proceedings of IEEE Conference on Computer Vision and Pattern Recognition.* IEEE Press doi:10.1109/CVPR.2013.337

Ross, T. J. (2008). *Fuzzy logic with Engineering Applications* (2nd ed.). New Delhi: Wiley India.

Roth, V., & Steinhage, V. (1999). Nonlinear discriminant analysis using kernel functions. In Advances in neural information processing systems.

Roudenko, S. (2004). *Noise and texture detection in image processing*. LANL report: W-7405-ENG-36.

Roussos, E. (2000). *Neural Networks for landslide hazard estimation*. (Master Thesis). Kings College.

Roychowdhury, M., Sarkar, S., Laha, S., & Sarkar, S. (2015, January). Efficient Digital Watermarking Based on SVD and PSO with Multiple Scaling Factor. In *Proceedings of the 3rd International Conference on Frontiers of Intelligent Computing: Theory and Applications (FICTA) 2014*. Springer International Publishing. doi:10.1007/978-3-319-11933-5_89

Roy, S., & Parekh, R. (2011). A Secure Keyless Image Steganography Approach for Lossless RGB Images. In *Proceedings of ACM ICCCS, Rourkela*. doi:10.1145/1947940.1948059

Ruanaidh, J. O., Dowling, W. J., & Boland, F. M. (1996). Watermarking of digital images for copyright protection. *Proc. IEEE Vision, Image and Signal Processing, 143*(4), 250–256. doi:10.1049/ip-vis:19960711

Rudin, L. I., & Osher, S. (1994). Total variation based image restoration with free local constraints. *Proc. IEEE Int. Conf. Image Processing, 1*, 31–35. doi:10.1109/ICIP.1994.413269

Rudin, L., Osher, S., & Fatemi, E. (1992). Nonlinear total variation based noise removal algorithms. *Physica D. Nonlinear Phenomena, 60*(1-4), 259–268. doi:10.1016/0167-2789(92)90242-F

Rui, Y., Huang, T. S., & Chang, S.-F. (1999). Image Retrieval: Current Techniques, Promising Directions, and Open Issues. *Journal of Visual Communication and Image Representation, 10*(1), 39–62. doi:10.1006/jvci.1999.0413

Ruparelia, S. (2012). *Implementation of watershed based image segmentation algorithm in FPGA*. Academic Press.

Ruspini, E. H. (1969). A new approach to clustering. *Information and Control, 15*(1), 22–32. doi:10.1016/S0019-9958(69)90591-9

Ryoo, M. S., Choi, S., Joung, J.-H., Lee, J.-Y., & Yu, W. (2013). Personal driving diary: Automated recognition of driving events from first-person videos. *Computer Vision and Image Understanding, 117*(10), 1299–1312. doi:10.1016/j.cviu.2013.01.004

Sah, N. K., Sheorey, P. R., & Upadhyama, L. W. (1994). Maximum Likelihood estimation of slope stability. *Int. J. Rock Mech. Min Sci. Geomech, 31*(1), 47–53. doi:10.1016/0148-9062(94)92314-0

Sahoo, A. J., & Kumar, Y. (2014, March). Modified Teacher Learning Based Optimization Method for Data Clustering. In Advances in Signal Processing and Intelligent Recognition Systems, 429-437. doi:10.1007/978-3-319-04960-1_38

Sahu, N. M., & Bhopal, S. H. (2012). Image Mining: a New Approach for Data Mining Based on Text Mining. *3rd International Conference on Computer and Communication Technology*.

Saikia, T., & Sarma, K. K. (2014), Multilevel-DWT based Image De-noising using Feed Forward Artificial Neural Network, in *Proceedings of 1st IEEE International Conference on Signal Processing and Integrated Networks (SPIN 2014)*. doi:10.1109/SPIN.2014.6777062

Sakellariou, M. G., & Ilias, P. (1997). Application of neural networks in the estimation of slope stability. *Proceedings of Third Hellenic Geotechnical Conference, 2*, 269-276.

Sakellariou, M. G., & Ferentinou, M. D. (2005). A study of slope stability prediction using neural networks. *Geotechnical and Geological Engineering, 23*(4), 419–445. doi:10.1007/s10706-004-8680-5

Salem, O., Guerassimov, A., Mehaoua, A., Marcus, A., & Furht, B. (2013). Sensor fault and patient anomaly detection and classification in medical wireless sensor networks. In *Proceedings of the IEEE International Conference on Communications (ICC)*. Budapest: IEEE.

Samir, C., Srivastava, A., Daoudi, M., & Klassen, E. (2009). An intrinsic framework for analysis of facial surfaces. *International Journal of Computer Vision, 82*(1), 80–95. doi:10.1007/s11263-008-0187-8

Sanjay, T., Gandhe, K. T., & Keskar. (2007). Image Mining Using Wavelet Transform. *LNAI, 4692*, 797–803.

Santosa, B., & Ningrum, M. K. (2009, December). Cat swarm optimization for clustering. In *IEEE International Conference of Soft Computing and Pattern Recognition.*

Sarma, K. K., & Mitra, A. (November, 2009). ANN based Rayleigh Multipath fading channel estimation of a MIMO-OFDM system. In *Proceedings of 1st IEEE Asian Himalayas International Conference on Internet (AH-ICI) - The Next Generation of Mobile, Wireless and Optical Communications Networks.* doi:10.1109/AHICI.2009.5340306

Sarma, K. K., & Mitra, A. (2011). *Estimation of MIMO Wireless Channels using Artificial Neural Networks. In Cross-Disciplinary Applications of Artificial Intelligence and Pattern Recognition: Advancing Technologies* (pp. 509–545). IGI Global.

Sarma, K. K., & Mitra, A. (2012, April). Modeling MIMO Channels using a Class of Complex Recurrent Neural Network Architectures. *International Journal of Electronics and Communications.*, *66*(4), 322–331. doi:10.1016/j.aeue.2011.08.008

Sarma, S. K. (1975). Seismic stability of earth dams and embankments. *Geotechnique*, *25*(4), 743–761. doi:10.1680/geot.1975.25.4.743

Satapathy, S. C., & Naik, A. (2011). Data clustering based on teaching-learning-based optimization. In *Swarm* (pp. 148–156). Evolutionary, and Memetic Computing, Springer Berlin Heidelberg.

Satone, M., & Kharate, G. (2014). Feature Selection Using Genetic Algorithm for Face Recognition Based on PCA, Wavelet and SVM. *International Journal of Electrical Engineering and Informatics*, *6*(1), 39–52. doi:10.15676/ijeei.2014.6.1.3

Sayood, K. (n.d.). Data Compression. *Encyclopedia of Information Systems, 1*, 423-444.

Schechner, Y. Y., Narasimhan, S. G., & Nayar, S. K. (2001). Instant dehazing of images using polarization. In *Computer Vision and Pattern Recognition, 2001. CVPR 2001. Proceedings of the 2001 IEEE Computer Society Conference on.* IEEE. doi:10.1109/CVPR.2001.990493

Schoenemann, T., & Cremers, D. (2010). A Combinatorial Solution for Model-based Image Segmentation and Real-time Tracking. *IEEE Transactions on Pattern Analysis and Machine Intelligence*, *32*(7), 1153–1164. doi:10.1109/TPAMI.2009.79 PMID:20489221

Scholkopf, B., & Smola, A. (2002). *Learning with Kernels.* Cambridge, MA: MIT Press.

Schulte, S., Nachtegael, M., De Witte, V., Van der Weken, D., & Kerre, E. E. (2006). A fuzzy impulse noise detection and reduction method. *IEEE Transactions on Image Processing, 15*(5), 1153–1162. doi:10.1109/TIP.2005.864179 PMID:16671296

Schwamberger, V., Le, P. H., Schölkopf, B., & Franz, M. O. (2010). The influence of the image basis on modeling and steganalysis performance. In: R. Böhme, & P. Fong (Ed.), *Proc. of the 12th Intl. Conf. on Information Hiding*, (pp. 133-144). Calgary. doi:10.1007/978-3-642-16435-4_11

Schweizer, S. M., & Moura, J. M. F. (2000). Hyperspectral imagery: Clutter adaptation in anomaly detection. *IEEE Transactions on Information Theory, 46*(5), 1855–1871. doi:10.1109/18.857796

Schyndel, V., Ron, G., Andrew, Z. T., & Charles, F. O. (1994). A digital watermark. *Image Processing, 1994. Proceedings. ICIP-94., IEEE International Conference.* IEEE.

Seal, A., Bhattacharjee, D., Nasipuri, M., & Basu, D. K., (2014). Thermal Face Recognition for Biometric Security System. In *Research Developments in Biometrics and Video Processing Techniques*, (pp. 1-24). Academic Press.

Seal, A., Bhattacharjee, D., Nasipuri, M., & Basu, D. K. (2011). Minutiae from Bit-Plane Sliced Thermal Images for Human Face Recognition. In *Proceedings of the International Conference on Soft Computing for Problem Solving, Advances in Intelligent and Soft Computing.*

Seddik, A. F., Hassan, R. A., & Fakhreldein, M. A. (2013). Spectral Domain Features for Ovarian Cancer Data Analysis. *Journal of Computer Science, 9*(8), 1061–1068. doi:10.3844/jcssp.2013.1061.1068

Selim, S. Z., & Alsultan, K. (1991). A simulated annealing algorithm for the clustering problem. *Pattern Recognition*, *24*(10), 1003–1008. doi:10.1016/0031-3203(91)90097-O

Senthilkumaran, N., & Suguna, J. (2011, February). Neural Network technique for Lossless Image Compression using X-Ray Images. *International Journal of Computer and Electrical Engineering*, *3*(1), 1793–8163.

Serre, D. (2002). *Matrices: Theory and applications.* Springer-Verlag.

Sfikas, G., Nikou, C., Galatsanos, N., & Heinrich, C. (2011). Majorization-minimization mixture model determination in image segmentation. *CVPR*, *2011*, 2169–2176.

Shannon, C. (1948). A mathematical theory of communication. Bell System Technical Journal, 27, 379–423, 623–656.

Sharma, M., & Kuamri, R. (2013, June). A Technique of Image Compression based on Discrete Wavelet Image Decomposition and Self Organizing Map. *International Journal of Computational Engineering Science*, *3*(8).

Sharma, O., & Bansal, S. K. (2013). Gait Recognition System for Human Identification Using BPNN Classifier. *International Journal of Innovative Technology and Exploring Engineering*, *3*(1), 217–220.

Shelokar, P. S., Jayaraman, V. K., & Kulkarni, B. D. (2004). An ant colony approach for clustering. *Analytica Chimica Acta*, *509*(2), 187–195. doi:10.1016/j.aca.2003.12.032

Shenbagavalli, R., & Ramar, K. (2014). Feature Extraction of Soil Images for Retrieval based on Statistics. *International Journal of Computers and Applications*, *88*(14), 8–12. doi:10.5120/15418-3822

Shen, C. (2011, December). Generalized random walks for fusion of multi-exposure images. *IEEE Transactions on Image Processing*, *20*(12), 3634–3646. doi:10.1109/TIP.2011.2150235 PMID:21550887

Shrivakshan, G. T., & Chandrasekar, C. (2012). A Comparison of various Edge Detection Techniques used in Image Processing. *International Journal of Computer Science Issues*, *9*(5), 269–276.

Shyu, M.-L., Chen, S.-C., Chen, M., & Zhang, C. (2004). Affinity Relation Discovery in Image Database Clustering and Content-based Retrieval. ACM.

Sicuranzi, G. L., Ramponi, G., & Marsi, S. (1990, March). Artificial Neural Network for Image Compression. *Electronics Letters*, *26*(7), 477–479. doi:10.1049/el:19900310

Singha, M., & Hemachandran, K. (2012). Content-Based Image Retrieval using Color and Texture, Signal & Image Processing. *International Journal (Toronto, Ont.)*, *3*(1). doi:10.5121/sipij.3104

Singh, M., Singh, S. B., & Singh, L. S. S. (2007). Hiding encrypted message in the features of images. *International Journal of Computer Science and Network Security*, *7*(4), 302–307.

Singh, S. P., Bansal, S., Ahuja, M., Parnami, S., & Singh, H. (2015). Classification of apples using neural networks. In *Proceedings of International Conference on Recent Trends in Engineering Science and Management.*

Singla, G., Cook, D. J., & Schmitter-Edgecombe, M. (2010). Recognizing independent and joint activities among multiple residents in smart environments. *Journal of Ambient Intelligence and Humanized Computing*, *1*(1), 57–63. doi:10.1007/s12652-009-0007-1 PMID:20975986

Sinha, N., & Ramakrishnan, A. G. (2003). Automation of differential blood count. In *Proceedings Conference on Convergent Technologies for Asia Pacific Region.* doi:10.1109/TENCON.2003.1273221

Siogkas, G. K., & Dermatas, E. S. (2006, May). Detection, tracking and classification of road signs in adverse conditions. In *Electrotechnical Conference, 2006. MELECON 2006. IEEE Mediterranean* (pp. 537-540). IEEE. doi:10.1109/MELCON.2006.1653157

Socolinsky, & Wolff, A. (2002). Multispectral image visualization through first-order fusion. *IEEE Trans. Image Process.*, *11*(8), 1109-1119 .

Solanki, U., Jaliya, U. K., & Thakore, D. G. (2015). A survey on detection of disease and fruit grading. *International Journal of Innovative and Emerging Research in Engineering*, *2*(2), 109–114.

Soliman, H. S., & Omari, M. (2006). A Neural Networks Approach to Image Data Compression.[Elsevier.]. *Applied Soft Computing*, *6*(3), 258–271. doi:10.1016/j.asoc.2004.12.006

Soltana, W. B., Ardabilian, M., Lemaire, P., Huang, D., Szeptycki, P., Chen, L., … Colineau, J. (2012). 3D face recognition: A robust multi-matcher approach to data degradations. In *Proc of ICB 2012*. doi:10.1109/ICB.2012.6199766

Sommer, C., Straehle, C., Koethe, U., & Hamprecht, F. (2011, March). ilastik: Interactive learning and segmentation toolkit. In *Biomedical Imaging: From Nano to Macro, 2011 IEEE International Symposium on*. IEEE.

Song, B., Kamal, A. T., Soto, C., Ding, C., Farrell, J. A., & Roy-Chowdhury, A. K. (2010). Tracking and activity recognition through consensus in distributed camera networks. *IEEE Transactions on Image Processing*, *19*(10), 2564–2579. doi:10.1109/TIP.2010.2052823 PMID:20550994

Sonka, M., Hlavac, V., & Boyle, R. (2014). *Image processing, analysis, and machine vision*. Springer.

Sorwar, G., Abraham, A., & Dooley, L. S. (2001). *Texture classification based on DCT and soft computing*. The 10th IEEE International Conference on Fuzzy Systems. doi:10.1109/FUZZ.2001.1009012

Spagnolo, P., Orazio, T. D., Leo, M., & Distante, A. (2006). Moving Object Segmentation by Background Subtraction and Temporal Analysis. *Image and Vision Computing, 24*, 411-423.

Spreeuwers, L. (2011). Fast and Accurate 3D Face Recognition Using registration to an Intrinsic Coordinate System and Fusion of Multiple Region Classifiers. Int. J. Comput Vis, 389–414. DOI doi:10.1007/s11263-011-0426-2

Sridevi, N., & Subashini, P. (2012). Moment Based Feature Extraction for Classification of Handwritten Ancient Tamil Scripts. *International Journal of Emerging trends in Engineering and Development, 7*(2), 106-115.

SriDevi, N., & Sunitha, V. (2012). WT through Differential Privacy. *International Journal Of Computational Engineering Research*, *2*(5), 1344–1351.

Srinivasan, G. N., & Shobha, G. (2008). Statistical Texture Analysis. Proceedings of World Academy of Science. *Engineering and Technology, 36*, 1264–1269.

Srinivasan, K. S., & Ebenezer, D. (2007). A new fast and efficient decision-based algorithm for removal of high-density impulse noises. *IEEE Signal Processing Letters*, *14*(3), 189–192. doi:10.1109/LSP.2006.884018

Srivastava, A. N., & Zane-Ulman, B. (2005). Discovering recurring anomalies in text reports regarding complex space systems. In *Proceedings of the IEEE Aerospace Conference*. Big Sky, MT: IEEE. doi:10.1109/AERO.2005.1559692

Stanchev, P. (2003). Using Image Mining for Image Retrieval. *IASTED Conf. Computer Science and Technology*.

Starik, S., & Werman, M. (2003, October). Simulation of rain in videos. In *Texture Workshop, ICCV*.

Stefan, W., Renaut, R., & Gelb, A. (2010). Improved total variation-type regularization using higher order edge detectors. *SIAM J. Imag. Sci.*, 232–251.

Steidl, G. (2006). A note on the dual treatment of higher-order regularization functionals. *Computing*, *76*(1-2), 135–148. doi:10.1007/s00607-005-0129-z

Stergiou, C., & Siganos, D. (n.d.). *Neural Networks*. Retrieved from: http://www.doc.ic.ac.uk/nd/surprise96/journal/vol4/cs11/report.html

Sthitpattanapongsa, P., & Srinark, T. (2011). A Two-Stage Otsu's Thresholding Based Method on a 2D Histogram. In *Proceedings of the 7th IEEE International Conference on Intelligent Computer Communication and Processing* (pp. 345-348). doi:10.1109/ICCP.2011.6047894

Stricker, M., & Orengo, M. (1995). Similarity of Color Images. *Proc. of the SPIE Conf.*, *2420*, 381–392. doi:10.1117/12.205308

Strong, D., & Chan, T. (2003). Edge-preserving and scale-dependent properties of total variation regularization. *Inverse Problems*, *19*(6), S165–S187. doi:10.1088/0266-5611/19/6/059

Sturm, J. (1999). Using SeDuMi 1.02, A MATLAB toolbox for optimization over symmetric cones. *Optimization Methods and Software*, *11-12*(1-4), 625–653. doi:10.1080/10556789908805766

Sudhir, R. (2011). A Survey of Image Mining Techniques: Theory and Applications. *Computer Engineering and Intelligent Systems, 2*(6), 44-53.

Suen, C. Y., Berthod, M., & Mori, S. (1980). Automatic Recognition of Hand Printed Characters- the State of the Art. *Proceedings of the IEEE, 68*(4), 469–487. doi:10.1109/PROC.1980.11675

Suganthy, M., & Ramamoorthy, P. (2012). Principal Component Analysis Based Feature Extraction, Morphological Edge Detection and Localization for Fast Iris Recognition. *Journal of Computer Science, 8*(9), 1428 – 1433.

Sumana, I. J., Islam, M. M., Zhang, D. S., & Lu, G. (2008). Content Based Image Retrieval Using Curvelet Transform. In *Proceedings of IEEE International Workshop on Multimedia Signal Processing (MMSP08)*. doi:10.1109/MMSP.2008.4665041

Sung, C. S., & Jin, H. W. (2000). A tabu-search-based heuristic for clustering. *Pattern Recognition, 33*(5), 849–858. doi:10.1016/S0031-3203(99)00090-4

Sung-Nien, Y., Chien-Nan, L., & Chun-Chieh, C. (2009). Emulation of salamander retina with multilayer neural network. In *Proceeding of IEEE International Symposium on Circuits and System* (ISCAP). IEEE.

Suriani, N. S., Hussain, A., & Zulkifley, M. A. (2013). Sudden event recognition: A survey. *Sensors (Basel, Switzerland), 13*(8), 9966–9998. doi:10.3390/s130809966 PMID:23921828

Sutaone, M. S., & Khandare, M. V. (2008). Image based steganography using LSB insertion technique. In *Proceedings of International Conference on Wireless, Mobile and Multimedia Networks*.

Suykens, J. A. K., & Vandewalle, J. (1999). Least squares support vector machine classifiers. *Neural Processing Letters, 9*(3), 293–300. doi:10.1023/A:1018628609742

Szeptycki, P., Ardabilian, M., & Chen, L. (2008). *A coarse-to-fine curvature analysis-based rotation invariant 3D faces landmarking*. Retrieved from http://liris.cnrs.fr/Documents/Liris-4503.pdf

Takagi, T., & Sugeno, M. (1985). Fuzzy identification of systems and its applications to modeling and control. *IEEE Transactions on Neural Networks, 15*, 116–132.

Talukder, K. H., & Harada, K. (2006). A Scheme of Wavelet Based Compression of 2D Image. In *Proceedings of IMECS-2006*.

Talukder, K. H., & Harada, K. (2007, February). Haar Wavelet Based Approach for Image Compression and Quality Assessment of Compressed Image, IAENG International. *Journal of Applied Mathematics, 36*(1), 1–8.

Tamilarasi, M., & Palanisamy, V. (2009, November). Fuzzy Based Image Compression on ROI using Optimized Directional Contourlet Transform. *International Journal of Recent Trends in Engineering, 2*(5), 217–212.

Tamura, H., Mori, S., & Yamawaki, T. (1978). Texture Features Corresponding to Visual Perception. *IEEE Transactions on Systems, Man, and Cybernetics, 8*(6), 460–473. doi:10.1109/TSMC.1978.4309999

Tamura, S., & Tateishi, M. (1997). Capabilities of a four layered feedforward neural network. *Four layer versus three. IEEE Transactions on Neural Networks, 8*(2), 251–255. doi:10.1109/72.557662 PMID:18255629

Tan, R. T. (2008, June). Visibility in bad weather from a single image. In *Computer Vision and Pattern Recognition, 2008. CVPR 2008. IEEE Conference on* (pp. 1-8). IEEE. doi:10.1109/CVPR.2008.4587643

Tang, H., Yin, B., Sun, Y., & Hua, Y. (2013). 3D face recognition using local binary patterns. *Signal Processing, 93*(8), 2190–2198. doi:10.1016/j.sigpro.2012.04.002

Tan, X., & Triggs, B. (2010). Enhanced local texture feature sets for face recognition under difficult lighting conditions. Image Processing. *IEEE Transactions on, 19*(6), 1635–1650.

Tarel, J. P., & Hautiere, N. (2009, September). Fast visibility restoration from a single color or gray level image. In *Computer Vision, 2009 IEEE 12th International Conference on* (pp. 2201-2208). IEEE. doi:10.1109/ICCV.2009.5459251

Tarel, J. P., Hautière, N., Caraffa, L., Cord, A., Halmaoui, H., & Gruyer, D. (2012). Vision enhancement in homogeneous and heterogeneous fog. *Intelligent Transportation Systems Magazine, IEEE, 4*(2), 6–20. doi:10.1109/MITS.2012.2189969

Taylor, D. W. (1937). Stability of earth slopes. *J. Boston Soc. Civil Eng, 24*, 197.

Teague, M. R. (1980). Image analysis via the general theory of moments. *Journal of the Optical Society of America, 70*(8), 920–930. doi:10.1364/JOSA.70.000920

Teppola, P., Mujunen, S. P., & Minkkinen, P. (1999). Adaptive Fuzzy C-Means clustering in process monitoring. *Chemometrics and Intelligent Laboratory Systems, 45*(1), 23–38. doi:10.1016/S0169-7439(98)00087-2

Tessens, L., Ledda, A., Pizurica, A., & Philips, W. (2007). Extending the depth of field in microscopy through curve-let-based frequency-adaptive image fusion. *Proc. IEEE Int. Conf. Acoust. Speech Signal Process., 1*, 861–864.

Texas 3D face database. (n.d.). Retrieved 23rd July, 2014, from http://live.ece.utexas.edu/research/texas3dfr/

Thai, R. (2003). *Fingerprint image Enhancement and Minutiae Extraction.* (Thesis). University of Western Australia.

The, C. -H., & Chin, R. T. (1988). On Image Analysis by the Methods of Moments. *IEEE Transactions on Pattern Analysis Machine Intelligent, 10*(4), 496-513.

Theodoridis, S., & Koutroumbas, K. (2009). *Pattern Recognition* (4th ed.). Singapore: Elsevier.

Thota, N. R., & Devireddy, S. K. (2008). Image Compression using Discrete Cosine Transform. *Georgian Electronic Scientific Journal: Computer Science and Telecommunications, 3*(17), 35–43.

Tian, D. P. (2013). A Review on Image Feature Extraction and Representation Techniques. *International Journal of Multimedia and Ubiquitous Engineering, 8*(4), 385–395.

Tian, J., & Chen, L. (2012, September). Adaptive multi-focus image fusion using a wavelet- based statistical sharpness measure. *Signal Processing, 92*(9), 2137–2146. doi:10.1016/j.sigpro.2012.01.027

Tian, L., Zheng, N., Xue, J., Li, C., & Wang, X. (2011). An integrated visual saliency based watermarking approach for synchronous image authentication and copyright protection. *Signal Processing Image Communication, 26*(8), 427–437. doi:10.1016/j.image.2011.06.001

Tibshirani, R. (1996). Regression shrinkage and selection via the lasso. *Journal of the Royal Statistical Society. Series B. Methodological, 58*, 267–288.

Tkachuk, C. D., & Hirschmann, J. V. (2007). Wintrobe's Atlas of Clinical Hematology. Lippincott Williams and Wilkins.

Toh, K., & Isa, N. (2010, March). Noise Adaptive Fuzzy Switching Median Filter for Salt and Pepper Noice Reduction. *IEEE Signal Processing Letters, 17*(3), 281–284. doi:10.1109/LSP.2009.2038769

Tripathi, A. K., & Mukhopadhyay, S. (2012). Single image fog removal using anisotropic diffusion. *Image Processing, IET, 6*(7), 966–975. doi:10.1049/iet-ipr.2011.0472

Truong, T.-K., Lin, C.-C., & Chen, S.-H. (2007). Segmentation of specific speech signals from multi-dialog environment using SVM and wavelet. *Pattern Recognition Letters, 28*(11), 1307–1313. doi:10.1016/j.patrec.2006.11.020

Tsai, C. F., Tsai, C. W., Wu, H. C., & Yang, T. (2004). ACODF: A novel data clustering approach for data mining in large databases. *Journal of Systems and Software, 73*(1), 133–145. doi:10.1016/S0164-1212(03)00216-4

Tsai, J. S., Huang, W. B., & Kuo, Y. H. (2011b). On the selection of optimal feature region set for robust digital image watermarking. *IEEE Transactions on Image Processing, 20*(3), 735–743. doi:10.1109/TIP.2010.2073475 PMID:20833602

Tsekeridou, S., & Pitas, I. (2000). Embedding self-similar watermarks in the wavelet domain. *IEEE International Conference on Acoustics, Speech, and Signal Processing.* doi:10.1109/ICASSP.2000.859216

Tsoumakas, G., & Vlahavas, I. (2009). Distributed Data Mining. IGI Global.

Tukey, J. W. (1974) Nonlinear (nonsuperposable) methods for smoothing data. In *Proceeding of Congressional Record EASCOM.*

Turk, M., & Pentland, A. (1991). Eigenfaces for recognition. *Journal of Cognitive Neuroscience, 3*(1), 71–86. doi:10.1162/jocn.1991.3.1.71 PMID:23964806

Turner, L. F. (1989). *Digital data security system.* Patent IPN wo 89: 08915.

Ukinkar, V. G., & Makrand. (2012). Object Detection in Dynamic Background Using Image Segmentation: A review. *International Journal of Engineering Research and Applications, 2*(3), 232–236.

UMB-DB face database. (n.d.). Retrieved 22nd July, 2014, from http://www.ivl.disco.unimib.it/umbdb/

Umpon, N. T. (2005). Patch based white blood cell nucleus segmentation using fuzzy clustering. *ECTI T Electr Electron Commun.*, *3*(1), 5–10.

Unay, D., & Gosselin, B. (2006). Automatic defect segmentation of Jonagold apples on multi-spectral images: A comparative study. *Postharvest Biology and Technology*, *42*(3), 271–279. doi:10.1016/j.postharvbio.2006.06.010

Univ. of York 1 database. (n.d.). Retrieved 22nd July, 2014, from http://www-users.cs.york.ac.uk/~tomh/3DfaceDatabase.html

Univ. of York 2 database. (n.d.). Retrieved 22nd July, 2014, from http://www-users.cs.york.ac.uk/~tomh/3DfaceDatabase.html

Upreti, K., Verma, K., & Sahoo, A. (2010). Variable Bits Secure System for Color Images. *Advances in Computing, Control and Telecommunication Technologies (ACT), 2010 Second International Conference on*. doi:10.1109/ACT.2010.58

Ursani, A. A., Kpalma, K., Ronsin, J., Memon, A. A., & Chowdhry, B. S. (2009). Improved Texture Description with Features Based on Fourier Transform. Wireless Networks. *Information Processing and Systems Communications in Computer and Information Science*, *20*, 19–28. doi:10.1007/978-3-540-89853-5_5

USF 3-D Database. (n.d.). Retrieved 15th July, 2014, from http://marathon.csee.usf.edu/GaitBaseline/USF-Human-ID-3D-Database-Release.PDF

Vamvakas, G., Gatos, B., & Perantonis, S. J. (2009). *A Novel Feature Extraction and Classification Methodology for the Recognition of Historical Documents.10th International Conference on Document Analysis and Recognition*. doi:10.1109/ICDAR.2009.223

Van der Merwe, D. W., & Engelbrecht, A. P. (2003, December). Data clustering using particle swarm optimization. In *IEEE Congress on Evolutionary Computation CEC-03*.

van Schyndel, R. G., Tirkel, A. Z., & Osborne, C. F. (1994). A digital watermark. *Proc. IEEE International Conference on Image Processing*, doi:10.1109/ICIP.1994.413536

VanHuffel, S., & Vandewalle, J. (1991). *The total least squares problem: computational aspects and analysis*. SIAM. doi:10.1137/1.9781611971002

Vapnik, V. (1995). *The nature of statistical learning theory*. New York: Springer Verlag. doi:10.1007/978-1-4757-2440-0

Veldkamp, W. J., Joemai, R. M., van der Molen, A. J., & Geleijns, J. (2010). Development and validation of segmentation and interpolation techniques in sinograms for metal artifact suppression in CT. *Medical Physics*, *37*(2), 620–628. doi:10.1118/1.3276777 PMID:20229871

Venu, G. A. (2011). Generative framework to investigate the underlying patterns in human activities. In *Proceedings of IEEE International Conference on Computer Vision Workshops* (pp. 1472–1479). IEEE Press.

Veracini, T., Matteoli, S., Diani, M., & Corsini, G. (2011). An anomaly detection architecture based on a data-adaptive density estimation. In *Proceedings of 2011 3rd Workshop on Hyperspectral Image and Signal Processing: Evolution in Remote Sensing (WHISPERS)*. Lisbon: IEEE. doi:10.1109/WHISPERS.2011.6080919

Verma, R., & Ali, J. (2012). A-Survey of Feature Extraction and Classification Techniques in OCR Systems. *International Journal of Computer Applications & Information Technology*, *1*(3), 1–3.

Vieira, M. A., Formaggio, A. R., Rennó, C. D., Atzberger, C., Aguiar, D. A., & Mello, M. P. (2012). Object Based Image Analysis and Data Mining applied to a remotely sensed Landsat time-series to map sugarcane over large areas, Elsevier. *Remote Sensing of Environment*, *123*, 553–562. doi:10.1016/j.rse.2012.04.011

Viola, P., & Jones, M. (2001). Rapid object detection using a boosted cascade of simple features. In *Proceedings of IEEE Computer Society Conference on Computer Vision and Pattern Recognition*. IEEE.

Vogel, C. R., & Oman, M. E. (1996). Iterative methods for total variation denoising. *SIAM J. on Scientiffic Computing*, *17*(1-4), 227–238. doi:10.1137/0917016

Vonesch, C., Blu, T., & Unser, M. (2007). Generalized Daubechies wavelet families. *IEEE Transactions on Signal Processing*, *55-9*(9), 4415–4429. doi:10.1109/TSP.2007.896255

VRML format. (n.d.). Retrieved 16th August, 2014, from http://www.nada.kth.se/~stefanc/VRML_lecture.pdf

Vyas, A. M., Talati, B., & Naik, S. (2014). Quality Inspection and classification of mangoes using color and size features. *International Journal of Computers and Applications*, *98*(1), 1–5. doi:10.5120/17144-7161

Wang, Zhang, Li, & Ma. (2007). Annotating Images by Mining Image Search Results. *IEEE Transactions on Pattern Analysis and Machine Intelligence*, 1-14.

Wang, J., Wang, S.-T., Deng, Z.-H., & Qi, Y.-S. (2010). Image thresholding based minimax probability criterion. *Pattern Recognition and Artificial Intelligence*, *23*(6), 880–884.

Wang, L., Gordo, M. D., & Ji Zhu, J. (2006). Regularized least absolute deviations regression and an efficient algorithm for parameter tuning.*Sixth International Conference on Data Mining*, (pp. 690–700). doi:10.1109/ICDM.2006.134

Wang, R., Chi-Fang, L., & Ja-Chen, L. (2001). Image hiding by optimal LSB substitution and genetic algorithm. *Pattern Recognition*, *34*(3), 671–683. doi:10.1016/S0031-3203(00)00015-7

Wang, X., Ding, X., & Liu, C. (2005). Gabor Filters-Based Feature Extraction for Character Recognition. *Pattern Recognition Letters*, *38*(3), 369–379. doi:10.1016/j.patcog.2004.08.004

Wang, Y., Doherty, J. F., & Van Dyck, R. E. (2001). A watermarking algorithm for fingerprinting intelligence images. In *Conference on Information Sciences and Systems*.

Wang, Y.-L., Zhao, Ch.-H., & Wang, Y. (2011). Anomaly detection using subspace band section based RX algorithm. In *Proceedings of 2011 International Conference on Multimedia Technology (ICMT)*. Hangzhou: IEEE.

Wang, Y., Yang, J., Yin, W., & Zhang, Y. (2008). A new alternating minimization algorithm for total variation image reconstruction. *Journal SIAM Journal on Imaging Sciences*, *1*(3), 248–272. doi:10.1137/080724265

Wang, Z., & Bovik, A. (2002, March). A universal image quality index. *IEEE Signal Processing Letters*, *9*(3), 81–84. doi:10.1109/97.995823

Wang, Z., Bovik, A., Sheikh, H., & Simoncelli, E. (2004, April). Image quality assessment: From error visibility to structural similarity. *IEEE Transactions on Image Processing*, *13*(4), 600–612. doi:10.1109/TIP.2003.819861 PMID:15376593

Wang, Z., & Hong, K. (2012). A Novel Approach for Trademark Image Retrieval by Combining Global Features and Local Features. *Journal of Computer Information Systems*, *8*(4), 1633–1640.

Wang, Z., & Zhang, D. (1999). Progressive switching median filter for the removal of impulse noise from highly corrupted images. *IEEE Transactions on Circuits and Systems II: Analog and Digital Signal Processing*, *46*(1), 78–80. doi:10.1109/82.749102

Weickert, J., & Schnörr, C. (2001). A theoretical framework for convex regularizers in PDE-based computation of image motion. *International Journal of Computer Vision*, *45*(3), 245–264. doi:10.1023/A:1013614317973

Wiskott, L., Fellous, J.-M., Kuiger, N., & von der Malsburg, C. (1997). Face recognition by elastic bunch graph matching. *IEEE Transactions on Pattern Analysis and Machine Intelligence*, *19*(7), 775–779. doi:10.1109/34.598235

Wolfgang, R. B., & Delp, E. J. (1999). Fragile watermarking using the VW2D watermark.*Proc. SPIE, Security and Watermarking of Multimedia Contents*. doi:10.1117/12.344670

Wong, K.-W., Lam, K.-M., & Siu, W.-C. (2001). An Efficient Algorithm for Human Face Detection and Facial Feature Extraction under Different Conditions. *Pattern Recognition*, *34*(10), 1993–2004. doi:10.1016/S0031-3203(00)00134-5

Woodford, B. J., Kasabov, K. K., & Wearing, C. H. (1999). *Fruit Image Analysis using Wavelets*. Research Gate Digital Library.

Woolley, A. W., Chabris, C. F., Pentland, A., Hashmi, N., & Malone, T. W. (2010). Evidence for a collective intelligence factor in the performance of human groups. *Science*, *330*(6004), 686–688. doi:10.1126/science.1193147 PMID:20929725

Wu, Kumar, Quinlan, Ghosh, Yang, Motoda, et al. (2008). The top 10 Data Mining Algorithms. *Knowl Inf Syst*. DOI 10.1007/s10115

Wu, L. Y., Cheng, L. Z., & Zhi-Hong, Y. X. (2004). Translucent DigitalWatermark Base on Wavelets and Error-Correct Code. *Chin. J. Comput., 11*(12), 533–1539.

Xia, J., Xiong, J., Xu, X., & Zhang, Q. (2010). An efficient two-state switching median filter for the reduction of impulse noises with different distributions. In *Proceedings of 3rd International Congress on Image and Signal Processing*. IEEE. doi:10.1109/CISP.2010.5647235

XiaoLi, C., Ying, Z., JunTao, S., & Jiqing, S. (2010). *Method of image segmentation based on fuzzy c-means clustering algorithm and artificial fish swarm algorithm.* In Intelligent Computing and Integrated Systems (ICISS), 2010 International Conference on.

Xia, X. G., Boncelet, C. G., & Arce, G. R. (1997). A multiresolution watermark for digital images. *Proc. International Conference on Image Processing.*

xm2vtsdb 3D face model. (n.d.). Retrieved 15th July, 2014, from http://www.ee.surrey.ac.uk/CVSSP/xm2vtsdb/

Xu, Z. W., Guo, X. X., Hu, X. Y., & Cheng, X. (2005). The Blood Vessel Recognition of Ocular Fundus. In *Proceedings of the 4th International Conference on Machine Learning and Cybernetics* (ICMLC05).

Xu, Z., Liu, X., & Chen, X. (2009, December). Fog removal from video sequences using contrast limited adaptive histogram equalization. In *Computational Intelligence and Software Engineering, 2009. CiSE 2009. International Conference on* (pp. 1-4). IEEE. doi:10.1109/CISE.2009.5366207

Xu, C., Li, S., Tan, T., & Quan, L. (2009). Automatic 3D face recognition from depth and intensity Gabor features. *Pattern Recognition, 42*(9), 1895–1905. doi:10.1016/j.patcog.2009.01.001

Xu, C., Tan, T., Wang, Y., & Quan, L. (2006). Combining local features for robust nose location in 3D facial data. *Pattern Recognition Letters, 27*(13), 1487–1494. doi:10.1016/j.patrec.2006.02.015

Xu, M., Chen, H., & Varshney, P. (2011, December). An image fusion approach based on markov random fields. *IEEE Transactions on Geoscience and Remote Sensing, 49*(12), 5116–5127. doi:10.1109/TGRS.2011.2158607

Xun, L., & Fang, Y. (2006). Anomaly Detection Based on High-order Statistics in Hyperspectral Imagery. In *Proceedings of the Sixth World Congress on Intelligent Control and Automation*. Dalia: IEEE.

Xydeas, C., & Petrovic´, V. (2000, February). Objective image fusion performance measure. *Electronics Letters, 36*(4), 308–309. doi:10.1049/el:20000267

Yang, C., Zhang, J., Wang, X., & Liu, X. (2008, April). A novel similarity based quality metric for image fusion. *Information Fusion, 9*(2), 156–160. doi:10.1016/j.inffus.2006.09.001

Yang, J., Zhang, D., Frangi, A. F., & Yang, J.-Y. (2004). Two-dimensional PCA: A new approach to appearance-based face representation and recognition. IEEE Tanns. *PAMI, 26*(1), 131–137. doi:10.1109/TPAMI.2004.1261097

Yang, L., Wang, L., Sun, Y., & Zhang, R. (2010). Simultaneous feature selection and classification via Minimax Probability Machine. *International Journal of Computational Intelligence Systems, 3*(6), 754–760. doi:10.1080/18756891.2010.9727738

Yang, L., You, X., Haralick, R. M., Phillips, I. T., & Tang, Y. Y. (2001). Characterization of Dirac Edge with New Wavelet Transform. *LNCS, 2251*, 129–138.

Yang, M., Kpalm, K., & Ronsin, J. (2008). A Survey of Shape Feature Extraction Techniques. *Pattern Recognition*, 43–90.

Yang, T.-H., & Lee, W.-P. (2011). Combining GRN modeling and demonstration-based programming for robot control. *Neural Computing & Applications, 20*(6), 909–921. doi:10.1007/s00521-010-0496-z

Yang, Y., & Huang, S. (2007). Image Segmentation by Fuzzy C-Means Clustering Algorithm with a Novel Penalty Term. *Computing and Informatics, 26*, 17–31.

Yasmin, M., Sharif, M., & Mohsin, S. (2013). Use of Low Level Features for Content Based Image Retrieval: Survey. *Research Journal of Recent Sciences, 2*(11), 65–75.

Yazdi, M., & Beaulieu, L. (2008). Artifacts in spiral x-ray CT scanners: Problems and solutions. *International Journal of Biological and Medical Sciences, 4*(3), 135–139.

Youssef, S. M., Elfarag, A. A., & Raouf, R. (2012). C7. A multi-level information hiding integrating wavelet-based texture analysis of block partition difference images. *Radio Science Conference (NRSC), 2012 29th National.* doi:10.1109/NRSC.2012.6208525

Yuan, J., Schnörr, C., & Steidl, G. (2009). Total-variation based piecewise affine regularization.*Proc. of the 2nd Int. Conf. Scale Space Variation. Methods in Comput. Vis. (SSVM)*, (pp. 552–564). doi:10.1007/978-3-642-02256-2_46

Yuan, Z., Sun, H., Ji, K., Li, Zh., & Zou, H. (2014). Local Sparsity Divergence for Hyperspectral Anomaly Detection. *IEEE Geoscience and Remote Sensing Letters*, *11*(10), 1697–1701. doi:10.1109/LGRS.2014.2306209

Yu, G., Lin, Y. Z., & Kamarthi, S. (2010). Wavelets-Based Feature Extraction for Texture Classification. *Advanced Materials Research*, *97*(101), 1273–1276. doi:10.4028/www.scientific.net/AMR.97-101.1273

Yun, F., & Runsheng, W. (2002). An Image Retrieval Method Using DCT Features. *Journal of Computer Science and Technology*, *17*(6), 865–873. doi:10.1007/BF02960778

Yu, Y., & Wu, H. (2012). Anomaly intrusion detection based upon data mining techniques and fuzzy logic. In *Proceedings of the IEEE International Conference on Systems, Man, and Cybernetics (SMC)*. Seoul: IEEE. doi:10.1109/ICSMC.2012.6377776

Zadeh, L. A. (1965). Fuzzy Sets. *Information and Control*, *8*(3), 338–353. doi:10.1016/S0019-9958(65)90241-X

Zadeh, L. A. (1994). Fuzzy logic, neural networks, and soft computing. *Communications of the ACM*, *37*(3), 77–84. doi:10.1145/175247.175255

Zainudin, M. N. S., Radi, H. R., Abdullah, S. M., Abd Rahim, R., Ismail, M. M., Idris, M. I., Sulaiman, H. A., & Jaafar, A. (2012). Face Recognition using Principle Component Analysis (PCA) and Linear Discriminant Analysis (LDA). *International Journal of Electrical & Computer Sciences, 12*(5), 50-55.

Ze-Feng, D., Zhou-Ping, Y., & You-Lun, X. (2007). High probability impulse noise-removing algorithm based on mathematical morphology. *IEEE Signal Processing Letters*, *14*(1), 31–34. doi:10.1109/LSP.2006.881524

Zeng, T., & Ng, M. K. (2010). On the total variation dictionary model. *IEEE Transactions on Image Processing*, *19*(3), 821–825. doi:10.1109/TIP.2009.2034701 PMID:19840910

Zhang, B., Hsu, M., & Dayal, U. (1999). *K-harmonic means-a data clustering algorithm.* Hewlett-Packard Labs Technical Report HPL-1999-124.

Zhang, D., Wong, A., Indrawan, M., & Lu, G. (2000). Content-Based Image Retrieval Using Gabor Texture Features. *Proceedings of the First IEEE Pacific- Rim Conference on Multimedia.*

Zhang, X., Li, H., Qi, Y., Leow, W. K., & Ng, T. K. (2006, July). Rain removal in video by combining temporal and chromatic properties. In *Multimedia and Expo, 2006 IEEE International Conference on* (pp. 461-464). IEEE. doi:10.1109/ICME.2006.262572

Zhang, Y. (2009). *User's Guide for YALL1: Your Algorithms for L1 Optimization.* Technical Report TR09-17, Department of Computational and Applied Mathematics, Rice University.

Zhang, Zhang, & Khanzode. (2004). *A Data Mining Approach to Modeling Relationships Among Categories in Image Collection.* ACM.

Zhang, D. S., Islam, M., & Lu, G. J. (2012). A review on automatic image annotation techniques. *Pattern Recognition*, *45*(1), 346–362. doi:10.1016/j.patcog.2011.05.013

Zhang, D., & Lu, G. (2004). Review of Shape Representation and Description Techniques. *Pattern Recognition*, *37*(1), 1–19. doi:10.1016/j.patcog.2003.07.008

Zhang, G. (2008). *Shape Feature Extraction Using Fourier Descriptors with Brightness in Content-Based Medical Image Retrieval.International Conference on Intelligent Information Hiding and Multimedia Signal Processing.* doi:10.1109/IIH-MSP.2008.16

Zhang, G., Jia, J., Wong, T.-T., & Bao, H. (2009). Consistent depth maps recovery from a video sequence. *IEEE Transactions on Pattern Analysis and Machine Intelligence*, *31*(6), 974–988. doi:10.1109/TPAMI.2009.52 PMID:19372604

Zhang, J., & Tan, T. (2002). Brief Review of Invariant Texture Analysis Methods. *Pattern Recognition, 35*(3), 735–747. doi:10.1016/S0031-3203(01)00074-7

Zhang, L., Xu, Y., & Wu, C. (2011). Features Extraction for Structured Light Stripe Image Based On OTSU Threshold. *Fourth International Symposium on Knowledge Acquisition and Modeling.* doi:10.1109/KAM.2011.32

Zhang, M., Raghunathan, A., & Jha, N. K. (2013). MedMon: Securing Medical Devices Through Wireless Monitoring and Anomaly Detection. *IEEE Transactions on Biomedical Circuits and Systems, 7*(6), 871–881. doi:10.1109/TBCAS.2013.2245664 PMID:24473551

Zhang, Q., & Guo, B. (2009, July). Multifocus image fusion using the non- subsampled contourlet transform. *Signal Processing, 89*(7), 1334–1346. doi:10.1016/j.sigpro.2009.01.012

Zhang, S., & Karim, M. A. (2002). A new impulse detector for switching median filters. *IEEE Signal Processing Letters, 9*(11), 360–363. doi:10.1109/LSP.2002.805310

Zhang, W., Huang, D., Wang, Y., & Chen, L. (2012). 3D Aided Face Recognition across Pose Variations. In *Proc of CCBR 2012.* doi:10.1007/978-3-642-35136-5_8

Zhang, X., & Xiong, Y. (2009). Impulse noise removal using directional difference based noise detector and adaptive weighted mean filter. *IEEE Signal Processing Letters, 16*(4), 295–298. doi:10.1109/LSP.2009.2014293

Zhang, X., Yin, L., Cohn, J. F., Canavan, S., Reale, M., Horowitz, A., & Liu, P. (2013). A High-Resolution Spontaneous 3D Dynamic Facial Expression Database. In *10th IEEE International Conference and Workshops on Automatic Face and Gesture Recognition (FG).* doi:10.1109/FG.2013.6553788

Zhang, Y., & Wu, L. (2012). Classification of Fruits Using Computer Vision and a Multiclass Support Vector Machine. *Sensors (Basel, Switzerland), 12*(12), 12489–12505. doi:10.3390/s120912489 PMID:23112727

Zhang, Z. (1994). Iterative point matching for registration of free-form curves and surfaces. *International Journal of Computer Vision, 13*(2), 119–152. doi:10.1007/BF01427149

Zhao, X., Liu, P., Liu, J., & Tang, X. (2013). Removal of dynamic weather conditions based on variable time window. Computer Vision, IET, 7(4).

Zhao, J., & Koch, E. (1995). Embedding robust labels into images for copyright protection. *Proc. International Congress on Intellectual Property Rights for Specialised Information, Knowledge and New Technologies.*

Zhao, J., Laganiere, R., & Liu, Z. (2007, December). Performance assessment of combinative pixel-level image fusion based on an absolute feature measurement. *International Journal of Innovative Computing, Information, & Control, 3*(6), 1433–1447.

Zhao, R., Du, B., & Zhang, L. (2014). A Robust Nonlinear Hyperspectral Anomaly Detection Approach. *IEEE Journal of Selected Topics in Applied Earth Observations and Remote Sensing, 7*(4), 1227–1234. doi:10.1109/JSTARS.2014.2311995

Zhao, W., Chellappa, R., & Phillips, P. J. (1999). *Subspace linear discriminant analysis for face recognition.* Computer Vision Laboratory, Center for Automation Research, University of Maryland.

Zhou, F., Feng, J.-F., & Shi, Q.-Y. (2001). Texture Feature Based on Local Fourier Transform. *IEEE Transactions on Image Processing, 2,* 610–613.

Zhou, H., & Liu, Y. (2008). Accurate integration of multi-view range images using k-means clustering. *Pattern Recognition, 41*(1), 152–175. doi:10.1016/j.patcog.2007.06.006

Zhou, X., S'anchez, S. A., & Kuijper, A. (2010). *3D Face Recognition with Local Binary Patterns.* In *2010 Sixth International Conference on Intelligent Information Hiding and Multimedia Signal Processing.* doi:10.1109/IIHMSP.2010.87

Zhou, Z. (2012). Cognition and removal of impulse noise with uncertainty. *IEEE Transactions on Image Processing, 21*(7), 3157–3167. doi:10.1109/TIP.2012.2189577 PMID:22389145

Zhou, Z., Wang, Z., & Sun, X. (2013). Face recognition based on optimal kernel minimax probability machine. *Journal of Theoretical and Applied Information Technology, 48*(3), 1645–1651.

Zhu, Y., Fang, B., & Zhang, H. (2009, December). Image de-weathering for road based on physical model. In *Information Engineering and Computer Science, 2009. ICIECS 2009. International Conference on* (pp. 1-4). IEEE. doi:10.1109/ICIECS.2009.5365298

Zhu, Q., Xu, Y., Lu, Y., Wen, J., Fan, Z., & Li, Z. (2014). Novel Matrix Based Feature Extraction Method for Face Recognition Using Gabor face Features. *Genetic and Evolutionary Computing Advances in Intelligent Systems and Computing, 238*, 349–357. doi:10.1007/978-3-319-01796-9_38

Zhu, W., Xiong, Z., & Zhang, Y. Q. (1999). Multiresolution watermarking for images and video. *IEEE Transactions on Circuits and Systems for Video Technology, 9*(4), 545–550. doi:10.1109/76.767121

Zulkifley, M. A., Moran, B., & Rawlinson, D. (2012). Robust foreground detection: A fusion of masked grey world, probabilistic gradient information and extended conditional random field approach. *Sensors (Basel, Switzerland), 12*(5), 5623–5649. doi:10.3390/s120505623 PMID:22778605

Zulkifli, Z., Iskandar, S., Saad, P., Skudai, & Mohtar, I. A. (2011). *Plant Leaf Identification using Moment Invariants & General Regression Neural Network.* 11th International Conference on Hybrid Intelligent Systems (HIS), Melacca. doi:10.1109/HIS.2011.6122144

Zuo, W. (2011). A generalized accelerated proximal gradient approach for total-variation-based image restoration. *IEEE Transactions on Image Processing, 20*(10), 2748–2759. doi:10.1109/TIP.2011.2131665 PMID:21435979

About the Contributors

Narendra Kumar Kamila is presently working as Professor, Department of Computer Science and Engineering, and Head (R&D Cell), C V Raman College of Engineering, Bhubaneswar, Odisha, India. He received his master degree from Indian Institute of Technology, Kharagpur and subsequently obtained his Ph. D. degree from Utkal University, Bhubaneswar. Prof. Kamila was also post-doctoral fellow to University of Arkansas, USA. He has published several research papers in the national/international journal of repute in the field of wireless sensor networking, Adhoc-networking, Image processing, meta cognition, data privacy/security. He has served as program committee members in many international conferences. He has completed many projects sponsored by various sponsoring agencies. He has guided many M.Tech. and Ph.D. students under different universities. Dr. Kamila has been rendering his best services as editorial board member to *American Journal of Intelligent System, American Journal of Advances in Networks, American Journal of Networks and Communications,* Reviewer of *International Journal of Intelligent Information System (USA),* Reviewer of *International journal of Automation Control and Intelligent Systems (USA),* Reviewer of *Elsevier Publication,* Reviewer of *AMSE, Modelling Simulation (France),* editor-in-chief of *International Journal of Advanced Computer Engineering and Communication Technology,* former editor-in-chief of *International Journal of Communication Network and Security (IJCNS)* and editor-in-chief of many international conference proceedings.

* * *

D. P. Acharjya received his Ph. D in computer science from Berhampur University, India; M. Tech. degree in computer science from Utkal University, India in 2002; and M. Sc. from NIT, Rourkela, India. He has been awarded with Gold Medal in M. Sc. Currently, he is working as a Professor in the school of computing sciences and engineering, VIT University, Vellore, India. He has authored many national and international journal papers, book chapters, and five books: Fundamental Approach to Discrete Mathematics; Computer Based on Mathematics; Theory of Computation; Rough Set in Knowledge Representation and Granular Computing; Introduction to Information Technology; and Computer Programming to his credit. In addition, he has edited three books with international publishers. He is associated with many professional bodies CSI, ISTE, IMS, AMTI, ISIAM, OITS, IACSIT, CSTA, IEEE, and IAENG. He was founder secretary of OITS Rourkela chapter. His current research interests include rough sets, formal concept analysis, knowledge representation, data mining, granular computing, and business intelligence.

Md. Imtiyaz Anwar did his Master of Technology from National Institute of Technology, Jalandhar, India and is currently pursuing his research in Image and video Processing towards completion of his

PhD from National Institute of Technology, Jalandhar, India. He has worked as Assistant Professor in Electronics and Communication department with Lovely Professional University, Phagwara, Punjab, India and other similar Institutions in India. His research interests include Image processing, Computer vision and WiMAX system. He is a student member of IEEE societies.

Debotosh Bhattacharjee received the MCSE and Ph.D. (Eng.) degrees from Jadavpur University, India, in 1997 and 2004 respectively. He was associated with different institutes in various capacities until March 2007. After that he joined his Alma Mater, Jadavpur University. His research interests pertain to the applications of computational intelligence techniques like Fuzzy logic, Artificial Neural Network, Genetic Algorithm etc. in Face Recognition, OCR, and Information Security. He is a life member of Indian Society for Technical Education (ISTE, New Delhi), Indian Unit for Pattern Recognition and Artificial Intelligence (IUPRAI), and Senior member of IEEE (USA).

Yi Chai is currently the Vis Director of College of Automation in Chongqing University. He holds a PhD degree major in Control theory and Engineering and Master's degree major in Industry Automation from Chongqing University, and his first degree from National University of Defense Technology major in Electronic Engineering, China. Professor Chai is a distinguished full professor in Chongqing University. He is a principal postgraduate courses' lecturer and PhD tutor, honorable academician and researcher in his field and in the college in general. Because of his deep academic scholastic, he innovated and running more than 40 national projects. Professor Chai is the famous and known academician, and in his successful achievement and patented work, he received more than 9 national awards. He is also a member and head of many professional and technical associations in the national level. He is therefore, highly respectful and honored by his collogues and students because of his immense and exemplary efforts and wishes to deliver applicable and scalable scientific techniques, methodologies, knowledge and experience to his followers. He published many academic and high standard journals, books, and other technical reports in both English and Chinese. His major research direction is information processing, fusion and control, industrial process control theory and technology, intelligent systems theory and applications, and others in the field of automation.

Abhijit Chandra received his B.E. in Electronics & Telecommunication Engineering in 2008 from Indian Institute of Engineering Science and Technology, Shibpur (Formerly Bengal Engineering & Science University, Shibpur) Howrah-711 103, India and M.E.Tel.E with specialization in Communication Engineering in 2010 from Jadavpur University, Kolkata-700 032, India. Presently, he is associated with the Department of Instrumentation & Electronics Engineering of Jadavpur University as an Assistant Professor. He has published more than 30 papers in International/National Journals and Conferences of good repute. His research area includes Digital Signal/Image Processing, Evolutionary Optimization Techniques, Digital/Mobile Communication Systems, Information and Coding Theory. Mr. Chandra has received President's Gold Medal from Bengal Engineering & Science University, Shibpur in 2010 for being First in the faculty of Engineering and Technology at B.E. examination 2008. He has also received University Medal in 2010 for standing First in order of merit at the M.E. Tel. E. examination 2010 from Jadavpur University.

Ankit Chaudhary is major in Computer Science & Engineering and received his PhD in Computer Vision. His current research interests are in Vision based applications, Intelligent Systems and Graph

Algorithms. He carried out his research work at Machine Vision Lab, CEERI–CSIR. Later, he was a Post-Doc at Dept. of Electrical and Computer Engineering, The University of Iowa.

Swaptik Chowdhury is an undergraduate majoring in Civil Engineering from Vellore Institute of Technology, Vellore. He is set to graduate in 2015 and hopes to specialize in Structural engineering. His interest lies in the alternate construction materials and soft computing model analysis in geotechnical and structural engineering.

Heba Elnemr was appointed to Electronics Research Institute in 1991. She has been an assistant research in computers and systems department. She received her PhD degree in computer engineering from Electronics and Communication Department, Faculty of Engineering, Cairo University, Egypt in 2003. She is presently an associate professor in computers and systems department and she is a member of the board of the department. Her research expertise lies mainly in image processing and analysis, pattern recognition, image retrieval, video processing and biometrics. She has supervised several masters and Ph. D. students in the field of image and video processing.

Vania Vieira Estrela, B.S. degree from Federal University of Rio de Janeiro (UFRJ) in Electrical and Computer Engineering (ECE); M.Sc. from the Instituto Tecnológico de Aeronáutica (ITA), Sao Jose dos Campos; M.Sc. degree in ECE at Northwestern University, Evanston, Illinois (IL), USA; and Ph.D. in ECE from the Illinois Institute of Technology (IIT), Chicago, IL, USA. Taught at: DeVry University; DePaul University; Universidade Estadual do Norte Fluminense (UENF), Campos de Goytacazes, Rio de Janeiro (RJ), Brazil; and for the Universidade Estadual da Zona Oeste (UEZO), Rio de Janeiro, RJ, Brazil. Visiting professor at the Polytechnic Institute of Rio de Janeiro (IPRJ)/State University of Rio de Janeiro (UERJ) in Nova Friburgo, RJ. Currently working at Universidade Federal Fluminense (UFF), Niterói, RJ for the Department of Telecommunications. Research interests include: signal/image/video processing, inverse problems, computational & mathematical modeling, stochastic models, multimedia, communications, motion estimation, machine learning and geoprocessing. Reviewer for the following journals/magazines: IMAVIS (Elsevier); Pattern Recognition (Elsevier); Computers & Electrical Engineering (Elsevier); IET Image Processing; IET Computer Vision and International Journal of Image Processing (IJIP). Engaged in topics such as technology transfer, engineering/math/computer education, environmental issues and digital inclusion. Member of IEEE, and ACM. Editor of IJIP.

Karim Saheb Ettabaa is a teacher researcher at the Hammam Sousse IsitCom and associate researcher at Telecom Breatgne since 2008.

Mahmoud Abdelmoneim Fakhreldein, Electronics Research Institute, Ministry of the higher education and the Scientific Research, Computers and Systems Department, the head of Biomedical engineering group. PhD in Electronics and communications engineering, Cairo University 2004. He has worked as a consultant since 1996. He is used to be responsible for delivering and supporting enterprise solutions, integrating systems and advising in technology direction. He has strong organizational, analytical and communications skills which are crucial to the success of any project. his expertise in multi-system environments, medical systems, development and networking will greatly benefit the organization. This experience includes project management, participating in project teams, leading committee's made up of third party vendors.He is working as a Consultant for the Egyptian Ministry of Communications and

Information Technology (MCIT) in many projects related to e-learning,ehealth, and e-business sectors to develop many projects in the field of Database, Networks, and Integrated systems. He has Shared in the developing and implementation about of 30 IT Projects

Suranjan Ganguly received the M.Tech (Computer Technology) degree from Jadavpur University, India, in 2014. He completed B-Tech (Information Technology) in 2011. His research interest includes image processing, pattern recognition. He was a project fellow of UGC, Govt. of India, sponsored major research project at Jadavpur University. Currently, he is a project fellow of DietY (Govt. of India, MCIT) funded research project at Jadavpur University.

Gebeyehu Belay Gebremeskel did his Master's degree in Advanced Information Technology in London South Bank University, UK, his PhD in Computer Science and Technology: Software Engineering in Chongqing University College of Computer Science, China, and now post doctoral fellow in Chongqing University, College of Automation. His research direction is An Integrating for Data Mining and Agent Systems towards Augmenting Big Data Analytics Performance in Sensor and Image Data. He had diversified research interests including Data mining, Big data, Business intelligence, Agents systems, Intelligent cloud systems, Artificial Intelligence, Decision Science and others in the field.

Pratik Goyal is a Research Student at VIT University, Vellore. He does work in Artificial Intelligence and has authored a few research papers in the field.

R. Hariharan is a Ph.D student in VIT University, Vellore.

Jhih-Yuan Hwang received his M.A. degree from the Department of Information Management, National Sun Yat-sen University, Kaohsiung, Taiwan. He is currently a software engineer. His research interests include data mining, image processing, multimedia broadcasting, and social networking.

Arun Khosla received his PhD degree from Indraprastha University, Delhi in the field of Information Technology. He is presently Associate Professor, Electronics & Communication Engineering and Dean Students Welfare National Institute of Technology, Jalandhar. India. His areas of interest are image processing, computer vision, fuzzy modeling, and high performance computing. Dr. Khosla is member, IEEE and has been reviewer for various IEEE and other National and International conferences and journals. He also serves on the editorial board of International Journal of Swarm Intelligence Research.

Sandeep Kumar, B.E. from Jaipur Rajasthan M.E. from BITS PILANI currently teaching at Govt. College of Engineering and Technology, Bikaner.

Wei-Po Lee received his Ph.D. in artificial intelligence from University of Edinburgh, United Kingdom. His is currently a professor at the Department of Information Management, National Sun Yat-sen University, Kaohsiung, Taiwan. He is interested in intelligent autonomous systems, machine learning, mobile multimedia, social networking, and entertainment computing.

Hermes Aguiar Magalhães, B.Sc. in Electrical Engineering from Universidade Federal de Minas Gerais (UFMG), Brazil; M.Sc. in Electronic Engineering and Computer Science from Instituto Tecnológico de Aeronáutica (ITA); MBA at Fundação Getúlio Vargas (FGV); and Ph.D. from UFMG, in Computer Engineering. Professor at UFMG´s Electronic Engineering Department, after completing a Post-Doc in Applied Electronics for Nuclear MRI at CTPMAG. Experience with underwater communications and robotics for oil industry, marine weapons, manned submersible life support, telephony, radar-sonar-vibration-voice-oceanographic and electric-measurements signal processing, software, circuits & system design with VHDL, integration and test, OOP, and UML/SysML, multidimensional signal processing, networking and distributed systems, computer architecture, stochastic processes, and system identification. Founder of DSP ART Hardware & Software Ltd. Member of Center for Research on Speech, Acoustic, Language and Music (CEFALA) and Magnetic Resonance Research and Technology Center (CTPMAG) at UFMG. Current interests: UML/SysML for real time embedded systems, signal and image processing for MRI.

Srideep Maity received his B.Tech. in Electronics & Communication Engineering in 2012 from College of Engineering & Management, Kolaghat, K.T.P.P Township, Kolaghat, Dist- Purba Medinipur, West Bengal. Presently, he is pursuing M.E. in Electronics & Telecommunication Engineering with specialization in Communication Engineering & Signal Processing from Indian Institute of Engineering Science and Technology, Shibpur, Howrah-711103, India. His research area includes Image Processing.

Pradeep Kumar Mallick received the Master of Computer Application(MCA) from F.M.University Balasore, India and Master of Technology(M.Tech) in Computer Science & Engineering from *Bijupatnaik Unversity of Technolgy(BPUT),Odisha India in 2008* and 2010, respectively, and pursuing PhD degree in Computer Engineering in St' Peters University Chennai, India. He is an Assistant Professor of Computer Science & Engineering Department, Balasore College of Engineering and Technology, Balasore, India. His current research interests are on Image Processing and Data Mining. He has been involved in organizing many conferences, workshop and FDP. He has several publications in national and International conference and journals and given invited talk in many workshops.

Mita Nasipuri received her B.E.Tel.E., M.E.Tel.E., and Ph.D. (Engg.) degrees from Jadavpur University, in 1979, 1981 and 1990, respectively. Prof. Nasipuri has been a faculty member of J.U since 1987. Her current research interest includes image processing, pattern recognition, and multimedia systems. She is a senior member of the IEEE, U.S.A., Fellow of I.E (India) and W.B.A.S.T, Kolkata, India.

Ramesh Chand Pandey is pursuing Ph.D from IIT(BHU). He has completed M.tech from Thapar University Patiala in Computer Science & Engineering. He has research interest in video and image forensic. He has both industrial and teaching experience.

Manel Ben Salem is a Research professor at the IsitCom Hammam Sousse and researcher since 2012.

Pijush Samui is working as a professor at VIT University.

V. Santhi is working as Associate professor in VIT University, Vellore, India. She has more than 20 years of experience in both academic and Industry. She has pursued her B.E. in Computer Science and Engineering from Bharathidasan University. She did her M.Tech. in Computer Science and Engineering, Pondicherry University, Puducherry. She has received her Ph.D. Degrees in Computer Science and Engineering from VIT University, Vellore, India. She has carried out her research in the domain of Multimedia Security. She is senior member of IEEE and she is holding membership in many professional bodies. Her areas of research include Image Processing, Digital Signal Processing, Digital Watermarking, Data Compression and Computational Intelligence. She has published many papers in reputed journals and International conferences. She is a reviewer for many refereed Journals.

Osamu Saotome, B.Sc. in Electronic Engineering from the Instituto Tecnológico de Aeronáutica - ITA (1974), M.Sc. (1984) and Ph.D. (1987) in Electrical and Electronic Engineering (EEE), emphasis on Digital Signal Processing (DSP) at the Tokyo Institute of Technology. Interests include electronic circuits, microprocessors, digital signal processors (DSPs), embedded electronic systems/software, FPGAs, intelligent sensors, real-time systems/algorithms, digital image processing and video systems projects with FPGA, radar receivers, global geo-positioning systems (GPS), global navigation satellite system (GNSS), mechatronics, aerial robotics/navigation, inertial systems, ultra-high, reliability systems, avionics, computers for artificial satellites.

Sanjay Kumar Singh completed his B. Tech. in Computer Engg., M. Tech. in Computer Applications and Ph.D. in Computer Science and Engineering. Currently he is an associated professor at the Department of Computer Science and Engineering, IIT BHU, Varanasi. He is a Certified Novell Engineer (CNE) from Novell Netware, USA and a Certified Novell Administrator (CNA) from Novell Netware, USA. He is a member of LIMSTE, IEE, International Association of Engineers and ISCE. His research areas include Biometrics, Computer Vision, Image Processing, Video Processing, Pattern Recognition and Artificial Intelligence. He has over 50 national and international journal publications, book chapters and conference papers.

Xu Su, 36, is currently the Lecturer of College of Computer Science and Information Engineering in Chongqing Technology and Business University. He holds his first degree from Electronic Engineering in Chongqing Technology and Business University, a Master Degree major in Communication Engineering from Chongqing Posts and Telecommunications University. He is currently doing his PhD in Chongqing University majoring in Automatic Control research streams. He published many academic and high standard journals, books, and other technical reports in both English and Chinese. His major research direction is information processing, fusion and control, industrial process control theory and technology, intelligent systems theory and applications, and others in the field of automation.

Santosh Tulsyani completed his M. Tech in Computer Science & Engineering from Birla Institute of Technology, Mesra Ranchi (Jharkhand, India) in 2012. He is currently pursuing his PhD at Indian Institute of Technology (BHU) Varanasi in Computer Science and Engineering. His research interests span a wide range of spectrum including Computer Vision, Swarm Intelligence, bio-inspired computing, Artificial Intelligence, operating systems and theoretical computer science.

Nourhan Zayed was born in Giza, Egypt in 1975. She received her B.Sc. and M.Sc. degrees from the Biomedical Engineering Department at Cairo University, Egypt in 1998 and 2003 respectively. She received her Ph.D. in Electrical and Computer Engineering, University of Calgary, Calgary, Canada in 2010 where she also worked as a teaching assistant. She worked as an instructor in the Center for Adult and Continuing Education Department, American University in Cairo, Egypt in 2000- 2006. She has been with the Computer Science and Systems Department at Electronics Research Institute, Cairo, Egypt since 1999 where she is currently a Researcher. Along her career, she received several awards and recognitions including the record for research studentship funded by the multiple sclerosis program of the Hotchkiss Brain Institute, Calgary, Alberta, Canada (2008), Scholarship for studying PhD funded by the Egyptian Government (2006-2010), The American University in Cairo selected her name to be placed in the CACE instructional affairs teaching honor roll for excellence in teaching as determined by the CACE selection criteria and students, Cairo, Egypt, (2003-2006) , Scholarship in software skills development, training focus was on Oracle developer funded by Ministry of Telecommunication, Egyptian Government, Egypt (1998-1999), as well as stipends for attending and training in Montreal 2008 World Congress on treatment and research in multiple sclerosis (ACTRIMS + ECTRIMS + LACTRIMS) conference (2008) form EndMS socity. She is a member of the IEEE, EMBS, ISMRM, and SPIE. Her research interests include medical imaging and in particular MRI and ultrasound, Neuroimaging, Multiple sclerosis and Optic neuritis imaging, multi-dimensional signal processing for biomedical applications, patter recognition, computer vision, and image processing.

Shangbo Zhou received his BSc degree from Gangxi National College in 1985, MSc degree from Sichuan University in 1991, both in math, and Ph.D. degree in circuit and system from Electronic Science and Technology University. From 1991 to 2003, he was with the Institute of Chongqing Aerospace Electronic and Mechanical Technology Design Researching. Currently, he is a full professor and one of the tops distinguished and honored senior instructors at the College of Computer Science and Engineering at Chongqing University. He is postdoctoral and PhD student tutors and senior researcher. His current research interests include artificial neural networks, video data mining and nonlinear dynamical system. His research is focusing on technologies and applications tools performance optimizations and precisions. In his research area is dynamic and the field of computer science in general performed many and top level accomplishments. He has explored and researches various complex issues, which has made numerous contributions to the field. Most of his work published in high standard journals, international conference proceeding, book chapters and other scientific and academic report bulletins. Moreover, he has given numerous invited talks and tutorials at the other universities too, currently running many projects. He is also working and gained solid experience in administrative positions.

Index

V

W

Become an IRMA Member

Members of the **Information Resources Management Association (IRMA)** understand the importance of community within their field of study. The Information Resources Management Association is an ideal venue through which professionals, students, and academicians can convene and share the latest industry innovations and scholarly research that is changing the field of information science and technology. Become a member today and enjoy the benefits of membership as well as the opportunity to collaborate and network with fellow experts in the field.

IRMA Membership Benefits:

- **One FREE Journal Subscription**
- **30% Off Additional Journal Subscriptions**
- **20% Off Book Purchases**
- Updates on the latest events and research on Information Resources Management through the IRMA-L listserv.
- Updates on new open access and downloadable content added to Research IRM.
- A copy of the Information Technology Management Newsletter twice a year.
- A certificate of membership.

IRMA Membership $195

Scan code to visit irma-international.org and begin by selecting your free journal subscription.

Membership is good for one full year.